appeared around 1800 in Paris. Early "velos" were powered by pu... ... the ground with the feet, and were not steerable until 1818. Velos were powered using treadles and rods by 1840 and by foot pedals in 1861, and finally a chain was used in approximately 1869, creating a machine that is recognizable as a modern bicycle.

In other situations, an invention's date was established by determining when the device or process was first depicted in illustrations or mentioned in writings. In yet other cases, the date of when a patent was issued is employed. Obviously, the date of recent discoveries are accurate as a result of better record keeping and documentation.

In some cases, two dates are shown matching the two places that those events/discoveries (or variations of the technology) took place. This may be useful in understanding the time that elapsed for a given technology in moving from one locale to another (technology diffusion) or in evolving separately in two different societies.

Event	Date	Event	Date
Chronometer	1735	Crayons (Crayola)	1902
Circumnavigation of globe	1589	Crop rotation (theory)	1804
Cities	5000 BC	Crystal radio	1901
Clock (pendulum)	1641	Cuisinart	1973
Clock (water)	1400 BC	DNA discovered	1953
Cloning (fish)	1981	Dinosaurs (era)	245 to 65 MYA
Coca-Cola	1866	Diaper (disposable)	1951
Codes/Cyphers	1623	Disk (floppy)	1970
Coffee	1400	DNA evolves	1.8 BYA
Coliseum	70	Drill (bow)	20000 BC
Compact discs	1982	Drill (dental)	1790
Compass	300 BC	Dynamite	1867
Computer (mechanical)	1832	Email	1987
Computer (electromechanical)	1942	Earth Day	1970
Computer (electronic)	1946	Electric generating station	1882
Computer (digital/binary)	1938	Electrocardiogram (EKG)	1924
Computer (personal)	1975	Electroencephalogram (EEG)	1929
Computer (programmable)	1941	Elevator (electric)	1887
Concrete	200 BC	Embryo transplant (cattle/human)	1950/1983
Coins	700 BC	Erector set	1901
Contact lens	1887	Escalator	1911
Container shipping (ships/trucks)	1954	Fastener (Velcro)	1948
Contraception (pill)	1956	Fastener (Zipper)	1923
Contraceptives	2000 BC	Fax machine	1902
Contracts (written)	2700 BC	Fetal surgery	1984
Copper	6400 BC	Fiber optics	1955
Copying (Xerography)	1937		
Crank handle	100 BC		

(continued at back of book)

SOCIETY, ETHICS, AND TECHNOLOGY

Second Edition

Morton Winston
The College of New Jersey

Ralph Edelbach
The College of New Jersey

THOMSON

WADSWORTH

Australia • Canada • Mexico • Singapore • Spain
United Kingdom • United States

Publisher: Holly J. Allen
Philosophy Editor: Steve Wainwright
Assistant Editor: Lee McCracken
Editorial Assistant: Anna Lustig
Marketing Manager: Worth Hawes
Advertising Project Manager: Bryan Vann
Print Buyer: Karen Hunt

Permissions Editor: Bob Kauser
Production Service: Robin Lockwood Productions
Copy Editor: Jennifer Gordon
Cover Designer: Bill Stanton
Text and Cover Printer: Transcontinental Printing, Louiseville
Compositor: TBH Typecast, Inc.

Printed in Canada

2 3 4 5 6 7 0   6 05 04 03

For more information about our products, contact us at:
Thomson Learning Academic Resource Center
1-800-423-0563
For permission to use material from this text,
contact us by
Phone: 1-800-730-2214
Fax: 1-800-730-2215
Web: http://www.thomsonrights.com

Library of Congress Control Number: 2002108440

ISBN 0-534-58540-X

Wadsworth Group/Thomson Learning
10 Davis Drive
Belmont, CA 94002-3098
USA

Asia
Thomson Learning
5 Shenton Way #01-01
UIC Building
Singapore 068808

Australia
Nelson Thomson Learning
102 Dodds Street
South Melbourne, Victoria 3205
Australia

Canada
Nelson Thomson Learning
1120 Birchmount Road
Toronto, Ontario M1K 5G4
Canada

Europe/Middle East/Africa
Thomson Learning
High Holborn House
50/51 Bedford Row
London WC1R 4LR

Latin America
Thomson Learning
Seneca, 53
Colonia Polanco
11560 Mexico D.F.
Mexico

Spain
Paraninfo Thomson Learning
Calle/Magallanes, 25
28015 Madrid, Spain

For Carla, Margaret, and Molly Winston
MORTON WINSTON

With great appreciation and love to my wife Maryann for her support, encouragement, and understanding during our years together.
RALPH EDELBACH

Contents

Part II: *Contemporary Technology and the Future*   161

INNOVATION, GLOBALIZATION, AND HUMAN RIGHTS

COMPUTERS, ROBOTICS, AND INFORMATION TECHNOLOGY

BIOTECHNOLOGY, GENETIC ENGINEERING, AND REPRODUCTION

POPULATION, ENERGY, AND THE ENVIRONMENT

Preface

The idea for this book began at The College of New Jersey in 1993 with the decision to introduce a new general education core course entitled "Society, Ethics, and Technology" (SET). Among the ideas that influenced the development of this course were the discussions of the "New Liberal Learning," the development of a vigorous "Science, Technology, and Society" (STS) movement under the auspices of the National Association for Science, Technology, and Society (NASTS), and the New Liberal Arts (NLA) program that was sponsored during the 1980s through grants made by the Sloan Foundation.

These trends made it clear that general education at the undergraduate level should include courses and curricula that help students to understand the profound role that science and technology play in shaping modern society, and which provide them with a method for evaluating the benefits and risks associated with technological change. The course and this reader were developed under the assumption that scientific and technological literacy remains an essential aspect of what it means to be an educated person in the twenty-first century.

The positive response to the first edition of this reader encouraged us to prepare this updated and revised second edition, which includes eleven new readings by authors such as: James Burke, David Noble, Andrew Feenberg, Bill Joy, Ray Kurzweil, Leon Kass, Mark Sagoff, and Hunter and Avory Lovins, among others. We have kept the basic organization of the book the same as in the first edition, but have expanded the topics covered in Part II of the book to provide better coverage of topics such as globalization, innovation, nanotechnology, human cloning, genetically engineered foods, and global climate change. However, as we noted in the preface to the first edition, the range of topics and issues related to the social and ethical implications of technological change is so broad, and is changing so quickly, no printed anthology can possibly do justice to all the topics that might be covered in courses dealing with these issues. We believe that the four-month subscription to InfoTrac on-line library that can be bundled with new copies of this text and which allows students and instructors to access more than 10 million articles from over 3,800 journals going back to 1980, provides an invaluable resource to be used along with this book.

The editors are grateful to our reviewers for comments on the first edition, and to the following reviewers of this second edition: Emund F. Byrne, Indiana University-Purdue University Indianapolis; Paul T. Durbin, University of Delaware; and Pat Munday, Montana Tech. Thanks to David Kaplan for helping us identify topics and readings for the second edition. We also thank Steve Wainwright, philosophy editor at Wadsworth, for his encouragement, as well as Robin Lockwood, our production editor, and Linda Rill, our permissions editor, for their assistance in bringing out this second edition.

M.W. & R.E.
August 2002

How to Use This Book

This book is designed for use in standard fifteen-week undergraduate Science, Technology, and Society (STS) courses. Such courses are intended to provide an interdisciplinary bridge between the humanities, particularly ethics, the social sciences, and the natural sciences and engineering, by developing a framework for analyzing the social, environmental, and ethical implications of contemporary science and technology. A principal goal of such courses is to empower students to think critically about contemporary technological issues such as privacy on the Internet, genetic engineering, and global warming, and to learn to accept the social responsibilities of educated citizens in a global technological society.

The key bridge idea that links science and technology with ethics and social science together is the dictum that "Ought Implies Can, but Can does not Imply Ought." The first half of this statement asserts that one cannot be obliged to do something that one cannot do, while the second half says that just because one can do something does not mean that one ought to do it. Science and technology, by enlarging the domain of what we humans know how to do, are continually enlarging the class of actions we humans can perform. As a consequence of this expansion of our power to do more things, we are obliged to ask ourselves whether we ought to be doing all the things that science and technology now allow us to do. "Ought questions" are ethical questions, and in order to answer these sorts of questions, one needs to understand how ethical values and traditional moral standards can be applied to evaluating past and present scientific and technological innovations.

The introductory essay, "Children of Invention," which has been written especially for this volume, is intended to provide students with a conceptual framework for thinking about the relationship between scientific and technological innovation, and the social and ethical issues that such innovations can create when new technologies are deployed and diffused in society. All too often, new technologies are developed and deployed without proper reflection as to their likely consequences for society. One reason for this is ignorance about the nature of technology and the processes by which new technologies are developed and deployed. Addressing the need for students to be scientifically and technologically literate has long been a primary goal of the STS movement, and it is also a primary goal of this book.

However, another reason for the failure to evaluate technology ethically is that traditional ethical theories were primarily intended to evaluate persons and their actions, rather than socio-technical practices employed by many persons in society. In order to correct for this, it is necessary for students to understand at least a little bit about ethics and to be familiar with the essential features of the major traditional ethical theories, such as ethical egoism, utilitarianism, natural law, and Kantian deontological ethics. It is also necessary to explain how these theories can be adapted to the evaluation of technology and to provide a method for applying familiar ethical principles to particular controversial issues surrounding contemporary science and technology. It is unusual to find books that serve these multiple purposes.

The introductory essay attempts to provide an ethical framework through which students can approach the evaluation of technology. It is advisable to assign the introductory essay early on in courses for which this book is adopted since it provides students who are new to STS with a comprehensive overview of the subject matter as well as a concise introduction to the ethical and social aspects of technology. The selections in Part I convey general perspectives on the historical, social, and philosophical aspects of technology, while those in Part II deal with several issues in specific fields of contemporary technology.

In selecting readings for this text the authors have tried to provide current selections on a number of standard STS topics, such as computers, automation, robotics, the Internet, genetic engineering, artificial reproduction, population, energy, and environmental policy issues. We have departed slightly from the standard set of topics by also including several articles dealing with the phenomenon of globalization. Each selection is preceded by a brief introduction describing the topic and major themes of the reading, mentioning something about its author, and providing several focus questions for students to keep in mind while reading the essay. Usually at least one of these focus questions asks the reader to compare the view in the present reading with that found in another selection that presents a competing or complementary perspective. This allows instructors to design their syllabus using such topical links instead of the standard organization.

However, one of the problems with edited readers is that no matter how careful the editors are in selecting the texts to be included, it is inevitable that some topics or issues will be omitted or given only cursory treatment and that some readings will soon become obsolete. This problem is especially difficult with respect to the field of science, technology, and society studies, because, given the dynamic nature of contemporary science and technology, new discoveries and developments are occurring constantly whose impacts on society need to be addressed and examined. Thus, even if the selections of an edited anthology are current at the time of publication, they soon lose their currency and must be updated with new materials.

While it is possible to use this book as a stand-alone course reader dealing with social and ethical issues related to technology, it is specially designed to be used along with Info-Trac College Edition, a searchable on-line full text library containing more than 10 million articles from over 3800 publications. By combining this text with InfoTrac, students and instructors can supplement the readings contained in this book with virtually any number of additional current readings dealing with the topics and issues that specifically interest them. Each reading introduction contains a set of suggested keywords that can be used in conjunction with InfoTrac, or other Web-based libraries, to search for articles on related themes or topics. By combining the readings in this book with the InfoTrac virtual library, it is possible for instructors to design their own units on topics or issues that are not addressed by the readings contained in this textbook. Instructors can choose a topic to discuss, search InfoTrac for suitable articles and references on that topic, and then ask students to access InfoTrac and retrieve and read the indicated selections. It is of course also possible to assign the task of searching InfoTrac to students and ask them to prepare reports on these supplementary course topics.

InfoTrac is easy to learn, and combining the readings in this book with the InfoTrac on-line library gives instructors considerable freedom in adapting this book to their particular course design and personal interests. Students will find that their InfoTrac subscription is useful not only for the course for which they bought this book, but for other courses as well. We believe that the combination of the *Society, Ethics, and Technology* reader with an InfoTrac subscription provides an exceptional resource for STS courses.

If this text was ordered with the InfoTrac option, a four-month subscription is bundled with this book. To access your InfoTrac account, point your web browser to:

http://www.Infotrac.thomsonlearning.com/

After you enter your account ID number, fill in your registration information. Once registered you can search the database for specific entries on precisely defined topics by subject or keyword, journal or date of publication (using Boolean operators, wildcards, and nested operators), or you can use the Easy Search to quickly compile a list of citations related to your topic. There is a complete on-line help index with InfoTrac that will guide you as you go.

The combination of a traditional print-media course reader together with the InfoTrac College Library transforms this text into what might be termed a "CyberReader"—literary amphibian that exists both in the print world and in cyberspace. In order to provide additional linkage between the text and the World Wide Web, the book is also supported by a course Web site:

http://www.tcnj.edu/~set/set.htm

that contains hyperlinks to various other sites on the Web dealing with topics and issues addressed in the reader. These links are continually being updated, but instructors may also want to create their own Web sites for their courses and link them to the Society, Ethics, and Technology site that supports this book. The site also provides the email addresses of the authors, who welcome comments and suggestions about this text.

M.W. & R.E.
August 2002

Children of Invention

IF NECESSITY IS THE MOTHER OF INVENTION, who is the father, and who, or what, are invention's children? Necessity, of course, is a matter of degree: We actually only *need* air, water, and food to survive. Shelter, clothing, and a few material possessions are also nice, as are companionship, affection, security, and several other psychological goods that we crave as social animals. But we humans learned how to satisfy these basic biological needs millions of years ago. Why then did we embark on the long journey that transformed us from cavemen into cosmonauts? What was it that made possible the ascent from the Stone Age to the Space Age?

Clearly, the leading answer to these questions is superior intelligence. But in what specific respects is human intelligence superior to that found in other species? Is it our capacity to learn from observation and experience and to transmit what we learn to others? Is it our ability to create and use language? Or might it be these general cognitive capacities for culture and language, together with our unique ability to discover new solutions to old problems and better ways of making and doing things, in short, our unique capacity as a species to form science and technology? Coupled with our needs and desires, which provide the motives that propel us to discover and invent, our scientific and technological creativity has guided the development of civilization through the development of theories, tools, inventions, and technologies that have transformed the ways we live and work.[1]

For most of us, a world without technology is inconceivable. The inventions that it has given us are all around us. In fact most of us spend most of our lives in completely artificial environments, wrapped in a technological cocoon that provides us with much more than merely food and protection from the elements. We are so wrapped up in our technological culture, in fact, that it takes an effort to distance ourselves from it in order to understand how technology has transformed human existence

from its natural state. Such a historical perspective also helps us to see how contemporary technologies, such as genetic engineering and the Internet, are now changing us in even more dramatic ways, creating new opportunities for humans to flourish, new ways of life, and also, in some cases, new social and ethical problems. These social and ethical issues arising from technological innovation are the "children of invention" that this book is about. In order to understand these issues, however, it is first necessary to get a clear view of their source—*technology*.

The Scope of Technology

When one ordinarily thinks of technology, what most likely comes to mind are artifacts, the manufactured objects, machines, structures, and devices that are the useful end products of technological design. Then, perhaps, one thinks of the less familiar, but potentially more impressive machines and industrial processes tucked away in the factories that manufacture the various gadgets and widgets that we use. Finally, one might visualize the scientists, engineers, and technicians in white laboratory coats, hard at work in the laboratories of the Research and Development Division, designing the next generation of technological devices and processes.

While it is true that technology is involved in each of these contexts—end-use, manufacturing, and design—we take the even broader view that technology consists not only of artifacts and the tools and processes needed to produce them, but also of the entire social organization of people and materials that permits the acquisition of the knowledge and skills needed to design, manufacture, distribute, use, repair, and eventually dispose of these artifacts. Technology is not a collection of things, but rather is a systematic and rational way of doing things; it is, in general, *the organization of knowledge, people, and things to accomplish specific practical goals.*[2]

Technology includes not only the obvious candidates, the mechanical, structural, and electronic technologies that direct the purposeful organization of materials, but also less obvious *invisible technologies* that control the purposeful organization of people. Few would doubt that the mechanical, chemical, and electrical know-how that goes into the design of the motors, transmissions, wheels, and dashboard of an automobile qualifies as technology, but so also does the assembly line, a technology for organizing the manufacturing environment, and the classroom, a technology for education. Looking farther afield, the monetary system, the banks, and the stock and commodity markets are technologies for the distribution of value that, whatever their faults, have long since displaced the competing technologies of barter and stuffing gold coins in a mattress. Free-market capitalism and centralized planned economies are competing technologies for organizing social production. Even governmental systems, ranging from varieties of representative democracy to theocracy and dictatorship, are competing political technologies for managing concerted societal action and resolving political conflicts. People ask, "Is there a better way to run the government?" no less frequently than "Is there a better way to design a mouse trap?" Both questions are requests to find a better technology.

The word *technology* is itself of fairly recent coinage; Harvard professor Jacob Bigelow first used it in the 1820s. Its root, "techne" is the ancient Greek word for art, craft, or skill, which itself is derived from an earlier Indo-European root, "teks," which means to weave or fabricate. ("Teks" is also the root of the word *textile*). Recent archeological evidence suggests that the weaving of cloth predates the birth of agriculture and the dawn of civilization, going back to about 35,000 B.C., making it one of the first technologies. As the etymology suggests, a "techne" is a method or craft or skill used in making things, not the things themselves, which are rather called *artifacts*. For instance, a woven object made from animal hairs twisted together into long strands, dyed with vegetable colors, and interlaced by a weaver is an artifact. Let us say that this object functions primarily as a blanket; a person

wraps her- or himself in it to stay warm. A typical use or function of an artifact is called its *purpose, end,* or *valence,* and the knowledge of how to gather the fibers, twist them, dye them, and weave them, are the individual *techniques* of which this particular technology is comprised.[3] Thus, the core meaning of the word *technology* refers to the ensembles of techniques by which humans make artifacts that serve certain useful ends. However, this original meaning is too restrictive for the contemporary context in which we think about the relationship between technology and modern society.

Technological Systems

Contemporary writers often speak of recent technologies as consisting of systems. Technological systems are complex things consisting of several distinguishable but interacting aspects: (1) techniques, human activity-forms, or socio-technical practices; (2) resources, tools, or materials; (3) technological products, or artifacts; (4) ends, functions, or valences; (5) background knowledge and skills; and (6) the social contexts or organization in which the technology is designed, developed, used, and disposed of. These six aspects are present in every technological system.

The first aspect of technological systems is the *human activity-form,* that is, the particular skills, techniques, methods, practices, or ways of doing things. We know that animals other than humans are able to make and use tools (for instance, chimpanzees strip the branches off tree limbs to make sticks that can be used for gathering insects), but for the purposes of our characterization of the technological system, we can restrict activity-forms or techniques to those employed by human beings. Some human activity-forms employ natural objects rather than tools to achieve ends; for instance, if one throws a rock in order to try to kill an animal for food, one is employing a particular technique. But, throwing rocks for hunting is a primitive and not very useful technique. Technologies for providing food have improved considerably. Nowadays there are complex ensembles of techniques for doing just about everything from planting and harvesting crops to figuring out the orbit of a moon of

Jupiter, from designing a house to conducting a leveraged hostile takeover, from cooking lasagna to programming a computer to sort sales data. Such complex techniques represent what is called procedural knowledge, or more commonly *know-how,* and is contrasted with factual or theoretical prepositional knowledge, or *know-that*. While both types of knowledge are necessary aspects of technological systems, techniques are its essence. Know-how forms the basis of technology since it provides the pattern for the socio-technical practices that we humans use to create artifacts of all kinds, and build and maintain our technological infrastructures.

One of the main consequences of technology is it increases our capacity to do things. Technologies, techniques, and tools extend, enhance, and sometimes even replace our natural powers such as sight, hearing, muscle, and even memory and thought. By using tools, we are able to accomplish things that we could not otherwise achieve, thus increasing our repertoire of human activity-forms. Tools are artifacts at our disposal that can be used to make other artifacts, but tools, even the *dawn stones* used by our distant ancestors, are themselves artifacts that have been transformed from their natural states in some way by means of human action.

The Earth itself is, of course, not an artifact, but has, for many centuries, been viewed by we humans as a *resource well* into which we can dip at will in order to satisfy our needs and desires. Technology requires resources of various kinds as inputs to technological processes, and by employing specific techniques or human activity-forms, we act upon and transform these resources from their original or natural states. Once a *built environment* has been created, however, everything in it can serve as a resource to further technological development. The term *infrastructure* describes elements of the built environment that are available to create or apply new technologies.

By acting upon either natural or artificial resources, through techniques, we alter them in various ways and thus create *artifacts,* which form the third aspect of technologies. A clay pot is an example of a material artifact, which, although transformed by human activity, is not all that far re-

moved from its natural state. A plastic cup, a contact lens, or a computer chip, on the other hand, are examples of artifacts that are far removed from the original states of the natural resources needed to create them. Artifacts can serve as resources in other technological processes. This is one of the important interaction effects within the technological system: Each new technology increases the stock of available tools and resources that can be employed by other technologies to produce new artifacts.

The fourth aspect concerns the typical use or *valence* of an artifact or technique. While most artifacts have typical or intended uses, there are, in fact, no artifacts that cannot be embedded in multiple contexts of use or which cannot serve multiple ends, a property of some artifacts referred to as *polypotency*. A toaster, for instance, designed in order to lightly burn slices of bread, can also be used as a hand warmer or as a murder weapon. There is a double ambiguity in the relations between artifacts and practices and between ends and practices, since the same artifacts can be used to achieve different ends, and different practices and their associated artifacts can be used to accomplish the same ends. For instance, I could have written this sentence with a quill pen, a pencil, a ballpoint pen, a typewriter, or a personal computer running text-editing software (in fact, I used the last). And I could have used my personal computer to play an adventure game or calculate my income tax instead of writing this sentence. Because artifacts are designed and created in order to serve certain intended functions, it is possible to talk about the ends of these objects, that is, their intended purpose, even though the objects themselves may often also be used in ways which were not intended by their designers. The *valences* of an artifact or technology are the ways it is typically used by most agents in most social contexts.

New technologies are developed in response to what we take to be our needs and desires. But as technologies develop they tend to change our needs and desires. Several years ago I had no need for floppy disks in order to save my written work, but now I do. Needs or ends come in two main varieties: *instrumental* and *intrinsic*. An instrumental end is one that is used to obtain or achieve something else that is perceived as valuable, that is, it is a means to another end or goal. An intrinsic end is something that is valued in and for itself. I have no intrinsic need for floppy disks, but I need them so that my writing on the screen will not disappear when I turn off my PC, and I need to write in order to do my job as a teacher and scholar, and I need to do my job in order to earn money, which I need to buy food and shelter for myself and my family, so that we can survive. The only thing in this example that is an intrinsic end (at least for me) is the survival of my family and myself; everything else is an instrumental end that is only valuable to the degree that it helps me to achieve this intrinsic end.

The fifth aspect of technological systems is *knowledge-that,* or factual knowledge about what the universe consists of and how it operates. In order to employ our technologies we need background knowledge of various kinds: knowledge about what resources to use and where to find them, knowledge about what techniques to employ to fabricate various artifacts, knowledge about the ends and purposes that are typically served by various techniques and objects, and knowledge about how all of these elements fit together in a systematic way. Both knowledge-how and knowledge-that have always been an important aspect of technologies, but, since the scientific revolution of the seventeenth century, scientific knowledge—both factual and theoretical knowledge about the universe and the way it works—has come to play an increasingly important role in technological development.

The sixth aspect of technology is the *social context* or organization in which technologies are developed, distributed, and employed. A division of labor in which different individuals perform different tasks or occupy different roles in order to accomplish common or coordinated ends characterizes technological societies. The schemes we use for organizing human labor represent a kind of technology that can be applied to the most important resource of all—ourselves. Complex schemes that have become more or less institutionalized can be called *social artifacts.* Examples of social artifacts include the stock market, battalions or divisions in an army, baseball teams, hospitals, schools, and corporations. In each case, human resources are organized in a particular way, according to a plan or

technique involving a division of labor in which different persons occupy different roles, and their labor is coordinated in order to be able to accomplish specific sorts of goals. It is important to see that technology encompasses not only material artifacts, but also the social and organizational forms, and even the cognitive techniques that produce the material and social infrastructure of human civilization. These *invisible technologies* frequently consist of formal, mathematical, or analytical techniques; for instance, the scientific method, statistical analysis, or procedures for creating a balance sheet, and many other specific high order thinking skills that are the content of higher education. Becoming a scientifically or technologically educated person consists mainly in the acquisition of a fairly extensive repertoire of such cognitive techniques.

The social and psychological aspects of technological systems are the <u>least obvious,</u> but also the <u>most important.</u> Technology is a human social construction. This is true in an obvious and straightforward sense when we speak of large technological structures, such as bridges, buildings, or dams, which obviously came into existence only by the coordination of the activities of numerous individuals, but it is equally true in the case of the lonely amateur inventor toiling in the attic. Inventions today are rarely the result of such solitary creativity, but even when they are, the resources and techniques employed and the knowledge by which they are put to use are themselves the products of prior social processes. Even the inventor's own knowledge and abilities have been shaped by her/his education in her/his society and by the repertoire of cognitive techniques s/he has acquired through her/his prior education. So there is really very little, only the raw materials and the laws of nature, which have not in some way resulted from a process of social production. Even when an inventor succeeds in inventing something new, it is still unlikely to be brought into production and placed on the market, unless it has some social value or is of use to other people. So all technologies must be seen as embedded in social contexts of development, deployment, and use.

To summarize this discussion, we can define technological systems as *the complex of techniques, knowledge, and resources that are employed by human beings in the creation of material and social artifacts that typically serve certain functions perceived as useful or desirable in relation to human interests in various social contexts.*

Technological Revolutions

The use of technologies to satisfy our needs is a fundamental feature of human nature. All human societies we know of, both those presently existing and those that existed hundreds of thousands of years before the dawn of civilization, were technological to some degree. For almost all of our species' evolution we lived in small, nomadic bands whose main means of livelihood were hunting, gathering, and scavenging. But we were also toolmakers and tool-users during this long period of human evolution, and tools were the principal means by which we satisfied our physiological needs for food, warmth, and shelter.

Our hominid ancestors first began chipping stones to make simple hand tools about 2.5 million years ago. Fire was used as early as 1.5 million years ago. If *homo sapiens sapiens* (literally, the wise human who knows s/he is wise) really is wise, it is in large part because s/he is also *homo faber* (human maker). Early human societies were organized as hunter-gatherer groups, gathering edible plants in season and supplementing their diet with the meat or marrow of hunted animals. Quite likely, these bands of hunter-gatherers were nomadic, following animal migrations and seasonal food plant distributions. As with the present-day hunter-gatherers, ancient nomadic societies were severely limited to only those objects they could take with them and thus tended to develop simple portable technologies for hunting, gathering, cooking, transportation, and defense. Perhaps surprisingly, life does not seem to have been especially hard for hunter-gatherers. The secrets of their success seem to have been populations that did not exceed the food supply, simple and limited material needs, and the ability to move to another area when the local food supply ran out. Nomadic hunter-gatherer societies have persisted into the twentieth century in such diverse environments as the African desert, the tropical rain forest, and the Arctic tundra. Remoteness might be the key to avoiding conversion to more technologically intensive ways of life. For the rest of us, our lives are deeply dependent on far-flung and complex technological systems.

About 8,000 B.C., the first great technological revolution occurred in several fertile river valleys of Asia Minor and North Africa. During the Agricultural Revolution humans learned how to domesticate animals and to plant, grow, and harvest crops to sustain their existence. This enabled humans to give up the nomadic lifestyle and to build permanent cities. *Civilization,* which means the building of cities, originates at this time, as do morality, law, religion, record keeping, mathematics, astronomy, class structures, patriarchy, and other social institutions that have since come to characterize the human condition. With the adoption of settled agriculture in the fertile river valleys, the history of humankind begins. Permanent houses could be built, tools and objects could be accumulated from year to year, and so humanity began the long climb toward the collections of miscellany and junk that now clutter people's closets, attics, and garages.

Settled agriculture had many advantages and a few disadvantages. The quantity of food that could be produced per acre was much higher, so population densities could also be much greater. With permanent dwellings, creature comforts could be made that did not have to be portable. With larger numbers of people together, specialization of activities could take place, and specialists were more likely to find better ways to do things. Larger concentrations of people could better share and perpetuate knowledge and band together to cooperate on projects that smaller groups could not attempt. Thus we see that even at this early stage of technological development, the organization of people, of information, and of accumulated resources were essential aspects of emerging technological societies.

The disadvantages of settled agriculture sprang from the fact that society had put all its eggs in one basket and had committed itself to living in one place. A settled society is prey to flood, drought, and insects. Persistent weeds must be removed from fields before they displace crops. Houses and farm implements must be maintained. Crop seeds must be gathered and sown. In short, the settled farmer has more, but must work harder to maintain her/his improved standard of living. Irrigated agriculture is even more technologically intensive and requires more complex social organization. Large irrigation projects demand larger groups to support them, and must be maintained throughout the year, not just during the growing season. Irrigated farms produce more food per acre more reliably than dry farms that rely on uncertain rainfall, but they also require more work per person fed. At the extreme are rice paddies in the river deltas of southeast China where three crops are grown per year. They are the most productive farmlands, but also the most labor intensive. The only exceptions to this unfortunate trend occur on large farms in industrialized countries where energy intensive farm machinery substitutes for human labor and chemical fertilizers maintain soil fertility.

The second great technological revolution took place many centuries later, beginning during the eighteenth century in Europe. The Industrial Revolution replaced the muscle power of animals with coal-fired steam energy, and then later, about 100 years ago, with gasoline-driven internal combustion engines. The machine age caused profound changes in economic and social relations; the number of people needed to produce food declined as the number of people engaged in factory work increased. People migrated from rural areas to cities in search of higher paying factory jobs, and new inventions such as the cotton gin, the locomotive, and the telegraph laid the groundwork for the emergence of the technological society that we live in today.

The methods a society uses to produce goods have a profound effect on what life is like in that society, both for the producers of goods and for the consumers. Prior to the industrial age, production was organized by crafts. Individual craftsmen designed and produced each individual product, usually guided by traditional techniques that were occasionally modified by creative innovations. The relative value of the product was largely determined by the skill of the craftsman. As a result, craftsmen were relatively autonomous, and production units often consisted of a single craftsman and several apprentices.

When the invention of the steam engine made power available on a scale never previously possible, it became feasible to concentrate larger numbers of workers in one place, and to have each worker perform only a small part of the production process, resulting in a much more specialized division of labor. Even more remarkable than the increased consolidation of people was the increased concentration and specialization of knowledge. In the early twentieth century, technological experts, working under the banner of "scientific management," studied the production process, learned what each worker knew about making the product, and then ordained the perfect way to produce a given product—what each worker would do, and at what pace they would do it. Each worker needed fewer skills and could be paid less per item. However, cheaper workers making larger numbers of products using specialized machinery resulted in less expensive goods. Lower prices resulted in an increased standard of living for consumers. Factory work may have become onerous, but a salary could buy more than it could previously.

In the search for increased productivity, working conditions in early factories were often harsh and dangerous. In response to the many abuses that existed, employees often battled tyrannical bosses for the right to form unions and bargain collectively, many times suffering injuries or even death for their actions. The sacrifices made in such organizing drives secured improved working conditions and raised the standard of living for millions of workers and their families. Despite the growth of the factory system, crafts did not vanish entirely. They survived in niches where no one could think of an economical way of applying mass production techniques, or to produce distinctive goods of high quality, or in some cases, because traditional cultural values prevailed over the lure of newer technologies.

The Industrial Revolution was characterized by the development of a new kind of technological system: the factory system. It required far greater concentrations of power, labor, and raw materials than either agriculture or cottage industries. It also required the development of an infrastructure for transportation of raw materials to the factory site and finished products from the site. Railroads and canals were as essential a part of the Industrial Revolution as the factories themselves. The industrial system also required a large labor force near the factory, so society's living patterns were reorganized to include factory towns and to supply them with food and other necessities. Factories were often located near sources of power or raw materials, resulting in net population shifts away from agricultural lands.

The technologies of power production were driving forces of the industrial system, and each new source of power required industrialized society to provide an accompanying infrastructure to make the system work. Water power, an ancient technology, was limited in availability and location, and required relatively little additional infrastructure beyond that already available in an agricultural and craft society. Coal could be more widely distributed, but coal-powered factories were large because efficient steam engines were large. Railroads and canals began to crisscross the countryside from mine to factory to market. Monetary supply and financial services had to expand to serve a system with increasing separation between producer and consumer.

Electricity is a more flexible source of power, capable of efficiently driving both large and small machines. Electricity permitted greater decentralization of industry, supported by a network of power grids that eventually reached nearly every house and factory in the country. Oil and gasoline revolutionized the transportation and distribution of goods. Internal combustion engines fueled by gasoline and diesel oil made it possible to use smaller vehicles, and smaller vehicles continued the trend toward decentralization. However, gas- and oil-powered vehicles required more and better roads. The U.S. Interstate Highway System (and similar systems in other industrialized countries) built in the 1960s–1980s, are society's most recent contributions to an industrial technology system based on oil.

Many people believe that in the late twentieth century we have been going through a third great technological transformation—from the *machine age* to the *information age*. Called by various names—"the Third Wave" or the "Knowledge Revolution"—it is clear that computers, communications satellites, and ubiquitous, global, high-capacity communications technologies such as the Internet are already profoundly changing the way in which we live, play, and work. Over the last two decades, revolutionary developments in computing and communications technology have transformed the workplace, faster than some would like, but slower than its visionaries had hoped for. The earliest successes of computers in industry were in payroll, inventory, and similar routine and repetitive kinds of record keeping. The processes automated were well understood, straightforward, and implemented exactly as they had been done before the advent of computers. In some cases, they didn't even save time or resources, but they were the wave of the future. The next stage gave decision makers more and better information to enhance efficiency, competitiveness, and other factors that are reflected in the bottom line. Computers made it possible to gather and organize data on an unprecedented scale. Also successful were the attempts to use computers to improve scheduling and reduce inventory in the production process. Goods stored in inventory cost money to store and contribute nothing to profit until they are used or sold. Being able to predict exactly how much of which raw materials and parts will be needed at which steps of the manufacturing process, and being able to schedule their arrival in the factory at precisely the right place at precisely the right time, was the "just-in-time" manufacturing technique developed in Japan, which led to real gains in productivity. It also made possible the kinds of geographically distributed production systems that are characteristic of *globalization*. In fact, without computers and rapid worldwide communications, our present-day global marketplace would not be possible.

As computers and computer programmers got better, computers became capable of doing jobs that were formerly thought to require human intelligence. Typically, computers proved capable of doing far more than most people would have predicted in advance and far less than their most vocal proponents claimed was possible. Although the conceptually most impressive achievements were in areas such as expert systems for medical diagnosis, the biggest successes of *artificial intelligence* were in the simpler applications, now so common that we take them for granted: automatic pilot, antilocking brakes, electronic fuel injection, and most important, more flexible, general purpose tools and machines for making other products. With flexible, modifiable, reprogrammable tools, it was no longer necessary to have long production runs to amortize the set-up time of the machinery. Computer-controlled machinery could switch quickly from one task to another, and customized production runs became in some cases economically viable. Supply could now more accurately follow demand, and both idle machinery and unproductive inventory were virtually eliminated in those industries adopting the new technology. More models and options could be made available to the consumer at substantially the same or lower price, unlike the early days of the assembly line when you could get a Model A Ford in any color you liked, as long as it was black.

Even more pervasive and far-reaching in its effects on society were the computer applications where the computer itself was the medium of interaction and communication. Computer word processing began in the late 1950s and early 1960s as a curious and amusing waste of computing resources that could only be tolerated in environments where the computers were severely underutilized; basically only the development programmers at a computer manufacturer could afford to write word processing programs to help edit their computer programs. However, in about 1980, when the Apple II computer hit the streets at a retail price of under $2000, and its more expensive imitator, the IBM PC, quickly followed, many people could afford to do word processing on a computer, and they soon did. Typewriters and typesetters hit the trash heap in record numbers, and the writing was on the wall that the secretarial pool would someday exit as well. The now ubiquitous Internet also arose partly by accident. During the Cold War with the USSR, the threat of a nuclear attack on the United States seemed plausible, and the Department of Defense

thought it prudent to establish electronic communications links between the supercomputers at the leading scientific laboratories so as to better share these resources. Soon it dawned on some people that having a decentralized communication system would allow those laboratories that survived a nuclear attack to still communicate with one another. The nuclear attack fortunately never happened, but no one who ever had access to the Internet (then called ARPA-net or DARPA-net) ever went back to using "snail-mail" (the U.S. Postal Service) for anything from computer programs and data files to personal notes, messages, recipes, jokes, trivia, animated cartoons, and whatever other new uses the future may bring. During the 1980s the Internet links expanded to most universities, and professors other than just those in computer science and engineering began using email for both professional and personal communications. Then in the mid-1990s the Internet went commercial and everybody signed up for America Online to get onto the World Wide Web.

The key technologies for an information society are those that support record keeping and communication. Tapes, disks, and computers are supplanting paper and printing. Telephones, modems, faxes, and communications satellites carry the data that are the lifeblood of a technological system based on information. Aware that continued growth of information technology in the United States depends on adequate infrastructure, national leaders have proposed a national, federally funded, fiber optic communications network, the information society's equivalent of the interstate highway system. Industrial societies, in general, require better education of their workers than do agricultural societies; however, more than ever before, an information society requires an adequate infrastructure of education and educated individuals. The whole system seems in danger of collapsing if there are not enough sufficiently educated techies to maintain the computers.

Technology and Science

In the modern world, technology and science often go together, with science supporting technology and technology supporting science. Although they now share a great deal in common, their goals have been historically quite different. Traditionally, science was viewed as an elevated activity involving "pure contemplation" and the "value-free" pursuit of knowledge, whereas technology was associated with more practical concerns and with the arts. It was not until the beginning of the modern period in the seventeenth century that there was a decisive shift, when the view that scientific knowledge was valuable because it was useful in gaining mastery over nature became prominent.

This shift was largely due to the writings of several influential philosophers, such as René Descartes and Francis Bacon. Bacon's works, particularly *Novum Organon* (1620) and *New Atlantis* (1624), are notable for their contempt for traditional speculative philosophy and their emphasis on the importance of empirical methods of investigation through which the secrets of nature could be revealed by means of judicious experiments. In 1637 Descartes wrote the *Discourse on Method,* in which he proclaimed that, "it is possible to attain knowledge which is very useful in life; and that, instead of speculative philosophy which is taught in the Schools, we may find a practical philosophy by means of which, knowing the force and the action of fire, water, air, stars, the heavens, and all other bodies that environ us, as distinctly as we know the different crafts of our artisans, we can in the same way employ them in all those uses to which they are adapted, and thus render ourselves masters and possessors of nature."[4] This change in the dominant view of the nature and bases of human knowledge set the stage for the modern belief in progress, which was expressed by Bacon as the belief that, "the improvement of man's mind and the improvement of his lot are one and the same thing."[5]

Despite the merger of science and technology in the modern period, there remain some significant differences between the two enterprises. Technologists primarily seek to answer the question, "How?" "How can we keep warm in the winter?" or "How can we see distant objects that are invisible to the naked eye?" Engineers seek to design and produce useful material objects and systems that will function under all expected circumstances for the planned lifetime of the product. Science, on the other hand, may be considered as a form of systematic inquiry, seeking to understand the underlying laws governing the behavior of natural objects. Scientists primarily try to answer the questions "What?" and "Why?" as in "What kind of thing is this?" and "Why does it behave the way it does?" In the early stages of a science, when little was known, the immediate goal of the science was to describe and classify the phenomena of the natural world. As more things became known, the sciences began asking, "How do these things change over time and interact with each other?" Scientists sought laws and principles that would enable them to predict and explain why things in nature behave as they do.

Science and technology have a symbiotic relationship, each one helping the other. Technology needs science to predict how its objects and systems will function so that it can tell if they will work. Science supplies predictive laws that apply to these objects and systems, a perfect match. However, although the laws of science are often simple, applying them to the complex objects of technology is often anything but simple. Sometimes the engineer must experiment with the complex objects that are the building blocks of a technology to find out what will happen. Perhaps the most important contribution that science makes to technology is in the education of the engineer, supplying the conceptual framework upon which s/he builds a body of more specific and practical knowledge.

Technology makes direct and obvious contributions to the progress of science. The laboratory equipment that the scientist uses is the product of technology. The biologist would discover little without a microscope, and the particle physicist even less without an accelerator. This direction of contribution is maintained throughout most of science. At the frontiers of science, however, the scientist may need equipment that has never been built before based on principles never been used before in applied contexts. The design of the Tokamak (magnetic confinement torus) to study controlled nuclear fusion in hydrogen plasmas is without a doubt the product of technology, but it is technology that can only be done by the scientists who understand and can predict the behavior of high temperature plasmas. Still, they do not do it alone; much of the design uses established technology, and this is the domain of the engineer.

But in recent years the lines between the role of the scientist and that of the engineer or technologist have become increasingly blurred. Much of the current research agenda is dictated by the possible practical applications of new scientific knowledge. This merging of science and technology has led some writers, such as Bruno Latour, to speak of contemporary research as *technoscience*.[6] The complex relationship that presently exists between science and technology can be exemplified in the contemporary field of biotechnology.

Genetics is the science that studies inherited characteristics. Genetic engineering, by contrast, is the application of the knowledge obtained from genetic investigations to the solution of such problems as infertility, treatments for diseases, food production, waste disposal, or the improvement of crop species. Among genetic-engineering techniques are procedures that can alter the reproductive and hereditary processes of organisms. Depending on the problem, the procedures used in genetic engineering may involve artificial insemination, cloning, *in vitro* fertilization, species hybridization, or molecular genetics. Recent discoveries in molecular genetics have permitted the direct manipulation of the genetic material itself by the recombinant-DNA technique. Is this a scientific discovery or a technological one? Both know-that and know-how are essential elements of modern biotechnology and both a part of the training of every working geneticist and genetic-engineer.

The genome of an organism is the totality of genes making up its hereditary constitution. The Human Genome Project (HGP) was designed to map the human genome, and in 1990 the U.S. National Institutes of Health and the Department of Energy created the National Center for Human Genome Research. The goal is to determine the exact location of all the genes—about 35,000 of them, plus regulatory elements—on their respective chromosomes, as well as establishing the sequence of nucleotides—estimated to be about 6 million pairs—of all human genes. The HGP has been completed ahead of schedule at an estimated

cost of $3 billion. It is highly doubtful that such a "Big Science" project would have been funded were it not for the expectation that it would result in new medical technologies for the treatment of diseases that currently afflict many people. Recently patents have been granted for the production of erythropoietin, a hormone that stimulates blood-cell formation; tissue-plasminogen activator, an anti-clotting agent used to treat heart attacks; and alpha-interferon, which has been found effective in treating hepatitis C.

Biotechnology also has nonmedical commercial applications. In 1980 a ruling by the U.S. Supreme Court permitted the U.S. Patent and Trademark Office to grant a patent on a genetically engineered oil-eating bacterium. The bacterium was categorized as a "nonnatural man-made microorganism." Over the following eight years, some 200 patents were granted for bacteria, viruses, and plants that had been genetically modified. In 1988 a patent was granted on a mouse strain in which the cells had been engineered to contain a cancer-predisposing gene sequence. Technically referred to as a "transgenic nonhuman eukaryotic animal," each mouse of this type can be used to test low doses of cancer-causing substances and to test the effectiveness of drugs considered as possibly offering protection against the development of cancer. In the field of agriculture a number of plants with genetically engineered traits have been patented, including maize (corn) plants rich in the amino acid tryptophan, cotton plants resistant to weed-killing herbicides, tobacco plants resistant to various insects, and potato plants resistant to various viruses.

The trial of O. J. Simpson has brought to light another application of DNA technology—its use in identifying the assailants in violent crimes when the victims are no longer able to do so themselves. Each person, with the exception of identical twins, has a unique DNA fingerprint that can be detected by matching patterns of restriction enzyme DNA fragments. Using this technique it is possible to extract samples of DNA from dried blood, hairs, or semen and produce a near certain match, with the DNA pattern obtained from cells of the accused. But the same technology also raises issues about personal privacy and genetic discrimination.

Each new application of biological knowledge to human reproduction has raised profound and troubling ethical questions. Already it is possible for children to be produced artificially by the use of *in vitro* fertilization (IVF), or gamete interfallopian transfer (GIFT). It is now possible for a child to have different genetic, gestational, and social parents, greatly complicating questions of custody. While it is still necessary to employ women's wombs in the gestational process, it may not be long before we have developed artificial wombs or incubators that will enable us to gestate mammals, such as ourselves, in an extra-uterine environment.

We already have the ability to create man-made plants and animals in the laboratory by splicing together strands of DNA taken from different organisms. How long will it be before we start applying these same techniques to ourselves? Germ-line genetic therapies offer the promise of eliminating many dreaded genetic diseases from the human gene pool, but they also raise the specter of our playing God by redesigning the human species to suit our dominant social values. Do we really want to live in a world where prospective parents can choose whether they will have a boy or a girl, and choose other characteristics such as height, body type, hair and eye color, or perhaps even intelligence and beauty? Do we really want to know what genetic diseases we are harboring? What will become of the notion of human dignity if we begin to clone ourselves, as if a person were just another man-made artifact built according to our specifications?

Technology and Ethics

In considering the ethical issues arising from technology, it is important to distinguish clearly between the specific products of technological development, such as clocks, internal combustion engines, digital computers, respirators, and nuclear bombs, and the typical ways that people use them, or what might be termed the associated *socio-technological practices*. The fact that a particular device or technology is available for human use does not, by itself, imply that we ought to adopt and use that technology nor does it tell us how the technology should or should not be used. A gun, for instance, can be used in many ways: as a paperweight, for recreational target practice, for hunting, for personal protection, or for the commission of a crime. Although the gun itself has many uses, its valence lies in the practices of use typically associated with it, which may or may not match its intended purpose. We can and do make moral judgments concerning the various socio-technological practices associated with different products of technology. We accept some uses as morally legitimate, find others to be morally questionable or problematic, and we take steps to restrict or outlaw certain other uses to which these devices may be put. In some cases, such as chemical or biological weapons, whose only valence is to produce mass death and destruction, we attempt to outlaw them entirely rather than to regulate their use. Other technologies are more benign, at least apparently so, and their introduction into society generates little concern or controversy.

Ethical concerns arising from technology can be divided into four kinds. The first and most basic kind of ethical problem associated with technology concerns questions about how traditional ethical values and norms apply in new technological contexts. Technological innovations enlarge the scope of possible human action by allowing us to do some things we could not do before (such as, perform liver transplants), and to do things we could do before in different ways (for example, reheat food in microwave ovens). Each new technology thus raises the implicit ethical questions: "Should we employ this new technique/technology?" and, if so, "How should we employ this new technique/technology?" In many cases, such questions are answered easily. However, in many other cases, decisions about whether, how, and when to use particular technologies can raise difficult and troubling ethical issues about how our traditional ethical values and rules apply in new technological contexts.

Ethical problems of this first kind are particularly evident in the field of medical technology where, for instance, the development and use of the respirator has made it possible to maintain heartbeat and respiration in patients who would certainly have died if this device were not available. Now that there is the option of placing a patient on such a device to prolong life, medical practitioners are faced with the moral choice about whether, and under what circumstances, they should do so, and whether, and under what conditions, they may ethically remove a patient from this device. Should patients with terminal illnesses be placed on respirators? What criterion should be used in determining when a person has died when that person's heart can be made to beat with the aid of a machine? Should physicians honor a patient's competent request to be removed from a respirator, even if that will bring death? Who makes such decisions for patients who are not able to decide for themselves? These are only a few of the difficult questions that present themselves when a life-prolonging technology such as artificial respiration comes into being. A different set of problems of this first kind arise with respect to modern computer and communications technologies that make it much easier to collect and analyze information about individuals. In this arena people are asking how the traditional value we place on *privacy* can be protected in the digital age.

A second kind of ethical problem arises concerning some socio-technological practices that, although innocuous in themselves when employed by individuals, raise serious concerns when their effects are aggregated across millions of users. There is, for instance, nothing intrinsically wrong in throwing empty bottles and cans into the trash to be carted off to the nearest landfill. But when millions of American households engage in this practice on a regular basis, we find that we are wasting recyclable resources and running rapidly out of space for new landfills. Similar sorts of *aggregation problems* arise with respect to causes of air and water pollution, over-fishing, suburban development, and many other cases in which the aggregate and cumulative effects of individual socio-technological choices threaten our collective long-term well-being.

A third class of ethical problems associated with technology concerns questions of *distributive justice* and social equality. New technologies generally benefit or advantage certain groups or members of society over others, namely those who have mastery over or access to the technology first. In many cases we think that because such advantages are earned

through hard work or special knowledge, they are therefore deserved. However, in other cases, we may feel that such restricted access to some technologies gives certain individuals or groups unfair advantages over others, and we seek to extend access to everyone in the society. Public libraries, for instance, were built in order to ensure that everyone could obtain access to books and learning. Today, we are putting computers and Internet connections into public schools for the same reason. Questions of social justice and equality of opportunity thus can be occasioned by technological innovation.

A fourth and final kind of ethical question raised by technology concerns the scope of modern technology's power to alter the world. In earlier and simpler times we humans had not the power to do very much to disturb the balance of nature or affect the life-prospects of other species or those of future generations of human beings. But when we entered the *nuclear age* all that changed. With nuclear weapons we now have the power to destroy virtually all life on Earth. Nuclear waste material from our reactors will last 10,000 years, posing a potential threat to unborn generations. Even apart from nuclear technology, we have been destroying natural habitats and thereby causing the extinction of other species at an alarming rate. Emissions from our cars and factories are filling the atmosphere with carbon dioxide, and we may be causing the earth to heat up. Issues and concerns of this type raise what are perhaps the most profound ethical questions about humankind's relationship to nature through technology. Should we continue down the course set for us by Bacon and Descartes who advised us to seek knowledge so that we could become the masters of nature, or should we change this course toward stewardship and long-term sustainability?

When we consider these sorts of questions about how the products of technology ought to be used, we are really asking questions about how people ought to behave or act. Questions about whether to use products of technology or how such products should be used are ethical questions; that is, they are questions concerning what we *ought* to do rather than about what we *can* do. Ethical questions related to technology are basically no different from other ethical questions that we ask about human conduct; in each case we must attempt to determine which action or policy, from among a range of alternative possible actions or policies, is the one we morally or ethically ought to choose. Viewed from the standpoint of technology, broadly defined, morality, ethics, and their cousin, law, are social techniques for regulating human behavior in society. They arose in human history at about the same time when most humans gave up the nomadic lifestyle and began building the permanent settlements that we call cities. Cities require the maintenance of high levels of social cooperation based on reliable expectations that others will act as they are required to. For instance, a simple commercial transaction, in which one person buys something from another at a mutually agreed upon price, presupposes that the buyer and seller cooperate in settling on a price and in exchanging the goods and money that the deal requires. Such economic exchanges are regulated by social custom, and in modern societies, by a complex system of laws that permit the drawing up of contracts legally binding individuals to the performance of the agreement terms. Other laws, such as those that prohibit theft of private property, or forbid others from committing assault, rape, and murder, are part of a social contract that we make with one another allowing us to live together in mass societies with a reasonable degree of freedom and security.

Many people are skeptical about whether there is a single, universally correct moral viewpoint. However, almost everyone believes that there is a difference between right and wrong, and most people understand that difference and can use that understanding to guide their behavior. Ethical decision making, like most other things in the modern age, is something that can be rationalized and practiced in accordance with a technique. The technique of ethical decision making consists in a conscious attempt to get a clear view of the issues, options, and arguments that present themselves in any situation calling for ethical judgment or decision. One should identify all of the *stakeholders,* that is, all of the individuals whose interests might be af-

fected by a decision. One should identify all possible courses of action; review all of the arguments, developing their pros and cons in terms of their potential risks and rewards for all stakeholders; and then, only after having carefully worked through such deliberations, make a rational choice from the available options that has the strongest set of moral reasons behind it.[7]

Moral reasons are those that involve ethical principles governing notions such as fairness, justice, equality, duty, obligation, responsibility, and various kinds of rights. In most ethical decisions, such reasons contend with other, non-moral reasons for actions based on prudence or self-interest, efficiency, and economy. From the moral point of view, ethical reasons ought always override non-moral reasons for action. Ethical decisions concerning the use of technologies involving judgments of value and obligation, responsibility and liability, and assessments of risk and benefit can arise at various levels: the personal level of individual behavior, the level of institutional or organizational policy, and at the social level of public policy. As individuals we are the consumers and users of the products of technology in our everyday lives; as workers or students we belong to and participate in institutions or organizations whose policies and practices can affect our health and well-being, and as citizens, we all must be concerned about the ethical issues we face because of modern technology.

Techno-Optimism Versus Techno-Pessimism

Our attitudes toward technology are complex and often ambivalent. We cannot but acknowledge and credit science and technology with delivering many wonders that have improved and extended our lives, and many people believe that these same agents will continue to solve our problems in the twenty-first century. Many people are, however, disturbed by what they view as technology being out of control and see technology as a threat to our traditional ways of life, to our environment, and even to our survival as a species. These two kinds of attitudes toward technology are often referred to as *techno-optimism* and *techno-pessimism.*

Techno-optimists tend to emphasize technology's benefits; they believe that science and technology are not the cause of society's current ills; they do not believe that technology needs to be controlled or regulated; and they have faith in "technological fixes" that will solve outstanding problems. Techno-pessimists, by contrast, tend to emphasize the risks and costs of technological changes; believe that many social ills are attributable to technology; think that technology needs to be controlled or is incapable of being controlled; and do not have faith in "technological fixes."[8]

Although there are some techno-pessimists around still, even some extreme Luddites and anti-technologists, the dominant view of contemporary society seems to be techno-optimism. The modern idea of scientific and technological progress continues to hold sway not only for people in the developed countries, but increasingly for those in the less developed nations of the world who tend to see development largely in terms of access to more sophisticated forms of technology. But although technological development can raise the standard of living, rapid technological and social change also brings with it social dislocation, confusion, and a sense of disappointment and alienation. Part of the problem is that technology has been allowed to assume an increasingly greater role in human affairs, without there being anyone in particular who is responsible for this change. Some writers see this as a problem, whereas others see uncontrolled or free technological innovation as the source of prosperity and human progress. These different reactions reflect broader differences among individuals in their general attitudes toward technology.

Among the ideas that are being questioned by critics of technology is the very idea of *progress*. Throughout most of history, societies believed strongly in tradition, and changes were presumed to be unwelcome and probably harmful. Kings sat comfortably (or uncomfortably) on their thrones, and when they were replaced through succession or conquest by other kings, it made little difference to the quality of life of the general populace. For most people as late as 1800, life was relatively little different than in Roman times. Then came the steam engine, the railroad, and the automobile. Science finally had something worthwhile to say to technology, and off they went together in an ever-widening spiral of discovery and innovation. Individual productivity exploded in factory and farm. New crop varieties and chemical fertilizers enabled fewer farmers to produce more food than ever before. New products offered unimagined comfort and convenience to everyone. Medical advances improved health and increased life span. In the industrialized world, progress was more than an idea, it was an everyday fact of life, and the cornerstone of progress was technological innovation.

But, in the industrialized world, over a century of uninterrupted belief in progress was disturbed by several rude surprises, starting in the 1960s. Technology could put a man on the moon, but the Cuban missile confrontation reminded the world that we were only a button's push away from global nuclear war. The miracle chemical DDT that promised to end crop damage by insects was found to accumulate in ever-larger amounts as it progressed up the food chain until eagles and peregrine falcons could no longer reproduce. DDT was making their eggshells too thin to keep from cracking. It did not take a genius to realize that humans are also high on the food chain, and DDT was hastily banned. Mountain lakes in the northeastern United States and Europe were found to be too acidic to support fish anymore, and the problem was traced back to acid rain and to automobile emissions and the exhaust of coal-burning electric power plants. Asbestos, our modern weapon against the age-old danger of fire, turned out to cause lung damage in asbestos workers and possibly in people living and working in asbestos-lined buildings. Radioactive by-products of nuclear power plants piled up, and no one could think of a foolproof way to keep them isolated and sealed for the thousands of years they were a hazard. One too many reactors melted down (Chernobyl) and the world was worried. Once the myth of technology as unmitigated blessing was destroyed, some people began looking for hazards posed by technology with as much fervor as had previously accompanied the search for benefits. They were not disappointed; there were heavy metals in the rivers and fish, farmland soil erosion and salinization, lead paint and pipes, houses built on industrial waste dumps, health problems of people processing radioactive materials, smog, ozone holes, radon, and global climate warming. Technology helped in the search for its own defects by supplying satellite photographs and instruments that could detect trace chemicals in parts per billion.

In the lesser developed countries of the world, the picture was often even worse. Some improvements in health care and new products trickled down, but they were expensive, and too often trickled no further than to the privileged elite of the country. When genuine improvements in farm productivity did trickle down to the masses, they fueled population growth that soon ate up the entire surplus. Industrialization proved harder to copy than expected. Industrialization would not work without infrastructure, and infrastructure could not be paid for without the surplus productivity of industrialization. Throughout most of the underdeveloped world, per capita investment is losing the race with population.

Technological Citizenship

Many potential threats to human well-being have been identified, and others no doubt soon will be. Some may be false alarms that are best ignored; some may be early warnings for which action will someday have to be taken; and some may be urgent last calls for which the optimum time to respond has already passed. Moreover, understanding these problems requires a level of scientific and technological literacy that few of our children are achieving in standard curricula. If technology is responsible for many of our present problems, it will likely be technology that will enable us to overcome them, sometimes in the narrow sense of finding a technological fix, but more often in the wider sense that the technologies of democratic decision making and economic restructuring will be used to address and resolve outstanding social problems.

Good citizenship is a kind of moral virtue: being a good citizen implies an understanding of mutual rights and responsibilities between oneself and other citizens, and between citizens and the state or government. Among our rights as citizens are the right to receive knowledge and information about technologies and how they might affect our lives, the right to express views and opinions about the development and use of technologies, and the right to participate in decisions concerning the development and deployment of potentially harmful technologies. In order to exercise any of these rights, however, citizens must first accept the responsibility to educate and inform themselves about the nature of the technologies that are changing their lives, and to understand the ethical and public policy dimensions of the decisions in which they claim the right to participate.[9]

Technologies are not value-neutral. Techniques are not developed and used for nothing, artifacts are not created without good reason, and social labor is not divided and organized for no purpose. In each case, there are human ends and values, which stand behind and direct the technological processes. Technology itself is perceived by most people as of positive value because they understand that through technology we are able to increase our powers and capabilities, and are therefore better able to satisfy our needs and desires. But most people also realize that technological innovations are seldom all for the good, and there are almost inevitably trade-offs that need to be considered: a new drug may help cure a disease, but it may also produce undesirable side effects in some patients and may in the long run promote the spread of new and more drug-resistant forms of the disease; car ownership may enable one to move about freely and comfortably, but it also entails loan payments, insurance payments, repairs, gasoline, atmospheric pollution, car accidents, and other negative side effects.

One of the main themes of this book is that when we evaluate which new technologies to develop, which to deploy, and how to deploy them, we need to consider carefully the benefits and costs, and the opportunities and risks that the technologies entail. Often doing this sort of *cost/benefit analysis* is very difficult because of the manifold aspects that need to be considered, because the costs and benefits often have no common measurement scale (if they can be measured at all), and because uncertainty exists in predicting a technology's long-term societal consequences. For instance, inventors and innovators often have no idea how their inventions and innovations will ultimately be used or what their effects will be. Gutenberg, inventor of the printing press and moveable metal type, was a devout Catholic who would have been horrified to know that his invention helped to stimulate the Protestant Reformation. Edison apparently believed that the phonograph would be mainly used for recording people's last wills and testaments, and would undoubtedly be amazed by today's tapes and CDs. Given enough experiences of this kind one gets the idea that every new technology has known and expected benefits and costs, but also unknown and unforeseen benefits and costs. They sometimes even produce consequences exactly the opposite of what they were intended to produce, "revenge effects." Powerful new technologies alter the social context in which they arise; they change the structure of our interests and values, they change the ways that we think and work, and they may even change the communities where we live. Who, until recently, would have thought that the chloroflourocarbons, which have been used for decades as refrigerants, would be eating away the ozone layer in the upper atmosphere?

Another political feature of technological change is the way that technological change produces winners and losers in society. If technology is a source of power over nature, it is also a means by which some people gain advantage over others. Every technological revolution has witnessed the competition among technologies, and the eventual replacement of one technology or technological system by another. Think of what happened to blacksmiths when the automobile came along, what happened to watchmakers when the quartz-electric digital watch came along, or what is today happening to bank tellers with the introduction of ATMs. In such processes of technological change, groups and individuals whose interests and livelihoods are connected to the older technology are usually the losers, whereas those whose interests are connected to the next wave of technological in-

novation are the winners. However, because the directions and effects of technological change are often unpredictable, it is difficult to tell in all cases whether any particular individual or group will come out as a winner or a loser.

Similar social phenomena are occurring today in the midst of the information and biotechnology revolutions, and the economic phenomenon known as *globalization*. Although the wealthier and better-educated people in society largely remain favorably disposed toward new technologies such as computers, the Internet, gene-splicing, and robots, and toward the globalization of production and distribution that these technologies have made possible, others see these developments as threatening to their jobs and livelihoods, even in some cases their ways of life. New technological elites are being created in each of these fields, while at the same time other people are becoming newly unemployed.

Population and Environmental Change

There is increasing evidence that our technological society is rapidly transforming the earth's environment, and probably not for the better. Hardly a day goes by that we do not hear of global environmental problems such as deforestation, species extinction, depletion of nonrenewable resources, desertification, overpopulation, acid rain, water pollution, ozone destruction, and atmospheric warming. In part, these problems represent the long-term and largely unforeseen effects of the Industrial Revolution, but, in part, they are caused by the sheer weight of human population growth and the increasing demands it places on the earth's ecosystem. The earth's human population now stands at roughly 6 billion. Demographers predict that there is likely to be a doubling of the human population to nearly 11 billion persons sometime within the next fifty years, so that by the middle of the twenty-first century, we will need twice the food, twice the water, and twice the resources we use now. At the same time, most of the world's population growth is taking place in the lesser-developed countries, while rates of resource consumption of everything from oil to personal computers is highest in the more developed countries. Given these trends, many analysts are predicting a widening gap between the "have" and the "have not" countries, accompanied by increasingly chaotic political, economic, and social conditions in the poorer nations where the environmental stress produced by population growth is greatest. Many believe it would be naïve to think that were such social unrest to grow and spread, the industrialized nations would not be affected.

Militarism, overpopulation, social inequality, poverty, environmental pollution, species extinction, global warming and other threats are not unrelated. The links and dependencies between them are all too obvious when we take a moment to think about them. Worldwide arms sales consume about $500 billion annually, or about the same amount as the total income of the world's poorest 2 billion people. Poverty amidst abundance breeds resentment and social unrest, which in turn fuels repression by the ruling elites, who turn to the developed nations to supply them with weapons. The industrialized societies, in order to provide for their own population's overheated consumption habits, are depleting the earth's natural resources and returning to the environment industrial wastes and poisons that are polluting the water, the air, and the soil. It has been estimated that the average person from a developed country has a fifty times greater impact on the environment in terms of resource consumption and pollution than does a person in a developing country. The uncontrolled growth of population in the less developed countries will place extreme strain on their already overtaxed economies and environments.

The threats we presently face all seem to share certain characteristics that distinguish them from standard threats we faced throughout most of our previous history. First, these threats arise not mainly from the consequences of individual acts or omissions, or from forces beyond mankind's control, but from our own collective action. Second, they do not involve direct harms, for the most part, but rather increased risks of harm that are distributed very broadly across individuals, often without their active participation or knowledge. Third, the threats affect not only the present, but also the future, often the distant, incalculable future. Fourth, they do not threaten only humans, but other animals, the natural environment, and life itself. Fifth, they are also to some degree the result of technology—they are problems that have arisen in part because of new powers given to us by technological progress, powers we have not always learned to use wisely and responsibly. Sixth, they do not affect single communities or even single nations, but threaten the whole of humankind.

Our previous ethics has not prepared us to cope with threats of these kinds. Traditional ethics has focused primarily on the moral requirements concerning individual action, on the direct dealings between persons, rather than on the remote effects of our collective action. This problem is particularly important with respect to widely distributed technologies such as the internal combustion engine, where the cumulative effects of individual decisions can have a major impact on air quality, even though no single individual is responsible for the smog. But traditional moral norms deal by and large with the present and near future effects of actions of individual human beings and do not prepare us to deal with cumulative effects and statistical deaths. Traditional ethics, above all, has been anthropocentric—the entire nonhuman world has been viewed as a thing devoid of moral standing or significance except insofar as it could be bent to satisfy human purposes. We have assumed that the natural world was our enemy and that it did not require our care (for what could we possibly do to harm it really?) and nature was not regarded as an object of human responsibility.

In the past we have attempted to fashion our ethical theories in terms of these assumptions. The traditional maxims of ethics such as "Love thy neighbor as thyself," "Do unto others as you would have them do unto you," and "Never treat your fellow man as a means only but always also as an end in himself" are in keeping with the individualistic, present-oriented, and anthropocentric assumptions of our ethical traditions. Even the Christian ethic of universal love, which instructs us to be our brother's keeper, does not transcend the barriers of time, and community, and species. Even more modern ethical theories such as utilitarianism and Kantian ethics do not provide particularly good guidance when it comes to the sorts of ethical concerns raised by technology. In part, this is because they were designed to be used to evaluate individual actions of particular moral agents. But the socio-technological practices that comprise our collective action is made up not only of many individual choices, such as the choice to have a child, or to eat a hamburger, or to invest in a mining stock, but it is also made up of the aggregate of these individual choices plus those of organized collectivities such as corporations and governments. In most cases, the individuals, or business executives, or politicians who are making the choices that add up to our collective insecurity do not intend harm, and neither they nor we consequently feel any sense of responsibility for it.

While individuals view themselves as moral agents, and consider themselves bearers of responsibility in all of the roles they participate in, the collectivities to which we belong do not. The threats we face are all in part the result of this diffusion of responsibility. How then should we citizens of the earth be responding to these environmental questions? Do people in richer countries have any responsibility to help those in poorer ones? Do we, in general, have any responsibilities to future generations concerning the long-term social and environmental effects of our present economic, lifestyle, and political choices?

These are essentially political issues. Political issues are ones in which different individuals and groups within society struggle to protect and enhance their interests against other individuals and groups who have different and often conflicting interests. Politics inevitably involves conflict and compromise. In democratic societies like ours, interest groups form around particular issues and each such group tries to influence the outcome of decisions that will affect many people. However, one's ability to participate politically in such decisions requires that one become informed about the technology involved and its likely or expected con-

sequences, and that one actively seek to have a voice in the way such decisions are made.

All too often, decisions that involve complex or unfamiliar technologies are left to the discretion of elites—scientists, engineers, policy "wonks," and corporate and government officials—even though the consequences of their decisions will usually affect the interests of others who are not themselves members of these elites. These other interested but often silent parties are sometimes called *stakeholders*. We are all stakeholders in decisions concerning technology, but not infrequently, the scientific, political, or corporate elites make decisions about these questions in ways that primarily benefit themselves at the expense of other stakeholders. It is often relatively easy for elites to "manufacture consent" for policies that they prefer by selectively sharing information about the possible risks and benefits of a particular technology policy with the other stakeholders whose interests might be adversely affected by it.[10] For instance, in the 1950s, U.S. soldiers were ordered to witness nuclear explosions and were told that there was no risk of harm due to radiation. In fact, there was a risk, and years later many of the soldiers who participated in these tests began developing lethal cancers.

In order to protect citizens against such unscrupulous practices, the government has established various special agencies, such as the Food and Drug Administration (FDA), the Environmental Protection Agency (EPA), and the Occupational Safety and Health Administration (OSHA), which are mandated to act as watchdogs looking out for the interests of the public and preventing people from being exposed to unnecessary or unreasonable risks without their informed consent. However, the operations of these very agencies often become politicized to some extent because they are funded by Congress and administered by the executive branch of government.

A second line of defense are the hundreds of nongovernmental organizations (NGOs), such as Common Cause, Greenpeace, the American Civil Liberties Union, and many lesser-known organizations, who lobby decision-makers to enforce and protect the stakeholder interests they represent, and produce public information that may enable citizens to more effectively protect their own interests. Such public interest groups play an important role in American politics, and provide a means, in addition to the ballot, by which ordinary citizens can participate in large-scale decisions that may affect their lives for good or for ill.

However, none of these groups could be effective without the support of an informed and attentive citizenry. In democratic societies, individuals and groups are given the right to inform themselves on the issues, associate with others having similar or common interests, and participate in the political discussions that will determine which laws and policies will be enacted. If we fail as individuals to exercise these rights, that is, if we shirk our responsibilities as technological citizens, it is likely that others will end up making these decisions for us, and when they do, they may not always have our best interests at heart or in mind. If we accept the responsibility to educate ourselves about the issues and to participate in the public conversations about them, then we will have some voice in how things will be decided, and some control over the future directions that our technological society will take. In the last analysis, there is no way for us to escape this responsibility, living as we do at the cusp of the third millennium, for we are all, in fact, the children of invention.

NOTES

1. For a rather long, but still incomplete, list of some of humankind's most significant inventions see the Timeline of Significant Technological Innovations.

2. Compare this definition to that found in Rudi Volti, *Society and Technological Change,* 2nd ed. (New York: St. Martin's Press, 1992), in which technology is defined as "a system based on the application of knowledge, manifested in physical objects and organizational forms, for the attainment of specific goals." (p. 6).

3. Corlann Gee Bush introduces the term *valence* to describe the way in which tools and technological systems have "a tendency to interact in similar situations in identifiable and predictable ways." The term "end" usually refers to the purpose in the mind of the designer of the artifact. Often the end is the same as the valence, but not always. See Selection I.5.

4. René Descartes, "Discourse on the Method of Rightly Conducting the Reason and Seeking for Truth in the Sciences" (1637). In *The Philosophical Works of Descartes,* Vol. I, translated by Elizabeth S. Haldane and G. R. T. Ross (Cambridge, England: Cambridge University Press, 1970), p. 119.

5. Francis Bacon, "Thoughts and Conclusions." In Benjamin Farrington (ed.), *The Philosophy of Francis Bacon* (Chicago: University of Chicago Press, 1964), p. 93.

6. See Bruno Latour, *Science in Action* (Cambridge, MA: Harvard University Press, 1987).

7. For more on ethical decision making see C. E. Harris Jr., *Applying Moral Theories,* 3rd ed. (Belmont, CA: Wadsworth, 1997).

8. The terms *techno-optimism* and *techno-pessimism* were suggested by the discussion of pessimism and optimism about technology found in Mary Tiles and Hans Oberdiek, *Living in a Technological Culture: Human Tools and Human Values* (New York: Routledge, 1995), pp. 14–31.

9. The idea of technological citizenship is based on the work of Phillip J. Frankenfeld. See especially "Technological Citizenship: A Normative Framework for Risk Studies," *Science, Technology, and Human Values,* Vol. 17, No. 4 (1992): 459–484.

10. The idea of manufacturing consent is based on the work of Noam Chomsky. See especially Noam Chomsky, "The Manufacture of Consent." In *The Chomsky Reader,* edited by James Peck (New York: Pantheon Books, 1987), pp. 121–136.

Part I

Perspectives on Technological Society

- Historical Perspectives
- Social Perspectives
- Philosophical Perspectives

JARED DIAMOND

The Great Leap Forward

Although modern DNA research and the Human Genome Project show that we are closely related to many animals in genetic terms, there appears to be a huge gap between us and other living creatures inhabiting our planet. Being able to trace the evolution of life using modern science has shed light on the different stages through which various life forms have passed; but Jared Diamond, with his background in physiology, considers the possibility that there was a major, significant event that accounts for the fact that humans became the dominant species on earth, with so much power and influence over everything else.

A MacArthur Foundation "Genius Award" recipient and Pulitzer Prize-winning author, Diamond proposes that a mutation of an upright walking ape occurred around 4 million years ago, which eventually led to modern humans—us. He discusses advances in various scientific fields that have permitted new insights into how different human societies evolved and possible reasons why some thrived while others languished or failed.

Tool making and hunting techniques, art, culture, and other aspects of how early protohumans lived are examined in this article. Diamond also reviews Neanderthals, *Homo erectus, Homo sapiens,* and the ways in which their developments and skills contributed to our lives today. The seminal event that Diamond feels nudged our ancestors onto a unique path will not be disclosed here; you will have to read his article to discover it. This article builds a strong case for the view that what we are today has been influenced to a large extent by our distant relatives and dispels some commonly held beliefs about them.

Focus Questions

1. What are the major developmental stages humans went through since our distance relatives diverged from chimps and gorillas? Approximately when did those stages occur?
2. What are some of the similarities and differences between Neanderthals and more modern humans discussed by Diamond?
3. What are some of the possible reasons that Cro-Magnons replaced Neanderthals as the dominant species?
4. What was the unique human capability proposed by Diamond that made the "Great Leap Forward" possible? When did this probably occur and what made it possible?

Keywords

aboriginal Australians, aesthetic sense, anatomically modern, compound tools, Cro-Magnons, cultural variation, ecological role, hominid, *Homo erectus, Homo habilis, Homo sapiens,* Ice Age, Neanderthals, protohuman

ONE CAN HARDLY BLAME nineteenth-century creationists for insisting that humans were separately created by God. After all, between us and other animal species lies the seemingly unbridgeable gulf of language, art, religion, writing, and complex machines. Small wonder, then, that to many people Darwin's theory of our evolution from apes appeared absurd.

Since Darwin's time, of course, fossilized bones of hundreds of creatures intermediate between apes and modern humans have been discovered. It is no longer possible for a reasonable person to deny that what once seemed absurd actually happened—somehow. Yet the discoveries of many missing links have only made the problem more fascinating without fully solving it. When and how did we acquire our uniquely human characteristics?

We know that our lineage arose in Africa, diverging from that of chimpanzees and gorillas sometime between 6 million and 10 million years ago. For most of the time since then we have been little more than glorified baboons. As recently as 35,000 years ago western Europe was still occupied by Neanderthals, primitive beings for whom art and progress scarcely existed. Then there was an abrupt change. Anatomically modern people appeared in Europe, and suddenly so did sculpture, musical instruments, lamps, trade, and innovation. Within a few thousand years the Neanderthals were gone.

Insofar as there was any single moment when we could be said to have become human, it was at the time of this Great Leap Forward 35,000 years ago. Only a few more dozen millennia—a trivial fraction of our 6-to-10 million-year history—were needed for us to domesticate animals, develop agriculture and metallurgy, and invent writing. It was then but a short further step to those monuments of civilization that distinguish us from all other animals—monuments such as the *Mona Lisa* and the Ninth Symphony, the Eiffel Tower and Sputnik, Dachau's ovens and the bombing of Dresden.

What happened at that magic moment in evolution? What made it possible, and why was it so sud-

den? What held back the Neanderthals, and what was their fate? Did Neanderthals and modern peoples ever meet, and if so, how did they behave toward each other? We still share 98 percent of our genes with chimps; which genes among the other 2 percent had such enormous consequences?

Understanding the Great Leap Forward isn't easy; neither is writing about it. The immediate evidence comes from technical details of preserved bones and stone tools. Archeologists' reports are full of such terms as "transverse occipital torus," "receding zygomatic arches," and "Chatelperronian backed knives." What we really want to understand—the way of life and the humanity of our various ancestors—isn't directly preserved but only inferred from those technical details. Much of the evidence is missing, and archeologists often disagree over the meaning of the evidence that has survived.

I'll emphasize those inferences rather than the technical details, and I'll speculate about the answers to those questions I just listed above. But you can form your own opinions, and they may differ from mine. This is a puzzle whose solution is still unknown.

To set the stage quickly, recall that life originated on Earth several billion years ago, the dinosaurs became extinct around 65 million years ago, and, as I mentioned, our ancestors diverged from the ancestors of chimps and gorillas between 6 and 10 million years ago. They then remained confined to Africa for millions of years.

Initially, our ancestors would have been classified as merely another species of ape, but a sequence of three changes launched them in the direction of modern humans. The first of these changes occurred by around 4 million years ago: the structure of fossilized limb bones shows that our ancestors, in contrast to gorillas and chimps, were habitually walking upright. The upright posture freed our forelimbs to do other things, among which toolmaking would eventually prove to be the most important.

The second change occurred around 3 million years ago, when our lineage split in two. As background, remember that members of two animal species living in the same area must fill different ecological roles and do not normally interbreed. For example, coyotes and wolves are obviously closely related and, until wolves were exterminated in most of the United States, lived in many of the same areas. However, wolves are larger, they usually hunt big mammals like deer and moose, and they often live in sizable packs, whereas coyotes are smaller, mainly hunt small mammals like rabbits and mice, and normally live in pairs or small groups.

Now, all modern humans unquestionably belong to the same species. Ecological differences among us are entirely a product of childhood education: it is not the case that some of us are born big and habitually hunt deer while others are born small, gather berries, and don't marry the deer hunters. And every human population living today has interbred with every other human population with which it has had extensive contact.

Three million years ago, however, there were hominid species as distinct as wolves and coyotes. On one branch of the family tree was a man-ape with a heavily built skull and very big cheek teeth, who probably ate coarse plant food; he has come to be known as *Australopithecus robustus* (the "robust southern ape"). On the other branch was a man-ape with a more lightly built skull and smaller teeth, who most likely had an omnivorous diet; he is known as *Australopithecus africanus* (the "southern ape of Africa"). Our lineage may have experienced such a radical division at least once more, at the time of the Great Leap Forward. But the description of that event will have to wait.

There is considerable disagreement over just what occurred in the next million years, but the argument I find most persuasive is that *A. africanus* evolved into the larger-brained form we call *Homo habilis* ("man the handyman").

Complicating the issue is that fossil bones often attributed to *H. habilis* differ so much in skull size and tooth size that they may actually imply another fork in our lineage yielding two distinct *habilis*-like species: *H. habilis* himself and a mysterious "Third Man." Thus, by 2 million years ago there were at least two and possibly three protohuman species.

The third and last of the big changes that began to make our ancestors more human and less apelike was the regular use of stone tools. By around 2.5 million years ago very crude stone tools appear in large numbers in areas of East Africa occupied by the protohumans. Since there were two or three protohuman species, who made the tools? Probably the light-skulled species, since both it and the tools persisted and evolved. (There is, however, the intriguing possibility that at least some of our robust relatives also made tools, as recent anatomical analyses of hand bones from the Swartkrans cave in South Africa suggest. . . .

With only one human species surviving today but two or three a few million years ago, it's clear that one or two species must have become extinct. Who was our ancestor, which species ended up instead as a discard in the trash heap of evolution, and when did this shakedown occur?

The winner was the light-skulled *H. habilis,* who went on to increase in brain size and body size. By around 1.7 million years ago the differences were sufficient that anthropologists give our lineage the new name *Homo erectus* ("the man who walks upright"—*H. erectus* fossils were discovered before all the earlier ones, so anthropologists didn't realize that *H. erectus* wasn't the first protohuman to walk upright). The robust man-ape disappeared somewhat after 1.2 million yeas ago, and the Third Man (if he ever existed) must have disappeared by then also.

As for why *H. erectus* survived and *A. robustus* didn't, we can only speculate. A plausible guess is that the robust man-ape could no longer compete: *H. erectus* ate both meat and plant food, and his larger brain may have made him more efficient at getting the food on which *A. robustus* depended. It's also possible that *H. erectus* gave his robust brother a direct push into oblivion by killing him for meat.

The shakedown left *H. erectus* as the sole protohuman player on the African stage, a stage to which our closest living relatives (the chimp and gorilla) are still confined. But around one million years ago *H. erectus* began to expand his horizons. His stone tools and bones show that he reached the Near

East, then the Far East (where he is represented by the famous fossils known as Peking man and Java man) and Europe. He continued to evolve in our direction by an increase in brain size and in skull roundness. By around 500,000 years ago some of our ancestors looked sufficiently like us, and sufficiently different from earlier *H. erectus,* to be classified as our own species, *Homo sapiens* ("the wise man"), although they still had thicker skulls and brow ridges than we do today.

Was our meteoric ascent to *sapiens* status half a million years ago the brilliant climax of Earth history, when art and sophisticated technology finally burst upon our previously dull planet? Not at all: the appearance of *H. sapiens* was a non-event. The Great Leap Forward, as proclaimed by cave paintings, houses, and bows and arrows, still lay hundreds of thousands of years in the future. Stone tools continued to be the crude ones that *H. erectus* had been making for nearly a million years. The extra brain size of those early *H. sapiens* had no dramatic effect on their way of life. That whole long tenure of *H. erectus* and early *H. sapiens* outside Africa was a period of infinitesimally slow cultural change.

So what was life like during the 1.5 million years that spanned the emergence of *H. erectus* and *H. sapiens?* The only surviving tools from this period are stone implements that can, charitably, be described as very crude. Early stone tools do vary in size and shape, and archeologists have used those differences to give the tools different names, such as hand-ax, chopper, and cleaver. But these names conceal the fact that none of these early tools had a sufficiently consistent or distinctive shape to suggest any specific function. Wear marks on the tools show that they were variously used to cut meat, bone, hides, wood, and nonwoody parts of plants. But any size or shape tool seems to have been used to cut any of these things, and the categories imposed by archeologists may be little more than arbitrary divisions of a continuum of stone forms.

Negative evidence is also significant. All the early stone tools may have been held directly in the hand; they show no signs of being mounted on other materials for increased leverage, as we mount steel ax blades on wooden handles. There were no bone tools, no ropes to make nets, and no fishhooks.

What food did our early ancestors get with those crude tools, and how did they get it? To address this question, anthropology textbooks usually insert a long chapter entitled something like "Man the Hunter." The point they make is that baboons, chimps, and some other primates prey on small vertebrates only occasionally, but recently surviving Stone Age people (like Bushmen) did a lot of big-game hunting. There's no doubt that our early ancestors also ate some meat. The question is, how much meat? Did big-game hunting skills improve gradually over the past 1.5 million years, or was it only since the Great Leap Forward—a mere 35,000 years ago—that they made a large contribution to our diet?

Anthropologists routinely reply that we've long been successful big-game hunters, but in fact there is no good evidence of hunting skills until around 100,000 years ago, and it's clear that even then humans were still very ineffective hunters. So it's reasonable to assume that earlier hunters were even more ineffective.

Yet the mystique of Man the Hunter is now so rooted in us that it's hard to abandon our belief in its long-standing importance. Supposedly, big-game hunting was what induced protohuman males to cooperate with one another, develop language and big brains, join into bands, and share food. Even women were supposedly molded by big-game hunting: they suppressed the external signs of monthly ovulation that are so conspicuous in chimps, so as not to drive men into a frenzy of sexual competition and thereby spoil men's cooperation at hunting.

But studies of modern hunter gatherers, with far more effective weapons than those of early *H. sapiens,* show that most of a family's calories come from plant food gathered by women. Men catch rats and other small game never mentioned in their heroic campfire stories. Occasionally they get a large animal, which does indeed contribute significantly to protein intake. But it's only in the Arctic, where little plant food is available, that big-game hunting becomes the dominant food source. And humans didn't reach the Arctic until around 30,000 years ago.

So I would guess that big-game hunting contributed little to our food intake until after we had evolved fully modern anatomy and behavior. I doubt the usual view that hunting was the driving force behind our uniquely human brain and societies. For most of our history we were not mighty hunters but rather sophisticated baboons.

To return to our history: *H. sapiens,* you'll recall, took center stage around half a million years ago in Africa, the Near East, the Far East, and Europe. By 100,000 years ago humans had settled into at least three distinct populations occupying different parts of the Old World. These were the last truly primitive people. Let's consider among them those whose anatomy is best known, those who have become a metaphor for brutishness: the Neanderthals.

Where and when did they live? Their name comes from Germany's Neander Valley, where one of the first skeletons was discovered (in German, *thal*—nowadays spelled *tal*—means "valley"). Their geographic range extended from western Europe, through southern European Russia and the Near East, to Uzbekistan in Central Asia, near the border of Afghanistan. As to the time of their origin, that's a matter of definition, since some old skulls have characteristics anticipating later "full-blown" Neanderthals. The earliest full-blown examples date from around 130,000 years ago, and most specimens postdate 74,000 years ago. While their start is thus arbitrary, their end is abrupt: the last Neanderthals died around 32,000 years ago.

During the time that Neanderthals flourished, Europe and Asia were in the grip of the last ice age. Hence Neanderthals must have been a cold-adapted people—but only within limits. They got no farther north than southern Britain, northern Germany, Kiev, and the Caspian Sea.

Neanderthals' head anatomy was so distinctive that, even if a Neanderthal dressed in a business suit or a designer dress were to walk down the street today, all you *H. sapiens* would be staring in shock. Imagine converting a modern face to soft clay, gripping the middle of the face from the bridge of the nose to the jaws, pulling the whole mid-face forward, and letting it harden again. You'll then have some idea of a Neanderthal's appearance. Their eyebrows rested on prominently bulging bony ridges, and their nose and jaws and teeth protruded far forward. Their eyes lay in deep sockets, sunk behind the protruding nose and brow ridges. Their foreheads were low and sloping, unlike our high vertical modern foreheads, and their lower jaws sloped back without a chin. Yet despite these startlingly primitive features, Neanderthals' brain size was nearly 10 percent greater than ours! (This does not mean they were smarter than us; they obviously weren't. Perhaps their larger brains simply weren't "wired" as well.) A dentist who examined a Neanderthal's teeth would have been in for a further shock. In adult Neanderthals front teeth were worn down on the outer surface, in a way found in no modern people. Evidently this peculiar wear pattern resulted from their using their teeth as tools, but what exactly did they do? As one possibility, they may have routinely used their teeth like a vise, as my baby sons do when they grip a milk bottle in their teeth and run around with their hands free. Alternatively, Neanderthals may have bitten hides to make leather or wood to make tools.

While a Neanderthal in a business suit or a dress would attract your attention, one in shorts or a bikini would be even more startling. Neanderthals were more heavily muscled, especially in their shoulders and neck, than all but the most avid bodybuilders. Their limb bones, which took the force of those big muscles contracting, had to be considerably thicker than ours to withstand the stress. Their arms and legs would have looked stubby to us, because the lower leg and forearm were relatively shorter than ours. Even their hands were much more powerful than ours; a Neanderthal's handshake would have been bone-crushing. While their average height was only around 5 feet 4 inches, their weight was at least 20 pounds more than that of a modern person of that height, and this excess was mostly in the form of lean muscle.

One other possible anatomical difference is intriguing, although its reality as well as its interpretation are quite uncertain—the fossil evidence so far simply doesn't allow a definitive answer. But a

Neanderthal woman's birth canal may have been wider than a modern woman's, permitting her baby to grow inside her to a bigger size before birth. If so, a Neanderthal pregnancy might have lasted one year, instead of nine months.

Besides their bones, our other main source of information about Neanderthals is their stone tools. Like earlier human tools, Neanderthal tools may have been simple hand-held stones not mounted on separate parts such as handles. The tools don't fall into distinct types with unique functions. There were no standardized bone tools, no bows and arrows. Some of the stone tools were undoubtedly used to make wooden tools, which rarely survive. One notable exception is a wooden thrusting spear eight feet long, found in the ribs of a long-extinct species of elephant at an archeological site in Germany. Despite that (lucky?) success, Neanderthals were probably not very good at big-game hunting; even anatomically more modern people living in Africa at the same time as the Neanderthals were undistinguished as hunters.

If you say "Neanderthal" to friends and ask for their first association, you'll probably get back the answer "caveman." While most excavated Neanderthal remains do come from caves, that's surely an artifact of preservation, since open-air sites would be eroded much more quickly. Neanderthals must have constructed some type of shelter against the cold climate in which they lived, but those shelters must have been crude. All that remain are post-holes and a few piles of stones.

The list of quintessentially modern human things that Neanderthals lacked is a long one. They left no unequivocal art objects. They must have worn some clothing in their cold environment, but that clothing had to be crude, since they lacked needles and other evidence of sewing. They evidently had no boats, as no Neanderthal remains are known from Mediterranean islands nor even from North Africa, just eight miles across the Strait of Gibraltar from Neanderthal-populated Spain. There was no long-distance overland trade: Neanderthal tools are made of stones available within a few miles of the site.

Today we take cultural differences among people inhabiting different areas for granted. Every modern human population has its characteristic house style, implements, and art. If you were shown chopsticks, a Schlitz beer bottle, and a blowgun and asked to associate one object each with China, Milwaukee, and Borneo, you'd have no trouble giving the right answers. No such cultural variation is apparent for Neanderthals, whose tools look much the same no matter where they come from.

We also take cultural progress with time for granted. It is obvious to us that the wares from a Roman villa, a medieval castle, and a Manhattan apartment circa 1988 should differ. In the 1990s my sons will look with astonishment at the slide rule I used throughout the 1950s. But Neanderthal tools from 100,000 and 40,000 years ago look essentially the same. In short, Neanderthal tools had no variation in time or space to suggest that most human of characteristics, *innovation*.

What we consider old age must also have been rare among Neanderthals. Their skeletons make clear that adults might live to their thirties or early forties but not beyond 45. If we lacked writing and if none of us lived past 45, just think how the ability of our society to accumulate and transmit information would suffer.

But despite all these subhuman qualities, there are three respects in which we can relate to Neanderthals' humanity. They were the first people to leave conclusive evidence of fire's regular, everyday use: nearly all well-preserved Neanderthal caves have small areas of ash and charcoal indicating a simple fireplace. Neanderthals were also the first people who regularly buried their dead, though whether this implies religion is a matter of pure speculation. Finally, they regularly took care of their sick and aged. Most skeletons of older Neanderthals show signs of severe impairment, such as withered arms, healed but incapacitating broken bones, tooth loss, and severe osteoarthritis. Only care by young Neanderthals could have enabled such older folks to stay alive to the point of such incapacitation. After my litany of what Neanderthals lacked, we've finally found something that lets us feel a spark of kindred spirit in these strange creatures of the Ice Age—human, and yet not really human.

Did Neanderthals belong to the same species as we do? That depends on whether we would have mated and reared a child with a Neanderthal man or woman, given the opportunity. Science fiction novels love to imagine the scenario. You remember the blurb on a pulpy back cover: "A team of explorers stumbles on a steep-walled valley in the center of deepest Africa, a valley that time forgot. In this valley they find a tribe of incredibly primitive people, living in ways that our Stone Age ancestors discarded thousands of years ago. Are they the same species as us?" Naturally, there's only one way to find out, but who among the intrepid explorers—male explorers, of course—can bring himself to make the test? At this point one of the bone-chewing cavewomen is described as beautiful and sexy in a primitively erotic way, so that readers will find the brave explorer's dilemma believable: Does he or doesn't he have sex with her?

Believe it or not, something like that experiment actually took place. It happened repeatedly around 35,000 years ago, around the time of the Great Leap Forward. But you'll have to be patient just a little while longer.

Remember, the Neanderthals of Europe and western Asia were just one of at least three human populations occupying different parts of the Old World around 100,000 years ago. A few fossils from eastern Asia suffice to show that people there differed from Neanderthals as well as from us moderns, but too few have been found to describe these Asians in more detail. The best characterized contemporaries of the Neanderthals are those from Africa, some of whom were almost modern in their skull anatomy. Does this mean that, 100,000 years ago in Africa, we have at last arrived at the Great Leap Forward?

Surprisingly, the answer is still no. The stone tools of these modern-looking Africans were very similar to those of the non-modern-looking Neanderthals, so we refer to them as Middle Stone Age Africans. They still lacked standardized bone tools, bows and arrows, art, and cultural variation. Despite their mostly modern bodies, these Africans were still missing something needed to endow them with modern behavior.

Some South African caves occupied around 100,000 years ago provide us with the first point in human evolution for which we have detailed information about what people were eating. Among the bones found in the caves are many seals and penguins, as well as shellfish such as limpets; Middle Stone Age Africans are the first people for whom there is even a hint that they exploited the seashore. However, the caves contain very few remains of fish or flying birds, undoubtedly because people still lacked fishhooks and nets.

The mammal bones from the caves include those of quite a few medium-size species, predominant among which are those of the eland, an antelope species. Eland bones in the caves represent animals of all ages, as if people had somehow managed to capture a whole herd and kill every individual. The secret to the hunters' success is most likely that eland are rather tame and easy to drive in herds. Probably the hunters occasionally managed to drive a whole herd over a cliff: that would explain why the distribution of eland ages among the cave kills is like that in a living herd. In contrast, more dangerous prey such as Cape buffalo, pigs, elephants, and rhinos yield a very different picture. Buffalo bones in the caves are mostly of very young or very old individuals, while pigs, elephants, and rhinos are virtually unrepresented.

So Middle Stone Age Africans can be considered big-game hunters, but just barely. They either avoided dangerous species entirely or confined themselves to weak old animals or babies. Those choices reflect prudence: their weapons were still spears for thrusting rather than bows and arrows, and—along with drinking a strychnine cocktail—poking an adult rhino or Cape buffalo with a spear ranks as one of the most effective means of suicide that I know. As with earlier peoples and modern Stone Age hunters, I suspect that plants and small game made up most of the diet of these not-so-great hunters. They were definitely more effective than baboons, but not up to the skill of modern Bushmen and Pygmies.

Thus, the scene that the human world presented from around 130,000 years ago to somewhat before 50,000 years ago was this: Northern Europe,

Siberia, Australia, and the whole New World were still empty of people. In the rest of Europe and western Asia lived the Neanderthals; in Africa, people increasingly like us in anatomy; and in eastern Asia, people unlike either the Neanderthals or Africans but known from only a few bones. All three populations were still primitive in their tools, behavior, and limited innovativeness. The stage was set for the Great Leap Forward. Which among these three contemporary populations would take that leap?

The evidence for an abrupt change—at last!—is clearest in France and Spain, in the late Ice Age around 35,000 years ago. Where there had previously been Neanderthals, anatomically fully modern people (often known as Cro-Magnons, from the French site where their bones were first identified) now appear. Were one of those gentlemen or ladies to stroll down the Champs-Elysées in modern attire, he or she would not stand out from the Parisian crowds in any way. Cro-Magnons' tools are as dramatic as their skeletons; they are far more diverse in form and obvious in function than any in the earlier archeological record. They suggest that modern anatomy had at last been joined by modern innovative behavior.

Many of the tools continue to be of stone, but they are now made from thin blades struck off a larger stone, thereby yielding roughly ten times more cutting edge from a given quantity of raw stone. Standardized bone and antler tools appear for the first time. So do unequivocal compound tools of several parts tied or glued together, such as spear points set in shafts or ax heads hafted to handles. Tools fall into many distinct categories whose function is often obvious, such as needles, awls, and mortars and pestles. Rope, used in nets or snares, accounts for the frequent bones of foxes, weasels, and rabbits at Cro-Magnon sites. Rope, fishhooks, and net sinkers explain the bones of fish and flying birds at contemporary South African sites.

Sophisticated weapons for killing dangerous animals at a distance now appear also—weapons such as barbed harpoons, darts, spear-throwers, and bows and arrows. South African caves now yield bones of such vicious prey as adult Cape buffalo and pigs, while European caves are full of bones of bison, elk, reindeer, horse, and ibex.

Several types of evidence testify to the effectiveness of late Ice Age people as big-game hunters. Bagging some of these animals must have required communal hunting methods based on detailed knowledge of each species' behavior. And Cro-Magnon sites are much more numerous than those of earlier Neanderthals or Middle Stone Age Africans, implying more success at obtaining food. Moreover, numerous species of big animals that had survived many previous ice ages became extinct toward the end of the last ice age, suggesting that they were exterminated by human hunters' new skills. Likely victims include Europe's woolly rhino and giant deer, southern Africa's giant buffalo and giant Cape horse, and—once improved technology allowed humans to occupy new environments—the mammoths of North America and Australia's giant kangaroos.

Australia was first reached by humans around 50,000 years ago, which implies the existence of watercraft capable of crossing the 60 miles from eastern Indonesia. The occupation of northern Russia and Siberia by at least 20,000 years ago depended on many advances: tailored clothing, as evidenced by eyed needles, cave paintings of parkas, and grave ornaments marking outlines of shirts and trousers; warm furs, indicated by fox and wolf skeletons minus the paws (removed in skinning and found in a separate pile); elaborate houses (marked by postholes, pavements, and walls of mammoth bones) with elaborate fireplaces; and stone lamps to hold animal fat and light the long Arctic nights. The occupation of Siberia in turn led to the occupation of North America and South America around 11,000 years ago.

Whereas Neanderthals obtained their raw materials within a few miles of home, Cro-Magnons and their contemporaries throughout Europe practiced long-distance trade, not only for raw materials for tools but also for "useless" ornaments. Tools of obsidian, jasper, and flint are found hundreds of miles from where those stones were quarried. Baltic amber reached southeast Europe, while

Mediterranean shells were carried to inland parts of France, Spain, and the Ukraine.

The evident aesthetic sense reflected in late Ice Age trade relates to the achievements for which we most admire the Cro-Magnons: their art. Best known are the rock paintings from caves like Lascaux, with stunning polychrome depictions of now-extinct animals. But equally impressive are the bas-reliefs, necklaces and pendants, fired-clay sculptures, Venus figurines of women with enormous breasts and buttocks, and musical instruments ranging from flutes to rattles.

Unlike Neanderthals, few of whom lived past the age of 40, some Cro-Magnons survived to 60. Those additional 20 years probably played a big role in Cro-Magnon success. Accustomed as we are to getting our information from the printed page or television, we find it hard to appreciate how important even just one or two old people are in preliterate society. When I visited Rennell Island in the Solomons in 1976, for example, many islanders told me what wild fruits were good to eat, but only one old man could tell me what other wild fruits could be eaten in an emergency to avoid starvation. He remembered that information from a cyclone that had hit Rennell around 1905, destroying gardens and reducing his people to a state of desperation. One such person can spell the difference between death and survival for the whole society.

I've described the Great Leap Forward as if all those advances in tools and art appeared simultaneously 35,000 years ago. In fact, different innovations appeared at different times: spear-throwers appeared before harpoons, beads and pendants appeared before cave paintings. I've also described the Great Leap Forward as if it were the same everywhere, but it wasn't. Among late Ice Age Africans, Ukrainians, and French, only the Africans made beads out of ostrich eggs, only the Ukrainians built houses out of mammoth bones, and only the French painted woolly rhinos on cave walls.

These variations of culture in time and space are totally unlike the unchanging monolithic Neanderthal culture. They constitute the most important innovation that came with the Great Leap Forward: namely, the capacity for innovation itself. To

us innovation is utterly natural. To Neanderthals it was evidently unthinkable.

Despite our instant sympathy with Cro-Magnon art, their tools and hunter-gatherer life make it hard for us to view them as other than primitive. Stone tools evoke cartoons of club-waving cavemen uttering grunts as they drag women off to their cave. But we can form a more accurate impression of Cro-Magnons if we imagine what future archeologists will conclude after excavating a New Guinea village site from as recently as the 1950s. The archeologists will find a few simple types of stone axes. Nearly all other material possessions were made of wood and will have perished. Nothing will remain of the multistory houses, drums and flutes, outrigger canoes, and world-quality painted sculpture. There will be no trace of the village's complex language, songs, social relationships, and knowledge of the natural world.

New Guinea material culture was until recently "primitive" (Stone Age) for historical reasons, but New Guineans are fully modern humans. New Guineans whose fathers lived in the Stone Age now pilot airplanes, operate computers, and govern a modern state. If we could carry ourselves back 35,000 years in a time machine, I expect that we would find Cro-Magnons to be equally modern people, capable of learning to fly a plane. They made stone and bone tools only because that's all they had the opportunity to learn how to make.

It used to be argued that Neanderthals evolved into Cro-Magnons within Europe. That possibility now seems increasingly unlikely. The last Neanderthal skeletons from 35,000 to 32,000 years ago were still full-blown Neanderthals, while the first Cro-Magnons appearing in Europe at the same time were already anatomically fully modern. Since anatomically modern people were already present in Africa and the Near East tens of thousands of years earlier, it seems much more likely that such people invaded Europe rather than evolved there.

What happened when invading Cro-Magnons met the resident Neanderthals? We can be certain only of the result: within a few thousand years no more Neanderthals. The conclusion seems to me inescapable that Cro-Magnon arrival somehow caused Neanderthal extinction. Yet many anthropologists recoil at this suggestion of genocide and invoke environmental changes instead—most notably, the severe Ice Age climate. In fact, Neanderthals thrived during the Ice Age and suddenly disappeared 42,000 years after its start and 20,000 years before its end.

My guess is that events in Europe at the time of the Great Leap Forward were similar to events that have occurred repeatedly in the modern world, whenever a numerous people with more advanced technology invades the lands of a much less numerous people with less advanced technology. For instance, when European colonists invaded North America, most North American Indians proceeded to die of introduced epidemics; most of the survivors were killed outright or driven off their land; some adopted European technology (horses and guns) and resisted for some time; and many of those remaining were pushed onto lands the invaders did not want, or else intermarried with them. The displacement of aboriginal Australians by European colonists, and of southern African San populations (Bushmen) by invading Iron Age Bantu speakers, followed a similar course.

By analogy, I suspect that Cro-Magnon diseases, murders, and displacements did in the Neanderthals. It may at first seem paradoxical that Cro-Magnons prevailed over the far more muscular Neanderthals, but weaponry rather than strength would have been decisive. Similarly, humans are now threatening to exterminate gorillas in central Africa, rather than vice versa. People with huge muscles require lots of food, and they thereby gain no advantage if less-muscular people can use tools to do the same work.

Some Neanderthals may have learned Cro-Magnon ways and resisted for a while. This is the only sense I can make of a puzzling culture called the Chatelperronian, which coexisted in western Europe along with a typical Cro-Magnon culture (the so-called Aurignacian culture) for a short time after Cro-Magnons arrived. Chatelperronian stone tools are a mixture of typical Neanderthal and Cro-Magnon tools, but the bone tools and art typical of Cro-Magnons are usually lacking. The identity of the people who produced Chatelperronian culture was debated by archeologists until a skeleton

unearthed with Chatelperronian artifacts at Saint-Césaire in France proved to be Neanderthal. Perhaps, then, some Neanderthals managed to master some Cro-Magnon tools and hold out longer than their fellows.

What remains unclear is the outcome of the interbreeding experiment posed in science fiction novels. Did some invading Cro-Magnon men mate with some Neanderthal women? No skeletons that could reasonably be considered Neanderthal-Cro-Magnon hybrids are known. If Neanderthal behavior was as relatively rudimentary and Neanderthal anatomy as distinctive as I suspect, few Cro-Magnons may have wanted to mate with Neanderthals. And if Neanderthal women were geared for a 12-month pregnancy, a hybrid fetus might not have survived. My inclination is to take the negative evidence at face value, to accept that hybridization occurred rarely if ever, and to doubt that any living people carry any Neanderthal genes.

So much for the Great Leap Forward in western Europe. The replacement of Neanderthals by modern people occurred somewhat earlier in eastern Europe, and still earlier in the Near East, where possession of the same area apparently shifted back and forth between Neanderthals and modern people from 90,000 to 60,000 years ago. The slowness of the transition in the Near East, compared with its speed in western Europe, suggests that the anatomically modern people living around the Near East before 60,000 years ago had not yet developed the modern behavior that ultimately let them drive out the Neanderthals.

Thus, we have a tentative picture of anatomically modern people arising in Africa over 100,000 years ago, but initially making the same tools as Neanderthals and having no advantage over them. By perhaps 60,000 years ago, some magic twist of behavior had been added to the modern anatomy. That twist (of which more in a moment) produced innovative, fully modern people who proceeded to spread westward into Europe, quickly supplanting the Neanderthals. Presumably, they also spread east into Asia and Indonesia, supplanting the earlier people there of whom we know little. Some anthropologists think that skull remains of those earlier Asians and Indonesians show traits recognizable in modern Asians and aboriginal Australians. If so, the invading moderns may not have exterminated the original Asians without issue, as they did the Neanderthals, but instead interbred with them.

Two million years ago, several protohuman lineages existed side-by-side until a shakedown left only one. It now appears that a similar shakedown occurred within the last 60,000 years and that all of us today are descended from the winner of that shakedown. What was the Magic Twist that helped our ancestor to win?

The question poses an archeological puzzle without an accepted answer. You can speculate about the answer as well as I can. To help you, let me review the pieces of the puzzle: Some groups of humans who lived in Africa and the Near East over 60,000 years ago were quite modern in their anatomy, as far as can be judged from their skeletons. But they were not modern in their behavior. They continued to make Neanderthal-like tools and to lack innovation. The Magic Twist that produced the Great Leap Forward doesn't show up in fossil skeletons.

There's another way to restate that puzzle. Remember that we share 98 percent of our genes with chimpanzees. The Africans making Neanderthal-like tools just before the Great Leap Forward had covered almost all of the remaining genetic distance from chimps to us, to judge from their skeletons. Perhaps they shared 99.9 percent of their genes with us. Their brains were as large as ours, and Neanderthals' brains were even slightly larger. The Magic Twist may have been a change in only 0.1 percent of our genes. What tiny change in genes could have had such enormous consequences?

Like some others who have pondered this question, I can think of only one plausible answer: the anatomical basis for spoken complex language. Chimpanzees, gorillas, and even monkeys are capable of symbolic communication not dependent on spoken words. Both chimpanzees and gorillas have been taught to communicate by means of sign language, and chimpanzees have learned to communicate via the keys of a large computer-controlled console. Individual apes have thus mastered "vocabularies" of hundreds of symbols. While scientists argue over the extent to which such communication resembles human language, there is little

doubt that it constitutes a form of symbolic communication. That is, a particular sign or computer key symbolizes a particular something else.

Primates can use as symbols not just signs and computer keys but also sounds. Wild vervet monkeys, for example, have a natural form of symbolic communication based on grunts, with slightly different grunts to mean *leopard, eagle,* and *snake.* A month-old chimpanzee named Viki, adopted by a psychologist and his wife and reared virtually as their daughter, learned to "say" approximations of four words: *papa, mama, cut,* and *up.* (The chimp breathed rather than spoke the words.) Given this capability, why have apes not gone on to develop more complex natural languages of their own?

The answer seems to involve the structure of the larynx, tongue, and associated muscles that give us fine control over spoken sounds. Like a Swiss watch, our vocal tract depends on the precise functioning of many parts. Chimps are thought to be physically incapable of producing several of the commonest vowels. If we too were limited to just a few vowels and consonants, our own vocabulary would be greatly reduced. Thus, the Magic Twist may have been some modifications of the protohuman vocal tract to give us finer control and permit formation of a much greater variety of sounds. Such fine modifications of muscles need not be detectable in fossil skulls.

It's easy to appreciate how a tiny change in anatomy resulting in capacity for speech would produce a huge change in behavior. With language, it takes only a few seconds to communicate the message, "Turn sharp right at the fourth tree and drive the male antelope toward the reddish boulder, where I'll hide to spear it." Without language, that message could not be communicated at all. Without language, two protohumans could not brainstorm together about how to devise a better tool or about what a cave painting might mean. Without language, even one protohuman would have had difficulty thinking out for himself or herself how to devise a better tool.

I don't suggest that the Great Leap Forward began as soon as the mutations for altered tongue and larynx anatomy arose. Given the right anatomy, it must have taken humans thousands of years to perfect the structure of language as we know it—to hit on the concepts of word order and case endings and tenses, and to develop vocabulary. But if the Magic Twist did consist of changes in our vocal tract that permitted fine control of sounds, then the capacity for innovation that constitutes the Great Leap Forward would follow eventually. It was the spoken word that made us free.

This interpretation seems to me to account for the lack of evidence for Neanderthal-Cro-Magnon hybrids. Speech is of overwhelming importance in the relations between men and women and their children. That's not to deny that mute or deaf people learn to function well in our culture, but they do so by learning to find alternatives for an existing spoken language. If Neanderthal language was much simpler than ours or nonexistent, it's not surprising that Cro-Magnons didn't choose to associate with Neanderthals.

I've argued that we were fully modern in anatomy and behavior and language by 35,000 years ago and that a Cro-Magnon could have been taught to fly an airplane. If so, why did it take so long after the Great Leap Forward for us to invent writing and build the Parthenon? The answer may be similar to the explanation why the Romans, great engineers that they were, didn't build atomic bombs. To reach the point of building an A-bomb required 2,000 years of technological advances beyond Roman levels, such as the invention of gunpowder and calculus, the development of atomic theory, and the isolation of uranium. Similarly, writing and the Parthenon depended on tens of thousands of years of cumulative developments after the Great Leap Forward—developments that included, among many others, the domestication of plants and animals.

Until the Great Leap Forward, human culture developed at a snail's pace for millions of years. That pace was dictated by the slowness of genetic change. After the Great Leap Forward, cultural development no longer depended on genetic change. Despite negligible changes in our anatomy, there has been far more cultural evolution in the past 35,000 years than in the millions of years before. Had a visitor from outer space come to Earth before the Great Leap Forward, humans would not have stood out as unique among the world's species. At most, we might have been mentioned along with beavers, bowerbirds, and army ants as examples of species with curious behavior. Who could have foreseen the Magic Twist that would soon make us the first species, in the history of life on Earth, capable of destroying all life?

JAMES BURKE

The Pinball Effect

Despite what is commonly believed, a great number of the innovations that make our lives easier and more comfortable today did not result from a "Eureka moment" when the proverbial lightbulb went off in some inventor's mind. Rather, as James Burke illustrates in this article, the technologies we now enjoy often evolved as a result of frequently tortuous routes, linking seemingly disparate discoveries employed by a succession of creative individuals to solve a myriad of problems or to salve their inquisitiveness.

Burke's BBC television series *Connections,* shown on PBS in the United States, illustrated the fascinating ways in which many things we presently take for granted came into existence. This article was a chapter in his book, *The Pinball Effect,* whose title implies a nonlinear, seemingly random path between early discoveries/inventions and modern artifacts and technological systems that we have come to depend on today. Burke demonstrates the ability to not only identify those foundational discoveries upon which future technologies were built but also to explain both the events and their circuitous paths in an entertaining and informative manner.

This selection follows a convoluted path, beginning with an English barrister who became a farmer in 1709 and was interested in how French vintners raised quality grapes without the use of fertilizers and ending with the destruction of a Pacific atoll in 1952. The evolutionary stories behind many of the interdependent technologies we take for granted today and revealed by Burke are both fascinating and far-ranging.

Focus Questions

1. What were some of the factors discussed in this article that helped propel humans from relatively isolated existences to lives where there was considerable interaction among nonrelatives?
2. Do the discoveries/inventions reviewed by Burke in this piece support or contradict Nobel's theory (selection I.3) of technology's masculine emphasis?
3. Discuss the extent to which you feel it is possible to view the paths of discovery described by Burke as comparable to the process of human evolution.
4. Consider how "the grand web of change" might perform in the future as well as the likelihood that we could collectively exercise sufficient control if a threat looms.

Keywords

artillery table, autonomic nervous system, common resources, deregulation, ENIAC, individualism, national market, nature-philosophy, "novel savage," Romanticism, *The Social Contract,* social groups, trigger effect

MAYBE ONE OF THE most fascinating things about the grand web of change is that it isn't so grand. Everybody's on the web, from world-altering geniuses to nobodies. Except, of course, on the web *nobody's* a nobody. On the web each one of us makes a contribution to the process of change. Sometimes even the most humdrum event, in an otherwise ordinary existence, ends in consequences that shake the planet.

Take, for instance, the case of Jethro Tull, a perfectly unexceptional, middle-class Englishman who was called to the bar, three hundred years ago,

at Gray's Inn, London, and prepared for a life of law. Nobody knows what happened next, but he began to suffer from ill health; so in 1709 he left the courts, bought a farm near the quiet English village of Hungerford and settled down to enjoy the less-stressful life of a gentleman farmer. Before long, his ill health caused him to seek recovery in a better climate, so in 1711 he left for Italy and France. By 1713 he was staying among the rolling green hills of Languedoc in southwestern France, near Frontignan.

It was here that events took a turn for the unexpected. Tull noticed the method local winegrowers were using to avoid the unpleasant taste they thought their wine would have if manure was used on the vines. Instead, they planted the vines in straight lines and deep hoed between them with a plow, at regular intervals through the growing season. This method had the effect of destroying the weeds and keeping the soil turned over. So the vines grew well, without the use of manure.

In time, Tull's health improved enough to go home, and when he arrived back in England he tried the same trick on his own farm. Initially, he limited the practice of hoeing to the land set aside for turnips and potatoes, but this proved so successful that he tried it for wheat. Tull discovered to his astonishment that he could grow the crop for thirteen years on the same land without the need for manure. What was more, the yield improved dramatically. Hoeing increased output (which made money) and reduced expenditure on manure (which saved money). In 1733 Tull published all the details of his experiments in one of those printed cures for insomnia, *The Horse-Hoeing Husbandry*. After initial resistance from the traditionally conservative English landowners, somebody translated the work into French. That did the trick. The English gentry thought all things fashionable began and ended with the French, so suddenly horse-hoeing was chic.

The new technique had one major thing going for it: it came along right in the middle of the great English Agricultural Revolution. This had kicked off nearly a century earlier, with ideas like crop rotation and the introduction from Holland of new plants (like clover) that would nitrogenate the soil. The practice of enclosure was also spreading fast. Fencing common land protected animals from predators and disease, kept livestock healthier and made possible the selective breeding of animals that would produce more meat. More food meant cheaper food, so people married younger and had more children. The surge in population generated a rapid rise in the demand for manufactured goods, which in turn triggered the Industrial Revolution.

It was ironic that in Tull's case the French should have had such a beneficial effect on English agriculture, since their own was in terminal decline. The appalling state of French roads made it impossible to develop a national market, so economic activity was fragmented and commerce was mostly local. The restrictive, feudal nature of French property rights meant there was little incentive for new industrial money to buy its way into land in the same way that had boosted agriculture in England. What few French freeholds there were tended to be small parcels of land, belonging to conservative peasant farmers living at subsistence level.

Even if a national market were to be established, trade was hamstrung by a dozen different regional systems of weights, measures and tariffs. The situation was a catch-22: because of a limited amount of industrialization, growing city populations couldn't feed themselves—and so the authorities were obliged to fix the price of bread. However, to ensure continuity of supply in this unprofitable market regime, the law also forced peasants to sell their produce at market within three days—at any price. So there was little incentive to increase production.

Into this mess came François Quesnay, a country doctor turned surgeon, with a boundless admiration for English land management, who might have risen without a trace had he not been in the right place at the right time and caught the eye of Louis XV's mistress, Jeanne-Antoinette Poisson (otherwise known as Madame de Pompadour). Quesnay's total lack of courtly manners and his uncompromisingly direct way of speaking must have had a certain curiosity value in an era of bow-and-scrape, because in 1749 Quesnay became Pompadour's personal physician and was installed on the mezzanine floor (just below her apartments) of the palace at Versailles. Since his new royal quarters were on the way up the stairs leading to Pompadour's rooms, Quesnay got to meet all the visiting notables and intellectuals of the day, including Voltaire (who was, incidentally, a fan of Tull's agricultural techniques). Quesnay's popularity with the royal family was rumored to have stemmed from the fact that he had cured Pompadour's frigidity by taking her off a diet of vanilla, truffles and celery and getting her to exercise.

Quesnay's staircase meetings soon included intellectual luminaries who turned up for Pompadour's regular salons. Among frequent visitors were liberal thinkers like Condillac, Buffon, Helvétius and, above all, Diderot, who was the editor of an amazing new encyclopedia that aimed to present all knowledge in modern, rational form. In 1756 Quesnay wrote two articles for the encyclopedia, one called "Farmers" (1756) and the other, "Rural Philosophy" (1763). In the articles he expounded his ideas on how to cure France of her economic malaise. Quesnay's theory became known as "physiocracy" because it linked the human condition directly to the physical conditions of life. Get agriculture and food production right, he said, and everything else would follow.

Quesnay based his ideas on the belief that the extraordinary advances happening in English agriculture were due to the existence of a national market, where individual producers were free to buy and sell without restriction. The disastrous situation in France proved Quesnay's point: that nature knew its own requirements and that any interference with the natural processes would only destroy the natural order. The results of such interference could be seen only too clearly from Paris to Marseilles. Quesnay's plans for deregulation appealed to land-owing aristocrats, who wanted to be able to sell their products or withhold them from the market, as they chose. However, the fundamental aim of the Physiocrats was to reduce the price of bread, which they considered to be the key factor controlling any country's political stability. "An honest loaf" would save France, but it would come only from the competition that free trade and a laissez-faire approach would encourage. Cheaper bread would generate economic recovery, as it had already done in England. The Physiocrats argued that the condition of the mob in France was so desperate that, if the government did not adopt these new policies, things could turn quite savage.

"Savage" was a new term introduced by philosopher and permanent Swiss exile Jean-Jacques Rousseau, whose influence on European thinking was considered by Napoleon and other movers and shakers to have been primarily responsible for the French Revolution. Rousseau had originally been obliged to leave Geneva for France because of his left-wing politics, spending much of his life flitting between France, England and Switzerland until his death in France in 1778.

In 1754 Rousseau wrote an essay in which he used the term "noble savage" for the first time. In the French world of kings by divine right, aristocrats with absolute power over their serfs, summary

justice and bureaucratic corruption on a vast scale, Rousseau looked back nostalgically on the simpler life of primitive man. Probably with the American Indian in mind, he referred to a savage living at one with nature amid the unspoiled beauties of forest and mountain. He described such an existence: "I saw him satisfying his hunger under an oak, quenching his thirst at the first stream, finding his bed at the foot of the same tree that furnished his meal; and therewith his needs were satisfied."

But from this natural, unfettered existence — self-sufficient and with no need of others — humans had then moved into social groups because of their rising numbers and the need to share resources. For organizational reasons, people had then been persuaded to place these common resources in the hands of a sovereign, who would enforce laws that would keep the people safe. Thus had appeared the concept of rights of possession, as well as laws to perpetuate such rights and to deny those without possessions the opportunity to express their views. For Rousseau this process of socialization had caused humankind to degenerate.

In *The Social Contract,* the work that did the most to inflame the republican passion of the French, Rousseau developed the theme. The original, natural freedoms should be every person's right and should be restored. Laws should only be the expression of the wishes of ordinary people, and it should be the people alone who sanctioned any government's existence by their vote. Those who drafted the laws should have no legislative power. Sovereignty was nothing more than the body politic in action and the "exercise of the general will." Above all, the only possession needed to qualify any individual to vote in such a democratic society was the possession of "feeling," the innate touchstone of truth and goodness that all individuals possessed.

These thoughts did not endear Rousseau's work to the royalist government in Paris. On the eve of the French Revolution, his message was being read aloud in the streets of Paris, smuggled copies of his books were everywhere and clandestine meetings discussed and helped to spread his ideas further. In 1789 he was hailed as the intellectual founder of the new republic. But it had taken more than

Rousseau's words to bring about the collapse of the French monarchy. The last straw was the disastrous effect on the French economy of another revolution happening on the other side of the Atlantic.

The American War of Independence offered France a great opportunity to do what she had wanted to do for years: damage Britain. The sugar-rich French West Indies were threatened by the British navy; French Canada had been lost to Britain; and with French industry suffering from the loss of Southern cotton thanks to the war, it was in French interests to help the American rebels in any way possible. So an already-famous playwright, Pierre Augustin Caron de Beaumarchais (whose works included *The Barber of Seville* and *The Marriage of Figaro*) was co-opted to arrange matters. Beaumarchais set up a fake company called Hortalez & Company to launder the money going to the American fighting fund. In case French ships were stopped by the British, he also doctored cargo manifests for French munitions being sent to America. He even hired agents provocateurs to whip up anti-British sentiment among the colonists.

French public opinion (among the literate few) was generally supportive of the venture. Penniless young aristocrats welcomed the opportunity for advancement and money that a transatlantic military operation would offer. The king backed the project because the prime minister, Necker, had cooked the national books to make it look as though France could afford the adventure.

But whatever the cost, France achieved her goal of detaching America from Britain. Thanks to the arrival of the French admiral de Grasse (with thirty ships and over three thousand troops) in Chesapeake Bay in September 1781 to back up the French siege artillery arriving at the same time from the French garrison in Newport, the British in Yorktown were outgunned and outmanned. Their surrender ended the war. But France would pay dearly for having supplied 90 percent of the rebels' guns and filling the American war chest. Between 1774 and 1789, as a direct consequence of the expenditure on America, interest on the French royal debt rose from about $150 million to about $500 million. Added to the problems caused by the king's unbe-

lievable extravagance, this debt was enough to push the state into bankruptcy and financial chaos. The French Revolution was the inevitable outcome.

But the Revolution did more than remove a corrupt political system. Together with what had happened in America, the new democracies gave birth to a different view of the world. Until then, thinkers and artists looked back to classical models for their inspiration. Science had shown, through the work of people like Newton and Leibniz, that the universe worked according to mechanistic laws. The new thinking of the Revolution saw this as further evidence that science and society had become too machinelike, with individuals reduced to cogs in the machine, and knowledge too fragmented and specialized to be socially valuable. The time had come for a new ethos that would be at the same time much more individualistic and concerned with the union of humankind with nature that Rousseau and others had talked about.

The first expression of these new ideas began to appear in Germany at the end of the eighteenth century. The movement was led by a twenty-three-year-old professor at the University of Jena. Friedrich von Schelling developed what became known as nature-philosophy. He attacked the old Cartesian, mechanistic view of the universe and tried to find a way of bringing all the sciences together in one unified theory. He probably got his initial ideas from K. F. Kielmeyer, a Jena biologist who was lecturing on the sensitivity of living organisms.

At this time it was beginning to look as if experiments with electricity and magnetism would reveal a single, indivisible force that worked together with gravity. The force obviously expressed itself in the life processes and in the will of the individual. So any science that separated the human spirit from nature and its forces was mistaken. Von Schelling's ideas drove the early Romantics to investigate the ways in which individualism expressed itself. What mattered was not a sterile, mechanistic theory of existence but how the senses perceived reality. In music, literature and art, individuals were to be portrayed alone with their feelings, free to seek communion with nature. True knowledge came from the experience of the heart, not the ratiocination of the head.

Naturally, all this imprecision got a very mixed reception from the scientific community. It was said among German medical researchers that nature-philosophy was "the Black Death of our century." But ironically, it was in medicine that Romanticism was to have the greatest effect. It was in reaction against the "mystery force" nature-philosophy school of thought that set Johannes Müller, professor of physiology (which he invented) at Bonn, to find out—physiologically—what actually happened during the process of "feeling." In 1840 he came up with the Law of Specific Nerve Energies. Whenever each organ was stimulated, it gave rise to its own specific sensation and no other. The ear reacted only to sound, the eye to light and so on. And it was the organ that determined the reaction to the stimulus, not the stimulus itself. To the organ it made no difference whether the external event affecting it was light or sound or electricity. It could even be that organs were stimulated by internal events, such as the activity of the imagination. This might explain why people saw ghosts. Müller also experimented on animals and theorized that there might be separate motor and sensory nerves present in the autonomic nervous system.

Müller's 1840 *Handbook of Physiology* made a great impression and got everybody interested in investigating the nervous system and how it worked. It may be because Müller had once said, "The will sets in activity the nervous fibers, like the keys of a piano," that one of his pupils, Hermann von Helmholtz (a surgeon who played the piano all day but didn't like the "new" Romantic music), looked closer at this concept. Beginning in 1856, he wrote a series of papers on sound: how tones are heard and how the mechanism of the inner ear works. Helmholtz was basically looking at an aspect of "feeling," expressed in the awareness of pitch, timbre and loudness, through which a hearer is able to identify one instrument or voice from another.

Helmholtz came to the conclusion that the inner ear contains vibrators, each tuned to different frequencies and exciting the appropriate nerve, so as to transfer into the brain the impulse relevant to that frequency. One day when he was working with a singer, he saw that if a sung note were held long enough, the string on the piano corresponding to that note would vibrate—as did certain others, at intervals above and below the note.

Helmholtz followed up this discovery with a series of sound-related experiments, using an electromagnet to make a tuning fork vibrate at different tones, to investigate what happens in the ear when tones combine. Helmholtz reckoned that the reason discordance is unpleasant is that sound waves from notes close to each other in pitch stimulate cochlear vibrators that are physically close to each other, causing a kind of discomfort. Helmholtz turned all his musical experiments into a highly successful lecture about how sound moves and is perceived, in which he said that all notes are really chords, of which the human ear hears only the primary note.

At the time there was another moving force which was also exciting great interest: electricity. Nobody knew what it was or how it traveled. Did it move, like sound, in waves? It had been known for some time that electricity had an effect across space. In the 1780s Luigi Galvani had used an electrostatic generator to make a frog's leg twitch at a distance. Joseph Henry had seen how a one-inch spark magnetized needles thirty feet way. In 1879 David Hughes, a teacher of natural science in Kentucky, had heard a microphone make a sound when sparks were created in a nearby generator. So when Helmholtz offered one of his pupils, Heinrich Hertz, the chance to write a dissertation, Hertz said he wanted to investigate the mystery of traveling electricity. In 1887, at Karlsruhe Technical College, Hertz gave his now-famous lecture-hall demonstration on how electricity propagates.

First, he generated a large spark between two metal balls. Two feet away, he set a wire shaped into an incomplete square, with the broken ends almost touching. When Hertz triggered the large spark, a tiny spark appeared in the distant wire gap. Hertz used reflectors of zinc to show that the electricity was moving in waves that interfered with one another, just as light did. He used prisms of coal tar pitch to show that the waves were refracted the way glass refracts light. The waves also went through a wooden door. Further tests showed that changes in the frequency of the current causing the spark made waves of different lengths. So electricity *did* behave like light.

In 1865 Hertz's demonstration would have effects nobody could possibly have ever foreseen, thanks to the elopement of an Irish whiskey heiress with her Italian lover. Annie Jamieson, the heiress, had a good singing voice, but her father disapproved of a musical career. To distract her ambition, he sent his daughter on a tour of Italy. During the trip she met and fell in love with another would-be opera star, called Giuseppe, whom she eventually married. The couple settled in a village near the northern Italian city of Bologna, and in 1874 Annie gave birth to a son she named William.

William was crazy about technical things and, as a teenager, was encouraged by a local physics teacher to start experimenting with the new traveling electric force. In 1895 he rigged up one of Hertz's spark-gap generators, linking it to a Morse telegraph key, which he used to make and break the connection so that the sparks were generated in sets of three (Morse code for the letter *S*). William found he could send these interrupted electric waves a kilometer, and with improved equipment the distance more than doubled. When the Italian authorities showed no interest in this trick, William went to England (he was bilingual and had attended school there); after a series of demonstrations for the British Post Office, he succeeded in transmitting a signal across the English Channel.

On December 12, 1901, using aerials held up by kites, he sent the Morse code signal for the letter *S* from England to St. John's, Newfoundland, over thirty-five hundred kilometers away. Thereafter, transmissions took place from captive balloons, from ship to shore, from airplanes and even from the *Titanic* (in time to save over seven hundred survivors). In 1910 the signals were used successfully in the manhunt for the world's most famous criminal, the wife-killer Dr. Crippen. And all the time William Marconi's signals went farther and farther around the Earth, at one point all the way from London to Buenos Aires. So electric waves were not behaving like light after all, since they were clearly being "bent" in some way, following the curvature of the Earth.

In 1902 Oliver Heaviside and A. E. Kennelly remarked that Hertz's electric waves had been reflected by zinc mirrors, and this suggested that there might be a kind of giant reflector in the sky. In 1925 Edward Appleton, an English physicist, used the new BBC radio transmitters to aim a number of signals straight up at the sky, to measure how long it took for them to return and in what ways they had been changed. The speed at which electricity moved (186,000 miles per second) told him that the reflector, whatever it was, operated about sixty miles high. A little later two Americans, Gregory Breit and Merle Tuve, found that signals of certain frequencies were also being reflected from even higher altitudes. Repeating these tests worldwide, they found that the frequencies that were reflected would vary with the time of day, the season and the geographic location.

There was only one thing that would reflect radio waves besides metal reflectors like the ones Hertz had used: ionized atoms, which had lost one or more of their electrons. These atoms became positively charged and would reflect electronic signals (which were negative). This theoretical explanation for signal reflection had already been confirmed in 1910, by the work of a French researcher, Theodore Wulf. Nine hundred feet up, at the top of the Eiffel Tower in Paris, Wulf had shown that the ionization was greater there than it was at the foot of the tower. Then between 1911 and 1912, an Austrian physicist, Victor Hess, took matters considerably further, with a number of balloon flights to an altitude of sixteen thousand feet. The flights revealed that the levels of ionization went on increasing, the higher Hess went. The following year a third intrepid researcher rose to twenty-eight thousand feet and found that levels of ionization there were twelve times what they were at sea level. It looked as if the source of the ionization was some kind of radiation coming from outer space. This radiation became temporarily known as Hess-rays.

Meanwhile, one of Appleton's problems with radio transmissions was that the signals would sometimes inexplicably fade. Fading occurred most often at night and when there were periods of high sunspot activity. Clearly, radiation from the Sun was knocking electrons from the gas atoms in the upper atmosphere and ionizing them. And since the loss of radio signals happened most of all

during the high point of the eleven-year cycle of solar activity, it looked as though when the Sun was
busy, it bombarded the Earth's atmosphere with increased levels of radiation, causing high levels of
radio-wave disruption.

This theory left one rather awkward, unexplained
problem. Hess and the others had found that at the
highest altitudes, the levels of ionization remained
unchanged night and day. So something out there,
other than the Sun, was generating constant, ionizing radiation. In 1933 an AT&T engineer, Karl Jan-
sky, who was looking for the source of interference
ruining radio reception on the latest luxury liners,
discovered that at certain frequencies constant static
was being caused by some kind of radiation coming
from all over the Milky Way. Four years later Grote
Reber, an unknown radio repairman in Wheaton,
Illinois, built a chicken-wire antenna in his back garden and made the first radio map of the sky. The radiation, he found, was coming from all over the universe. Radio astronomy was born, and "Hess-rays"
had now become "cosmic rays."

One of the other things that had been noticed
about the eleven-year solar cycle was that it seemed
to cause the weather to behave in a similar, cyclical
pattern. In the early 1930s a young American physicist, John Mauchly, teaching at Ursinus College,
became interested in correlating the data on this behavior. During summer vacations, while he was still
a student at Johns Hopkins University in Baltimore, Mauchly had worked at the Weather Bureau
and the National Bureau of Standards. There he
learned that although weather forecasting data had
been collected in the United States for over a hundred years, nothing had been done to analyze them.
Mauchly decided that the figures might help to
provide information on long-term weather patterns—perhaps making it possible to predict
droughts, rainy spells and other such agriculturally
ruinous phenomena.

However, it would take too long to process the
massive amount of data, unless some faster method
were found to do the tedious calculations. In 1934
Mauchly happened to be in Chicago visiting the
Barthold Institute, whose director had been a
friend of Mauchly's father for some years. There he
saw a group of cosmic-ray-particle researchers using

vacuum tubes that would react extremely quickly to
signal input. These physicists were using the tubes
to register up to one hundred thousand cosmic-ray-
particle impacts a second. Mauchly realized this
technique might be adapted to do the calculations
he needed for his weather-data work. But before he
could do much about it, World War II would involve him and his ideas in something very far removed from weather forecasting.

The problem with the war effort early on was
that it was way too successful. Allied research and
development produced different weapons almost
every week. These armaments involved new kinds
of explosives, guns, aiming devices, propellants and
so on. All these new technologies complicated even
further the already-complicated business of firing a
weapon, which involves a great deal more than just
pulling the trigger.

When any weapon fires, many factors interact to
influence the accuracy with which the projectile
reaches the target. These factors include a truly
mind-boggling number of considerations: type of
gun, type of shell, type of propellant, type of barrel,
rate of propellant burn, type of primer, type of
cartridge case, pressure of gases in the barrel, pressure of gases outside the barrel, pressure of back
shock, projectile velocity, friction created by the
shell leaving the barrel, gun-barrel bore, barrel distortion from the heat of the explosion, density of
the air, near-muzzle blast-absorption system, resistance on the shell in flight, forebody drag on the
shell, shock waves created by the shell, shell-skin
friction, shape of the shell, angle of trajectory, rate
of shell spin, shell mass, ambient air temperature,
wind direction and speed, humidity, force of gravity, relative height of target, type of target, impact
type required, target penetration required and impact angle. And most of these factors were also affected by the terrain in which the gun sat, the
movement of the Earth at the time and the position
of the Moon!

With these inconveniences in mind, it must be
clear that the principal problem involved in firing a
gun was not the shot but the arithmetic needed to
work out how to do it. The sums came in the form
of a small booklet delivered with each weapon. It
contained artillery tables that would tell the gunner

how the weapon should be fired, under all possible conditions. In the United States, these tables were being prepared at the Ballistic Research Labs in Aberdeen, Maryland, by a number of women mathematicians.

Their task was daunting in the extreme. A typical single trajectory required 750 multiplications, and a typical artillery table for one gun included over three thousand trajectories. Working round the clock, with the mechanical calculators then available, the mathematicians at Aberdeen took thirty days to complete one table. By 1944 requests would be arriving at the lab for six new tables a day. Some faster way to do arithmetic had to be found if the Allies were to go on firing their guns to victorious effect.

In 1942 some of the women table makers started taking courses at the nearby Moore School of Electrical Engineering in Philadelphia, where John Mauchly was then teaching (one of the mathematicians married him). It occurred to Mauchly that the arithmetic anxiety might be assuaged with a device that could add, subtract, multiply and divide, and then store the number until it was needed for further calculation. Storage was the key to success because his earlier work on statistics had shown him that most mistakes are made at the point where a previously calculated number is picked up again, to be used in the next stage of calculation. So what Mauchly had in mind would need to work extremely fast. He had briefly used just such a device in his weather-data calculations. It was the vacuum tube the cosmic-ray researchers had been using, which could react to input one hundred thousand times a second.

In 1942 he sent a memo to his military superiors, with the war-winning title "The Use of High-Speed Vacuum Tubes for Calculating." The Army lost or ignored it. In 1943 the proposal was resubmitted and, this time, was accepted. From then on, Mauchly and a colleague, J. Presper Eckert, worked on the project. The result of their efforts was a giant machine, switched on for the first time at the Moore School, in 1946, too late to speed up wartime calculation of artillery tables. The machine was called the electronic numerical integrator and calculator (ENIAC). It had cost $800,000; was one

hundred feet long, ten feet high and three feet deep; contained almost eighteen thousand vacuum tubes; and consumed 174 kilowatts of power. The joke at the time was that when ENIAC switched on, the lights of Philadelphia dimmed.

Because of the tedious and time-consuming way ENIAC had to be wired up for each job, it was known by its operators as the "machine from hell." Tedious it may have been, but within a few years ENIAC would affect the lives of everybody on the planet. Meanwhile, the tedium: ENIAC used groups of ten vacuum tubes, each "decade" representing units, tens, hundreds and so on. These decade groups could each be fed with an electronic pulse. In any decade a number of pulses would turn on the same number of vacuum tubes. So four pulses sent into the "units" decade would activate four tubes. Two pulses sent into the "tens" decade would activate two tubes. The number now stored was twenty-four. To add another fifteen, you simply turned on five more tubes in the units decade and one in the tens decade. Then to retrieve the sum, all that was needed was to find out how many pulses it took to return the entire system to zero (by turning all the tubes off). In this case, the relevant pulses required would be three in the tens decade and nine in the units decade, so the sum was thirty-nine. Each pulse took only 0.02 milliseconds.

In spite of how complicated the process sounds, once it was wired up, ENIAC was able to calculate in a day what would have taken one of the Aberdeen mathematicians a year. In honor of the women it replaced, the machine was called by the name used in their job description: "computer." ENIAC's very first task was the one that changed the world. It was used to mathematically model the process of detonating the first hydrogen bomb. The calculations took several months, and the result of the work (thanks ultimately to Jethro Tull's agricultural interests) vaporized the Pacific atoll of Elugelab on November 1, 1952. Plowshares had been turned into swords.

In one of history's fascinating pieces of minutiae, it was not so much the hydrogen bomb that would change the world as the fact that ENIAC's fragile vacuum tubes left much to be desired. . . .

I.3   DAVID NOBLE

A Masculine Millennium:
A Note on Technology and Gender

In this reading from the book *The Religion of Technology: The Divinity of Man and the Spirit of Invention* (Knopf 1997), historian of technology David Noble provides a startling account of why contemporary scientific and technological elites tend to be mainly male. Up through the Middle Ages, women played a major role in the practical arts, but they gradually lost ground to men as scientists and technologists came to be seen as a kind of secular priesthood, engaged in an essentially spiritual pursuit of re-creating the world in the divine likeness. Noble traces the development of the masculine image of the technologist in Western culture—from its biblical origins in the Genesis story of Adam and Eve, through the Carolingian renaissance of the late Middle Ages—and shows that women were viewed as imperfect descendants of Eve and therefore as unfit to participate with men in the contemplation of spiritual aspects of the useful arts. Under the influence of Christian theology, human technological innovation was seen as activity reflecting the likeness of men to the Divine Creator.

The association between technology and masculinity continued through the Enlightenment and was highlighted in the works of the seventeenth-century philosopher Francis Bacon, who is viewed as the prophet of the coming age of science and technology. As Noble demonstrates, misogyny pervades Bacon's writings, and partly due to his influence, the devaluation and exclusion of women became a constant theme in subsequent development of scientific societies. Other influential philosophers and authors, such as Auguste Comte and Jules Verne, continued the tradition of excluding women from the world of science and technology.

By the time of the Industrial Revolution, the association between the idea of technology as a spiritualized means of re-creating the world and the masculine image was firmly entrenched. According to Noble, contemporary fields of technology such as artificial intelligence research and genetic engineering continue to be seen as exclusively male preserves, reflecting a 1,000-year-old image of a gendered technoculture.

Focus Questions

1. How has the association between masculinity and spirituality helped to perpetuate male dominance in modern technological society?
2. In the late twentieth century women gained entry in greater numbers to higher education and therefore were able to acquire the knowledge and skills required to succeed as scientists and engineers. Although many women have entered technical fields that are still to a large extent male dominated, are there remaining cultural barriers that prevent more women from entering and flourishing in these professions?
3. Compare the point of view of this essay with those of Bush (selection I.5) and Wajcman (selection II.10). To what extent has modern feminist scholarship been able to successfully challenge and deconstruct the masculine image of technology?

Keywords

Francis Bacon, Auguste Comte, Freemasonry, masculinity, misogyny, Jules Verne

PERSISTENT EFFORTS BY WOMEN in recent years to breach the so-called traditionally masculine bastions of science and technology have consistently proved less than successful. In order to understand why, it might be helpful to learn how these vital fields of human endeavor became traditionally masculine in the first place, and how the history that shaped them continues to haunt and hamper such efforts. In an earlier book, *A World Without Women,* I tried to account for the gendered construction of science by tracing the ideology and institutions of Western science to their roots in the celibate, misogynist, and homosocial clerical culture of the Latin Church, and to suggest that the legacy of this lineage persists in today's scientific milieu.

I want now to suggest that the religion of technology described here might help us to account for the powerful cultural affinity between technology and masculinity in Western society. For, if the religion of technology elevated the arts, it at the same time masculinized them. By investing the arts with spiritual significance and a distinctly transcendent meaning, the religion of technology provided a compelling and enduring mythological foundation for the cultural representation of technology as a uniquely masculine endeavor, evocative of masculinity and exclusively male. Insofar as the technological project was now aimed at the recovery of Adam's prelapsarian perfection, the image-likeness of man to God, it looked back to a primal masculine universe and forward to the renewal of that paradise in a masculine millennium.

Adam signified the ideal of restored perfection, and that ideal was male. So too were the apostles of the religion of technology, the successive generations of monks, friars, explorers, magi, virtuosi,

Masons, and engineers. And so too are their ideological descendants who have designed the hallmark technologies of our own age and given the name "Adam" to the first manned spaceflight, the seed programs of Artificial Life, and the composite human genome. Of course, women might participate, but only marginally at best, because, by definition, they could never aspire to, much less hope to achieve, the ultimate transcendent goal.

In reality, women have always been actively involved in the actual advancement of the useful arts, contributing daily and significantly to the practical activities of human sustenance, security, and survival. As technology came to be mythologically defined as masculine, however, their presence, efforts, and achievements became ideologically invisible. "Women invent, but are not . . . recognized as inventors. This . . . is the whole of the story," observed Autumn Stanley, author of the first encyclopedic study of women's historic and enduring contributions to the development of the useful arts. Stanley has amply documented the full range of female invention from the dawn of human society to the present age, and has concluded, "Women invent. Women have always invented. . . . Women still invent. They invent significant things. They create breakthroughs and fundamental inventions. . . . And they do all this in the full range of human endeavor and technology." "The real question," she argues, "is not, why so few? but why do we know so few?" The exclusive identification of technology with men, on the one hand, and the invisibility of women as agents of technological development, on the other, are, she insists, but reverse sides of the same cultural coin: "the stereotypes separating women and technology." The religion of technology contributed significantly to the creation of such stereotypes.[1]

As late as the Middle Ages, the useful arts were identified as much with women as with men, and women were engaged in almost all aspects of

---

technological practice. Indeed, it was in part because of that female association that the arts were disdained and disregarded by elite men. Carolingian legislation refers to "women's workshops" for the making of linen, wood products, wool combs, soap, oils, and vessels. In a twelfth-century description of the crafts, women were identified not only as weavers and spinners but also as metalworkers and goldsmiths. Parisian guild regulations of the thirteenth century refer to female apprentices, and even craft masters, particularly in the silk and woolen trades. Moreover, the distaff, primarily a woman's tool, was emblematic not only of women's work but of the useful arts and productive labor in general. If some technologies were traditionally identified with men—especially those relating to hunting, warfare, toolmaking, and metalworking, and the ornamental arts associated with religion and state power—others were identified with women; as Ivan Illich has argued, technological activities, including the use of specific tools, were traditionally divided between gendered domains.[2]

In short, the totality of the useful arts belonged to neither domain. Likewise, though guild regulations often specified male hegemony, they at the same time acknowledged respected roles for daughters, wives, and widows of guild members. Men dominated the craft, but they never altogether defined it. Finally, as women steadily lost ground to men, for numerous reasons (including politicized guild regulations, new social legislation, extended markets, the increasing separation of public and private spheres, the diminished importance of household production, the exclusion of women from educational institutions, etc.), their role was relatively diminished in many crafts, although women remained, and even increased their numbers, in others. But this meant merely that men became predominant in certain areas, not that the useful arts per se became totally male. The actual participation and status of women relative to men in the arts, therefore, do not by themselves account for the emergence of so exclusive an ideological identification of technology with men. The relative exclusion of women from the arts did not cause, but more than likely followed from, the cultural representation of technology as uniquely masculine, an ex-

treme and totalistic notion that reflected rather the rise of the religion of technology. In short, the alleged exclusive "masculinity" of technology historically had no reference in reality (at least up until the relatively recent monopolization of the useful arts by professional engineering), only in mythology. It was a mythic rather than a social construct, but one with profound social implications.[3]

The ideological masculinization of the useful arts and the ideological elevation of the useful arts were two sides of the same coin, and both were the product of the belated association of the most humble and worldly of human activities with the other-worldly spirit of transcendence. For it was only when the arts came to be invested with spiritual significance that they became worthy of the attention of and identification with elite males, and the specific Adamic content of that spiritualization reinforced that identification.

Throughout recorded history, men had monopolized the transcendent realms, through their exclusive identification with the ritualized activities of hunting, warfare, religion, and magic. The arts related to such activities—especially metalworking and goldsmithing—had also been associated with the transcendent. Now, for the first time, this transcendent realm was extended to encompass the useful arts in general. At the heart of this change was a renewed emphasis in the early-medieval West, a time of significant advance in technology, on its core monotheistic Judeo-Christian male creation myth, whereby men consciously sought to imitate their male god, master craftsman of the universe, either directly, by assuming a new God-like posture vis-à-vis nature, or indirectly, through a reassertion of their image-likeness to God. The latter reflected a renewed identification not only with Christ—the mythic male Son of God, the last Adam, who symbolized the promise of redemption and the prospect of new beginnings—but also with the first Adam, the mythic first man, whose original but lapsed image-likeness to God inspired efforts toward its recovery.[4]

Just as the Judeo-Christian story of the creation and Fall betrays a decidedly masculine bias, so the recovery of mankind's image-likeness to God was understood by orthodox Christians from the outset to be restricted to males—those whom Augustine called "the sons of promise." God is the male Father of the universe, who creates a son in his image, and it is this masculine divine image which is lost and restored.[5]

In the first chapter of Genesis there is some ambiguity on this point ("So God created man in his own image, in the image of God created he him; male and female created he them"—Genesis 1:27). But however much heterodox commentators used this passage to assert a positive female role in the story of redemption, orthodox commentary, which became the dominant interpretation in the West, either ignored it or treated it allegorically (Augustine interpreted "female" and "male" in a spiritual rather than corporeal sense and argued that the former signified the Church, the latter Christ). In what became the dominant interpretation of the creation story, Church fathers referred instead either to the preceding passage ("Let us make man in our image, after our likeness"—Genesis 1:26) or to the quite different account of creation in the second chapter of Genesis—which thus became far more familiar—in which Adam is created before Eve. Here Adam receives the breath of life directly from God, whereas Eve is created from Adam. (In Christian iconography, God's role in the creation of Eve becomes more remote over time. Initially God is seen removing Adam's rib and transforming it into Eve. In medieval representations, however, God has become a mere midwife, removing a fully formed Eve from the side of Adam, who has, in effect, given birth to her—a procreative reversal common to male creation myths.) Here only Adam, the male, was created in the image of God. This was made explicit by Paul in his first letter to the Corinthians, in which he insisted that women who pray or prophesy must cover their heads, whereas men who do likewise should not: "For a man indeed ought not to cover his head, forasmuch as he is the image and glory of God: but the woman is the glory of the man" (I Corinthians 11:7).[6]

Thus Eve did not share in the original divine likeness. Indeed, it was because of her that Adam, and all the sons of Adam thereafter, lost their divine likeness. According to the fathers of the Church, woman, through her vulnerability to Satan and her temptation of Adam, brought about the Fall and destroyed man's original perfection. "You are the devil's gateway," Tertullian wrote of woman. "You desecrated the fatal tree, you first betrayed the law of God, you softened up with your cajoling words the man against whom the devil could not prevail by force. The image of God, Adam, you broke him as if he were a plaything." Thus did woman bring desolation and death to mankind and take from man his once-exalted role in creation. Because of her he lost his immortality, his share in divine knowledge, and his divinely ordained dominion over nature.[7]

If Eve did not share in original perfection, neither could she lose or recover it: the restoration of perfection was a project for men only. According to the Book of Revelation, the guidebook for two thousand years of such expectation, the possibility of resurrection in the millennium is restricted to those "which were not defiled with women, for they are virgins" (Revelation 14:4). As one recent commentator on this passage noted, not only does it indicate the importance of chastity, or at least continence, but it is "expressed . . . from an exclusively male point of view."[8]

As woman was the proximate cause of the Fall and hence of the loss of man's original perfection, so she remained the perpetual impediment to its recovery. Thus, insofar as the useful arts came to be viewed as a vehicle of such a recovery, they were deemed to be, by definition, for men only, just as the presence of women was, by definition, perceived as antithetical to the entire project. For the restoration of perfection was a male-only pursuit, an exclusively masculine means back to a primordially masculine beginning: Eden before Eve.

The pursuit of the masculine millennium began within a culturally contrived world without women, a celibate monastic environment which prefigured the promised return of this primordial patriarchal paradise. (Ernst Benz described celibacy as "an anticipation of impending perfection.") This masculine milieu had its origins in the rise of monasticism from the fourth through the sixth centuries, but it had lost much of its ascetic rigor and gender purity in the centuries thereafter. In the ninth century, however, under the imperial auspices of the Carolingians, the spirit of monasticism underwent a thoroughgoing reform and revitalization and became institutionalized as a social force as never before, its ethos extending beyond the cloister into the imperial court itself. It was thus during the so-called Carolingian renaissance that men, through the power of the reformed imperial state, were able to monopolize many social spaces formerly shared with women, from the monasteries themselves to the rarefied realms of higher learning. The Carolingian sponsors of such efforts at strict sexual segregation were also avid supporters of development in the useful arts, and it was under their protection, in the writings of court philosopher John Scotus Erigena, that the ideological transformation of the useful arts began.[9]

Erigena inhabited a world without women, a single-sex environment which was reflected in his contemplation on the spiritual significance of the useful arts. In his revision of Capella's allegory of the marriage of Mercury and Philology, where he first coined the generic term "mechanical arts" to signify all of the useful arts and crafts—the totality of technology—Erigena not only elevates them to the "celestial" level of the liberal arts but assigns them exclusively to Mercury. If Erigena was also the first Christian to identify the useful arts as a means of restoring Adamic perfection, which accounted for their elevation, he understood that such a recovery, in overcoming "the sin of the first man," was restricted to men, that paradise would be a world without women. "At the Resurrection," he proclaimed, "sex will be abolished and nature made one. There will then be only man, as if he had never sinned." With Christ's return, as Georges Duby explained the full meaning of Erigena's words, "the end of the world would do away with dual sexuality or, more precisely, with the female part of it. When the heavens opened in glory, femininity, that imperfection, that stain on the purity of creation, would be no more."[10]

It was among the celibate monks themselves, elite men who had isolated themselves from women and assumed the burdens of female labor, that this ideological transformation of the useful arts proved most influential. For the Benedictines, especially the Cistercians, the spiritual elevation and masculiniza-

tion of the arts defined their life, transforming what had heretofore been the most worldly of human activities into an other-worldly obsession. In pursuit of perfection, they mechanized myriad crafts by substituting water-power for woman-power, and thereby launched an industrial revolution of the Middle Ages. In their earthly masculine milieu, they aspired toward another, turning their heavenly attention to the useful arts, as Hugh of St. Victor indicated, "to restore within us the divine likeness."[11]

It was a rigorously reform-minded member of the Cistercian order, an austerely ascetic male enclave which strictly forbade any woman ever to cross their threshold, who gave millenarian significance and hence historical meaning and momentum to this practical project of salvation. Guided by the explicit prescriptions of the early Christian celibate John of Patmos as well as by those of his own masculine cloister, Joachim of Fiore well understood that millenarian redemption was restricted to males—and only those not "defiled by women." In his tripartite millenarian scheme, the vanguard of salvation, the *viri spirituales,* were exclusively and explicitly men only (the word *viri* being unambiguously masculine). Indeed, he identified his own brethren, the Cistercians, as the agents of transition to the new age of spiritual illumination.

If the gender identity of these saints of the millennium was not already clear enough in the writings of John of Patmos and Joachim of Fiore, it became obvious in practice less than a century after Joachim's death, as various self-anointed groups attempted to assume for themselves the mantle of the new spiritual elite. Among these were the upperclass followers of Guglielma, prophetess of Milan. Inspired by Joachim and led by Manfreda and her spiritual companion Andreas Saramita, they allotted the saintly roles of the new age to women only, thereby to ensure an absolute transformation of the corrupt world. Manfreda was to be the new pope, and her cardinals would all be women. They declared that, as the Word had become incarnate in a man, Christ, so the Holy Spirit, guide of the third stage, had become incarnate in a woman, their deceased Guglielma. But for all their zeal, their efforts were stillborn. Manfreda and her companions were burned alive, together with the disinterred bones of their prophetess. And a century later, the female Joachimite Prous Boneta, who likewise believed herself to be the incarnation of the Holy Spirit and the embodiment of the third age—the female agent of redemption as Eve had been the female agent of the Fall—met the same somber fate. There was clearly no place for women in the march toward the masculine millennium.[12]

If for Joachim the new age was represented by his fellow monks, that spiritual mantle was soon after his death claimed by another cadre of like-minded celibate males, the mendicant friars. As scholars in the forefront of learning, the friars inhabited the new celibate male cloisters of the universities. This was the setting in which the Joachimite friar Roger Bacon contemplated the past and future of the arts and sciences. Predictably, he too viewed them as exclusively male activities. From biblical accounts he traced the evolution of the arts as a strictly male affair, the remnant of Adamic perfection inherited by the "Sons of Adam," and he speculated about how their further development might contribute to a full recovery of mankind's divine birthright in a masculine millennium.[13]

As missionaries too the friars roamed the world spreading their message of salvation, as well as knowledge of the arts, and all the while maintained their distance from women. In this they were joined by the great explorers themselves—epitomized by the inspired Columbus—whose voyages excluded women. As these intrepid Westerners extended their horizons through global travel and conquest, they measured the worth of the people they encountered in exclusively male terms, not only by religious but also by technological standards. For four centuries, from 1500 to 1900, Michael Adas observed, these Westerners "assumed that the unprecedented achievements in experiment and invention which they invoked to demonstrate Western superiority"—as well as the native knowledge and tools with which these were compared— "were the products of male ingenuity and male artifice" alone.[14]

In the same spirit, Renaissance advocates of the useful arts, humanists and magi alike, pursued their antiquarian and esoteric studies in an elite male subculture and assumed that only men could hope to recapture the divine illumination they promised. Thus Marsilio Ficino and Pico della Mirandola, whose labors unearthed the ancient hermetic lore that inspired a rebirth of hermetic investigations and astrological imaginings, revived as well the ancient homoerotic ideal of intellectual purity and fraternity that came to define humanist scholarship, an impulse that meshed well with the occult pursuit of Adamic innocence and perfection. Only the "purified soul" of the magus, Agrippa argued, could hope to return to "the condition before the Fall of Adam."[15]

In the manner of Erigena, the great alchemist Paracelsus envisioned perfection in the form of a reconstructed primordial universe before the advent of sexual duality, when Eve still remained within, and merely a part of, Adam. Indeed, Paracelsus believed that he himself had attained this primal sexual reunification within his own person, which accounted for his untroubled "natural celibacy." For Paracelsus, such purity was a precondition of the pursuit of perfection, in emulation and anticipation of its promised end. Thus, although he acknowledged that he had learned some of his knowledge of healing from wise women, he called only men to alchemical study. "Blessed be those men whose reason will reveal itself," he wrote, expressly excluding women from the art of perfection and the perfection of art. Likewise, his apocalyptically minded contemporary Albrecht Dürer addressed his inspirational instructional primer on the arts: "to our German young men I appeal alone." In his famous illustration of the Rapture from Revelation, his first great work, as the lamb appears on Mount Sion, men only await their saintly ascent.[16]

If the Reformation rekindled millenarian hopes as never before, and in the process heightened expectations of a restoration of Adamic dominion, it also aroused a resurgence of related misogynist sentiment. The same early-modern moment that spawned the intellectual ferment of the scientific revolution was also the "burning times" when countless women were persecuted as witches and perished at the stake. From the time of Luther, Steven Ozment observed, "women and marriage were widely ridiculed" and, in particular, "the biblical stories of the downfall of Adam, Samson, and

David at the hands of women had gained popularity." "Oh, why did the Creator wise, /that people'd highest Heaven with spirits masculine," lamented Milton in his *Paradise Lost*, "create at last this Noveltie on Earth, this fair defect of Nature, /and not fill the World at once with men as Angels without Feminine, /or find some other way to generate Mankind?" There were no women in his *Paradise Regained*.[17]

Inspired by the Reformation, the Rosicrucians proclaimed a glorious new age of redemption through the advancement of knowledge but, like the monks and friars before them, excluded women from their blessed brotherhood. Their manifestos heralded the arrival only of "men"—not women— "embued with great wisdom, who might renew all arts and reduce them all to perfection," and thereby restore the "truth, light, life, and glory" that "the first man Adam had, which he lost in Paradise." As in all such masculine invocations of original perfection, Eve has vanished.[18]

The torch of the Rosicrucian enlightenment, and with it the pursuit of the masculine millennium, was confidently carried forth by Francis Bacon. Bacon also believed that the recovery of perfection through the arts and sciences was an exclusively male affair. Like the earlier Bacon, he assumed from biblical accounts that only men had contributed to the historical evolution of the useful arts, and also that only in chastity—"washed and clean"—would they be able to bring about their full recovery. Bacon first wrote of such a restoration in a fragment that early anticipated his magnum opus, *The Great Instauration*. Subtitled "The Great Restoration of the Power of Man over the Universe," its title, "The Masculine Birth of Time," heralded the advent of the masculine millennium. Interestingly, this provocative work, which the Bacon scholar Benjamin Farrington considered "the strongest, and from a personal angle, one of the most illuminating of all his works," was written just at the moment when the misogynist James I, whose patronage Bacon sought, succeeded Elizabeth I, who had ignored Bacon's reform proposals. Written in an avuncular style, the early essay is addressed throughout to "my son," and prescribes the means by which "to create a blessed race of Heroes

and Supermen" able to "stretch the deplorable narrow limits of man's dominion over the universe to their promised bounds." "Take heart, then, my son, and give yourself to me so that I may restore you to yourself," wrote Bacon to the sons of Adam, teaching them how they might regain their rightful reign over nature and recover their prelapsarian powers. Bacon's technological utopia, *The New Atlantis*, one of his latest works, displays the same overtly masculine spirit. No women disturb the serene scientific sanctity of Solomon's House.[19]

The seventeenth-century savants who reverently followed Bacon's lead shared the same masculine millenarian mentality. If utopian educational reformers like Comenius and Hartlib allowed that women should have access to some forms of advanced education, "it was understood," as Frank Manuel noted, "that as a rule they would be excluded from exalted studies." Robert Boyle, the virtuoso who most inspired the generation that founded the Royal Society, was a model saint as well as a model scientist and early committed himself to the celibate life. As a practitioner of the arts, he resolved in his investigations to overcome the "feminine squeamishness" that he assumed had heretofore handicapped inquiry. In the same spirit, the founding fathers of the Royal Society emphasized the quintessentially masculine nature of their enterprise. Henry Oldenburg, the society's secretary, declared that its aim was "to raise a Masculine Philosophy"; Thomas Sprat, the society's historian and chief propagandist, dubbed its domain "the Masculine Arts of Knowledge."[20]

From the perspective of this masculine enclave, women were viewed as a threat to the entire enterprise. Walter Charleton, an early advocate of the mechanistic philosophy and a founding member of the Royal Society, gave voice to the primitive anxieties of the new men of science. "When folly hath brought us within your reach," he wrote of women, "you leap upon us and devour us. You are the traitors to Wisdom, the impediment to Industry, the clogs to virtue, and goads that drive us all to Vice, Impiety, and ruine. You are the Fools Paradise, the Wiseman's Plague, and the grand Error of Nature." Joseph Glanvill, another leading society founder and propagandist, who outlined the Baconian enterprise of Adamic restoration in his treatise on the vanity of dogmatizing, likewise cautioned the "sons of Adam" that "the Woman in us still prosecutes a deceit, like that begun in the Garden," and that their most earnest efforts were for naught so long as "our understandings are wedded to an Eve, as fatal as the mother of our Miseries." With his fellow Royal Society founder Henry More, mentor of Isaac Newton, Glanvill vigorously insisted on the existence of witches, and thereby supported the persecution of women, who were often themselves lay practitioners of the useful and healing arts. Newton himself, meanwhile, another celibate, steadfastly avoided any contact with women as he piously strove, through the study of nature and prophecy, to become one of those he called the "sons of the Resurrection."[21]

The religion of technology and its corollary myth of the masculine millennium were carried into the eighteenth century by the Freemasons, a fraternity that excluded women with a vigor worthy of monks. In its review of the history of the arts, the Freemason *Constitutions* referred only to the contributions made by men. Indeed, the opening sentence ascribed to mankind as well as to the arts an exclusively male parentage, describing Adam alone as "our first parent" in the singular, "created in the image of God," as if Eve had played no role whatever in the story of creation. Later it acidly assailed Elizabeth I for discouraging the development of the Art "because, being a WOMAN, she could not be made a Mason." Although Masonic lodges, like Cistercian monasteries, were called "mothers" and "sisters," the *Constitutions* explicitly and repeatedly excluded women from membership. Masonic practice went further, again in imitation of the Cistercians, preventing women from ever crossing the thresholds of these sacred male redoubts, which were predicated upon male-bonding rites of resurrection.[22]

A few women were briefly admitted to some lodges in revolutionary France, as Margaret Jacob has shown, but these were rare and officially condemned exceptions to the rule according to which women were excluded as "profane." A French Masonic almanac strongly advised "banishing in our assemblies the Sexe Enchanteur," and a pro-

posal on admitting women evoked a Masonic outburst decrying women as "a vain sex, indiscreet and fickle . . . possessed of dangerous instincts. . . . We know women, their foolish spirit, their inconsequential heart. . . . Inconstancy is her only element." (This negative image of woman was represented by the Queen of the Night, who made war against the Solomonic Sarastro in Mozart's Masonic opera *The Magic Flute*.)[23]

In an initiation ritual in a Masonic lodge in Amsterdam, the initiate was asked, "In what place was the first Lodge formed?" To this he was instructed to reply, in true monastic fashion, "Upon a mountain inaccessible to the profane, where a Cock was never heard to crow, a lion to roar, or a woman to babble." When the wife of the Spanish ambassador managed to pay a brief visit to another Amsterdam lodge, as one member later recounted, the brothers were instructed, in the same monastic spirit, steadfastly to avoid the contagion. "Finally she was permitted. But before she entered, the Grand Masters asked us to cover ourselves by putting on our hats; not to look at the lady, in order to signal our disdain at all that is profane. And she entered and exited without anyone having looked at her or having given any attention to her." In the words of one late-eighteenth-century Freemason from Exeter, women were banned "because their presence might insensibly alter the purity of our maxims." "Only the friendship of men," declared the members of a new French lodge in 1761, "could produce the harmony sought in Masonic society."[24]

Thus, in Freemasonry too the mythology of the masculine millennium inspired and defined the technological imagination, which was now to become incarnate, largely through Masonic agency, in engineering. By the end of the eighteenth century, Nicholas Hans observed, it was assumed that "any sound knowledge of 'useful arts and sciences' was definitely intended for boys only," and engineering was from the outset a decidedly male occupation. No doubt the formative military influence on engineering contributed to its overtly masculine character, as did the determinedly masculine mentality of the men of science who shared in its parentage and monopolized the institutions of higher learning. But ideology, specifically the religion of technology, shaped it too. As the personification of the Baconian union of science and the useful arts and the embodiment of the religion of technology that inspired it, the engineers epitomized the mythology of the masculine millennium. Held together by their own male-bonding rituals of initiation, which they inherited from the Masons, they displayed a vigorous and vigilant disdain for women and the feminine, and kept their distance lest they too, as the new Adam, forfeit their God-given powers.[25]

The culture of engineering has remained emphatically male-centered. "Engineering contains the smallest proportion of females of all major professions," sociologist Sally Hacker wrote, "and projects a heavily masculine image hostile to women." In her extended studies of the collective psychology of engineers, Hacker found that as a group they shared a starkly stratified Cartesian outlook, devaluing the body and the earth (identified with the feminine) in favor of the mind, the abstract, the mathematical. Through sacrifice, she suggested—a "second nature" fashioned in their own image—they sought to compensate for their social, sexual, and procreative anxieties, secure their command over the earth, and confirm their unrivaled centrality in creation.[26]

Auguste Comte, their true herald, identified the engineers as the magi of modern industry, destined to restore mankind's dominion over nature and regain the presumed primal male monopoly over the arts. Although Comte displayed a sentimental reverence for women and, late in his life, based his new religion upon the bizarre worship of his dear departed Clothilde, he nevertheless firmly believed that women were inferior beings incapable of either industrial leadership or scientific thought. In identifying women as the wellspring of love and compassion, he consigned them solely to the domestic sphere, and emphatically disqualified them from participation in the advance of modern industry, of which engineering was emblematic. Indeed, he confidently assumed, as he wrote to John Stuart Mill, that "the natural movement of our industry certainly tends gradually to pass to men the professions long exercised by women."[27]

It was at this moment that the term "technology" came into use to describe the realm of the useful arts, reshaped by science, and from the start the idea of technology became the modern measure of elite masculine identity. In the exaggeratedly masculine image of engineering especially, technological development assumed its modern appearance as a "traditionally masculine" enterprise—a mythic male affair against which women would forever have to struggle to reassert even a semblance of their former role in the useful arts. Since technology was defined from the outset as masculine, rooted as it was in the religion of technology and, hence, in the myth of a masculine millennium, women were, by definition, excluded, and whatever women did was, by definition, not included. Thus emerged what Autumn Stanley called "the stereotypes separating woman and technology," which legitimized the displacement of women, rendered their continuing contributions all but invisible, and left an indelible masculine imprint on the hallmark technological achievements of the age.

When William Broad visited the high-technology, high-security compound of the "Star Warriors" at the Lawrence Livermore Laboratories, he found that "there were no women. . . . The offices and hallways were alive with young men [but] women were nowhere to be seen." ("Just like the engineering or physics departments of any major university in America," he added.) Robert Jay Lifton noted that there was a hierarchy of esteem as well as power in this community, with the highest regard accorded the "'sons' and 'grandsons'" of Edward Teller, direct descendants of the patriarch of doom. In her study of the "nuclear language" of the "defense intellectuals," Carol Cohn described the vivid vocabulary of male competition and sexual domination that routinely came into play in discussions of nuclear warfare, and the overt phallic imagery of missiles. She and others, particularly Brian Easlea, also noted the recurring pseudo-maternal metaphors used to describe the development and detonation of atomic and hydrogen bombs from the beginning, a rhetorical masculine appropriation of the female powers of procreation which is a tell-tale reflection of a womanless world.[28]

If the engineers of Armageddon described the creation and "delivery" of their weapons as births, Wernher von Braun described at least one birth, that of his secretary's child, as a "successful blastoff."

His world too, the enchanted enclave of space enthusiasts, was a preponderantly male domain equally marked by imagery of exclusively patriarchal procreation. This was not merely an artifact of its military origins. At the height of NASA activities, in the 1960s and 1970s, women constituted only between 2 and 3 percent of the scientific and engineering workforce (and 92 percent of clerical staff). Ian Mitroff observed an ethos of "intense masculinity" that characterized the culture of the Apollo Project. Until the space-shuttle program, all of the astronauts were men. A study on the social and psychological implications of the space program done for NASA by the Brookings Institution noted that the risk-defying "macho" astronauts were "not models for other women's husbands," and that "part of the feeling about space, which spreads right throughout the country, is women's objection to men's going there."[29]

The thoroughly masculine milieu and spirit of the space program faithfully brought to life the fantasies of its foremost visionary and inspiration, Jules Verne, "a man whom his family biographers call a misogynist." Throughout his life, Verne betrayed "a bitterness about women." Early in his career, he was a member of an elite literary dining club which called itself "onze sans Femmes," eleven without women, and throughout his long married life, he kept his distance from both his wife and his child. Verne viewed the world of science especially as an exclusively male endeavor. In a speech at a girls' school late in his life, he warned his female audience to steer clear of science and concentrate instead upon their domestic duties and destiny. "Little girls and big ones, be careful not to lose your way by running after the sciences," said Verne. "Do not plunge too deeply into science, that 'sublime emptiness' . . . wherein a man may sometimes lose himself."[30]

Verne's writings resounded with the enticements of that "sublime emptiness" as well as not a little "misogynist streak." His heroes were "peripatetic voyagers" perpetually in flight from hearth and home (and women) and steadfastly in search of some supreme fulfillment. The members of his notorious Gun Club were all men, and they exuded a mentality, inhabited a milieu, and expressed themselves in metaphors (particularly the "pre-eminently male expulsive form of the cannon") that were all at once militaristic, misogynist, monkish, apocalyptic, and transcendent—the epitome of masculine millenarianism. This was most explicit in *Sans Dessus Dessous,* the sequel and fulfillment of his *From the Earth to the Moon.*[31]

In this incredible story, the Gun Club's inspired effort to correct the earth's axis by firing off an enormous cannon buried deep into the earth ends in failure because of the ill-timed act of a woman. Distracted by a call from Mrs. Scorbitt proposing marriage, the Gun Club's leader, Maston, miscalculates the measurement of the earth's circumference, thereby dooming the mission. "Thus the fault from which the savant's downfall follows can be attributed to a woman," Verne critic Andrew Martin noted. "From the beginning of the novel, woman is denounced as the antithesis of the scientist. Maston, invoking the figure of Eve, identifies woman with the earthy, the material, the sensual, whereas man, in the figure of Newton, is credited with transcendence: while the one merely eats the apple, the other derives from it the fundamental laws of nature. . . . The text can thus be read as a re-enactment of the Fall to which it alludes at its opening: the proud and celibate Vernian bachelor succumbs to feminine guile and sheer persistence. The male paradise of perfect knowledge and control over the environment is shattered by less abstract desire."[32]

In short, in his "juvenile technological utopias," Verne offered perhaps the quintessential modern evocation of the mythology of the masculine millennium, a mythology that resonated especially in the impressionable adolescent minds of earnest young men eager to prove their manhood. This most likely explains his appeal, the remarkable fact that, by their own testimony, nearly all of the pioneers of spaceflight, and a good many later enthusiasts, were as youths so inspired by Verne's vision that they resolved to dedicate their lives to making it a reality.[33]

The same mentality was also abundantly evident in the masculine domain of Artificial Intelligence, where it was simply assumed that the immortal mind was male. ("There was a standard saying in our family about Newell men, and how they were somehow so much greater than the women," Allen Newell later remembered.) Steven Levy found that the reclusive world of the computer "hackers" who developed Artificial Intelligence was characterized by "an exclusively male culture." "There were women programmers and some of them were good," he noted, "but none seemed to take hacking as a holy calling the way [the men] did. Even the substantial cultural bias against women getting into serious computing does not explain the utter lack of female hackers."[34]

At least one hacker attributed their absence "to 'genetic' or 'hardware' differences," but the close-knit, male-only cliques that typically formed the core of academic Artificial Intelligence centers probably posed the real barrier, along with the obsessive masculine computer culture these reflected. "Men tend to be seduced by the technology itself," said Oliver Strimpel, executive director of the Computer Museum in Boston. "To the truly besotted, computers are a virtual religion. . . . This is not something to be trifled with by mere females, who seem to think that machines were meant to be *used* . . . interesting and convenient on the job but not worthy of obsession." This same culture was evident among the "postpubescent men" of cyberspace, as well as those who inhabited the rarefied realm of Artificial Life. "Many of the engineers currently debating the form and nature of cyberspace," sociologist Allucquere Rosanne Stone noted, "are the young turks of computer engineering, men in their late teens and twenties. . . ." The programmers, she found, were "almost exclusively male."[35]

"While there are certainly exceptions, many of the people doing the work of A-life simulation at the Santa Fe Institute are men, while most of the staff supporting the bodily and worldly needs of the researchers are women," observed anthropologist Stefan Heimreich. These men tended to hold a "spermist view of procreation," and were partial to patrilinear lines of descent, which were evident in their simulations and nomenclature. One researcher disdainfully described the actual woman-centered process of pregnancy and parturition as "an implementation problem."[36]

Finally, the brave new world of genetic engineering reflected the same masculine millenarian culture, not only in its masculine ideal of Adamic perfection (and parallel preoccupation with artificial reproduction) but also in its own patterns of social relations. The woeful experience of X-ray crystallographer Rosalind Franklin, who died before her crucial contribution to the deciphering of the structure of DNA was ever acknowledged, testified to the plight of women in this essentially masculine world. Only much later, in the epilogue of his account of the discovery of the double helix, did James Watson pay belated tribute to Franklin and her work (which he had used without her knowledge or consent), "realizing years too late the struggles that the intelligent woman faces to be accepted by a scientific world which often regards women as mere diversions from serious thinking." But the situation had hardly changed. Nearly all of the acknowledged pioneers of recombinant DNA technology were men, as were the foremost architects of the Human Genome Project and practitioners of gene therapy. Such are the new spiritual men of our age, bearers of ancient masculine millenarian dreams now about to be realized. And with the advent of human cloning at hand, human reproduction may at last become their own preserve, a chaste male affair, "not defiled with women."[37]

"The changes which have taken place during the last centuries and which we sum up under the compendious term 'modern civilization,'" wrote the early-twentieth-century feminist Olive Schreiner in her classic *Woman and Labour,* "have tended to rob woman, not merely in part but almost wholly, of the more valuable part of her ancient domain of production and social labour." If women still labored mightily for human survival and continued to invent useful ways to lighten the load of mankind, their efforts went unnoticed, unrewarded, and unsung. For the advance of technology was now aimed at loftier, more transcendent, goals. As Schreiner's contemporary Sherwood Anderson observed, in an insightful essay about the mystical marriage between men and machines: "In a factual age, woman will always rule. . . . But let her come over into my own male world, the world of fancy, and surely I will lose her there."[38]

NOTES

1. Autumn Stanley, *Mothers and Daughters of Invention* (Metuchen, N.J.: Scarecrow Press, 1993), pp. 747, xxxvii.

2. Paola Tabet, "Hands, Tools, Weapons," *Feminist Issues,* vol. 2, no. 2 (Fall 1982), pp. 3–62; Emilie Amt, ed., *Women's Lives in Medieval Europe* (New York: Routledge, 1993), pp. 179, 194, 197; Martha C. Howell, *Women, Production, and Patriarchy in Late Medieval Cities* (Chicago: University of Chicago Press, 1986), pp. 2–5; see also Ivan Illich, *Gender* (New York: Pantheon, 1982), pp. 88–102.

3. Howell, *Women, Production, and Patriarchy,* passim; see also Olive Schreiner, *Woman and Labour* (Cape of Good Hope, South Africa: Frederick A. Stokes, 1911); Ivy Pinchbeck, *Women Workers and the Industrial Revolution* (London: Cass, 1969).

4. Tabet, "Hands, Tools, Weapons"; Jacques Le Goff, *Time, Work, and Culture in the Middle Ages* (Chicago: University of Chicago Press, 1980), p. 186.

5. St. Augustine, *The City of God* (Garden City, N.Y.: Doubleday, 1958), pp. 526–27.

6. Book of Genesis 1:27, 1:26; Gerhart B. Ladner, *The Idea of Reform* (New York: Harper and Row, 1967), pp. 173, 233, 59; Arnold Williams, *The Common Expositor: An Account of the Commentaries on Genesis, 1527–1633* (Chapel Hill: University of North Carolina Press, 1948), p. 26.

7. Tertullian, "Disciplinary, Moral, and Ascetical Works," quoted in Marina Warner, *Alone of All Her Sex* (New York: Alfred A. Knopf, 1976), p. 58.

8. Adela Yerbro Collins, *Crisis and Catharsis: The Power of the Apocalypse* (Philadelphia: Westminster Press, 1984), pp. 127, 129, 131; Kevin Harris, *Sex, Ideology and Religion: The Representation of Women in the Bible* (Totowa, N.J.: Barnes and Noble, 1984), pp. 112–13.

9. Ernst Benz, *Evolution and Christian Hope* (Garden City, N.Y.: Doubleday, 1975), p. 13; on the historical evolution of this clerical world without women, see David F. Noble, *A World Without Women: The Christian Clerical Culture of Western Science* (New York: Alfred A. Knopf, 1992), part two.

10. Erigena, quoted in Georges Duby, *The Knight, The Lady, and the Priest* (New York: Pantheon, 1983), p. 50; ibid., p. 51.

11. Jean Gimpel, *The Medieval Machine: The Industrial Revolution of the Middle Ages* (London: Penguin, 1977), passim; Hugh, quoted in George Ovitt, *The Restoration of Perfection* (New Brunswick, N.J.: Rutgers University Press, 1986), p. 120.

12. Marjorie Reeves, *The Influence of Prophecy in the Later Middle Ages: A Study in Joachimism* (Oxford: Oxford University Press, 1969), pp. 248–50.

13. Roger Bacon, *The Opus Majus of Roger Bacon* (New York: Russell and Russell, 1962), pp. 52, 56.

14. Michael Adas, *Machines as the Measure of Men: Science, Technology and Ideologies of Western Dominance* (Ithaca, N.Y.: Cornell University Press, 1989), pp. 13–14.

15. Charles G. Nauert, Jr., *Agrippa and the Crisis of Renaissance Thought* (Urbana: University of Illinois Press, 1965), pp. 48, 284.

16. Franz Hartmann, *The Life and Doctrines of Philippus Theophrastus* (New York: Theosophical Publishing Company, 1910), pp. 99–101; Wilhelm Waetzgoldt, *Dürer and His Time* (London: Phaidon Press, 1950), p. 207.

17. Steven Ozment, *Protestants: The Birth of a Revolution* (New York: Doubleday, 1992), pp. 151–52; John Milton, *Paradise Lost* (New York: Macmillan, 1993), p. 571 (bk. 10, lines 888–95).

18. Frances Yates, *The Rosicrucian Enlightenment* (Boulder: Shambala Press, 1978), p. 47.

19. Francis Bacon, "De Augmentis," quoted in Williams, *Common Expositor,* p. 81; Francis Bacon, "The Masculine Birth of Time," in Benjamin Farrington, *The Philosophy of Francis Bacon* (Chicago: University of Chicago Press, 1964), pp. 533–54; Francis Bacon, "History of Winds," in Benjamin Farrington, ed., *The Works of Francis Bacon* (Philadelphia: Carey and Hart, 1848), vol. 1, p. 54; Carolyn Merchant, *The Death of Nature* (New York: Harper and Row, 1980), pp. 172–74, 181.

20. Frank E. Manuel, *Freedom from History* (New York: New York University Press, 1971), p. 109; Robert Boyle, "Of the Usefulness of Natural Philosophy," in *Works of the Honorable Robert Boyle* (London, 1772), vol. 2 p. 14; Robert Boyle, *On Seraphic Love: Motives and Incentives to the Love of God* (London: Henry Herrington, 1661); Oldenburg, quoted in Evelyn Fox Keller, *Reflections on Gender and Science* (New Haven: Yale University Press, 1985), p. 52; Sprat, quoted in Londa Schiebinger, *The Mind Has No Sex? Women in the Origins of Modern Science* (Cambridge, Mass.: Harvard University Press, 1989), p. 138.

21. Walter Charleton, quoted in Brian Easlea, *Witch-Hunting, Magic, and the New Philosophy* (Brighton, England: Harvester Press, 1980), p. 242; Joseph Glanvill, *The Vanity of Dogmatizing* (New York: Columbia University Press, 1931), p. 6; Frank E.

Manuel, *The Religion of Isaac Newton* (Oxford: Oxford University Press, 1974), pp. 99, 100.

22. *The Constitutions of the Free-Masons* (New York: J. W. Leonard, 1855), pp. 1, 38, 51; Abner Cohen, "The Politics of Ritual Secrecy," *Man,* vol. 6 (Sept. 1977), p. 121.

23. Margaret Jacob, *Living the Enlightenment* (New York: Oxford University Press, 1991), pp. 21, 122, 126–27, 121.

24. Ibid., pp. 135, 139, 125, 122; Margaret Jacob, "Freemasonry and the Utopian Impulse," in Richard H. Popkin, ed., *Millenarianism and Messianism in English Literature and Thought, 1650–1800* (Leiden: E. J. Brill, 1988), p. 141.

25. Nicholas Hans, *New Trends in Education in the Eighteenth Century* (London: Routledge and Kegan Paul, 1951), p. 208.

26. Sally Hacker, "The Culture of Engineering: Women, Workplace and Machine," *Women's Studies International Quarterly,* vol. 4, no. 3 (1981), pp. 341–43.

27. Auguste Comte to John Stuart Mill, Oct. 5, 1843, reprinted in Kenneth Thompson, *Auguste Comte: The Foundation of Sociology* (New York: John Wiley and Sons, 1975).

28. William J. Broad, *Star Warriors: A Penetrating Look into the Lives of the Young Scientists Behind Our Space Age Weaponry* (New York: Simon and Schuster, 1985), p. 25; Robert Jay Lifton and Eric Markusen, *The Genocidal Mentality* (New York: Basic Books, 1988), p. 118; Carol Cohn, "Nuclear Language," *Bulletin of the Atomic Scientists,* June 1987, p. 68.

29. Erik Bergaust, *Wernher von Braun* (Washington, D.C.: National Space Institute, 1976), p. 499; *Historical Data Book IV* (Washington, D.C.: NASA, 1994), p. 104; Ian Mitroff, *The Subjective Side of Science* (Amsterdam: Elsevier, 1974), p. 144; Donald N. Michael et al., "Summary of Proposed Studies on the Implications of Peaceful Space Activities for Human Affairs," report to NASA by Brookings Institution, Dec. 1960.

30. Jean Chesneaux, *The Political and Social Ideas of Jules Verne* (London: Thames and Hudson, 1972), pp. 82, 16; Peter Costello, *Jules Verne, Inventor of Science Fiction* (London: Hodder and Stoughton, 1978), pp. 31, 35.

31. Costello, *Jules Verne,* p. 35; Andrew Martin, *The Knowledge of Ignorance: From Genesis to Jules Verne* (Cambridge: Cambridge University Press, 1985), p. 189.

32. Martin, *Knowledge,* p. 189.

33. Ibid., p. 215.

34. Newell, quoted in Pamela McCorduck, *Machines Who Think* (San Francisco: W. H. Freeman, 1979), p. 122; Steven Levy, *Hackers* (Garden City, N.Y.: Bantam Doubleday, 1994), p. 83.

35. Levy, *Hackers,* p. 84; Allucquere Rosanne Stone, "Will the Real Body Please Stand Up," in Michael Benedikt, ed., *Cyberspace: First Steps* (Cambridge, Mass.: MIT Press, 1991), p. 103; Sherry Turkle, *The Second Self* (New York: Simon and Schuster, 1984), p. 108; Strimpel, quoted in Barbara Kantrowitz, "Men, Women, and Computers," *Newsweek,* May 16, 1994, p. 50.

36. Stefan Helmreich, "Anthropology Inside and Outside the Looking-Glass Worlds of Artificial Life," unpublished manuscript, Department of Anthropology, Stanford University, pp. 37, 19, 20.

37. James B. Watson, *The Double Helix* (New York: Atheneum, 1968), p. 225; Revelation 14:4.

38. Schreiner, *Woman and Labour,* pp. 45–46; Sherwood Anderson, *Perhaps Women* (Mamaroneck, N.Y.: Paul P. Appel, 1970), p. 56.

I.4   RUTH SCHWARTZ COWAN

Industrial Society and Technological Systems

As the Civil War came to an end, America began the transition from a pre-industrial society into the industrial age. The period from 1870 to 1920 saw many changes in America and at the end of that era, we had become the largest economy in the world—one that was far less dependent on nature than it once had been.

While we currently use many different technological systems, Ruth Cowan discusses five developed during that fifty-year period to demonstrate the increasing complexity of life and the development of infrastructure we now largely take for granted. Eventually this increasing complexity spread across the world. The characteristics of an industrialized society can now be found in even the most remote corners of the globe.

The increased levels of productivity in manufacturing, including agriculture, had economic as well as political ramifications. As these changes occurred, few thought about what was happening or what the long-range implications would be. Today's globalized world is vastly different than it once was, with many people more reliant and interdependent on one another. Our lives are increasingly more intertwined than ever before.

Focus Questions

1. Explain the rationale behind Cowan's assertion that industrialization has made us less independent and more closely connected to many other people than ever before.
2. Consider the key points of this article in relation to the ethical issues raised in the Jonas piece (selection I.9). What new individual responsibilities might arise from the new networks extending far beyond the normal family?
3. If technology continues to improve the quality of life for many more people in the world, what might our future look like if the networks discussed by Cowan become larger and more common, linking even greater numbers of people throughout the world?

Keywords

balance of trade, entrepreneurs, hunter-gatherers, industrialization, infrastructure, international trade, investment banking, manufacturing, productivity, transportation

BETWEEN 1870 AND 1920, the United States changed in ways that its founders could never have dreamed possible. Although American industrialization began in the 1780s, the nation did not become an industrialized society until after the Civil War had ended. The armistice agreed to at Appomattox signaled, although the participants probably did not realize it, the beginning of the take-off phase of American industrialization. Having begun as a nation of farmers, the United States became a nation of industrial workers. Having begun as a financial weakling among the nations, by 1920 the

United States had become the world's largest industrial economy.

What did this transformation mean to the people who lived through it? When a society passes from preindustrial to industrial conditions, which is what happened in the United States in the years between 1870 and 1920, people become less dependent on nature and more dependent on each other. This is one of history's little ironies. In a preindustrial society, when life is unstable, the whims of the weather and the perils of natural cycles are most often to blame. In an industrial society, when life is unstable, the whims of the market and the perils of social forces are most often to blame. Put another way, this means that in the process of industrialization individuals become more dependent on one another because they are linked together in large, complex networks that are, at one and the same time, both physical and social: technological systems.

Industrialization, Dependency, and Technological Systems

Many Americans learned what it means to become embedded in a set of technological systems in the years between 1870 and 1920. Today we have become so accustomed to these systems that we hardly ever stop to think about them; although they sustain our lives, they nonetheless remain mysterious. In the late twentieth century, people have tended to think that, if anything, industrialization has liberated them from dependency, not encased them in it, but that is not the case. We can see this clearly by imagining how a woman might provide food for a two-year-old child in a nonindustrialized society.

In a hunter-gatherer economy, she might simply go into the woods and collect nuts or walk to the waterside and dig for shellfish. In a premodern agricultural community (such as the one that some of the native peoples of the eastern seaboard had created), she might work with a small group of other people to plant corn, tend it, harvest it, and shuck it. Then she herself might dry it, grind it into meal, mix it with water, and bake it into a bread for the child to eat. In such a community, a woman would be dependent on the cooperation of several other people in order to provide enough food for her child, but all of those people would be known to her and none of them would be involved in an activity in which she could not have participated if necessity had demanded.

In an industrialized economy (our own, for example), an average woman's situation is wholly different. In order to get bread for a child, an average American woman is dependent on thousands of other people, virtually all of them totally unknown to her, many of them living and working at a considerable distance, employing equipment that she could not begin to operate, even if her life (quite literally) depended on it and even if she had the money (which isn't likely) to purchase it. A farmer grew the wheat using internal combustion engines and petroleum-derivative fertilizers. Then the wheat was harvested and transported to an organization that stored it under stable conditions, perhaps for several years. Then a milling company may have purchased it and transported it (over thousands of miles of roads or even ocean) to a mill, where it was ground by huge rollers powered by electricity (which itself may have been generated thousands of miles away). Then more transportation (all of this transportation required petroleum, which itself had to be processed and transported) was required: to a baking factory, where dozens of people (and millions of dollars of machinery) were used to turn the flour into bread. Then transportation again: to a market, where the woman could purchase it (having gotten herself there in an automobile, which itself had to be manufactured somewhere else, purchased at considerable expense, and supplied with fuel)—all of this before a slice of it could be spread with peanut butter to the delight of a two year old.

The point should, by now, be clear. People who live in agricultural societies are dependent on natural processes: they worry, with good reason, about whether and when there will be a drought or a flood, a plague of insects or of fungi, good weather or bad. People who live in industrial societies are not completely independent of such natural processes, but are more so than their predecessors (many floodplains have been controlled; some droughts can be offset by irrigation). At the same time, they are much more dependent on other people and on the technological systems that other people have designed and constructed. The physical parts of these systems are networks of connected objects: tractors, freight cars, pipelines, automobiles, display cases. The social parts are networks of people and organizations that make the connections between objects possible: farmers, bakers, and truck drivers; grain elevators, refineries, and supermarkets.

Preindustrialized societies had such networks of course, but in industrialized societies, the networks are more complex and much denser—all of which makes it much harder for individuals to extricate themselves. A small change very far away can have enormous effects very quickly. Daily life can be easily disrupted for reasons that ordinary people can find hard to understand, and even experts can have difficulty comprehending.

People live longer and at a higher standard of living in industrial societies than in preindustrial ones, but they are not thereby rendered more independent (although advertising writers and politicians would like them to think they are) because, in the process of industrialization, one kind of dependency is traded for another: nature for technology. Americans learned what it meant to make that trade in the years between 1870 and 1920. We can begin understanding what they experienced if we look at some of the technological systems that were created or enlarged during those years.

The Telegraph System

The very first network that Americans experienced really looked like a network: the elongated spider's web of electric wires that carried telegraph signals. The fact that electricity could be transmitted long distances through wires had been discovered in the middle of the eighteenth century. Once a simple way to generate electric currents had been developed (a battery, or voltaic pile, named after the man who invented it, Alessandro Volta) many people began experimenting with various ways to send messages along the wires. An American portrait painter, Samuel F. B. Morse, came up with a practiceable solution. Morse developed a transmitter that emitted a burst of electric current of either short or long duration (dots and dashes). His receiver, at the other end of the wire, was an electromagnet, which, when it moved, pushed a pencil against a moving paper tape (thus recording the pattern of dots and dashes). The most creative aspect of Morse's invention was his code, which enabled trained operators to make sense out of the patterns of dots and dashes.

In 1843, after Morse had obtained a government subvention, he and his partners built the nation's first telegraph line between Baltimore and Washington. By 1845, Morse had organized his own company to build additional lines and to license other telegraph companies so that they could build even more lines, using the instruments he had patented. In a very short time, however, dozens of competing companies had entered the telegraph business, and Morse had all he could do to try to collect the licensing fees to which he was entitled. By 1849, almost every state east of the Mississippi had telegraph service, much of it provided by companies that were exploiting Morse's patents without compensating him.

Beginning around 1850, one of these companies, the New York and Mississippi Valley Printing Telegraph Company, began buying up or merging with all the others; in 1866, it changed its name to the Western Union Telegraph Company. In the decades after the Civil War, Western Union had an almost complete monopoly on telegraph service in the United States; a message brought to one of its offices could be transmitted to any of its other offices in almost all fairly large communities in the United States. Once the message was delivered, recipients could pick it up at a Western Union office. During these decades, only one company of any note succeeded in challenging Western Union's almost complete monopoly on telegraph service. The Postal Telegraph Company specialized in providing pick-up and delivery services for telegrams; yet even at the height of its success, it never managed to corner more than 25 percent of the country's telegraph business.

In 1866, when Western Union was incorporated, it already controlled almost 22,000 telegraph offices around the country. These were connected by 827,000 miles of wire (all of it strung from a virtual forest of telegraph poles, many of them running along railroad rights of way), and its operators were handling something on the order of 58 million messages annually. By 1920, the two companies (Western and Postal) between them were managing more than a million miles of wire and 155 million messages. Yet other companies (many of the railroads, for example, several investment banking houses, several wire news services) were using Western Union and Postal Telegraph lines on a contractual basis to provide in-house communication services (the famous Wall Street stock ticker was one of them).

As a result, as early as 1860, and certainly by 1880, the telegraph had become crucial to the political and economic life of the nation. Newspapers had become dependent on the telegraph for quick transmission of important information. The 1847 war with Mexico was the first war to have rapid news coverage, and the Civil War was the first in which military strategy depended on the quick flow of battle information over telegraph lines. During the Gilded Age (1880–1900), the nation's burgeoning financial markets were dependent on the telegraph for quick transmission of prices and orders. Railroad companies used the telegraph for scheduling and signaling purposes since information about deviations in train times could be quickly transmitted along the lines. The central offices of the railroads utilized telegraph communication to control the financial affairs of their widely dispersed branches. When the Atlantic cable was completed in 1866, the speed and frequency of communication between nations increased, thereby permanently changing the character of diplomatic negotiations. The cable also laid the groundwork for the growth of international trade (particularly the growth of multinational corporations) in the later decades of the century.

In short, by 1880, if by some weird accident all the batteries that generated electricity for telegraph lines had suddenly run out, the economic and social life of the nation would have faltered. Trains would have stopped running; businesses with branch offices would have stopped functioning; newspapers could not have covered distant events; the president could not have communicated with his European ambassadors; the stock market would have had to close; family members separated by long distances could not have relayed important news—births, deaths, illnesses—to each other. By the turn of the century, the telegraph system was both literally and figuratively a network, ranking together various aspects of national life—making people increasingly dependent on it and on one another.

The Railroad System

Another system that linked geographic regions, diverse businesses, and millions of individuals was the railroad. We have already learned about the technical developments (the high-pressure steam-engine, the swivel truck, the T-rail) that were crucial to the development of the first operating rail lines in the United States in the 1830s. Once the technical feasibility of the railroad became obvious, its commercial potential also became clear. The railroad, unlike canals and steamboats, was not dependent on proximity to waterways and was not (as boats were) disabled when rivers flooded or canals froze.

During the 1840s, American entrepreneurs had began to realize the financial benefits that railroading might produce and railroad-building schemes were being concocted in parlors and banks, state houses, and farm houses all across the country. By the 1850s, a good many of those schemes had come to fruition. With 9,000 miles of railroad track in operation, the United States had more railroad mileage than all other western nations combined; by 1860, mileage had more than trebled, to 30,000 miles.

The pre–Civil War railroad system was not yet quite a technological system because, large as it was, it still was not integrated as a network. Most of the existing roads were short-haul lines, connecting such major cities as New York, Chicago, and Baltimore with their immediate hinterlands. Each road was owned by a different company, each company owned its own cars, and each built its tracks at the gauge (width) that seemed best for the cars it was going to attempt to run and the terrain over which the running had to be done. This lack of integration created numerous delays and additional expenses. In 1849, it took nine transshipments between nine unconnected railroads (and nine weeks of travel) to get freight from Philadelphia to Chicago. In 1861, the trip between Charleston and Philadelphia required eight car changes because of different gauges. During and immediately after the Civil War, not a single rail line entering either Philadelphia or Richmond made a direct connection with any other, much to the delight of the local teamsters, porters, and tavern keepers.

The multifaceted processes summed up under the word "integration" began in the years just after the Civil War and accelerated in the decades that followed. The rail system grew ever larger, stretching from coast to coast (with the completion of the Union Pacific Railroad in 1869), penetrating into parts of the country where settlement did not yet even exist. There were roughly 53,000 miles of track in 1870, but there were 93,000 miles by the time the next decade turned, and 254,000—the all-time high—by 1920. In that half century, the nation's population tripled, but its rail system grew sevenfold; the forty-eight states of the mainland United States became physically integrated, one with the other.

The form of the rail system was just as significant as its size. By 1920, what had once been a disjointed collection of short (usually north-south) lines had been transformed into a network of much longer trunk lines (running from coast to coast, east-west), each served by a network of shorter roads that connected localities (the limbs) with the trunks. Passengers could now travel from New York to San Francisco with only an occasional change of train and freight traveled without the necessity of trans-shipments. What had made this kind of integration possible was not a technological change, but a change in the pattern of railroad ownership and management.

From the very beginning of railroading, railroad companies had been joint-stock ventures. Huge amounts of capital had been required to build a railroad: rights of way had to be purchased, land cleared, bridges built, locomotives ordered, passenger cars constructed, freight cars bought. Once built, railroads were very expensive to run and to maintain: engines had to be repaired, passengers serviced, freight loaded, tickets sold, stations cleaned. Such a venture could not be financed by individuals, or even by partnerships. Money had to be raised both by selling shares of ownership in the company to large numbers of people and by borrowing large sums of money by issuing bonds.

As a result, both American stockbroking and American investment banking were twin products of the railroad age. Some of America's largest nineteenth-century fortunes were made by people who knew not how to build railroads, but how to finance them: J. P. Morgan, Leland Stanford, Jay Gould, Cornelius Vanderbilt, and George Crocker.

These businessmen consolidated the railroads. They bought up competing feeder lines; they sought control of the boards of directors of trunk lines; they invested heavily in the stock of feeder roads until the feeders were forced to merge with the trunks. When they were finished, the railroads had become an integrated network, a technological system. In 1870, there had been several hundred railroads, many of which were in direct competition with each other. By 1900, virtually all the railroad mileage in the United States was either owned or controlled by just seven (often mutually cooperative) railroad combinations, all of which owed their existence to the machinations of a few very wealthy investment bankers.

As railroad ownership became consolidated, the railroad system became physically integrated. The most obvious indicator of this integration was the adoption of a standard gauge, which made it unnecessary to run different cars on different sets of tracks. By the end of the 1880s, virtually every railroad in the country had voluntarily converted to a gauge of 4 feet, 8½ inches in order to minimize both the expense and the delays of long distance travel. On this new integrated system, the need for freight and passengers to make repeated transfers was eliminated; as a result, costs fell while transportation speed increased.

The railroad system had a profound impact on the way in which Americans lived. By 1900, the sound of the train whistle could be heard in almost every corner of the land. Virtually everything Americans needed to maintain and sustain their lives was being transported by train. As much as they may have grumbled about freight rates on the railroads (and there was much injustice, particularly to farmers, to grumble about) and as much as they may have abhorred the techniques that the railroad barons had used to achieve integration, most Americans benefited from the increased operational efficiency that resulted.

In the years in which population tripled and rail mileage increased seven times, freight tonnage on the railroads went up elevenfold. Cattle were going by train from the ranches of Texas to the slaughterhouses of Chicago; butchered beef was leaving

Chicago in refrigerated railroad cars destined for urban and suburban kitchens. Lumber traveled from forests to sawmills by train; two-by-four beams to build houses on the treeless plains left the sawmills of the Pacific Northwest on flatcars. Some petroleum went from the well to the refinery by train; most kerosene and gasoline went from the refinery to the retailer by train. Virtually all the country's mail traveled by train, including cotton cloth and saddles, frying pans and furniture ordered from the mail-order companies that had begun to flourish in the 1880s.

Even as fundamental and apparently untransportable a commodity as time was affected by the integration of the rail system, for scheduling was an important facet of integration. People who were going to travel by train had to know what time their trains would leave, and if connections had to be made, trains had to be scheduled so as to make the connections possible. Schedules also had to be constructed, especially on heavily trafficked lines, to ensure that trains did not collide. But scheduling was exceedingly difficult across the long distances of the United States because communities each established their own time on the basis of the position of the sun. When it was noon in Chicago, it was 12:30 in Pittsburgh (which is to the east of Chicago) and 11:30 in Omaha (to the west). The train schedules printed in Pittsburgh in the early 1880s listed six different times for the arrival and departure of each train. The station in Buffalo had three different clocks.

Sometime in the early 1880s, some professional railroad managers and the editors of several railroad publications agreed to the idea, first proposed by some astronomers, that the nation should be divided into four uniform time zones. By common agreement among the managers of the country's railroads, at noon (in New York) on Sunday, November 18, 1883, railroad signalmen across the country reset their watches. The zones were demarcated by the 75th, 90th, 105th, and 120th meridians. People living in the eastern sections of each zone experienced, on that otherwise uneventful Sunday, two noons, and people living in the western sections, skipped time. Virtually everyone in the country accepted the new time that had been established

by the railroads, although Congress did not actually confirm the arrangement by legislation for another thirty-five years. Such was the pervasive impact of the integrated rail network.

The Petroleum System

In 1859, a group of prospectors dug a well in a farmyard in Titusville, Pennsylvania. Although they appeared to be looking for water, the prospectors were in fact searching for an underground reservoir of a peculiar oily substance that had been bubbling to the surface of nearby land and streams. Native Americans had used this combustible substance as a lubricant for centuries. The prospectors were hoping that if they could find a way to tap into an underground reservoir of this material, they could go into the business of selling it to machine shops and factories (as a machine lubricant, an alternative to animal fat) and to households and businesses (as an illuminant, an alternative to whale oil and candles).

The prospectors struck oil—and the American petroleum industry was born. Within weeks the news had spread, and hundreds of eager profiteers rushed into western Pennsylvania, hoping to purchase land, drill for oil, or find work around the wells. The Pennsylvania oil rush was as massive a phenomenon as the California gold rush a decade earlier.

The drillers soon discovered that crude petroleum is a mixture of oils of varying weights and characteristics. These oils, they learned, could be easily separated from one another by distillation, an ancient and fairly well-known craft. All that was needed was a fairly large closed vat with a long outlet tube (called a still) and a fire. The oil was heated in the still and the volatile gases produced would condense in the outlet tube. A clever distiller (later called a refiner) could distinguish different portions (fractions) of the distillate from each other, and then only the economically useful ones needed to be bottled and sent to market.

The market for petroleum products boomed during the Civil War: northern factories were expanding to meet government contracts; the whaling industry was seriously hampered by naval operations; railroads were working overtime to transport men and material to battlefronts. By 1862, some 3 million barrels of crude oil were being processed every year. Under peacetime conditions the industry continued to expand; by 1872, the number of processed barrels had trebled.

Transportation of petroleum remained a problem, however. The wells were located in the rural, underpopulated Appalachian highlands of Pennsylvania, not only many miles away from the cities in which the ultimate consumers lived, but also many miles away from railroad lines that served those cities. Initially crude oil had been collected in barrels and had been moved (by horse and cart or by river barges) to railroad-loading points. There the barrels were loaded into freight cars for the trip to the cities (such as Cleveland and Pittsburgh) in which the crude was being refined and sold. The transportation process was cumbersome, time-consuming, and wasteful; the barrels leaked, the barges sometimes capsized, the wagons—operating on dirt roads—sometimes sank to their axles in mud.

Pipelines were an obvious solution, but a difficult one to put into practice given that no one had ever before contemplated building and then maintaining a continuous pipeline over the mountainous terrain and the long distances that had to be traversed. The first pipeline to operate successfully was built in 1865. Made of lap-welded cast-iron pipes, two inches in diameter, it ran for six miles from an oil field to a railroad loading point and had three pumping stations along the way. This first pipeline carried eighty barrels of oil an hour and had demonstrated its economic benefits within a year. Pipeline mileage continued to increase during the 1870s and 1880s (putting thousands of teamsters out of business), but virtually all of the lines were relatively short hauls, taking oil from the fields to the railroads. Throughout the nineteenth century and well into the twentieth, the railroads were still the principal long-distance transporters of both crude and refined oil. After the 1870s, the drillers, refiners, and railroads gradually dispensed with barrels (thus putting thousands of coopers out of business) and replaced them with specially built tank cars, which could be emptied into and loaded from specially built holding tanks. As it was being constructed, the network of petroleum pipelines was thus integrated

into the network of railroad lines. It was also integrated into the telegraph network. Oil refineries used the telegraph system partly to keep tabs on prices for oil in various localities and partly to report on the flow of oil through the lines.

The most successful petroleum entrepreneurs were the ones who realized that control of petroleum transportation was the key ingredient in control of the entire industry. The major actor in this particular economic drama was John D. Rockefeller. Rockefeller had been born in upstate New York, the son of a talented patent medicine salesman, but he had grown up in Cleveland, Ohio, a growing commercial center (it was a Great Lake port and both a canal and railroad terminus), and had learned accountancy in a local commercial college. His first job was as a bookkeeper for what was then called a commission agent, a business that collected commissions for arranging the shipment of bulk orders of farm products. A commission agent's success depended on getting preferential treatment from railroads and shipping companies. Rockefeller carried this insight with him, first when he went into a partnership as his own commission agent and then, in 1865, when he became the co-owner of an oil refinery in Cleveland.

Rockefeller and his associates were determined to control the then chaotic business of oil refining. They began by arranging for a secret rebate of oil shipments from one of the two railroads then serving Cleveland. Then in the space of less than a month, using the rebate as an incentive, they managed to coerce other Cleveland refiners into selling out and obtained control of the city's refining. Within a year or two, Rockefeller was buying up refineries in other cities as well. He had also convinced the railroads that he was using that they should stop carrying oil to refineries owned by others, so that he was in almost complete control of the price offered to drillers. In the early 1870s, a group of drillers banded together to build pipelines that would take their oil to railroads with which Rockefeller wasn't allied. Rockefeller responded to this challenge by assembling a monopoly on the ownership of tank cars (since the pipelines did not go all the way to the refineries and railroad tank cars were still necessary), and by 1879, he had been so successful in squeezing the finances of the pipeline companies that their stockholders were forced to sell out to him. In that year, as a result of their control both of refineries and pipelines, Rockefeller and his associates controlled 90 percent of the refined oil in the United States.

Having bought up the competing pipelines (having let other people take the risks involved in developing new technologies for building and maintaining those lines), Rockefeller was quick to see their economic value. In 1881, one of his companies completed a six-inch line from the Pennsylvania oil fields to his refinery in Bayonne, New Jersey—the first pipeline that functioned independently of the railroads. By 1900, Rockefeller had built pipelines to Cleveland, Philadelphia, and Baltimore, and Standard Oil (Rockefeller's firm) was moving 24,000 barrels of crude a day (he still used the railroads to move the oil after it had been refined).

By that point, hundreds of civil and mechanical engineers were working for Rockefeller's pipeline companies (which held several patents on pipeline improvements), and several dozen chemists and chemical engineers were working in his refineries (and developing new techniques, such as the Frasch process for taking excess sulfur out of petroleum). In addition, Standard Oil was pioneering financial, management, and legal techniques for operating a business that had to control a huge physical network, spread out over several states. Since the laws dealing with corporations differed in each state and since some of them prevented a corporation in one state from owning property in another, one of Rockefeller's attorneys worked out a corporate arrangement so that Standard Oil had a different corporation in each state in which it operated (Standard Oil of New Jersey, Standard Oil of Ohio, and so forth). The stockholders in each corporation turned their stock over to a group of trustees, who managed the whole enterprise from New York— the famous Standard Oil Trust, of which Rockefeller himself was the single largest stockholder and therefore the major trustee. (The trust, as a way to organize a complex business, was soon picked up in tobacco and sugar refining and other industries involved in large-scale chemical processing, leading

Congress, worried about the monopolistic possibilities, to pass the Sherman Anti-Trust Act in 1890.)

By 1900, the Standard Oil Trust (which had successfully battled antitrust proceedings in court) controlled most of the oil produced in Pennsylvania, and it owned most of the new oil fields that had been discovered in Ohio and Indiana. Rockefeller's almost complete stranglehold on the industry wasn't broken until oil was discovered early in the twentieth century in Texas, Oklahoma, Louisiana, and California, outside the reach of the pipelines he controlled and the railroads with which he was associated. Increased competition was accompanied by the continued growth not only of the pipeline network, but also of the industry as a whole: 26 million barrels of petroleum were processed in 1880, 45 million in 1890, 63 million in 1900, 209 million in 1910 (as gasoline was just beginning to edge out kerosene as the most important petroleum product), and 442 million in 1920 (when the Model T had been in production for almost eight years).

Like the telegraph and the railroad (and in combination with the telegraph and the railroad), the oil pipeline network had become a pervasive influence on the American economy and on the daily life of Americans. In the last decades of the nineteenth century, a very large number of Americans, especially those living outside of the major cities, used one of its products, kerosene, for heating and lighting their homes and for cooking. During the same decades, American industry became dependent on other fractions of petroleum to lubricate the machinery with which it was producing everything from luxurious cloth to common nails. Finally, in the early decades of the twentieth century, with the advent first of the internal combustion engine fueled by gasoline and then of automobiles and trucks powered by that engine, Americans discovered that access to petroleum was becoming a necessary condition not only of their working lives but also of their leisure time.

The Telephone System

Technologically the telephone was similar to the telegraph, but socially it was very different. The device patented by Alexander Graham Bell in 1876 was rather like a telegraph line: voices rather than signals could be transmitted by electric current because the transmitter lever and the receiving pencil had been replaced by very sensitive diaphragms. Aware of the difficulties that Morse had encountered in reaping profits from his patents—and aware that he had no head for business—Bell decided to turn over the financial and administrative details of creating a telephone network to someone else.

The businessmen and the attorneys who managed the Bell Telephone Company did their work well. While the railroad, telegraph, and petroleum networks had been integrated by corporate takeovers, the telephone system was integrated, from the very beginning, by corporate design. A crucial decision had been made early on: Bell Telephone would manufacture all the telephone instruments, then lease the instruments to local companies, which would operate telephone exchanges under license to Bell. This meant that for the first sixteen years of telephone network development (sixteen years was then the length of monopoly rights under a patent), the Bell Telephone Company could dictate, under the licensing agreements, common technologies for all the local telephone systems. Bell could also control the costs of telephone services to local consumers.

Because of this close supervision by one company, the telephone system was integrated from the very beginning. Between 1877 and 1893, the Bell Telephone Company, through its affiliated local operating companies, controlled and standardized virtually every telephone, every telephone line, and every telephone exchange in the nation. Indeed in the 1880s, the officers of Bell were confident that they could profitably begin long-distance service (that is, service that would connect one local operating company with another) precisely because all of the operating companies were using its standardized technology. Bell needed to hire physicists and electrical engineers to solve the technical problems involved in maintaining voice clarity over very long wires, but the organizational problems involved in connecting New York with Chicago and Chicago with Cleveland turned out to be minimal.

On the assumption that the telephone system would end up being used very similarly to the telegraph network, the officers of Bell had decided that their most important customers would be other businesses, particularly those in urban areas. They decided, as a marketing strategy, to keep rates fairly high, in return for which they would work to provide the clearest and most reliable service possible. By the end of the company's first year of operation, 3,000 telephones had been leased, 1 for every 10,000 people. By 1880, there were 60,000 (1 per 1,000), and when the Bell patents expired in 1893, there were 260,000 (1 per 250). About two thirds of these phones were located in businesses. Most of the country's business information was still traveling by mail and by telegraph (because businessmen wanted a written record of their transactions), but certain kinds of businesses were starting to find the telephone very handy: in 1891, the New York and New Jersey Telephone Company served 937 physicians and hospitals, 401 pharmacies, 363 liquor stores, 315 stables, 162 metalworking plants, 146 lawyers, 126 contractors, and 100 printing shops.

After the Bell patents expired, independent telephone companies entered the business despite Bell's concerted effort to keep them out. By 1902, there were almost 9,000 such independent companies, companies not part of the Bell system. When the organizers of the Bell system had analogized the telephone to the telegraph, they had made a crucial sociological mistake. They understood that in technological terms the telephone was similar to the telegraph, but they failed to understand that in social terms it was quite different. The telephone provided user-to-user communication (with the telegraph there were always intermediaries). In addition, the telephone was a form of voice communication; it facilitated emotional communication, something that was impossible with a telegraph. In short, what the organizers of the Bell system had failed to understand was that people would use the telephone to socialize with each other.

The independent companies took advantage of Bell's mistake. Some of them offered services that Bell hadn't thought to provide. Dial telephones were one such service, allowing customers to contact each other without having to rely on an operator (who sat at a switchboard, manually connecting telephone lines, one to another, with plugs). Operators were notorious for relieving the boredom of their jobs by listening in on conversations, something many customers wanted to avoid. Party lines were another such service. Anywhere from two to ten residences could share the same telephone line and telephone number, which drastically lowered the costs of residential services. Many lower-income people turned out to be willing to put up with the inconvenience of having to endure the ringing of telephones on calls meant for other parties in exchange for having telephone service at affordable rates.

Yet other independent companies served geographic locales that the Bell companies had ignored. This was particularly the case in rural areas where there were farm households. Bell managers apparently hadn't thought that farmers would want telephones, but it turned out that they were wrong. Farm managers used telephones to get prompt reports on prices and weather. Farm households used telephones to summon doctors in emergencies and to alleviate the loneliness of lives lived far from neighbors and relatives. In 1902, relatively few farm households had telephones, but as the independent companies grew, so did the number of farm-based customers; by 1920, just under 39 percent of all farm households in the United States had telephone service (while only 34 percent of nonfarm households did).

All this competition in telephone service had the net effect that any economist could have predicted: prices for telephone service fell, even in the Bell system. In order to keep the system companies competitive, the central Bell company had to cut the rates that it charged its affiliates for the rental of phones, and these savings were passed on to consumers. In New York City, as just one example, rates fell from $150 for 1,000 calls in 1880 to $51 in 1915 (figures adjusted for inflation).

As a result, in the period between 1894 and 1920, the telephone network expanded profoundly. Middle-class people began to pay for telephone service to their homes. Farm households became part of the telephone network (in record numbers). Retail businesses began to rely on telephones in their relations with their customers. By 1920, there were 13 million telephones in use in the country, 123 for every 1,000 people. Eight million of those 13 million phones belonged to Bell and 4 million to independent companies that connected to Bell lines. In just forty years, the telephone network, which provided point-to-point voice communication, had joined the telegraph, railroad, and petroleum networks as part of the economic and social foundation of industrial society.

The Electric System

Like the telegraph and telephone systems, the electric system was (and still is) quite literally a network of wires. Physicists, who had been experimenting with electricity since the middle of the eighteenth century, knew that under certain conditions electricity could produce light. Unfortunately, the first devices invented for generating a continuous flow of electricity—batteries—did not create a current strong enough for illumination. However, in 1831 the British experimenter Michael Faraday perfected a device that was based on a set of observations that scientists had made a decade earlier: all electric current will make a magnet move and a moving magnet will create an electric current. Faraday built an electric generator (a rotating magnet with a conducting wire wound around it)—a device that could, unlike the battery, create a continuous flow of current strong enough to be used for lighting.

Within a short time, the generator was being used to power arc lamps in which the light (and a lot of heat) was produced by sparking across a gap in the conducting wires. Arc lamps were first used in British and French lighthouses in the 1860s; the generator that created the electricity was powered by a steam engine. A few years later, arc lamps were also being used for street lighting in some American cities. Unfortunately, arc lamps were dangerous; they had to be placed very far away from people and from anything that might be ignited by the sparks. By the mid-1870s, several people in several different countries were racing with each other to find a safer form of electrical lighting, the incandescent lamp. In such a lamp, light would be derived from a glowing, highly resistant filament and not a spark; but the filament had to be kept in a vacuum so that it wouldn't oxidize (and disappear) too fast.

Thomas Alva Edison won the race. In 1878, when Edison started working on electrical lighting, he already had amassed a considerable reputation (and a moderate fortune) as an inventor. His first profitable invention had been the quadruplex telegraph, which could carry four messages at once, and he had also made successful modifications to the stock ticker, the telegraph system for relaying stock prices from the floor of the stock exchange to the offices of investors and brokers. These inventions had enhanced his reputation with Wall Street financiers and attorneys. In 1876, when he decided to become an independent inventor, building and staffing his own laboratory in Menlo Park, New Jersey, and again in 1878, when he decided that he wanted his laboratory to crack the riddle of electric lighting, he had no trouble borrowing money to invest in the enterprise.

Actually, they were enterpris*es*. From the beginning, Edison understood that he wanted to build a technological system *and* a series of businesses to manage that system. The first of these businesses was the Edison Electric Light Company, incorporated for the purpose of financing research and development of electric lighting. Most of the stock was purchased by a group of New York financiers; Edison received stock in return for the rights to whatever lighting patents he might develop. Once Edison had actually invented a workable lightbulb (it had a carbonized thread as its filament), he proceeded to design other devices, and create other companies, that would all be parts of the system. The Edison Electric Illuminating Company of New York, founded in 1880, was created to build and maintain the very first central generating station providing electric service to customers. When this station opened its doors in 1882 (as its site Edison chose the part of Manhattan with the highest concentration of office buildings), it contained several steam-driven generators (built to Edison's design by the Edison Machine Company) and special cables to carry the electricity underground (made by the Edison Electric Tube Company). Customers who signed up for electric service had their usage measured by meters that Edison had invented; their

offices were outfitted with lamp sockets that Edison had designed into which they were to place lightbulbs that another Edison company manufactured.

Information about this new system spread very fast (thanks to publicity generated by the Edison Electric Light Company), and within a few months (not even years), entrepreneurs were applying to Edison for licenses to build electric generating plants all over the country, indeed all over the world. Having been designed as a system, the electrical network grew very fast. There was only one generating plant in the country in 1882, but by 1902, there were 2,250, and by 1920, almost 4,000. These plants had a total generating capacity of 19 million kilowatts. Just over a third of the nation's homes were wired for electricity by 1920, by which time electricity was being used not only for lighting but also for cooling (electric fans), ironing (the electric iron replaced the so-called sad iron quickly), and vacuuming (the vacuum cleaner was being mass-produced by 1915).

The Edison companies (some of which eventually merged with other companies to become the General Electric Company) were not, however, able to remain in control of the electric system for as long (or as completely) as the Bell companies were able to dominate the telephone business or Standard Oil the petroleum business. Part of the reason for this lay in the principles of electromagnetic induction, which can be used to create electric motors as well as electric generators. The same experimenters who were developing electric generators in the middle years of the nineteenth century were also developing electric motors, and one of the first applications of those motors was in a business very different from the lighting business: electric traction for electric intraurban streetcars, often known as trolley cars. The first of these transportation systems was installed in Richmond, Virginia, in 1888 by a company owned by Frank Sprague, an electrical engineer who had briefly worked for Edison.

Sprague had invented an electric motor that, he thought, would be rugged enough to power carriages running day in and day out on city streets. As it turned out, the motor had to be redesigned, and redesigned again, before it worked very well, and Sprague also had to design trolley poles (for conducting the electricity from the overhead wires to the carriage) and a controlling system (so that the speed of the motor could be varied by the person driving the carriage). In the end, however, the electric streetcar was successful, and the days of the horse-pulled carriage were clearly numbered. Fourteen years after Sprague's first system began operating, the nation had 22,576 miles of track devoted to street railways.

Electric motors were also being used in industry. The earliest motors, like the streetcar motors, had been direct current (d.c.) motors, which needed a special and often fragile device (called a commutator) to transform the alternating current (a.c.) produced by generators. In 1888, an a.c. motor was invented by Nikola Tesla, a Serbian physicist who had emigrated to the United States. Tesla's patents were assigned to the Westinghouse Company, which began both to manufacture and to market them. At that point, the use of electric motors in industry accelerated. The very first factory to be completely electrified was a cotton mill, built in 1894. As electric motors replaced steam engines, factory design and location changed; it was no longer necessary to build factories that were several stories high (to facilitate power transmission from a central engine) or to locate them near water sources (to feed the steam boilers). The first decade of the twentieth century was a turning point in the use of electric power in industry as more and more factories converted; by 1901, almost 400,000 motors had been installed in factories, with a total capacity of almost 5 million horsepower.

In short, the electrical system was more complex than the telephone and petroleum systems because it consisted of several different subsystems (lighting, traction, industrial power) with very different social goals and economic strategies; because of its complexity, no single company could dominate it. By 1895, when the first generating plant intended to transmit electricity over a long distance became operational (it was a hydroelectric plant built to take advantage of Niagara Falls, transmitting electricity twenty miles to the city of Buffalo), there were several hundred companies involved in the electric industry: enormous companies such as Westinghouse and General Electric that made everything from generators to lightbulbs; medium-sized companies, such as the ones that ran streetcar systems or that provided electric service to relatively small geographic areas; and small companies, which made specialized electric motors or parts for electric motors. Despite this diversity, the electric system was unified by the fact that its product, electric energy, had been standardized. By 1910, virtually all the generating companies (which, by now, had come to be called utility companies) were generating alternating current at sixty cycles per second. This meant that all electric appliances were made to uniform specifications and all transmission facilities could potentially be connected to one another. By 1920, electricity had supplanted gas, kerosene, and oils for lighting. In addition, it was being used to power sewing machines in ready-made clothing factories, to separate aluminum from the contaminants in its ores, to run projectors through which motion pictures could be viewed, to carry many thousands of commuters back and forth, and to do dozens of other chores in workplaces and residences. As transmission towers marched across the countryside and yet another set of wire-carrying poles were constructed on every city street, few Americans demonstrated any inclination to decline the conveniences that the youngest technical system—electricity—was carrying in its wake.

The Character of Industrialized Society

As inventors, entrepreneurs, and engineers were building all these multifarious technological systems, Americans were becoming increasingly dependent on them. Each time a person made a choice—to buy a kerosene lamp or continue to use candles, to take a job in an electric lamp factory or continue to be a farmer, to send a telegraph message instead of relying on the mail, to put a telephone in a shop so that customers could order without visiting—that person, whether knowingly or not, was becoming increasingly enmeshed in a technological system. The net effect of all that construction activity and all those choices was that a wholly new social order, and wholly different set of social and economic relationships between people, emerged: industrial society.

In industrial societies, manufactured products play a more important economic role than agricultural products. More money is invested in factories than in farms; more bolts of cloth are produced than bales of hay; more people work on assembly lines than as farm laborers. Just over half (53 percent) of what was produced in the United States was agricultural in 1869 and only a third (33 percent) was manufactured. In 1899 (just thirty years later), those figures were reversed: half the nation's output was in manufactured goods and only a third was agricultural, despite the fact that the nation's total farm acreage had increased rapidly as a result of westward migration. Manufacturing facilities were turning out products that were becoming increasingly important aspects of everyday life: canned corn and lightbulbs, cigarettes and underwear.

In a preindustrial society, the countryside is the base for economic and political power. In such societies, most people live in rural districts. Most goods that are traded are agricultural products; the price of fertile land is relatively high; and wealth is accumulated by those who are able to control that land. Industrialized societies are dominated by their cities. More people live and work in cities than on farms; most goods are manufactured in cities; most trade is accomplished there; wealth is measured in money and not in land. Furthermore, the institutions that control money—banks—are urban institutions.

As the nineteenth century progressed, more and more Americans began living either in the rural towns in which factories were located (which, as a result, started to become small cities) or in the older cities that had traditionally been the center of artisanal production and of commerce. Native-born Americans began moving from the countryside to the city; many newly arrived Americans (and there were millions of newcomers to America in the nineteenth century) settled in cities. Just over half of all Americans (54 percent) were farmers or farm laborers in 1870, but only one in three was by 1910. Some American families underwent the rural–

urban transition slowly: a daughter might move off the farm to a rural town when she married, and then a granddaughter might make her fortune in a big city. Others had less time: a man might be tending olive groves in Italy one day and working in a shoe factory in Philadelphia two months later.

During the 1840s, the population of the eastern cities nearly doubled, and several midwestern cities (St. Louis, Chicago, Pittsburgh, Cincinnati) began to grow. In 1860, there were nine port cities that had populations over 100,000 (Boston, New York, Brooklyn, Philadelphia, Baltimore, New Orleans, Chicago, Cincinnati, and St. Louis)—by 1910, there were fifty. Just as significantly, the country's largest cities were no longer confined to the eastern seaboard or to the Midwest. There were several large cities in the plains states, and half the population of the far west was living not in its fertile valleys or at the feet of its glorious mountains, but in its cities: Los Angeles, Denver, San Francisco, Portland, and Seattle. By 1920, for the first time in the nation's history, just slightly over half of all Americans lived in communities that had more than 10,000 residents.

Money was flowing in the same direction that people were; by 1900, the nation's wealth was located in its cities, not in its countryside. The nation's largest businesses and its wealthiest individuals were in its cities. J. P. Morgan and Cornelius Vanderbilt controlled their railroad empires from New York; Leland Stanford and Charles Crocker ran theirs from San Francisco; John D. Rockefeller operated from Cleveland and New York; Andrew Carnegie, at least initially, from Pittsburgh. Probably by 1880, and certainly by 1890, stock exchanges and investment bankers had become more important to the nation's economic health than cotton wharves and landed gentry.

This transition to an urban society had political consequences because political power tends to follow the trail marked out by wealth (and, in a democracy, to some extent by population). In the early years of the nineteenth century, when the independent political character of the nation was being formed, most Americans still lived on farms and American politics was largely controlled by people who earned their living directly from the land. After the Civil War, city residents (being both more numerous and more wealthy) began to flex their political muscles and to express their political interests more successfully. The first twelve presidents of the United States had all been born into farming communities, but from 1865 until 1912, the Republican party, then the party that most clearly represented the interests of big business and of cities, controlled the White House for all but eight years, and those eight years were the two terms served by Grover Cleveland, who before becoming president had been the mayor of Buffalo, New York.

The transition to an urban society also had economic and technological consequences. In a kind of historical feedback loop, industrialization caused cities to grow and the growth of cities stimulated more industrialization. Nineteenth-century cities were, to use the term favored by urban historians, walking cities. Since most residents could not afford either the cost or the space required to keep a horse and carriage, they had to be able to walk to work or to work in their own homes. Since businesses also had to be within walking distance of each other, this meant that as cities grew they became congested; more and more people had both to live and to work within the same relatively limited space. With congestion came disease; all nineteenth-century American cities were periodically struck by devastating epidemics: cholera, dysentery, typhoid fever.

Even before they understood the causes of these epidemics, city governments became convinced that they had to do something both to relieve the congestion and to control the diseases. Streets had to be paved, running water provided, sewers constructed, new housing encouraged. This meant that reservoirs had to be built, aqueducts and pumping stations constructed, trenches dug, pipes purchased, brickwork laid, new construction techniques explored. All of this municipal activity not only stimulated American industry but also served as a spur to the growth of civil engineering.

In addition, in the years between 1870 and 1920, many American cities actively stimulated industrialization by seeking out manufacturing interests and

offering operating incentives to them. Many of the nation's older cities found themselves in economic trouble as railroad depots become more important than ports as nodes in the country's transportation system. In their distress, these cities decided that their futures lay not in commerce but in manufacturing, and they began to seek out manufacturing entrepreneurs to encourage industrial growth. By that time, the steam engine having been perfected and its manufacture made relatively inexpensive, manufacturers had ceased to depend on waterwheels as a power source, which meant that they could easily (and profitably) establish their enterprises in cities rather than in the countryside; the development of the electric motor only served to increase this potential.

Minneapolis became a center of flour milling, Kansas City of meatpacking, Memphis of cotton seed oil production, Rochester of shoe manufacturing, Schenectady of electric equipment, New York of ready-made clothing, Pittsburgh of steel and glass manufacture. Local banks helped manufacturers start up in business and local politicians helped recruit a docile labor force, all in the interests of stabilizing or augmenting a city's economy. Nationwide the net result was a positive impetus to the growth of industry; the processes of industrialization and urbanization are mutually reinforcing.

If American cities grew prodigiously during the second half of the nineteenth century, so, too, did the American population as a whole: between 1860 and 1920, the population of the United States more than tripled (from 31 million to 106 million). Some of the increase was the result of a high natural birthrate; in general, American families were larger than what is needed to keep a population at a stable size from one generation to the next. In addition, as the result of improvements in public health and improvements in the food supply, the death rate was declining and life expectancy was rising. People were living longer and that meant that in any given year a declining proportion of the total population was dying. On top of this, immigrants were arriving in record numbers. The figures are astounding; the total, between the end of the Civil War and the passage of the Immigration Restriction Acts (1924), came to over 30 million people. Like their native-born contemporaries, immigrants had a high birth-rate and a declining death rate and more of their children lived past infancy and then enjoyed a longer life expectancy, all of which further contributed to the mushrooming size of the American population. This startling population increase—almost 20 percent—reflects another crucial difference between societies that have become industrialized and those that have not. In a preindustrialized society the size of the population changes in a more or less cyclical fashion. If the weather cooperates and the crops are bounteous and peace prevails, people remain reasonably healthy and many children live past infancy; over the course of time the population will grow. But eventually the population will grow too large to be supported by the available land or the land itself will become infertile. Droughts may come or heavy rains; locusts may infest the fields or diseases may strike the cattle. Men will be drawn off to battle just when it is time to plow the fields or soldiers engaged in battles will trample the wheat and burn the barns. Then starvation will ensue. People will succumb to disease; fewer children will be born, and more of them will die in infancy. The population will shrink.

Under preindustrial conditions, such population cycles have been possible. Sometimes the cycle will take two generations to recur, sometimes two centuries, but it has recurred as long as there have been agricultural peoples who have been keeping records of themselves. Industrialization breaks this cyclical population pattern. Once a country has industrialized, natural disasters and wars do not seem to have a long-term effect on the size of its population; the rate of increase may slow for a few years or so, but there is still an increase. And the standard of living keeps rising as well. People stay relatively healthy; they live longer lives. Generally speaking, they can have as many (or as few) children as they want, knowing that, also generally speaking, most of their children will live past infancy. This is the salient characteristic that makes underdeveloped countries long for development: industrialized countries seem able to support extraordinarily large populations without any long-term collapse either in the size of the population or in the standard of living.

Industrialized countries can do this because agriculture industrializes at the same time that manufacturing does. In the transition to industrialization, what is happening on the farm is just as important as what is happening in the factories since, to put it bluntly, people cannot work if they cannot eat. These social processes—sustained growth of the population and the industrialization of agriculture—are interlocked. Both were proceeding rapidly in the United States between the years 1870 and 1920 as American farmers simultaneously pushed west and industrialized, settling new territory and developing more productive farming techniques. As the frontier moved westward, roughly 400 million new acres were put under cultivation: virgin prairies became farms, fertile mountain valleys were planted in orchards, grassy hills became grazing land for sheep and cattle. The total quantity of improved acreage (meaning land that had been cleared or fenced or otherwise made suitable for agricultural use) in the United States multiplied two and a half times between 1860 and 1900.

This alone would have considerably expanded the nation's agricultural output, but newly introduced agricultural implements profoundly altered the work process of farming (particularly grain growing) and increased its productivity. The first of these was the reaper (patented by Cyrus McCormick in 1834 and in limited use even before the Civil War). The reaper, which was pulled by horses, replaced hand labor. Once a reaper had been purchased, a farm owner could quadruple the amount of acreage cut in one day or fire three day laborers who had previously been employed for the harvest or greatly increase the acreage put to plow (since the number of acres planted had always been limited by what could be reaped in the two prime weeks of harvest).

The reaper was followed by the harvester (which made binding the grain easier), followed by the self-binder (which automatically bound the grain into shocks), and—in the far west—followed by the combine, a steam-driven tractor (which cut a swath of over forty feet, then threshed and bagged the grain automatically, sometimes at the rate of three 150-pound bags a minute). In those same years, haymaking was altered by the introduction of automatic cutting and baling machinery, and plowing was made considerably easier by the invention of the steel plow (John Deere, 1837) and the chilled-iron plow (James Oliver, 1868), both of which had the advantage of being nonstick surfaces for the heavy, wet soils of the prairies.

The net result, by 1900, was that American farmers were vastly more productive than they had been in 1860. Productivity has two facets: it is a measure both of the commodities being produced and of the labor being used to produce them. Statistics on wheat production indicate how radically American agriculture was changing in the second half of the nineteenth century. In 1866, there were roughly 15.5 million acres devoted to wheat production in the United States; farmers achieved average yields of 9.9 bushels per acre, resulting in a total national production of about 152 million bushels. By 1898, acreage had roughly trebled (to 44 million), yields had almost doubled (to 15.3 bushels per acre), and the total production was 675 million bushels.

All this was accomplished with a marked saving of labor. By the hand method, 400 people and 200 oxen had to work ten hours a day to produce 20,000 bushels of wheat; by the machine method, only 6 people (and 36 horses) were required. Farms were getting larger, ownership was being restricted to a smaller and smaller number of people and more machinery was required for profitable farming (between 1860 and 1900, the annual value of farm implements manufactured in the United States went from $21 million to $101 million)—at the same time, the firms were becoming more productive.

What this means, put another way, was that a smaller proportion of the nation's people were needed to produce the food required by its ever larger population. Some people left their farms because they hated the farming life, some because they could not afford to buy land as prices began to rise, some because they were forced off the land by the declining profitability of small farms. The farming population (this includes both owners and laborers) began to shrink in relation to the rest of the population.

New transportation facilities and new food-based industries made it easier and cheaper for the residents of cities and towns to eat a more varied diet. The fledgling canning industry was spurred by the need to supply food for troops during the Civil War. After the war, the canners turned to the civilian market, and by the 1880s, urban Americans had become accustomed to eating canned meat, condensed milk (invented by Gail Borden in 1856), canned peas, and canned corn. The Heinz company was already supplying bottled ketchup and factory pickles to a vast population, and the Campbell's company was just about to start marketing soups. By 1900, cheese and butter making had become largely a factory operation, made easier and cheaper by the invention of the centrifugal cream separator in 1879.

After the Civil War, the railroads replaced steamboats and canal barges as the principal carriers of farm products (from wheat to hogs, from apples to tobacco), thus both shortening the time required to bring goods to market and sharply lowering the cost of transportation. After the 1880s, when refrigerated transport of various kinds was introduced, this trend accelerated: even more products could be brought to market (butchered meat, for example, or fresh fish) in an even shorter time. New refrigeration techniques transformed beer making from a home to a factory operation; by 1873, there were some 4,000 breweries in the United States with an output of 10 million barrels a year. Commercial baking had also expanded and Americans were becoming fond of factory-made crackers and cookies. In the end, then, another historical feedback loop had been established, a loop connecting industrialization with agricultural change. Industrialization made farming more productive, which made it possible for the population to increase, which created a larger market for manufactured goods, which increased the rate of industrialization.

Conclusion: Industrialization and Technological Systems

By 1920, a majority of Americans had crossed the great divide between preindustrial and industrial societies. The foods they ate, the conditions under which they worked, the places in which they lived—all had been transformed. The majority of Americans were no longer living on farms. They were eating food that had been carried to them by one technological system (the railroad) after having been processed by machines that were powered by a second (electricity) and lubricated by a third (petroleum). If they wanted to light their domiciles at night or heat their dwelling places during cold weather, they could not avoid interacting with one or another technological system for distributing energy—unless they were willing to manufacture their own candles (even then, they might have ended up buying paraffin from Standard Oil). The social ties that bound individuals and communities together—someone has been elected, someone else has died, young men are about to be drafted, a young woman has given birth—were being carried over, communicated through, and to some extent controlled by technological networks that were owned by large, monopolistically inclined corporations. More people were living longer lives; fewer babies were dying in infancy; the standard of living for many Americans (albeit not for all) was rising. And at the very same time, because of the very same processes, people were becoming more dependent on each other.

Early in the nineteenth century the process of industrialization had appeared (to those who were paying attention) as a rather discrete undertaking: a spinning factory in a neighboring town, a merchant miller up the river, a railroad station a few miles distant. By the end of the century, virtually all Americans must have been aware that it had become something vastly different: a systematic undertaking that had created interlocking physical and social networks in which all Americans—rich or poor, young or old, urban or rural—were increasingly enmeshed.

CORLANN GEE BUSH　　　　　　　　　　　　　　　　　　　I.5

Women and the Assessment of Technology

In this reading author Corlann Gee Bush develops a feminist analysis of technology. In doing so she tries to "unthink" and "rethink" several popular assumptions about technology, particularly ones that suggest that technological fixes can cure social problems that afflict women. She distinguishes the design, user, environmental, and cultural contexts in which technologies operate, and provides examples of how technological innovations such as the washing machine have had unexpected impacts on the cultural context of women. She then develops what she calls an equity analysis approach to technology assessment that aims to consider all of the various types of impacts that a technological innovation can have on different groups in society, and she illustrates this analysis with the example of refrigeration technology. She warns against oversimplifying new technologies into "triumphs" or "threats" and suggests a new way of looking at the multifaceted impacts of technology on society.

Focus Questions

1. What does the author mean when she uses the term *valence* to describe a particular property of technologies? What are some examples of the valences of particular technologies?

2. What are the four contexts in which technologies operate?
3. How does Bush's approach to understanding the social and ethical impacts of technology compare with that of Freeman Dyson (selection I.10) and Virginia Postrel (selection II.2)?

Keywords

constructivism, design, feminism, Native Americans, progress, refrigeration, social equality, welfare

"Everything is what it is, what it isn't, and its direct opposite. That technique, so skillfully executed, might help account for the compelling irrationality . . . *double double think is very easy to deal with if we just realize that we have only to double double unthink it.*"
—Dworkin 1974, p. 63.

Although Andrea Dworkin is here analyzing Pauline Reage's literary style in the *Story of O,* her realization that we can "double double unthink" the mind fetters by which patriarchal thought binds women is an especially useful one. For those of us who want to challenge and change female victimization, it is a compelling concept.

Something Else Again

The great strength of the women's movement has always been its twin abilities to unthink the source of oppression and to use this analysis to create a new and synthesizing vision. Assertiveness is, for example, something else again: a special, learned behavior that does more than merely combine attributes of passivity and aggressiveness. Assertiveness is an unthinking and a transcendence of those common, control-oriented behaviors.[1]

Similarly, in their books *Against Our Will* and *Rape: The Power of Consciousness,* Susan Brownmiller (1974) and Susan Griffin (1979) unthink rape as a

From *Machina Ex Dea,* pp. 151–170, Joan Rothschild, ed. (New York: Teacher's College Press). Copyright © 1983 by Joan Rothschild. All rights reserved. Reprinted by permission of the author.

crime of passion and rethink it as a crime of violence—insights which led to the establishment of rape crisis and victim advocacy services. But a good feminist shelter home-crisis service is something else again: it is a place where women are responsible for the safety and security of other women, where women teach self-defense and self-esteem in each other. In like manner, women's spirituality is something else again. Indebted both to Mary Daly for unthinking Christianity in *Beyond God the Father* (1973) and *The Church and the Second Sex* (1968) and to witchcraft for rethinking ritual, women's spirituality is more than a synthesis of those insights, it is a transformation for them.

In other words, feminist scholarship and feminist activism proceed not through a sterile, planar dialectic of thesis, antithesis, synthesis, but through a dynamic process of unthinking, rethinking, energizing, and transforming. At its best, feminism creates new life forms out of experiences as common as seawater and insights as electrifying as lightning.

The purpose of this chapter is to suggest that a feminist analysis of technology would be, like assertiveness, something else again. I will raise some of the questions that feminist technology studies should seek to ask, and I will attempt to answer them. Further, I hope to show how scholars, educators, and activity can work together toward a transformation of technological change in our society.

The endeavor is timely not least because books such as this, journal issues, articles, and conferences are increasingly devoting time and energy to the subject or because technologically related political issues such as the anti-nuclear movement and genetic engineering consume larger and larger amounts of both our news space and our consciousness. The most important reason why feminists must unthink and rethink women's relationship to technology is that the tech-fix (Weinberg 1966, p. 6) and the public policies on which it is based are no longer working. The tech-fix is the belief that technology can be used to solve all types of problems, even social ones. Belief in progress and the tech-fix has long been used to rationalize inequity: it is only a matter of time until technology extends material benefits to all citizens, regardless of race, sex, class, religion, or nationality.

> Technology has expanded our productive capacity so greatly that even though our distribution is still inefficient, and unfair by Marxian precepts, there is more than enough to go around. Technology has provided a "fix"—greatly expanded production of goods—which enables our capitalistic society to achieve many of the aims of the Marxist's social engineer without going through the social revolution Marx viewed as inevitable. Technology has converted the seemingly intractable social problem of *widespread* poverty into a relatively tractable one (Weinberg 1966, p. 7).

While Weinberg himself advocates cooperation among social and technical engineers in order to make a "better society, and thereby, a better life, for all of us who are part of society" (Weinberg 1966, p. 10), less conscientious philosophers and politicians have seen in the tech-fix a justification for laissez-faire economics and discriminatory public policy. Despite its claim to the contrary, the tech-fix has not worked well for most women or for people of color; recent analyses of the feminization of poverty, for example, indicate that jobs, which have always provided men with access to material goods, do not get women out of poverty.

> Social welfare programs based on the old male model of poverty do not consider the special nature of women's poverty. One fact that is little understood and rarely reflected in public welfare policy is that women in poverty are almost invariably productive workers, participating fully in both the paid and the unpaid work force. The inequities of present public policies molded by the traditional economic role of women cannot continue. Locked into poverty by capricious programs designed by and for male policy makers . . . women who are young and poor today are destined to grow old and poor as the years pass. Society cannot continue persisting with the male model of a job automatically lifting a family out of poverty . . . (McKee 1982, p. 36).

As this example illustrates, the traditional social policies for dealing with inequity—*get a job*—and traditional solutions—*produce more efficiently*—have not worked to make a better society for women. Therefore, it is essential that women begin the unthinking of these traditions and the thinking of new relationships between social and technical engineering.

Unthinking Tech-Myths

In her poem "To An Old House in America," Adrienne Rich describes the attitude that women should take toward the task of unthinking public policy in regard to technology: "I do not want to simplify/Or: I would simplify/By naming the complexity/It has been made o'er simple all along" (Rich 1975, p. 240). Partly because it is in their best interest to do so and partly because they truly see nothing else, most politicians and technocrats paint the canvas of popular opinion about technology with the broadest possible brushstrokes, rendering it, in pure type, as TOOL, as THREAT, or as TRIUMPH.[2] From each of these assumptions proceed argument, legislation, public policy, and, ironically, powerlessness. In order to develop a feminist critique of technology, we must analyze these assumptions and unthink them, making them simpler by naming their complexity.

The belief that technology represents the triumph of human intelligence is one of America's most cherished cultural myths; it is also the easiest to understand, analyze, and disprove. Unfortunately, to discuss it is to resort to cliches: "There's nothing wrong that a little good old American ingenuity can't fix"; "That's progress"; or "Progress is our most important product." From such articles of faith in technology stemmed Manifest Destiny, the mechanization of agriculture, the urbanization of rural and nomadic cultures, the concept of the twentieth as the "American Century," and every World's Fair since 1893. That such faith seems naive to a generation that lives with the arms race, acid rain, hazardous waste, and near disasters at nuclear power plants is not to diminish one *byte* either Western culture's faith in the tech-fix or its belief that technological change equal material progress. And, indeed, like all generalizations, this myth is true—at least partially. Technology *has* decreased hardships and suffering while raising standards of health, living, and literacy throughout the industrialized world.

But, not without problems, as nay-sayers are so quick to point out. Those who perceive technology as the ultimate threat to life on the planet look upon it as an iatrogenic disease, one created, like nausea in chemotherapy patients, by the very techniques with which we treat the disease. In this view, toxic wastes, pollution, urban sprawl, increasing rates of skin cancer, even tasteless tomatoes, are all problems created through our desire to control nature through technology. Characterized by their desire to go cold turkey on the addiction to the tech-fix, contemporary critics of technology participate in a myriad of activities and organizations (Zero Population Growth, Friends of the Earth, Sierra Club, the Greenpeace Foundation) and advocate a varsity of goals (peace, arms limitation, appropriate technology, etc.). And, once again, their technology-as-threat generalization is true, or at least as true as its opposite number: in truth, no one, until Rachel Carson (1955), paid much attention to the effects of technology on the natural world it tried to control; indeed, technology has created problems as it has set out to solve others.

Fortunately, the inadequacy of such polarized thinking is obvious: technology is neither wholly good nor wholly bad. "It has both positive and negative effects, and it usually has the two *at the same time and in virtue of each other*" (Mesthene 1970, p. 26). Every innovation has both positive and negative consequences that pulse through the social fabric like waves through water.

Much harder to unthink is the notion that technologies are merely tools: neither good nor bad but neutral, moral only to the extent that their user is moral. This, of course, is the old saw "guns don't kill people, people kill people" writ large enough to include not only guns and nuclear weapons but also cars, televisions, and computer games. And there is truth here, too. Any given person can use any given gun at any given time either to kill another person for revenge or to shoot a grouse for supper. The gun is the tool through which the shooter accomplishes his or her objectives. However, just as morality is a collective concept, so too are guns. As a class of objects, they comprise a technology that is designed for killing in a way that ice picks, hammers, even knives—all tools that have on occasion been used as weapons—are not. To believe that technologies are neutral tools subject only to the motives and morals of the user is to miss completely their collective significance. Tools and technologies have what I can only describe as *valence*, a bias or "charge" analogous to that of atoms that have lost or gained electrons through ionization. A particular technological system, even an individual tool, has a tendency to interact in similar situations in identifiable and predictable ways. In other words, particular tools or technologies tend to be favored in certain situations, tend to perform in a predictable manner in these situations, and tend to bend other interactions to them. Valence tends to seek out or fit in with certain social norms and to ignore or disturb others.

Jacques Ellul (1964) seems to be identifying something like valence when he describes "the specific weight" with which technique is endowed:

> It is not a kind of neutral matter, with no direction, quality, or structure. It is a power endowed with its own peculiar force. It refracts in its own specific sense the wills which make use of it and the ends proposed for it. Indeed, independently of the objectives that man pretends to assign to any given technical means, that means always conceals in itself a finality which cannot be evaded (pp. 140–41).

While this seems to be overstating the case a bit— valence is not the atom, only one of its attributes—

tools and techniques do have tendencies to pull or push behavior in definable ways. Guns, for example, are valenced to violence; the presence of a gun in a given situation raises the level of violence by its presence alone. Television, on the other hand, is valenced to individuation; despite the fact that any number of people may be present in the same room at the same time, there will not be much conversation because the presence of the TV itself pulls against interaction and pushes toward isolation. Similarly, automobiles and microwave ovens are individuating technologies while trains and campfires are accretionary ones.

Unthinking tech-myths and understanding valence also requires greater clarity of definition (Winner 1977, pp. 10–12). Several terms, especially *tool, technique,* and *technology,* are often used interchangeably when, in fact, they describe related but distinguishable phenomena. *Tools* are the implements, gadgets, machines, appliances, and instruments themselves. A hammer is, for example, a tool as is a spoon or an automatic washing machine. *Techniques* are the skills, methods, procedures, and processes that people perform in order to use tools. Carpentry is, therefore, a technique that utilizes hammers, baking is a technique that uses spoons, and laundering a technique that employs washing machines. *Technology* refers to the organized systems of interactions that utilize tools and involve techniques for the performance of tasks and the accomplishment of objectives. Hammers and carpentry are some of the tools and techniques of architectural or building technology. Spoons and baking, washing machines and laundering are some of the tools and techniques of domestic or household technology.

A feminist critique of the public policy debate over technology should, thus, unthink the tripartite myth that sees technology in simple categories as tool, triumph, or threat. In unthinking it, we can simplify it by naming its complexity:

- A tool is not a simple isolated thing but is a member of a class of objects designed for specific purposes.
- Any given use of tools, techniques, or technologies can have both beneficial and detrimental effects at the same time.

- Both use and effect are expressions of a valance or propensity for tools to function in certain ways in certain settings.
- Polarizing the rhetoric about technology enables advocates of particular points of view to gain adherents and power while doing nothing to empower citizens to understand, discuss, and control technology on their own.

"Making it o'er simple all along" has proven an excellent technique for maintaining social control. The assertion that technology is beneficial lulls people into believing that there is nothing wrong that can't be fixed, so they do nothing. Likewise, the technophobia that sees technology as evil frightens people into passivity and they do nothing. The argument that technology is value-free either focuses on the human factor in technology in order to obscure its valence or else concentrates on the autonomy of technology in order to obscure its human control. In all cases, the result is that people feel they can do nothing. In addition, by encouraging people to argue with and blame each other, rhetoric wars draw public attention away from more important questions such as: Who is making technological decisions? On what basis? What will the effects be?

Context, Context, Whither Art Thou, Context?

In unthinking the power dynamics of technological decision making, a feminist critique needs to pay special attention to the social messages whispered in women's ears since birth: mother to daughter, "Don't touch that, you'll get dirty"; father to daughter, "Don't worry your pretty little head about it"; teacher to young girl, "It doesn't matter if you can't do math"; woman to woman, "Boy, a man must have designed this."

Each of these statements is talking about a CONTEXT in which technological decisions are made, technical information is conveyed, and technological innovations are adopted. That such social learning is characterized by sex role stereotyping should come as no surprise. What may be surprising is not the depths of women's ignorance—after all, women have, by and large, been encouraged to be ignorant—but the extent to which men in general, inventors, technocrats, even scholars, all share an amazing ignorance about the contexts in which technology operates. There are four:

1. *The design or developmental context* which includes all the decisions, materials, personnel, processes, and systems necessary to create tools and techniques from raw materials.

2. *The user context* which includes all the motivations, intentions, advantages, and adjustments called into play by the use of particular techniques or tools.

3. *The environmental context* that describes non-specific physical surroundings in which a technology or tool is developed and used.

4. *The cultural context* which includes all the norms, values, myths, aspirations, laws, and interactions of the society of which the tool or technique is a part.

Of these, much more is known about the design or developmental context of technology than about the other three put together. Western culture's collective lack of knowledge about all but the developmental context of technology springs in part from what Langdon Winner calls technological orthodoxy: a "philosophy of sorts" that has seldom been "subject to the light of critical scrutiny" (Winner 1979, p. 75). Standard tenets of technological orthodoxy include:

- That men know best what they themselves have made.
- That the things men make are under their firm control.
- That technologies are neutral: they are simply tools that can be used one way or another; the benefit or harm they bring depends on how men use them (Winner 1979, p. 76).

If one accepts these assumptions, then there is very little to do except study processes of design and invent ever-newer gadgets. The user and environmental contexts become obscured if not invisible, an invisibility further confirmed by the fact that,

since the Industrial Revolution, men have been inventors and designers while women have been users and consumers of technology. By and large, men have created, women have accommodated.

The sex role division of labor that characterizes Western societies has ensured that boys and girls have been brought up with different expectations, experiences, and training, a pattern that has undergone remarkably little change since the nineteenth century.

> Games for girls were carefully differentiated from boys' amusement. A girl might play with a hoop or swing gently, but the "ruder and more daring gymnastics of boys" were outlawed. Competitive play was also anathema: A "little girl should never be ambitious to swing higher than her companions." Children's board games afforded another insidious method of inculcating masculinity and femininity. On a boys' game board the player moved in an upward spiral, past temptations, obstacles, and reverses until the winner reached a pinnacle of propriety and prestige. A girl's playful enactment of her course in life moved via circular ever-inward path to the "mansion of happiness," a pastel tableau of mother and child. The dice of popular culture were loaded for both sexes and weighted with domesticity for little women. The doctrine of (separate) spheres was thereby insinuated in the personality of the child early in life and even during the course of play (Ryan 1979, p. 92).

It is difficult to invent a better mousetrap if you're taught to be afraid of mice; it is impossible to dream of becoming an engineer if you're never allowed to get dirty.

As compared to women, men do, indeed, know a great deal about what they would call the "design interface" of technology; they know more about how machines work; they discovered the properties of elements and the principles of science. They know math, they develop cost-benefit risk analyses; they discover, invent, engineer, manufacture, and sell. Collectively, men know almost everything there is to know about the design and development of tools, techniques, and systems; but they understand far less about how their technologies are used—in part because there is less money in understanding than in designing, in part because the burden of adjusting to technological change falls more heavily on women. What is worse, however, is that most men do not know that they do not know anything about women and the user context.

> From the preliminary conceptualization to the final marketing of a product, most decision making about technology is done by men who design, usually subconsciously, a model of the physical world in which they would like to live, using material artifacts which meet the needs of the people—men—they best know. The result is technological development based on particular sets of male conditioning, values, and roles . . . (Zimmerman 1981, p. 2).

Ironically, until very recently, most women did not realize that they possessed information of any great significance. With all the cultural attention focused on the activity in the developmental context, it was hard to see beyond the glare of the spotlights into the living rooms and kitchens and laundries where women were working and living out the answers to dozens of unverbalized questions: How am I spending my time here? How is my work different from what I remember my mother doing? Am I really better off? Why does everything seem so out of control? Rephrased, these are the questions that will comprise a feminist assessment of technology: How have women's roles changed as a result of modern technology? Has women's status in society kept pace with the standard of living? Do women today have more opportunities or merely more expectations? What is the relationship of material possessions to personal freedom?

Think for a moment about washing machines. Almost every family in the United States has access to one; across the country, women spend thousands of hours each day in sorting, washing, drying, folding, and ironing clothes. The automatic washing machine has freed women from the pain and toil described so well by Agnes Smedley (1973) in *Daughter of Earth*. But as washing technology has changed, so too has clothing (it gets dirtier faster) and wardrobes (we own more clothes) and even standards of cleanliness (clothes must be whiter

than white), children change clothes more often, there are more clothes to wash. Joan Vanek (1974, p. 118), in her work on time spent in housework, asserts that women spent as much time in household-related tasks in 1966 as they did in 1926.

More has changed, however, than just standards of cleanliness. Doing laundry used to be a collective enterprise. When I was a child in the late 1940s and early 1950s, my mother and grandmother washed the family's clothes together. My grandmother owned a semiautomatic machine but she lived 45 miles away; my mother had hot water, a large sink, and five children. Every Sunday, we would dump the dirty clothes in a big wicker basket and drive to my grandmother's house where all the womenfolk would spend the afternoon in the basement, talking and laughing as we worked. By evening, the wicker basket would again be full, but this time with neatly folded, clean smelling piles of socks, sheets, towels, and underwear that would have to last us a week. Crisply ironed dresses and slacks, on hangers, waited to be hung, first on those little hooks over the side doors of the car, then in our closets at home.

Nostalgic as these memories are, doing laundry was not romantic. It was exhausting, repetitious work, and neither my mother nor I would trade in our own automatic washers to go back to it (Armitage 1982, pp. 3–6). Yet, during my childhood, laundry was a communal activity, an occasion for gossip, friendship, and bonding. Laundering was hard work, and everyone in the family and in the society knew it and respected us as laborers. Further, having laundry and a day on which to do it was an organizing principle (Monday, wash day; Tuesday, iron; Wednesday . . .) around which women allocated their time and resources. And, finally, there was a closure, a sense of completion and accomplishment impossible to achieve today when my sister washes, dries, folds, and irons her family's clothes every day or when I wash only because I have nothing to wear.

Admittedly, this homey digression into soap opera (One Woman's Wash) is a far cry from the design specification and cost-benefit analyses men use to describe and understand the developmental context of washing machines, but it is equally valid for it describes the user context in the user's terms. Analyzing the user context of technological change is a process of collecting thousands and thousands of such stories and rethinking them into an understanding of the effects of technological change on women's lives.[3] From unthinking the developmental context as such and rethinking the user context, it is only a short step to studying the environmental and cultural contexts of technological change. Of these, our knowledge of the environmental context is the better developed, partly because we have given it more serious attention but mostly because environmental studies has been a legitimate career option for men.

While concern about the effects of technology on the natural environment is an idea that can be traced back to de Crevecoeur (1782) and James Fenimore Cooper (1832), Rachel Carson (1955, 1961, 1962) is the person most responsible for our current level of ecological awareness and for the scientific rather than aesthetic basis on which it rests. As we learn more about the fragile reciprocity within ecosystems, we begin to unthink the arrogance of our assumption that we are separate from and superior to nature. In an ecosystem, it is never possible to do only *one* thing; for every action there are chain reactions of causes and effects. The continued survival of the world depends upon developing more precise models of the environment so we can predict and prevent actual catastrophe without being immobilized by the risking of it.

Perhaps no one could have foreseen that the aerosol sprays we used to apply everything from paint to antiperspirant would degrade the earth's ozone layer, but no one seems to have asked. That drums for burying toxic waste would eventually corrode and leak seems so obvious that millions ought to have been able to predict the risk, yet no one seems to have had the desire or the clout to deal with the problem of hazardous waste before it became a crisis. In pursuit of progress, we have been content to ignore the ecological consequences of our technological decisions because, until it was pointed out to us, we did not realize that there *was* an environmental context surrounding the tools we use.

The environmental impact analysis (EIA) has become the most popular means by which governments and industries attempt to predict and assess the ecological impact of technological change. While most EIAs are long, tedious, and nonconfrontive, the idea behind them and much of the work that has gone into them is sound. In her articles on appropriate technology, Judy Smith (1978, 1981) from the Women and Technology Projection in Missoula, Montana, has suggested that sex-role impact reports could be used to improve our understanding of the cultural context of technology in much the same way that the EIA has improved our knowledge of the environmental context.

And we do need something, for we know next to nothing about the interactions of culture and technology, having always seen these as separate phenomena. Most people welcome technological change because it is *material*, believing that it makes things better, but it doesn't make them different. They resist social change because it is *social* and personal; it is seen as making things different . . . worse. The realization that technological change stimulates social change is not one that most people welcome.

Feminists need to unthink this cultural blindness. Because women are idealized as culture carriers, as havens of serenity in a heartless world (Lasch 1977), women are supposed to remain passive while the rest of the culture is allowed, even encouraged, to move rapidly ahead. Women are like the handles of a slingshot whose relatively motionless support enables the elastic and shot to build up energy and to accelerate past them at incredible speeds. The culture measures its progress by women's status. When women do try to move, when they try to make changes rather than accommodations, they are accused of selfishness, of me-ness, of weakening the family, of being disloyal to civilization (Rich 1979, pp. 275–310).

However, it is crucial that feminists continue to unthink and rethink the cultural contexts of technology for a reason more significant than our systematic exclusion from it: it is dangerous not to. Technology always enters into the present culture, accepting and exacerbating the existing norms and values. In a society characterized by a sex-role division of labor, any tool or technique—it has valence, remember—will have dramatically different effects on men than on women.

Two examples will serve to illustrate this point. Prior to the acquisition of horses between the late sixteenth and mid-seventeenth centuries, women and dogs were the beasts of burden for Native American tribes on the Great Plains. Mobility was limited by both the topography and the speed at which people and dogs could walk. Physical labor was women's province in Plains culture, but since wealth in those societies was determined by how many dogs a person "owned" and since women owned the dogs, the status of women in pre-equestrian tribes was relatively high—they owned what men considered wealth (Roe 1955, p. 29). Women were central to the economic and social life of their tribes in more than the ownership of the dogs. They controlled the technology of travel and food: they were responsible for the foraging, gathering, and preserving of food for the tribe and, in many cases, determined the time and routes of tribal migration. They had access to important women's societies and played a central part in religious and community celebrations (Liberty 1982, p. 14).

Women's roles in Plains Indian societies changed profoundly and rapidly as horses were acquired and domesticated. In less than two centuries—for some tribes in less than a generation—a new culture evolved. The most immediate changes were technological and economic; horses became the technology for transportation and they were owned by men. Women could still own dogs, but this was no longer the measure of wealth it had been.

With their "currency" debased, women's status slipped further as important economic, social, and religious roles were reassigned to men. As the buffalo became a major source of food and shelter, the value of women's foraging activities decreased. Hunting ranges were expanded, causing more frequent moves with women doing more of the packing up and less of the deciding about when and where to go. As each tribe's hunting range increased, competition for land intensified; and warfare, raiding, and their concomitants for women—rape and slavery—also increased.

Of course, not all the effects were negative. Technologies are substitutes for human labor: horses made women's work easier and more effective. Also, several tribes, including the Blackfeet, allowed a woman to retain ownership of her own horse and saddle. However, a woman was seldom allowed to trade or raid for horses, and her rights to her husband's herd usually ended with his death.

Thus, for Native American women, the horse was a mixed blessing. It eased their burdens and made transportation easier. But it also added new tasks and responsibilities without adding authority over those tasks or increasing autonomy. The opposite was true for men; the horse provided few new tasks and responsibilities—men had always been responsible for hunting, defense, and warfare—but it did enhance these traditional roles, giving men more decision-making authority, more autonomy, and more access to status. Paradoxically, while a woman's absolute status was greatly improved by the changes from dog to horse culture, her status relative to men actually declined. In this manner, horses changed the nature of Native American culture on the high plains, but women and men were affected in profoundly different ways.

A similar phenomenon occurred at the end of the horse farming era in the Palouse region of Idaho and Washington in the United States. During the 1920s, it was common for a farmer to employ fifteen to twenty-five hired men and to use twenty-five to forty-four horses to harvest his crops; farmers and their hands worked back-breaking, twenty-hour days. On the other hand, women also worked long days during harvest, cooking five meals a day for as many as forty people. During the year, women were responsible for a family's food, nutrition, health, safety, and sanitation. Women's work had economic value. Performing their traditional roles as wives, mothers, and homemakers, women were economically crucial to the survival of the labor intensive family farm (Bush 1982). Unfortunately, in the same manner that the horse made a Plains Indian woman's work easier even as it lowered her status relative to men, so too did the conversion from horses to diesel power and electricity ease the farm wife's hardships while it decreased the economic significance of her labor. In both cases, technological innovation had profoundly different consequences for men's and women's work. In both cases, the innovation was coded or valenced in such a way that it loaded the status of men's roles while eroding status for women.

Technology and Equity

Technology is, therefore, an equity issue. Technology has everything to do with who benefits and who suffers, whose opportunities increase and whose decrease, who creates and who accommodates. If women are to transform or "re-valence" technology, we must develop ways to assess the equity implications of technological development and develop strategies for changing social relationships as well as mechanical techniques. To do this, we must have a definition of technology that will allow us to focus on such questions of equity.

Not surprisingly, there are no such empowering definitions in the existing literature. Equity has not been a major concern of either technophobes or technophiles. In fact, most definitions of technology fall short on several counts. The most commonly accessible definitions, those in dictionaries, tell us little: Webster's "the science of the industrial arts" and "science used in a practical way," and the American Heritage Dictionary's "the application of science, especially to industrial and commercial objectives" and "the entire body of methods, and materials used to achieve such objectives" are definitions so abstract as to be meaningless. Other attempts clarify function but lose the crucial connection to science, as in James Burke's (1980, p. 23) "the sum total of all the objects and systems used to produce goods and perform services."

Better definitions connect technology to other categories of human behavior and to human motivation.

A form of cultural activity devoted to the production or transformation of material objects, or

the creation of procedural systems, in order to expand the realm of practical human possibility (Hannay & McGinn 1980, p. 27).

On rare occasions, definitions do raise equity questions as in John McDermott's attempt:

Technology, in its concrete, empirical meaning, refers fundamentally to systems of rationalized control over large groups of men, events, and machines by small groups of technically skilled men operating through organizational hierarchy (McDermott 1969, p. 29).

However, this definition is really defining *technocracy* rather than *technology*. More often, there are romantic definitions that enmesh us in cotton candy:

[Technology's task] is to employ the earth's resources and energy income in such a way as to support all humanity while also enabling all people to enjoy the whole earth, all its historical artifacts and its beautiful places without any man enjoying life around earth at the cost of another (Fuller 1969, p. 348).

While no one could argue with such ideals, Buckminster Fuller leaves us where the boon and bane theorists leave us—confounded by doublethink. It is impossible to ask tough questions of such a definition or to examine closely why technology does not now support all humanity equally.

More distressing is the tendency of scholars to use the generic "he/man" to represent all of humanity. For example, "without one man interfering with the other, without any man enjoying life around the earth at the cost of another" is a statement that completely disregards the fact that, around the earth, men enjoy their lives at *women's* cost. Similarly, statements such as "because of the autonomy of technique, man cannot choose his means any more than his ends" (Ellul 1964, p. 40) and "the roots of the machine's genealogical tree is in the brain of this conceptual man. . . after all it was he who made the machine" (Usher 1954, p. 22) grossly mislead us because they obscure the historical and contemporary roles that women have played in technological development. Worse, they reinforce the most disabling myth of all, the assumption that men and women are affected similarly by and benefit equally from technological change.

Therefore, because of the oversimplification of some definitions and the exclusion of women from others, feminists need to rethink a definition of technology that both includes women and facilitates an equity analysis. Such a definition might be:

> Technology is a form of human cultural activity that applies the principles of science and mechanics to the solution of problems. It includes the resources, tools, processes, personnel, and systems developed to perform tasks and create immediate particular, and personal and/or competitive advantages in a given ecological, economic, and social context (Bush in *Taking Hold of Technology* 1981, p. 1).

The chief virtue of this definition is its consideration of advantage; people accept and adopt technology to the extent that they see advantage for themselves and, in competitive situations, disadvantage for others. Thus, an equity analysis of an innovation should focus on benefits and risk within the contexts in which the technology operates. An equity analysis of a technology would examine the following:

The developmental context:

- the principles of science and mechanics applied by the tool or technique
- the resources, tools, processes, and systems employed to develop it
- the tasks to be performed and the specific problems to be solved

The user context:

- the current tool, technique, or system that will be displaced by its use
- the interplay of this innovation with others that are currently in use
- the immediate personal advantage and competitive advantage created by the use of technology
- the second and third level consequences for individuals

The environmental context:

- the ecological impact of accepting the technology versus the impact of continuing current techniques

The cultural context:

- the impact on sex roles
- the social system affected
- the organization of communities
- the economic system involved and the distribution of goods within this system

A specific example will serve to illustrate how an equity analysis might be approached. Refrigeration was "invented" in the 1840s in Apalachicola, Florida, by John Gorrie as a by-product of his work on a cure for malaria (Burke 1980, p. 238). Gorrie's invention was a freezing machine that used a steam-driven piston to compress air in a cylinder that was surrounded by salt water. (As the piston advances, it compresses air in the cylinder; as the piston retracts, the air expands.) An expanding gas draws heat from its surroundings; after several strokes of the piston, the gas has extracted all the heat available from the surrounding brine. If a flow of continuously cold air is then pumped out of the cylinder into the surrounding air, the result is air conditioning; if the air is continuously allowed to cool the brine solution, the brine itself will draw heat from water, causing it to freeze and make ice. If the gas (air) or brine is allowed to circulate in a closed system, heat will be drawn from the surrounding air or matter (food), causing refrigeration.

THE DEVELOPMENTAL CONTEXT

Thus, refrigeration applies the laws of science (especially the properties of gases) and the principles of mechanics (thermodynamics and compression) to perform the tasks of making ice, preserving and freezing food, and cooling air. Refrigeration also solves the problems of retarding food spoilage and coping with heat waves, thereby creating personal advantage. The resources and tools used include a gas, a solution, a source of energy, and a piston-driven compressor.

The developmental context is enormously complex and interconnected; however, a general analysis would include all the supply, manufacture, and distribution systems for the refrigeration units themselves—everything from the engineers who design the appliances, to the factory workers who make, inspect, and pack them, to the truckers who transport them, to the clerk who sells them. A truly expansive analysis of the development context would also include the food production, packing, and distribution systems required to make available even one box of frozen peas as well as the artists, designers, paper producers, and advertisers who package the peas and induce us to buy them.

THE USER CONTEXT

Refrigeration has affected our lives in such a myriad of ways that elaborating on them all would require another paper in itself. Refrigeration has important commercial uses as well as medical ones, and it would not be overstating the case to assert that there is no aspect of modern life that has not been affected by refrigeration. Nonetheless, a more limited analysis of refrigeration as it has affected domestic and family life in the United States is both revealing and instructive.

To the self-sufficient farm family of the early twentieth century, refrigeration meant release from the food production and preservation chores that dominated much of men's and women's lives: canning garden produce to get the family through the winter; butchering, smoking, and drying meat from farm-raised hogs and cattle; milking cows daily and churning butter. The advantages of owning a refrigerator in such a situation were immediate and dramatic: food could be preserved for longer periods of time so there was less spoilage; food could be cooked ahead of serving time allowing women to spend less time in meal preparation; freezing produce and meat was a faster, easier, and more sanitary process than canning or smoking, again, saving women time and improving the family's health. The refrigerator thus generated positive changes for women, freeing them from hard, hot work and improving their absolute status. However, the second and third level effects of refrigera-

tion technology were not as benign for women as the primary effects.

Since refrigeration kept food fresh for long periods of time, fresh produce could be shipped across country, thus improving nutrition nationwide. Food processing and preservation moved out of the home, and new industries and services paid workers to perform the duties that had once been almost solely women's domestic responsibilities. Within the home, the nature of women's work changed from responsibility for managing food production to responsibility for managing food consumption. Also, farmers stopped growing food for family subsistence and local markets and started growing cash crops for sale on national and international markets. Opportunities for employment shifted from farm labor to industrial labor, and families moved from rural areas to cities and suburbs. Thus, the use of refrigeration changed the work roles of individual women and men and, through them, the economy, the content of work, and the nature of culture and agriculture.

THE ENVIRONMENTAL CONTEXT

An analysis of the environmental context of refrigeration technology would examine the effects of the developmental and user contexts on the environment by asking such questions as: Since refrigeration affects agriculture, what are the ecological effects of cash crop monoculture on, say, soil erosion or the use of pesticides? Since refrigeration retards the growth of bacteria and preserves blood and pharmaceuticals, what are the consequences for disease control? What are the effects of increased transportation of food on energy supplies and air pollution?

THE CULTURAL CONTEXT

Finally, an examination of the sex role impact of refrigeration technology would reveal a disparate effect on men and women. In the United States, men have been largely responsible for food production, women for food preservation and preparation. Refrigerators were a valenced technology that affected women's lives by, generally, removing food preservation from their domestic duties and relocating it in the market economy. Women now buy what they once canned. Women's traditional roles have been eroded, as their lives have been made easier. On the other hand, men, who originally had very little to do with food preservation, canning, or cooking, now control the processes by which food is manufactured and sold. Men's roles and responsibilities have been loaded and their opportunities increased, although their work has not necessarily been made easier. Refrigeration has, thus, been adopted and diffused throughout a sexist society; we should not be surprised to learn that its effects have been dissimilar and disequitable.

The Great Chain of Causation

Of course, not one of us thinks about the effects of refrigeration on soil erosion or women's status when we open the fridge to get a glass of milk. We are gadget-rich and assessment-poor in this society, yet each private act connects us to each other in a great chain of causation. Unfortunately, to think about the consequences of one's actions is to risk becoming immobilized; so the culture teaches us to double think rather than think, and lulls us into believing that individual solutions can work for the collective good.

Of course, we can continue to double think such things only so long as we can foist negative effects and disadvantages off onto someone else: onto women if we are men, onto blacks if we are white, onto youth if we are old, onto the aged if we are young. Equity for others need not concern us as long as *we* are immediately advantaged.

Feminists, above all, must give the lie to this rationale, to unthink it; for if the women's movement teaches anything, it is that there can be no individual solutions to collective problems. A feminist transformation of technological thought must include unthinking the old myths of technology as threat or triumph and rethinking the attendant rhetoric. A feminist unthinking of technology should strive for a holistic understanding of the contexts in which it operates and should present an unflinching analysis of its advantages and disadvantages. Above all, a feminist assessment of technology must recognize technology as an equity issue. The challenge to feminists is to transform society in order to make technology equitable and to transform technology in order to make society equitable. A feminist technology should, indeed, be something else again.

NOTES

1. I am indebted for this insight to Betsy Brown and the other students in my seminar "The Future of the Female Principle," University of Idaho, Spring 1982.
2. In *Technological Change: Its Impact on Man and Society* (1970), Emmanuel Mesthene identifies "three unhelpful views about technology: technology as blessing, technology as curse, and technology as unworthy of notice." He does not mention the "technology as neutral tool argument," perhaps because he is one of its leading proponents.
3. Obviously, oral history is the only way that scholars can accumulate this data. Oral historians should ask respondents questions about their acquisition of and adaptation to household appliances. Such questions might include: "When did you get electricity?"; "What was the first appliance you bought?"; "What was your first washing machine like?"; "How long did it take you to learn how to use it?"; "What was your next machine like?"; "When did you get running water?"; "Are you usually given appliances for presents or do you buy them yourself?," etc.
4. This situation is slowly changing thanks to much good work by Elise Boulding (1976), Patricia Draper (1975), Nancy Tanner and Adrienne Zihlman (1976), and Autumn Stanley (1984, and the volume from which this chapter was taken.)

REFERENCES

Armitage, Susan. 1982. Wash on Monday: The housework of farm women in transition. *Plainswoman* VI, 2:3–6.

Boulding, Elise. 1976. *The underside of history: A view of women through time.* Boulder, Colo.: Westview Press.

Brownmiller, Susan. 1974. *Against our will: Men, women and rape.* New York: Simon and Schuster.

Burke, James. 1980: *Connections.* Boston: Little, Brown

Bush, Corlann Gee. 1982. The barn is his; the house is mine: Agricultural technology and sex roles. *Energy and transport.* Eds. George Daniels and Mark Rose, Beverly Hills, Calif.: Sage Publications, 235–59.

Carson, Rachel. 1955. *The edge of the sea.* Boston: Houghton Mifflin.

Carson, Rachel. 1961. *The sea around us.* New York: Oxford University Press.

Carson, Rachel. 1962. *Silent spring.* Boston: Houghton Mifflin.

Cooper, James Fenimore. 1832. *The pioneer.* Philadelphia: Carey & Lea.

Daly, Mary. 1968. *The church and the second sex.* New York: Harper & Row.

Daly, Mary. 1973. *Beyond God the father: Toward a philosophy of women's liberation.* Boston: Beacon Press.

de Crevecoeur, Michel Guillaume St. Jean. 1968. *Letters from an American farmer: Reprint of 1782 edition.* Magnolia, Mass.: Peter Smith.

Draper, Patricia. 1975. Kung women: Contrasts in sexual egalitarianism in foraging and sedentary contexts. *Toward an anthropology of women.* Ed. Rayna Reiter. New York: Monthly Review Press: 77–109.

Dworking, Andrea, 1974. *Woman hating.* New York: E. P. Dutton.

Ellul, Jacques. 1964. *The technological society.* New York: Knopf.

Fuller, R. Buckminster. 1969. *Utopia or oblivion: The prospects for humanity.* New York: Bantam Books.

Griffin, Susan. 1979. *Rape: The power of consciousness.* New York: Harper & Row.

Hannay, N. Bruce; and McGinn, Robert. 1980. The anatomy of modern technology. *Daedalus* 109, 1:25–53.

Lasch, Christopher. 1977. *Haven in a heartless world: The family besieged.* New York: Basic Books.

Liberty, Margot, 1982. Hell came with horses: Plains Indian women in the equestrian era. *Montana: The Magazine of Western History* 32, 3:10–19.

McDermott, John. 1969. Technology: The opiate of the intellectuals. *New York Review of Books* XVI, 2 (July):25–35.

McKee, Alice. 1982. The feminization of poverty. *Graduate Woman* 76, 4:34–36.

Mesthene, Emmanuel G. 1970. *Technological change: Its impact on man and society.* Cambridge, Mass.: Harvard University Press.

Rich, Adrienne. 1975. *Poems: Selected and new 1950–1974.* New York: W. W. Norton.

Rich, Adrienne. 1979. Disloyal to civilization. *On lies, secrets and silence: Selected prose.* New York: W. W. Norton.

Roe, Frank Gilbert, 1955. *The Indian and the horse.* Norman, Okla.: University of Oklahoma Press.

Ryan, Mary P. 1979. *Womanhood in America: From colonial times to the present.* 2nd ed. New York: Franklin Watts.

Smedley, Agnes. 1973. *Daughter of earth.* Old Westbury, N.W.: The Feminist Press.

Smith, Judy. 1978. *Something old, something new, something borrowed, something due: Women and appropriate technology.* Butte, Mont.: National Center for Appropriate Technology.

Smith, Judy. 1981. Women and technology: What is at stake? *Graduate Woman* 75, 1:33–35.

Stanley, Autumn. 1984. *Mothers of invention. Women inventors and innovators through the ages.* Metuchen, N.J.: Scarecrow Press.

Taking hold of technology: Topic guide for 1981–83. 1981. Washington, D.C.: American Association of University Women.

Tanner, Nancy; and Zihlman, Adrienne. 1976. Women in evolution: Part I. Innovation and selection in human origins. *Signs* 1 (Spring): 585–608.

Usher, Abbott Payson. 1954. *A history of mechanical inventions.* Cambridge: Harvard University Press.

Vanek, Joann. 1974. Time spent in housework. *Scientific American* 231 (November): 116–20.

Weinberg, Alvin M. 1966. Can technology replace social engineering? *University of Chicago Magazine* 59:6–10.

Winner, Langdon. 1977. *Autonomous technology: Technics-out-of-control as a theme in political thought.* Cambridge: MIT Press.

Winner, Langdon. 1979. The political philosophy of alternative technology. *Technology in Society* 1:75–86.

Zimmerman, Jan. 1981. Introduction. *Future, technology and woman: Proceedings of the conference.* San Diego, Calif.: Women's Studies Department, San Diego State University.

RICHARD SCLOVE   I.6

I'd Hammer Out Freedom: Technology as Politics and Culture

Even though technologies are usually developed to meet a particular need or solve a specific problem, they often have secondary functions or unintended effects on our lives. In this article, Richard Sclove is interested in how technologies exist within, are influenced by, and in turn, exert influence on society. He claims that they often work in subtle ways, to both define and set limits on human interaction.

The view of "technology as society" discussed in this article states that although technology influences the social experience, it is not the sole determinant of how society develops. As a technology goes through various evolutionary stages, it assumes a greater role in our lives, and we become less aware of its influence and less likely to seek alternative ways of doing something. It is important, claims Sclove, for societies to look for alternative technologies more in keeping with humane ideals and aspirations.

Focus Questions

1. Identify one modern technology and discuss its development. In what ways has this technology changed the way you live from both a positive and negative perspective, and what future changes might occur that could have even more impact on your life?
2. Identify one environmental and organizational background imperative of a contemporary technology. How might those conditions have influenced that technology's development and its influence on our lives?
3. What are some ways in which Sclove's concept of "polypotency" relates to the issues of "freedom, power, authority, community and justice" raised in the reading by Langdon Winner (selection I.9)?

Keywords

artifact, citizenship, democracy, primary function, social consequences, social structure

WHAT IS TECHNOLOGY? People ordinarily think of technology as machinery or gadgetry, as an economic factor of production, as know-how, as what engineers do, or as progress. Often they characterize technologies in terms of a single intended function. What is a hammer? It's what someone uses to pound nails into boards. What is a telephone? It's a device that enables people to converse at a distance. Some technologies, however, have more than one intended function. Hammers, for example, can pound nails into boards but can also extract them. This is the core of the contemporary view of technology. People understand technologies in terms of a primary function—or, occasionally, several functions—that each is intended to accomplish.

Beyond this, our society has in the past few decades come to acknowledge that technologies tend to produce at least two general kinds of "secondary" or "unintended" effects. First, they generate environmental consequences: pollution, resource depletion, and ecosystem modification. Each of these may, in turn, have direct or indirect effects on human life. Second, they promote unintended social consequences—consequences that are generally mediated by economic markets (e.g., the replacement of workers by machines or the emergence of boomtowns). Thus common knowledge has it that technologies perform one or perhaps a few intended functions, while also producing a limited range of unintended social and environmental consequences.

Although this view of technology is straightforward, it is also incomplete and misleading. It diverts attention from many significant aspects of technology, including some of central concern to democracy. By synthesizing recent technological criticism, the alternative view of technology introduced here incorporates the accepted view's sound insights but situates these within a broader perspective that recognizes technologies as a species of social structure.

The phrase "social structure" refers to the background features that help define or regulate patterns of human interaction. Familiar examples include laws, dominant political and economic institutions, and systems of cultural belief. Technologies qualify as social structures because they function politically and culturally in a manner comparable to these other, more commonly recognized kinds of social structures.

Technologies as Social Structures

Ibieca, a Spanish village, found that its indoor plumbing came at the expense of community integration. That is an instance of a technology helping to structure social relations. Upsetting a traditional pattern of water use compromised important means through which the village had previously perpetuated itself as a self-conscious community.[2] In the United States the automobile has played a somewhat similar role in disrupting prior patterns of community life.[3]

These are not isolated cases; technologies designed for such mundane tasks as commuting to work or cooking food also routinely help constitute social systems of cooperation, isolation, or domination.[4]

> Technology often embodies and expresses political value choices that, in their operations and effects, are binding on individuals and groups, whether such choices have been made in political forums or elsewhere. . . . Technological processes in contemporary society have become the equivalent of a form of law—that is, an authoritative or binding expression of social norms and values from which the individual or a group may have no immediate recourse.[5]

COERCIVE COMPLIANCE

Technologies help regulate social behavior in part because they are themselves governed by both physical and political laws. For example, the operation of many technologies—such as automobiles, medical X-ray machines, or guns—is legally regulated. Thus their misuse can entail a socially enforced penalty.

However, whether or not they are governed by legal regulations, technologies generally embody a variety of other kinds of coercive mandates. The penalty for resisting these mandates may range from an informal reprimand ("Don't lick the food off your knife!") to economic loss or systemic failure (e.g., the gears in a conveyor belt jam, or a worker's hand is injured). These latter results are akin to the consequences befalling those who ignore physical laws (e.g., when someone literally walks on thin ice). Thus physical constraints, or accompanying legal and social sanctions, are among the obvious means through which technologies help structure human behavior.

SUBCONSCIOUS COMPLIANCE

Sometimes technologies shape behavior and relationships less through brute compulsion than via subtle, psychological inducement. For example, social scientists have shown that the physical arrangement of chairs and tables strongly influences the kind of social interaction that occurs in schools, nursing homes, and hospitals. Yet the staff in those institutions had previously attributed behavior (including their own) entirely to the mix of personalities and psychological capabilities. They were surprised to learn that simply shifting the furniture could, for instance, help reanimate a seemingly moribund group of mentally impaired hospital inmates.[6]

OPPORTUNITIES AND CONSTRAINTS

Social structures are also ambiguous in that while they can restrict opportunities in some respects, they can—when appropriately designed—enhance them in others.[7] For example, well-crafted laws help protect basic civil rights and, by providing a relatively stable and well-ordered social context, make it easier for people to realize their life plans.

Besides creating novel opportunities and constraints, technologies also reconfigure prior patterns. For instance, within some offices and factories the proliferation of personal computer networks has enhanced lower level workers' chances to contribute to production decisions while simultaneously challenging midlevel managers' former domains of authority and autonomy.[8] Once deployed, technologies can also aid or hinder the use of other technologies. For instance, telephone systems gradually displaced telegraph services but have more recently facilitated development of computer networks and long-distance data processing.

BACKGROUND CONDITIONS
AS IMPERATIVES

In order to function, technologies require various environmental and organizational background conditions. A television set is only useful so long as viewers know how to operate it, it is protected from inclement weather, there is access to electricity, programs are being produced and distributed, and so on.

Frequently when individuals or groups acquire new technologies or technological facilities, they are at best only dimly conscious of the demands that effective operation will impose or require to be developed. Several years ago a town near mine in western Massachusetts approved construction of an industrial research center, hoping thereby to realize tax benefits. But no one asked beforehand the eventual costs (financial, environmental, and emotional) that

the town would one day bear in order to accommodate both new research activities and the concomitant growth in commuting, ancillary employment, and residential population. These costs could include hazards associated with toxic waste disposal, future loss of open space to new housing, and the burden of upgrading roads, sewer lines, snowplowing capabilities, schools, and school bus lines.

To the extent that a given technology plays only a small part in one's life, maintaining the conditions needed for its operation may be of no particular concern. But as a person or society grows dependent on a technology, the necessary conditions of its operation loom as practical imperatives. The need to support these conditions represents a way in which technologies exert a profound structural social influence.

TECHNOLOGY AS STRUCTURAL
FOR NONUSERS

Often technologies exert comparably significant effects on people who neither operate nor use the technology in question. One clear example involves phenomena that economists label "spillover effects" or "externalities."[9] Homeowners hear neighbors' radios, lawn mowers, or air conditioners; whole communities breathe noxious fumes from an industrial facility. Each person lives in an aesthetic landscape that reflects the aggregate technological choices made by other people or organizations. The psychological texture of our everyday life reflects the influence of countless technological choices and practices in which we did not participate.

Moreover, often such spillover effects exert a structural influence that is dynamic and transformative. For instance, someone might choose not to purchase a power lawn mower to avoid its noise. However, after a few neighbors have bought theirs, this person may reconsider, thinking, "Since I'm suffering from the noise anyway, why not buy my own power mower and at least benefit from the convenience?" In this way each mower purchased contributes to a cycle that gradually transforms a neighborhood of quiet into one rent by the sound of churning engines.

Next reconsider the background conditions necessary for a technology to operate. Many of those conditions have a tremendous impact on lives even if individuals do not own the technology or use the technological service that establishes their raison d'être. Suppose, to state the case dramatically, that as a citizen of a modern nation a woman opts for a relatively self-sufficient mode of life: She refuses to own a car, uses solar collectors on the roof of her home, and plants a large vegetable garden in her yard. What has she accomplished? Something,[10] certainly, but the texture of her world still reflects the existence not only of cars and their immediate culture, but of roadways, automobile manufacturing and marketing systems, oil refineries, electric generating facilities, agribusiness, the private or public bureaucracies that manage these things, and their often tumultuous politics. That is part of what it means to say that technologies are social structures. The aggregate result of a society's many technological choices in one way or another affects every member.

COMMUNICATIVE AND CULTURAL SYSTEMS

Apart from materially influencing social experience, technologies also exert symbolic and other cultural influences. This is true not only of technologies explicitly called communications devices (e.g., cellular phones, televisions, and radios), but of all technologies.

For example, modern sofas generally have two or three separate seat cushions. There is no compelling technical or economic rationale for this design (an affordable, seamless sofa is an easily conceived alternative—as seamless mattresses and Japanese futon sofa-beds attest). Rather, separate sofa cushions define distinct personal spaces and thus respect—but also help to perpetuate—modern Western culture's emphasis on individuality and privacy.[11]

Technologies even play transformative roles within psychological development. For example, earlier this century Swiss psychologist Jean Piaget determined that young children distinguish living from nonliving things according to whether or not the things move, and—as the children develop psychologically—then according to whether things move by themselves or are moved by an outside force. However, more recently, social psychologist Sherry Turkle found that children who play with

computer toys that appear to "talk" and "think" develop different criteria for distinguishing "alive" from "not alive." Instead of relying on physical criteria (such as motion), they invent psychological criteria and hypotheses ("Computers are alive because they cheat" or "Computers are not alive because they don't have feelings"). Children's developmental trajectories, including their conceptions of self and moral reasoning, are transformed as a result of their interactions with these machines.[12]

The process that Turkle described with respect to computer toys is a specific instance of a much more general phenomenon. As they reconfigure opportunities and constraints for action, and function simultaneously as symbols and latent communicative media, technologies also reconfigure opportunities and constraints for psychological development.[13]

MACROPOLITICS: TECHNOLOGY
AND SOCIETY VERSUS TECHNOLOGY
AS SOCIETY

Many scholars have described cases in which technologies exert a macrolevel influence on societies. Consider historians who focus on the social role of just one or two important technologies at a time. Large scale dams and irrigation systems may have played a decisive role in the creation and maintenance of states in antiquity. Lynn White, Jr. told a now-famous story of the role of the stirrup in the development of European feudalism: stirrups made possible mounted shock combat, which led in turn to heavy full-body armor, heraldry, chivalry, stronger horse breeds, more efficient plowing methods, and so forth.[14] In America, railroads helped establish national markets; promoted coal mining, steelmaking, and the widespread adoption of steam power; provided an influential model of geographically dispersed, hierarchically managed corporate organization; contributed to the adoption of standardized timekeeping; and served as a dominant metaphor with which Americans interpreted their entire civilization.[15]

More recently in the United States one role of new technologies has been to provide grounds for the growth of the federal government, through the proliferation of such agencies as the Federal Communications Commission for regulating telecommunications, the Federal Aviation Administration for regulating the airline industry, the Nuclear Regulatory Commission and the Department of Energy for administering aspects of national energy production and nuclear weapons development, and the like.

In each of these instances, technological innovation plays a role in establishing, transforming, or maintaining states or societies at the macrolevel. Langdon Winner has explored the further hypothesis that the entire ensemble of modern technological systems—including the background conditions required to keep them operating—tends to promote centrally coordinated, technocratic social administration.[16]

Hence there are numerous examples in which technologies affect societies or states in ways that have macrostructural implications. However, this formulation—while both true and dramatic—nonetheless misses the force of this chapter's earlier analysis. Technologies function politically and culturally as social structures by coercing physical compliance; prompting subconscious compliance; constituting systems of social relations; establishing opportunities and constraints for action and self-realization; promoting the evolution of background conditions; affecting nonusers; shaping communication, psychological development, and culture generally; and constituting much of the world within which lives unfold.

Considering all of the preceding functions and effects together, it would be fairer to say that technologies do not merely *affect* society or states, they also *constitute* a substantial portion of societies and states. That, too, is part of what it means to be a social structure. Recognizing the many respects in which technologies contribute to defining who people are, what they can and cannot do, and how they understand themselves and their world should dispel the common myth that technologies are morally or politically neutral.[17]

INFLUENTIAL, NOT DETERMINING

Technologies "structure" social relations in that they shape or help constitute—but do not fully determine—social experience.[18] Water pipes and washing machines did not, for example, literally force Ibiecans to stop gathering at their village's central fountain and washbasin, but instead altered the system of inducements and interdependencies that formerly made such gathering occur naturally.

Aside from the possibility of rejecting or retiring a particular technology, there is always a margin of flexibility in how existing technological artifacts may be used or operated, or in what activities may occur in conjunction with them. This margin is finite, and its extent varies from one technology to the next and over time, but it nevertheless exists. For example, while a conventional assembly line provides only highly restricted opportunities to vary work routines at each station, it does not materially prevent workers from rotating jobs among work stations.[19]

CONTEXT-DEPENDENCY

Developing a railroad network helped catapult the United States to global economic preeminence, but Britain developed railroads earlier and yet nonetheless gradually lost its world economic predominance. Thus railroads (or other technologies) are socially consequential, but how and why they matter depends on the precise technologies in question in each particular context of use.

Moreover, just as social context—including, among other things, a society's preexisting technological order—regulates each technology's material functions and effects, it also regulates a technology's communicative functions and cultural meanings. A few decades ago a belching smokestack symbolized progress. Today—in a different historical context—the same smokestack is more likely to evoke distress or even outrage.

Finally, one important influence on a technology's functions and effects is the minds and culture of people.[20] Nineteenth-century high-wheeler bicycles were perceived by athletic young men as virile, high-speed devices. But to some women and elderly men the same devices signified personal danger. Indeed, conflicting perceptions of the high-wheeler proved consequential to its subsequent technological development. Its perception as a "macho machine" prompted new bicycle designs with ever higher front wheels. The competing perception of the high-wheeler as an "unsafe machine" prompted designs with smaller front wheels, different seat placement, or higher rear wheels.[21] Thus to understand the social function, meaning, and evolution of the high-wheeler, it is essential to explore its psychological and cultural context.

Public controversies concerning technology offer another occasion for observing the role of culture and cognition in establishing a technology's context, and hence its social role. For example, during the 1970s nuclear engineers and electric utility executives generally viewed centralized production of electricity as a critical social need and essential to the concept of commercial nuclear power. To them an alternative to nuclear power needed to be another means of performing this critical function.[22] But other energy policy analysts saw the expanded production of electricity as so inessential that a perfectly viable alternative could be a panel of foam wall insulation that did not generate any electricity.[23]

In evidence here are fragments of a social process of contesting or negotiating what is or is not to count as an essential function of a technology and hence as an alternative.[24] Thus, when technological consequences or meanings become controversial, processes through which technologies are culturally constituted may emerge openly.

CONTINGENT SOCIAL PRODUCTS

There is residual variability in the structural effects associated with any deployed technology—*within a particular social context and even more so among different contexts.* However, a technology's greatest flexibility exists before its final deployment, when artifacts and their accompanying social organization are being conceived and designed.

Technologies do not just appear or happen; they are contingent social products. Thus it is possible, both before and after the fact, to imagine alternative designs. The process by which one set of designs rather than another comes to fruition is influenced by prevailing social structures and forces, including the preexisting technological order. However, this process also reflects explicit or tacit social choices, including political negotiations or struggles.[25]

For example, it is hard to imagine a modern home without an electric refrigerator, but had the accidents of competing corporate resources played out slightly differently, gas-powered refrigerators that would have run more reliably and quietly could have been the norm.[26] Other feasible alternatives in household technology harbored the potential for even more dramatic social effects.[27] Moreover, although today people think of the guiding impulses behind technological development as necessarily being profit, convenience, or military advantage, throughout history religious or aesthetic motivations have often been just as significant.[28]

Thus there are many potential, competing technological pathways, and each is socially developed. But the flexibility associated with a given technology, or with other social structures, tends to diminish with time. After a society has habituated itself to one technology, alternatives tend to become less accessible. Once designed and deployed, a technology, like a law or a political institution tends—if it is going to endure—gradually to become integrated into larger systems of functionally interdependent artifacts and organizations and then to influence the design of subsequent technologies, laws, and institutions such that the latter all tend to depend on the continued existence of the former. Thus, owing to the accompanying evolution of supporting custom, entrenched interest, and various sunk costs, it is often difficult to achieve radical design alterations once an initial decision has been implemented.[29] A further factor reducing the flexibility of technologies is that they exhibit some of the pure physical recalcitrance that comes with material embodiment. Hence, both technologies and other social structures, once they have come into existence, tend to endure. However, technologies exhibit a remaining characteristic that tends to distinguish them from other social structures and to increase their relative political salience: polypotency.

Polypotency

Technologies function as social structures, but often independently of their (nominally) intended purposes. This is one of the phenomena that the conventional view of technology obscures. The same obfuscation is reflected in studies that profess a broad interest in the political effects of technology but that discuss only technologies designed explicitly to function politically (such as telecommunications, military and police technologies, voting machines, or computer databases).[30] Such technologies indeed function politically, but everyone knows that. That is these technologies' announced purpose. Harder to grasp is the truth that all technologies are associated with manifold latent social effects and meanings, and that it is largely in virtue of these that technologies come to function as social structures. In other words, technologies exhibit superfluous efficacy or "polypotency" in their functions, effects, and meanings. (The word *polypotency,* meaning "potent in many ways," is introduced here for want of a better existing term. The unfamiliarity wears off quickly if one contrasts it with omnipotence, meaning, literally, "potent in all ways.")

For example, when a man uses an ordinary hammer to pound nails, he also learns about the texture and structural properties of materials, he exercises and develops his muscles, he improves his hand-eye coordination, and he generates noise, all while stressing and wearing the hammer itself. As his competence at hammering grows, he feels his self-respect affirmed and approved. At another level, his activity resonates with half-conscious memories of primeval myths about Vulcan and Thor. He is also reminded of the blacksmith and the mythology of the American frontier. He thinks of a judge's gavel, the hammer as a symbol of justice, and a song popularized by the folksinging trio Peter, Paul, and Mary.

Where did the hammer come from? Somebody chopped down a tree and fashioned the handle. Others located and extracted iron ore. Some of that ore was refashioned into a hammer head. If a man touches his tongue to the hammer, with the taste of oxidized iron he senses fleetingly a former age when once-independent craftsmen and farmers first found themselves working under strict supervision in a factory. When he was a child, an uncle first taught him to use a hammer. Now when he hefts a

hammer, he feels embedded in a historical relationship with this and other hammers and with the development of the concept of hammers and technology in general.

The hammer's immediate social context of use can vary. The man may work alone, on a project with others, or in a room where each person pursues a different project. He may or may not choose his task; he may or may not earn a wage. Depending on the precise social context of its use, the hammer means different things to him, he sees it differently, and it helps disclose the world to him in different ways. Likewise, his style of using the hammer discloses to others much about his character, competence, and mood.

The hammer differs from a partially automated assembly line in that the latter requires and helps coordinate the simultaneous efforts of many workers. But a hammer also establishes certain limiting possibilities on the social conditions of its use. Hammers have only one handle. They are not designed to permit the type of close collaboration that is possible through computer networks or necessary when using a long, two-handled saw.

The material result of the man's activity is likely to include some bent nails, scrap wood, a hearty appetite, maybe a bruised thumb, a few sore but marginally strengthened muscles, some excess exhalation of carbon dioxide, perspiration, and a product that becomes part of the humanly shaped world. So, is the nail entering the board necessarily the most important feature of the activity called "hammering"? Hammers, like all technologies, are polypotent in their social functions, effects, and meanings.

Today's accepted view of technology takes a step toward acknowledging polypotency by speaking of technologies' unintended or secondary consequences. However, the term "polypotency" is helpful in not presuming that one knows automatically which of a technology's many functions or meanings are the most important or even which are intended. Many social historians of technology have, for example, argued that a latent but intended function of some innovations in manufacturing technology has been to substitute low-paid unskilled workers for higher-paid skilled workers, discipline the remaining workforce, and weaken unions.[31]

It is furthermore useful to introduce the term "focal function" to refer to a technology's (ostensibly) intended purpose. "Nonfocal" then denotes its accompanying complex of additional—but often recessive—functions, effects, and meanings. Thus, 19th-century New England schoolhouses' focal function was to provide a space for educational instruction, whereas one of their nonfocal functions was to help generate—in part via the symbolism of churchlike architectures—a relatively docile workforce.[32]

Occasionally technologies function as social structures precisely by virtue of their focal purpose. For instance, weapons function coercively because they are designed to do just that. But more often and more subtly, it is technologies' latent polypotency that accounts for their structural performance. This is illustrated by many previous examples, ranging from sofa cushions (which help to latently reproduce our culture's sense of privacy) to computer toys (which unexpectedly alter children's psychological development). Even technologies focally designed to function structurally are apt to structure nonfocally as well.

For instance, nuclear weapons are designed focally to coerce, deter, or destroy other societies, but they contribute nonfocally to legitimating authoritarian government institutions within the societies that possess them.[33] Marshall McLuhan popularized this truth as it applies specifically to technologies focally designated as communications devices: "The medium *is* the message."[34] In other words, the technical means of focally delivering a message can, owing to polypotency, matter more than the message itself.

Moreover, often groups of focally unrelated technologies interact latently to produce a structural effect that no one of them could accomplish alone. Distinct sofa cushions would not help establish cultural norms of privacy and individualism were they not part of a complex of artifacts and ritual behavior that contribute jointly toward that same result. (Other artifacts in the complex with sofa cushions include individual eating utensils, private bed-

rooms, telephone receivers designed to accommodate one person at a time, and so forth.[35]) In short, to achieve social insight and efficacy, it is essential to consider all the different artifacts and practices that comprise a society's technological order.

There are important functional equivalences between technologies and nontechnological social structures (e.g., legal statutes, government agencies, and large corporations). All represent enduring social products that shape subsequent social experience. However, there are also differences, revolving around contrasting levels of social understanding with respect to each.

First, laws and political and economic institutions are contingent social products, and at some level everyone knows this truth. Societies evolve these things through formal political or juridical processes, and it is commonly understood that alternative choices are possible. In contrast, people are prone to misperceive a society's technologies as inevitable, that is, as naturally determined rather than socially shaped and chosen.

Second, laws and other formally evolved social structures are commonly understood to function as social structures. That is their explicit purpose. Certainly, they can also be implicated in the production of various unintended social consequences. Prohibition-era laws were enacted to stop alcohol production, not to drive it underground and contribute to the expansion of organized crime. However, people at least expect that legal statutes and institutions will—because that is their intent—in some way shape social interaction and history. In contrast, people ordinarily expect most technologies to prove structurally inconsequential, and—because focally most of them do—this expectation appears confirmed. But here is where appearances deceive, insofar as it is frequently a technology's nonfocal aspects alone that conspire to manifest profound structural consequences.

Hence, although technologies are as consequential as other social structures, people tend to be more blind both to the social origins of technologies and to their social effects. This dual blindness is partly due to certain myths or misconceptions, such as the myth that technologies are autonomous self-contained phenomena and the myth that they are morally neutral.[36] It is also inculcated through modern technologies themselves, via both their style and their social process of design.

These dual misperceptions concerning technologies actually enhance their relative structural significance, because they enable technologies to exert their influence with only limited social awareness of how, or even that, they are doing so. This helps explain why people are prone to resign themselves to social circumstances established through technological artifice and practices that they might well reject if the same results were proposed through a formal political process.[37]

So long as their social origin, effects, and dynamics remain so badly misperceived, technologies will not suffer the same liability as would, say, functionally comparable laws or economic institutions, of being challenged on the grounds that they are politically or culturally unacceptable. Furthermore, societies will fail to develop the capacity to seek other technologies more consonant—both focally and nonfocally—with their members' ideals and aspirations.

NOTES

1. Winner (1986, p. 29).
2. The story of Ibieca is not unique. I will refer to it repeatedly because it vividly illustrates some general lessons concerning technology's social dimensions.
3. Jackson (1985).
4. For illustrative examples, see Part II, especially Chapters 4 and 5.
5. Carroll (1977, pp. 338–339).
6. Sommer (1969).
7. Giddens (1979, pp. 69–70).
8. Zuboff (1988).
9. In economic theory these are impacts imposed on someone without the mediation of a perfect competitive market. See Chapters 7 and 10.
10. See Borgmann (1984).
11. Lee (1959, p. 31).
12. Turkle (1984).
13. Luria (1976) and Elias (1978).
14. White (1962).
15. Chandler (1977), Kasson (1977), and Stephens (1989).
16. Winner (1977; 1986, chap. 2).

17. See also Balabanian (1980).
18. On structures shaping, but not determining, social reality, see, for example, Unger (1987).
19. Schrank (1978, pp. 221–222).
20. Sclove (1982).
21. Bijker et al. (1987, pp. 42–44).
22. E.g., Goldsmith et al. (1976).
23. E.g., Lovins (1977).
24. See Callon (1980, 1987) and compare Pfaffenberger (1992).
25. See, in addition to the examples cited in the succeeding text, Piore and Sabel (1984), Bijker et al. (1987), and Feenberg (1991).
26. Cowan (1983, chap. 5).
27. Hayden (1984, chap. 4).
28. Smith (1970) and Pacey (1976).
29. Collingridge (1980), Hughes (1989), and Callon (1994, pp. 407–408). For a case where late-stage design change did take place, see the Dutch damn example in Chapter 8.
30. E.g., OTA (1987).
31. See, for example, Zimbalist (1979).
32. The example is from Professor Merrit Roe Smith's fall 1979 M.I.T. lectures on "Technology in America."
33. E.g., Falk (1984).
34. McLuhan (1964, chap. 1).
35. On the contingent historical development of privacy and individualism, and its relation to material artifacts, see, for example, White (1974) and Elias (1978).
36. Winner (1977). One curious fact about these two prevalent myths is that not only is each false, but they are also mutually exclusive. That is, if technologies were indeed neutral, they could not also be an autonomous force that determines the course of history. While false, these myths are nevertheless socially consequential. Each helps deflect the critical political scrutiny that technologies warrant. The myth of neutrality does so by saying that artifacts themselves are irrelevant; one need only be concerned about the people who use them. The myth of autonomy does so by saying, in contrast, that technologies matter very much, but that people can have no choice in the matter; technologies themselves are running the show. By competing with one another, these myths comprise a unified ideological system that deflects attention from the relatively simple insight that technologies are contingent social structures.
37. Winner (1986).

Artifacts/Ideas and Political Culture

Although technology usually offers us a bright and rosy future, Langdon Winner suggests that we should be considering what type of technological future we want to build and the extent to which it will be kind to human society. As our modern political culture has evolved, it is important that we be aware of the ways in which advancing technology has affected our common experiences of "freedom, power, authority, community, and justice." Even though the artifacts and processes associated with technological systems are taken for granted or thought to be politically neutral, this article examines technology as a major force on our lives, changing relationships between people in subtle but significant ways. This is evident in secondary influences from inventions of the Industrial Revolution, which created an entirely new society that continues to evolve today, even though we might not be conscious of the change. Whether these changes are for the better will be determined by our commitment to building a society in which more people share in the benefits.

Focus Questions

1. Describe the seven concepts mentioned by Winner that are present in the structure of contemporary technology, and give an example of two specific technologies utilized today that embody those ideas.
2. Identify a contemporary technology and discuss one probable answer to each of the three questions normally focused on by individuals, groups, and nations. With the benefit of hindsight, how has that particular technology influenced the kind of world that has developed since its inception?
3. Consider the three guiding maxims proposed by Winner to focus discussion about the relationship between technological choice and the future of political culture. How do these concepts relate with the issue of spreading capitalism discussed in the Sachs reading (selection II.1)?

Keywords

capitalism, culture, democracy, feudalism, politics, public policy, UTOPIA

THIS IS A TIME OF GREAT EXCITEMENT about the fruitful possibilities of new technology, but also a time of grave concern about what those possibilities mean for the future of our society. Horizons visible in microelectronics and photonics, biotechnology, composite materials, computing, and other fields hold out prospects of sweeping change in our way of life. How should we regard these prospects?

As individuals, groups, and nations anticipate technological change nowadays, they usually focus upon three questions.

Selection from Whole *Earth Review, No. 73* (Winter 1991), pp. 18–24. *Whole Earth Review*, San Rafael, CA 94901. Subscription available: subs@wholeearthmag.com Reprinted by permission.

First: How will the technology be used? What are its functions and practical benefits?

Second: How will the technology change the economy? What will it contribute to the production, distribution, and consumption of material wealth?

Third: How will the technology affect the environment? What will its consequences be for global climate change, pollution of the biosphere, and other environmental problems?

While these are important issues, another crucial question is seldom mentioned: What kind of world are we building here? As we develop new devices, techniques and technical systems, what qualities of social, moral, and political life do we create in the process? Will this be a world friendly to human sociability or not?

These are questions about the relationship of technological change to the evolution of modern political culture. In what ways do the development, adoption, and use of instrumental things affect our shared experience of freedom, power, authority, community, and justice? How might we respond creatively to the role technology plays in contemporary political life?

In the titles of a great many books, articles, and conferences these days, the topic is often described as "technology and society" or "technology and culture" or "technology and politics." But if one takes a closer look, such distinctions no longer have much validity. In the late twentieth century, technology and society, technology and culture, technology and politics are by no means separate. They are closely woven together in a multiplicity of settings in which many forms of human living are dependent upon and shaped by technological devices and systems of various kinds. Our useful artifacts reflect who we are, what we aspire to be. At the same time, we ourselves mirror the technologies which surround us; to an increasing extent social activities and human consciousness are technically mediated.

In this light, any attempt to understand the matter might well begin from either of two basic starting points: (1) the technological world seen from the point of view of human beings and (2) the same world seen from the point of view of the artifacts.

Although it may seem perverse to do so, I shall begin with the second perspective.

Many of the things that we like to think of as mere tools or instruments now function as virtual members of our society. It makes sense to ask: Which roles, responsibilities, and possibilities for action have been delegated to technological things? Which social features are associated with a particular artifact? For example, does a computer in the workplace function as a servant, slave, controller, guard, supervisor, etc.?

The social roles delegated to the phone answering machine provide a good illustration. It used to be that only executives in business and government could afford to keep a full-time secretary answering the phone, screening calls, and taking messages. Now it is possible to buy a small, inexpensive answering machine that does at least some of that work. An alternative would be to answer the phone yourself, have someone else do it for you, or simply miss some calls. The machine serves as a surrogate, a kind of nonhuman agent that has been given certain kinds of work to do.

An interesting fact about these machines is that their initial use often brings some embarrassment. In the little taped message that precedes the beep, there is often something like an apology. "I'm sorry I can't be here to answer your call . . ." or "I'm sorry you have to talk to this machine, but . . . ." What one sees in cases like this is, I believe, quite common in modern life: the uneasy feeling that accompanies the renegotiation of social and moral boundaries around a technological change. But what is sometimes at first a source of discomfort eventually becomes a widely accepted pattern—"second nature," if you will.

It is clear that in decades to come a great many things like telephone answering machines and automatic bank tellers will become, in effect, members of our society. As their use spreads, the tone of embarrassment that surrounds their early introduction will gradually vanish. For better or worse, the renegotiation of boundaries will be complete. When I phoned a friend recently, I heard a recorded message that said simply: "It's 1991. You know what to do!"

One can also consider technological innovations from the alternate viewpoint—noticing the roles, responsibilities, and possibilities for action delegated to human beings within and around technological systems of various kinds. Now one can ask: Is a person's guiding hand required for the system to function? Does the human give orders or receive them? Is the person active or acted upon? What social qualities accompany the human presence?

I will offer some illustrations in a moment. But first I want to call attention to the fact that once one has entered the twofold perspective I've suggested, one has the beginning of a social and political vision of technology quite different from the one that economists, engineers, and technology policy makers usually employ. One recognizes, first and foremost, that technologies are not merely tools that one "picks up and uses." They can be seen as "forms of life" in which humans and inanimate objects are linked in various kinds of relationships. The interesting question becomes: How can we describe and evaluate technologies seen as "forms of life"?

By comparison, in the conventional view of things, the story usually goes that people employ technologies as simple tools for rather specific instrumental purposes, attempting to wrest new advantages over nature and to gain various economic benefits. Once these instrumental advantages and economic benefits have been obtained, other things may happen. There are what are called secondary, tertiary, and other distant consequences of our actions, often called the "impacts" or "unintended" consequences, the broader social, cultural, political, and environmental effects of technological applications of various kinds.

For some purposes, it is perfectly acceptable to view technological change in the conventional manner. However, if you take a longer view of history, an interesting fact soon emerges. In the fullness of time, the so-called "secondary" consequences or impacts of technological change are often far more significant than the results thought to be "primary" at the time. This is certainly true, for example, of the kinds of changes we associate with the Industrial Revolution of the eighteenth and nineteenth centuries. One could list the thousands upon thousands of instrumental advantages and economic benefits obtained during that period—techniques for making textiles, extracting coal, making locomotives run, etc. But that is not what is truly important about the Industrial Revolution. What matters is the fact that a whole new kind of society was created. The truly enduring part of that revolution, the truly significant aspect is the multiplicity of relationships between people and between humans and technology we call Industrial Society, results many of which arose largely as so-called "secondary" consequences of technological change.

If one looks carefully at contemporary technological innovations in their broader human context, one often finds emerging forms of political culture. Several years ago Maevon Garrett, a woman who had worked as a telephone operator in Baltimore for 18 years, was called into her supervisor's office and abruptly fired. She was informed that a computer had been installed to monitor the performance of telephone operators and that data gathered by the computer showed that she was less efficient than the average worker in processing phone calls. At that moment Maevon Garrett became the victim of norms of productivity and efficiency embodied in the workings of a new technological system.

What is interesting, however, is not only the fact of Ms. Garrett's firing, but her response to it. She pointed out that some portion of her time each day was spent talking with people who dial a telephone operator because they are lonely or in distress— elderly people who live alone, or "latchkey children," youngsters who come home after school to an empty house because their parents are still at work. Ms. Garrett argued she would not hang up on such people just to meet the phone company's hourly quota.

It is reasonable to conclude that she was behaving responsibly, serving a role in civic culture, but not a role recognized by the norms of efficiency and productivity in the system that employed her. This is a case in which conditions of technical rationality and cultural rationality meet in flagrant conflict.

The good news is that after a union protest Maevon Garrett's job was restored. The bad news, however, is that the system's design, the technopolitical regime that caused the problem, still exists and looms before us a rapidly spreading form of life. A study released by the Office of Technology Assessment of the U.S. Congress several years ago noted that approximately seven million American workers now live under rapidly spreading systems of computerized surveillance, an unhappy spin-off of office automation. The title of that report is, appropriately, *The Electronic Supervisor.* To an increasing extent in today's workplaces, computers are delegated the role of supervising; human beings have been assigned roles that involve working faster and faster while ending in less social conversation—all in the name of a system called "communications," but one that drastically limits people's ability to communicate in a human sense.

The term "regime" seems perfectly appropriate in such cases. For once they have been designed, built, and put in operation, sociotechnical systems comprise regimes with features that can be described in a political way. It makes perfect sense to talk about freedom or its absence, equality or inequality, justice or injustice, authoritarianism or democracy, and the kinds of power relationships technological instruments and systems contain.

This is true of extremely simple as well as complex technologies. For example, if one visits the agricultural fields of the southwestern U.S.A., one finds workers using a hoe, "el cortito," a tool with a short handle. There's nothing political about the length of a wooden handle, is there? Well, that depends on the broader social relationships and activities in which it plays a part. To use "el cortito" you must bend over or get down on your knees. A casual observer might say: If you're digging in the ground, isn't it sometimes more comfortable to stand up?

Why, then, has the handle been shortened? The reason is, in large part, that the foremen who manage the work can look across a field, even at a great distance, and tell who is working and who is not. Those who are bending over are the ones working; those standing upright are not and the foreman can apply discipline accordingly. In that light, even the length of the handle of a hoe expresses a regime, a regime of power, authority, and control.

Embodied in the tools and instruments of modern technology is a political world. I am suggesting that we use metaphors and rhetorical devices of political speech to unpack the meaning of various technologies for how we live.

Everyone understands that political ideas can be expressed in language. But ideas of this kind present themselves in material objects as well. In this form they might be called artifact/ideas. In their very silence, artifact/ideas have a great deal to say. They tell us who we are, where we are situated in the social order, what is normal, what is possible, what is excluded. The technological world is filled with artifact/ideas of great consequence for modern political culture. Things often speak louder than words. Among the main ideas present in the structure of contemporary technological devices and systems are the following:

- Power is centralized.
- The few talk and the many listen.
- There are barriers between social classes.
- The world is hierarchically structured.
- The good things are distributed unequally.
- Women and men have different kinds of competence.
- One's life is open to continual inspection.

As they are expressed in the shape of material objects, ideas of this kind are covert. They seldom become topics for discussion in the political sphere as it is usually understood. One reason that artifact/ideas tend to be covert is that most people buy the functional account of the meaning of material things. We are inclined to say: "This is a car which enables us to go from point A to point B." "This is a hoe which helps us to dig in the fields."

Another reason why ideologies in things tend to be covert is that they have been implanted there by those who do not wish those ideas to be known or widely discussed. The apparent solidity of useful things sometimes provides a mask for persons and groups who wish to exercise power while avoiding responsibility. Their alibi is usually something like: "This is the most effective way to do things" or "This is most efficient."

But whatever the source of specific beliefs and instrumental conditions, it is often true that ideas embodied in material things are painful or even dangerous to acknowledge. Artifact/ideas can involve astonishing contradictions. In particular, the mapping of the world encountered in the shape of things frequently contradicts the political ideology to which most people in Western societies claim to be committed.

In particular, many of the artifact/ideas prevalent in our time stand in flagrant contradiction to the ideology of modern democracy. That ideology holds that human beings flourish, achieving what is best in their potential, under conditions of freedom, equality, justice, and self-government. In that light, societies ought to create social conditions and political institutions that make it possible for each human being's potential to develop. Both victories and setbacks in this regard are clearly visible in the laws, constitutions, and political practices that prevail in each historical period.

From this vantage point a technological society is unique only in the sense that it presents new and seemingly unlikely domains—domains of instrumentality—in which the ends of democratic freedom, equality, and justice must somehow be recognized and realized. I take it to be the fundamental failure of modern civilization to have ignored again and again how such questions present themselves in the guise of what appear to be "neutral" technologies. To a considerable extent the ideas embodied in the realm of material things and in opposition to the central ideas that we believe describe and guide our political culture.

There is an important way in which freedom and justice depend in human communities upon the existence of suitable material environments— the creation and maintenance of arrangements in which the goal of becoming free, self-determining individuals is nurtured rather than destroyed. As we look at the kinds of sociotechnical innovations being introduced today, it is often beside the point to ask whether or not they are optimally efficient; by someone's definition they are usually very efficient indeed. Instead the crucial questions concern the kinds of cultural environments such technologies present to us. What one finds are far too many instances of developments of the following kind:

1. communications technologies employed in attempts to control people's thoughts, desires and behaviors;
2. computer technologies used to whittle away people's privacy and erode freedom;
3. information technologies that eliminate what were formerly places of community life;
4. energy systems that make people dependent upon, or even hostage to, sources of fuel over which they exercise no control;
5. systems of manufacturing that seek control by eliminating as much human initiative and creativity as possible.

The appropriate moment to examine and debate conditions such as these is the time during which they are designed and first introduced into the fabric of human activity. At present our society persists in designing a great many technical artifacts in ways that make people feel passive, superfluous, stupid, and incapable of initiating action. Such systems bear the cultural embryos of tomorrow's citizenry. For as we invent new technical systems, we also invent the kinds of people who will use them and be affected by them. The structures and textures of future social and political life can be seen in the blueprints of technologies now on the drawing board.

We often hear these days that the world is engaged in a "technology race" in which nations rise or fall according to their ability to use technologies to competitive advantage. Unfortunately, some of the design strategies that look fabulous from the point of view of efficiency, productivity, and global competitiveness involve what mounts to an ingenious synthesis of oriental feudalism and capitalism. Many people in freedom-loving countries like the United States seem eager to embrace repressive models of social integration expressed in automation, electronic surveillance, and pseudo-democratic "quality circles." But must we embrace these merging patterns of technofeudalism as "the wave of the future"? Would it not be a wiser approach to resist, choosing to explore ways of extending our ideas about freedom and a just society into the realm of technology itself?

In fact, one obvious path that may still be open to us is to cultivate ways of democratizing the process of technology policymaking and, indeed, the process of technological innovation. If this is to be done, both citizens and experts will need to become aware of the social, moral, and political dimensions of choices made in technological policy and technological design. They will need to find ways to act directly and democratically within settings in which the important choices are made.

In that light I would offer three guiding maxims as a way to focus discussion about the relationship between technological choices and the future of political culture. These maxims can be raised at times in which unquestioned assumptions about "productivity," "competitiveness," "the need to innovate," or "technology transfer" seem to provide the only language for talking about the choices at hand.

1. *No innovation without representation.* This suggests that all the groups and social interests likely to be affected by a particular kind of technological change ought to be represented at a very early stage in defining what that technology will be. Yes, let us accept the idea that particular technologies are social creations that arise through a complex, multi-centered process. But let us see to it that all the relevant parties are included rather than kept in the dark in this process. If we find that we do not have the kinds of social institutions that make this possible, then let's change our institutions to create such opportunities.

2. *No engineering without political deliberation.* Proposed technological projects should be closely examined to reveal the covert political conditions and artifact/ideas their making would entail. This ought to become an interpretive skill of people in all modern societies. It is especially important for engineers and technical professionals whose wonderful creativity is often accompanied by an appalling narrow-mindedness. The education of engi-

neers ought to prepare them to evaluate the kinds of political contexts, political ideas, political arguments, and political consequences involved in their work. Skill in the arts of democratic citizenship ought to become part of the "tool kit" that engineers master in their education.

3. *No means without ends.* Many of the varieties of innovation now pushed on the public these-days amount to "tools looking for uses," "means looking for ends." Those who have dealt with the introduction of computers into the schools in recent years can give many colorful examples of this phenomenon. The current promotion of high definition television and renewed efforts to push President Reagan's Star Wars project offer even more stark illustration. For HDTV and SDI bear little relationship to any significant human need. As we study the prospects offered by new technologies, it is always essential to ask: Why? Why are we doing this? What are the ends we have chosen and how well do they fit the pattern of means available? In many cases of high tech planning, suitable background music would be the theme from *The Twilight Zone.*

If you were to look for examples of places in which something similar to these three maxims are actually being put to work, I would begin by pointing to some recent experiments in the Scandinavian democracies where a positive, creative politics of technology has recently become a focus of research and development. In one such project, workers in the Swedish newspaper industry—printers, typographers, lithographers, and the like—joined with representatives from management and with university computer scientists to design a new system of computerized graphics used in newspaper layout and typesetting. The name of the project was UTOPIA, a Swedish acronym that means "training, technology, and products from a skilled worker's perspective."

UTOPIA's goal was to fashion a system that would be highly advanced technically, but also one designed in ways that would take into account the skills, needs, and perspectives of all those who would eventually be using it. Rather than develop a system under management directives and then impose it on workers, the project included representation of the people concerned. UTOPIA became the focus of a rigorous program of research and development at a government-sponsored laboratory: The Center for Working Life in Stockholm. Here was a case in which the purely instrumental and economic thrust of a technological innovation encountered a legitimate set of political ends and enlightened artifact/ideas. The result was democratization expressed in hardware, software, and human relationships.

The technological world of the twenty-first century beckons. Will it be better than the one we now inhabit or worse? Will it realize the promise of human freedom or curtail it? And whose interest will be decisive?

If ordinary citizens are to be empowered in shaping the world to come, we must become very skillful in areas where we are now profoundly ignorant, using ideas and abilities that enable us to define and realize human freedom and social justice within the realm of technology itself: within things like new machines for the workplace, computerized systems of information management, biotechnologies in agriculture and medicine, communications devices introduced into our homes. If we cannot develop these skills or do not care to, if we fail to confront the world-shaping powers that new technologies present, then human freedom and dignity could well become obsolete remnants of a bygone era.

I.8   ANDREW FEENBERG

Democratic Rationalization

In the reading from his book *Questioning Technology,* Andrew Feenberg defends the idea that social values play a role in shaping the direction of technological development in modern society. He questions the assumptions involved with the idea of technological determinism and argues for a constructivist theory of technological change in which social values affect the final shapes of the technologies that are adopted. He illustrates his theory by means of several examples that show how technological design has responded to social pressures based on moral or ethical considerations.

When we look back on successful technological designs, they seem to have an air of inevitability about them. But in fact the "fit" that is finally achieved is the product of a process of social negotiation in which technological designs come to embody social values. Given this, Feenberg is hopeful that new forms of energy-efficient, environmentally friendly designs for buildings and vehicles will eventually come to be seen as representing technological progress.

Focus Questions

1. What does Feenberg mean by the "ambivalence of technology"?
2. What are the two assumptions associated with the view called "technological determinism"? What arguments and examples does Feenberg use to refute these assumptions?

3. What is the alternative explanation of the adoption of new technologies provided by the constructivist theory? How does constructivism support a redefinition of the humanistic study of technology that interprets technologies as possessing meanings?

4. How does Feenberg account for the tendency of technological elites to view their own activities as autonomous and socially neutral? Do you find this explanation convincing?

5. Compare Feenberg's argument in this selection with those of Senge and Carstedt (selection II.3) and Lovins, Lovins, and Hawken (selection II.16). How does Feenberg's theory of democratic rationalization support the possibility of the kinds of technological innovations that these other authors are recommending?

Keywords:

constructivism, democracy, hermeneutics, paradigms, rationalization, regimes, technological determinism

Technology and Democracy

A great deal of 20th century social thought has been based on a pessimistic view of modernity that achieved its classic expression in Max Weber's theory of rationalization. According to Weber, modernity is characterized by the increasing role of calculation and control in social life, a trend leading to what he called the "iron cage" of bureaucracy. This notion of enslavement by a rational order inspires pessimistic philosophies of technology according to which human beings have become mere cogs in the social machinery, objects of technical control in much the same way as raw materials and the natural environment. While this view is overdrawn, it is true that as more and more of social life is structured by technically mediated organizations such as corporations, state agencies, prisons, and medical institutions, the technical hierarchy merges with the social and political hierarchy.

The idea and (for some) ideal of technocracy grows out of this new situation. Technocracy represents a generalization to society as a whole of the type of "neutral" instrumental rationality supposed to characterize the technical sphere. It assumes the existence of technological imperatives that need only be recognized to guide management of society as a system. Whether technocracy is welcomed or abhorred, these deterministic premises leave no room for democracy. . . . "Democratic" rationalization is a contradiction in Weberian terms. On those terms, once tradition has been defeated by modernity, radical struggle for freedom and individuality degenerates into an affirmation of irrational life forces against the routine and drab predictability of a bureaucratic order. This is not a democratic program but a romantic anti-dystopian one, the sort of thing that is already foreshadowed in Dostoievsky's *Notes from Underground* and various back to nature ideologies. The new left and all its works have been condemned repeatedly on these grounds.

No doubt the new left is rightly criticized for the excesses of its romanticism, but . . . [this is not the whole story]. Modern societies experienced real crises in the late 1960s that marked a turning point in the willingness of the public to leave its affairs in the hands of experts. Out of that period came not just regressive fantasies but a new and more

From *Questioning Technology* by Andrew Feenberg, 1999, pp. 75–99. Copyright © 1999 by Routledge. Reprinted by permission of Taylor & Francis and the author. (Footnotes and references have been omitted.)

democratic conception of progress. I have attempted in several previous books to articulate that conception in a third position that is neither technocratic nor romantic. The crux of the argument is the claim that technology is ambivalent, that there is no unique correlation between technological advance and the distribution of social power. The ambivalence of technology can be summarized in the following two principles.

1. Conservation of hierarchy: social hierarchy can generally be reserved and reproduced as new technology is introduced. This principle explains the extraordinary continuity of power in advanced capitalist societies over the last several generations, made possible by technocratic strategies of modernization despite enormous technical changes.

2. Democratic rationalization: new technology can also be used to undermine the existing social hierarchy or to force it to meet needs it has ignored. This principle explains the technical initiatives that often accompany the structural reforms pursued by union, environmental, and other social movements.

This second principle implies that there will generally be ways of rationalizing society that democratize rather than centralize control. We need not go underground or native to escape the iron cage. In this chapter . . . I will show that this is in fact the meaning of the emerging social movements to change technology in a variety of areas such as computers, medicine, and the environment.

But does it make sense to call the changes these movements advocate *rationalizations*? Are they not irrational precisely to the extent that they involve citizens in the affairs of experts? The strongest objections to democratizing technology come from those experts, who fear the loss of their hard-won freedom from lay interference. Can we reconcile public participation with the autonomy of professional technical work? Perhaps, as advocates of technocracy argue, we should strive not to politicize technology but to technicize politics in order to overcome the irrationality of public life. The counter-argument in favor of democratization must establish the rationality of informal public involvement in technical change.

From Determinism to Constructivism

DETERMINISM DEFINED

Faith in progress has been supported for generations by two widely held deterministic beliefs: that technical necessity dictates the path of development, and that that path is discovered through the pursuit of efficiency. So persuasive are these beliefs that even critics of progress such as Heidegger and Ellul share them. I will argue here that both beliefs are false, and that, furthermore, they have antidemocratic implications.

Determinism claims that technologies have an autonomous functional logic that can be explained without reference to society. Technology is presumably social only through the purpose it serves, and purposes are in the mind of the beholder. Technology would thus resemble science and mathematics by it intrinsic independence of the social world. Yet unlike science and mathematics, technology has immediate and powerful social impacts. Society's fate seems to be at least partially dependent on a nonsocial factor which influences it without suffering a reciprocal influence.

Determinism is based on two premises which I will call *unilinear progress* and *determination by the base*.

1. Technical progress appears to follow a unilinear course, a fixed track, from less to more advanced configurations. Each stage of technological development enables the next, and there are no branches off the main line. Societies may advance slowly or quickly, but the direction and definition of progress is not in question. Although this conclusion seems obvious from a backward glance at the history of any familiar technical object, in fact it is based on two claims of unequal plausibility: first, that technical progress proceeds from lower to higher levels of development; and second, that that development follows a single sequence of necessary stages. As we will see, the first claim

is independent of the second and not necessarily deterministic.

2. Technological determinism also affirms that social institutions must adapt to the "imperatives" of the technological base. This view, which no doubt has its source in a certain reading of Marx, is long since the common sense of the social sciences. Adopting a technology necessarily constrains one to adopt certain practices that are connected with its employment. Railroads require scheduled travel. Once they are introduced people who formerly could live with rather approximate notions of time—the day marked out by church bells and the sun—need watches. So the imperative consequence of railroads is a new organization of social time. Similarly factories are hierarchical institutions and set the tone for social hierarchy throughout modern societies. Again, there is something plausible about this view, namely that devices and practices are congruent, but the stream of influence is not unidirectional.

These two theses of technological determinism present decontextualized, self-generating technology as the foundation of modern life. And since we in the advanced countries stand at the peak of technological development, the rest of the world can only follow our example. Determinism thus implies that our technology and its corresponding institutional structures are universal, indeed, planetary in scope. There may be many forms of tribal society, many feudalisms, even many forms of early capitalism, but there is only one modernity and it is exemplified in our society for good or ill. . . .

UNDERDETERMINATION

The implications of determinism appear so obvious that it is surprising to discover that neither of its two premises withstand close scrutiny. Yet contemporary sociology undermines the idea of unilinear progress while historical procedures are unkind to determination by the base.

Recent constructivist sociology of technology grows out of the new social studies of science. The "strong program" in sociology of knowledge challenges the exemption of scientific theories from the sort of sociological examination to which we submit nonscientific beliefs. The "principle of symmetry" holds that all contending beliefs are subject to the same type of social explanation regardless of their truth or falsity. This view derives from the thesis of underdetermination, the so-called Duhem-Quine principle in philosophy of science, which refers to the inevitable lack of logically compelling reasons for preferring one competing scientific theory to another. Rationality, in other words, does not constitute a separate and self-sufficient domain of human activity.

A similar approach to the study of technology denies that a purely rational criterion such as technical effectiveness suffices to account for the success of some innovations and the failure of others. Of course it remains true that some things really work and others do not: successful design respects technical principles. But there are often several possible designs with which to achieve similar objectives and no decisive technical reason to prefer one to the others. Here, underdetermination means that technical principles alone are insufficient to determine the design of actual devices.

What then does decide the issue? A commonplace reply is "economic efficiency." But the problem is trickier than it seems at first. Before the efficiency of a process can be measured, both the type and quality of output have to be fixed. Thus economic choices are necessarily secondary to clear definitions of both the problems to which technology is addressed and the solutions it provides. But clarity on these matters is often the outcome rather than the presupposition of technical development. For example, MS DOS lost the competition with the Windows graphical interface, but not before the very nature of computing was transformed by a change in the user base and in the types of tasks to which computers were dedicated. A system that was more efficient for programming and accounting tasks proved less than ideal for secretaries and hobbyists interested in ease of use. Thus economics cannot explain but rather follows the trajectory of development.

Constructivism argues, I think correctly, *that the choice between alternatives ultimately depends neither on technical nor economic efficiency, but on the "fit" between devices and the interests and beliefs of the various social groups that influence the design process.* What singles out an artifact is its relationship to the social environment, not some intrinsic property.

Pinch and Bijker illustrate this approach with the early evolution of the bicycle. In the late 19th Century, before the present form of the bicycle was fixed, design was pulled in several different directions. The object we take to be a self-evident "black box" actually started out as two very different devices, a sportsman's racer and a means of transportation. Some customers perceived bicycling as a competitive sport, while others had an essentially utilitarian interest in getting from here to there. Designs corresponding to the first definition had high front wheels that were rejected as unsafe by riders of the second type, who preferred designs with two equal-sized low wheels. The large diameter front wheel of the sportsman's racer was faster, but it was unstable. Equal-sized wheels made for a safer but less exciting ride. These two designs met different needs and were in fact different technologies with many shared elements. Pinch and Bijker call this original ambiguity of the object designated as a "bicycle," "interpretative flexibility."

Eventually the "safety" design won out, and it benefited from subsequent advances in the field. The entire later history of the bicycle down to the present day stems from that line of technical development. In retrospect, it seems as though the high wheelers were a clumsy and less efficient stage in a progressive development leading through the old "safety" bicycle to current designs. In fact the high wheeler and the safety shared the field for years and neither was a stage in the other's development. The high wheeler represented a possible alternative path of bicycle development that addressed different problems.

The bicycle example is reassuringly innocent as are, no doubt, the majority of technical decisions. But what if the various technical solutions to a problem have different effects on the distribution of power and wealth? Then the choice between them is political and the political implications of

that choice will be embodied in some sense in the technology. Of course the discovery of this connection did not await constructivism. Langdon Winner offers a particularly telling example of it. Robert Moses' plans for an early New York expressway included overpasses that were a little too low for city buses. Poor people from Manhattan, who depended on bus transportation, were thereby discouraged from visiting the beaches on Long Island. In this case a simple design specification contained a racial and class bias. We could show something similar with many other technologies, the assembly line for example, which exemplifies capitalist notions of control of the work force. Reversing these biases would not return us to pure, neutral technology, but would simply alter its valuative content in a direction more in accord with our own preferences and therefore less visible to us.

Determinism ignores these complications and works with decontextualized temporal cross-sections in the life of its objects. It claims implausibly to be able to get from one such momentary configuration of the object to the next on purely technical terms. But in the real world all sorts of attitudes and desires crystallize around technical objects and influence their development. Differences in the way social groups interpret and use the objects are not merely extrinsic but make a difference in the nature of the objects themselves. Technology cannot be determining because the "different interpretations by social groups of the content of artifacts lead via different chains of problems and solutions to different further developments." *What* the object *is* for the groups that ultimately decide its fate determines what it *becomes* as it is modified. If this is true, then technological development is a social process and can only be understood as such.

Determinism is a species of Whig history which makes it seem as though the end of the story were inevitable from the beginning. It projects the abstract technical logic of the finished object back into it origins as a cause of development, confounding our understanding of the past and stifling the imagination of a different future. Constructivism can open up that future, although its practitioners have hesitated so far to engage the larger social issues implied in their method.

Selection Criteria	Partially Substitutable Artifacts	Shared Effects (e.g. uses)	Unique Effects

HOW ARTIFACTS HAVE POLITICS

Artifacts 1–4 share certain effects but each also has its own unique effects which distinguish it from the others. Effects in this sense include uses, contextual requirements that must be met to employ the artifacts, and their unintended consequences. Criteria 1–4 all select the shared effects of the artifacts and each also valorizes one or another of the unique effects. Where different unique effects have different political consequences, competing groups will have preferred criteria corresponding to the fit between their goals and the various artifacts. The criteria can also be combined in the course of the evolution of the artifacts through design changes that adapt one of them to also delivering the unique effects of one or several others. In a political context such combinations correspond to alliances.

INDETERMINISM

If the thesis of unilinear progress falls, the collapse of the notion of determination by the technological base cannot be far behind. Yet it is still frequently invoked in contemporary political debates. I shall return to these debates later in this chapter. For now, let us consider the remarkable anticipation of current conservative rhetoric in the struggle over the length of the workday and child labor in mid-19th Century England. Factory owners and econo-

mists denounced regulation as inflationary; industrial production supposedly required children and the long workday. One member of parliament declared that regulation is "a false principle of humanity, which in the end is certain to defeat itself." The new rules were so radical, he concluded, as to constitute "in principle an argument to get rid of the whole system of factory labor." Similar protestations are heard today on behalf of industries threatened with what they call environmental "Luddism."

Yet what actually happened once limitations were imposed on the workday and children expelled from the factory? Did the violated imperatives of technology exact a price? Not at all. Regulation led to an intensification of factory labor that was incompatible with the earlier conditions in any case. Children ceased to be workers and were redefined socially as learners and consumers. Consequently, they entered the labor market with higher levels of skill and discipline that were soon presupposed by technological design and work organization. As a result no one is nostalgic for a return to the good old days when inflation was held down by child labor. That is simply not an option.

This case shows the tremendous flexibility of technical systems. They are not rigidly constraining but on the contrary can adapt to a variety of social demands. The responsiveness of technology to social redefinition explains its adaptability. On this account technology is just another dependent social variable, albeit an increasingly important one, and not the key to the riddle of history.

Determinism, I have argued, is characterized by the principles of unilinear progress and determination by the base; if determinism is wrong, then research must be guided by two contrary principles. In the first place, technological development is not unilinear but branches in many directions, and could reach generally higher levels along several different tracks. And, secondly, social development is not determined by technological development but depends on both technical and social factors.

The political significance of this position should also be clear by now. In a society where determinism stands guard on the frontiers of democracy, indeterminism is political. If technology has many unexplored potentialities, no technological imperatives dictate the current social hierarchy. Rather, technology is a site of social struggle, in Latour's phrase, a "parliament of things" on which political alternatives contend.

Critical Constructivism

TECHNOLOGY STUDY

The picture sketched so far requires a significant change in our definition of technology. It can no longer be considered as a collection of devices, nor, more generally, as the sum of rational means. These definitions imply that technology is essentially nonsocial.

Perhaps the prevalence of such tendentious definitions explains why technology is not generally considered an appropriate field of humanistic study; we are assured that its essence lies in a technically explainable function rather than a hermeneutically interpretable meaning. At most, humanistic methods might illuminate extrinsic aspects of technology, such as packaging and advertising, or popular reactions to controversial innovations such as nuclear power or surrogate motherhood. Of course, if one ignores most of its connections to society, it is no wonder technology appears to be self-generating. Technological determinism draws its force from this attitude.

The constuctivist position has very different implications for the humanistic study of technology. They can be summarized in the following three points:

1. Technical design is not determined by a general criterion such as efficiency, but by a social process which differentiates technical alternatives according to a variety of case-specific criteria;
2. That social process is not about fulfilling "natural" human needs, but concerns the cultural definition of needs and therefore of the problems to which technology is addressed;
3. Competing definitions reflect conflicting visions of modern society realized in different technical choices.

The first point widens the investigation of social alliances and conflicts to include technical issues which, typically, have been treated as the object of a unique consensus. The other two points imply that culture and ideology enter history as effective forces not only in politics, but also in the technical sphere. These three points thus establish the legitimacy of applying the same methods to technology that are employed to study social institutions, customs, beliefs, and art. With such a hermeneutic approach, the definition of technology expands to embrace its social meaning and its cultural horizon.

FUNCTION OR MEANING

The role of social meaning is clear in the case of the bicycle. The very definition of the object was at stake in a contest of interpretations: was it to be a sportsman's toy or a means of transportation? It might be objected that this is merely a disagreement over function with no hermeneutic significance. Once a function is selected, the engineer has the last word on its implementation and the humanist interpreter is out of luck. This is the view of most engineers and managers; they are at home with "function" but have no place for "meaning."

. . . I . . . propose a very different model of the essence of technology based not on the distinction of the social and the technical, but crosscutting the customary boundaries between them. In this conception, technology's essence is not an abstraction from the contingencies of function, a causal structure that remains the same through the endless uses to which devices are subjected in the various systems that incorporate them. Rather, the essence of technology is abstracted from a larger social context within which functionality plays a specific limited role. Technologies do of course have a causal aspect, but they also have a symbolic aspect that is determining for their use and evolution. From that standpoint, I would like to introduce Bruno Latour's and Jean Baudrillard's quite different but complementary proposals for what I call a *hermeneutics of technology.*

Latour argues that norms are not merely subjective human intentions but that they are also realized in devices. This is an aspect of what he calls the symmetry of humans and nonhumans which he adds to the constructivist symmetry of true or false theories, successful and unsuccessful devices.

According to Latour, technical devices embody norms that serve to enforce obligations. He presents the door closer as a simple example. A notice posted on a door can remind users to close it, or a mechanism can close it automatically. The door closer, in some sense, does the work of the notice but more efficiently. It materializes the moral obligation to close the door too easily ignored by passersby. That obligation is "delegated" to a device in Latour's sense of the term. According to Latour,

the "morality" in this case can be allocated either to persons—by a notice—or to things—by a spring. This Latourian equivalent of Hegelian *Sittlichkeit* opens the technical world to investigation not simply as a collection of functioning devices determined by causal principles but also as the objectification of social values, as a cultural system.

Baudrillard suggests a useful approach to the study of the aesthetic and psychological dimensions of this "system of objects." He adapts the linguistic distinction between denotation and connotation to describe the difference between the functions of technical objects and their many other associations. For example, automobiles are means of transportation—a function; but they also signify the owner as more or less respectable, wealthy, and sexy—connotations. The engineer may think these connotations are extrinsic to the device he or she is working on, but they too belong to its social reality.

Baudrillard's approach opens technology to quasi-literary analysis. Indeed, technologies are subject to interpretation in much the same way as texts, works of art, and actions. However, his model still remains caught in the functionalist paradigm insofar as it takes the distinction between denotation and connotation for granted. In reality, that distinction is a product not a premise of technical change. There is often no consensus on the precise function of new technologies. The personal computer is a case in point; it was launched on the market with infinite promise and no applications. The story of Chinese sea faring in the 15th century offers another marvelous example of prolonged suspense regarding function. The Chinese built the largest fleet composed of the biggest ships the world had ever seen, but could not agree on the purpose of their own naval achievements. Astonishingly, they dismantled the fleet and retreated into their borders, paving the way for the European conquest of Asia.

In the case of well established technologies, the distinction between function and connotation is usually fairly clear. There is a tendency to project this clarity back into the past to imagine that the technical function of a device called it into being. However, as we have seen, technical functions are not pregiven but are discovered in the course of development and use. Gradually they are locked in by the evolution of the social and technical environment, as for example the transportation functions of the automobile have been institutionalized in low-density urban designs that create the demand for transportation automobiles satisfy. So long as no institutional lock-in ties it decisively to one of its several possible functions, these ambiguities in the definition of a new technology pose technical problems which must be resolved through interactions between designers, purchasers and users.

TECHNOLOGICAL HEGEMONY

Technical design responds not only to the social meaning of individual technical objects, but also incorporates broader assumptions about social values. The cultural horizon of technology therefore constitutes a second hermeneutic dimension. It is one of the foundations of modern forms of social hegemony. As I will use the term, hegemony is domination so deeply rooted in social life that it seems natural to those it dominates. One might also define it as that aspect of the distribution of social power which has the force of culture behind it.

The term "horizon" refers to culturally general assumptions that form the unquestioned background to every aspect of life. Some of these support the prevailing hegemony. For example, in feudal societies, the "chain of being" established hierarchy in the fabric of God's universe and protected the caste relations of the society from challenge. Under this horizon, peasants revolted in the name of the King, the only imaginable source of power. Technocratic rationalization plays an equivalent role today, and technological design is the key to its cultural power.

Technological development is constrained by cultural norms originating in economics, ideology, religion, and tradition. I discussed earlier how assumptions about the age composition of the labor force entered into the design of 19th century production technology. Such assumptions seem so natural and obvious they often lie below the threshold of conscious awareness. When one looks at old photos of child factory workers, one is struck by the adaptation of machines to their height. The

images disturb us, but were no doubt taken for granted until child labor became controversial. Design specifications simply incorporated the sociological fact of child labor into the structure of devices. The impress of social relations can be traced in the technology.

The assembly line offers another telling instance. Its technologically enforced labor discipline increases productivity and profits by increasing control through deskilling and pacing work. However, the assembly line only appears as technical progress in a specific social context. It would not look like an advance in an economy based on workers' councils in which labor discipline was largely self-imposed by the work group rather than imposed from above by management. In such a society engineers would seek different ways of increasing productivity. Here again design mirrors back the social order. Thus what Marcuse called "technological rationality" and Foucault the "regime of truth" is not merely a belief, an ideology, but is effectively incorporated into the machines themselves.

Technologies are selected by the dominant interests from among many possible configurations. Guiding the selection process are social codes established by the cultural and political struggles that define the horizon under which the technology will fall. Once introduced, technology offers a material validation of that cultural horizon. Apparently neutral technological rationality is enlisted in support of a hegemony through the bias it acquires in the process of technical development. The more technology society employs, the more significant is this support. The legitimating effectiveness of technology depends on unconsciousness of the cultural-political horizon under which it was designed. A critical theory of technology can uncover that horizon, demystify the illusion of technical necessity, and expose the relativity of the prevailing technical choices.

TECHNICAL REGIMES AND CODES

Disputes over the definition of technologies are settled by privileging one among many possible configurations. This process, called closure, yields an "exemplar" for further development in its field. The exemplar reacts back on the technical discipline from which it originated by establishing standard ways of looking at problems and solutions. These are variously described by social scientists as "technological frames" or "technological regimes" or "paradigms." Rip and Kemp, for example, define a regime as:

> The whole complex of scientific knowledge, engineering practices, production process technologies, product characteristics, skills and procedures, and institutions and infrastructures that make up the totality of a technology. A technological regime is thus the technology-specific context of a technology which prestructures the kind of problem-solving activities that engineers are likely to do, a structure that both enables and constrains certain changes.

Such regimes incorporate many social factors expressed by technologists in purely technical language and practices. I call those aspects of technological regimes which can best be interpreted as direct reflections of significant social values the "technical code" of the technology. *Technical codes define the object in strictly technical terms in accordance with the social meaning it has acquired.* These codes are usually invisible because, like culture itself, they appear self-evident. For example, if tools and workplaces are designed today for adult hands and heights, that is only because children were expelled from industry long ago with design consequences we now take for granted. Technological regimes reflect this social decision unthinkingly, as is normal, and only social scientific investigation can uncover the source of the standards in which it is embodied.

Technical codes include important aspects of the basic definition of many technical objects insofar as these too become universal culturally accepted features of daily life. The telephone, the automobile, the refrigerator and a hundred other everyday devices have clear and unambiguous definitions in the dominant culture: we know exactly what they are insofar as we are acculturated members of our society. Each new instance of these standard technologies must conform to its defining code to be recognizable and acceptable. But there is nothing obvious about this outcome from a historical point of view. Each of these objects was selected from a series of alternatives by a code reflecting specific social values.

The bicycle reached this point in the 1890s. A technical code defining the bicycle as a safe means of transportation required a seat positioned well behind a small front wheel. The bicycle produced according to this code, known at the time as a "safety," became the forebear of all future designs. The safety connoted women and mature riders, trips to the store, and so on, rather than racing and sport. Eventually the safety was able to incorporate the racing connotations of the bicycle in specialized designs and the old high wheeler was laid to rest. Note that in this typical case the choice of the exemplary design reflected the privilege granted the specific code defining for it, i.e., designating objects as "safe" or "unsafe." The high wheelers could only have won out by a similar privileging of "fast" and "slow."

Because technologies have such vast social implications, technical designs are often involved in disputes between ideological visions. The outcome of these disputes, a hegemonic order of some sort, brings technology into conformity with the dominant social forces, insuring the "isomorphism, the formal congruence between the technical logics of the apparatus and the social logics with which it is diffused." These hermeneutic congruencies offer a way to explain the impact of the larger sociocultural environment on the mechanisms of closure, a still relatively undeveloped field of technology studies.

KUHNIAN PERSPECTIVES ON TECHNICAL CHANGE

This analysis leads to an obvious question: if all this is true, why aren't we more aware of the public interventions that have shaped technology in the past? Why does it appear apolitical? It is the very success of these interventions that gives rise to this illusion. Success means that technical regimes change to reflect interests excluded at earlier stages in the design process. But the eventual internalization of these interests in design masks their source in public protest. The waves close over forgotten struggles and the technologists return to the comforting belief in their own autonomy which seems to be verified by the conditions of everyday technical work.

The notion of the "neutrality" of technology is a standard defensive reaction on the part of professions and organizations confronted by public protest and attempting to protect their autonomy. But in reality technical professions are never autonomous; in defending their traditions, they actually defend the outcomes of earlier controversies rather than a supposedly pure technical rationality. Informal public intervention is thus already an implicit factor in design whatever technologists and managers may believe.

Lay initiatives usually influence technical rationality without destroying it. In fact, public intervention may actually improve technology by addressing problems ignored by vested interests entrenched in the design process. If the technical professions can be described as autonomous, it is not because they are truly independent of politics but rather because they usually succeed in translating political demands into technically rational terms.

With some modifications, Kuhn's famous distinction between revolutionary and normal science can be reformulated to explain these aspects of the design process. The alternation of professional and public dominance in technical fields is one of several patterns that correspond roughly to the distinction between normal and revolutionary scientific change. There is, however, a significant difference between science and technology. Natural science eventually becomes far more independent of public opinion than technology. As a result, democratic interventions into scientific change are unusual, and revolutions explode around tensions within the disciplines. Of course even mature science is responsive to politics and culture, but their influence is usually felt indirectly through administrative decisions and changes in education. By contrast, ordinary people are constantly involved in technical activity, the more so as technology advances. It is true that they may be objects rather than subjects of the technologies that affect them, but in any case their closeness offers them a unique vantage point. Situ-

ated knowledges arising from that vantage point can become the basis for public interventions even in a mature technological system.

These situated knowledges are usually viewed with skepticism by experts guided by the pursuit of efficiency within the framework of the established technical codes. But in Kuhnian terms, efficiency only applies within a paradigm; it cannot judge between paradigms. To the extent that technical cultures are based on efficiency, they constitute the equivalent of Kuhn's normal science and as such they lack the categories with which to comprehend the paradigmatic changes that will transform them in the course of events. And since democratic interventions are often responsible for such changes, they too remain opaque to the dominant technical culture.

. . .

Progress and Rationality

THE TRADEOFF MODEL

The anti-deterministic arguments of the previous sections of this chapter undermine one basis of the technical professions' claims to autonomy. If they have succeeded in incorporating public concerns in the past, why reject participation on principle today? However, even if the democratic position is granted this much, it is still possible to argue that participation has unreasonable costs. Thus the autonomy thesis still has another leg to stand on. This is the notion that technical rationality can supply the most efficient solution to economic problems when it suffers the least interference. On this basis one might argue that there is an inevitable tradeoff between ideology and technology.

. . . The claims of technical purity were denied most vigorously by anti-technocratic movements . . . that challenged the direction of progress. And the environmental debate turns ultimately on whether environmental goals are compatible with technological advance. Is a democratic alternative to technocracy conceivable? Can a technological society pursue environmental goals without sacrificing prosperity? Many would answer these questions in the negative, claiming that public involvement in technology risks slowing progress to a halt, that democratization and environmental reform are tantamount to Luddite reaction. In this section I will address this objection through an analysis of the limits of technical rationality in social policy.

Let me begin by acknowledging that public fear of technology sometimes results in costly changes or even abandonment of controversial innovations. And of course there is the famous NIMBY ("not in my backyard") syndrome that has greeted nuclear power, toxic waste incinerators, genetic engineering facilities, and other harbingers of a future lived on a higher plane of anxiety.

I call the public's response to new and imponderable risks it is not equipped to evaluate "rational dread." Childhood dread of the monster under the bed can usually be stilled by more information—a simple glance may suffice. But the dread of modern technologies such as atomic energy resists information strategies. On the contrary, often more information leads to still greater concern. To make matters worse, the hope that expert advice could unburden the public has long since been disappointed as general skepticism overtakes the authority of knowledge. The problem is occasionally resolved by forcing a return to an already accepted level of risk rather than achieving habituation to the higher level involved in new technologies.

The American nuclear power industry has indeed been the victim of just such a response. The significance of this case cannot be overestimated: the nuclear industry was one of the major technological projects of modern times. Nuclear power promised to free industrial society from dependence on the fragile bottleneck of fossil fuels. But the industry became fixated on unsafe designs in the 1960s and was unable to adapt to the standards of the 1970s and 1980s. In the head on confrontation with public opinion that followed, technology lost, at least in the US. Today conversion initiatives multiply as the owners of old nuclear plants switch back to fossil fuels.

What is the moral of this story? One can conclude with bitter irony that technology is in fact democratically controlled because "the very irrationality that has come to dominate the nuclear debate confirms that the public will is still what

counts." But it is a good question where the "irrationality" lay, in the government and utility industries which pushed for impracticable goals or in the public which called them to account out of unverified fears. Clearly, we would be much better off if the many billions of research dollars spent to develop nuclear power had been employed in other ventures, for example, in the fields of solar energy and energy storage.

In any case, this example is not typical. Fear usually does not kill new technology; for the most part, it simply changes the regulatory environment and the orientation of development. Automotive safety and emission is a good example. Regulation gradually effected changes that were well within the technical capabilities of manufacturers. The results are much safer and less polluting vehicles, not the disaster foreseen by the foes of government "interference."

These issues appear with particular force in the environmental movement. Arguably, this is the single most important domain of democratic intervention into technology. Environmentalists want to reduce harmful and costly side effects of technology to protect nature and human health. This program can be implemented in different ways. As Commoner has argued, in a capitalist society there is a tendency to deflect criticism from technological processes to products and people, from a priori prevention to a posteriori cleanup. The preferred strategies are generally costly and reduce efficiency, with unfortunate political consequences.

Restoring the environment after it has been damaged is a form of collective consumption financed by taxes or higher prices. Because this approach to environmentalism dominates public awareness, it is generally perceived as a cost involving tradeoffs, and not as a rationalization with long-term benefits. But in a modern society, obsessed by economic well-being, that perception is damning. Economists and businessmen are fond of explaining the price we must pay in inflation and unemployment for worshipping at Nature's shrine instead of Mammon's. Poverty awaits those who will not adjust their social and political expectations to technological imperatives.

. . .

The tradeoff model confronts us with dilemmas—environmentally sound technology vs. prosperity, workers' control vs. productivity, etc.—where what we need are syntheses. Unless the problems of modern industrialism can be solved in ways that both enhance public welfare and win public support, there is little reason for hope.

But how can technological reform be reconciled with prosperity when it places a variety of new limits on the economy? The child labor case shows how apparent dilemmas arise on the boundaries of cultural change, specifically where major technological regimes are in transition. In such situations, social groups excluded from the original design network articulate their unrepresented interests politically. New values the outsiders believe would enhance their welfare appear as mere ideology to insiders who are adequately represented by the existing designs.

This is a difference of perspective, not of nature. Yet the illusion of essential conflict is renewed whenever social changes affect technology. At first, satisfying the demands of new groups after the fact has visible costs and, if it is done clumsily, will indeed reduce efficiency until better designs are found. But usually better designs can be found and apparent barriers to growth dissolve in the face of technological change.

This situation indicates the essential difference between economic exchange and technique. Exchange is all about tradeoffs: more of A means less of B. But the aim of technical advance is precisely to avoid such dilemmas by devising what the French philosopher of technology, Gilbert Simondon, called "concrete" designs that optimize several variables at once. A single cleverly conceived mechanism then corresponds to many different social demands, one structure to many functions. . . . [D]esign is not a zero-sum economic game but an ambivalent cultural process that serves a multiplicity of values and social groups without necessarily sacrificing efficiency.

REGULATION OF TECHNOLOGY

That these conflicts over social control of risk are not new can be seen from the interesting case of the "bursting boilers." Steamboat boilers were the first

technology the US Government subjected to safety regulation. Over 5000 people were killed or injured in hundreds of steamboat explosions from 1816, when regulation was first proposed, to 1852, when it was actually implemented. Is this many casualties or few? Consumers evidently were not too alarmed to continue traveling by riverboat in ever increasing numbers. Understandably, ship owners interpreted this as a vote of confidence and protested the excessive cost of safer designs. Yet politicians also won votes demanding safety.

The accident rate fell dramatically once technical improvements were mandated. Legislation would hardly have been necessary to achieve this had these improvements been technically determined. But in fact boiler design was relative to a social judgment about safety. That judgment could have been made on market grounds, as the shippers wished, or politically, with differing results. In either case, those results *constitute* a proper boiler. What a boiler "is" was thus defined through a long process of political struggle culminating finally in uniform codes issued by the American Society of Mechanical Engineers.

This example shows how the technical code responds to the changing cultural horizon of the society. Quite down-to-earth technical parameters such as the choice and processing of materials are *socially* specified by the code. The illusion of technical necessity arises from the fact that the code is thus literally "cast in iron" (at least in the case of the boilers.)

Conservative anti-regulatory social philosophies are based on this illusion. They forget that the design process always already incorporates standards of safety and environmental compatibility; similarly, all technologies support some basic level of user or worker initiative and skill. A properly made technical object simply *must* meet these standards to be recognized as such. Conformity is no ideological extravagance but an intrinsic production cost. Raising the standards means altering the definition of the object, not paying a price for an alternative good or value as the tradeoff model holds.

THE FETISHISM OF EFFICIENCY

But what of the much discussed cost/benefit ratio of design changes such as those mandated by environmental or other similar legislation? These calculations have some application to transitional situations, before technical advances responding to new demands fundamentally alter the terms of the problem. But it is important not to overestimate their scientific value simply because they are expressed in numbers. All too often, the results depend on economists' very rough estimates of the monetary value of such things as a day of trout fishing or an asthma attack. If made without prejudice, these estimates may well help to prioritize policy alternatives, but one cannot legitimately generalize from such pragmatic applications to a universal theory of the cost of regulation.

Such fetishism of efficiency ignores our ordinary understanding of the concept which is primarily of relevance to social philosophy. In that everyday sense, efficiency concerns those values with which economic actors are routinely concerned. The plumber may compare plastic to copper pipe as to their efficiency; he may even consider septic tanks vs. sewer hookups. But he is not expected to calculate the value of the night soil modern plumbing wastes. Such unproblematic aspects of technology can be safely ignored.

In theory one can decompose any technical object and account for each of its elements in terms of the costs it imposes and the goals it meets, whether it be safety, speed, reliability, etc., but in practice no one is interested in opening the "black box" to see what is inside. For example, once the boiler code is established, such things as the thickness of a wall or the design of a safety valve appear as essential to the object. The cost of these features is not broken out as the specific "price" of safety and compared unfavorably with a more "efficient" but less secure design. Violating the code in order to lower costs is a crime, not a tradeoff.

Design is only controversial while it is in flux. Resolved conflicts over technology are quickly forgotten. Their outcomes, a welter of taken-for-granted technical and legal standards, are embodied in a stable code, and form the background against which economic actors manipulate the unstable portions of the environment in the pursuit of efficiency. The code itself is not normally varied in real world economic calculations, and as further advance occurs on the basis of it, movement backward no longer seems technically feasible.

Anticipating the stabilization of a new code, one can often ignore contemporary arguments that will soon be silenced by the emergence of a new horizon of efficiency calculations. This is what happened with boiler design and child labor; presumably, current debates on the environment will have a similar history and we will someday mock those who object to cleaner air and water as a "false principle of humanity" that violates technological imperatives.

There is a larger issue here. Non-economic values intersect the economy in the technical code. The examples we are dealing with illustrate this point clearly. The legal standards that regulate workers' economic activity have a significant impact on every aspect of their lives. In the child labor case, regulation widened educational opportunities with consequences that are not primarily economic in character. In the riverboat case, the choice of high levels of security was no tradeoff of one good for another, but a non-economic decision about the value of human life and the responsibilities of government.

Technology is thus not merely a means to an end; technical design standards define major portions of the social environment, such as urban and built spaces, workplaces, medical activities and expectations, life patterns, and so on. The economic significance of technical change often pales beside its wider human implications in framing a way of life. In such cases, regulation defines the cultural framework *of* the economy; it is not an act *in* the economy.

THE CONCEPT OF POTENTIALITY

The false dilemmas of technical politics arise from a peculiarity of change in the technical sphere. Technical resources can be configured in many different patterns. Any given configuration realizes a certain fraction of the well-being potentially available at the achieved technical level. Unrealized technical potential stands as a measure of the existing system. Where the contrast between what is and what might be becomes a political issue, technical resources are reconfigured in response to public pressure.

Looking back, the new configuration may seem obvious, but looking forward it is often very difficult to imagine radical technical solutions to contemporary problems. Worse still, without a clear idea of a solution, it is difficult even to formulate the problems clearly in their technical aspect. Thus often only after innovations have been introduced does it become entirely clear to what demand they respond.

Not only is it difficult to anticipate future technical arrangements, it is all too easy to think up utopias that cannot be realized under the existing ones. Thoroughgoing social changes are often inspired by such large ideological visions. In such cases, the long-term success of the new vision depends on its ability to deliver a better life over an extended period. That in turn depends on the technical changes necessary for its realization. Once success has been achieved, it is possible to look back and argue that the older way of life obstructed progress. In anticipation, theory may situate itself imaginatively on the boundary of the new civilizational configuration that will give a concrete content to its speculations, judging this society from the standpoint of a possible successor. However, so long as its hopes remain contingent for their realization on still unimagined technical advances, they can only take an ethical or ideological form. Their concrete formulation depends ultimately on the advances that will someday realize them by locking in the sort of irreversible sequence we call progress. As progress unfolds on the basis of the constrained choices that have shaped technology in the past, lines of development emerge with a clear direction. What were once values posited in the struggle for the future, become facts inherited from the past as the technical and institutional premises of further advance.

In economics the failure to actualize the full potential of a resource is called "suboptimization." Where suboptimizations are rooted in the technical code, we are dealing not with a specific or local failure but with the generalized wastefulness of a whole technological system. In economic terms, unrealized civilizational potentialities appear as systematic underemployment of major resources due to the restrictions the dominant economic culture places on technical and human development. A new culture is needed to shift patterns of investment and consumption and to open up the imagination to technical advances that transform the horizon of economic action.

The speculative claims of morality become ordinary facts of life through such civilizational advances. The child labor example illustrates these points clearly. Reforms based on ethical demands led to social changes so profound that eventually those demands became self-evident facts of life. At the time, businessmen worried about the economic costs of the reforms, but today these costs seem trivial, even irrelevant, in the light of the enormous human gain that results from the modern practices of child rearing and education. Of course time is of the essence in such cases. The point of view of contemporaries is not arbitrary, just subject to radical reinterpretation in a wider historical context. Something similar seems to be occurring today in the movements for environmental reform and for the equality of women and racial minorities.

Where the struggle for new ideals succeeds in restructuring society around a new culture, it will not be perceived as trading off wealth against morality, but as realizing the economic potentialities associated with its ethical claims. The dilemma of virtue and prosperity is not absolute, but can be mediated in the course of technological developments. . . . To some extent this redefinition has actually taken hold. As it sinks down into the structure of technology itself, through advances that adapt technical systems to the natural environment, it will become "obvious" that environmentalism represents progress.

Because economic culture is not fixed once and for all, and because a population's socially relative goals may be served by a variety of technological means, it is possible to link ideals and interests in a progressive process of technical change. In that progress potentialities that appear at first in ethical or ideological form are eventually realized in an effective consciousness of self-interest. This link makes possible a radical democratic politics of technology.

HANS JONAS   I.9

Technology and Responsibility: Reflections on the New Task of Ethics

Hans Jonas is one of a relatively small number of twentieth-century philosophers who have reflected carefully on the relationship between technology and ethics. He is also known for his writing on topics in biomedical ethics. He ended his professional career as Alvin Johnson Professor Emeritus of Philosophy at the New School for Social Research.

In this essay that originally appeared in *Social Research* in 1973, Jonas develops the view that traditional ethics is incapable of handling the kinds of ethical problems that are being created by our contemporary global technological civilization. His view is that in order to adequately evaluate the ethical significance of contemporary science and technology, we need to do so through the lens of a new kind of ethics, what he terms an "ethics of responsibility." He subsequently expanded the ideas presented in this essay in a book published in 1984 entitled *The Imperative of Responsibility: In Search of an Ethics for the Technological Age.*

Focus Questions

1. What are the three characteristics of traditional "neighbor ethics" that Jonas isolates, and in what respects has modern technology made traditional ethics obsolete?
2. How does Jonas' view that "man himself has been added to the objects of technology" compare to the discussion of the ethics of human cloning by Robert Wachbroit (selection II.9)?
3. What do you think Jonas means when he says, "We need wisdom the most when we believe in it the least"?

Keywords

behavior control, environmental ethics, ethics, genetic engineering, morality, utopia

ALL PREVIOUS ETHICS—whether in the form of issuing direct enjoinders to do and not to do certain things, or in the form of defining principles for such enjoinders, or in the form of establishing the ground of obligation for obeying such principles—had these interconnected tacit premises in com-

mon: that the human condition, determined by the nature of man and the nature of things, was given once for all; that the human good on that basis was readily determinable; and that the range of human action and therefore responsibility was narrowly circumscribed. It will be the burden of my argument to show that these premises no longer hold, and to reflect on the meaning of this fact for our moral condition. More specifically, it will be my contention that with certain developments of our powers the *nature of human action* has changed, and since ethics is concerned with action, it should follow that the changed nature of human action calls for a change in ethics as well: this not merely in the sense that new objects of action have added to the case material on which received rules of conduct are to be applied, but in the more radical sense that the qualitatively novel nature of certain of our actions has opened up a whole new dimension of ethical relevance for which there is no precedent in the standards and canons of traditional ethics.

I

The novel powers I have in mind are, of course, those of modern *technology*. My first point, accordingly, is to ask how this technology affects the nature of our acting, in what ways it makes acting under its dominion *different* from what it has been through the ages. Since throughout those ages man was never without technology, the question involves the human difference of *modern* from previous technology. Let us start with an ancient voice on man's powers and deeds which in an archetypal sense itself strikes, as it were, a technological note— the famous Chorus from Sophocles' *Antigone*.

> Many the wonders but nothing more wondrous
>   than man.
> This thing crosses the sea in the winter's storm,
> making his path through the roaring waves.
> And she, the greatest of gods, the Earth—
> deathless she is, and unwearied—he wears her away
> as the ploughs go up and down from year to year
> and his mules turn up the soil.
>
> The tribes of the lighthearted birds he ensnares, and
>   the races
> of all the wild beasts and the salty brood of the sea,
> with the twisted mesh of his nets, he leads captive,
>   this clever man.
> He controls with craft the beasts of the open air,
> who roam the hills. The horse with his shaggy mane
> he holds and harnesses, yoked about the neck,
> and the strong bull of the mountain.

> Speech and thought like the wind
> and the feelings that make the town,
> he has taught himself, and shelter against the cold,
> refuge from rain. Ever resourceful is he.
> He faces no future helpless. Only against death
> shall he call for aid in vain. But from baffling
>   maladies
> has he contrived escape.
>
> Clever beyond all dreams
> the inventive craft that he has
> which may drive him one time or another to well
>   or ill.
> When he honors the laws of the land the gods'
>   sworn right
> high indeed in his city; but stateless the man
> who dares to do what is shameful.

This awestruck homage to man's powers tells of his violent and violating irruption into the cosmic order, the self-assertive invasion of nature's various domains by his restless cleverness; but also of his building—through the self-taught powers of speech and thought and social sentiment—the home for his very humanity, the artifact of the city. The raping of nature and the civilizing of himself go hand in hand. Both are in defiance of the elements, the one by venturing into them and overpowering their creatures, the other by securing an enclave against them in the shelter of the city and its laws. Man is the maker of his life *qua* human, bending circumstances to his will and needs, and except against death he is never helpless.

Yet there is a subdued and even anxious quality about this appraisal of the marvel that is man, and nobody can mistake it for immodest bragging. With all his boundless resourcefulness, man is still small by the measure of the elements: precisely this makes his sallies into them so daring and allows those elements to tolerate his forwardness. Making free with the denizens of land and sea and air, he yet leaves the encompassing nature of those elements unchanged, and their generative powers undiminished. Them he cannot harm by carving out his little dominion from theirs. They last, while his schemes have their short lived way. Much as he harries Earth, the greatest of gods, year after year with his plough—she is ageless and unwearied; her enduring patience he must and can trust, and he must conform. And just as ageless is the sea. With all his netting of the salty brood, the spawning ocean is inexhaustible. Nor is it hurt by the plying of ships, nor sullied by what is jettisoned into its deeps. And no matter how many illnesses he contrives to cure, mortality does not bow to cunning.

All this holds because man's inroads into nature, as seen by himself, were essentially superficial, and powerless to upset its appointed balance. Nor is there a hint, in the *Antigone* chorus or anywhere else, that this is only a beginning and that greater things of artifice and power are yet to come—that man is embarked on an endless course of conquest. He had gone thus far in reducing necessity, had learned by his wits to wrest that much from it for the humanity of his life, and there he could stop. The room he had thus made was filled by the city of men—meant to enclose and not to expand—and thereby a new balance was struck within the larger balance of the whole. All the well or ill to which man's inventive craft may drive him one time or another is inside the human enclave and does not touch the nature of things.

The immunity of the whole, untroubled in its depth by the importunities of man, that is, the essential immutability of Nature as the cosmic order, was indeed the backdrop to all of mortal man's enterprises, between the abiding and the changing: the abiding was Nature, the changing his own works. The greatest of these works was the city, and on it he could offer some measure of abidingness by the laws he made for it and undertook to honor. But no long-range certainty pertained to this contrived abidingness. As a precarious artifact, it can lapse or go astray. Not even within its artificial space, with all the freedom it gives to man's determination of self, can the arbitrary ever supersede the basic terms of his being. The very inconstancy of human fortunes assures the constancy of the human condition. Chance and luck and folly, the great equalizers in human affairs, act like an entropy of sorts and make all definite designs in the long run revert to the perennial norm. Cities rise and fall, rules come and go, families prosper and decline; no

change is there to stay, and in the end, with all the temporary deflections balancing each other out, the state of man is as it always was. So here too, in his very own artifact, man's control is small and his abiding nature prevails.

Still, in this citadel of his own making, clearly set off from the rest of things and entrusted to him, was the whole and sole domain of man's responsible action. Nature was not an object of human responsibility—she taking care of herself and, with some coaxing and worrying, also of man: not ethics, only cleverness applied to her. But in the city, where men deal with men, cleverness must be wedded to morality, for this is the soul of its being. In this intra-human frame dwells all traditional ethics and matches the nature of action delimited by this frame.

II

Let us extract from the preceding those characteristics of human action which are relevant for a comparison with the estate of things today.

1. All dealing with the non-human world, i.e., the whole realm of *techne* (with the exception of medicine), was ethically neutral—in respect both of the object and the subject of such action: in respect of the object, because it impinged but little on the self-sustaining nature of things and thus raised no question of permanent injury to the integrity of its object, the natural order as a whole; and in respect of the subject it was ethically neutral because *techne* as an activity conceived itself as a determinate tribute to necessity and not as an indefinite, self-validating advance to mankind's major goal, claiming in its pursuit man's ultimate effort and concern. The real vocation of man lay elsewhere. In brief, action on non-human things did not constitute a sphere of authentic ethical significance.

2. Ethical significance belonged to the direct dealing of man with man, including the dealing with himself: all traditional ethics is *anthropocentric*.

3. For action in this domain, the entity "man" and his basic condition was considered constant in essence and not itself an object of reshaping *techne.*

4. The good and evil about which action had to care lay close to the act, either in the praxis itself or in its immediate reach, and were not a matter for remote planning. This proximity of ends pertained to time as well as space. The effective range of action was small, the time-span of foresight, goal-setting, and accountability was short, control of circumstances limited. Proper conduct had its immediate criteria and almost immediate consummation. The long run of consequences beyond was left to change, fate, or providence. Ethics accordingly was of the here and now, of occasions as they arise between men, of the recurrent, typical situations of private and public life. The good man was he who met these contingencies with virtue and wisdom, cultivating these powers in himself, and for the rest resigning himself to the unknown.

All enjoinders and maxims of traditional ethics, materially different as they may be, show this confinement to the immediate setting of the action. "Love thy neighbor as thyself"; "Do unto others as you would wish them to do unto you"; "Instruct your child in the way of truth"; "Strive for excellence by developing and actualizing the best potentialities of your being *qua* man"; "Subordinate your individual good to the common good"; "Never treat your fellow man as a means only but always *also* as an end in himself"—and so on. Note that in all those maxims the agent and the "other" of his action are sharers of a common present. It is those alive now and in some commerce with me that have a claim on my conduct as it affects them by deed or omission. The ethical universe is composed of contemporaries, and its horizon to the future is confined by the foreseeable span of their lives. Similarly confined is its horizon of place, within which the agent and the other meet as neighbor, friend or foe, as superior and subordinate, weaker and stronger, and in all the other roles in which humans interact with one another. To this proximate range of action all morality was geared.

III

It follows that the *knowledge* that is required—besides the moral will—to assure the morality of action, fitted these limited terms: it was not the knowledge of the scientist or the expert, but knowledge of a kind readily available to all men of good will. Kant went so far as to say that "human reason can, in matters of morality, be easily brought to a high degree of accuracy and completeness even in the most ordinary intelligence";[1] that "there is no need of science or philosophy for knowing what man has to do in order to be honest and good, and indeed to be wise and virtuous. . . . [Ordinary intelligence] can have as good a hope of hitting the mark as any philosopher can promise himself";[2] and again: "I need no elaborate acuteness to find out what I have to do so that my willing be morally good. Inexperienced regarding the course of the world, unable to anticipate all the contingencies that happen in it," I can yet know how to act in accordance with the moral law.[3]

Not every thinker in ethics, it is true, went so far in discounting the cognitive side of moral action. But even when it received much greater emphasis, as in Aristotle, where the discernment of the situation and what is fitting for it makes considerable demands on experience and judgment, such knowledge has nothing to do with the science of things. It implies, of course, a general conception of the human good as such, a conception predicated on the presumed invariables of man's nature and condition, which may or may not find expression in a theory of its own. But its translation into practice requires a knowledge of the here and now, and this is entirely non-theoretical. This "knowledge" proper to virtue (of the "where, when, to, whom, and how") stays with the immediate issue, in whose defined context the action *as the agent's own* takes its course and within which it terminates. The good or bad of the action is wholly decided within that short-term context. Its moral quality shines forth from it, visible to its witnesses. No one was held responsible for the unintended later affects of his well-intentioned, well-considered, and well-performed act. The short arm of human power did not call for a long arm of predictive knowledge; the shortness of the one is as little culpable as that of the other. Precisely because the human good, known in its generality, is the same for all time, its relation or violation takes place at each time, and its complete locus is always the present.

IV

All this has decisively changed. Modern technology has introduced actions of such novel scale, objects, and consequences that the framework of former ethics can no longer contain them. The *Antigone* chorus on the *deinotes,* the wondrous power, of man would have to read differently now; and its admonition to the individual to honor the laws of the land would no longer be enough. To be sure, the old prescriptions of the "neighbor" ethics—of justice, charity, honesty, and so on—still hold in their intimate immediacy of the nearest, day by day sphere of human interaction. But this sphere is overshadowed by a growing realm of collective action where doer, deed, and effect are no longer the same as they were in the proximate sphere, and which by the enormity of its powers forces upon ethics a new dimension of responsibility never dreamt of before.

Take, for instance, as the first major change in the inherited picture, the critical *vulnerability* of nature to man's technological intervention—unsuspected before it began to show itself in damage already done. This discovery, whose shock led to the concept and nascent science of ecology, alters the very concept of ourselves as a causal agency in the larger scheme of things. It brings to light, through the effects, that the nature of human action has *de facto* changed, and that an object of an entirely new order—no less than the whole biosphere of the planet—has been added to what we must be responsible for because of our power over it. And of what surpassing importance an object, dwarfing all previous objects of active man! Nature as a human responsibility is surely a *novum* to be pondered in ethical theory. What kind of obligation is operative in it? Is it more than a utilitarian concern? Is it just prudence that bids us not to kill the goose that lays the golden eggs, or saw off the branch on which we sit? But the "we" that here sits and may fall into the abyss is all future mankind, and the survival of the species is more than a prudential duty of its present members. Insofar as it is the fate of *man,* as affected by the condition of nature, which makes us care about the preservation of nature, such care admittedly still retains the anthropocentric focus of all classical ethics. Even so, the difference is great. The containment of nearness and contemporaneity is gone, swept away by the spatial spread and timespan of the cause-effect trains which technological practice sets afoot, even when undertaken for proximate ends. Their irreversibility conjoined to their aggregate magnitude injects another novel factor into the moral equation. To this take their cumulative character: their effects add themselves to one another, and the situation for later acting and being becomes increasingly different from what it was for the initial agent. The cumulative self-propagation of the technological change of the world thus constantly overtakes the conditions of its contributing acts and moves through none but unprecedented situations, for which the lessons of experience are powerless. And not even content with changing its beginning to the point of unrecognizability, the cumulation as such may consume the basis of the whole series, the very condition of itself. All this would have to be co-intended in the will of the single action if this is to be a morally responsible one. Ignorance no longer provides it with an alibi.

Knowledge, under these circumstances, becomes a prime duty beyond anything claimed for it heretofore, and the knowledge must be commensurate with the causal scale of our action. The fact that it cannot really be thus commensurate, i.e., that the predictive knowledge falls behind the technical knowledge which nourishes our power to act, itself assumes ethical importance. Recognition of ignorance becomes the obverse of the duty to know and thus part of the ethics which must govern the ever more necessary self-policing of our out-sized might. No previous ethics had to consider the global condition of human life and the far-off future, even existence, of the race. There now being an issue demands, in brief, a new concept of duties and rights, for which previous ethics and metaphysics provide not even the principles, let alone a ready doctrine.

And what if the new kind of human action would mean that more than the interest of man alone is to be considered—that our duty extends farther and the anthropocentric confinement of former ethics no longer holds? It is at least not senseless anymore to ask whether the condition of extra-human nature, the biosphere as a whole and in its parts, now subject to our power, has become a human trust and has something of a more claim on us not only for our ulterior sake but for its own and in its own right. If this were the case it would require quite some rethinking in basic principles of ethics. It would mean to seek not only the human good, but also the good of things extra-human, that is, to extend the recognition of "ends in themselves" beyond the sphere of man and make the human good include the care for them. For such a role of stewardship no previous ethics has prepared us—and the dominant, scientific view of *Nature* even less. Indeed, the latter emphatically denies us all conceptual means to think of Nature as something to be honored, having reduced it to the indifference of necessity and accident, and divested it of any dignity of ends. But still, a silent plea for sparing its integrity seems to issue from the threatened plenitude of the living world. Should we heed this plea, should we grant its claim as sanctioned by the nature of things, or dismiss it as a mere sentiment on our part, which we may indulge as fair as we wish and can afford to do? If the former, it would (if taken seriously in its theoretical implications) push the necessary rethinking beyond the doctrine of action, i.e., ethics, into the doctrine of being, i.e., metaphysics, in which all ethics must ultimately be grounded. On this speculative subject I will here say no more than that we should keep ourselves open to the thought that natural science may not tell the whole story about Nature.

V

Returning to strictly intra-human considerations, there is another ethical aspect to the growth of *techne* as a pursuit beyond the pragmatically limited terms of former times. Then, so we found, *techne* was a measured tribute to necessity, not the road to mankind's chosen goal—a means with a finite measure of adequacy to well-defined proximate ends. Now, *techne* in the form of modern technology has turned into an infinite forward-thrust of the race, its most significant enterprise, in whose permanent, self-transcending advance to ever greater things the vocation of man tends to be seen, and whose success of maximal control over things and himself appears as the consummation of his destiny. Thus the triumph of *homo faber* over his external object means also his triumph in the internal constitution of *homo sapiens,* of whom he used to be a subsidiary part. In other words, technology, apart from its objective works, assumes ethical significance by the central place it now occupies in human purpose. Its cumulative creation, the expanding artificial environment, continuously reinforces the particular powers in man that created it, by compelling their unceasing inventive employment in its management and further advance, and by rewarding them with additional success—which only adds to the relentless claim. This positive feedback of functional necessity and reward—in whose dynamics pride of achievement must not be forgotten—assures the growing ascendancy of one side of man's nature over all the others, and inevitably at their expense. If nothing succeeds like success, nothing also entraps like success. Outshining in prestige and starving in resources whatever else belongs to the fullness of man, the expansion of his power is accompanied by a contraction of his self-conception and being. In the image he entertains of himself—the potent self-formula which determines his actual being as much as it reflects it—man now is evermore the maker of what he has made and the doer of what he can do, and most of all the preparer of what he will be able to do next. But not you or I: it is the aggregate, not the individual doer or deed that matters here; and the indefinite future, rather than the contemporary context of the action, constitutes the relevant horizon of responsibility. This requires imperatives of a new sort. If the realm of making has invaded the space of essential action, then morality must invade the realm of making, from which it had formerly stayed aloof, and must do so in the form of public policy. With issues of such inclusiveness and such lengths of anticipation public policy has never had to deal before. In fact, the changed nature of human action changes the very nature of politics.

For the boundary between "city" and "nature" has been obliterated: the city of men, once an enclave in the non-human world, spreads over the whole of terrestrial nature and usurps its place. The difference between the artificial and the natural has vanished, the natural is swallowed up in the sphere of the artificial, and at the same time the total artifact, the works of man working on and through himself, generates a "nature" of its own, i.e., a necessity with which human freedom has to cope in an entirely new sense. Once it could be said *Fiat justitia, pereat mundus,* "Let justice be done, and may the world perish"—where "world," of course, meant the renewable enclave in the imperishable whole. Not even rhetorically can the like be said anymore when the perishing of the whole through the doings of man—be they just or unjust—has become a real possibility. Issues never legislated on come into the purview of the laws which the total city must give itself so that there will be a world for the generations of man to come.

That there *ought* to be through all future time such a world fit for human habitation, and that it ought in all future time to be inhabited by a mankind worthy of the human name, will be readily affirmed as a general axiom or a persuasive desirability of speculative imagination (as persuasive and undemonstrable as the proposition that there being a world at all is "better" than there being none): but as a *moral* proposition, namely, a practical *obligation* toward the posterity of a distant future, and a principle of decision in present action, it is quite different from the imperatives of the previous ethics of contemporaneity; and it has entered the moral scene only with our novel powers and range of prescience.

The *presence of man in the world* had been a first and unquestionable given, from which all idea of obligation in human conduct started out. Now it has itself become an *object* of obligation—the obligation namely to ensure the very premise of all obligation, i.e., the *foothold* for a moral universe in the physical world—the existence of mere *candidates* for a moral order. The difference this makes for ethics may be illustrated in one example.

VI

Kant's categorical imperative said: "Act so that you *can* will that the maxim of our action be made the principle of a universal law." The "can" here invoked is that of reason and its consistency with itself: *Given* the existence of a community of human agents (acting rational beings), the action must be such that it can without self-contradiction be imagined as a general practice of that community. Mark that the basic reflection of morals here is not itself a moral but a logical one: The "I *can* will" or "I *cannot* will" expresses logical compatibility or incompatibility, not moral approbation or revulsion. But there is no self-contradiction in the thought that humanity would once come to an end, therefore also none in the thought that the happiness of present and proximate generations would be bought with the unhappiness or even non-existence of later ones—as little as, after all, in the inverse thought that the existence or happiness of later generations would be bought with the unhappiness or even partial extinction of present ones. The sacrifice of the future for the present is *logically* no more open to attack than the sacrifice of the present for the future. The difference is only that in the one case the series goes on, and in the other it does not. But that it *ought to go on,* regardless of the distribution of happiness or unhappiness, even with a persistent preponderance of unhappiness over happiness, nay, even of immorality over morality[4]—this cannot be derived from the rule of self-consistency *within* the series, long or short as it happens to be: it is a commandment of a very different kind, lying outside and "prior" to the series as a whole, and its ultimate grounding can only be metaphysical.

An imperative responding to the new type of human action and addressed to the new type of agency that operates it might run thus: "Act so that the effects of your action are compatible with the permanence of genuine human life"; or expressed negatively: "Act so that the effects of your action are not destructive of the future possibility of such life"; or simply: "Do not compromise the conditions for an indefinite continuation of humanity on earth"; or most generally: "In your present choices, include the future wholeness of Man among the objects of your will."

It is immediately obvious that no rational contradiction is involved in the violation of this kind of imperative. I *can* will the present good with sacrifice of the future good. It is also evident that the new imperative addresses itself to public policy rather than private conduct, which is not in the causal dimension to which that imperative applies. Kant's categorical imperative was addressed to the individual, and its criterion was instantaneous. It enjoined each of us to consider what would happen *if* the *maxim* of my present action were made, or at this moment already were, the principle of a universal legislation; the self-consistency or inconsistency of such a *hypothetical* universalization is made the test for my *private* choice. But it was no part of the reasoning that there is any probability of my private choice *in fact* becoming universal law, or that it might contribute to its becoming that. The universalization is a thought-experiment by the private agent not to test the immanent morality of his action. Indeed, real consequences are not considered at all, and the principle is one not of objective responsibility but of the subjective quality of my self-determination. The new imperative invokes a different consistency: not that of the act with itself, but that of its eventual *effects* with the continuance of human agency in times to come. And the "universalization" it contemplates is by no means hypothetical—i.e., a purely logical transference from the individual "me" to an imaginary, causally unrelated "all" ("*if* everybody acted like that"); on the contrary, the actions subject to the new imperative— actions of the collective whole—have their universal reference in their actual scope of efficacy: they "totalize" themselves in the progress of their momentum and thus are bound to terminate in shaping the universal dispensation of things. This adds a *time* horizon to the moral calculus which is entirely absent from the instantaneous logical operation of the Kantian imperative: whereas the latter extrapolates into an ever-present order of abstract compatibility, our imperative extrapolates into a predictable real *future* as the open-ended dimension of our responsibility.

VII

Similar comparisons could be made with all the other historical forms of the ethics of contemporaneity and immediacy. The new order of human action requires a commensurate ethics of foresight and responsibility, which is as new as are the issues with which it has to deal. We have seen that these are the issues posed by the works of *homo faber* in the age of technology. But among those novel works we haven't mentioned yet the potentially most ominous class. We have considered *techne* only as applied to the non-human realm. But man himself has been added to the objects of technology. *Homo faber* is turning upon himself and gets ready to make over the maker of all the rest. This consummation of his power, which may well portend the overpowering of man, this final imposition of art on nature, calls upon the utter resources of ethical thought, which never before has been faced with elective alternatives to what were considered the definite terms of the human condition.

a. Take, for instance, the most basic of these "givens," man's mortality. Who ever before had to make up his mind on its desirable and *eligible* measure? There was nothing to choose about the upper limit, the "three score years and ten, or by reason of strength fourscore." Its inexorable rule was the subject of lament, submission, or vain (not to say foolish) wish-dreams about possible exceptions— strangely enough, almost never of affirmation. The intellectual imagination of a George Bernard Shaw and a Jonathan Swift speculated on the privilege of not having to die, or the curse of not being able to die. (Swift with the latter was the more perspicacious of the two.) Myth and legend toyed with such themes against the acknowledged background of the unalterable, which made the earnest man rather pray "teach us to number our days that we may get a heart of wisdom" (Psalm 90). Nothing of this was in the realm of doing, and effective decision. The question was only how to relate to the stubborn fact.

But lately, the dark cloud of inevitability seems to lift. A practical hope is held out by certain advances in cell biology to prolong, perhaps indefinitely extend the span of life by counteracting biochemical processes of aging. Death no longer appears as a necessity belonging to the nature of life, but as an avoidable, at least in principle tractable and long-delayable, organic malfunction. A perennial yearning of mortal man seems to come nearer fulfillment. And for the first time we have in earnest to ask the question "How desirable is this? How desirable for the individual, and how for the species?" These questions involve the very meaning of our finitude, the attitude toward death, and the general biological significance of the balance of death and procreation. Even prior to such ultimate questions are the more pragmatic ones of who should be eligible for the boon: persons of particular quality and merit? of social eminence? those that can pay for it? everybody? The last would seem the only just course. But it would have to be paid for at the opposite end, at the source. For clearly, on a population-wide scale, the price of extended age must be a proportional slowing of replacement, i.e., a diminished access of new life. The result would be a decreasing proportion of youth in an increasingly aged population. How good or bad would that be for the general condition of man? Would the species gain or lose? And how *right* would it be to preempt the place of youth? Having to die is bound up with having been born: mortality is but the other side of the perennial spring of "a natality" (to use Hannah Arendt's term). This had always been ordained; now its meaning has to be pondered in the sphere of decision.

To take the extreme (not that it will ever be obtained): if we abolish death, we must abolish procreation as well, for the latter is life's answer to the former, and so we would have a world of old age with no youth, and of known individuals with no

surprises of such that had never been before. But this perhaps is precisely the wisdom in the harsh dispensation of our mortality: that it grants us the eternally renewed promise of the freshness, immediacy, and eagerness of youth, together with the supply of otherness as such. There is no substitute for this in the greater accumulation of prolonged experience: it can never recapture the unique privilege of seeing the world for the first time and with new eyes, never relive the wonder which, according to Plato, is the beginning of philosophy, never the curiosity of the child, which rarely enough lives on as thirst for knowledge in the adult, until it wanes there too. This ever renewed beginning, which is only to be had at the price of ever repeated ending, may well be mankind's hope, its safeguard against lapsing into boredom and routine, its chance of retaining the spontaneity of life. Also, the role of the *memento mori* in the individual's life must be considered, and what its attenuation to indefiniteness may do to it. Perhaps a non-negotiable limit to our expected time is necessary for each of us as the incentive to number our days and make them count.

So it could be that what by intent is a philanthropic gift of science to man, the partial granting of his oldest wish—to escape the curse of mortality—turns out to be to the detriment of man. I am not indulging in prediction and, in spite of my noticeable bias, not even in valuation. My point is that already the promised gift raises questions that had never to be asked before in terms of practical choice, and that no principle of former ethics, which took the human constants for granted, is competent to deal with them. And yet they must be dealt with ethically and by principle and not merely by the pressure of interest.

b. It is similar with all the other, quasi-utopian powers about to be made available by the advances of biomedical science as they are translated into technology. Of these, *behavior control* is much nearer to practical readiness than the still hypothetical prospect I have just been discussing, and the ethical questions it raises are less profound but have a more direct bearing on the moral conception of man. Here again, the new kind of intervention exceeds the old ethical categories. They have not equipped us to rule, for example, on mental control by chemical means or by direct electrical action of the brain via implanted electrodes—undertaken, let us assume, for defensible and even laudable ends. The mixture of beneficial and dangerous potentials is obvious, but the lines are not easy to draw. Relief of mental patients from distressing and disabling symptoms seems unequivocally beneficial. But from the relief of the *patient,* a goal entirely in the tradition of the medical art, there is an easy passage to the relief of *society* from the inconvenience of difficult individual behavior among its members: that is, the passage from medical to social application; and this opens up an indefinite field with grave potentials. The troublesome problems of rule and unruliness in modern mass society make the extension of such control methods to non-medical categories extremely tempting for social management. Numerous questions of human rights and dignity arise. The difficult question of preemption care versus enabling care insists on concrete answers. Shall we induce learning attitudes in school children by the mass administration of drugs, circumventing the appeal to autonomous motivation? Shall we overcome aggression by electronic pacification of brain areas? Shall we generate sensations of happiness or pleasure or at least contentment through independent stimulation (or tranquilizing) of the appropriate centers—independent, that is, of the objects of happiness, pleasure, or content and their attainment in personal living and achieving? Candidacies could be multiplied. Business firms might become interested in some of these techniques for performance-increase among their employees.

Regardless of the question of compulsion or consent, and regardless also of the question of undesirable side-effects, each time we thus bypass the human way of dealing with human problems, short-circuiting it by an impersonal mechanism, we have taken away something from the dignity of personal selfhood and advanced a further step on the road from responsible subjects to programmed behavior systems. Social functionalism, important as it is, is only one side of the question. Decisive is the question of what kind of individuals the society is composed of to make its existence valuable as a whole. Somewhere along the line of increasing

social manageability at the price of individual autonomy, the question of the worthwhileness of the human enterprise must pose itself. Answering it involves the image of man we entertain. We must think it anew in light of the things we can do to it now and could never do before.

c. This holds even more with respect to the last object of a technology applied on man himself—the genetic control of future men. This is too wide a subject for cursory treatment. Here I merely point to this most ambitious dream of *homo faber,* summed up in the phrase that man will take his own evolution in hand, with the aim of not just preserving the integrity of the species but of modifying it by improvements of his own design. Whether we have the right to do it, whether we are qualified for that creative role, is the most serious question that can be posed to man finding himself suddenly in possession of such failed powers. Who will be the image-makers, by what standards, and on the basis of what knowledge? Also, the question of the moral right to experiment on future human beings must be asked. These and similar questions, which demand an answer before we embark on a journey into the unknown, show most vividly how far our powers to act are pushing us beyond the terms of all former ethics.

VIII

The ethically relevant common feature in all the examples adduced is what I like to call the inherently "utopian" drift of our actions under the conditions of modern technology, whether it works on non-human or on human nature, and whether the "utopia" at the end of the road be planned or unplanned. By the kind and size of its snowballing effects, technological power propels us into goals of a type that was formerly the preserve of Utopias. To put it differently, technological power has turned what used and ought to be tentative, perhaps enlightening, plays of speculative reason into competing blueprints for projects, and in choosing between them we have to choose between extremes of remote effects. The one thing we can really know of them is their extremism as such—that they concern the total condition of nature on our globe and the very kind of creatures that shall, or shall not, populate it. In consequence of the inevitably "utopian" scale of modern technology, the salutary gap between everyday and ultimate issues, between occasions, closing. Living now constantly in the shadow of unwanted, built-in, automatic utopianism, we are constantly confronted with issues whose positive choice requires supreme wisdom—an impossible, and in particular for contemporary man, who denies the very existence of its object: viz., objective value and truth. We need wisdom most when we believe in it least.

If the new nature of our acting then calls for a new ethics of long-range responsibility, coextensive with the range of our power, it calls in the name of that very responsibility also for a new kind of humility—a humility not like former humility, i.e., owing to the littleness, but owing to the excessive magnitude of our power, which is the excess of our power to act over our power to foresee and our power to evaluate and to judge. In the face of the quasi-eschatological potentials of our technological processes, ignorance of the ultimate implications becomes itself a reason for responsible restraint—as the second best to the possession of wisdom itself.

One other aspect of the required new ethics of responsibility for and to a distant future is worth mentioning: the insufficiency of representative government to meet the new demands on its normal principles and by its normal mechanics. For according to these, only *present* interests make themselves heard and felt and enforce their condition. It is to them that public agencies are accountable, and this is the way in which concretely the respecting of rights comes about (as distinct from their abstract acknowledgement). But the *future* is not represented, it is not a force that can throw its weight into the scales. The non-existent has no lobby, and the unborn are powerless. Thus accountability to them has no political reality behind it yet in present decision-making, and when they can make their complaint, then we, the culprits, will no longer be there.

This raises to an ultimate pitch the old question of the power of the wise, or the force of ideas not allied to self-interest, in the body politic. What *force* shall represent the future in the present? However, before *this* question can become earnest in practical terms, the new ethics must find its theory, on which dos and don'ts can be based. That is: before the question of what *force,* comes the question of what *insight* or value-knowledge shall represent the future in the present.

IX

And here is where I get stuck, and where we all get stuck. For the very same movement which put us in possession of the powers that have now to be regulated by norms—the movement of modern knowledge called science—has by a necessary complementarity eroded the foundations from which norms could be derived; it has destroyed the very idea of norm as such. Not, fortunately, the feeling for norm and even for particular norms. But this feeling, become uncertain of itself when contradicted by alleged knowledge or at least denied all sanction by it. Anyway and always does it have a difficult enough time against the loud clamors of greed and fear. Now it must in addition blush before the frown of superior knowledge, as unfounded and incapable of foundation. First, Nature has been "neutralized" with respect to value, then man himself. Now we shiver in the nakedness of a nihilism in which near-omnipotence is paired with near-emptiness, greatest capacity with knowing least what for. With the apocalyptic pregnancy of our actions, that very knowledge which we lack has become more urgently needed than at any other stage in the adventure of mankind. Alas, urgency is no promise of success. On the contrary, it must be avowed that to seek for wisdom today requires a good measure of unwisdom. The very nature of the age which cries out for an ethical theory makes it suspiciously look like a fool's errand. Yet we have no choice in the matter but to try.

It is a question whether without restoring the category of the sacred, the category most thoroughly destroyed by the scientific enlightenment, we can have an ethics able to cope with the extreme powers which we possess today and constantly increase and are almost compelled to use. Regarding those consequences imminent enough still to hit ourselves, fear can do the job—so often the best substitute for genuine virtue or wisdom. But this means fails us towards the more distant prospects, which here matter the most, especially as the beginnings seem mostly innocent in their smallness. Only awe of the sacred with its unqualified veto is independent to fit computations of mundane fear and the solace of uncertainty about distant consequences. But religion as a soul-determining force is no longer there to be summoned to the aid of ethics. The latter must stand on its worldly feet—that is, on reason and its fitness for philosophy. And while of faith it can be said that it either is there or is not, of ethics it holds that it must be there.

It must be there because men act, and ethics is for the reordering of actions and for regulating the power to act. It must be there all the more, then, the greater the powers of acting that are to be regulated; and with their size, the ordering principle must also fit their kind. Thus, novel powers to act require novel ethical rules and perhaps even a new ethics.

"Thou shalt not kill" was enunciated because man has the power to kill and often the occasion and even inclination for it—in short, because killing is actually done. It is only under the *pressure* of real habits of action, and generally of the fact that always action already takes place, without *this* having to be commanded first, that ethics as the ruling of such acting under the standard of the good or the permitted enters the stage. Such a *pressure* emanates from the novel technological powers of man, whose exercise is given with their existence. *If* they really are as novel in kind as here contended, and if by the kind of their potential consequences they really have abolished the moral neutrality which the technical commerce with matter hitherto enjoyed—then their pressure bids to seek for new prescriptions in ethics which are competent to assume their guidance, but which first of all can hold their own theoretically against that very pressure. To the demonstration of those premises this paper was devoted. If they are accepted, then we who make thinking our business have a task to last us for our time. We must do it in time, for since we act anyway we shall have some ethic or other in any case, and without a supreme effort to determine the right one, we may be left with a wrong one by default.

NOTES

1. Immanuel Kant, *Groundwork of the Metaphysics of Morals,* preface.
2. *Op. cit.,* chapter 1.
3. *Ibid.* (I have followed H. J. Paton's translation with some changes.)
4. On this last point, the biblical God changed his mind to an all-encompassing "yes" after the Flood.

I.10   FREEMAN DYSON

Technology and Social Justice

Freeman Dyson was born in England and educated at Cambridge University. He served in World War II as an operations research specialist for the RAF. Following the war he did graduate training in physics and became professor of physics at Cornell University. In 1953 he joined the faculty at the Institute for Advanced Study in Princeton, New Jersey, where he remains. He is a Fellow of the Royal Society of London and a member of the National Academy of Sciences.

The text reprinted here was delivered as the fourth Louis Nizer Lecture on Public Policy for the Carnegie Council on Ethics and International Affairs on November 5, 1997. It relates to themes that he has developed more fully in his book *The Sun, the Genome, and the Internet* (1999). In this lecture Dyson addresses the issue of whether technological innovation tends to increase or decrease social justice and equality.

There are many who believe that technological innovation is a force for increasing social inequality. New technologies tend to benefit those who are already rich enough to afford them or powerful enough to control them, and because technology is a source of power, its control by elites only serves to enhance their dominance over other members of society. On the other side of this argument there are those who believe that technological progress is the engine of human progress and that technological innovation acts as a great leveler of society by breaking down the barriers erected by privilege and allowing for a more equitable distribution of knowledge and power.

Dyson examines the evidence for each of these general perspectives and ends up endorsing a qualified "techno-optimist" answer—that "ethics must guide technology toward social justice." Dyson supports his conclusion through a combination of historical reflection, personal anecdotes, and the exercise of technological and moral imagination.

Focus Questions

1. Dyson begins his discussion by giving some historical examples of technological innovations that he claims have increased social justice. What are his examples? Can you think of any others?
2. Why does Dyson believe that "The advent of electrical appliances liberated the servants and shackled their mistresses"?
3. Dyson argues that ethical and religious values can and should influence technological change, and he mentions Max Weber's seminal work *The Protestant Ethic and the Spirit of Capitalism* as providing evidence that this is possible. Do you agree?
4. In the concluding section, Dyson presents a vision in which the nascent technologies of solar energy, genetic engineering, and global Internet communications are combined to help billions of poor people all over the earth to attain a higher standard of living. Do you think that this vision is attainable? Why or why not?

Keywords

biomass energy, genetic engineering, high-tech medicine, the Human Genome Project, inequality, the Internet, national health care, social justice, solar energy

---

IT IS EASY TO FIND historical examples illustrating the thesis that technology may have something to contribute to social justice. In the fourteenth century the new technology of printing changed the

From "Technology and Social Justice," a Carnegie Council on Ethics and International Affairs lecture, delivered November 5, 1997, by Freeman Dyson. Copyright © 1998 Carnegie Council on Ethics and International Affairs. Reprinted by permission.

face of Europe, bringing books and education out of the monasteries and spreading them far and wide among the people. Printing gave power to the Bible and led directly to the Protestant Reformation in Northern Europe. One may question whether Luther's Germany and Shakespeare's England enjoyed social justice, but they were certainly closer to it than the medieval Germany and England out of which they grew. Luther and Shakespeare brought at least the idea of justice—if not the reality—to ordinary citizens outside the nobility and the priesthood. The Protestant ethic, which took root in Germany, England, Holland, and Scandinavia with the help of printed books, carried with it a perpetual striving for social justice, even if the Utopian visions were seldom achieved.

More recent technologies that contributed in a practical way to social justice were those of public health—clean water supplies, sewage treatment, vaccination, and antibiotics. These technologies could only be effective in protecting the rich from contagion and sickness if they were also available to the poor. Even if the rich and powerful receive preferential treatment, as they usually do, the benefits of public health technology are felt to some extent by everybody. In countries where public health technologies are enforced by law, there is no large gap in life expectancy between rich and poor.

The technology of synthetic materials has also helped to erase differences between rich and poor. Throughout history, until the nineteenth century, only the rich could afford to dress in brilliant colors, furs, and silk. Fine clothes were a badge of privilege and wealth. In the nineteenth century the chemical industry produced artificial dyestuffs. The twentieth century added artificial fur and silk and many other synthetic fabrics cheap enough for working-class women to afford. No longer can one tell a woman's social class by her clothes. It is a measure of social justice in modern societies that the children of the rich now dress down, imitating the style of the majority both in clothes and in behavior.

Household appliances are another technology with a tendency towards social justice. When I was a child in England in the 1920s, my mother employed four full-time servants: a cook, a housemaid, a nursemaid, and a gardener. We didn't consider ourselves rich. My father was a schoolteacher. We were an average middle-class family. In those days an average middle-class family needed four servants to do the hard manual work of cooking, cleaning, child care, and gardening. To do all this work a whole class of people existed who spent their lives as domestic servants. The professional and intellectual classes to which we belonged were riding on the backs of the servant class. Because of

the servants, my mother had leisure to organize socially useful projects, such as a club for teenage girls and a birth control clinic. The birth control clinic was undoubtedly a godsend to the women who came to it for instruction in the art of not having unwanted babies. But it did not in any way narrow the gulf between her and them. She always spoke of her birth control clientele like a mistress speaking of servants.

My mother was a kind mistress and treated the servants well, according to the standards of the time, but the servants knew their place. They knew that if they disobeyed orders or answered back, they would be out on the street. Now, like the antebellum South, the servant class in England is gone with the wind, and the wind that blew it away was not the ravaging invasion of Sherman's army, but the peaceful invasion of an army of electric stoves, gas heaters, vacuum cleaners, refrigerators, washing machines, drying machines, garbage disposals, freezers, microwave ovens, juicers, choppers, and disposable diapers. The technology of household appliances made servants unnecessary, and, at the same time, the children of the servant class began to go to college and make the transition to the middle class. The transition was not painless, but it was less painful than a civil war. It was a big step on the road to social justice.

I remember with great fondness the nursemaid, Ethel, who cared for me as a young child. She had left school, as girls of the servant class did in those days, at the age of fourteen. When my sister and I were safely in bed in the night nursery, we sometimes heard the "putt, putt, putt" of a motorbike approaching the house, stopping, and then driving away into the night. That was Ethel's young man taking her out for the evening. The motorbike was the first harbinger of the approaching social revolution. The motorbike was the technology of upward mobility. After Ethel left us and married the young man, she had three daughters of her own, and all of them went to college. One of her grandsons is now a university professor.

Those are enough examples to show that technology can be helpful in the struggle for social justice. But in each case, as Edward Tenner tells us in his book *Why Things Bite Back,* a step forward in technology tends to bring with it an unexpected step backward. A step forward for some people frequently brings with it a step backward for others. And it often happens that when an old privileged class of people is dispossessed and the blessings of wealth and power are spread more equally, the burdens of equalization fall disproportionately upon women. When the revolutions accompanying the technology of printing destroyed the wealth and power of the monasteries over much of Europe, both male and female orders were dispossessed, but the nuns lost more than the monks. Nuns in the old convents were in many ways more free than wives in the new Protestant communities. The old monastic society provided a refuge where women of outstanding ability—for example, Hildegard of Bingen—had access to higher education. Sheltered and supported by the monastic orders, women could follow their vocations as scholars and artists. When the monasteries were dissolved, nuns had to find shelter in other people's homes, either as wives or as servants. The new secular society replaced the monasteries with colleges and universities. In the universities men scholars could find shelter and security, but there was no place for women.

The technology of household appliances, likewise, brought a step backward to the stratum of society to which my mother belonged, the women of the middle class. My mother would be considered by the standards of today a thoroughly liberated woman. Trained as a lawyer, she helped to write the Act of Parliament that opened the professions in England to women. With the help of her servants, she could take care of her husband and children without being confined to the home. She was free to pursue her interests outside the home—her girls' club and birth control clinic. But she was by no means the most liberated of the women in our family. I had a collection of aunts who were in various ways more liberated than my mother. All of them had husbands and most of them had children, but this did not stop them from being liberated. All of them were more adventurous than their husbands. My Aunt Margaret was trained as a nurse and rose to become a matron, which meant that she was the managing administrator of a large hospital. My Aunt Ruth was a figure skater of international re-pute who kept an Olympic silver medal among her trophies. My Aunt Dulcibella was the first woman in England to receive an airplane pilot's license. She and her husband had an airplane which they used for traveling around in Africa. They loved Africa, and their lifestyle would have fit in very well with the group of adventurers that Michael Ondaatje describes in his novel *The English Patient*. My Aunt Dulcibella was also a professional actress, and if she had only been eighty years younger, she might have had a starring role in *The English Patient* movie. We did not consider these aunts of ours to be unusual. It was normal at that time for middle-class women to do something spectacular. My mother, with her birth control clinic, was the quiet one, the least daring of the four.

Now, consider what happened to the next generation of middle-class women in England and the United States. Thirty years later, in the 1950s, the servants were gone and the electrical appliances were taking their place. For wives and mothers of the middle class, this was a big step backward. Appliances do not cook the dinner, clean the house, do the shopping, and mind the baby. The middle-class women of the 1950s were far less liberated than their mothers. The liberation that my mother's generation achieved had to be fought for all over again. Even now, in the 1990s, women are only partially liberated. To achieve partial liberation, they have replaced the old domestic servants with day care centers, cleaning ladies, and *au pair* girls imported from overseas. Electrical appliances help, but they only do a small part of the job.

The Institute of Advanced Study, where I have spent my working life, is a peculiar institution with a small permanent faculty. The faculty is supposed to be representative of the most distinguished men and women in academic life. Unfortunately, we have always found it difficult to appoint women to the faculty. The original faculty, appointed in the 1930s, contained one woman, the archaeologist Hetty Goldman. I remember her vividly. She was a formidable lady, small in stature and large in spirit, who led excavations of ancient sites in Turkey, ruling over small armies of Turkish laborers with an iron hand. Her colleagues used to say she was the equal of any two male archaeologists. There was never the slightest doubt that she had the "right stuff" to be an Institute professor. She was a natural leader in her own eyes and in ours. She belonged to my mother's generation of liberated women. She grew up, like my mother, in a society of women with servants. When she retired in 1947, she was not replaced. For almost forty years the Institute faculty was entirely male. In 1985, the sociologist Joan Scott became the second woman to join the faculty. And in 1997 the historian Patricia Crone became the third.

The history of our faculty encapsulates in a nutshell the history of women's liberation: a glorious beginning in the 1920s; a great backsliding in the 1950s; a gradual recovery in the 1980s. It is not altogether fanciful to blame the technology of household appliances for the backsliding. The advent of electrical appliances liberated the servants and shackled their mistresses.

High-Tech Medicine and Computers

I have discussed four technologies that led to large expansions of social justice. Although each of them had compensating negative effects, especially on women, the overall effects of all of them were predominantly positive. It will be just as easy to find examples of technologies that had negative effects. One could mention the technologies of gas chambers and nuclear weapons, useful for the convenient extermination of people to whom we do not wish to extend the benefits of social justice. But the more troubling examples are two of the technologies that are making the most rapid progress today: high-tech medicine and high-tech communication.

All of us who live in the United States are familiar with the ugly face that high-tech medicine presents to the patient: the initial telephone call answered by a machine rather than a human voice; the filling out of forms in the office; the repetitive answering of questions; the battery of routine chemical and physical tests carried out by technicians wearing rubber gloves; and finally, the abbreviated contact with the physician. It is all very different from the old-fashioned practice of medicine, when doctors were personal friends and advisers to pa-

tients and sometimes even made house calls. The face of high-tech medicine is ugly even when the patient is rich, and uglier still when the patient is poor. The ugliness results from many factors working together. First, the prevalence of malpractice litigation, which destroys trust, compelling doctors to conform to rigid rules and surrounding them with layers of bureaucratic documentation. Second, the high cost of the equipment that high-tech medicine demands, forcing medical centers to adopt elaborate cost-accounting systems. Third, the size of the staff needed to operate a high-tech center, with many doctors qualified in narrow specialties so that the patient rarely gets to see the same doctor twice. Fourth, the overwhelming cost of hospitalization, allowing patients a bare minimum of days for rest and recuperation after major illness or surgery. These factors, together, led to the situation that confronts the patient today. What the patient needs most, but finds least, is personal attention.

Since personal attention has become the scarcest resource in high-tech medicine, it is inevitable that it should be distributed unequally. The majority of advanced countries have national health services that attempt, with varying degrees of success, to distribute medical attention fairly. In countries with national health services, medical attention is theoretically available to everybody. This is what the ethic of social justice demands. But the escalating cost of medical attention makes social justice more and more difficult to achieve. One way or another, as personal attention becomes scarcer, people of status tend to receive more of it and people without status to receive less. The national health services in countries where they exist make valiant efforts to preserve the ideal of social justice, but the march of medical technology and the concomitant increase of costs constantly erode the ideal. In the United States, which never had a national health service and does not pretend to distribute medical resources equally, the prospects for social justice are far worse. In the United States a medical system based on the ethic of the free market inevitably favors the rich over the poor, and the inequalities grow sharper as the costs increase.

I have seen in my own family a small example of the dilemma that the growth of high-tech medicine presents to physicians. One of my daughters is a cardiologist. For many years she worked in state-supported hospitals taking care of patients as they flowed through the system, working brutally long hours and still having little time for personal contact with her patients. Her patients in the public hospitals were predominantly poor and uninsured. Many of them had AIDS or gunshot wounds in addition to cardiac problems. The public health system, such as it was, was designed to get these patients out of the hospital and back on the streets as fast as possible. Last year my daughter was offered a job in a private cardiology practice with far shorter hours, better pay and working conditions, and an expectation of long, continued care of her patients. She accepted the offer without much hesitation. She is much happier in her new job. Now, for the first time, she knows her patients as individuals and can tailor their treatments to their individual histories and personalities. She feels that she is a better doctor, and her new job gave her the flexibility to take time off to have her first baby last July. From almost every point of view, her jump into private practice was a wise move. Her only problem was a small twinge of conscience for having abandoned the poor to take care of the rich. In the private practice her patients are not all rich, but they are all paying for the personal attention that she is now able to give them. She was forced to make a choice between social justice and professional satisfaction, and social justice lost. I don't blame her. But in a socially just society, physicians would not be forced to make such choices.

Similar dilemmas, not so stark as the dilemmas of medical practice but equally important, exist in the world of high-tech computing and communications. Here, too, there is a clash between the economic forces driving the technology and the needs of poor people. Access to personal computers and the Internet is like medical insurance: almost everybody needs it, but most poor people don't have it. The people who are wired, the people who browse the World Wide Web and conduct their daily lives and businesses on the Net, have tremendous economic and social advantages. Increasingly, jobs and business opportunities are offered through the Internet. Access to the Internet means access to well-paying jobs. People who are not wired in are in danger of becoming the new servant class. The gulf between the wired and the unwired is wide, and growing wider.

The computer and software industries are driven by two contradictory impulses. On the one hand, they sincerely wish to broaden their market by making computers accessible to everybody. On the other hand, they are forced by competitive pressures to upgrade their products constantly, increasing their power and speed and adding new features and new complications. The top end of the market drives the development of new products, and the new products remain out of the reach of the poor. In the tug of war between broadening the market and pampering the top-end customer, the top-end customer usually wins.

The problem of unequal access to computers is only a small part of the problem of inequality in our society. Until the society is willing to attack the larger problems of inequality in housing, education, and health care, attempts to provide equal access to computers cannot be totally successful. Nevertheless, in attacking the general problems of inequality, computer access might be a good place to start. One of the virtues of the new technology of the Internet is that it has an inherent tendency to become global. The Internet easily infiltrates through barriers of language, custom, and culture. No technical barrier stops it from becoming universally accessible. To provide equality of access to the Internet is technically easier than providing equality of access to housing and health care. Universal access to the Internet would not solve all our social problems, but it would be a big step in the right direction. The Internet could then become an important tool for alleviating other kinds of inequality.

The Protestant Ethic and the Spirit of Capitalism

Up to now I have been talking as if technology came first and ethics second. I have been describing historical events in which technological changes occurred first and then increases or decreases of social justice occurred as a consequence. I depicted technological change as the cause of ethical improvement or deterioration. This view of history is opposed to the view propounded by Max Weber in his seminal book *The Protestant Ethic and the Spirit of Capitalism*. Weber argued that the Protestant ethic came first and the rise of capitalism and the technologies associated with it came second. Weber's view has become the prevailing view of modern historians. Weber said that ethics drove technology. I say that technology drives ethics.

I am not trying to prove Weber wrong. His historical vision remains profoundly true. It is true that the religious revolutions of the sixteenth century engendered an ethic of personal responsibility and restless inquiry, an ethic that encouraged the growth of capitalistic enterprise and technological innovation. It was no accident that Isaac Newton, the preeminent architect of modern science, was also a Protestant theologian. He took his theology as seriously as his science. It was no accident King Henry VIII, the man who brought the Protestant revolution to England, also endowed the college where Newton lived and taught. Henry and Isaac were kindred spirits—both were rebels against authority, enemies of the Pope, tyrants, supreme egoists, suspicious to the point of paranoia, believers in the Protestant ethic, and in love with technology. Henry loved to build ships and Isaac loved to build telescopes. It is true that ethics can drive technology. I am only saying that this is not the whole truth, that technology can also drive ethics, that the chain of causation works in both directions. The technology of printing helped to cause the rise of the Protestant ethic just as much as the Protestant ethic helped to cause the rise of navigation and astronomy.

I am not the first to take issue with Weber on this question. The historian Richard Tawney also studied the interrelationships of religion and capitalism and came to conclusions similar to mine. He held Weber in high esteem and contributed a foreword to the English translation of *The Protestant Ethic and the Spirit of Capitalism*. Here are the concluding sentences of Tawney's foreword: "It is instructive to trace with Weber the influence of religious ideas on economic development. It is not less important to grasp the effect of economic arrange-ments accepted by an age on the opinion which it holds of the province of religion." Tawney's view is that technology influenced religion as strongly as religion influenced technology. Since my view of history is closer to Tawney's than to Weber's, I now ask the question: How can we push new technologies into directions conducive to social justice? How can we make ethics drive technology in such a way that the evil consequences are minimized and the good maximized? I shall hope to persuade you that the situation we are in is not hopeless, that new technologies offer us real opportunities for making the world a happier place.

The Sun, the Genome, and the Internet

Finally, I turn to the positive side of my message. Technology guided by ethics has the power to help the billions of poor people all over the earth. My purpose is to help push technology in a new direction, away from toys for the rich and toward necessities for the poor. The time is ripe for this to happen. Three huge revolutionary forces are being harnessed just in time for the new century: the sun, the genome, and the Internet. These three forces are strong enough to reverse some of the worst evils of our time. The evils I am hoping to reverse are well known to you all. All over the earth, and especially in the poor countries to the south of us, millions of desperate people leave their villages and pour into overcrowded cities. There are now ten megacities in the world with populations twice as large as New York City. Soon there will be more. We all know that the increase of human population is one of the causes of the migration to cities. The other cause is the poverty and lack of jobs in villages. Both the population explosion and the poverty must be reversed if we are to have a decent future. Many experts on population say that if we can mitigate the poverty, the population will stabilize itself, as it has done in Europe and Japan. I am not an expert on population, so I won't say any more about that. I am saying that poverty can be reduced by a combination of solar energy, genetic engineering, and the Internet. Our task in the next century is to put the new technologies to work in the cause of social justice. Social justice means making the new technologies accessible to everyone, to bring wealth to poor countries and hope to poor people.

I have seen with my own eyes what happens to a village when the economic basis of life collapses, and I have seen how the economic basis of village life can be revived. My wife grew up in Westerhausen, a village in East Germany that was under Communist management. The Communist regime took care of the village economy, selling the output of the farms to Russia at fixed prices, which gave the farmers economic security. The village remained beautiful and, on the whole, pleasant to live in. Nothing much had changed in the village since 1910. One thing the Communist regime did was organize a zoo, with a collection of animals maintained by a few professionals with a lot of help from the local school children. The village was justly proud of its zoo. The zoo was subsidized by the regime so it did not need to worry about being unprofitable. I visited the village under the old regime in 1975 and found it very friendly. Then came 1990 and the unification of Germany. Overnight, the economy of the village was wrecked. The farmers could no longer farm because nobody would buy their products. Russia could not buy because the price had to be paid in West German marks. German consumers would not buy because the local produce was not as good as that available in the supermarkets. The village farmers could not compete with the goods pouring in from France and Denmark. So the farmers were out of work. Most of the younger generation moved out of the village to compete for jobs in the cities, and most of the older generation remained. Many of them, both old and young, are still unemployed. The zoo, deprived of its subsidy, collapsed.

The sad exodus that I saw in the village of Westerhausen when I visited there in 1991 is the same exodus that is happening in villages all over the world. Everywhere the international market devalues the work of the village. Without work, the younger and the more enterprising people move out.

In the seven years since the unification, Westerhausen has slowly been recovering. Recovery is possible because of the process of gentrification. Wealthy people from the local towns move in and modernize the homes abandoned by the farmers. Cottages are demolished to make room for two-car garages. Ancient and narrow roads are widened. The village will survive as a community of nature lovers and commuters. Lying on the northern edge of the Harz Mountains, it is close to the big cities of northern Germany and even closer to unspoiled mountain forests. Its permanent asset is natural beauty.

Two months ago my wife and I were back in the village. The change since we had last visited in 1991 was startling. We stayed in the elegant new home of a friend who had been in my wife's class in the village elementary school fifty years earlier. The village now looks well cared for and prosperous. The recovery from the disaster of 1990 has been slow and difficult, but it has been steady. The government did two things to mitigate the harshness of the free market: it allowed every homeowner to borrow money with almost zero interest from the government to modernize houses, and it allowed every farming cooperative to borrow money with almost zero interest to modernize farms. As a result, the houses that were not bought by outsiders are being modernized, and the few farmers who remained as farmers are flourishing. The zoo has been revived. In addition, there are some new enterprises. A Western immigrant has planted a large vineyard on a south-facing hillside and will soon be producing the first Westerhausen wines. My wife's family and many of her friends still live in the village. They gave us a warm and joyful welcome.

The probable future of Westerhausen can be seen in a thousand villages in England. The typical English village today is not primarily engaged in farming. The typical village remains beautiful and prosperous because of gentrification. Wealthy homeowners pay large sums of money for the privilege of living under a thatched roof. The thatching of roofs is one of the few ancient village crafts that still survives. The thatchers are mostly young, highly skilled, and well paid. The farmers who remain are either gentlemen amateurs, who run small farms as a hobby, or well-educated professionals, who run big farms as a business. The old population of peasant farmers, who used to live in the villages in poverty and squalor, disappeared long ago. Discreetly hidden in many of the villages are offices and factories engaged in high-tech industry. One of the head offices of IBM Europe is in the English village of Hursley not far from where I was born. In the villages of France, at least in the area I know around Paris, the picture is much the same. Wealth came to the villages because they have what wealthy people seek: peace, security, and beauty.

What would it take to reverse the flow of jobs and people from villages to megacities all over the world? I believe the flow can be reversed by the same process of gentrification that is happening in Westerhausen. To make gentrification possible, the villages themselves must become sources of wealth. How can a godforsaken Mexican village become a source of wealth? Three facts can make it possible. First, solar energy is distributed equitably over the earth. Second, genetic engineering can make solar energy usable everywhere for the local creation of wealth. Third, the Internet can provide people in every village with the information and skills they need to develop their talents. The sun, the genome, and the Internet can work together to bring wealth to the villages of Mexico, just as the older technologies—electricity and automobiles— brought wealth to the villages of England. Let me talk briefly about each of the three new technologies, in turn.

Solar energy is most available where it is most needed—in the countryside rather than in cities, and in tropical countries, where most of the world's population lives, rather than in temperate latitudes. The quantity of solar energy is enormous compared with all other energy resources. Each square mile in the tropics receives about 1,000 megawatts averaged over day and night. This quantity of energy would be ample to support a dense population with all modern conveniences. Solar energy has not yet been used on a large scale for one simple reason: it is too expensive. It cannot compete in a free market with imported coal, oil, and natural gas. The country that has used solar energy on the largest scale is Brazil, where sugar was grown as an energy crop to make alcohol as a substitute for gasoline in cars and trucks. Brazil protected and subsidized the local alcohol industry. The experiment was technically successful, but the cost was high. Brazil has now re-

verted to free-market policies, and the experiment is at an end. What the world needs is not high-cost subsidized solar energy, but solar energy cheap enough to compete with oil.

Solar energy is expensive today because it has to be collected from large areas and there is not yet a technology that covers large areas cheaply. One of the virtues of solar energy is the fact that it can be collected in many ways. It is adaptable to local conditions. The two main tools for collecting it are photoelectric panels, which convert sunlight directly into electricity, and energy crops, like the Brazilian sugar plantations, which convert sunlight into fuel. Roughly speaking, photoelectric collection is the method of choice for deserts, and energy crops are the method of choice for farmland and forests. Each method has its advantages and disadvantages. Photoelectric systems have high efficiency, typically between 10 percent and 15 percent, but are expensive to deploy and maintain. Energy crops have low efficiency, typically around 1 percent, and are expensive and messy to harvest. The electricity produced by photoelectric systems is intermittent and cannot be cheaply converted into storable forms of energy. Fuels produced from energy crops are storable and, therefore, more convenient.

To make solar energy cheap, we need a technology that combines the advantages of photovoltaic and biological systems. Two technical advances would make this possible. First, crop plants could be developed that convert sunlight into fuel with efficiency comparable to photovoltaic collectors, in the range of 10 percent rather than 1 percent. This would reduce the costs of land and harvesting by a large factor. Second, crop plants could be developed that do not need to be harvested at all. An energy crop could be a permanent forest with trees that convert sunlight to liquid fuel and deliver the fuel directly through their roots to a network of underground pipelines. If those two advantages could be combined, we would have a supply of solar energy that was cheap, abundant, ubiquitous, and environmentally benign.

The energy supply system of the future might be a large area of forest with species of trees varying from place to place to suit the local climate and topography. We may hope that substantial parts of the forest would be nature reserves closed to human settlement and populated with wildlife so as to preserve the diversity of the natural ecologies. But the greater part could be open to human settlement, with teeming towns and villages under the trees. Landowners outside the nature reserves would be encouraged, but not compelled, to grow trees for energy. If the trees converted sunlight into fuel with 10 percent efficiency, landowners could sell the fuel for $10,000 per acre per year and easily undercut the present price of gasoline. Owners of farmland and city lots alike would have a strong economic incentive to grow trees. The future energy plantation need not be a monotonous expanse of identical trees in regular rows. It could be as varied and as spontaneous as a natural woodland, interspersed with open spaces and houses, villages, towns, factories, and lakes.

To make this dream of a future landscape come true, the essential tool is genetic engineering. At present, large sums of money are being spent on sequencing the human genome. The Human Genome Project is motivated primarily by its medical applications. It will contribute enormously to the understanding and treatment of human diseases. It does not contribute directly to the engineering of trees. But alongside the human genome many other genomes are being sequenced—bacteria, yeast, worms, and fruit flies. For advancing the art of genetic engineering the genomes of simpler organisms are more useful than the human genome. Before long, we shall also have sequenced the genomes of the major crop plants—wheat, maize, and rice—and after that will come trees. Within a few decades, we shall have achieved a deep understanding of the genome, an understanding that will allow us to breed trees that will turn sunlight into fuel and still preserve the diversity that makes natural forests beautiful.

As soon as we can genetically engineer trees to use sunlight efficiently to make fuel, we shall learn to breed trees that convert sunlight into useful chemicals of other kinds, including silicon chips for computers and gasoline for cars. Economic forces will then move industries from cities to the country. Mining and manufacturing could be economically based on locally available solar energy, with geneti-

cally engineered creatures consuming and recycling the waste products. It might even become possible to build roads and buildings biologically, breeding little polyps to lay down durable structures on land in the same way as their cousins build coral reefs in the ocean.

But the third, and most important, of the triad of new technologies is the Internet. The Internet is essential to enable businesses and farms in remote places to function as part of the modern global economy. The Internet will allow people in remote places to make business deals, buy and sell, keep in touch with their friends, continue their education, and follow their hobbies and avocations, with full knowledge of what is going on in the rest of the world.

This will not be the Internet of today, accessible only to computer-literate people in rich countries and to the wealthy elite in poor countries. It will be a truly global Internet, using a network of satellites in space for communication with places that fiber optics cannot reach and connected to local networks in every village. The new Internet will end the cultural isolation of poor countries and poor people.

Two technical problems have to be solved to make the Internet accessible to almost everybody on a global scale: large-scale architecture and the problem of the "last mile." Large-scale architecture means choosing the most efficient combination of landlines and satellite links to cover every corner of the globe. The Teledesic system of satellite communication now under development is intended to be a partial answer to this problem. The Teledesic system has 280 satellites in a dense network of low orbits, allowing any two points on the globe to be connected with minimum delay. If the Teledesic system fails, some other system will be designed to do the job. The problem of the "last mile" is more difficult. This is the problem of connecting homes and families, wherever they happen to be, with the nearest Internet terminal. The problem of the last mile has to be solved piecemeal, with methods depending on the local geography and the local culture. An ingenious method of solving the last-mile problem in urban American neighborhoods has been introduced recently by Paul Baran, the original inventor of the Internet. Baran's system is called Ricochet and consists of a multitude of small, wireless transmitters and receivers. Each user has a modem that communicates by radio with a local network. The feature that makes the system practical is that the transmitters constantly switch their frequencies so as not to interfere with one another. The system is flexible and cheap, avoiding the large expense of laying cable from the Internet terminal to every apartment and every house. It works well in the environment of urban America. It remains to be seen whether it is flexible and cheap enough to work well in the environment of a Mexican village or a Peruvian barrio.

Suppose, then, we can solve the technical problems of cheap solar energy, genetic engineering of industrial crop plants, and universal access to the Internet. What will follow? My thesis is that the solution of those three problems will bring about a worldwide social revolution, similar to the revolution we have seen in the villages of England and Germany. Cheap solar energy and genetic engineering will provide the basis for primary industries in the countryside. After that, the vast variety of secondary and tertiary economic activities that use the Internet for their coordination—food processing, publishing, education, entertainment, and health care—will follow the primary industries as they move from overgrown cities to country towns and villages. And as soon as the villages become rich, they will attract people and wealth back from the cities.

I am not suggesting that in the brave new world of the future everyone will be compelled to live in villages. Many of us will always prefer to live in large cities or in towns of moderate size. I am suggesting only that people should be free to choose. When wealth has moved back to villages, people who live there will no longer be forced by economic necessity to move out, and people who live in megacities will no longer be compelled by economic necessity to stay there. Many of us who have the freedom to choose, like the successful stockbrokers and business executives in England and Germany, will choose to live in villages.

So this is my dream: Solar energy, genetic engineering, and the Internet will work together to create a socially just world in which every Mexican village is as wealthy as Princeton. Of course, that is only a dream. Inequalities will persist. Poverty will not disappear. But I see a hope that the world will move far and fast in the directions I have been describing. Ethics must guide technology toward social justice. Let us all help to push the world in that direction as hard as we can. It does no harm to hope.

I.11   ROBERT E. MCGINN

Technology, Demography, and the Anachronism of Traditional Rights

Many of the ethical issues surrounding the forms of technology found in modern society are not simply analyzable as involving harms traceable to the actions of an individual moral agent. In a great many cases, it is only the cumulative effects of many people using a particular kind of technology, or engaging in what author Robert McGinn calls a "sociotechnical practice," that carries with it harmful consequences for society.

In this selection, McGinn, the Director of the Science, Technology, and Human Values Program at Stanford University, develops a conceptual framework for understanding these kinds of problems associated with some technologies. In his analysis, a "troubling triad" arises when there is a conjunction of three factors: technological maximality, the traditional notion of individual rights, and ever-increasing numbers of right holders.

His controversial proposal for avoiding these kinds of problems would change the way in which we think about human rights, by replacing the Enlightenment's idea of "natural" or "God-given" and inalienable rights with a more "contextualized" theory of individual rights. This theory would be designed to limit the kinds of moral claims that individuals can advance against society in light of the effects of changing technologies and demographics.

Focus Questions

1. What does McGinn mean by a "technologically maximal sociotechnical practice"? What are some factors that explain why we tend to employ such practices?
2. What is the importance of the aggregation principle? How does the idea of simple aggregation relate to the question of evaluating the ethics of individual uses of technology?
3. How does McGinn's proposal for avoiding the troubling effects of technological maximality compare to Garrett Hardin's suggestions (selection II.13) concerning how we might avoid the tragedy of the commons?

Keywords

abortion, biomedical ethics, euthanasia, freedom of speech, gun control, human rights, natural rights, population planning, the right to life, urban planning, waste disposal

Introduction

Critics of the influence of technology on society debit the unhappy outcomes they decry to different casual accounts. Some target *specific characteristics or purposes* of technologies that they hold are inherently objectionable. For example, certain critics believe biotechnologies such as human *in vitro* fertilisation and the genetic engineering of transgenic animals to be morally wrong, regardless of who controls or uses them, and attribute what they see as the negative social consequences of these innovations to their defining characteristics or informing purposes. Others, eschewing the technological determinism implicit in such a viewpoint, find fault with the *social contexts* of technological developments and hold these contexts—more precisely, those who shape and control them—responsible for such unhappy social outcomes as result. For example, some critics have blamed the tragic medical consequences of silicone gel breast implants on a profit-driven rush to market these devices and on lax government regulation. Still other critics focus on *users* of technologies, pointing to problematic aspects of the use and operation of the technics and technical systems at their disposal. For example, some attributed the fatal crash of a DC-10 in Chicago in 1979 and the rash of reports in the mid 1980s of spontaneous acceleration of Audi

Originally published as "Technology, Demography, and the Anachronism of Traditional Rights," *Journal of Applied Philosophy*, Vol 11, No. 1, 1994. Copyright © 1994 Society for Applied Philosophy, Blackwell Publishers, 108 Cowley Road, Oxford, OX4 1JF, UK and 3 Cambridge Center, Cambridge, MA 02142, USA.

automobiles upon braking to the alleged careless-ness of maintenance workers and consumers.

Questions of the validity and relative value of these theory-laden approaches aside, this paper identifies and analyses an important source of prob-lematic technology-related influence on society of a quite different nature. Neither wholly technical, nor wholly social, nor wholly individual in nature, the source discussed below combines technical, so-cial, and individual elements.

The source in question is a recurrent pattern of sociotechnical practice characteristic of contempo-rary Western societies. The pattern poses a chal-lenge to professionals in fields as diverse as medi-cine, city planning, environmental management, and engineering. While not intrinsically problem-atic—indeed, the pattern sometimes yields benefi-cial consequences—the pattern is *potentially* prob-lematic. Its manifestations frequently dilute or jeopardise the quality of life in societies in which they unfold. Unless appropriate changes are forth-coming, the pattern's effects promise to be even more destructive in the future. In what follows, I shall describe and clarify the general pattern, ex-plore its sources of strength, elaborate a concep-tual/theoretical change that will be necessary to bring the pattern under control and mitigate its negative effects, and survey some conflicts over re-cent efforts to do just that in two social arenas: ur-ban planning and medicine.

The Pattern: Nature and Meaning

The pattern in question involves the interplay of technology, rights, and numbers. It may be charac-terised thus:

> 'technological maximality,' unfolding under the auspices of 'traditional rights' supposedly held and exercised by a large and increasing number of parties, is apt to dilute or diminish contempo-rary societal quality of life.

Let us begin by defining the three key expressions in this formulation.

First, in speaking of an item of technology or a technology-related phenomenon as exhibiting,

'technological maximality' (TM), I mean the *qual-ity of embodying in one or more of its aspects or dimen-sions the greatest scale or highest degree previously at-tained or currently possible in that aspect or dimension.*

Thus understood, TM can be manifested in var-ious forms. Some hinge on the characteristics of technological products and systems, while others have to do with aspects of their production, diffu-sion, use, or operation. Making material artifacts (technics) and sociotechnical systems of hitherto unequaled or unsurpassed scale or performance might be viewed as paradigmatic forms of TM. However, the TM concept is also intended to en-compass maximalist phenomena having to do with processes as well as products. Examples of techno-logical maximality of process include producing or diffusing as many units as possible of a technic in a given time interval or domain, and using a technic or system as intensively or extensively as possible in a given domain or situation. It is important to rec-ognize that technological maximality can obtain even where no large-scale or super-powerful tech-nics or technical systems are involved. Technologi-cal maximality can be reflected in *how* humans inter-act with and use their technics and systems as much as in technic and system characteristics proper. TM, one might say, has adverbial as well as substantive modes. In sum, technology can be maximalist in one or more of the following nine senses:

- product size or scale
- product performance (power, speed, efficiency, scope, etc.)
- speed of production of a technic or system
- volume of production of a technic or system
- speed of diffusion of a technic or system
- domain of diffusion of a technic or system
- intensity of use or operation of a technic or system
- domain of use or operation of a technic or system
- duration of use or operation of a technic or system

Secondly, 'traditional rights' are entitlements of individuals as traditionally conceived in modern Western societies. For example, in the traditional

Western conception individual rights have been viewed as timelessly valid and morally inviolable. Traditional individual rights often interpreted in this absolutist way include the right to life as well as liberty, property, and procreative rights.

Thirdly, the 'large and increasing number of parties' factor refers to the presence in most kinds of context in contemporary Western societies of many, indeed also a growing number of, parties—usually individual humans—each of whom supposedly holds rights of the above sort and may exercise them in, among other ways, technologically maximalist behaviour.

Before proceeding, I want to stress that this paper is neither a critique of 'technological maximality' per se nor a celebration of E. F. Schumacher's 'small is beautiful' idea. For, like the above triadic pattern, TM (or, for that matter, technological minimality) per se is not inherently morally objectionable or problematic. Specimens of technological maximality such as the then unprecedentedly large medieval Gothic cathedrals and the mammoth Saturn V rockets of the kind that took Apollo XI toward the moon suffice to refute any such claim. Rather, it is the *conjunction* of the three above-mentioned factors in repeated patterns of sociotechnical practice—*large and increasing numbers of parties engaged in technologically maximalist practices as something that each party supposedly has a morally inviolable right to do*—that is apt to put societal quality of life at risk. With this in mind, in what follows we shall refer to the combustible mixture of these three interrelated factors as 'the troubling triad.'

The triadic pattern is surprisingly widespread. Consider the following examples:

1. the intensive, often protracted use of life-prolonging technologies or technological procedures in thousands of cases of terminally ill or irreversibly comatose patients, or in the case of those needing an organ transplant or other life-sustaining treatment, such uses supposedly being called for by the inviolable right to life;
2. the proliferation of mopeds, all-terrain, snowmobile, and other kinds of versatile transport

vehicles in special or fragile environmental areas, such use supposedly being sanctioned by rider mobility rights; and
3. the erection of growing numbers of high-rise buildings in city centers, as supposedly permitted by owner or developer property rights.

As suggested by these examples, our pattern of sociotechnical practice unfolds in diverse spheres of human activity. Problematic phenomena exemplifying the pattern in other arenas include the infestation of American national parks by tens of thousands of small tourist aircraft overflights per year; the depletion of ocean fishing areas through the use of hundreds of enormous, mechanically operated, nylon monofilament nets; and the decimation of old-growth forests in the northwestern U.S. through the use of myriad potent chain saws. The untoward effects exacted by the unfolding of our triadic pattern include steep financial and psychological tools, the depletion and degradation of environmental resources, and the dilution and disappearance of urban amenities. In short, the costs of the ongoing operation of the triadic pattern are substantial and increasing.

To this point, the pattern identified above makes reference to a number of individual agents, each of whom engages in or is involved with a specimen of technologically maximal behaviour, e.g., having life-prolonging technologies applied intensively to herself or himself, using a technic 'extensively'—meaning either 'in a spatially widespread manager' or 'frequently'—in a fragile, limited, or distinctive domain; or erecting a megastructure.

However, as characterised above, our pattern obscures the fact that TM can be present in *aggregative* as well as non-aggregative situations. Each of a large number of individuals, acting under the auspices of a right construed in traditional fashion, can engage in behaviour that while not technologically maximal in itself becomes so when aggregated over all relevant agents. Of course, aggregating over a number of cases each of which is *already* technologically maximal compounds the maximality in question, and probably also its effects on society. We may say, therefore, that there is *individual* TM (where the individual behaviour in question is technologically maximal) and *aggregative* TM, the latter having two subspecies: *simple-aggregative,* where the individual behavior is *not* technologically maximal, and *compound-aggregative,* where the individual behavior is *already* technologically maximal.

One reason why simple-aggregative TM is troubling is that individual agents may have putative rights to engage in specimens of non-technologically-maximal behaviour that, taken individually, seem innocuous or of negligible import. However, contemporary environments or contexts do not automatically become larger or more robust in proportion to technic performance improvements, increasing costs of contemporary technics and systems, or the increasing number of those with access to or affected by these items. Hence, the aggregation of individually permissible behaviour over all relevant agents with access to technics can result in substantial harm to societal quality of life. One can therefore speak of 'public harms of aggregation.' For example, the failure of each of a large number of people to recycle their garbage is technological behaviour that when aggregated provides an instance of problematic technological maximality of use. Aggregating the individually innocuous effects of a large number of people driving motor vehicles that emit pollutants yields the same story: individually innocuous behaviour can, when aggregated over a large group, yield a significant, noxious outcome.

The Pattern: Sources of Strength

How is the power of the pattern under discussion to be accounted for? Put differently, why does the troubling triad come under so little critical scrutiny when it has such untoward effects on individual and societal quality of life? In the case of simple-aggregate TM, the reason is that the effects of the behaviour of the individual agent are negligibly problematic. It is difficult to induce a person to restrict her or his behaviour when it is not perceivably linkable to the doing of significant harm to some recognised protectable individual or societal interest.

More generally, the strength of the pattern derives from the effects of factors of various sorts that lend impetus to its constituent elements. Let us examine each element in the pattern in turn.

TECHNOLOGICAL MAXIMALITY

The modern drive to achieve increases in efficiency and economies of scale and thereby reap enhanced profits is unquestionably an important factor that fuels various modes of technological maximality. One thinks in this connection of maximalist technics such as the Boeing 747 and the Alaska pipeline as well as the diffusion speed and scope modes of TM for personal technics like the VCR and CD player.

However, economic considerations do not tell the entire causal story. Cultural phenomena also play an important role and help explain the low level of resistance to our pattern. Technological maximality is encouraged by the 'technological fix' mentality deeply entrenched in Western countries. Should anything go awry as a result of some technological maximalist practice, one can always, it is assumed, concoct a technological fix to remedy or at least patch up the situation in time. Moreover, there is much individual and group prestige to be garnered in modern Western societies by producing, possessing, or using the biggest, fastest, or more potent technic or technological project; more generally, by being, technologically speaking, 'the-firstest-with-the-mostest.' Further, influential sectors of Western opinion gauge societal progress and even a society's level of civilisation by the degree to which it attains and practises certain forms of technological maximality. Small-scale, appropriate technology may be fine for developing countries but resorting to it would be seen as culturally retrogressive for a technologically 'advanced' society such as the U.S.

Technological maximality is often associated with construction projects. In 1985, American developer Donald Trump announced what proved to be abortive plans for a 150-story, 1,800-foot-tall Television City on the West Side of Manhattan, a megastructure that he revealingly called 'the world's greatest building.'[1] The demise in contemporary Western society of shared qualitative standards for making comparative value judgments has created a vacuum often filled by primarily quantitative standards of value. This in turn has fueled technological maximality as a route to invidious distinction. If a building is quantitatively 'the greatest,' it must surely be qualitatively 'the best,' a convenient confusion of quality and quantity.

TM in the sense of virtually unrestricted technic use throughout special environments is greatly encouraged by modern Western cultural attitudes toward nature. Unlike in many traditional societies, land and space are typically perceived as homogeneous in character. No domains of land or space are sacred areas, hence possibly off limits to certain technological activity. On the contrary, in the contemporary U.S., nature is often regarded more as playground for technology-intensive human activity. Dune buggy riders were incensed when environmentalists sued to force the National Park Service to ban off-road vehicles from the fragile dunes at Cape Cod National Seashore. The leader of the Massachusetts Beach Buggy Association lamented that 'it seems like every year they come up with more ways to deprive people of recreational activities,'[2] a comment that comes close to suggesting that rider rights have been violated.

The U.S. has no monopoly on TM. For example, France has a long tradition of technological maximality. The country's fascination with 'grands travaux,' large-scale technical projects conceived by politicians, public engineers, or civil servants, is several centuries old.[3] Encompassing classic projects such as Napoleon's Arc de Triomphe, Hausmann's transformation of central Paris, and Eiffel's Tower, the maximalist trend has also been manifested in the nation-wide SNCF electric railroad system and the Anglo-French Concorde supersonic transport airplane. More recent specimens suggesting that TM is alive and well in France include audacious undertakings such as the Channel Tunnel, ever more potent nuclear power stations, the T.G.V. (*très grand vitesse*) train, and the Mitterand government's plan for building the world's largest library, dubbed by critics the 'T.G.B.' (*très grand bibliothèque*).[4] Such projects are not pursued solely or primarily for economic motives but for reasons of national prestige and grandeur, certification of governmental power and competence, as symbols

of cultural superiority, and as monuments to individual politicians.

Another cultural factor that fosters certain modes of TM is the relatively democratic consumer culture established in the U.S. and other Western countries in the twentieth century. For the American people, innovative technics should not be reserved for the competitive advantage and enjoyment of the privileged few. Rather, based on experience with technics such as the automobile, the phone, and the television, it is believed and expected that such items should and will become available to the great mass of the American people. This expectation, cultivated by corporate advertising in order to ensure sufficient demand for what industry has the capacity to produce, in turn greatly facilitates technological maximality of production and diffusion.

TRADITIONAL RIGHTS

Many modern Western societies are founded on belief in what were once called the 'rights of man,' a term that succeeded the earlier phrase 'natural rights.' Building on Locke's thought about natural rights, the Bill of Rights enacted by the British Parliament in 1689 provided for rights to, among other things, life, liberty, and property. The U.S. Declaration of Independence of 1776 declared that 'all men . . . are endowed by their Creator with certain inalienable rights; that among these are life, liberty, and the pursuit of happiness.' The French 'Declaration des droits de l'homme et du citoyen' of 1789 asserts that 'the purpose of all political association is the conversation of the natural and inalienable rights of man: these rights are liberty, property, security and resistance to oppression.' In the 1940s Eleanor Roosevelt promoted use of the current expression 'human rights' when she determined through her work in the United Nations 'that the rights of men were not understood in some parts of the world to include the rights of women.'[5] Although later articles of the 1948 U.N. universal Declaration of Human Rights make reference to novel 'economic and social rights' that are more clearly reflections of a particular stage of societal development, the document's Preamble refers to inalienable human rights and its early articles are couched in the language of 'the old natural rights tradition.'[6] Thus, in the dominant modern Western conception, individual rights are immutable, morally inviolable, and, for many, God-given.

What has this development to do with technological maximality? Things are declared as rights in a society under particular historical circumstances. When the declaration that something is a fundamental right in a society is supported by that society's dominant political-economic forces, it is safe to assume that recognition of and respect for that right is congruent with and adaptive in relation to prevailing social conditions. However, given the millennial history of the perceived close relationship between morality and religion, to get citizens of a society to take a declared 'right of man' seriously, it has often seemed prudent to represent rights thus designated as having some kind of transcendental seal of approval: e.g., God's blessing, correspondence with the alleged inherent fabric of the universe, or reference to them in some putatively sacred document. The right in question is thereby imbued with an immutable character, as if, although originating in specific historical circumstances, the right was nevertheless timelessly valid. Such a conception of rights can support even technologically maximal exercises of particular rights of this sort.

However, the specific sets of social-historical circumstances that gave birth to such rights eventually changed, whereas, on the whole, the perceived nature of the rights in question has not. Continuing to affirm the same things as categorical rights can become dysfunctional under new, downstream social-historical conditions; in particular, when the technics and systems to which citizens and society have access have changed radically. Endowing traditional rights with a quasi-sacred status to elicit respect for them has made it more difficult to delimit or retire them as rights further down the historical road, e.g., in the present context of rampant technological maximality. In essence, the cultural strategy used to legitimate traditional rights has bestowed on them considerable intellectual inertia, something which has proved difficult to alter even though technological and demographic changes have radically transformed the context in which those rights are exercised and take effect.

A recent example of how continued affirmation of traditional rights in the context of unprecedented technological maximality can impede or disrupt societal functioning is that of the automated telephone dialer. These devices can systematically call and leave prerecorded messages at every number in a telephone exchange, including listed and unlisted numbers, cellular telephones, pagers, corporate switchboards, and unattended answering machines. By one estimate, at least 20,000 such machines are likely to be at work each day dialing some 20 million numbers around the United States. As a consequence of the potency and number of autodialers, significant communications breakdowns have already occurred.[7]

When Oregon legislators banned the commercial use of autodialers, two small-business owners who used the devices in telemarketing brought suit to invalidate the legislation on the grounds that, among other things, it violated their right to free speech. One issue here is whether U.S. society should leave its traditional robust right to free speech intact when threats to or violations of other important protectable interests, e.g., privacy, emergency preparedness, and efficient organisational operation, result from exercise of this right in revolutionary technological contexts such as those created by the intensive commercial use of autodialers and fax machines for 'junk calls' and 'junk mail.' Significantly, the American Civil Liberties Union, which supported the plaintiffs in the Oregon case, argued for preserving the traditional free speech right unabridged.

In November 1991 Congress passed the Telephone Consumer Protection Act that banned the use of autodialers for calling homes, except for emergency notification or if a party had explicitly agreed to receive such calls. However, the decision to ban turned on the annoying personal experiences of Congressional representatives and their constituents with unsolicited sales calls, not on any principled confrontation with the tension between traditional rights, technological maximality, and increasing numbers.[8] Not surprisingly, in 1993 a U.S. District Court Judge blocked enforcement of the law, ruling that it violated the constitutional right to free speech.[9]

INCREASING NUMBERS

The positive attitude in the U.S. toward an increasing national population was adaptive in the early years of the Republic when more people were needed to settle the country and fuel economic growth. Today, even while evidencing concern over rapid population increases in less developed counties, the U.S. retains strongly pronatalist tax policies and evidences residues of the long-standing belief that when it comes to population 'more is better.' The 'land of unlimited opportunity' myth, belief that America has an unlimited capacity to absorb population increases without undermining its quality of life, and conviction that intergenerational fairness requires that just as America opened its doors widely to earlier generations of impoverished or persecuted peoples so also should it continue to do so today; these and other beliefs militate against taking the difficult steps that might decrease or further slow the rate of increase of the American population. Hence of the number of rights claimants.

The Pattern as Self-Reinforcing

Not only do powerful cultural factors foster each of the three elements of the pattern, it is also self-reinforcing. For example, reproductive freedom, derived from the right of freedom or liberty, is sacrosanct in contemporary Western societies. This belief aids and abets the increasing number factor, something that in turn fuels technological maximality (e.g., in technic and system size and production and diffusion rates) to support the resultant growing population. Put differently, the increasing numbers factor intensifies the interaction of the elements of the troubling triad. Under such circumstances the latter can undergo a kind of chain reaction: increases in any of its elements tend to evoke increases in one or both of the other two, and so forth. The rights to life, liberty, property, and the pursuit of happiness have traditionally been construed as 'negative rights,' i.e., as entitlements *not to be done to* in certain ways: not to be physically attacked, constrained, deprived of one's property, etc. But, in the context of new technologies, some such rights have also taken on a positive facet: entitle-

ment of the individual *to be done to* in certain ways, e.g., to be provided with access to various kinds of life-sustaining medical technologies and to be provided with certain kinds of information in possession of another party. A positive-faceted right to life encourages further technological maximality in both development and use, something that in turn increases the number of rights holders.

Toward a Contextualized Theory of Human Rights

A society that generates an ever more potent technological arsenal and, in the name of democratic consumerism, makes its elements available in ever larger numbers to a growing citizenry whose members believe they have inviolable rights to make, access, and use those items in individually or aggregatively technologically maximalist ways, risks and may even invite progressive impairment of its quality of life. Substantial changes will be necessary if this scenario is to be avoided, especially in the U.S.

What changes might help avoid this outcome?

Decrease, stabilize, or at least substantially cut the rate of increase in the number of rights holders. To think that any such possibility could be achieved in the foreseeable future is utopian at this juncture in Western cultural history. In spite of projections about the environmental consequences of a doubled or trebled world population, no politician of standing has raised the question of population limitation as a desirable goal for the U.S. or any other Western society. For this possibility to be realisable, it would seem that certain traditional rights, viz., those relating to reproductive behaviour and mobility, would have to be significantly reined in, a most unlikely prospect.

Put a tighter leash on individual technologically maximal behaviour. As with the previous possibility, this option too would seem to require abridging certain traditional exercise rights or changing the underlying, quasi-categorical traditional conception of individual rights to a more conditional one.

Alternatively, if one could demonstrate that un-trammeled operation of the pattern is producing effects that undermine various intangible individual or societal interests, this might furnish a reason for leash-tightening. However, for various reasons, such demonstrations, even if feasible, are rarely socially persuasive.[10]

This situation suggests that one thing that may be crucial to avoiding the above scenario is elaboration and diffusion of a *new theory of moral rights*. While detailed elaboration and defense of such a theory is not feasible here, an acceptable theory should at least include accounts of the basis, function, status, and grounds for limitation of individual rights. Brief remarks on these components follow.

BASIS

Western intellectual development has reached a stage in which individual moral rights can be given a more empirical, naturalistic basis. It should be acknowledged that the epistemological plausibility of rights talk need not, indeed should not, depend upon untestable beliefs in the existence and largesse of a deity interested in protecting the vital interests of individual human beings by endowing them with inalienable rights. Human rights can be plausibly anchored in basic human needs, i.e., universal features of human 'wiring' that must be satisfied to an adequate degree if the individual is to survive or thrive.[11] The notion then would be that something qualifies as an individual human right if and only if its protection is vital to the fulfillment of one or more underlying basic human needs. This *bottom-up* approach has the virtue of making discourse about moral rights more empirically grounded than traditional top-down theological or metaphysical approaches.

FUNCTION

In the new theory I propose, moral rights have a mundane though important function: to serve as conceptual spotlights that focus attention on aspects of human life that are essential to individual survival or thrival. The reason why such search-

lights are needed is that such aspects of human life are ever at risk of being neglected because of political or social inequalities, socially conditioned pre-occupation with ephemera, or the tendency of human agents to overlook or discount the interests of parties outside of their respective immediate geographical and temporal circles.

STATUS

Joel Feinberg has distinguished three degrees of absoluteness for individual moral rights.[12]

1. a right can be absolute in the sense of 'bounded exceptionlessness,' i.e., binding without exception in a finite, bounded domain, as with, e.g., the right to freedom of speech;
2. a right can be absolute in the (higher) sense of an 'ideal directive,' i.e., always deserving of respectful, favourable consideration, even when, after all things have been considered, it is concluded that the right must regrettably be overridden, as with, e.g., the right to privacy, and
3. a right can be absolute in the (still higher) sense of 'unbounded exceptionlessness' and 'non-conflictability,' i.e., binding without exception in an unbounded domain and not intrinsically susceptible to conflict with itself or another right, in the way that, e.g., the right to free speech is conflictable, as exemplified in the hectoring of a speaker. The right not to be subjected to gratuitous torture is a plausible candidate for a right that is absolute in this third sense.

In the theory we propose, individual moral rights will not be absolute in the third, highest degree, only in the first or second degree, depending on technological and demographic circumstances and on the effects on societal quality of life of aggregated maximalist exercise of the right in question.

GROUNDS FOR DECREASING THE ABSOLUTENESS OF INDIVIDUAL RIGHTS

There are at least six kinds of circumstantial grounds that may justify restriction or limitation of individual moral rights because of the bearing of its technologically maximal exercise on societal quality of life:

1. if the very existence of society is called into question by the exercise of a putative right, e.g., exercise of the right to self-defense by the acquisition of the capability of making and using weapons or other technologies of mass destruction;

2. if continued effective social functioning is threatened by the exercise of a right, e.g., the disruption of telecommunication by the operation of automatic phone dialers operated under the auspices of the right of free speech;

3. if some natural resource vital to society is threatened through the exercise of a right, e.g., the reduction of fishing areas or forests to non-sustainable conditions by technologically maximal harvesting practices;

4. if a seriously debilitating financial cost is imposed on society by the widespread or frequent exercise of a right, as with mushrooming public health care payments for private kidney dialysis treatment in the name of the right to life;

5. if some phenomenon of significant aesthetic, cultural, historical, or spiritual value to a people is jeopardised by the exercise of a right, e.g., the destruction of a recognised architectural landmark by affixing its facade to a newly built, incongruous, megastructure under the aegis of a private property right; and

6. if some highly valued social amenity would be seriously damaged or eliminated through the exercise of a right. For example, between 1981 and 1989 convivial public space at the Federal Plaza in downtown Manhattan was effectively eliminated by the installation of an enormous sculpture (Richard Serra's 120 ft. long by 14 ft. high 'Tilted Arc'). The artist unsuccessfully sued the government, attempting to halt removal of the work as a violation of his First Amendment right of free speech, while many of his supporters cited the right to free artistic expression.[13]

In the case of simple-aggregative TM, the only option to acquiescence is to demonstrate the signifi-cant harm done to a protectable societal interest by the aggregated act and attempt to effect an ethical revaluation of putatively harmless individual behaviour; in other words, to lower the threshold of individual wrongdoing to reflect the manifest wrong effected by aggregation. With such a revaluation, the individual would have no right to act as he or she once did because of the newly declared immorality of the individual act. This process may be underway vis-a-vis the individual's disposal of home refuse without separation for recycling.

In sum, we need a *contextualized theory of human rights*. An acceptable theory of rights in contemporary technological society must be able to take on board the implications of their exercise in a context in which a rapidly changing, potent technological arsenal is diffused throughout a populous, materialistic, democratic society. Use of such a technological arsenal by a large and growing number of rights holders has considerable potential for diluting or diminishing societal quality of life. Indeed, insistence on untrammeled, entitled use of potent or pervasive technics by a large number of individuals can be self-defeating, e.g., by yielding a state of social affairs incompatible with other social goals whose realisation the group also highly values.

At a deeper level, what is called into question here is the viability of modern Western individualism. Can, say, contemporary U.S. society afford to continue to promote technology-based individualism in the context of the diffusion and use of multiple potent technics by a large and ever growing population? Or is the traditional concept of individualism itself in need of revision or retirement? The ideology of individualism in all areas of life may have been a viable one in the early modern era, one with a less potent and diverse technological arsenal and a less populous society. But can contemporary Western societies have their ideological cake and eat it too? Can individualism continue to be celebrated and promoted even as a greater and greater number of citizens have access to powerful technics and systems that they, however technologically unsocialised, believe themselves entitled to use in maximalist ways?

Recent Struggles to Adapt Individual Rights to Technological Maximality and Increasing Numbers

In recent years, struggles to adapt individual rights to the realities of technological maximality in populous democratic societies have been waged incessantly on several professional fronts. Let us briefly discuss some pertinent developments in two such fields: urban planning and medicine.

URBAN PLANNING

Two urban planning concerns involving our pattern, over which there were protracted struggles in the 1980s, are building construction and the unrestricted movement of cars. In 1986, the city of San Francisco, California, became the first large city in U.S. history to impose significant limits on the proliferation of downtown high-rise buildings. After several unsuccessful previous efforts, a citizen initiative was finally approved that established a building height limit and a cap on the amount of new high-rise floor space that can be added to the downtown area each year. The majority of San Francisco voters came to believe that the aggregate effects of the continued exercise of essentially unrestricted individual property rights by land owners and developers in technologically maximal ways—entitled erection of numerous high rises—was undermining the quality of city life. In 1990, voters of Seattle, Washington, reached the same conclusion and approved a similar citizen initiative.

As for cars, the 1980s saw the adoption in a few Western countries of substantial limits on their use in cities. For example, to combat air pollution and enhance the quality of urban social life, citizens of Milan and Florence voted overwhelmingly in the mid 1980s to impose limits on the use of cars. In Milan, they are prohibited from entering the *centro storico* between 7:30 a.m. and 6:30 p.m., while in Florence much of the *centro storico* has been turned into a pedestrians-only zone. In California, the cities of Berkeley and Palo Alto installed barriers to prevent drivers from traversing residential streets in the course of crosstown travel. Revealingly, in a debate in the California State Senate over legislation authorising Berkeley to keep its barriers, one sena-

tor argued that 'We should be *entitled* to use all roadways . . . Certain individuals think they're too good to have other people drive down their streets' (emphasis added).[14] The phenomenon combated by the road barriers is a clear instance of aggregative TM of use unfolding under the auspices of traditional mobility rights exercised by large numbers of car drivers. The senator's mind reading notwithstanding, it would seem that citizens, perceiving this pattern as jeopardising the safety of children and diluting the neighbourhood's residential character (read: quality of social life), prevailed on authorities to diminish the long-established domain of driver mobility rights.

Efforts to restrict individual property and mobility rights in urban settings in light of the quality-of-life consequences of their aggregated, technologically maximalist exercise have initiated a high-stakes struggle that promises to grow in importance and be vigorously contested for the foreseeable future.

MEDICINE

An important issue in the area of medicine that involves our pattern is the ongoing tension between the right to life and the widespread intensive use of life-prolongation technology. Following World War II, the change in the locus of dying from the home to the technology-intensive hospital enabled the full arsenal of modern medical technology to be mobilized in service of the right to life. However, the quality of the prolonged life was often so abysmal that efforts to pull back from application of technologically maximal life-extending medical care eventually surfaced.

The Karen Ann Quinlin case (1975–1985) was a landmark in the United States. The Quinlins asked their comatose daughter's doctor to disconnect her respirator. He refused, as did the New Jersey Court of Appeals.[15] The latter argued, significantly for our purposes, that 'the right to life and the preservation of it are "interests of the highest order."' In other words, in the Appeals Court's view, respecting the traditional individual right to life was held to require ongoing provision of technologically maximal medical care. The New Jersey Supreme Court eventually found for the Quinlins, not by revoking this idea but by finding that a patient's privacy interest grows in proportion to the invasiveness of the medical care to which the patient is subjected, and that that interest can be exercised in a proxy vein by the patient's parents.[16]

The equally celebrated Nancy Cruzan case (1983–1990) was essentially an extension of Quinlin, except that the technological means of life extension that Nancy's parents sought to terminate were her food and hydration tubes. Many who opposed the Cruzans believed that removal of those tubes were tantamount to killing their comatose daughter, i.e., to violating her right to life. In their views, respect for Nancy's right to life required continued application of these technological means without limitation of time, regardless of the quality of life being sustained. The Missouri Supreme Court concluded that the state's interest in the preservation of life is 'unqualified,' i.e., that the right to life is inviolable. The court held that in the absence of 'clear and convincing evidence' that a patient would not want to be kept alive by machines in the state into which he or she had fallen, i.e., would not wish to exercise her or his right to life under such circumstances, the perceived absoluteness of the right to life drove continued application of the life-prolonging technology.[17]

The 1990 case of Helga Wanglie, seemingly commonplace at the outset, took on revolutionary potential. Hospitalised after fracturing her hip, Mrs. Wanglie suffered a respiratory attack that cut off oxygen to her brain. By the time she could be resuscitated, the patient had incurred severe brain damage and lapsed into a vegetative state believed irreversible by hospital doctors. Despite this prognosis and after extensive consultation with the doctors, Mrs. Wanglie's family refused to authorise disconnection of the respirator that prolonged her life, asserting that the patient 'wants everything done.' According to Mr. Wanglie, 'she told me, "Only He who gave life has the right to take life."'[18]

Unprecedently, believing that further medical care was inappropriate, the hospital brought suit in court to obtain authorisation to disconnect the patient's respirator against her family's wishes. Predictably, this suit was unsuccessful, but Mrs. Wanglie died shortly thereafter.[19,20] Had the suit succeeded, it would have marked a significant departure from traditional thinking and practice concerning the right to life. Care would have been terminated not at the behest of patient or guardians, something increasingly familiar in recent years, but rather as the result of a conclusion by a care-providing institution that further treatment was 'futile.' Projected quality of patient life would have taken precedence over the patient's inviolable right to life as asserted by guardians, and the absoluteness of the right to life would have been diminished. Consensus that further treatment, however intensive or extensive, offered no reasonable chance of restoring cognitive functioning would have been established as a sufficient condition for mandatory cessation of care.

There are thousands of adults and children in the U.S. and other Western societies whose lives of grim quality are sustained by technological maximality in the name of the right to life, understood by many as categorically binding.[21] The financial and psychological tolls exacted by this specimen of compound-aggregative TM are enormous and will continue to grow until the right to life—its nature and limits—is adapted to the individual and aggregative implications of the technologies used on its behalf.

The troubling triadic pattern should be of concern to many kinds of professional practitioners, not just public officials. Professionals such as urban designers, environmental managers, engineers, and physicians are increasingly confronted in their respective practices with problematic consequences of the continued operation of the troubling triad. Each such individual must decide whether to conduct her or his professional practice—processing building permits, managing natural resource use, designing technics and sociotechnical systems, and treating patients—on the basis of traditional individualistic conceptions of rights unmodified by contemporary technological capabilities and demographic realities, or to alter the concepts and constraints informing her or his practice to reflect extant forms of technological maximality. The fundamental reason why the triad pattern should be of concern to practising professionals is that failure to combat it is tantamount to acquiescing in the increasingly serious individual and social harms apt to result from its predictable repeated manifestations. Professionals have an important role to play in raising societal consciousness about the costs of continuing to rely on anachronistic concepts of individual rights in contemporary technological societies. To date, doctors have made some progress in this effort but other professional groups have not even begun to rise to the challenge.

Conclusion

In the coming years U.S. citizens and other Westerners will face some critical choices. If we persist in gratifying our seemingly insatiable appetite for technological maximality, carried out under the auspices of anachronistic conceptions of rights claimed by ever increasing numbers of people, we shall pay an increasingly steep price in the form of a diminishing societal quality of life. Consciousness-raising, through education and responsible activism, though maddeningly slow, seems the most viable route to developing the societal ability to make discriminating choices about technological practices and their aggregated effects. However accomplished, developing that ability is essential if we are to secure a future of quality for our children and theirs. Taming the troubling triadic pattern would be an excellent place to begin this quest. The technodemographic anachronism of selected traditional rights should be recognised and a new, naturalistic, non-absolutist theory of human rights should be elaborated, one that stands in dynamic relationship to evolving technological capabilities and demographic trends. Whether or not such a new theory of rights emerges, becomes embodied in law, and lathers the contours of professional practice in the next few decades will be critically important to society in the twenty-first century and beyond.

NOTES

1. *New York Times,* 19 November, 1985, p. 1.
2. *Newsweek,* 25 July, 1983, p. 22.
3. See for example: Cecil O. Smith Jr (1990) The Longest Run: Public Engineers and Planning in France, *American Historical Review,* 95, No. 3 pp. 657–692.
4. *New York Times,* Section II, 22 December, 1991, p. 36.
5. Maurice Cranston (1983) Are There Any Human Rights?, *Daedalus,* 112, No. 4, p. 1.
6. Maurice Cranston (1973) *What Are Human Rights?* (New York, Taplinger), pp. 53–54.
7. *New York Times,* 30 October, 1991, p. A1.
8. *New York Times,* 28 November, 1991, pp. D1 and D3.
9. *New York Times,* 23 May, 1993, I, p. 26.
10. Robert E. McGinn (1979) In Defense of Intangibles: The Responsibility-Feasibility Dilemma in Modern Technological Innovation, *Science, Technology, and Human Values,* No. 29, pp. 4–10.
11. See for example, David Braybrooke (1968) Let Needs Diminish That Preferences May Prosper, in *Studies in Moral Philosophy* (Oxford, Blackwell), pp. 86–107, and the same author's (1987) *Meeting Needs* (Princeton, Princeton University Press) for careful analysis of the concept of basic human needs. For discussion of the testability of claims that something is a bona fide basic human need, see Amatai Etzioni (1968), Basic Human Needs, Alienation, and Inauthenticity, *American Sociological Review,* 33, pp. 870–885. On the relationship between human rights and human needs, see also C. B. Macpherson, quoted in D. D. Raphael (1967), *Political Theory and the Rights of Man* (London, MacMillan). p. 14.
12. Joel Feinberg (1973), *Social Philosophy* (Englewood Cliffs, NJ: Prentice-Hall), pp. 85–88.
13. See for example: J. Hitt, (ed.) The Storm in the Plaza, *Harper's Magazine,* July 1985, pp. 27–33.
14. *San Francisco Chronicle,* 2 July, 1983, p. 6.
15. *In re Quinlin,* 137 N.J. super 227 (1975).
16. *In re Quinlin,* 70 N. J. 10,335 A. 2d 647 (1976).
17. After the U.S. Supreme Court decision upholding the Missouri Supreme Court was handed down, three of the patient's friends provided new evidence of her expressed wish to be spared existence in a technologically sustained vegetative state. This led, in a lower court rehearing, to a judgment permitting parental exercise of the patient's recognised privacy interest through the withdrawal of her food and hydration tubes. Nancy Cruzan expired twelve days after this decision was announced. See *New York Times,* 15 December, 1990. A1 and A9, and 27 December, 1990, A1 and A13.
18. *New York Times,* 10 January, 199, A16.
19. Ibid., 2 July, 1991, A12.
20. Ibid., 6 July, 1991, I8.
21. U.S. Congress, Office of Technology Assessment (1987) *Technology-Dependent Children: Hospital v. Home Care Sustaining Technologies and the Elderly* (Washington, D.C., U.S. Government Printing Office).

DAVID STRONG   I.12

Technological Subversion

This reading, taken from the author's book *Crazy Mountains: Learning from Wilderness to Weigh Technology,* philosopher David Strong asks us to consider the basic question, "Why do we value technology?"

In his analysis, we value technological devices because they disburden us of toilsome labor, discomfort, and bother. Technological innovations beckon us with the promise of freedom and happiness. We want things to be easy so that we are freer to pursue our ends without having to worry too much about the means we use to do so, and we believe that being "free" in this sense—that is, disburdened—will make us happy.

Using as his examples the replacement of the hearth by the central heating system and television viewing as a primary form of entertainment, Strong argues that this quest for freedom and happiness through technologically provided ease and comfort often alters the nature of human experience in ways that disconnect us from nature and other people, and ironically produces not happiness but alienation. While some readers may find this philosophical meditation somewhat demanding, those who study it carefully will find that it rewards their effort.

Focus Questions

1. What does the author mean by the term *technological availability*? What specific values does this concept embody?
2. What is the vision of the "good life" that our modern technological society offers us? Why does the author question the goodness of this way of life?
3. What are the main differences between what Strong calls "things" and what he calls "devices"? What values do we sacrifice when we choose the device paradigm over engagement with things?

Keywords

alienation, commodification, environmental ethics, heating systems, television, wilderness

THE UNDERLYING ETHIC OF TECHNOLOGY

Some have argued that we live in an invisible iron cage. Indeed, technological forces are shaping peo-

ple's lives in ways that they have little or no control over, especially if the basic framework of technology goes unchallenged; but, as Charles Taylor points out, the conquest of nature had a benevolent point to it. It was to serve humanity. So, he finds that, along with other forces, there are moral forces of work here shaping our lives. We live neither in an iron cage nor in an arena of unconstrained choice; we inhabit a possibility space where some moral choices are being made. There is a kind of ethical appeal to not letting our resources go to waste. So what ethical forces might be called upon to reform technology in a deep way? How should we understand the basic choice we face? For developing what I call the vision and underlying ethic of technology, I will draw heavily upon Albert Borgmann's theory of technology, the best account of the character of the technological culture we have so far. Then we will use this vision of technology to show that the concerns of environmental ethics and people's better concerns for nature generally will be subverted by technology unless we as a culture come to grips with the irony of this vision and begin to make a fundamentally different choice, that is, choose things over consumption.

MAKING THE APPEAL OF TECHNOLOGY INTELLIGIBLE: THE PROMISE OF TECHNOLOGY

Neither Heidegger nor Thoreau makes clear what it is about technology that is attractive to people. Claiming that we delight in the exercise of power seems correct enough when we think of the enormous amount of power we wield with technology, yet this view does not address our more intelligible motives and, therefore, does not really address many of the proponents of technology without trivializing their concerns. In one way or another, most of us, if not all, see technology as good. What is at the heart of our petty homocentrism? What good is technology?

Typically people articulate what good technology is when they say that something is better or improved and demonstrate that "that's progress." Advertisements are continually pointing out what is better about the product advertised, even if the chief "advantage" is two for the price of one. Although they may well dupe us, these advertisements normally appeal to standards that at least on a deep and general level are already in place and widely shared in consumer culture. We hear everywhere around us, not just in advertisements, what better is. "It means less work." "It's more comfortable." "It's convenient." "It's healthier." "It's faster and more productive." "It's less of a hassle." "Sleeker looks better." "It's lighter." "It doesn't get in your way." "You don't have to wait on anyone else." "It's

exciting." When we see the very latest devices, often our expression are on the order of "Wow!" or "That's great!" or "Look at that, would you?" So, at deeper levels, there seems to be a good deal of like-mindedness about what constitutes better in our culture.

Another approach is to consider what people think of as clear examples of progress. Television today is far different from what it was in the past. In the early 50s, one was lucky to own a television. Reception was poor, the picture rough and in black and white; the screen was small, the set large; the number of programs was very limited. In addition to other obvious improvements, now the sets come on instantly, are controlled from the couch, can be found in all sizes and nearly everywhere, and have access to a vast number and variety of programs, especially with video cassette recorders. Even if they are not willing to pay the price for all of them, most count these changes as improvements, and rarely do we find people watching a black and white set any longer. What are the standards which make these changes count as improvements?

Television as a clear example of technology will play a key role in our understanding of the nature of the fundamental choice we face, but Borgmann uses another paradigmatic example of technology, the central heating system, to disclose most of these standards of technology. We can easily trace the development of central heating systems back to the wood-burning stove or the hearth. The chief advantages of the heating system over these latter two are various. Central heating *is easier.* We do not have to gather, stack, chop, or carry the wood. An automatic thermostat means that we not have to trouble ourselves in the morning or evening with setting a thermostat. Central heating is more *instantaneous.* We do not have to wait for the house to warm up. It's *ubiquitous.* Warmth is provided to each corner of the room, to every room, and everywhere equally well. Finally, a central heating system is *safer* than a hearth. My grandmother was born in a newly built chicken coop because three weeks earlier her family's house burnt down from a chimney fire. So the standards by which people judge central heating to be better than a wood-burning stove are ease, instantaneity, ubiquity, and safety or some combination of these, for example, convenience. These four "technological standards" can be collected under the more general notion of technological availability. To be more *available* is to be an improvement, then, in terms of one or more of the four above standards.

Why does it seem to people that this availability is good? From one perspective, this availability relieves people of burdens: less effort, less time, and less learning skills are required. Available anytime and anyplace, they are disburdened of the constraints of time and place. They are disburdened of having to take risks. Historically, modern technology was envisioned as enabling people not just to subjugate nature, but to do so for the purpose of freeing humanity from misery and toil. To be relieved of these burdens then, fulfills this vision of technology. *To the degree people personally share this vision,* they will also see its concrete manifestations, such as central heating, as unquestionably good. Compared to older versions, the latest portable computers exemplify this relief from burdens and are attractive to many for this reason.

By overcoming nature, technology would, as some in the seventeenth century foresaw, not only relieve humans of burdens, but it would make available to them—easier, safer, quicker, and more ubiquitous—all the goods of the Earth. So, technological availability negatively disburdens people of misery and toil, and positively enriches their lives, makes them happy, it seems. So seen, technology has an attractive glow about it.

> Technology promises to bring the forces of nature and culture under control, to liberate us from misery and toil, and to enrich our lives . . . [More accurately], implied in the technological mode of taking up with the world there is a promise that this approach to reality will, by way of the domination of nature, fuel liberation and enrichment.

Borgmann calls this "the promise of technology."

Clearly those below the middle-class of advanced industrialized countries and those outside those countries do not derive the benefits of technology, although many do feel the pull of its promise. The claims of social justice will not likely be met until the more privileged ones, the middle and higher classes of these industrialized countries, come to terms with the questionable character of technology's promise. So, the critique of technology I am developing here does not apply to those in poverty. It applies only to those who have too much.

For these latter, technology has made good on its promise in important ways. My grandmother's father died from what she believes was pneumonia when she was eleven, leaving her and her younger sister to perform heroic feats to save the cattle from starvation in the drought times of an extended winter that followed. Often hitching the team up before dawn and returning hours after dark, especially in winter, her family took an entire day to get to and from town sixteen miles away. For the privileged, then, many past hardships have now been conquered. Although we may have legitimate concerns about whether there is too much medical technology, no one could reasonably refuse every advance of modern medical technology. The weather will never be brought under control, but, via comfortable structures, nature's heat and cold, rain and snow are controlled as well as darkness and drought. Toilsome labor is largely eliminated within the culture of technology.

A reasonable person may reject motorcycles in favor of horses to do ranch work, but that person still rides to town on paved roads in a car, has parts shipped by air, reads a newspaper and books, transacts business over the phone, and owns at least a radio. No thoughtful person will want to turn her back on technology entirely. Thus, technology, by conquering nature, has relieved humans of severe burdens. Today we are still working to overcome those, such as cancer and AIDS, that remain. So, if technology does not saddle us in the long run with more than it has relieved us from, it will have made good on this aspect of what at first seemed and still does seem promising about it. It could turn out that ozone depletion, global warming, ecosystem destruction, the population explosion, polluted land, air, streams and oceans, and human and mechanical errors will impose burdens far greater than those we were relieved from in the first place. To meet these problems certainly calls for a reform of present practices. We read or hear of these calls for reform nearly every day. More common critiques of technology, such as David Ehrenfeld's *The Arrogance of Humanism,* attempt to show that technology will fail its own standards, bringing disaster upon us.

Much as reform in these areas is needed and much as these pessimistic critiques deserve thoughtful consideration, the present work will turn to a uniquely different task. It grants and, in fact, seeks to have the reader appreciate, the genuine success of modern technology. Technology has relieved, and technology will, I assume for the purposes at hand, continue to relieve, humans of many hardships of the human condition.

So what is wrong with technology for those within the realm of its benefits? Underlying these standards of availability is really a vision of a good life that is free and prosperous. What is at the bottom of concern with technological availability is an aspiration for freedom and happiness. Most people, at least in the Western tradition, are concerned with liberty and prosperity. For Aristotle only the Greek free man was able to have sufficient time and sufficient wherewithal to develop the moral and intellectual virtues he thought to be required for happiness or eudaemonia. The Hebrew people's understanding of the covenant centered on an idea of prosperity. Jesus preached of a free and abundant life. The Enlightenment, as we see its results in "the pursuit of happiness" in our Declaration of Independence, is fully within this tradition. But to find agreement at this high level of abstraction is not to see that the crucial differences lie with the particular versions of freedom and prosperity. For Socrates living well had to do with human excellence and living a just life, not with materialism. The blessed life and the abundant life of the Hebrews and of Jesus was not commodity happiness. So, too, we must look carefully at the particular idea of freedom and prosperity governing people's attraction to technology, for only at this level of particularity will its misleading and harmful features begin to show. In other words, one can criticize the trivialized forms of freedom and prosperity on which the technological society is centered without, at the same time, criticizing freedom and prosperity more generally as a vision of the good life. Quite the contrary, we can call

technology into question even more sharply by showing that technology fails to provide the free, prosperous, and good life we want in our waking moments.

Technological society offers a flattened vision of freedom and prosperity. The more disburdened, the better off I am according to this vision. So, the technological idea of freedom is really one of disburdenment. What about prosperity? Cellular phones are currently a status symbol. These devices which disburden people of the constraints of place are taken to be a sign of affluence because, generally, only the more prosperous have them. So, in part, to be prosperous is to have the latest, most refined device. A sign of affluence, too, is to be able to go to an undiscovered exotic place, have the most channels and compact discs, own specially designed clothing, own what no one else has yet. Thus, in part, to be prosperous is to own the most varied, the widest assortment of commodities. Finally, when people buy a product on sale they get both the commodity they purchased and still have money left over. Why is that attractive? Because they can buy something else with the money saved. They are better off that way, they think, because they get more items for the money. Thus people pursue prosperity through the standards of owning the *most numerous, widest variety, and the very latest (most refined)* commodities. The powers that be in the technological society own and control most of these items. Such is the picture of the good life envied by those keeping up with the Joneses. Our culture's vision of the good life is the goods life.

Does this vision really deliver a good life? If we say no merely because it differs from the blessed life according to Abraham, Moses, and the prophets, or from the Greeks' eudaemonia, our analysis would be dogmatic and presumptuous. Technology must be thought through; it will not be met by simply reacting against it. So, if we answer "no," as I will, then we must be able to provide good reasons.

THE TECHNOLOGICAL MEANS TO FREEDOM AND HAPPINESS: THE DEVICE

The ironic consequences of this vision of freedom and prosperity can be drawn out through a careful analysis of the peculiar way technology transforms, or more specifically, dominates nature and culture. Technology does not dominate these in the traditional manner of lording it over them; rather, as Albert Borgmann shows, technology follows a pattern, unique to the modern era, in the way it gets everything under control. We can expose this pattern by examining instances of it.

The central heating system dominates warmth; it brings warmth under control in ways that the wood-burning stoves do not. To show its unique form of domination, Borgmann distinguishes between "things" and "devices." A thing in his sense

> is inseparable from its context, namely its world, and from our commerce with the thing and its world, namely, engagement. The experience of a thing is always and also a bodily and social engagement with the thing's world . . . Thus a stove used to furnish more than mere warmth. It was a *focus,* a hearth, a place that gathered the work and leisure of a family and gave the house a center. Its coldness marked the morning, and the spreading of its warmth marked the beginning of the day. It assigned to various family members tasks that defined their place in the household . . . It provided the entire family a regular and bodily engagement with the rhythm of the seasons that was woven together with the threat of cold and the solace of warmth, the smell of wood smoke, the exertion of sawing and carrying, the teaching of skills, and the fidelity to daily tasks . . . Physical engagement is not simply physical contact but the experience of the world through the manifold sensibility of the body. That sensibility is sharpened and strengthened in skill. Skill is intensive and refined world engagement.

Here, in his retrieval of the thing's world and our engagement with the thing, Borgmann has been influenced by Heidegger's fourfold account of things. Obviously, Earth and sky are woven together with mortals. He points out that in Roman times the hearth was the abode of household gods, though he does not make much of it. Borgmann's account goes beyond Heidegger in emphasizing social and bodily engagement to a degree to which Heidegger seems insensitive. He also steps beyond Heidegger

by highlighting the way things focus practices. Practices call for skills and the development of character; the diversity of different characters is joined to each other through participating in a world of practices. In our terms developed earlier, the hearth is the correlational coexistent thing which establishes the world of the household and, correlatively, calls forth its members and calls on their deeper capacities.

Today the hearth, if it exists at all, is no longer the central location in the house although the mantel still remains a place of honor. What has replaced the thing is the "device." The device (the central heating system) provides a commodity, one element of the original thing (warmth alone) and disburdens people of all the elements that compose the world and engaging character of the thing. This world of the thing, its ties to the natural and cultural world and our engagement with that many-dimensional world on bodily, cerebral, and social levels, is taken over by the *machinery* (the central heating plant itself) of the device.

> The machinery makes no demands on our skill, strength, or attention, and it is less demanding the less it makes its presence felt. In the progress of technology, the machinery of the device has therefore a tendency to become concealed or to shrink. Of all the physical properties of a device, those alone are crucial and prominent which constitute the commodity that the device procures.

To make the commodity even more technologically available, the machinery varies radically in the history of technology (wood or coal or oil or electricity or gas). Owing to this radical variability and to this concealment, the machinery becomes necessarily *unfamiliar.* I probably do not know by what means the water is heated in a building. But the device is not just machinery or even most importantly machinery. The device makes available a commodity—warmth. Warmth is what the central heating system is for. Just the opposite of the machinery, the commodity tends to *expand* (become ubiquitous in the house), to remain relatively *fixed* as the means change (from coal to electricity) and to be *familiar.* It follows that—unlike with things—there is a wide division between what a device provides, the commodity, and how it provides this commodity, the machinery. Hence, and this is Borgmann's central insight we saw illustrated earlier with second homes, devices *split* means and ends into mere means and mere ends.

Even though these claims that a thing makes on people are not always experienced as burdensome (as we see from the above account), this very world of the thing and the engagement it calls for can be felt at times as a burden or hassle. The technological device and its refinement *disburdens* people of all these problems by expanding the commodity, so that the world of the thing no longer determines when, in what way, and where it is available. Thus, it disburdens them of the claims that call for engagement. In short, the technological device disburdens people of the thing's world and its claims upon them. The device is considered the more refined the more it lifts these burdens from them. The ideal device is one where, from an experiential standpoint, a commodity can be enjoyed unencumbered by means. A reliable self-regulating central heating system whose maintenance and energy bill are taken care of by a management agency can be taken as a paradigmatic example.

The peculiar way technology dominates things is not limited, of course, to the central heating system. Considering how household technologies have changed, Witold Rybczynski in *Home: A Short History of An Idea* writes:

> The evolution of domestic technology . . . demonstrates that the history of physical amenities can be divided into two major phases: all the years leading up to 1890, and the three following decades. If this sounds outlandish, it is worth reminding ourselves that tall "modern" devices that contribute to our domestic comfort—central heating, indoor plumbing, running hot and cold water, electric light and power and elevators—were unavailable before 1890, and were well known by 1920. We live, like it or not, on the fair side of a great technological divide. As John Lukacs reminds us, although the home of 1930 would be familiar to us, it would have been unrecognizable to the citizen of 1885.

Just as with household technologies, so too with other features of our surroundings and our cultural and natural environment generally. This thing-to-device example is representative of the pattern of the technological transformations of the Earth. Generally then, this transformation is one in which:

> Devices . . . dissolve the coherent and engaging character of the pre-technological world of things. In a device, the relatedness of the world is replaced by a machinery, but the machinery is concealed, and the commodities, which are made available by a device, are enjoyed without the encumbrance of or the engagement with a context [that is, the world of the thing].

Borgmann calls this pattern the *device paradigm*. At times I will call it the separation pattern of technology.

We can understand our age as one in which we reduce everything to resources that we want to control. Now we can see that the device pattern is used to get control of these resources. The purpose of the device is to supply people with unencumbered commodities. So now we can develop this picture of our age further. The fuller vision is one in which everything gets reduced to resources, machinery and commodities.

IRONIC CONSEQUENCES

So far we have developed a theory by which we can interpret what has taken and is taking place with regard to the technological transformation in our time. Using this theory we can pass from technological object to technological object, seeing how they more or less fit the pattern. The illustration of the pattern does not commit us as yet to an evaluation of the good or bad of what has taken place. Now we are in a position to begin that task. What are the consequences of this change from things to devices?

Don Ihde finds that technologies transform experience in a "non-neutral" manner. A tool always amplifies in some way certain aspects of normal embodied experience while simultaneously reducing other aspects. A dentist's probe shows the hardness and cavities in a tooth to a degree fingers miss, while the wetness and warmth of the tooth felt by the fingers go undetected by probe. This change

Ihde finds is non-neutral because the amplified features are heightened, drawing our attention, while the reduced features tend to go unheeded and are overlooked and often forgotten. Asked what a hearth is for, we find it logical, after having experienced central heating, to answer that it supplies heat, ignoring or not even seeing its other aspects. Extending Ihde's insight makes it more intelligible why we become fascinated with commodities, heedless of what has been reduced. Yet pointing out that this change is non-neutral is not enough. We now want to comprehend what exactly has been hidden from us. We need a language which articulates what is overlooked and forgotten, for then we can see in what ways this change is non-neutral. Our language of things retrieves and focuses this loss. It reveals the general pattern that things are transformed into devices, detaching people from things, their world, and each other.

Ihde further argues that these lost features only tend to recede, thus, implying that they are retrievable. With certain kinds of instruments (not all technological objects are devices, splitting means and ends), this is true. We can easily retrieve the features missed by the dentist's probe. With devices, however, these features do not just tend to withdraw, so that a change of attitude, perception, or act of will could retrieve them. Notice that mere warmth, no matter how expanded the commodity has become, is not a substitute for the thing of the wood-burning stove. Mere warmth could not be the essence of a household; it does not warrant the kind of attention or care, of heeding. Indeed the source itself is concealed and the warmth is suffused throughout the house so that it fails to provide a focus. So warmth is no substitute for the thing because it lacks a world with which to become engaged. More than this, because it is impossible to recover in the mere warmth of the central heating plant, the full-bodied experience of the hearth, the machinery of devices ineluctably withdraws the world from people. A device is necessarily unfamiliar in the ways that the context of the thing was familiar. Thus the transformation of the thing into a device does not merely tend to obscure possibilities of experience, but its very material structure makes the rich experience of the thing impossible.

Another way of putting this is that devices allow the possibility of only slim points of contact with "narrowly defined aspects of what used to be things of depth." Devices force people to take them as commodity bearers; they leave them no choice. So our way of taking commodities is not a psychological matter, but a real matter. Technology is not only a way of seeing (and for this reason characterizing technology as a vision is perhaps misleading), it is more importantly a way of *shaping*. The very material structure of a device is such that it can be experienced only as holding up a commodity calling for consumption and nothing more.

The implication of this change of shape is alienation. What seemed promising at the outset—relieving people of burdens—leads ironically to disengagement, diversion, distraction, and loneliness. In short, we become not-at-home in the universe. But clearly, simply finding ourselves free from the exclusive use of candles and outhouses does not place us in this alienated position. So how can such positive events as electric lighting and indoor plumbing lead to these ironic results?

To be relieved of famine, cold, darkness, confinement, and other genuine adversities of the human condition was an intelligible and urgent demand for the early phase of modern technology. For the middle-classes of advanced industrialized countries, most, not all, of these kinds of challenges have been met for some time. At the stage of mature technology, the challenges can be quite frivolous. Food processors, electric pencil sharpeners, prepared fishing leaders, automatic cameras, electric knives, and some pain relievers are typical. The basic question here is: Do we need to be relieved of every last and least burden? Aren't some of these burdens actually good in senses that touch our very humanity? When people reflect on these questions they may answer them differently, but when they act, they tend to act in agreement with a vision that seeks to bring everything under control. Ironically, in the wake of such technological success, in the wake of the initial excitement over owning the latest item, the item falls back into the ordinary every day and they become bored. Being bored, they become disengaged and alienated from what may have been a vital practice, such as preparing meals or gardening or photography. Accordingly, they seek diversion. Thus, ironic consequences follow from the disburdenment of every hassle, problem, or felt demand. If we pursue disburdenment in this unchecked and unreflective manner, as people are doing in the stage of mature technology, then these are the results we should expect.

However, it may seem as though we have been just too nostalgic. The disbursement devices yield "frees us up for other things" as people commonly say. Yet this perspective makes us think that technology is mostly about freedom, as Charles Taylor thinks, when the promise and vision of technology are mostly a promise of happiness. The most unique and devastating critique of technology is not centered on technological freedom, but on the fact that technology *fails most where it succeeds most* at procuring happiness, at procuring the good things of life. As a culture, we think not only that we can use technology to liberate us, but also that we can use it to fill that new possibility space with technologically available goods. In short, what people are freed up for are not other things, but *more commodities.* Then too when people imagine what they are doing as they throw food into the microwave as freeing themselves up for other and more important things, they ignore how pervasive the technological order is. The totality of technological devices is far more consequential than any particular device. The former point can be advanced best by developing the latter first.

Extensively yet unobtrusively this technological way of taking up with the world pervades and informs what people think, say and do. We need an account of technology as *correlational environment.* Organizations, institutions, the ways nature and culture are arranged and accessible all become modeled on the device. As people make more decisions for consumption against engagement, our average, everyday world is stamped more deeply with the pattern of the device. In other words, devices do not simply liberate people from some things and free them for other and better things. We are surrounded. The things enabling correlational coexistence have nearly disappeared. As the totality of our daily environment changes from an environment of things to an environment of devices, from an environment making demands on people to an environment that is more at their fingertips, this change necessarily entails heedlessness and evokes an attitude of cultural petty homocentrism. So it is important to consider not just the appropriateness of this or that device in a particular context, but to consider what the consequences are of the totality of these devices and people's *typical* use of them. We would expect the consumptive ways of life in such surroundings to be disburdened and disengaged.

So what are people finally freed up for? How do they attempt to use technological means to positively enrich their lives? Typically people use devices to procure entertainment commodities. Hence our culture treats tradition, culture, and nature as resources to be mined. Just as ubiquitously available warmth is not a substitute for the hearth, entertainment commodities are at best insubstantial aspects of the original things. Because they use devices here to procure the delights that matter, final things, these entertainment commodities can be thought of as final commodities. In this respect, to consume a final commodity is no different from consuming an instrumental one that disburdens us of a chore.

THE IRONIC CONSEQUENCES OF FINAL CONSUMPTION

Television is a clear example of a final commodity. Its refinements from the first sets to those of today fit the same pattern as the refinements in central heating and the refinements of devices in accordance with Borgmann's device paradigm in general. So television is an instance of the vision of domination, liberation, and enrichment. It does not make demands on people and is a window of the world, making all the goods of the Earth available, technologically available, to them in their living rooms.

Understandably, television has tremendous appeal to us as a culture. It's where technology comes home to people. The amount of time they spend watching it indicates its power.

The A.C. Nielsen Company (1989) currently estimates that people in the United States view upwards of 4 hours of television each day. Given the likelihood that such estimates are inflated, let us assume a more conservative estimate of 2 1/2 hours of television viewing per day over the period of a lifetime. Even at this more conservative rate, a typical American would spend more than 7 full years watching television out of the approximately 47 waking years each of us lives by age 70—this assuming an average of 8 hours of sleep per day. Such a figure is even more striking when we consider that Americans have about 5 1/2 hours a day of free time, or approximately 16 years available for leisure of the same 47-year span. From this point of view and based on a conservative estimate, Americans are spending nearly half of their available free time watching television.

Since it is the most popular way people enjoy final consumption, it is worthwhile to examine in detail the *experience* of this form of consumption as we develop the ironic consequences of final consumption. *Television and the Quality of Life* by Robert Kubey and Mihaly Csikszentmihalyi (cited above) do just that, examining systematically the reported experience of television in contrast to the reported experience of other activities people spend time on in their daily life. So we need to look closely at their findings with a view to showing how technology in the form of TV does not fulfill its promise.

Kubey and Csikszentmihalyi find that television is inexpensive and is easily and quickly available for those who have time for it. It helps people to relax and, at times, may help some to retreat before gathering themselves to face a difficulty. People can watch it for prolonged periods without wearing themselves out physically. It tends to bring families together and family members normally do talk with each other while watching. They also feel better than when watching alone. It is used for news programs, for nature shows, and to present dramas such as *Death of a Salesman*. It could be used to present lectures in chemistry and Plato. It helps connect us with our culture and some of its common stories. On the other hand, "viewing is almost always mildly rewarding in that it provides relaxation, distraction, and escape with minimal effort." It gives people something to do with their time and most report they do want to watch it. With so much

of our leisure time taken up with television and with so many benefits, one might mistakenly conclude that people choose to watch because it is better than anything else they could be doing. Yet the actual cumulative benefits they receive from television are rather low and often negative.

Ironically, the reported experience of people viewing television often turns out to be one of disappointment. Not only are chemistry courses not aired because few would watch them, not only do most people gravitate toward watching movies with light and escapist content rather than challenging dramas, but, just as important, half the people who watch television do not use television guides to help them decide what to watch. The stories viewers share, then, are not those shown on public television. The shows tend to support existing beliefs. As Stu Silverman told Kubey, "Television reassures us, it's 'nice,' it doesn't offend or challenge an audience. It is designed to do just the opposite of art, to reassure rather than excite. That often is what people want." Although television does help people to relax, it does not do so any more than other activities such as reading. Moreover, it helps people relax only while watching it and not later as sports and other activities do. Although this study found that television is not a completely passive activity, it is comparatively so. It is not usually challenging, requires little mental alertness, and is reported to exact fewer skills than eating. Only idling was reported to be more passive. Unlike activities that gather and restore a person, a "passive spillover effect" tended to follow watching television, making people feel duller, more passive, and less able to concentrate. Families for which television provides a center also experience this spillover effect carried over into other family activities. Finally, the positive benefits one receives from television tend to be enjoyed less the more one watches. Heavy viewers are not made happy by watching it; they generally feel worse than light viewers both before and after viewing. Even light viewers do not report themselves to be any happier than average while watching.

Aristotle found amusement, like sleep, to be therapeutic as long as life is oriented around exertion. So, too, Kubey and Csikszentmihalyi find that those who stand to benefit most from television use and need it least. More often television is used to disburden people of problems in ways that do not go to the roots of the problems, are only marginally effective, and, hence, are entirely inappropriate. People disburden themselves of the problem of leisure time that their time-saving and labor-saving devices have created by killing time watching television. They disburden themselves of the problem of loneliness when devices leave them isolated by turning on a device, the television set. Heavy use is higher among singles. Such an answer to loneliness is only a diversion from genuine forms of social engagement. On the other hand, television is often used as a way for family members, usually fathers, to avoid talking with other family members and avoid dealing with family problems. Television resolves the problem of independently ordering one's life, of giving shape to the day. It takes care of boredom. Heavy television viewing is likely driven by a wish to escape, to be disburdened of bad days and bad moods, of personal problems and of alienation from self. Diverting one's attention, it tend to mask the deeper and more real problems a person is having and, hence, leaves these problems unintelligently resolved. Does it meet the task of leading a more rewarding and meaningful life? No. "Happiness is a more complex state than relaxation. It requires a more elusive set of conditions, and is therefore more difficult to obtain." Television seems to "encourage a false sense of well-being in some people," distracting them from and becoming an obstacle to the hard work it takes to realize one's potentials.

More indirectly, we can ask what people are missing when they watch television. When viewers are not pleased with the amount of time they watch television, the entire reason is not only that it is a low-grade activity, one that many think best fits the phrase "Am I lazy!" Part of the reason, too, has to do with what television is displacing. Many report that they feel as though they should have been doing something else. College educated viewers felt this way more often than other people because "they should have been doing something more productive." Television rearranges life through de-creasing the amount of time spent involved with other activities. It at times provides a center for the household, but such a center seems flimsy at best, especially in comparison with other potential centers or centers of the past. In another context, Kubey and Csikszentmihalyi speak of these kinds of centers of life.

> When people are asked what they enjoy most, and enough time is left for a genuine answer to emerge, we often find that the most enjoyable things involve doing something, and usually something rather complex and demanding. Rarely does watching television get mentioned, or any other passive or consummatory activity . . . The first reflex for many people is to say that one most enjoys going on vacations, going to movies or restaurants—the typical "leisure" responses in our culture. But as people think more deeply about their real feelings they will mention enjoyable times with their families, and then there is often a point when their faces light up and they say something like: "Actually, the best times in my life have . . ." and start talking with great enthusiasm about designing and sewing quilts, rock climbing, playing music, working on a basement lathe, or about other activities that require concentrated skill, that do not separate the individual from the end result of his or her effort, and that provide the kind of exhilaration and high focused attention of flow. So . . . we are still able to keep in sight those *vivid signposts* that show what it is that makes life worth living . . . [On] reflecting on such occasions, people often say that not only was the experience enjoyable at the time, but that it helped them grow and become more than they had been. Compared to such optimal experiences, much television watching could be deemed a waste of time . . . wasting it amounts to wasting life.

Casting television in terms of the symmetrical relationship of correlational coexistence developed earlier, we can see that the medium is just not enough for humans to make the center of their lives. It does not call forth their humanity in any depth. Hence, Kubey and Csikszentmihalyi worry that by spending so much time viewing television "one may well lose opportunities to grow as a human being."

Kubey and Csikszentmihalyi find that a mistaken cultural assumption underlies much of the appeal of television. For them the mistaken cultural assumption is narrowly one of thinking that physical and mental exertion are bad, and that they are unrelated to human growth and living a worthwhile life. In contrast, for us, the more comprehensive mistaken assumption is that technology generally can fulfill our aspirations for freedom and enrichment. Considered from the standpoint of the vision of technology, television is a paradigmatic example of and not an exception to the unimpeded development of technological culture. As for liberation, it is a commodity which does not make demands—in dress, transportation, or manners, or even having to be at home when a program is aired. Following the device's split between means and ends, people exert themselves in labor and expect to relax completely in leisure. They want amusement, not challenge or disturbance. In terms of prosperity, with video cassette players and hundreds of channels, the most, the most varied, and the latest programs can be watched. Advertisements, too, and the settings of the programs themselves celebrate this prosperity of technology. In short, the incredible attraction of television is that it is the homeplace of the vision people are still spellbound by. It confirms them in that vision and tells them what's what in the universe. Its glamour binds and soothes while simultaneously disappointing them with the flatness and shallowness of its nourishment, its ironic unfulfillment. Television as an exemplar of a final commodity represents the ultimate appeal of the promise of technology. It is, then, the success story of the technology. Television is the vision of technological culture.

So while technology is successful on its own terms when it make goods available, its success is merely a pyrrhic victory. What makes good things rich and involving has been lost. We have been seduced by a shallow semblance. Thus, technology fails to deliver happiness, not because it fails to make goods available, but because such goods as it does make available turn out to be merely ironic goods. What seemed promising in the appearance is disappointing in the reality. Our aspirations for freedom and happiness go awry when we attempt to procure them with devices.

So does technology deliver the goods? Does technology help people live more rewarding and meaningful lives? As people make the things that count in their lives technologically available, they empty them of depth and they lose them. It is a lesson our culture has to learn yet when we let television turn us into something less than members of the animal kingdom.

Part II

Contemporary Technology and the Future

- Innovation, Globalization, and Human Rights
- Computers and Information Technology
- Biotechnology, Genetic Engineering, and Reproduction
- Population, Energy, and the Environment

II.1   JEFFREY SACHS

International Economics: Unlocking the Mysteries of Globalization

Although there have been previous economic cycles of boom and bust, today's generally improving global economy is built on new relationships that create an interdependent structure in which we are all, to a certain extent, dependent on each other. Jeffrey Sachs, a professor of international trade at Harvard University, looks at the many ways in which countries at various levels of technological development have joined forces to improve their economic well-being. The recent shifts in the economic policies of many countries and rapid technological advances are, claims Sachs, bringing changes that are not predictable and only dimly understood today. One critical issue to be decided is how decisions will be made in our new world where multinational corporations exercise greater and greater influence. What will be the future roles of citizens and governments in deciding whether a particular economic policy will be beneficial or not and in exercising control over their portion of the global marketplace?

Focus Questions

1. What are the four major issues related to globalization's impact on both developed and developing countries raised by Sachs in this reading?
2. In what ways does this article suggest it is possible that the "increasingly dense network of economic interactions" between countries could prove to be problematic?
3. What might be some long-range impacts on employment and the environment if globalization continues at its present rate?

Keywords

division of labor, G-7 countries, GDP, globalization, imperialism, income inequity, International Monetary Fund, macroeconomics, World Trade Organization

INTERNATIONAL ECONOMICS IS CONCERNED with the trade and financial relations of national economies, and the effects of international trade and finance on the distribution of production, income, and wealth around the world and within nations. In recent years, international economics has been

Reprinted with permission from *Foreign Policy* 110 (Spring 1998). © 1998 by the Carnegie Endowment for International Peace.

increasingly taken up with one central question: How will national economies perform now that nearly all of the world is joined in a single marketplace? As a result of changes in economic *policy* and technology, economies that were once separated by high transport costs and artificial barriers to trade and finance are now linked in an increasingly dense network of economic interactions. This veritable economic revolution over the last 15 years has come upon us so suddenly that its fundamental ramifications for economic growth, the distribution of income and wealth, and patterns of trade and finance in the world economy are only dimly understood.

The most notable features of the new world economy are the increasing links between the high- and low-income countries. After all, the advanced income economies of Europe, Japan, and the United States have been linked significantly through trade flows at least since the 1960s. The great novelty of the current era is the extent to which the poorer nations of the world have been incorporated in the global system of trade, finance, and production as partners and market participants rather than colonial dependencies. For *globalization* enthusiasts, this development promises increased gains from trade and faster growth for both sides of the worldwide income divide. For skeptics, the integration of rich and poor nations promises increasing inequality in the former and greater dislocation in the latter.

National economies are becoming more integrated in four fundamental ways—through trade, finance, production, and a growing web of treaties and institutions. The increased trade linkages are clear: In almost every year since World War II, international trade has grown more rapidly than global production, resulting in a rising share of exports and imports in the GDP of virtually every country. In the past 15 years, cross-border financial flows have grown even more rapidly than trade flows. Foreign direct investment (in which foreign capital gains a controlling interest in a cross-border enterprise), in particular, has grown even more rapidly than overall capital flows.

The sharp rise in foreign direct investment underscores the enormous and increasing role of multinational corporations in global trade, and especially in global production. As scholars such as Peter Dicken have shown, with falling transport and communications costs, it is possible to "divide up the value chain" of production. Different stages of the production process of a single output can be carried out in different parts of the world, depending on the comparative advantages of alternative production sites. Semiconductor chips might be designed in the United States, where the basic wafers are also produced; these are then cut and as-

sembled in Malaysia; and the final products are tested in and shipped from Singapore. These cross-border flows often occur within the same multinational firm. One stunning fact about current trade flows is that an estimated one-third of merchandise trade is actually composed of shipments among the affiliates of a single company, as opposed to arms-length transactions among separate exporters and importers.

The fourth major aspect of globalization is the increased harmonization of economic institutions. Part of this is a matter of imitation. Most of the developing world chose nonmarket, economic strategies of development upon independence after World War II. These state-led models of development came crashing down in the 1980s, followed by a massive shift toward market-based, private sector-led growth. Beyond mere imitation, however, has come a significant rise in international treaty obligations regarding trade, investment policy, tax policy, intellectual property rights, banking supervision, currency convertibility, foreign investment policy, and even the control of bribery. A growing web of treaties ties nations together through multilateral obligations (such as the G-7 group, with 132 member countries), regional obligations (the European Union and other trade blocs), and bilateral obligations (for example, binational tax treaties between the United States and dozens of other governments).

The Implications of Globalization

The implications of globalization for both the developed and developing countries are currently the subject of intensive research and heated policy debates. Four main sets of issues are now under investigation. First, will globalization promote faster economic growth, especially among the four-fifths of the world's population (4.5 billion people) still living in developing countries? Second, will globalization promote or undermine macroeconomic stability? Are the sudden and unexpected collapses of emerging market economies in recent years (such as Mexico in 1994 and East Asia in 1997) the result of deep flaws in the globalization process, or are they manageable, perhaps avoidable bumps in the road to greater prosperity? Third, will globalization promote growing income inequality, and, if so, is the problem limited to low-skilled workers in the advanced economies, or is this inequality a deeper result of intensifying market forces in all parts of the world? Fourth, how should governmental institutions at all levels—regional, national, and international—adjust their powers and responsibilities in view of the emergence of a global market?

Economic Growth

Adam Smith famously declared in the *Wealth of Nations* that "the discovery of America, and that of a passage to the East Indies by the Cape of Good Hope are the two greatest and most important events recorded in the history of mankind." He reasoned that by "uniting, in some measure, the most distant parts of the world, by enabling them to relieve one another's wants, to increase one another's enjoyments, and to encourage one another's industry, their general tendency would seem to be beneficial." The discoveries, of course, were not enough to guarantee these benefits. Smith himself recognized that the depredations of imperialism had deprived the native inhabitants of the New World and the East Indies of most of the benefits of globalization in his day. In our century, two world wars, the Great Depression, and 40 years of post–World War II protectionism in most of the developing world again frustrated Smith's vision of mutual gains from trade. Now, finally, can we envision the Smithian mechanism operating to worldwide advantage?

Much current theorizing on economic growth, such as the research by Gene Grossman and Elhanan Helpman, offers reasons for cheer. Smith's conjectures of dynamic gains to trade are at the core of many new mathematical models of "endogenous growth." These models stress that long-term growth depends on increased productivity and innovation, and that the incentives for both depend (as Smith conjectured) on the scope of the market. If innovators are selling into an expanded world market, they will generally have more incentive to innovate. If productivity is raised by refining the production process among a larger number of specialized sub-

units, and if each subunit faces fixed costs of production, then a larger market will allow these fixed costs to be spread over a larger production run.

One part of the argument has found strong empirical support in recent years. The fastest-growing developing countries in the past two decades have been those that succeeded in generating new export growth, especially in manufactured goods. Andrew Warner and I have demonstrated that economies that tried to go it alone by protecting their economies from imports through high trade barriers grew much less rapidly than more open export-oriented economies. Moreover, the manufactured exports of the developing countries have themselves exemplified the Smithian principle of division of labor. Steven Radelet and I found that in almost all cases of developing-country, export-led growth, the exports themselves have been part of a highly refined division of labor, in which final goods (e.g. automobiles, avionics, electronic machinery) are produced in multisite operations, with the labor-intensive parts of the production process reserved for the developing countries.

This kind of "new division of labor" in manufacturers was inconceivable to early postwar development economists such as Raul Prebisch, who counseled protectionism as the preferred path for industrialization in poor countries. These economists simply could not conceive of the production process being a complementary relationship between advanced and developing countries. In the standard theory, then, both sides of the great income divide stand to benefit from globalization: the developed countries by reaching a larger market for new innovations and the developing economies by enjoying the fruits of those innovations while sharing in global production via multinational enterprises.

Modern theorizing still stresses, however, that the gains in growth might not in fact be shared by all. Two major theoretical exceptions that do find some supporting empirical evidence are most often discussed. The first exception is based on geography. The gains from trade depend on the transport costs between a national economy and the rest of the world being low enough to permit an extensive interaction between the economy and world markets. If the economy is geographically isolated—for example, landlocked in the high Andes or the Himalayas or Central Africa, as in the cases of Bolivia, Nepal, and Rwanda—the chances for extensive trade are extremely limited. Also, as MIT economist Paul Krugman has shown, the combination of increasing returns to scale and high transport costs may cause economic activity to concentrate somewhat accidentally in some areas at the expense of others. Climate may also have serious adverse effects. Generally speaking, the tropics impose additional burdens of infectious disease and often poor agricultural conditions (involving soil, water, and pests) not found in the temperate zones. For these reasons, a significant portion of the world's population may face severe geographical obstacles to development, despite the overall beneficial effects of globalization.

The second major theoretical exception, recognized in development thinking at least since Alexander Hamilton's call for protection of nascent U.S. industry, is the risk that producers of natural resources might get "trapped" into an unsatisfactory specialization of trade, thereby delaying or blocking the improvements in industry necessary for economic development. Kiminori Matsuyama was among the first to formulate a mathematical model to test this idea. Early evidence, derived from studies Warner and I conducted, gives some support to the "dynamic Dutch Disease" effect. Dutch Disease occurs when a boom in the natural resources that a country exports causes a national currency to strengthen, thereby undermining the profitability of nonresource-based industries. (The name comes from the de-industrialization that allegedly followed Holland's development of North Sea gas fields in the 1960s.) The "dynamic" effect is the supposed long-term loss of growth coming from the specialization in primary goods (e.g. gas exports) rather than manufactured products, which supposedly offer better opportunities for long-term productivity growth.

The findings suggest that countries with large natural resource bases, such as the Persian Gulf oil exporters, find themselves uncompetitive in most

manufacturing sectors. This condition, in turn, seems to be consistent with lower long-term growth, possibly because manufacturing rather than primary production (agriculture and mining) offers better possibilities for innovation, learning by doing, and productivity improvement in the long term. Economic theory suggests that some form of nonmarket intervention—ranging from the protection of nascent industries to the subsidization of manufacturing—could have beneficial effects in these circumstances. The practicalities of such real-world interventions, however, are heatedly debated and open to question.

Macroeconomic Stability

In a famous cry of despair in the middle of the Great Depression, John Maynard Keynes, in his essay "National Self-Sufficiency," argued that economic entanglements through trade and finance added to global destabilization. He went so far as to declare "let goods be homespun whenever it is reasonably and conveniently possible; and, above all, let finance be primarily national."

After the depression, Keynes changed his mind and championed a postwar return to open trade based on convertible currencies. In his design of the new IMF, however, he kept to his view that financial flows ought to remain restricted so as to minimize the chance that international financial disturbances would create global macroeconomic instabilities. For this reason, the Articles of Agreement of the IMF call on member countries to maintain currencies that are convertible for current transactions (essentially trade and the repatriation of profits and interest) but not necessarily for capital flows.

As globalization has taken off in the past two decades, many forms of international capital flows have risen dramatically. Foreign direct investment, portfolio investment through country funds, bank loans, bond lending, derivatives (swaps, options, forward transactions), reinsurance, and other financial instruments, have all grown enormously. Both developed and developing countries have increasingly opened their capital markets to foreign participation. In 1997, the IMF endorsed a move toward amending the Articles of Agreement to call for open capital flows. The Organization for Economic Cooperation and Development, World Trade Organization (WTO), and Bank for International Settlements have also increasingly sought international standards for the liberalization and supervision of international investment flows.

Economic theory generally asserts that trade in financial assets will benefit individual countries in ways analogous to trade in goods. Financial transactions, in theory, allow two kinds of gains from trade: increased diversification of risk and intertemporal gains (a better ability to borrow and lend over time, more consistent with desired patterns of investment and consumption). The theory, however, also hints at some limits to this optimistic view, and the experience of international financial liberalization gives real reason for pause. Perhaps Keynes' skepticism should still apply, despite our supposedly much enhanced capability to identify and manage financial risks.

The real meaning of the Mexican crash and the East Asian financial crisis is still far from clear, but both experiences have shown that unfettered financial flows from advanced to emerging markets can create profound destabilization. The problem, it seems, is that financial markets are subject to certain key "market failures" that are exacerbated, rather than limited, by globalization. One kind of failure is the tendency of underregulated and undercapitalized banks to gamble recklessly with depositor funds, since from the owner/management point of view, bank profits accrue to themselves, while bank losses get stuck with the government. Thus, international financial liberalization of a poorly capitalized banking system is an invitation to overborrowing and eventual financial crisis.

The second kind of failure is financial panic, which comes when a group of creditors suddenly decides to withdraw loans from a borrower, out of fear that the other creditors are doing the same thing. Each lender flees for the exit because the last one out will lose his claims, assuming that the borrower does not have the liquid assets to cover a sudden withdrawal of loans. This kind of panic was once familiar in the form of bank runs, which used to afflict U.S. banks before the introduction of federal deposit insurance in 1934. It seems to be prevalent in international lending, especially in international bank loans to emerging markets. Both in Mexico in late 1994 and several East Asian economies in 1997 (Indonesia, Malaysia, the Philippines, and South Korea), once enthusiastic international bankers suddenly pulled the plug on new credits and the rollover of old credits. This withdrawal of funding sent the emerging markets into a tailspin, with falling production and the risk of outright international default. Emergency bailout loans led by the IMF aimed to block the defaults, but did not address the core causes of the crises.

These dramatic experiences are giving second thoughts in many quarters to the pressures for rapid liberalization of international capital flows. While the official Washington community still presses for liberalization of the capital market, voices are being raised for putting a "spanner in the works" to slow capital movements with an aim toward preventing financial market panics. Ideas include the taxation of international transactions (such as the famous proposal of James Tobin to tax foreign exchange transactions to deter short-term currency speculation, or Chile's taxation of capital inflows); the direct limitation of short-term bank borrowing from abroad as a banking supervisory standard; and increased disclosure rules. Both the theory and practice of capital market liberalization are therefore in limbo.

Income Distribution

Perhaps no aspect of globalization has been more controversial than the alleged effects of increased trade on income distribution. A series of claims are made that it is a major factor in increasing inequality, both in advanced and developing countries. Of course, within the United States, the main focus of debate is on advanced countries, especially the United States itself.

Over the past 25 years, international economics theory has mostly focused on two kinds of trade:

intra-industry and inter-industry. The first kind, in which the United States sells cars to Europe while also importing European cars, is ostensibly based on gains from specialization under conditions of increasing returns to scale. The United States could itself produce "European style" cars, so the argument goes, but chooses not to because it is less costly to have longer production runs of U.S. models, selling some of them to Europe to finance imports of the European models. Intra-industry trade, the theory holds, is a win-win situation for all. Consumers in both Europe and the United States enjoy an expanded range of products, and nobody suffers a loss of income, either absolute or relative.

Inter-industry trade involves the U.S. export of high technology goods to Asia, in return for inexpensive labor-intensive goods imported from Asia. In this case, trade is motivated by differing factor proportions. The United States produces goods that are intensive in physical capital and skills—advanced telecommunications equipment, for example—and imports goods that are intensive in labor, such as footwear and apparel. The theory suggests that both regions can gain overall from this kind of trade, though workers within each country may well lose. In the United States, for example, workers in the footwear and apparel sectors may lose their jobs in the face of increased low-wage competition, while skilled workers in Asia could conceivably lose out when skill-intensive goods are imported from the United States. More generally, according to basic Heckscher-Ohlin-Samuelson trade theory, unskilled U.S. workers may suffer relative and even absolute income declines, while skilled workers in the developing countries could similarly suffer a loss of relative and/or absolute income.

Since intra-industry trade is generally strongest among similar-income countries (e.g. U.S./European trade), while inter-industry trade is strongest among dissimilar countries (e.g. U.S./developing Asia), the income-distributional ramifications of trade between rich and poor countries are ostensibly more threatening to particular social groups, a point stressed early on by Krugman. It is therefore the increasing linkages of rich and poor countries

that have become the cornerstone of political challenges to globalization.

Despite the hard work of researchers, there is still no consensus on the effects of the globalized economy on income distribution within the advanced and emerging markets. Clearly, the period of dramatic globalization (especially during the 1980s and 1990s) has also been one of rising income inequality within the United States, and especially of a loss of relative income for low-skilled workers, consistent with basic trade theory. However, as with many important economic phenomena, the cause of this widening income inequality is almost surely multifaceted. While trade might be one culprit, changes in technology such as the computer revolution might also favor skilled workers over unskilled ones, thereby contributing to the rising inequality. Most researchers agree that a combination of factors has played a role in the widening inequality, and the majority of them, including Krugman and Robert Lawrence, put the preponderant weight on technology rather than trade. They do this for one main reason: The share of U.S. workers that are in direct competition with low-skilled workers in the emerging markets seems to be too small to explain the dramatic widening of inequalities since the end of the 1970s. Less than 5 percent of the U.S. labor market—in apparel, footwear, toys, assembly operations, and the like—appears to be in the "direct line of fire" of low-wage goods from Asia. If the United States is already out of the low-skill industries, then increased globalization in such goods cannot widen inequalities in the United States, and, in fact, would tend to benefit all households by offering less expensive consumer goods.

One problem with such estimates, however, is that they tend to be based on rather simple theoretical models of international trade. Conventional trade measures may not pick up the additional channels through which globalization affects income distribution. Some researchers argue, for example, that increased globalization limits the ability of union workers to achieve a "union wage premium" in collective bargaining because of the risk that firms will simply move overseas in response to higher union wages. Thus, the opening of international trade may have changed the bargaining power of workers vis-à-vis capital in ways not measured by trade flows. More generally, the export of capital to low-wage countries can exacerbate inequalities caused by increased trade. Researchers have not yet uncovered large effects on wages and income distribution through these additional channels, but the scholarship devoted to these topics is still rather sparse.

Some sporadic evidence suggests that growing inequalities are not simply a problem of developed economies but also of developing economies. If the salary premium of skilled workers is rising in both developing and developed economies, something more than inter-industry trade effects are at work. Part of the story could be technological change. Another possible factor (suggested recently by Robert Frank and Philip Cook) is that globalization is supporting a new "winner-take-all" approach in labor markets. The argument holds that skilled workers of all kinds, whether in sports, industry, science, or entertainment, find an expanding world market for their skills, while unskilled workers see no particular gains in an expanding market. Therefore, the scale of the world market would affect skilled workers differently from unskilled ones, leading to a worldwide rise in the market premium for skills. This hypothesis remains as yet almost completely unexamined empirically.

Economic Governance

Without question, globalization is having a deep effect on politics at many levels. Most important, the national marketplace is losing its salience relative to international markets. This is causing a sea change in the role of the nation-state, relative to both local and regional governments on the one side, and multinational political institutions on the other.

In Smith's day, part of the market revolution was the removal of barriers to trade within nations and proto-nations. The freeing of trade among the German states in the Zollverein of 1834, and then the full unification of the German market with the establishment of the German Reich in 1871, exemplify the historical process. In most cases, nineteenth-century market capitalism and the importance of the national marketplace rose hand in hand, even as international trade was itself expanding. Generally speaking, the spread of capitalism within Europe, Japan, and North America gave impetus to the increasing importance of the national economy and thereby of the national government.

At the end of the twentieth century, the national market is being increasingly displaced by the international marketplace. After decades of experimentation, almost all countries have realized that the national market is simply too small to permit an efficient level of production in most areas of industry and even in many areas of services. Efficient production must be geared instead toward world markets. Moreover, globalization has proved a catalyst for internationally agreed-upon rules of behavior in trade, finance, taxation, and many other areas, thus prompting the rise of the WTO and other international institutions as the new bulwarks of the emerging international system. At the same time, communities, local governments, and regions within nations are increasingly asserting their claims to cultural and political autonomy. The nation is no longer their economic protector, and in peaceful regions of the world, the national government is no longer seen as a critical instrument of security. Consequently, regions as far-flung as Catalonia, Northern Italy, Quebec, and Scotland, as well as oblasts in Russia, provinces in China, and states in India, have taken globalization as their cue to pursue greater autonomy within the nation-state.

We are therefore in the midst of a startling, yet early, tug of war between polities at all levels. Where will the future of decision making, tax powers, and regulatory authorities reside: with localities, subnational regions, nation-states, or multilateral institutions (both within geographic regions such as the European Union and at the international level)? To the extent that increased regulatory, tax, and even judicial powers shift to the international setting, how should and will international institutions be governed in the future? Will there be a democracy deficit, as is now charged about decision making in the European Union? What will be the balance of political power between the developed and developing countries, especially as population and economic balances shift over time in favor of the new developing world? And crucially, what will be the balance of power between democratic and non-democratic polities at the world level? All of these issues are fresh, urgent, and likely to loom large on the research radar screens.

VIRGINIA POSTREL   II.2

The One Best Way

Virginia Postrel is the editor of *Reason* magazine and a regular columnist for *Forbes*. This selection, taken from her book *The Future and Its Enemies,* takes on the chorus of "techno-pessimism" rising from both the political Left and Right and argues for an optimistic view of an open technological future.

Postrel develops a contrast between "stasist reactionaries," those who seek stability, predictability, and control, and "dynamists," those who welcome change, innovation, and an open future. She points to many examples of how contemporary political debates turn out to "take place between competing technocratic schemes," and how they amount to competing schemes of how to impose order and predictability on what is in fact an open and dynamic system. Dynamists, on the other hand, "are often drawn to biological metaphors, symbols of unpredictable growth and change, variety, and of experiment, feedback, and adaptation." And although "stasists see nothing but trouble in the exuberant, unruly, kaleidoscopic, post–Cold War world—with its fluid international trade, border-leaping communications, and ever-more audacious scientific discoveries—dynamists are delighted." For dynamists the evolving world order cannot be controlled by a humanly constructed plan, but will develop in a decentralized fashion through a process of experimentation, adaptation, feedback, and creative destruction of the old. An unpredictable and uncontrolled process of innovation is not something to fear: It is something to embrace. It is just part of the wild joy-ride into the future that scientific and technological ingenuity has been giving us for the past several centuries, and it is what will carry us into a future ripe with possibilities that we cannot now imagine.

Focus Questions

1. What are the characteristics of the unusual Left/Right alliances that Postrel discusses?
2. Where do you stand politically on the various contemporary issues mentioned in this reading? Are you personally more attracted to the "stasist" or the "dynamist" point of view?

Keywords

deregulation, free trade, national health care, planned economies, the Progressive Era, scientific management, Sierra Club, technocrats

ONE OF THE MOST COMMON RITUALS in American political life is the television debate between right and left. Producers round up conservative and liberal representatives and set them to arguing with each other: about the federal budget, campaign finance, gun control, or whatever other issue is hot that particular day. Since the purpose is as much to entertain as to inform, and since many shows like to feature politicians, these debates tend to be predictable. They rehash familiar arguments, repeat familiar sound bites, and confirm traditional views of the political landscape.

Nowhere is the ritual more established than on CNN's *Crossfire*. The hosts and their guests are stuffed into familiar boxes—even positioned on the right or left of the TV screen according to political convention—and are expected to behave predictably.

Which is why the first *Crossfire* of 1995 was so remarkable.

For starters, the subject was an unusual one for a Washington show: the future. Not the future of the new Republican-led Congress or of welfare reform or of Bill Clinton's political career, but the future in general. The guests were Jeremy Rifkin, the well-known antitechnology activist, and Ed Cornish, the president of the World Future Society. Rifkin sat on the left, aligned with Michael Kinsley; Cornish on the right, aligned with Pat Buchanan.

Or at least that was how the producers planned it. That was how conventional politics prescribed it. Rifkin, the former antiwar protester and darling of environmentalists, clearly belongs to the left. Cornish, a technophile, becomes a right-winger by default. And hosts Kinsley and Buchanan were, of course, hired for their political positions.

But as soon as the discussion began, the entire format broke down. Buchanan and Rifkin turned out to be soulmates. Rifkin answered Buchanan's opening question with a fearful description of "this new global high-tech economy" as a cruel destroyer

of jobs. "You sound like a Pat Buchanan column," replied his interrogator. "I agree."

Both men were deeply pessimistic about the future, upset about changes in the world of work, and desperate to find government policies to restore the good old days. Both spoke resentfully of the "knowledge sector." Neither had anything good to say about new technologies. Neither could imagine how ordinary people could possibly cope with economic changes. "There are many, many Americans who are not equipped to do this kind of work. They're the ones losing their jobs," said Buchanan. Responded Rifkin: "Let me say I find myself in a position of agreeing with Pat once again, which gives me alarm, but I really do agree with you on this one."

It was surely a bad day for the *Crossfire* bookers. They had managed to call the show's entire premise into question. How could such a thing happen? How could *Crossfire* become a love-in between Jeremy Rifkin and Pat Buchanan?

The problem lay not in the bookers' Rolodexes but in the conventional categories. Like a geographical territory, our political, cultural, and intellectual landscape can be divided many different ways. The features may be fairly stable, but the boundary lines change. A defining question in one era—whether to nationalize the railroads, give women the vote, outlaw racial segregation, or abolish the draft—may be settled, and therefore meaningless, in another. Or questions may be important to individuals without creating meaningful political divisions: Nowadays, "conservatives" may support careers for women, and "liberals" may back the death penalty; not since Walter Mondale's disastrous presidential bid have Democrats made raising taxes a defining "liberal" position. Similarly, the economic issues that have divided the American political landscape matter little in Israel, where defense and foreign policy dominate the debate.

Once upon a time, before the Berlin Wall came down, Buchanan and Rifkin did indeed belong on opposite sides of the *Crossfire* table. Whatever agreements they might have had about the evils of corporate restructuring, the dangers of new technologies, or the rigidity of job skills paled in com-

Reprinted with permission of The Free Press, a Division of Simon & Schuster from *The Future and Its Enemies* by Virginia Postrel. © 1998 by Virginia Postrel. Footnotes omitted. Interested readers should consult the original.

parison to their fundamental disagreements about how to deal with the Soviet Union. That defining issue has now vanished, and others have faded. Government spending is no longer seen, even by most liberals who support it, as a simple solution to the problems of poverty. Nor do conservatives all agree that expansive military spending and vigorous engagement abroad are the best approach to American defense. There are plenty of practical policy differences over such issues, but they no longer define clear ideological camps. People can change their minds without changing their political identities.

Meanwhile, seemingly strange alliances have popped up on subjects no one paid much attention to until recently. Treaties to loosen trade restrictions, once uncontroversial beyond a few protection-seeking industries, draw fierce opposition from a left-right coalition that includes both Rifkin and Buchanan. Indeed, the subtitle of Buchanan's latest book is *How American Sovereignty and Social Justice Are Being Sacrificed to the Gods of the Global Economy,* a bid to woo both "conservatives" (worried about "sovereignty") and "liberals" (concerned about "social justice"). In its lobbying efforts, the antitrade alliance emphasizes its apparent breadth; it has described itself as "a strikingly broad cross-section" and the "broadest range of [the] American political spectrum ever to jointly petition a president." In 1994, for example, a motley collection of activists—including not only Buchanan and Rifkin but consumerist Ralph Nader and New Right organizer Paul Weyrich, feminist Gloria Steinem and antifeminist Phyllis Schlafly—all signed a letter opposing the General Agreement on Tariffs and Trade.

Immigration attracts similar left-right opposition. In 1998, many leftists were shocked when the Sierra Club held a membership vote on whether to take an official stance supporting "an end to U.S. population growth . . . through reduction in net immigration," essentially an immigration moratorium. "Zealots Target Sierra Club," read a headline in the left-leaning *L.A. Weekly.* "The specter of xenophobic anti-immigrant sentiment now threatens to swallow the Green movement whole," said the article. (The measure was defeated, 60 percent to 40

percent.) The movement to drastically curtail U.S. legal immigration levels has vocal conservative supporters, including Buchanan, former *National Review* senior editor Peter Brimelow, and Reagan administration immigration commissioner Alan Nelson. But the Sierra Club measure was supported by such leading environmentalists as Worldwatch Institute head Lester Brown, Earth Day founder Gaylord Nelson, former Interior Secretary Stewart Udall, and Earth First! founder Dave Foreman. The foremost anti-immigration group, the Federation for American Immigration Reform, was founded by population-control advocates from the green movement. And many smaller anti-immigration groups, such as the Carrying Capacity Network, draw almost entirely from the environmentalist left.

We have also seen increasing numbers of "conservatives" and "liberals" uniting in opposition to new technologies. Thus Neil Postman, the left-wing media and technology critic, writes in the neoconservative magazine *First Things* that "our technological ingenuity transformed information into a form of garbage, and ourselves into garbage collectors. . . . Information is now a commodity that is bought and sold." To oppose genetic patents, Rifkin, in 1995, rallied nearly two hundred religious leaders, prominently including representatives of the conservative Southern Baptist Convention. Self-styled neo-Luddite Kirkpatrick Sale, a well-known environmentalist, concludes antitechnology speeches by smashing computers with a sledgehammer; the cover of the conservative *Weekly Standard* magazine features a sledgehammer crashing into a computer screen, with the headline "Smash the Internet."

Economic and cultural dynamism get similar treatment. The *Standard* praises cultural critic Tom Frank, an anticommerce leftist, for promoting the idea that "both free speech and a free market did much to democratize values and attitudes that previous generations would have largely dismissed as pernicious or infantile." Attacking management guru Tom Peters for his emphasis on change, flexibility, and innovation, Frank himself waxes conservative. He denounces markets for disrupting the social order: "Capitalism is no longer said [by management thinkers] to be a matter of enforcing order, but of destroying it. This new commercial ethos, not a few movies and rap albums, is the root cause of the unease many Americans feel about the culture around them." Former Clinton aide William Galston praises Republican Bill Bennett for his attacks on market-driven popular culture: "The invisible hand," says Galston, "no more reliably produces a sound cultural environment than it does a sound natural environment."

What all these left-right alliances have in common is a sense of anguish over the open-ended future: a future that no Galston, Bennett, Frank, or Buchanan can control or predict, a future too diverse and fluid for critics to comprehend. Their anguish is not always coherent, nor is it expected to be. If statist criticisms are impossibly vague, they seem all the more profound. What matters is the general message: The world has gone terribly wrong, and someone needs to take control and make things right.

"The task of finding true meaning in a hyper-technological and increasingly pointless society becomes ever more difficult. A gnawing feeling of hopelessness grows from the sense that living as a hero, or heroine, in one's own life is no longer possible," writes Gary Chapman, the former executive director of Computer Professionals for Social Responsibility and now a technology critic. "The all-pervasive 'system' we've created closes off both the value of ordinary virtue and any escape routes. . . . How do we smash this particular system and build an alternative we can be proud of?"

A mere three decades ago, "the system" looked very different. Technology, its critics believed, was oppressive; even its supporters said it demanded predictability and order. Back then, what young leftists like Chapman wanted to smash was not the dynamic, out-of-control future but the static, hyper-controlled present. Technocracy and repression, not dynamism and creativity, were the enemy embodied in technology. Conventional wisdom had declared the market an obsolete myth, too fragmented and unpredictable to manage or produce advanced technology. Bigness, stability, and planning ruled the imagination of sophisticates.

To see how dramatically attitudes have changed, consider the following 1974 news report on the Nixon administration's plans to deal with energy shortages:

What happens when spring's heavy driving begins depends on when word can be passed to U.S. refineries to start cutting back on production of heating oil and increasing output of gasoline. . . . That decision, which could come at any time, is up to Federal Energy Office chief William E. Simon. One of his aides says:

"It's absolutely critical. If we decide to trigger the switch to gasoline and a long cold wave hits, heating-oil stocks might not last to spring. Heaven help us if we're wrong."

Meanwhile Simon and his staff are putting finishing touches on the Administration's gasoline-rationing plan. . . .

The number of gallons a driver would be allotted is to depend on where he lives. Those in rural areas, or in urban communities of less than 100,000 people, would get the most. Drivers in large cities with good mass transit would get the least.

Present estimates by the Federal Energy Office show a gasoline shortage of 1.2 million barrels a day, or about 20 per cent below normal demand. At that rate, officials say the maximum ration per driver would be 41 gallons a month. Residents of cities with fair mass-transit facilities would get 37 gallons, while those in areas with good mass transit would get 33 gallons.

As a description of the U.S. government at work—under a Republican administration, no less—this perfectly routine news story reads like science fiction. Only a quarter-century ago, however, it was an obvious truth that central bureaucrats could efficiently decide when refineries should switch from heating oil to gasoline and could wisely allocate gasoline supplies, carefully differentiating between drivers who needed thirty-seven gallons a month and those who required forty-one. Such technocratic manipulations were not limited to Soviet-style planning.

"The enemies of the market are . . . not the socialists," wrote the economist John Kenneth

Galbraith in his influential 1967 book, *The New Industrial State*. "It is advanced technology and the specialization of men and process that this requires and the resulting commitment of time and capital. These make the market work badly when the need is for greatly enhanced reliability—when planning is essential." We lived, critics and supporters agreed, in what Galbraith called "the technostructure," an oligopolistic industrial state where the future was carefully planned in advance, either through government or private bureaucracy. "With the rise of the modern corporation," wrote Galbraith, "the emergence of the organization required by modern technology and planning and the divorce of the owner of the capital from control of the enterprise, the entrepreneur no longer exists as an individual person in the mature industrial enterprise."

In the era of Bill Gates, Ted Turner, and Andy Grove, no one much believes that any more. The efficient capital markets and entrepreneurship that Galbraith consigned to the crazed imagination of free-market ideologues are all too real and disruptive. Contrary to his confident claims, technology generates change, not predictability, and corporations cherish flexibility, leanness, and just-in-time management. The small and adaptable flourish. And the quest for freedom and authenticity that once inspired many of Chapman's friends on the left has mutated into the cultural—and business—dynamism that today disconcerts stasists from Pat Buchanan and Bill Bennett to Jeremy Rifkin and Tom Frank.

Our new awareness of how dynamic the world really is has united two types of stasists who would have once been bitter enemies: *reactionaries,* whose central value is stability, and *technocrats,* whose central value is control. Reactionaries seek to reverse change, restoring the literal or imagined past and holding it in place. A few decades ago, they aimed their criticism at Galbraithean technocracy. Today they attack dynamism, often in alliance with their former adversaries. Technocrats, for their part, promise to manage change, centrally directing "progress" according to a predictable plan. (That plan may be informed by reactionary values, making the categories somewhat blurry; al-

though they are more technocrats than true reactionaries, Bennett and Galston inhabit the border regions.) Despite their shared devotion to stasis, reactionaries and technocrats are sufficiently distinct that it makes sense to examine each category separately.

Buchanan expresses reactionary ideas when he yearns for "the kind of social stability, rootedness . . . we all used to know," the world in which his father lived in the same place and worked at the same job his whole life. International trade, he warns, disrupts that stability and should be controlled. In his book *The Way,* the influential British green Edward Goldsmith similarly emphasizes stability, imagining a quiet and peaceful past in contrast to dynamic, progress-driven modernity: "It is the failure of modern man to observe the constraints necessary for maintaining the integrity and stability of the various social and ecological systems of which he is a part that is giving rise to their disintegration and destabilization, of which the increased incidence of discontinuities such as wars, massacres, droughts, floods, famines, epidemics and climatic change are but the symptoms."

On a more violent note, the Unabomber echoes countless environmentalist tracts: "For primitive societies the natural world (which usually changes only slowly) provided a stable framework and therefore a sense of security. In the modern world it is human society that dominates nature rather than the other way around, and modern society changes very rapidly owing to technological change. Thus there is no stable framework. . . . The technologies are taking us all on an utterly reckless ride into the unknown."

Technocrats, by contrast, are less likely to emphasize the problem of social instability when they criticize the unruly vitality of contemporary life. They do not celebrate the primitive or traditional. Rather, they worry about the government's inability to control dynamism. Their nostalgia is for the era of Galbraithean certainties. In a 1997 essay for *Foreign Affairs,* the historian Arthur Schlesinger, Jr., condemns the "onrush of capitalism" for its "disruptive consequences." While the economist Joseph Schumpeter depicted the "creative destruction" of the market as a strength, emphasizing its creativity,

Schlesinger sees it as a horror. He warns of dire results from the dynamism of global trade and new technologies:

> The computer turns the untrammeled market into a global juggernaut crashing across frontiers, enfeebling national powers of taxation and regulation, undercutting national management of interest rates and exchange rates, widening disparities of wealth both within and between nations, dragging down labor standards, degrading the environment, denying nations the shaping of their own economic destiny, accountable to no one, creating a world economy without a world polity.

Across the Atlantic, the French bureaucrat-turned-consultant Jacques Attali warns that "the market economy today is more dynamic than democracy" and that its dynamism is dangerous. Abetted by the decentralizing power of the Internet and the mobility of "high-tech nomads," he argues, the dynamic marketplace erodes the ability of political elites to enforce collective decisions—a power he equates with "democracy": "Under such circumstances, Western civilization is bound to collapse." What terrifies technocrats is not that the future will depart from a traditional ideal but that it will be unpredictable and beyond the control of professional wise men.

The characteristic values of reactionaries are continuity, rootedness, and geographically defined community. They are generally anticosmopolitan, antitechnology, anticommercial, antispecialization, and antimobility. They draw on a powerful romantic tradition that gives their politics a poetic, emotional appeal, especially to people with literary sensibilities. With some exceptions, they oppose not only the future but the present and the recent past, the industrial as well as the postindustrial era. The reactionary vision is one of peasant virtues, of the imagined harmonies and, above all, the imagined predictability of traditional life. It idealizes life without movement. In the reactionary ideal, people know and keep their places, geographically as well as socially, and tradition is undisturbed by ambition or invention. "The central concept of wisdom is permanence," wrote E. F. Schumacher, the environmentalist guru, in *Small Is Beautiful.*

In part because they do not fit neatly into left-right categories, reactionary thinkers are rarely acknowledged in conventional discussions. But their ideas regularly turn up in books from major publishers, in influential magazines such as *Harper's* and *The Atlantic Monthly,* and on the opinion pages of leading newspapers. Their work shapes the worldview of the yuppie-green consumers of the *Utne Reader* and of the trade-hawk followers of Pat Buchanan. The most hackneyed speech about "sustainable development," "national sovereignty," or "preserving community" is but one or two footnotes away from the work of reactionary intellectuals such as Schumacher.

Although they represent a minority position, reactionary ideas have tremendous cultural vitality. Reactionaries speak directly to the most salient aspects of contemporary life: technological change, commercial fluidity, biological transformation, changing social roles, cultural mixing, international trade, and instant communication. They see these changes as critically important, and, as the old *National Review* motto had it, they are determined to "stand athwart history, yelling, 'Stop!'" Merely by acknowledging the dynamism of contemporary life, reactionaries win points for insight. And in the eyes of more conventional thinkers, denouncing change makes them seem wise.

By personal history or political background, many reactionaries are classified as leftists. Whether cultural critics or environmentalists, however, that label fits them awkwardly. Their tradition-bound views of the good life make them true conservatives. And they frequently voice disappointment that their views aren't shared by mainstream Republicans. The late social critic Christopher Lasch, a scourge of the left from which he came, complained, "A movement calling itself conservative might have been expected to associate itself with the demand for limits not only on economic growth but on the conquest of space, the technological conquest of the environment, and the ungodly ambition to acquire godlike powers over nature. Reaganites, however, condemned the demand for limits as another counsel of doom."

As Buchanan's political career suggests, however, there is indeed a strong reactionary strain among elements of the Cold War right. Fred Iklé, the undersecretary of defense for policy in the very Reagan administration Lasch denounces, now attacks as "Jacobins" those conservatives who support "the philosophy of perpetual growth" and scorns as "xenophilia" the notion that individuals should ideally be free to trade across national borders. He laments that "the intellectuals' jubilation throughout the world about our ever-expanding, homogenizing, perpetually-GNP-increasing global market creates a sense of inevitability even among the wisest of conservative thinkers." Another conservative defense intellectual, Edward N. Luttwak, calls for "re-regulation and other measures to stabilize the economy, thus favoring *Gemeinschaft* over efficient *Gesellschaft*"—traditional, geographically settled life over cosmopolitan choice and fluidity. He endorses the Unabomber's critique of conservatives as "fools [who] whine about the decay of traditional values, yet they enthusiastically support technological progress and economic growth."

Similarly, the journalist Charlotte Allen excoriates fellow conservatives who support the "creative destruction" of market processes. She writes in the liberal *Washington Monthly*:

> Most of today's conservatives refuse to support the traditional social and economic arrangements—small towns, extended families, generational roots, secure livelihoods, and respect for the land—that create the stability in which a sense of duty to others thrives. Instead, conservatives function as shills for big business and, as if America weren't already the most prosperous country on Earth, "growth"—a perpetual frenzy of economic development designed to make life ever more expensive and transform people into slaves of consumption.

By "support" traditional arrangements, Allen does not mean simply "favor" or "adhere to" but rather "enforce through political action." Among her prescriptions: "Conservatives should work to destroy agribusiness" and "don't let Wal-Mart wreck *your* downtown." Both issues have in fact catalyzed coalitions of reactionaries from the "left" and the "right."

Intellectually, the roots of many conservative reactionaries lie in the antimodern writings of traditionalists such as Russell Kirk and the Southern Agrarians of the 1920s and 1930s, who anticipated many green arguments against the open-ended future: "The tempo of the industrial life is fast, but that is not the worst of it; it is accelerating," complained the Agrarians in their 1930 manifesto, *I'll Take My Stand*. "The ideal is not merely some set form of industrialism, with so many stable industries, but industrial progress, or an incessant extension of industrialization. *It never proposes a specific goal; it initiates the infinite series*" (emphasis added).

This reactionary fear of the "infinite series" produces a conservativism more familiar to Europeans than to Americans. Unlike the striving descendants of American pioneers, wrote John Crowe Ransom in *I'll Take My Stand,* Europeans "have elected to live their comparatively easy and routine lives in accordance with the tradition which they inherited, and they have consequently enjoyed a leisure, a security, and an intellectual freedom that were never the portion of pioneers. The pioneering life is not the normal life, whatever some Americans may suppose." (Such "comparatively easy and routine lives" are, of course, the privilege of a static upper class, while the "pioneering life" assumes upward mobility.)

Stasist reactionaries have in fact made greater inroads among British and European conservatives than among Americans. Before his death in 1997, the Anglo-French billionaire Sir James Goldsmith—known in the the 1980s as a swashbuckling takeover artist and political Tory—had become a prominent opponent of international trade, immigration, and Third World development, arguing that such dynamic forces are too disruptive of traditional societies. His manifesto *Le Piège (The Trap)* was a best-seller in France. "Families are broken, the countryside is deserted and social stability in towns is destroyed" when modern agriculture increases crop yields, he wrote. Goldsmith's brother Edward, the author of *The Way* and founder of *The Ecologist* magazine, shares Sir James's antitrade, antitechnology views but not his conservative political associations. On a more scholarly note, the Oxford philosopher John Gray, whom James

Goldsmith thanks as one of his advisers and who in turn praises Edward Goldsmith's *The Way* for its attack on progress, has called for an alliance between greens and conservatives.

Such ideas are indeed influential among environmentalists, who include most of the reactionaries of the "left." (Some leftist reactionaries, such as Rifkin, actually engage a broad range of issues, but are often called "environmentalists" for lack of a better term.) Most green theorists, as opposed to garden-variety Sierra Club members or Washington-based lobbyists and regulators, are reactionaries. Their ruling metaphor for the ideal society is that of an ecosystem that has reached an unchanging "climax" stage where its flora and fauna remain constant. Environmental historian Donald Worster thus idealizes "a stable, enduring rural society in equilibrium with the processes of nature" and deplores the "constant innovation, constant change, constant adjustment [that] have become the normal experience of this culture."

Green reactionaries celebrate premodern and, in some cases, prehistoric life. "Back to the Pleistocene!" is a popular, semiserious slogan among radical greens. Edward Goldsmith writes romantically of hunter-gatherer societies with "no history" and, he presumes, with no "wars, invasions, massacres, revolutions, assassinations, and intrigues." He marvels at the stability of these cultures: "During the old stone age, for instance, flint-chipping techniques did not change for some 200,000 years." In his many books, the sledgehammer-wielding Kirkpatrick Sale praises various prehistoric cultures, including "the Paleolithic hunter-gatherers of prehistory—the 'cavemen.'"

"The darkness is all around us: it is called industrial civilization," says Sale. In his 1980 book *Human Scale,* Sale proposed the ideal of self-sufficient towns of five thousand to ten thousand residents, arguing that self-sufficiency—the absence of any trade with the outside world—helps a community "to create stability and balance and predictability." Rifkin, a moderate by comparison, envisions cities that "once again return to their preindustrial size of 50,000 to 100,000 citizens," and an autarkic economy. In his ideal world, if a product "cannot be made locally by the community, using readily avail-

able resources and technology, then it is most likely unnecessary that it be produced at all."

The friendly, popular version of this ideal is the "radical localism" espoused by Sierra Club president Adam Werbach, a self-described former "Valley boy" who calls for "self-sufficiency" without sacrifice. He wouldn't ban wheat from Cape Cod or much of anything from Los Angeles, but, he writes, "We should demand that the Safeway in Idaho carry only native potatoes. And we should draw the line when department stores bottom out prices, muscle out local businesses, and eradicate local culture." Once transformed into a platform bland enough for yuppie consumption, the stability of self-sufficiency becomes the stability of economic protectionism. The goal is to eliminate price-cutting competition, tacky merchandise, and international trade. Along these lines, Werbach zealously attacks Wal-Mart, which sells, he says, "row upon row of imported, low-quality junk—anything you might need for your work, home, or pleasure."

Even in Werbach's suburbanized vision, however, the ideal remains the static peasant village, where "whatever is produced in the village must be used, first and foremost, by the members of the village." This peasant ideal—the good life imagined as hand-spinning and subsistence farming—runs through much green thought. Drawn originally from the writings of Mohandis Gandhi, it was popularized by one of the most influential environmentalist works ever, *Small Is Beautiful.* In that book, E. F. Schumacher praises peasant societies, singling out Burma in particular, for having less "pressure and strain of living" than developed countries. He sharply criticizes modern transportation and communications for making people "footloose":

> Everything in this world has to have a *structure,* otherwise it is chaos. Before the advent of mass transport and mass communications, the structure was simply there, because people were relatively immobile. . . . Now a great deal of structure has collapsed, and a country is like a big cargo ship in which the load is in no way secured. It tilts, and all the load slips over, and the ship founders. . . . Everything and everybody

has become mobile. All structures are threatened, and all structures are *vulnerable* to an extent that they have never been before.

Lurking in the background, such reactionary attitudes exercise a powerful, though sometimes indirect, influence on most discussions of environmental policy. And they help explain trends that have puzzled observers who see environmentalism as simply a "left-wing" phenomenon. A cultural–political movement opposed to mobility and change will, over time, come to support restrictions on immigration, technology, and trade, regardless of what its leftist allies think.

It may even come to extol values and people "the left" has traditionally scorned. The Marxist historian Eugene Genovese, once a supporter of Soviet socialism, now praises the southern conservative tradition represented by the Agrarians as the "most impressive native-born critique of our national development, of liberalism, and of the more disquieting features of the modern world." Among its other virtues, he notes, southern traditionalism has been "critical of capitalism's cash-nexus, recognizing it as a revolutionary solvent of social relations."

Looking at a different traditionalist model, Lasch wrote fondly of the parochialism of urban ethnic neighborhoods:

Lower-middle-class culture, now as in the past, is organized around the family, church, and neighborhood. It values the community's continuity more highly than individual advancement, solidarity more highly than social mobility. Conventional ideals of success play a less important part in lower-middle-class life than the maintenance of existing ways. . . . [Anthony] Lukas [in his chronicle of the Boston busing battles] contrasted the "Charlestown ethic of getting by" with the "American imperative to get ahead." The people of Charlestown, deserted by the migration of more amibitious neighbors to the suburbs, had renounced "opportunity, advancement, adventure" for the "reassurance of community, solidarity, and camaraderie."

Buchanan's stump speeches and columns similarly invoke the stability of such neighborhoods and of

industrial work—the Washington parish of his childhood, the steel mills of western Pennsylvania, the forges and factories of the industrial heartland. And Buchanan inspires disconcerted praise on the left: "I've been waiting my whole life for someone running for president to talk about the Fortune 500 as the enemy," *Village Voice* writer Tom Carson told him, "and when I finally get my wish, it turns out to be you."

As Buchanan illustrates, in practical political terms the craving for stability translates most prominently into reactionary alliances against freer international trade—a stasist cause that neatly aligns the nationalism of Buchananites with the anticommerce instincts of greens. (It also draws ordinary interest-group support from unions and protection-seeking industries.) Analyzing the 1997 defeat of a bill to extend the president's "fast track" authority to negotiate trade agreements, *New Republic* writer Peter Beinart found many seemingly strange currents:

I interviewed Congressman Cliff Stearns, a hard right, anti–fast track Florida Republican who last year held a press conference with Pat Buchanan to oppose the Mexican bailout. "The administration cannot make the argument that the North American Free Trade Agreement [NAFTA] has been a winner," he said. "Public Citizen says 500,000 jobs have been lost." I wasn't sure that I had heard him correctly. "You're quoting Public Citizen, Ralph Nader's group?" I asked. "Oh," he replied, "let's not use that." Then, 30 seconds later, he noted that "the Economic Policy Institute says 11,300 jobs have been lost in Florida [as a result of NAFTA]." The Economic Policy Institute is a liberal think tank heavily funded by unions.

The exchange points to the most peculiar aspect of the nationalist transformation. In myriad small ways, the boundaries between right-wing anti–free traders and left-wing anti–free traders are blurring. . . . Last year, Pat Choate [a leading trade critic and Ross Perot's running mate in 1996] convinced the United Auto Workers to put up money for the United Broadcasting Network (UBN). The network, which now reaches 200 markets, boasts shows hosted by [Pat's sister] Bay Buchanan; nationalist San Diego Republican Duncan Hunter; Representative Marcy Kaptur, a passionate anti–fast track Democrat from Toledo; and populist Jim Hightower, the former Democratic Agriculture Commissioner of Texas.

Despite intense lobbying by both the Clinton administration and the Republican congressional leadership, fast track went down to a shocking defeat, beaten by a reactionary coalition that defied the old categories.

Such victories are relatively rare, because the full reactionary package is a tough sell in contemporary America. Even trade protection, which enjoys support from interest groups that stand to benefit, has proven a consistent loser in presidential campaigns. And few people want to smash their computers, give-up off-season fruits and vegetables, turn their backs on modern medicine, move in with their cousins and in-laws, or forgo higher incomes. Even fewer resonate to slogans like "Back to the Pleistocene!" But if, like Allen and Werbach, you want to stifle agribusiness and shut down Wal-Mart; if, like Schumacher and Sale, you want to make people less footloose and limit the size of cities; if, like Rifkin, you want to ban genetic engineering or, like Buchanan, you want to keep out foreign people and foreign goods; if, like Frank and Bennett, you want to rein in advertising and control popular culture, you can find powerful allies—and a friendly political system. If exhortation and polemics aren't enough to rally the public to voluntarily adopt your favored form of stasis, government help is available. Ever since the Progressive Era, when Theodore Roosevelt defined the mission of public officials as "to look ahead and plan out the right kind of civilization," technocrats have dominated American politics. And technocrats know how to stop things.

Running for reelection in 1996, Bill Clinton and Al Gore promised again and again to build a "bridge to the twenty-first century." The slogan cast them as youthful builders and doers, the sort of people with whom forward-looking voters would identify. It contrasted them nicely with Bob Dole's nostalgic convention pledge to build a bridge to a better past.

But a bridge to the future is not just a feel-good cliché. It symbolizes technocracy. Regardless of its destination, a bridge is a quintessentially static structure. It goes from known point A to known point B. Its construction requires big budgets and teams of experts, careful planning and blueprints. Once completed, it cannot be moved. "A bridge to the twenty-first century" declares that the future must be brought under control, managed and planned by experts. It should not simply evolve. The future (and the present) must be predictable and uniform: We will go from point A to point B, with no deviations. Fall off that one bridge—let alone jump—and you're doomed.

Technocrats are "for the future," but only if someone is in charge of making it turn out according to plan. They greet every new idea with a "yes, but," followed by legislation, regulation, and litigation. Like Schlesinger and Attali, they get very nervous at the suggestion that the future might develop spontaneously. It is, they assume, too important and too dangerous to be left to undirected evolution. "To conceive of a better American future as a consummation which will take care of itself—as the necessary result of our customary conditions, institutions, and ideas—persistence in such a conception is admirably designed to deprive American life of any promise at all," wrote Herbert Croly, among the most influential Progressive Era thinkers, in *The Promise of American Life,* published in 1909.

Technocracy is the ideology of the "one best way," an idea that spread from Frederick Taylor's "scientific management" techniques to encompass the regulation of economic and social life. Turn-of-the-century technocrats, notes the historian John M. Jordan, used images of engineering to promise efficiency and order amid social and economic change: "In an era when the term *progressive* connoted a steady, teleological, restrained pace of improvement, *efficiency* implied change while at the same time suggesting security. The smoothly humming social machine envisioned by these reformers promised harmonious eradication of social problems. . . . This peculiarly American paradox of kinetic change made stable appears to have contributed to the ubiquity of efficiency claims in this era." By design, technocrats pick winners, establish standards, and impose a single set of values on the future. Only through such uniform plans can they hope to deliver "kinetic change made stable."

Consider this statement from a CNN interview: "As the president said, we need a comprehensive system, one that's been worked out, that's affordable and has national standards." Is this a legislator discussing national health insurance? A governor promoting education reform? An environmentalist proposing recycling mandates? The speaker is, in fact, a magazine editor talking about child care, but the prescription would fit just about any subject. To technocrats, institutional forms must be uniform and "comprehensive"; goals must be established once and for all; behavior must be molded to the proper pattern. In his 1998 State of the Union address, for instance, Bill Clinton denounced "untargeted tax cuts," which would reduce rates regardless of how taxpayers choose to spend their money, and he bragged about the complex "targeted tax cuts" passed the previous year.

Accustomed to technocratic governance, we take for granted that each new development, from the contents of popular entertainment to the latest in medical equipment, deserves not only public discussion but government scrutiny. Every new idea seems to spark a campaign to ban or control it: breast implants and mobile phones, aseptic juice boxes and surrogate mothers, Japanese cars and bovine growth hormone, video games and genetic engineering, quality circles and no-haggle car pricing, telecommuting and MRIs, data encryption and book superstores—the list goes on forever.

Most political arguments thus take place between competing technocratic schemes. Should there be a mandatory "family viewing" hour on TV, or ratings and a V-chip? Should the tax code favor families with children, or people attending college? Should a national health insurance program enroll everyone in managed care, or should we regulate health maintenance organizations so they act more like fee-for-service doctors? The issue isn't *whether* the future should be molded to fit one static ideal. It's what that static ideal should be. There must be a single blueprint for everyone.

Technocracy declares that if automobile air bags are a good idea for some people, they must be re-quired for everyone. If they turn out to injure children and small adults, planners may make an exception, but only if given a "good reason." Safety regulators "can't even consider a letter from somebody who says, 'Well, I'm scared, and I want to disconnect the air bag,'" a spokesman told *The New York Times*. "We've had somebody who said, 'I have claustrophobia, and I'm afraid.' That's not a medical condition that would require an air bag disconnection."

The ill-fated Clinton health care plan, with its complicated price controls and monopoly health alliances, was a model of technocratic governance. It combined a role for private providers with extensive regulation of what could be sold, at what price, to and by whom, and in what quantities. It set up an appointed National Health Board, with subsidiary advisory committees, and local boards to govern the alliances. It fixed the form of health care delivery, down to the ratio of specialists to primary care physicians, leaving little room for evolution or experimentation. It assumed that health care institutions would not and should not change significantly over time. It expressed egalitarian values by opposing a "tiered system." And it was called, not coincidentally, the Health Security Plan.

Comprehensive, neutrally administered plans are the technocratic dream. William Henry Smyth, who coined the term *technocracy* based on his experience with World War I planning, described it this way: "We became, for the time being, a real Industrial Nation. This we did by organizing and coordinating the Scientific Knowledge, the Technical Talent, and the Practical Skill of the entire Community; focussed them in the National Government, and applied this Unified National Force to the accomplishment of a Unified National Purpose." Smyth wanted technocracy to continue in peacetime, to "organize our scientists, our technologists, our exceptionally skilled."

While reactionaries often denigrate learning and mock experts (witness Iklé's scorn for "intellectuals"), technocrats celebrate their own knowledge and hoard their expertise. They are social engineers, tinkerers who seek "rational solutions" to public problems. Those rational solutions are supposed to be above politics and ideology, the pure results of science. Hence the multiplication of appointed boards and independent agencies. If the ideal of reactionaries is the self-sufficient family farm or the urban ethnic enclave, the ideal of technocrats is the regulated monopoly or the independent administrative agency—a rule-bound entity run by experts.

True to its Progressive Era origins, the pure technocratic vision combines the frisson of futurism—a combination of excitement and fear—with the reassurance that some authority will make everything turn out right. In 1984, amid the personal computer revolution, Newt Gingrich marveled at its creativity, but he worried that such uncoordinated enterprise lacked the focus necessary for national greatness. "These developments are individually striking," he wrote. "Taken together, they form a kaleidoscope that is difficult to develop into a coherent picture. Yet it is by sweeping dreams that societies shape themselves."

For technocrats, a kaleidoscope of trial-and-error innovation is not enough; decentralized experiments lack coherence. "Today, we have an opportunity *to shape technology*," wrote Gingrich in classic technocratic style (emphasis added). His message was that computer technology is too important to be left to hackers, hobbyists, entrepreneurs, venture capitalists, and computer buyers. "We" must shape it into a "coherent picture." That is the technocratic notion of progress: Decide on the one best way, make a plan, and stick to it. Looking for a model, Gingrich had kind words for the French Minitel system of terminals run by the state phone company—a centrally administered system whose rigidity has stifled Internet development in France.

In recent years, Gingrich has become more skeptical—and so has the rest of the country. In 1984, he expressed his enthusiasm for space exploration in demands for new heroic technocratic programs like the moon landing. By 1995, he was musing about the great things that could happen "if we got the government out of the business of designing space shuttles and space stations. . . . The challenge for us is to get government and bureaucracy out of the way and put scientists, engineers, entrepreneurs, and adventurers back into the business of exploration and discovery." Far from creating a promising future, technocracy had stifled its spontaneous revolution.

II.3   PETER M. SENGE AND GORAN CARSTEDT

Innovating Our Way to the Next Industrial Revolution

When past innovations, such as the steam engine, factory system, and interchangeable parts, were developed, it is not likely that there was much thought or planning about how those developments would impact either our lives or the planet on which we live. Even newer innovations, such as the computer, space travel, and genetic engineering, were developed with similar lack of consideration. It is more likely that business decisions were made on economic grounds rather than taking into account the importance of being in harmony with nature. This view regards various types of resources primarily as means to advance the goals of humans and sees these resources as unlimited in quantity.

In this article, Senge and Carstedt raise the issue of how responsible our economic system is in converting natural and social capital into the financial and productive capital that characterizes our world. They feel that New Economy products have the same fate as those produced in the Old Economy and express serious concerns about the future of the natural world if current production and consumption practices continue unabated.

While moving to a sustainable production model for ethical reasons might seem noble to some, the authors suggest that doing it because it would be a smart business decision will accomplish the same goal. Both authors have backgrounds in business management and see the future to be one where companies will provide services rather than only sell more products. This shift from a linear production model to one that mimics nature and is circular would mean that the next Industrial Revolution will benefit and not harm our environment—an important consideration.

Focus Questions

1. What are the major differences and similarities between the Old and New Economies, and what possible reasons are there for any shifts?
2. What are some of the factors described by the authors for the negative ecological impact of many enterprises, and do they propose this trend be reversed?
3. How is the term *sustainability* used by the authors, and why ought we strive to achieve this goal?
4. Discuss the relationship between the circular flow of living system cycles and the ways in which the authors propose corporations function in the future.

Keywords

biological diversity, biomimicry, W. Edwards Deming, discontinuous technological change, ecoefficient, humanism, hybrid car, naturalism, photovoltaics, postindustrial age, prosumer, rationalism, stewardship, sustainability, transparency, World Bank

MUCH OF WHAT IS BEING SAID about the New Economy is not all that new. Waves of discontinuous technological change have occurred before in the industrial age, sparked by innovations such as the steam engine in the 18th century; railroads, steel, electrification and telecommunications in the 19th century; and auto and air transport, synthetic fibers and television in the first half of the 20th century. Each of those technologies led to what economist Joseph Schumpeter called "creative destruction," in which old industries died and new ones

Reprinted from "Innovating Our Way to the Next Industrial Revolution" by Peter M. Senge & Goran Carstedt, *MIT Sloan Management Review, Vol 42*, No. 2, 2001, pp. 24–38, by permission of publisher. Copyright © 2001 by Massachusetts Institute of Technology. All rights reserved.

were born. Far from signaling the end of the industrial era, these waves of disruptive technologies accelerated and extended it.

What would constitute the beginnings of a truly postindustrial age? Only fundamental shifts in how the economic system affects the larger systems within which it resides—namely, society and nature. In many ways, the industrial age has been an era of harvesting natural and social capital in order to create financial and productive capital. So far there is little evidence that the New Economy is changing that.

The industrial-age assault on natural capital continues. Vague hopes about "bits for atoms" and "demassification" are naïve at best, echoes of talk about "paperless offices" 20 years ago. The rate of losing species has not slowed. Most New Economy products end up where Old Economy products do:

in increasingly scarce landfills. Globalization is destroying the last remnants of stewardship for natural resources in industries such as forest products: Today, buy-and-sell decisions are executed by faceless agents living on the other side of the world from the people and ecosystems whose futures they decide. Moreover, New Economy growth stimulates related growth in Old Economy industries—along with the familiar pattern of suburban sprawl, pollution, loss of habitat and competition for natural resources.

The New Economy's effects on social capital are more complex but no less disturbing.[1] Industrial progress has tended to destroy cultural as well as biological diversity, despite the protests of marginalized groups like the Provençal farmers who oppose the globalization of food production. Likewise, although changes in traditional family and community structures have brought greater freedom for women and many ethnic groups, the past decade also has brought worldwide increases in divorce rates, single-parent families and "street" children. Global markets, capital flows and e-commerce open up new opportunities for emerging economies, but they also create new generations of technological haves and have-nots. According to the World Bank, the poorest quartile of humankind has seen its share of global income fall from 2.5% to 1.25% over the past 25 years. More immediately, eroding social capital manifests in the isolation, violence and frenzy of modern living. Individuals and small circles of friends carve out increasingly private lives amidst increasingly distrustful strangers, preferring to "bowl alone." We almost take for granted road rage, deaths of spectators at sporting matches and kids shooting kids at school.[2] The "24-7" job has become the norm in many industries, the latest step in subjugating our lives to the clock, a process begun with the mechanization of work at the outset of the industrial era.

Judged by its impact on natural and social capital, so far the New Economy looks more like the next wave of the industrial era than a truly post-industrial era. Why should we care? Because the basic development patterns of the industrial era are not sustainable. As U.S. National Academy of Sci-

ences home secretary Peter Raven says, quoting the Wildlife Conservation Society's George Schaller, "We cannot afford another century like the last one." Plus, there are other possibilities.

CORPORATE HERETICS

"Is genuine progress still possible? Is development sustainable? Or is one strand of progress—industrialization—now doing such damage to the environment that the next generation won't have a world worth living in?"[3]

Those are not the words of the Sierra Club or Greenpeace, but of BP chairman John Browne. In 1997, Browne broke rank with the oil industry to declare, "There is now an effective consensus among the world's leading scientists and serious and well-informed people outside the scientific community that there is a discernible human influence on the climate." Moreover, he argued that "the time to consider the policy dimensions of climate change is not when the link between greenhouse gases and climate change is conclusively proven, but when the possibility cannot be discounted."[4]

Equally important, BP looks at the situation as a business opportunity. "There are good commercial reasons for being ahead of the pack when it comes to issues to do with the environment," says Browne. Since 1997, the company has become active in public forums on global climate, has begun to reduce emissions in exploration and production, has started to market cleaner fuels and has invested significantly in alternative sources of energy (such as photovoltaic power and hydrogen). All the while, Browne has led an effort to build a more performance-oriented culture, and company profits have been at an all-time high.

The Dimensions of Sustainability

Rationalism, the belief in reason, has dominated society throughout modern times. It remains the dominant perspective in business and education. Yet it has limits. It cannot explain the passion that motivates entrepreneurs committed to a new product idea nor the imagination of scientists testing an intuition. Nor does it explain why a quiet walk on a beach or a hike into the mountains may inspire both. These can only be understood by seeing how naturalism, humanism and rationalism infuse one another. Naturalism arises from our innate sense of being part of nature. Humanism arises from the rich interior life that connects reason, emotion and awareness—and ultimately allows us to connect with one another. Epochs in human history that have nurtured all three have stood out as golden ages.

BP is but one example of the shift in thinking that is becoming evident in many companies and industries. Appliance maker Electrolux uses water- and powder-based paints (rather than hazardous solvent-based paints), prioritizes the use of recycled materials, and has introduced the world's first family of refrigerators and freezers free of the chlorofluorocarbons that contribute to ozone depletion. In 1999, Toyota and Honda began selling hybrid cars that combine internal combustion and electric propulsion, perform comparably to competitors— and can achieve up to 70 miles per gallon today, with prospects for two to three times that mileage in a few years.[5] In 1998, Xerox introduced its first fully digitized copier, the Document Centre 265, which is more than 90% remanufacturable and 97% recyclable. The product has only about 200 parts, an order of magnitude less than its predecessor. Its sales have exceeded forecasts. According to Fortune, remanufacturing and waste reduction saved Xerox $250 million in 1998. Some firms, such as Interface Inc., a $1.3 billion manufacturer of commercial carpet tiles, which saved about $140 million in sustainable waste reductions from 1995 to 1999, are even rethinking their basic business model. Interface's goal is to stop selling product altogether. Instead, it will provide floor-covering services, leasing products and later taking them back for 100% recycling. Assessing the environmental impact of the carpeting industry, chairman Ray Anderson says bluntly, "In the future, people like me will go to jail."[6]

These examples are all just initial steps, as each of these companies would readily admit. Ultimately, sustainability is a challenge to society as a whole. Nonetheless, business can play a legitimate leadership role as a catalyst for larger changes. We believe that a new environmentalism is emerging, driven by innovation, not regulation—radical new technologies, products, processes *and* business models. More and more businesses are recognizing the opportunities this creates. "Sustainability not only helps improve the world, but also energizes the company," says ABB's CEO Goran Lindahl.

The good news is that change through market-driven innovation is the type of change our society understands best. The problem is that much in today's business climate appears to run in the opposite direction. Short-term financial pressures, the free-agent work force, dramatic opportunities to start new companies and get rich quickly, often cynical mass media, and industrializing countries aspiring to catch up to the industrialized world's consumption standards—these hardly seem like the conditions for increasing stewardship of the earth.

The challenge today is to develop sustainable businesses that are compatible with the current economic reality. Innovative business models and products must work financially, or it won't matter how good they are ecologically and socially. To explore how to achieve this, the SoL Sustainability Consortium was formed to bring together like-minded corporate executives experienced in organizational learning who also see sustainability becoming a cornerstone of their business strategy.[7] Together, we are asking: Can organizations committed to sustainability work with the forces propelling most of the New Economy in the opposite direction? And, can organizational-learning principles and tools help in realizing the changes that this will require?

BETWEEN TWO STORIES

The first reality confronting businesses that are serious about sustainability is ambiguity, starting with the question: What do we mean by *sustainability*? The ambiguity inherent in sustainability has deep cultural roots.

"We are in trouble just now because we do not have a good story," says cultural historian Thomas Berry. "We are in between stories. The old story, the account of how the world came to be and how we fit into it . . . sustained us for a long period of time.

It shaped our emotional attitudes, provided us with life purposes and energized our actions. It consecrated our suffering and integrated our knowledge. We awoke in the morning and knew where we were. We could answer the questions of our children."[8] In a sense, sustainability requires letting go of the story of the supremacy of the human in nature, the story that the natural world exists as mere "resources" to serve human "progress." But most of us grew up with this story, and it is still shared by the vast majority of modern society. It is not easy to let it go, especially when we are uncertain about what the new story will be. Businesses seeking sustainability can easily feel like a trapeze artist suspended in the air. They have let go of a secure worldview without knowing what they can hang on to.

Yet the dim outlines of a new story are emerging. At its root are two elements: a new picture of the universe and a new sense of human possibility. "We are just beginning to explore what it means to be part of a universe that is alive . . . not just cosmos but cosmogenesis," in the words of Barry and physicist Brian Swimme. Moreover, the new universe story "carries with it a psychic-spiritual dimension as well as a physical-materialistic dimension. Otherwise, human consciousness emerges out of nowhere . . . an addendum [with] no real place in the story of the universe."[9] Echoing Barry, Roger Saillant, former Ford executive and now Visteon vice president, says, "The new story will have to do with personal accountability . . . new communities in business and elsewhere based on knowing that there is no parent to take care of us and that we have a stewardship responsibility for future generations." Saillant adds that gradually "a larger intelligence will emerge. Those special moments when we glimpse that our actions are informed by a larger whole will become more frequent." Interface marketing vice president Joyce LaValle foresees a similar shift: "I think this will actually get easier as we proceed. But first we must go through a kind of eye of the needle."

According to John Ehrenfeld, president of the International Society for Industrial Ecology, the challenge arises because sustainability "is a radical concept that stretches our current ideas about rationality. It has often been framed as environmentalists against business. But this generates polarization and misses the three very different worldviews needed to move forward: rationalism, naturalism and humanism." Only by embracing all three can we begin to understand what sustainability actually means. (See "The Dimensions of Sustainability.")

NATURALISM: BIOMIMICRY AND THE LOGIC OF NATURAL SYSTEMS

The diverse innovations that created the first Industrial Revolution sprang from the same guiding image that inspired the preceding scientific revolution—the image of the machine. "My aim," wrote 17th-century scientist Johannes Kepler, "is to show that the celestial machine is to be likened not to a divine organism but rather to a clockwork."[10] The assembly line became the prototypical organization—with managers as controllers and workers operating in rigid routines, all coordinated by bells, whistles and production schedules. The assembly line was so successful it became the model for other types of organizations, including the 19th-century urban school system. Although the machine-age organization achieved previously unimaginable productivity, it also created a mechanized organizational environment that dehumanized and fragmented how people worked together.

If the machine inspired the industrial age, the image of the living system may inspire a genuine postindustrial age. This is what life-sciences writer Janine Benyus calls "biomimicry," innovation inspired by understanding how living systems work. "What is consistent with life is sustainable," says Benyus. For example, in nature there is no waste. All byproducts of one natural system are nutrients for another. Why should industrial systems be different? We would not ask engineers to build bridges that defy the laws of gravity nor chip designers to violate laws of physics. Why should we expect businesses to violate the law of zero waste?

All living systems follow cycles: produce, recycle, regenerate.

By contrast, industrial-age systems follow a linear flow of extract, produce, sell, use, discard—what "Ecology of Commerce" author Paul Hawken calls "take-make-waste.". . .

Indeed, the primary output of today's production processes is waste. Across all industries, less than 10% of everything extracted from the earth (by weight) becomes usable products. The remaining 90% to 95% becomes waste from production.[11] Moreover, what is sold creates still more waste—from discard and from use (for example, from auto exhaust). So, while businesses obsess over labor and financial capital efficiency, we have created possibly the most inefficient system of production in human history.

What would industrial systems that conform to natural principles look like? First, they would be circular rather than linear, with significant reductions in all waste flows. . . . This implies three specific waste-reduction strategies: resource productivity, clean products, and remanufacturing, recycling and composting."[12]

Strategy 1 Resource productivity reduces waste from production through ecoefficient production technologies and the design of production processes in which wastes from one process become nutrients for another.

Strategy 2 Clean products (say, hybrid cars) reduce waste from goods in use through nonpolluting product technologies.

Strategy 3 Remanufacturing and recycling (creating "technical nutrients") and designing more products that are biodegradable (creating "natural nutrients") reduce waste from discard.

Architect William McDonough and chemist Michael Braungart summarize the three strategies with a simple dictum: "Waste equals food."

Second, companies would invest in nature's regenerative processes. They would do fewer things that compromise regeneration, such as paving over wetlands, and would invest some surpluses in restoring natural capital—for example, companies like Interface plant trees to match business miles traveled because increasing forest cover reduces greenhouse gases.

Third, following Buckminster Fuller's dictum, companies would "learn how to live on our energy income [solar, wind, hydrogen] rather than off our principal [oil and gas]." Living on our income would not only reduce resource extraction, but also eliminate the side effects of using minerals, like auto emissions.

Thinking in more systemic terms may appear simple, but it raises important questions about current corporate environmentalism. For example, ecoefficiency has become a goal for companies worldwide, with many realizing significant cost savings from eliminating waste from production. That is good in some ways, but troubling in others. Thinking about the larger system shows that ecoefficiency innovations alone could actually worsen environmental stresses in the future.

Ecoefficiency innovations reduce waste from production, but this does not alter the number of products produced nor the waste generated from their use and discard. Indeed, most companies investing in cost-reducing ecoefficiency improvements are doing so with the aim of increased profits and growth. Moreover, there is no guarantee that increased economic growth from ecoefficiency will come in similarly ecoefficient ways. In today's global capital markets, greater profits show up as investment capital that could easily be reinvested in old-style eco-inefficient industries.

To put it another way, nature does not care about the industrial system's efficiency. Nature cares about its impact in *absolute terms*. If a vastly more ecoefficient industrial system grows much larger, it conceivably could generate more total waste and destroy more habitat and species than a smaller, less ecoefficient economy.

The answer is not necessarily zero growth. The implications of naturalism are more subtle: We can sustain growth only by reducing total material throughput and total accumulated waste. Ecoefficiency gains are laudable but dangerously incomplete, as is any strategy that fails to consider the industrial-natural system as a whole. A systemic approach would reduce all sources of waste: from production, use and discard.

Managers' faith in ecoefficiency also illustrates the power of mental models. Industrial-age managerial practice has always been about increasing efficiency. Increased natural-resource productivity that translates directly into lower costs offers a compelling business case, one that does not challenge established thinking deeply. However, focusing on ecoefficiency may distract companies from pursuing radically different products and business models—changes that require shifts in mental models, not just shifting attention within existing mental models.

This is unlikely to happen without mastering the human dimensions of learning and change.

HUMANISM: THE LOGIC OF LEARNING

"The prevailing system of management has destroyed our people," said total-quality pioneer W. Edwards Deming. "People are born with intrinsic motivation, self-esteem, dignity, curiosity to learn, joy in learning." Echoing Deming, anthropologist Edward Hall declares, "Humans are learning organisms *par excellence*. The drive to learn is as strong as the sexual drive—it begins earlier and lasts longer." The premise of work on learning organizations has been that thriving in today's knowledge-based marketplaces means reversing the destructiveness that Deming speaks about and cultivating people's drive to learn.

In fall 1999 the sustainability consortium was hosted by the Xerox "Lakes" team that had developed the Document Centre 265 copier. Already aware of the team's innovations in design for remanufacture (more than 500 patents came from the Lakes project) and the product's success in the marketplace, we learned about how the team's zero-waste vision translated into a manufacturing facility with virtually no waste and eventually became embraced by many of the team's suppliers. But it still wasn't clear *how* the team had achieved those accomplishments.

Late in the day, Rhonda Staudt, a young engineer who was one of the lead designers, was talking about the team's innovations when she was interrupted by David Berdish, veteran of many organizational-learning projects at Ford. "Rhonda," Berdish said, "I understand what a great opportunity this was for you and how exciting it was. I work with engineers, and I know the excitement of pushing the technological envelope. But what I really want to know is why you did this. What I mean

is: 'What was the stand you took and who were you taking that stand for?'"

Rhonda looked at David for a long time in silence and then, in front of many peers and a few superiors, began to cry. "I am a mom," she answered. We had all heard of the Lakes motto, "Zero to landfill, for the sake of our children." But now we were in its presence. Roger Saillant of Visteon turned to Peter and whispered, "Seamlessness." Peter knew exactly what he meant: when what we do becomes inseparable from who we are.

We have all spent much of our lives in institutions that force us to be someone we are not. We commit ourselves to the company's agenda. We act professionally. After a while, we have lived so long in the house of mirrors that we mistake the image we are projecting for who we really are. The poet David Whyte quotes an AT&T manager who wrote, "Ten years ago, I turned my face for a moment . . . and it became my life."

Over the past decade, many companies have attempted to build learning organizations with little grasp of the depth of the changes required. They want to increase imagination and creativity without unleashing the passion that comes from personal vision. They seek to challenge established mental models without building real trust and openness. They espouse systems thinking, without realizing how threatening that can be to established "quick fix" management cultures. There is a difference between building more-sustainable enterprises because there is profit in it and because it is one' life's work. The journey ahead will require both.

If understanding natural systems establishes the guiding ideas for sustainability innovations, then learning provides the means to translate ideas into accomplishments. But, just as the logic of natural systems conflicts with take-make-waste industrial systems, so too does the logic of a learning culture conflict with traditional, control-oriented organizational cultures. To a controlling culture, a learning culture based on passion, curiosity and trust appears to be out of control. But, in fact, it is based on a different type of control. "We are not trying to eliminate control and discipline in our organizations," says retired CEO William O'Brien, formerly with Hanover Insurance Co. "We are trying to substitute top-down discipline based on fear with self-discipline. This does not make life easier for people in organizations. It makes it more demanding—but also more exciting."

These two tensions—between natural systems and industrial systems on the one hand and between learning and controlling on the other—may appear to make sustainable enterprises impossible. However, deeper currents in the New Economy could also cause those tensions to become immutable forces transforming traditional industrial-age management.

A NEW BUSINESS LOGIC

Kevin Kelly, editor at large of Wired, observes that the "emerging new economic order . . . has three distinguishing characteristics. It is global. It favors intangibles—ideas, information and relationships. And it is intensely interlinked." Kelly sees electronic networks generating new patterns of "organic behavior in a technological matrix." But he suggests that the real changes are not ultimately about technology but communication. According to Kelly, in the world that is emerging, "Communication is the economy."[13]

Today, perhaps the earth as a living system is communicating to us through increasingly turbulent weather patterns. Perhaps our frayed social structures are communicating to us through increasing acts of child violence. Are we listening? If the New Economy is revolutionizing communication, can it enable deeper listening? If so, we may discern a new business logic emerging, one that starts with rethinking how firms create value and continues by redefining "customers," "employees," "suppliers"—and ultimately the company itself.

From Things to the Value Provided by Things

"Production is increasingly not where value is created," says Ting Ho, vice president of strategy for global-logistics Internet startup Zoho. "The traditional company produced something that it then had to sell. Today, w must understand a customer and serve a genuine need."

At the heart of the industrial-age growth machine was a kind of mass hypnosis—convincing consumers that happiness meant owning a new thing. A new washing machine. A new computer. A new car. However, people do not want a hunk of steel in the driveway. They want the benefits it provides—whether they are tangible benefits like transport or intangible benefits like freedom or fun.

What does it mean to create new business models on the basis of that understanding? For Interface, it means shifting from selling carpets to providing floor-covering services, automatically taking back worn carpet tiles or replacing entire sections if a customer wants a different color. For Dow Chemical, it means leasing "dissolving services," then reusing the solvents. For Carrier, the world's leading manufacturer of air-conditioning equipment, it means renting cooling services rather than selling air conditioners. For IKEA, according to its published mission statement, it means providing services to help people "make a house or apartment into a home" rather than selling furniture. All these firms believe that "higher profits will come from providing better solutions rather than selling more equipment," in the words of "Natural Capitalism" authors Amory and Hunter Lovins and Paul Hawken.

From the standpoint of sustainability, providing services rather than just selling products creates a potential new alignment between what is sound economically and what is sound environmentally. A company's business model no longer requires designed-in obsolescence to push customers into buying new products. Instead, producers have an incentive to design for longevity, efficient servicing, improved functioning, and product take-back. Such design allows for maintaining relationships with customers by continually ensuring that products are providing the services that people desire—at the lowest cost to the provider.

The shift from "the value is in the stuff" to "the value is in the service the stuff provides" also may lead to a radical shift in the concept of ownership. Swiss industry analyst Walter Stahel and chemist Braungart have proposed that, in the future, producers will own what they produce forever and therefore will have strong incentives to design products to be disassembled and remanufactured or recycled, whichever is more economical. Owning products forever would represent a powerful step toward changing companies' attitudes about product discard.

Such ideas signal a radical shift in business models, one that will not come easily. It starts with how a company thinks of itself in relation to its customers: as a producer of things people buy or a provider of services through products made and remade? Marketing strategist Sandra Vandermerwe argues that such a view is essential to true customer focus, providing value *for* customers as well as obtaining value from customers.[14] It also shifts producers' time horizons. As Volvo discovered years ago, when a company is only selling cars, its relationship with the customer ends with the purchase. When it is providing customer satisfaction, it just begins.

From Producers and Consumers to Cocreators of Value Focusing on the services provided by products also shifts the very meaning of "customer." Customers are no longer passive; they are cocreators of value. Thirty years ago, futurist Alvin Toffler coined the term "prosumer," people who actively participate in generating the value they derive from any product.[15] "Today, prosumers are everywhere," says Kelly, "from restaurants where you assemble your own dinner to medical self-care arenas, where you serve as doctor and patient." As Kelly says, the essence of prosumerism today is that "customers have a hand in the creation of the product."[16]

Prosumerism is infiltrating diverse marketplaces, especially those where Internet technology is strong. One of Amazon.com's most popular Website features is customer reviews of books, CDs and other products. The five-year-old magazine Fast Company now rivals Business Week, Fortune and Forbes, partly because of its "Company of Friends," a Web-site feature that allows subscribes to get together to discuss common concerns, form support networks for projects, or tell the magazine their interests. "I can go to our Web site and determine which are the 10 most frequently forwarded articles," says editor Alan Webber. "Our readers are no longer just an audience but cocreators of product."

How does that shift to prosumers relate to sustainability? It starts with activist customers who think for themselves. And activist customers are organizing themselves. "Thanks largely to the Internet," say C. K. Prahalad and V. Ramaswamy, "consumers have increasingly been engaging themselves in an active and explicit dialogue with manufacturers of products and services."[17] They add, "The market has become a forum." Or, as the popular "Cluetrain Manifesto" puts it, the market is becoming "a community of discourse."[18] With the inmates running the asylum, will they start to change the rules? What if people start talking to one another? What if they talk about the state of the world and how different types of products affect the quality of people's lives?

Leading Web-based companies, because they relate to their customers differently, also gain a different sense of what truly concerns customers. "Without a doubt, sustainability of our current lifestyle—personally and environmentally—matters to a lot of our readers," says Webber. "These were among the concerns that motivated us to start the magazine, and we've seen nothing to persuade us otherwise."

At this stage, it is speculation whether self-organizing networks of customers will unearth the deeper values essential to building sustainable societies. But it is no speculation that shifts in consumer behavior will be essential in creating such societies. One of the most significant concentrations of power in the industrial era has been the growth of a massive advertising industry applying psychological savvy to manipulate consumer preferences. "Soap operas" acquired their name because they were devised by Procter & Gamble and other consumer-goods companies to market soap. Could this be another form of centralized control that becomes history, the victim of the freer flow of information and interaction that allows people to know more and learn faster?

Homo sapiens has been around longer than *Homo consumer.* People still care deeply about the world their children will live in. Building sustainable enterprises will require tapping and harnessing that caring.

Many market-oriented companies sense just such a shift emerging in consumer preferences. For example, Nike has a host of recycled and recyclable products coming to market. For a company that sells the image of fitness, it is not surprising that Darcy Winslow, general manager of sustainable products and services, says: "Corporations in the 21st century cannot be fit if we don't prioritize and neutralize our impact on the environment."

From Compliant Employees to Committed Members of Social Networks There are few companies today that do not struggle with the implications of the free-agent work force. The traditional employment contract based on good pay and benefits in exchange for loyalty is vanishing in many industries. Entrepreneurial opportunities are enticing, especially to young people. Most companies respond by trying to rework the old contract. They increase salary and benefits. They offer stock. They invent creative new perks. But in so doing, they miss entirely the change that might make the greatest difference: a mission worthy of people's commitment.

In 1991, IKEA faced the daunting challenge of extending its European business success to North America, the "graveyard of European retailers." It was clear from the outset that IKEA managers could not say, 'Here's how we do it in Sweden,' and expect much enthusiasm. Achieving strong returns for a distant corporate office was not enough. Being part of a proud and widely imitated European firm had limited meaning. It became clear that IKEA's North American management team had to find ways to truly engage people.

It turned out that North Americans, like Europeans, were concerned about the environment. Eventually, some 20,000 IKEA employees in North America and Europe participated voluntarily in a two-day training session on "The Natural Step," an intuitive introduction to the system conditions that must be met by a sustainable society. Not only did that engage people in selling the company's environmentally oriented products and creating related product and service ideas, it engaged them in working for IKEA. From 1990 through 1994, North American sales increased 300%.

The free-agent image connotes to many employers lack of commitment, people seeking a purely transactional relationship with a company. Perhaps the opposite is true. It may be a unique opportunity for organizations that truly value commitment.

If we actually thought of people as free, we would have to approach them with respect, knowing that they can choose where to work. "It is amazing the commitment that people feel toward our focus on sustainability and the environment," says Vivienne Cox, BP vice president for marketing. "In a very tough business environment, it really matters to people who have many options in their lives."

Most industrial-age companies wanted what *they* regarded as committed employees. Today, the definition of commitment is changing, and paternalism is giving way to more-adult relationships. "People stay with a firm, in many instances, because they see an alignment between their personal values and those they perceive the firm to be committed to," says Ged Davis, who is Shell's vice president for global business environment. If enterprises are not committed to anything beyond making money, why should managers be surprised that workers make transactional commitments?

Kelly also notes that in the competitive labor markets found in fast-growing industries, people change companies but maintain their loyalty "to advancing technology or to the region."[19] And to trusted colleagues. One key person may take groups of people from employer to employer like the Pied Piper.[20] Project teams form, un-form and then re-form like the teams of writers, actors and technical specialists that make movies. Yet larger social networks remain intact. Increasingly, such networks are the keepers of values and commitments and the subtle know-how that makes winners and losers. Longer-term relationships embedded in fluid but enduring social networks are a new phenomenon that most companies have not yet understood.

"Companies have felt that workers needed them more than they needed workers," says Peter Drucker. "This is changing in ways that most companies still do not seem to grasp."[21]

From Separate Businesses to Ecological Communities "The great benefits reaped by the New Economy in the coming decades," says Kelly, "will be due in large part to exploring and exploiting the power of decentralized and autonomous networks," which in many ways now resemble "an ecology of organisms, interlinked and coevolving, constantly in flux, deeply entangled, ever expanding at its edges."

"In traditional businesses, everything was piecework," says Zoho's Ho. "Now we are all part of larger systems, and our success depends on understanding those systems." For example, the traditional relationship between producer and supplier was neat and tidy. Producers wanted reliable supply at the lowest possible cost. Today, cost may be only one of several criteria that shape successful producer-supplier relationships. "Both as a supplier and with our suppliers, we are continually co-designing and co-innovating," says Ho. "There is no other way to keep pace with rapid changes and expanding knowledge."

Paradoxically, the realization that all enterprises are part of complex, evolving systems imparts new meaning to relationships and trust. As Webber has said, "The New Economy starts with technology and ends with trust."[22] People who are co-innovating must know each other and trust each other—in ways unnecessary in traditional relationships between providers and customers. That leads to the question: Can partners in complex supply networks co-innovate more-sustainable practices?

For example, Nike has programs in place with six of its material suppliers to collect 100% of their scrap and recycle it into the next round of products. The goal is to scale this up to all material suppliers. Similarly, all the big steps in design for remanufacture require intense cooperation up and down supply chains. "If you don't have suppliers hooked in, the whole thing will fail," says former Lakes chief engineer John Elter. The Xerox team hosted "supplier symposiums" where "we taught suppliers what remanufacturing means and gave them the basic tools for remanufacture," says Elter. Even more important, they assured suppliers that they would share in the cost savings—because used parts would go back to the suppliers for remanufacture. "The key is that suppliers participate in the economic benefit of remanufacturing because they don't have to make everything new. This is a big deal. Plus, they are developing new expertise they can apply with other customers."

Building the necessary alignment for product take-back among networks of wholesalers, retailers and customers is equally daunting. "Without doubt, one of the biggest challenges with our 'Evergreen Service Contract' [Interface's model for selling floor-covering services rather than carpeting]," says chairman Ray Anderson, "is transforming mental models built up over generations"—such as those of purchasing departments in big companies whose incentives are based purely on cost of purchase, rather than on lifetime costs and aesthetic benefits.

Intense cooperative learning will never occur unless companies view their fates as linked. That is why the shift from seeing a world of suppliers and customers to one in which "we are all part of larger systems" is essential. Companies that do not recognize their interdependence with suppliers, distributors and customers will never build the trust needed to shift established mental models.

"Tennyson had it only half right when he said nature was 'red in tooth and claw,'" writes Janine Benyus. "In mature ecosystems, cooperation seems as important as competition. [Species cooperate] in order to diversify and . . . to fully use the habitat." Companies that see one another only as competitors may likewise find their habitat disappearing as the world around them changes.

From Closed Doors to Transparency   The world in which key corporate decisions could be made behind closed doors is disappearing. In 1995, Shell encountered a dramatic and unexpected reaction to its plans to sink in the North Sea its Brent Spar oil platform, which was approaching the end of its productive lifetime. Despite the fact that the company had gone through a three-year process to identify the best environmental option and had the concurrence of the U.K. government, the situation became a public-relations nightmare when other governments objected to the plan. Shell had failed to realize that its private decision had become a public one, a harsh lesson learned by many other companies, from Nike to Ford to Microsoft, in recent years.

There is an old saying in the field of ecology: "There is no 'away.'" The old world of corporate inner sanctums isolated managers from many of their decisions' social and environmental consequences, distant in time and space from those who made the decisions. As transparency increases, these feedback loops are closing, and consequences must be faced. In this sense, transparency is a powerful ally to naturalism and may drive many of the changes needed to implement more-naturalistic, circular business processes and models.

Growing transparency already has led to the inclusion of voices traditionally outside the inner circle. Several years ago, Greenpeace objected to the chlorides IKEA used in the printing of catalogs. Few in the industry thought there was any cost-effective alternative. But working together, Greenpeace and IKEA found a Finnish printing company that could produce catalogs without chlorides. IKEA presented its chloride-free catalog at an environmental conference in Washington and set a new industry standard. This experience showed that Greenpeace and IKEA could work together productively by focusing on tangible problems and by believing that breakthroughs were possible. Such trust can only be built over time.

Growing transparency is also leading to new accounting and performance-management practices. Shell and others are moving toward "triple-bottom-line" accounting—assessing economic, environmental and social performance in a balanced way. The Global Reporting Initiative provides practical guidelines for such changes. "Adopting GRI guidelines and triple-bottom-line practices is an enormously difficult step," says consultant John Elkington. "But companies like Shell, Ford and many others feel they must do this if they want to lead, rather than just react to change."

But the path toward broader accountability is fraught with perils. Last spring, Ford's first "Corporate Citizenship Report," based loosely on GRI guidelines, was greeted with as much cynicism as appreciation. The New York Times ignored most of the report (which included lengthy sections on reducing emissions and radical redesign of manufacturing processes) to announce that "Ford Is Conceding SUV Drawbacks."[23] The article focused on a three-page section of the 98-page report that discussed the dilemma of having a profitable product line that had environmental and safety problems. The Wall Street Journal was more personal, suggesting that chairman William Clay Ford was a

hypocrite for both making and criticizing SUVs, a "guilt-ridden rich kid" who should either embrace his customers' preferences or leave the business to those who do.[24]

Ultimately, transparency is about awareness. With increasing awareness will come pressures for greater accountability for social and natural capital as well as financial capital. Gradually, this will lead to innovations in the larger social context as well.

It is impossible to predict the range of social innovations that growing transparency will ultimately foster. Perhaps new collaborative action-research networks will create the right climate of objectivity and compassion, tough standards and fair reporting combined with a spirit of learning together. . . . Perhaps more-participative media, building on successful experiments such as those of Fast Company, will enable new levels of collaborative innovation. It may even be time to question the traditional limited-liability status of corporations, which uniquely favors owners of financial capital. Today's world of abundant financial capital and limited natural and social capital differs profoundly from the world of a century ago, when there was a need to protect individual investors. "In a world where learning and knowledge generation are the basis for corporate survival and wealth creation, managers must see a company as a living being, a human community," says writer and former Shell executive Arie de Geus. "Yet, today's managers inherit a very different worldview, focused on the optimism of financial capital. Is it not inconsistent to emphasize knowledge creation, on the one hand, and then treat a company as a machine for producing money, which is owned by its financial investors on the other?"

Perhaps when we are able to rediscover "company" (from the Latin *com-panis,* sharing of bread) as "living community," we will also rediscover its place within the larger community of living systems where it rightfully resides.

THE LOGIC OF REVOLUTIONS

The New Economy is both not new and new. It continues industrial-age patterns, yet it also may hold the seeds for a truly postindustrial world. As such, it brings us to a crossroads. We can either continue moving ever more rapidly in a direction that cannot be sustained, or we can change. Perhaps, no time in history has afforded greater possibilities for a collective change in direction.

"Creative engineers understand the role of constraints," says Elter of his Lakes experience. "Design engineers always deal with constraints: time, weight, operability. These are all real. The extraordinary creativity of [our] team had its source in recognizing a different constraint—the constraint of nature, to produce no waste. Zero to landfill is an uplifting constraint. It's worth going after. It's not manmade." Constraint and creativity are always connected. No artist paints on an infinite canvas. The artist understands that rather than just being limits, constraints can be freeing, especially when those constraints that have genuine meaning are recognized. What if product and business designers everywhere recognized that their constraints came from living systems? What if they adhered to the simple dictums: waste equals food; support nature's regenerative processes; live off energy income, not principal; and, borrowing from Elter's team, do it for the children. As occurred with the Lakes engineers, might this not free everyone's creativity in previously unimaginable ways?

Such rethinking will not happen all at once. It will not arise from any central authority. It will come from everywhere and nowhere in particular. The first Industrial Revolution, according to author Daniel Quinn, was "the product of a million small beginnings. [It] didn't proceed according to any theoretical design [and] was not a utopian undertaking."[25] Likewise, the next Industrial Revolution, if it is to happen, will have no grand plan and no one in charge. It will advance, in Quinn's words, on the basis of "an outpouring of human creativity," innovations not just in the technological but in the human landscape as well—the only way a new story can arise.

Acknowledgments

Most of the ideas and many of the examples above come from the practitioners, researchers and consultants in the SoL Sustainability Consortium, many of whom are quoted above. In addition, the authors would like to thank other consortium members who read the manuscript and offered helpful suggestions: Bernie Bulkin of BP, Amory and Hunter Lovins of the Rocky Mountain Institute, Otto Scharmer of MIT, Debbie Zemke of Ford, and Sara Schley and Joe Laur of Seed Systems, coordinators for the Consortium.

To support those interested in building more-sustainable enterprises, there are several Web sites focused on environmental education and planning (The Natural Step at www.naturalstep.org), natural capitalism and hybrid cars (the Rocky Mountain Institute at www.rmi.org), ecoefficiency (the World Business Council for Sustainable Development at www.WBCSD.org), triple-bottom-line reporting (www.sustainability.co.uk and www.globalreporting.org) and organizational learning (SoL at www.SoLonline.org).

REFERENCES

1. Social capital refers to "connections among individuals—social networks and the norms of reciprocity and trustworthiness that arise with them." See: R. D. Putnam, "Bowling Alone" (New York: Simon & Schuster, 2000), p. 19. It is also the necessary context for developing human capital—skills and knowledge embedded in people. See: J. S. Coleman, "Social Capital and the Creation of Human Capital," *American Journal of Sociology* 94 (1988): 95–120.

2. "Why Is Everyone So Short-Tempered?" *USA Today,* July 18, 2000, sec. A, p. 1.

3. J. Browne, "Respect for the Earth," a 2000 BBC Reith Lecture, available from BP, London.

4. J. Browne, "Rethinking Corporate Responsibility," *Reflections* 1.4 (summer 2000): 48–53.

5. See www.rmi.org/sitepages/pid175.asp for Rocky Mountain Institute publications about the hypercar.

6. E. P. Gunn, "The Green CEO," *Fortune,* May 24, 1999, 190–200.

7. The SoL (Society for Organizational Learning) Sustainability Consortium was established by BP and Interface and now includes established SoL members Royal Dutch/Shell, Ford, Xerox, Harley-Davidson, Detroit-Edison, Visteon and the World Bank, along with new members Nike and Northeast Utilities. The group's current projects—on product development, innovation across complex

supply networks, new energy sources, and leadership and cultural change—are described at www.SoLonline.org and are being studied through a National Science Foundation grant.

8. T. Berry, "The Dream of the Earth" (San Francisco: Sierra Club Books, 1990), 123.

9. Ibid., 131–132.

10. D. Boorstin, "The Discoverers: A History of Man's Search To Know His World and Himself" (New York: Random House, 1985), 108–109.

11. See P. Hawken, A. B. Lovins and L. H. Lovins, "Natural Capitalism" (New York: Little Brown and Co., 1999), p. 14; R. U. Ayers, "Industrial Metabolism," in J. S. Ausubel and H. E. Sladovich, eds., "Technology and Environment" (Washington, D.C.: National Academy Press, 1989); and A. B. Lovins, L. H. Lovins and P. Hawken, "A Road Map for Natural Capitalism," *Harvard Business Review 77* (May–June 1999): 145–158.

12. These three strategies, in concert with ideas below, relate closely to the four strategies of "natural capitalism," three of the four "system conditions" of the "the natural step" described in J. Holmberg and K.-H. Robert, "Backcasting From Nonoverlapping Sustainability Principles—A Framework for Strategic Planning," *International Journal of Sustainable Development and World Ecology* 7 (2000): 1–18; and William McDonough, "Hannover Principles: Design for Sustainability" (New York: William McDonough Architects, 1992). Available through McDonough Braungart Design Chemistry, Charlottesville, Virginia (info@mbdc.com) or downloadable from www.mcdonough.com/principles.pdf.

13. K. Kelly, "New Rules for the New Economy" (New York: Penguin Books, 1999), 2, 5, 31.

14. S. Vandermerwe, "How Increasing Value to Customers Improves Business Results," *MIT Sloan Management Review* 42 (fall 2000): 28.

15. A. Toffler, "The Third Wave" (New York: William Morrow, 1980).

16. Kelly, "New Rules," 121–122.

17. C. K. Prahalad and V. Ramaswamy, "Co-Opting Customer Competence," *Harvard Business Review* 78 (January–February 2000): 79–87.

18. R. Levine, C. Locke, D. Searls and D. Weinberger, "The Cluetrain Manifesto: The End of Business as Usual" (Cambridge, Massachusetts: Perseus Press, 2000), xiv.

19. Kelly, "New Rules," 28.

20. B. Wysocki Jr., "Yet Another Hazard of the New Economy: The Pied Piper Effect," *Wall Street Journal*, March 30, 2000, sec. A, p. 1.

21. P. F. Drucker and P. Senge, "Becoming a Change Leader," video conversations, Peter F. Drucker Foundation for Nonprofit Management, New York, and SoL (the Society for Organizational Learning), Cambridge, Massachusetts, forthcoming.

22. A. Webber, "What's So New About the New Economy?" *Harvard Business Review* 71 (January–February 1993): 24–42.

23. K. Bradsher, "Ford Is Conceding SUV Drawbacks," *New York Times*, May 12, 2000, sec. A, p. 1.

24. B. Yates, "On the Road: Pecksniffs Can't Stop SUV," *Wall Street Journal Europe*, May 19, 2000, sec. A, p. 26.

25. D. Quinn, "My Ishmael" (New York: Bantam Books, 1997), 200–201.

UNITED NATIONS   II.4

Globalization and Its Impact on the Full Enjoyment of All Human Rights

This report, prepared for the United Nations General Assembly in August 2000, discusses the effects of advances in communications and transportation technologies on the global economy. It warns that because the benefits of globalization are not being distributed equitably among the world's peoples, the continued development of a technologically advanced economy may have adverse consequences for the enjoyment of human rights.

The editors thought it important to include this selection in the reader in order to draw attention to the interdependence between technology and the rules of international trading and financial systems and to highlight the role of multinational corporations in the global economy. The report highlights the wide disparities in the access to advanced communications technologies between people in the richer, more developed countries and those in poor countries—the so-called digital divide. It also contains data showing that trade liberalization and financial deregulation do not necessarily result in a fairer distribution of the benefits of economic growth and are sometimes accompanied by illegal trade, such as black market weapons, drugs, and even human beings.

In conclusion, the authors argue that although technological innovation and globalization have the potential to lift millions of people out of dire poverty, this promise will not be realized unless human rights are factored into our economic policies.

Focus Questions

1. The report discusses trade-related aspects of intellectual property rights (TRIPS) under the World Trade Organization (WTO) agreements. Do the authors of this report believe that the current trading rules strike the appropriate balance between the rights of corporations and those of people? Explain.
2. What are some facts cited in the report that indicate that the benefits of technological innovation and international trade are not being distributed equitably among the world's peoples? To what extent should be we be concerned about the disparities mentioned in this report?
3. What is the Global Compact initiative about? Do you think that it is sensible to ask multinational corporations to assume some responsibility for protecting human rights, labor rights, and the environment? Discuss the idea of corporate social responsibility in light of globalization.
4. Compare this reading with those by Senge and Carstedt (selection II.3) and Brown and Flavin (selection II.15). Do you believe that technological innovation and economic growth can be organized so as to benefit everyone?

Keywords

development, direct foreign investment, globalization, human rights, multinational corporations, structural adjustment, trade liberalization, trafficking, TRIPS, UN Global Compact, WTO

Globalization—Issues and Challenges

Globalization is a term often used without any formal definition. The United Nations Development Programme *Human Development Report 1999* noted

From "Globalization and Its Impact on the Full Enjoyment of All Human Rights," Preliminary report of the Secretary-General, United Nations, *General Assembly 31 August 2000,* pp. 2–12.

that globalization is not new, but that the present era of globalization has distinctive features. Shrinking space, shrinking time and disappearing borders are linking people's lives more deeply, more intensely, more immediately than ever before.[1] The present report assumes that globalization is multidimensional. It can be broken down into numerous complex and interrelated processes that have a dynamism of their own, resulting in both varied and often unpredictable effects. While there have been previous eras that have experienced globalization, the present era has certain distinctive features, including, although not limited to, advances in new technology, in particular information and communications technology, cheaper and quicker transport, trade liberalization, the increase in financial flows and the growth in the size and power of corporations. In order to advance a constructive exchange of views on globalization, States might consider conveying to the Secretary-General their views on how globalization might best be defined and approached from the perspective of human rights.

While many people are benefiting from new opportunities for travel and from new communications technology, new levels of wealth through increased trade, investment and capital flows, others are being left behind, in poverty, effectively marginalized from the hopes that globalization holds out.

Globalization therefore presents an important challenge to the international community. Over 50 years ago, the international community agreed, within the framework of the Universal Declaration of Human Rights, that, "Everyone is entitled to a social and international order in which the rights and freedoms set forth in this Declaration can be fully realized." According to the norms and standards of international human rights law, such an international and social order is one that promotes the inherent dignity of the human person, respects the right of people to self-determination and seeks social progress through participatory development and by promoting equality and non-discrimination in a peaceful, interdependent and accountable world.[2]

The norms and standards of international human rights law have an important role in providing principles for globalization. At the same time, the international rules established under the General Agreement on Tariffs and Trade (GATT) and the World Trade Organization (WTO), and the macroeconomic policies of the International Monetary Fund (IMF) and the World Bank play a significant role in shaping and directing globalization. While the norms and standards of international human rights law stress participation, non-discrimination, empowerment and accountability, the global economy stresses economic objectives of free trade, growth, employment and sustainable development. The challenge facing the international community is to ensure that these two sets of objectives can be brought together to meet the commitment to a social and international order conducive to the enjoyment of all human rights. "The Global Compact" with business proposed by the Secretary-General in 1999 is an example of a strategy designed to address issues such as these.

The present report begins with an examination of the framework of international economic rules and policies from the perspective of the principles and goals of human rights law. This examination is followed by an overview of the principal effects of globalization as they have so far been identified by the reports of United Nations organizations, programmes and agencies, specifically as a result of trade liberalization, the increase in international financial flows, the advances in information and communications technology and the growth in the size and power of transnational corporations. The report concludes that the norms and standards of human rights are crucial to a full assessment of the cultural, political, social, environmental and economic dimensions of globalization.

The Global Economy and Human Rights

While various national, regional as well as international rules and policies drive many of the processes of globalization, in particular liberalization, deregulation and privatization, the trade rules established within the framework of the World Trade Organization (WTO) Agreement (the WTO agreements) and the macroeconomic policies of international financial institutions have a particularly strong influence in shaping the workings of the global economy. A review of the global economy as it functions within the framework of the policies of the international financial institutions and the rules of WTO will assist in establishing the extent to which an enabling environment supportive of the enjoyment of human rights exists.

The global economy is of course only one aspect in the creation of a social and international order conducive to the enjoyment of human rights. A just, efficient and equitable social order must also exist at the national level. Good governance at the national level is therefore an essential element. Good governance is important, not only from the perspective of ensuring respect for human rights at the national level, but as a means of incorporating and implementing international norms faithfully. The following issues are raised to solicit responses from States on the diverse effects of globalization at the national, regional and international levels, as a means of developing understanding for a constructive exchange of views on globalization.

THE WORLD TRADE ORGANIZATION AGREEMENTS

On 15 April 1995, the Members of the General Agreement on Tariffs and Trade (GATT) signed the Final Act of the Uruguay Round of Multilateral Trade Negotiations, a document including the various agreements setting rules relevant to trade in goods, services and intellectual property. The various agreements set the principles for trade liberalization, as well as the permitted exceptions, and established a procedure for settling disputes. As a result of the Uruguay Round, WTO, the organization responsible for strengthening the rule of law governing international trade, was created.

There is an unavoidable link between the international trading regime and the enjoyment of human rights. Economic growth through free trade can increase the resources available for the realization of human rights. However, economic growth does not automatically lead to greater promotion and protection of human rights. From a human rights perspective, questions are raised: does economic growth entail more equitable distribution of income, more and better jobs, rising wages, more gender equality and greater inclusiveness? From a human rights perspective, the challenge posed is how to channel economic growth equitably to ensure the implementation of the right to development and fair and equal promotion of human well-being.

There are points of potential convergence between trade principles and objectives and the norms and standards of international human rights law. Looking at the WTO agreements themselves,

the guiding principles can be said to mirror, to some extent, the principles of human rights law and, as such, to provide an opening for a human rights approach to the international trade regime.

The WTO agreements seek to create a liberal and rules-based multilateral trading system under which enterprises from Member States can trade with each other under conditions of fair competition. The goals of WTO itself link the objectives of increasing living standards, full employment, the expansion of demand, production and trade in goods and services with the optimal use of the world's resources, in accordance with the objective of sustainable development. The agreements seek to achieve these ends by establishing rules geared towards reducing barriers to trade and ensuring respect for the principle of non-discrimination among Member States. The WTO agreements also encourage preferential treatment in favour of developing countries and least developed countries in the form of special assistance and longer implementation periods, the non-prohibition on export subsidies and the obligation to consider constructive remedies in anti-dumping actions against imports from developing countries.

The goals and principles of the WTO agreements and those of human rights law do, therefore, share much in common. Goals of economic growth, increasing living standards, full employment and the optimal use of the world's resources are conducive to the promotion of human rights, in particular the right to development.[3] Parallels can also be drawn between the principles of fair competition and non-discrimination under trade law and equality and non-discrimination under human rights law. Furthermore, the special and differential treatment offered to developing countries under the WTO rules reflects notions of affirmative action under human rights law.

These parallels can even be traced to the origins of GATT. It will be recalled that, in 1945, the United Nations was established to uphold peace on the foundations of respect for human rights and economic and social progress and development. The International Trade Organization, which was envisaged in the Havana Charter for an International Trade Organization of 1947, included the International Bank for Reconstruction and Development (IBRD) and IMF as part of that vision. Article XX of the original GATT recognized non-trade public interest values in particular cases where values and rules conflict. Article XX provided that nothing in the Agreement should be construed to prevent the adoption or enforcement by any contracting party of measures necessary to protect public morals, necessary to protect human, animal or plant life or health, relating to the products of prison labour, relating to the conservation of exhaustible natural resources if such measures were made effective in conjunction with restrictions on domestic production or consumption or essential to the acquisition or distribution of products in general or local short supply. The exceptions referred to call to mind the protection of the right to life, the right to a clean environment, the right to food and to health, the right to self-determination over the use of natural resources and the right to development and freedom from slavery, to mention a few. The exceptions under GATT give rise to the question: to what extent does article XX indicate a point of convergence between trade rules and international human rights law? The challenge ahead is to develop the human rights aspects incorporated in international trade law, in particular as a result of the inclusion of article XX, so that the development and implementation of trade rules promote the social and international order envisaged under article 28 of the Universal Declaration of Human Rights.

While the goals and principles of the WTO agreements and international human rights law converge to some extent, the rules which have been adopted to achieve the goals of the former do not always produce results that are consistent with human rights imperatives. To take a case in point, specific issues arise in relation to the standards set concerning intellectual property rights.

First, the minimum standards for the protection and enforcement of intellectual property rights included under the Agreement on Trade-Related Aspects of Intellectual Property Rights (the TRIPS agreement) have led to the expression of concerns of balance and fairness.[4] Issues have been raised in relation to the protection of the intellectual property of indigenous peoples and local communities. It has been said that, while some of the standards in

the TRIPS agreement are relevant to the protection of the knowledge and technology of these groups, the question arises whether the standards established under the TRIPS agreement are sufficient to provide comprehensive protection to the intellectual property of indigenous peoples and local communities. It has been pointed out, for example, that, in spite of the relevance of intellectual property of indigenous peoples to the development of modern technology, including biotechnology and technology relevant to the protection of the environment, universities and companies have taken and developed traditional medicines and other knowledge, protecting the resulting technology with intellectual property rights, without the equitable sharing of the benefits and profits with the original holders of that knowledge. It has also been contended that the TRIPS agreement, in its present form, has not been effective in preventing such uses of culture and technology. One question that has been raised from a human rights perspective is: how can international rules be adapted to protect and promote the cultural rights of indigenous peoples and other groups?[5]

Similarly, questions have been raised over the adequacy of the TRIPS agreement in addressing the needs of developing countries, generally technology users, to access needed technology for development and the protection of the environment.[6] Figures related to patent applications demonstrate an overwhelming presence of technology holders in developed countries.[7] Furthermore, an examination of the flow of royalty fees indicates that the overwhelming proportion of payments and receipts of royalties and licence fees flow between countries with high incomes. For example, in 1998, while sub-Saharan Africa paid US$ 273 million in royalty and licensing fees, and Europe and Central Asia paid US$ 723 million, high-income countries paid US$ 53,723 million. To put this in perspective, high-income countries dwarf the rest of the world in royalty and licencing fee receipts, with high-income countries receiving US$ 63,051 million and the rest of the world only US$ 1,283 million.[8]

While there are many complex reasons explaining the concentration of technology holders and technology transfer in and among developed countries, the figures are significant. Given the importance of technology to development, the TRIPS agreement has implications for the enjoyment of human rights, in particular the right to development, which need to be explored further.

The Committee on Economic, Social and Cultural Rights issued a statement to the Third Ministerial Conference of WTO noting that human rights norms must shape the process of international economic policy formulation so that the benefits for human development of the evolving international trading regime will be shared equitably by all, in particular the most vulnerable sectors.[9] The Committee stated its willingness to collaborate with WTO in the realization of economic, social and cultural rights.

THE POLICIES OF INTERNATIONAL FINANCIAL INSTITUTIONS

The implementation of macroeconomic policies, in particular through the projects and programmes of the international financial institutions, has also played a significant role in shaping globalization. The design and implementation of structural adjustment programmes has heightened concerns that macroeconomic policies do not sufficiently accommodate the need to promote and protect human rights. The special rapporteur of the working group on structural adjustment programmes established by the Economic and Social Council has noted that, while such programmes might be necessary and in fact beneficial for economic growth and social development, their design has generally been motivated by the objective of ensuring repayment of interest on debts owed to international creditor institutions and not by the promotion and protection of human rights.[10] The Committee on Economic and Social Rights has underlined the importance of including the promotion and protection of human rights within the framework of structural adjustment programmes.[11]

The Effects of Globalization: Preliminary Remarks

While the rules and policies of the global economy are important in shaping an international and so-

cial order conducive to the protection of human rights, the active features of globalization, the growth in trade and financial flows, the new information and communication technology and the growth in size and power of corporations, have a dynamism of their own which affect human rights in ways beyond the rules and policies referred to above. The following section identifies issues needing further research concerning some of the possible impacts of these processes on the enjoyment of human rights. The summary of issues is built on recognition of the many positive effects that the processes of globalization have on the enjoyment of human rights for many. However, from a human rights perspective, the principles of equality and non-discrimination underline the importance of promoting the human rights of all. This concern forms the basis for the identification of the issues that follow. The issues are identified in order to assist States in identifying factors relevant for a continuing dialogue on globalization.

ADVANCES IN COMMUNICATIONS AND INFORMATION TECHNOLOGY

One of the most influential elements in the globalization process has been the explosion of information and communications technology. The Internet has enabled people from different regions and cultures to communicate rapidly and across great distances and to access information quickly. Indeed, the Internet is the fastest growing communications tool, with more than 140 million users as at mid-1998, and the number of users expected to pass 700 million by 2001.[12]

In addition, communications networks can foster advances in health and education. The Internet has enabled the interconnection of civil society, which has had a direct impact on the promotion and protection of human rights. The successful organization of civil society has been assisted by the interconnection of individuals and interested groups made possible through modern telecommunication and information technology.

In spite of the benefits flowing from information and communications technology, the uneven spread of new technology can also result in the marginalization of people. World Bank figures indicate that while in high-income countries there are 607 Internet hosts per 10,000 people, in sub-Saharan Africa and in South Asia there are, respectively, only 2 and 0.17 hosts per 10,000 people. Similarly, while in high-income countries, there are, on average, 311 people per 1,000 with personal computers, in Latin America and the Caribbean, there are only 34, and in South Asia there are only 2.9 per 1,000.[13] In the *Human Development Report, 1999,* it has been noted that, in spite of the positive effects of the new technology, it also introduces problems of marginalization. The report characterizes marginalization in the form of divisions by geographical location (countries of the Organisation for Economic Cooperation and Development (OECD) have 91 per cent of connections), education (30 per cent of users have at least one university degree), income (only wealthy people and countries can afford Internet connections) and language (80 per cent of web sites are in English).[14]

The new technology can also be used to abuse human rights, in particular through the spread of hate speech. The Internet, in particular, has been used for the propagation of racism, child pornography and religious intolerance through the spread of violent, sexist, pornographic, anti-minority and anti-religious hate speech and images. The technical difficulty of regulating the content of messages broadcast through the Internet makes it a particularly effective means of misusing the freedom of expression and inciting discrimination and other abuses of human rights. This aspect of the Internet poses particular problems for Governments as protectors of human rights. It will be one of the key issues at the World Conference against Racism, Racial Discrimination, Xenophobia and Related Intolerance, which is to be held in Durban, South Africa, in 2001.

LIBERALIZATION OF TRADE AND FINANCIAL FLOWS

In recent years, many countries, spurred on by liberalizing international and regional trade policies, have based their development strategies on increasing integration into the global financial and trading systems. This has led to a dramatic increase in world exports of goods and services, from $4.7 tril-lion in 1990 to $7.5 trillion in 1998.[15] Today, nearly one fifth of all goods and services produced are being traded internationally.[16] The results have generally been an increase in capital inflows and outflows and a growth in the share of external trade relative to national income.

Increased trade and investment has brought significant benefits to many nations and people. There is evidence to suggest that increased trade and investment are related to higher rates of economic growth and productivity.[17] A recent WTO study suggests that trade provides an important contribution to the economic growth of nations and may ultimately lead to the alleviation of poverty.[18]

However, dismantling trade barriers and the growth of international trade does not always have a positive impact on human rights.[19]

For example, while some nations have benefited from impressive increases in trade and financial flows over the past decade, other countries have not fared so well.[20] The *Human Development Report 2000* noted that, in 1998, least developed countries, with 10 per cent of the world population, accounted for only 0.4 per cent of global exports, representing a consistent fall from 0.6 per cent in 1980 and 0.5 per cent in 1990. Sub-Saharan Africa's share declined to 1.4 per cent, down from 2.3 per cent in 1980 and 1.6 per cent in 1990.[21] Similarly, capital flows tended to remain highly concentrated between developed countries, or to a limited number of developing countries. For example, in 1998, the 10 top developing country recipients accounted for 70 per cent of foreign direct investment (FDI) flows.[22] In 1998, the 48 least developed countries received only $3 billion of the total FDI flow of $600 billion that year.

These figures raise several questions for further consideration: to what extent are the figures connected to trade and financial liberalization? To what extent are they related to a failure to liberalize trade and finance effectively? What other factors cause the low rates of foreign direct investment? To what extent do they identify the benefits of globalization being shared unevenly or at different rates? Finally, how could a human rights approach to trade liberalization correct perceived inequalities in international trade and investment?

It should be recognized that the trade protectionism, which the liberalization of trade is now replacing, can have a negative impact on the promotion and protection of human rights. The uneven distribution of trade and finance is not helped by the significant restrictions on trade that often face developing countries. Indeed, as developing countries open up their economies, they are often faced with significant trade barriers or restricted access in their areas of natural comparative advantage, such as agriculture or textiles.[23] For example, a report of the Department of Economic and Social Affairs notes that, in the agricultural sector, the total level of support in the form of subsidies for agriculture in OECD countries averaged $350 billion during the period from 1996 to 1998, a figure that represents double the agricultural exports from developing countries over the same period. This makes it difficult for developing countries to compete, which is particularly harmful, given the importance of the agricultural sector as a source of income and employment. Ironically, sub-Saharan Africa has one of the most liberal agricultural sectors in the world, in spite of its small share of the global market.[24]

While dismantling barriers to trade and investment opens up markets to new opportunities, a recent study on the social impact of globalization carried out by the International Labour Organization (ILO) found that it can also leave countries vulnerable to global economic changes in exchange rates, wages and commodity prices.[25] This vulnerability to external shocks is exacerbated by a lack of sophisticated economic and social structures in many developing countries.

Ultimately, trade liberalization and financial deregulation have diverse impacts that are often difficult to assess. Country studies undertaken by ILO also indicate that, while it has the potential to improve people's welfare, globalization occurs in a context of rising inequalities.[26] For example, the final ILO report on country studies states that there is a trend towards wider income inequalities, not only in most of the countries under study, but also in other member States. The report goes on to state that there is little evidence that trade is the main direct factor at work.[27] Further research is needed to clarify any linkages between the processes of globalization, trade liberalization and inequality.

While globalization has led to the dismantling of barriers to the trade in goods and services, labour is increasingly restricted inside national and ethnic boundaries. The increasing barriers to trade in labour, and migration in general, have been coupled with a resistance to promote and protect the human rights of migrants. Although the General Assembly adopted the International Convention on the Protection of the Rights of All Migrant Workers and Their Families in 1990, 10 years ago, it still lacks the sufficient number of ratifications by States for it to come into force.

The effect of the growth in trade on workers rights is difficult to assess. A study of nine countries undertaken by the Department of Economic and Social Affairs noted that trade liberalization was accompanied by reduced wages, underemployment, informalization of labour and adverse impacts on unskilled labour, particularly in the manufacturing sector.[28] In relation to women's workers' rights, globalization seems to have had the effect of repeating existing patterns of discrimination against women, but on an international scale. The *World Survey on the Role of Women in Development* indicates that, on the positive side, the orientation of manufacturing production towards exports has led to a significant increase in the share of female workers in export industries. In the international financial services sector, women enjoy high rates of employment, increasingly even at higher levels. However, the report also shows that, in the export manufacturing sector, women workers are generally confined to low skill wage occupations, and it appears that, as jobs and wages improve in quality, women tend to be excluded from them.[29] In the informal sector, it appears that women suffer as a result of the growth of trade with imports displacing women, as workers and as small entrepreneurs, disproportionately to men.[30] This is occurring, in spite of the significant role that women play in the globalization process. As the survey states, "it is now a well-known fact that industrialization in the context of globalization is as much female-led as it is export led."[31]

It is also important to highlight certain negative aspects of international trade in a globalizing world. In doing so, a distinction is made between the rules and policies of the international community concerning trade liberalization and particular international trade practices in a globalizing world. While the globalization of trade has been accompanied by the growth in particular types of trade that lead to human rights abuses, these should not be confused with international rules and policies that are intended to produce trade liberalization. Nonetheless, a report of the Subcommission on the Promotion and Protection of Human Rights notes that, in some instances, and particularly in impoverished and undemocratic societies, globalization has facilitated trade in the form of international arms transfers, which, in turn, provide the necessary tools for armed conflict.[32] The same report links globalization with an increase in the dumping of environmental waste near the homes of low income or minority groups and notes significant dumping in developing countries. Globalization has also been accompanied by the rise in the international trafficking of drugs, diamonds and even human beings, including children. Such aspects of international trade raise issues of the right to life, the right to a clean environment, and the right to development. Further research is needed into the links between the processes of globalization and negative aspects of international trade and the ways in which policies may be formulated to promote and protect human rights in this regard.

The growth of trafficking in women and girls and the sex industry are causes of major concern. Each year, millions of individuals, the vast majority of them women and children, are tricked, sold or coerced into situations of exploitation from which they cannot escape.[33] The causes and effects of trafficking are complex, however several observations are relevant to the discussion of trafficking. First, trafficking in women and girls reflects global inequalities, as it invariably involves movement from a poorer country to a wealthier one.[34] Secondly, trafficking, in particular for prostitution, is becoming more widespread. Crime cartels, operating transnationally, are often the mediator for traf-

ficking, and trafficking for prostitution can be traced to the demand caused by the rapidly expanding global sex industry.[35] As a result, trafficked people suffer abuses of their human rights, in particular freedom from slavery, freedom of movement, freedom from fear, discrimination and injustice.

GROWTH OF CORPORATIONS

The need to compete in new and often distant markets has led to a wave of mergers and acquisitions, which have enabled companies to specialize in core competencies that ensure international competitive advantages in particular areas. This, in turn, has led to the phenomenon of the mega-corporation, with cross-border mergers and acquisitions exceeding the value of $1,100 billion in 1999. As a result, some transnational corporations have greater economic wealth than States. A report by the United Nations Research Institute for Social Development (UNRISD) noted that the annual sales of one transnational corporation exceeds the combined gross domestic product of Chile, Costa Rica and Ecuador.[36]

The comparative size and power of transnational corporations raises issues that need to be considered. In a worst case scenario, transnational corporations may be able to use their position of comparative power over States to play nations and communities off against each other in an effort to receive the most advantageous benefits.[37] The relative power of transnational corporations must not detract from the enjoyment of human rights.

Questions have been raised about the social costs of schemes to attract foreign investment such as economic processing zones. Questions have also been raised about the employment practices of transnational corporations and their effects on the human rights of their employees. Greater attention is needed in order to devise strategies that link investment policy with the protection of workers' rights. In this regard, ILO has been active in developing strategies for the protection of workers rights, in particular through the development and implementation of the Declaration on Fundamental Principles and Rights at Work, as well as the ILO Convention (No. 182) concerning the Prohibition and Immediate Action for the Elimination of the Worst Forms of Child Labour. In the outcome document of the World Summit for Social Development of July 2000, States committed themselves to improving the quality of work in the context of globalization, including through the promotion of these and other ILO initiatives.[38]

Concerns about the impact of the operations of transnational corporations in relation to the protection of cultural diversity were also expressed in the *Human Development Report 1999*.[39] Some commentators fear that failure to give appropriate attention and support to the cultures of local and indigenous peoples, as a counterbalance to foreign influence, could result in pressures on local cultures.[40] Moreover, media control in the hands of a limited number of transnational media corporations can also have implications for the freedom of expression. Highly concentrated media ownership vests powers of censorship in the hands of media owners to determine where and what they publish.[41]

At the same time, transnational corporations can play an important role in promoting and protecting human rights. The Global Compact initiative of the Secretary-General was first proposed in 1999 to challenge business leaders to promote and apply, within their own domains, nine principles derived from international instruments, including the Universal Declaration of Human Rights, to advance human rights, labour and environmental standards.[42] At a meeting held at United Nations Headquarters on 26 July 2000, global leaders from business, labour and civil society met with the Secretary-General to formally launch this initiative. They agreed to work together within the common framework of the Global Compact to strengthen responsible corporate citizenship and the social pillars of globalization through dialogue and operational activities. While the Global Compact is not a substitute for effective action by Governments, or for the implementation of existing or future international agreements, it is a significant step in the direction of voluntary cooperation between the United Nations and the private sector in order to ensure that corporations have a positive impact on the enjoyment of human rights.

Conclusions

POVERTY

The above preliminary overview of globalization identifies evidence to suggest that while globalization provides potential for the promotion and protection of human rights through economic growth, increased wealth, greater interconnection between peoples and cultures and new opportunities for development, its benefits are not being enjoyed evenly at the current stage. Indeed, many people are still living in poverty. On the positive side, World Bank figures indicate that the number of people living on less than $1 a day has been relatively stable in the past decade, in spite of an increase in the world's population, and, as a percentage rate, the percentage of people living in extreme poverty decreased from 29 per cent to 24 per cent between 1990 and 1998. Nonetheless, poverty alleviation is uneven. While East Asia and the Pacific, the Middle East and North Africa have had significant reductions in poverty, poverty rates in South Asia, Latin America and the Caribbean and sub-Saharan Africa have remained relatively stable, while Europe and Central Asia have experienced significant increases in poverty.[43] Statistics also reveal that 790 million people suffer from malnutrition, 880 million have no access to basic health services, 900 million adults are illiterate and 20 per cent of the world's population lacks access to safe drinking water. In sub-Saharan Africa, 51 per cent of the population lives in absolute poverty. The majority of people living in poverty are women.[44]

Poverty is both a cause and effect of human rights abuses. The Vienna Declaration and Programme of Action, adopted at the World Conference on Human Rights in 1993, affirmed that extreme poverty and social exclusion constitute a violation of human dignity. It is difficult to assess the extent to which the various agents of globalization, trade liberalization, deregulation of finance and the growth of corporations and new technology, lead to or alleviate poverty. A study commissioned by WTO indicates that domestic policy in areas such as education and health has a greater impact on poverty than trade does, and concludes that trade liberalization is generally a positive contributor to poverty alleviation.[45] Nonetheless, it is clear that poverty is still a part of the present era of globalization. Given the potential for growth that is offered by globalization, there is a need for more effective strategies to harness this potential as a means of alleviating poverty for all nations and regions.

A SOCIAL AND INTERNATIONAL ORDER

The challenge of article 28 of the Universal Declaration of Human Rights, to ensure the entitlement of everyone to a social and international order supportive of the realization of human rights, remains. At the heart of the challenge is the need to examine the social, political, cultural and economic, dimensions of globalization, and the impact they have on the rights of every human being. As the Secretary-General said in his report to the Millennium Assembly:

> "The economic sphere cannot be separated from the more complex fabric of social and political life, and sent shooting off on its own trajectory. To survive and thrive, a global economy must have a more solid foundation in shared values and institutional practices—it must advance broader, and more inclusive, social purposes."[46]

The keys to achieving these goals exist. The world conferences of the 1990's set out commitments and programmes for the promotion and protection of human rights, the advancement of women and social development. In June 2000, States agreed on new initiatives to achieve social development during the present era of globalization, including through the constant monitoring of the social impacts of economic policies, the reduction of negative impacts of international financial turbulence on social and economic development, the strengthening of the capacities of developing countries, in particular through the strengthening of capacities for trade as it relates to health, and the integration of social as well as economic aspects in the design of structural adjustment and reform programmes.[47]

The goals and programmes are already formulated. The strategy to achieve them lies in acknowledging that the principles and standards of human rights should be adopted as an indispensable framework for globalization. Human rights embody universal shared values and are the common standard of achievement for all peoples and all nations.[48] By adopting a human rights approach, globalization can be examined in its civil, cultural, political, social and economic contexts so that the international community can meet its commitment to an international and social order conducive to respect for human rights. This must be the strategy of governance at all levels—to secure respect of all human rights for everyone.

NOTES

1. United Nations Development Programme (UNDP), *Human Development Report 1999,* Oxford University Press, New York, 1999, p. 1. The report goes on to note that globalization is not a new phenomenon in historical terms, but that it is different today. Some of the characteristics are new markets—foreign exchange and capital markets linked globally, operating 24 hours a day, with dealings at a distance in real time; new tools—Internet links, cellular phones, media networks; new actors—the World Trade Organization (WTO) with authority over national Governments, the multinational corporations with more economic power than many States, the global network of non-governmental organizations (NGOs) and other groups that transcend national boundaries; new rules—multilateral agreements on trade, services and intellectual property, backed by strong enforcement mechanisms and more binding for national governments reducing the scope for national policy.

2. See articles 1, 2 and 28 of the Universal Declaration of Human Rights, parts I and II of the International Covenant on Economic, Social and Cultural Rights and the International Covenant on Civil and Political Rights and article 1 of the United Nations Declaration on the Right to Development.

3. See also articles 3 (Right to life), 23 (Right to work) and 25 (Right to an adequate standard of living) of the Universal Declaration of Human Rights.

4. It should be noted that the protection of intellectual property is a human right under article 27 of

the Universal Declaration of Human Rights and article 15 of the International Covenant on Economic, Social and Cultural Rights. In particular, article 15 (1) (c) notes that "The States Parties to the present Covenant recognize the right of everyone . . . to benefit from the protection of the moral and material interests resulting from any scientific, literary or artistic production of which he is the author." Intellectual property rights themselves, as for example those established according to the minimum standards contained in the TRIPS agreement, are not themselves human rights. However they could be a means of promoting and protecting the human right to intellectual property, so long as the granting of such intellectual property rights achieves the balance and fairness required by article 27 of the Universal Declaration and article 15 of the Covenant.

5. There is of course nothing in the TRIPS agreement that prevents States taking individual action to protect the technology and knowledge of indigenous peoples and local communities.

6. While article 7 of the TRIPS agreement states that the protection and enforcement of intellectual property rights should contribute to the transfer and dissemination of technology, the agreement does not develop any mechanism to achieve this.

7. For example: in 1997, patent applications numbered 2,785,420 in high-income countries, while in East Asia and the Pacific they numbered 290,630; in the Middle East and North Africa there were only 1,716 applications; and in sub-Saharan Africa, 392,959, with only 38 of those being filed by residents. See World Bank, *World Development Indicators 2000*, World Bank, Washington, D.C., 2000, table 5.12.

8. World Bank, op. cit., table 5.12.

9. See E/CN.12/1999/9, para. 5.

10. See E/CN.4/1999/47.

11. See E/1999/22, paras. 378-393. See also, E/C.12/1/Add.7/Rev.1, para. 21.

12. UNDP, op. cit., p. 5.

13. World Bank, op. cit., table 5.12.

14. UNDP, 1999, op. cit., p. 6.

15. UNDP, *Human Development Report 2000*, Oxford University Press, New York, 2000, p. 82.

16. UNDP, 1999, op. cit., p. 1.

17. International Labour Office, *Country studies on the social impact of globalization: final report,* ILO, Governing Body, 276th Session, GB. 276/ WP/SDL/1, para. 30.

18. Ben-David, D. and L. Alan Winters, "Trade, Income Disparity and Poverty," *Special Studies No. 5,* World Trade Organization, WTO Publications, Geneva, 1999.

19. See E/CN.4/Sub.2/1999/11, para. 3.

20. Even those countries that have experienced impressive increases in trade and financial flows have suffered downturns and reversals in fortune as a result of financial crises, such as the Asian financial crisis of 1997.

21. UNDP, 2000, op. cit., p. 82.

22. A/AC.253/25, para. 41.

23. See the comments of Joseph Stiglitz, former World Bank chief economist, quoted in E/CN.4/Sub.2/2000/13, para. 14.

24. A/AC.253/25, para. 21.

25. International Labour Office, op. cit., para. 68 (f).

26. Ibid., para. 3.

27. Ibid.

28. See Janine Berg and Lance Taylor, "External liberalization, economic performance and social policy," New School for Social Research, Working Paper Series: Globalization, Labour Markets and Social Policy, February 2000. Cited in A/AC.253/25, para. 9.

29. See E/1999/44, para. 52.

30. Ibid., para. 55.

31. Ibid., para. 50.

32. E/CN.4/Sub.2/1999/8, para. 16.

33. E/ECE/RW.2/2000/3, para. 1.

34. Ibid., para. 11.

35. Ibid., para. 17.

36. United Nations Research Institute for Social Development, *States of Disarray: The Social Effects of Globalization,* report on the World Summit for Social Development, Geneva, March 1995, p. 153. Similarly, according to the *Human Development Report 1999,* the assets of the top three billionaires are more than the combined gross national product of all least developed countries.

37. See E/CN.4/Sub.2/1995/11, para. 53.

38. A/S-24/8/Rev.1, para. 38.

39. UNDP, 1999, op. cit., para. 4 (f).

40. E/CN.4/Sub.2/1999/8, para. 19. Also, UNDP 1999, op.

41. Ghai, Y., "Rights, Markets and Globalization: East Asian Experience," *Report of the Symposium on Human Development and Human Rights,* UNDP and the Office of the United Nations High Com-

missioner for Human Rights, Royal Ministry of Foreign Affairs, Oslo, Norway, 2–3 October 1998, p. 130.

42. See Mary Robinson, United Nations High Commissioner for Human Rights, *Putting principles into practice: creating a Global Compact with the business sector, 2000.*

43. World Bank, 2000, op. cit., p. 4.

44. See UNDP, 1999, op. cit.; *United Nations Action Strategy for Halving Poverty* (25 May 2000); and

United Nations Bulletin on the Eradication of Poverty (Nos. 1–5).

45. Ben-David, D. and L. Alan Winters, op. cit.

46. A/54/2000, para. 25.

47. See A/S-24/2/Add.2 (Parts I and III), paras. 6 bis, 10, 82, 82 bis and 103 ter.

48. See *Universal Declaration of Human Rights,* preamble.

STACEY L. EDGAR

II.5

Computers and Privacy

This reading, taken from the author's book *Morality and Machine: Perspectives in Computer Ethics,* describes how various new information technologies are posing new threats to personal privacy. The initiatives that have been taken to preserve privacy in face of these threats are also discussed.

At several points in her discussion, Edgar conjures up the image of a society like that described in George Orwell's classic *1984* in which all of us are constantly being watched by Big Brother. Although our present society is different in significant ways from Orwell's dystopian vision, there are also, Edgar suggests, some disturbing similarities in the scale and type of information about oneself that can be obtained by others. The main difference is that citizens in our society still enjoy the protection of a right to privacy that serves as a counterbalance to the new threats to our privacy being created by information technologies. The legal and constitutional basis for this important right is examined by Edgar.

Focus Questions

1. How does the author define the concept of privacy? What is the value of privacy? Is there a right to privacy?

2. Computers and related information technologies have, in the author's view, made invasions of people's privacy easier and more likely. What are some examples she uses to establish this claim? Do you agree?

3. Compare the point of view in this reading to that developed by Langdon Winner (selection I.7). What political values are embodied in many of the new forms of surveillance and screening technologies that Edgar discusses?

Keywords

caller ID, Clipper chip, computerized criminal history system, computer matching, confidentiality, consolidated databases, credit reporting, electronic surveillance, employment screening, market research, medical records, privacy

HUMAN BEINGS MAY INVADE your privacy, but in our modern technological society it is a variety of fancy monitoring devices and computerized record-keeping and record-processing procedures—initiated, run, and analyzed by humans—that pose the greatest threats to personal privacy. One cannot help but think of the two-way telescreens in George Orwell's *1984* or the "Boss" monitoring Charlie Chaplin's bathroom break in *Modern Times,* if the potential of much of today's technology is examined closely.[1]

. . . Defenders of the right to own guns say, "It is not guns that kill people—people kill people." Similarly, "it is not computers that invade privacy—people invade privacy." However, the storage, processing, and monitoring capabilities of today's computers make these invasions of privacy much easier and perhaps more likely.

Why Is Privacy of Value?

John Locke, in the *Second Treatise of Government,* argued that anyone who threatens your (private) property potentially threatens your life, and so you are justified in using the same measures against such a person (including killing him or her) that are permissible in protecting your life. To Locke, the most fundamental human rights were to life, liberty, and property. The defense of private property put forward by Locke connected it with one's right to own one's own body and any natural extensions of that body through one's labor.

The right to one's own, if valid, can be interpreted to include one's thoughts and actions. Thus one would seem to have a right to protect those thoughts and actions against unwanted intrusions, in the same way that no one should violate someone else's body (by rape or murder, for example). The logical exceptions to this are if one's actions infringe on another's rights; then they are subject to control by others. We have a notion of having a

personal "space" into which we can invite others but into which no one should trespass unbidden. Yet modern surveillance techniques and methods of record analysis and "matching" pose a threat to invade our personal spaces, often without our knowledge and certainly without our permission.

The Stoics found, in bad times, that even though their bodies might be in chains, their minds could still be free, and it was on this presupposition that they turned inward to engage in the freedom of their thoughts. If one's mental activity is also threatened, there is nothing left to make life worthwhile.

In order to be fully developed human beings, we must be free to choose. Kant says that the moral individual must be rational and *autonomous.* I cannot be autonomous if there are outside forces directing my decisions. My choices must be private to be truly *mine,* to be truly *choices.* One of the highest-level goods is the exercise of the will, displaying courage or fortitude. These are not group activities. One's courage, one's knowledge, and even one's pleasure are all personal, private. They could not exist without privacy. Your courage may help others, and you can share your knowledge, but they originate and develop in your own private world. Thus if privacy is not intrinsically valuable in itself, it makes possible achievements that *are* intrinsically good.

Kant also stressed the value of a *person* as an end in itself, and that persons should never be used as means. Constant surveillance diminishes your personhood. The world is no longer as you think it is, but rather a mini-world under the microscope of some larger world. You become a *means* to some other end—that of governmental power or corporate profit. Even if you do not ever know you are being observed, the value of what you hold in high regard is diminished, made into a cold statistic. If you *do* realize that you are being observed, then this affects your actions and you are no longer autonomous.

Charles Fried argues that privacy is essential to the fundamental good of friendship. Friendship entails love, trust, and mutual respect, and these can only occur in a *rational context* of privacy.[2] Trust presumes that some things are secret or confidential and will not be revealed; if there is no privacy,

From *Morality and Machine: Perspectives in Computer Ethics* by Stacey L. Edgar. Copyright © 1997, Sudbury, MA: Jones and Bartlett Publishers. www.jbpub.com. Reprinted with permission.

there can be no such confidences. A love relationship involves a certain intimacy that is just between two people; if all of their actions, conversations, and special gifts are made public, something valuable has been lost.

Privacy may simply be necessary to mental survival, just as the body needs sleep. Much of the time we are on a public stage, performing in class, in front of a classroom, at work for an employer, or acting in a play. This requires concentration and effort; we work hard to put forward a certain appearance and a high level of performance to others. It would be very difficult, if not impossible, to do this all of the time. Thus we need some privacy in which to rest, to kick off our shoes, put our feet up, and do and think what we please, *in private*. We are talking about preservation of mental health here.

A utilitarian argument can be made that invasions of privacy cause, overall, more harm than good. There is the potential for inaccurate information being spread around about a person, or even information that is accurate, but is no one else's concern, being misused. Think carefully about the sorts of instances in which you value your privacy. Your bank account? Your grades? (Of course, you may have to disclose them to a potential employer or graduate school, and the administration knows; but colleges, under federal law, must protect your records from casual prying.) Your bathroom activities? (Presumably, you would prefer not to have these broadcast over the airwaves.) Your sex life, or lack thereof? (There are legal protections in most states for what consenting adults do in the privacy of their own homes; these legal protections are grounded in fundamental ethical principles, which recognize privacy as a good, or as contributing to other goods.) Your medical records? Your private fantasies? What else would you add to the list?

Just what is it about each of the preceding cases that you value and that would be compromised if your privacy in these respects was invaded? A totalitarian government, like that of Nazi Germany or in Orwell's *1984*, might want to know everything about its citizens. Those citizens would then cease to be autonomous, freely choosing beings; they would be more like animals in a laboratory or cogs in a machine.

Alexis de Tocqueville, writing about his observations of the United States in 1832, described the sort of despotism that he feared could overcome democratic nations:

> Above this race of men stands an immense and tutelary power, which takes upon itself alone to secure their gratifications, and to watch over their fate. That power is absolute, minute, regular, provident, and mild. It would be like the authority of a parent, if, like that authority, its object was to prepare men for manhood; but it seeks, on the contrary, to keep them in perpetual childhood: it is well content that the people should rejoice, provided they think of nothing but rejoicing. For their happiness such a government willingly labors, but it chooses to be the sole agent and the only arbiter of that happiness; it provides for their security, foresees and supplies their necessities, facilitates their pleasures, manages their principal concerns, directs their industry, regulates the descent of property, and subdivides their inheritances: what remains, but to spare them all the care of thinking and all the trouble of living? . . .
>
> It covers the surface of society with a network of small complicated rules, minute and uniform, through which the most original minds and the most energetic characters cannot penetrate, to rise above the crowd. The will of man is not shattered, but softened, bent, and guided; men are seldom forced by it to act, but they are constantly restrained from acting: such a power does not destroy, but it prevents existence; it does not tyrannize, but it compresses, enervates, extinguishes, and stupefies a people, till each nation is reduced to be nothing better than a flock of timid and industrious animals, of which the government is the shepherd. (Tocqueville, 1956, pp. 303–304)

You probably remember what it was like to be a young child. You don't get any privacy. Adults are constantly hovering over you, afraid you will hurt yourself or some object and telling you "no" a lot. As one grows up, one is given more and more autonomy, control of one's own life, and *privacy*. Who would want to give this up by going back to total surveillance?

"I'll Be Watching You"

Gary T. Marx uses the lyrics from the rock song "Every Breath You Take" (The Police) to point out the scope of current surveillance in our society:

every breath you take	[breath analyzer]
every move you make	[motion detection]
every bond you break	[polygraph]
every step you take	[electronic anklet]
every single day	[continuous monitoring]
every word you say	[bugs, wiretaps, mikes]
every night you stay . . .	[light amplifier]
every vow you break . . .	[voice-stress analyzer]
every smile you fake	[brain wave analysis]
every claim you stake . . .	[computer matching]
I'll be watching you.	[video surveillance][3]

This is a very dramatic way to point up what Marx calls "the new surveillance." This might also be called *dataveillance;* we are living in a world where data, or information, has become the most active commodity. One buys and sells information—on which products the affluent neighborhoods are buying, on the "best buys" in goods (*Consumer Reports*), on who are the most likely prospects to buy into a land deal, and so on.

Information about you is sold; the magazine you subscribe to sells your mailing address to other magazines, or to those who sell products that connect with the theme of the magazine. There is an increasing demand for information that can be found in government records, and a recent *New York Times* article comments that, "for government, selling data can provide extra revenue in times of tight budgets."[4] Vance Packard had noted as early as 1964, in *The Naked Society,* that privacy was becoming harder to maintain, and surveillance was becoming more pervasive.

Some Noteworthy Violations of Privacy Involving Computers

Ed Pankau, the president of Inter-Tect, a Houston investigative agency, wrote a book called *How to Investigate by Computer.* In it, he describes how easy it is to sit at a computer terminal and gather information about someone, and how lucrative it can be for an agency like his. He says that much of his business comes from single women who want potential romantic partners investigated. "For $500, Inter-Tect investigative agency in Houston promises to verify within a week a person's age, ownership of businesses, history of bankruptcies, if there are any tax liens, appearance in newspaper articles, as well as divorces and children."[5]

Procter & Gamble, disturbed when they discovered that someone had leaked confidential company information to the *Wall Street Journal,* got a court order for the phone company in Cincinnati, Ohio, to turn over the phone numbers of anyone who had called the home or office of the *Journal* reporter on the article. This involved scanning millions of calls made by 650,000 phone units.[6] However, this sort of search is made incredibly easy by computerization. What is scary is the impact on private lives of the ease of getting such information.

In California in 1989, Rebecca Schaeffer, a television actress, was murdered by a man who got her home address through the Department of Motor Vehicles records. Since then, California has restricted access to DMV files, but they can still be accessed readily by car dealers, banks, insurance companies, and process servers. Since anyone can register as a process server for under $100, this does not afford much protection of such files.[7]

Although this is not an invasion of *personal* privacy, it makes an interesting example of the power of computer correlation. The scholars who have been working with the Dead Sea Scrolls had very slowly been releasing the documents as they finished working with them and had denied other groups any access to them. However, they did publish concordances of some of the scrolls that had not yet been published. The concordances list all the significant words and their place of occurrence in the text. A group at Union Hebrew College in Cincinnati "reverse-engineered" the concordance, by computer, to recreate one of the unreleased texts.[8] Again, this would not have been possible without the use of a computer. What the Dead Sea Scrolls scholars had hoped to keep private until they were ready to publish was made public through the use of a program that simply was able to manipulate and correlate the partial information they had released.

Software Engineering Notes reported on a middle-school computer in Burbank that calls the homes of absent students each night until it gets a live voice or an answering machine, to check on the validity of the absences.[9] This kind of surveillance could easily be extended to other areas—the workplace in particular.

Records disclosed in 1992 indicate that many employees ("dozens") of the Los Angeles Police Department had been using the police computer files to investigate babysitters, house sitters, and others (potential dates?) for personal reasons.[10] When we think of people in the police departments and in the tax return offices[11] *snooping* into our files for their own personal reasons, when they are not the ones authorized to process those records, it should send chills up and down our spines. Who is snooping into our bank records, our charge-card records, and our phone records, and for what reasons?

In *The Naked Consumer,* Erik Larson describes an interview he had with Jonathan Robbin, president of the Virginia "target-marketing company" Claritas. The company uses computerized *cluster analysis* of census data into different neighborhood types and then examines (and predicts) their consumer habits. They call this analysis *geodemographics;* some of the categories identified are Blue Blood Estates (the richest), Gray Power (the oldest), Public Assistance (the poorest), Pools & Patios, Shotguns & Pickups, Tobacco Roads, and Bohemian Mix (Larson, 1992, pp. 46–47). Claritas has many customers, including the U.S. Army, ABC, American Express, Publishers Clearing House, and big manufacturers of consumer goods such as Coca-Cola, Colgate-Palmolive, and R.J. Reynolds Tobacco. Robbins calls his computer system "a 'proesthetic' device for the mind" (Larson, 1992, p. 47)—one that allows corporate minds to "perceive" new targets. For example, the new Saturn division of GM used the Claritas program PRIZM (Potential Rating Index for Zip Markets) "as part of its vast market research campaign to figure out what kind of car to build and how to sell it" (Larson, 1992, p. 48).

Lotus Corporation was going to market a software package called Lotus Marketplace: Households, which was a database containing information on 120,000,000 Americans, including names, addresses, incomes, consumer preferences, and other personal data. In January 1991, however, Lotus withdrew the package due to an avalanche of complaints about its invasion of privacy.

In *Privacy for Sale,* Jeffrey Rothfeder describes how easy it is to access credit rating information on anyone; he was able to get extensive information on Dan Quayle and Dan Rather. He describes how Oral Roberts was able to buy lists of debtors whose accounts were overdue sixty days or more. Roberts used these lists to send letters addressing the person by first name, saying that he is a friend, and that "it's time to get out from under a load of debt, a financial bondage." The letter continued, commiserating with the recipient's financial burden, and then gets to the point: to plant a seed to get out of the financial bondage by sending a gift of $100 to Oral Roberts, so he could intercede with God and "begin the war on your debt" (Rothfeder, 1992, pp. 23–24).

Rothfeder discusses the fact that your credit reports might not be private, but your video-rental records are. This is because of a personal incident involving a government official. When Robert Bork was a candidate for the Supreme Court in 1987, "an enterprising reporter" at *City Paper,* a Washington weekly, went to Bork's local video store and got a list of the movies that Bork had rented recently (nothing salacious; mostly John Wayne). The paper published the list of titles anyway, and "lawmakers were outraged—and quickly passed the Video Privacy Protection Act of 1988" (Rothfeder, 1992, p. 27).

Rothfeder describes a service called PhoneFile where, for a fee, you can get the address, telephone number, and "household makeup" of almost anyone in the United States, from just the name and the state of residence (1992, p. 29). A New York City woman named Karen Hochmann received a call in Fall of 1988 from a salesman for ITT who wanted her to choose their long-distance service. When she said no, that she didn't make many out-of-town calls, the salesman said, "I'm surprised to hear you say that; I see from your phone records that you frequently call Newark, Delaware, and Stamford, Connecticut." Hochmann was "shocked" and "scared" by this blatant invasion of her personal records (Rothfeder, 1992, p. 89).

Rothfeder reports on the case of a young man whose American Express card was cancelled because the company determined that he did not have enough money in his bank balance to pay his March bill (1992, p. 17). Apparently, American Express made regular checks into people's financial accounts to determine the likelihood of their being able to pay their AmEx tabs.

There exist databases on employees in heavy industries like construction, oil, and gas which are accessed regularly by employers (for example, EIS—Employers Information Service in Louisiana). They contain information such as which employees have demanded worker's compensation; the employer consulting such a database may then decide not to hire such a potential employee (Rothfeder, 1992, pp. 154–157). There also apparently are databases maintained by landlords which can be used to determine that they do not want to rent to people who show up in the database as having complained to previous landlords (even if such complaints are legitimate about lack of heat or water or rodent control).

The coming together of the information superhighway and the proposals for national health care are going to raise serious problems in terms of the confidentiality of medical records. There is a principle that goes back to Hippocrates in the fifth century B.C. that a doctor should hold a patient's medical information to be confidential. But the movement to store patient records in electronic form, and to transfer them from one computer to another, perhaps across considerable physical distances, raises all of the difficulties that we have already seen with the security of any electronic data. A report was produced in 1991 called *The Computerized Patient Record: An Essential Technology for Health Care;* this raises serious issues about the accuracy, access, and privacy of such a record.[12]

Some people are so disturbed by the dehumanization they believe is being brought about by computers that they mount physical attacks against the machines. A "Committee for the Liquidation of Computers" bombed the government computer center in Toulouse, France (January 28, 1983) and there were bombings of the Dusseldorf, Germany, offices of IBM and Control Data Corporation in 1982; the Sperry Rand office in West Berlin; and a Harrison, New York, office of IBM (Eaton, 1986, p. 133).

In 1974, Senators Barry Goldwater and Charles Percy proposed an amendment to a bill in Congress to stop the use of a Social Security number as a universal identifier, to "stop this drift towards reducing each person to a number":

> Once the social security number is set as a universal identifier, each person would leave a trail of personal data behind him for all of his life which could be immediately reassembled to confront him. Once we can be identified to the administration in government or in business by an exclusive number, we can be pinpointed wherever we are, we can be more easily manipulated, we can be more easily conditioned and we can be more easily coerced.[13]

The Pythagoreans thought that everything was number, especially souls (or personal identities). There is an old phrase, "I've got your number!", which implies that you know everything there is to know about that person. In the cases of concern here, the government and big business would have our numbers and so control of our personal destinies.

In Aleksandr Solzhenitsyn's *Cancer Ward,* a view from the Stalinist Soviet Union gives us a chilling, but similar picture:

> As every man goes through life he fills in a number of forms, each containing a number of questions. . . . There are thus hundreds of little threads radiating from every man, millions of threads in all. If these threads were suddenly to become visible, the whole sky would look like a spider's web, and if they materialized like rubber bands, buses and trams and even people would lose the ability to move and the wind would be unable to carry torn-up newspapers or autumn leaves along the streets of the city.

This is also reminiscent of the network of rules that Tocqueville described; is it today the network of computers containing information on all the members of our society?

A National Computerized Criminal History (CCH) System?

In 1986, Kenneth C. Laudon wrote a book called *Dossier Society: Value Choices in the Design of National Information Systems*. His purpose was primarily to examine the FBI's plan for a national computerized criminal history (CCH) system, and the impact it would have on our society and on personal privacy. He first examines the positive side of such a proposal—"the professional record-keeper vision," as he calls it. This would foresee "a more rational world in which instantly available and accurate information would be used to spare the innocent and punish the guilty" (Laudon, 1986, p. 18). He says that this vision is held primarily by police, district attorneys, and criminal courts.

The question of whether such information could be accurate and instantly available should be examined in the light of the performance of similar smaller systems; the odds of increasing errors and decreasing reliability go up alarmingly as the size of a system increases.

As Laudon points out:

> The significance of a national CCH extends beyond the treatment of persons with a prior criminal record. Creating a single system is a multijurisdictional, multiorganizational effort which requires linking more than 60,000 criminal justice agencies with more than 500,000 workers, thousands of other government agencies, and private employers, from the local school district to the Bank of America, who will use the system for employment screening. (Laudon, 1986, p. 16)

Two questions immediately come to mind about such a system: (1) What kind of reliability can it possibly have (and what will be the magnitude of the consequences of system failures or reporting errors)? (2) Is it appropriate, or even legal, for a system designed for one purpose (criminal record-keeping for the justice system) to be used for such a different purpose (employment screening)?

Laudon also notes that, in addition to the fingerprint records on roughly 36 million people with criminal records, the FBI has fingerprints of over twice as many citizens who do not have any criminal record, but have had their fingerprints taken for the armed forces, work in nuclear plants, work on defense contracts, for any work requiring a security clearance for a job, and others. With the amazing capabilities of computerized fingerprint identifications, it would be quite feasible to run *all* of these prints, and not just those of people with criminal records, in any investigation. This would greatly increase the chances of "false positives" and the resulting invasion of innocent people's privacy and equanimity.

The second perspective regarding the national CCH, Laudon writes, is the "dossier society vision," held by members of the ACLU (American Civil Liberties Union), state and federal legislative research staffs, and defense lawyers. Proponents of this vision think in terms of a system with "imperfect information and incomplete knowledge," a "runaway" system that would be out of anyone's control. Linking this information (see the upcoming section on "computer matching") with that from other agencies such as the Social Security Administration, the IRS, and the Department of Defense, could create "a caste of unemployable people, largely composed of minorities and poor people, who will no longer be able to rehabilitate themselves or find gainful employment in even the most remote communities" (Laudon, 1986, pp. 20–21). He also points out that the present system already discriminates against those who live in poor and ghetto neighborhoods, where the police may regularly make a pass down the street in the summer and haul everyone in for questioning, thus creating "criminal records" for many who violated no laws (Laudon, 1986, pp. 226–227).

Laudon pessimistically concludes, "In the absence of new legislation, it is clear that national information systems . . . will continue to develop in a manner which ensures the dominance of efficiency and security over freedom and liberty" (Laudon, 1986, p. 367). This is a frightening prospect. Those running these systems would claim that they are the guards of our domestic and national security; but the old question echoes, "Who will guard the guards?" Hobbes would respond that it must be the Leviathan. What other possibilities are there?

The FBI Wiretap Law

A hotly contested FBI proposal called the Wiretap Bill, or the DT (Digital Telephony) bill, finally passed the Congress *unanimously* on October 7, 1994. The bill mandates that all communications carriers must provide "wiretap-ready" equipment. The purpose of this is to facilitate the FBI's implementation of any wiretaps that are approved by the courts. The bill was strongly opposed by the Computer Professionals for Social Responsibility (CPSR), the Voters Telecomm Watch (VTM), the ACLU, and the Electronic Privacy Information Center (EPIC), among others, and much support for this opposition was marshaled in terms of letters and e-mail messages to congressional representatives.

CPSR sent out a list of "100 Reasons to Oppose the FBI Wiretap Bill"; for example, Reason 29 was that the bill contains inadequate privacy protection for private e-mail records. The estimated cost of enacting the law is (according to a CPSR report) $500 million, which will be borne by "government, industry, and consumers." This is just another instance of an action of government that will infringe on a right of the public (in this case, privacy) and require the public to pay for it.

The Clipper Chip Proposal

Another recent government proposal is the "Clipper chip," a device to establish a national data encryption standard. The device would sell for $30 (or less in large quantities) and allow the encoding of messages sent electronically, to avoid tampering. The objectors (some of whom are referred to as "cypherpunks") fear that the standard, developed by NSA, will have a "trap door" that will allow the government to eavesdrop on any transmissions it chooses.[14]

Some fear that the Clipper chip will create an "information snooperhighway," but NSA assures that Clipper is "your friend." CPSR is at the forefront of the opposition, and made available an electronic petition against Clipper; the petition goes to the president, because the proposal does not require congressional approval, and states reasons for the opposition.

The Clipper petition says that the proposal was developed in secret by federal agencies (NSA and the FBI) whose main interest is in surveillance, not in privacy. The plan will create obstacles to businesses wanting to compete in international markets and discourage the development of better technologies to enhance privacy. "Citizens who anticipate that the progress of technology will enhance personal privacy will find their expectations unfulfilled." The petition goes on to say that the signees fear that if the proposal and the standard are adopted, "even on a voluntary basis, privacy protection will be diminished, innovation will be slowed, government accountability will be lessened, and the openness necessary to ensure the successful development of the nation's communications infrastructure will be threatened" (CPSR, Clipper petition).

There is a moral dilemma arising between the desire for an open society and the need to reduce crime and disorder. This tension is never easily resolved. The ideal would be to have a society in which all people minded their own business, supported the state, and were truly just (Plato's ideal state). Since the real world is not like that, there must be some laws and restrictions to control wrongdoing. However, the laws must not suppress all freedom and undermine what openness is possible. The Wiretap Bill and the Clipper chip lean too far in the direction of suppressing fundamental goods such as freedom. If all communications can in principle be monitored, that creates a closed society, not an open one. All of the arguments against invasions of privacy in the beginning of this chapter apply.

Computerized Credit

Many people today use credit cards to buy various products and services. Credit cards can even be used in many grocery stores and liquor stores now. The information from any of these credit cards, plus data on any loans from banks or other financial institutions, goes into several huge centralized credit bureaus. An institution (or, as Rothfeder demonstrated, an individual) can request this information on someone, usually if it is considering giving the person a loan or a credit line.

The Federal Trade Commission puts out informational pamphlets on credit bureaus so that individuals will know what they are, how they operate, and what the individual's rights are with respect to credit bureaus. A credit bureau is a kind of "clearinghouse" for information on a person's financial history. The Fair Credit Reporting Act of 1971 attempted to regulate the credit bureaus' operation and provide some privacy for the personal information they handle. However, in reality there is very little private about this data. The regulations *do* allow an individual access to the information and the opportunity to request correction of any errors.

One of the largest credit bureaus is TRW. It will provide you, on request, with one free copy of your credit report per year (but a free one might take three to four weeks to reach you; one you pay for [$8.68 last time I checked] comes within a week). To request a copy of your credit report, you must send a letter (with your check) indicating your full name, current mailing address (and other addresses within the past five years), your Social Security number, and your date of birth. Send this to TRW, P.O. Box 2106, Allen, Texas 75002. The report comes with a copy of your credit rights and how to go about resolving any disputes.

The report I received contained a listing of recent (it seemed to cover about the past six years) charge accounts and bank loans. It contained a description of each account (revolving credit, car loan, mortgage, etc.), the current balance, and whether all payments had been made on time. It also contained a list of inquiries made into the credit record. Most of them were inquiries from financial institutions determining whether to send me an offer of a new charge card ("to develop a list of names for a credit offer or service"). Thus TRW does not have to notify you every time an inquiry is made, but when you receive a credit report you get a listing of recent inquirers into your record.

Rothfeder says that TRW "upgrades and expands its files with information it purchases from the Census Bureau, motor vehicle agencies, magazine subscription services, telephone white pages, insurance companies, and as many as sixty other sources. 'We buy all the data we can legally buy,' says Dennis Benner, a TRW vice president" (Rothfeder, 1992, p. 38). TRW also has a Highly Affluent Consumer database, from which it sells names, phone numbers, and addresses of people categorized by income to anyone (catalog company, telemarketer, or political group) that will pay for it (Rothfeder, 1992, p. 97). TRW will also screen out names of those who are late in payments or likely to go bankrupt!

The storage, transfer, and analysis of all of this information is made possible by computers. Computers have thus presented us with the ethical concern of whether the handling and disseminating of this information creates a breach of our moral rights—in this case, the right of privacy.

Caller ID

A new service called "Caller ID" *sells* information on who you are (your phone number) when you make a phone call. Some states (such as California) have prohibited "Caller ID," but it is in place in many other states, including New York. The original idea behind "Caller ID" was to track nuisance callers (but they can just call from pay phones), and perhaps to allow call recipients to screen their calls. However, in practice it represents an invasion of the caller's privacy, the right not to have one's number identified; many people pay to have unlisted phone numbers for just that reason. CPSR has spoken out against it: "Caller ID, for example, reduced the privacy of telephone customers and was opposed by consumers and state regulators."[15]

There also is an option called "Call Return," which allows anyone you have called to call you back, whether they answered your call or not. In New York, there is a feature called "Per-Call Restrict," where you can block display of your number on the recipient's "Caller-ID" device, if you press *67 on a touch-tone phone, or dial 1167 on a rotary phone, before you place your call. That seems like an annoyance at the very least. In something that should by rights be private, you have to go to an extra effort every time you place a call to ensure that privacy. And, given that feature, what nuisance caller (against whom the ID system was initially devised) would not use the Call-Restrict option to prevent identification?

To those who think that Caller ID is just an innocent convenience, consider some cases where it might be damaging. (1) A professor, who values her privacy and quiet time, out of decency calls a student who has left a message of panic regarding tomorrow's exam. After the professor spends half an hour on the phone answering questions, the student lets others know that the professor helped and gives out her (unlisted) phone number, obtained through Caller ID. The professor (who had more than adequate office hours all semester to help students) is harassed all evening with phone calls from other students in the class. (2) A consumer calls to make a telephone inquiry about the price of a product, but decides not to buy. The organization that took the call begins phoning her every week, trying to talk her into other products. (3) An informant, who wishes to remain anonymous, calls the police department to report a crime. The police record from Caller ID is used to track down the informant, and the phone number and address also are picked up by a nosy reporter, who puts the person's name in a newspaper article.

Computer Matching

Computer matching involves combining information from several databases to look for patterns—of fraud, criminal activity, and so on. Generally, it is used to detect people who illegally take government money from more than one source—they are termed "welfare double-dippers."

The Reagan Administration was quick to capitalize on the capabilities of computer matching. In March 1981, President Reagan issued an executive order establishing a President's Council on Integrity and Efficiency (PCIE) to "revitaliz[e] matching to fight waste, fraud and abuse" (*Computer Matching and Privacy,* 1986, p. 56). This government committee has seemed to be primarily concerned with assessing the cost-effectiveness of matching pro-

grams, rather than with looking into how they may constitute serious invasions of personal privacy. The Long-Term Computer Matching Project has published a quarterly newsletter, developed standardized formats for facilitating matching, created a "manager's guide" to computer matching, established Project Clean Data (a program that identifies incorrect or bogus Social Security numbers), and looked into problems of security with the systems in which matching takes place, in order to promote "efficient and secure matches" (*Computer Matching,* 1986, pp. 59–60).

Some of the government agencies involved in computer matching include Defense, Veterans Affairs, HEW, HUD, the Postal Service, Agriculture, Health and Human Services, Justice, Social Security, Selective Service, NASA, and Transportation. Examples of matches performed include locating wanted and missing persons files with federal and state databases, detecting underreporting of income by those receiving mortgage or rent subsidies (or food stamps or other aid), locating absent parents with child support obligations, checking wage reports against those receiving unemployment, and so on (*Computer Matching,* 1986, pp. 236–246). One can see that the possibilities are practically limitless. Some of these matches may be perfectly justifiable, as in cases where Social Security fraud is being perpetrated against the government. But it will be so easy to cross the line into blatant invasions of personal privacy, and the lines are not clearly drawn, or are not drawn at all.

The American Bar Association (ABA) has identified seven distinct areas in which computer matching programs impinge on privacy:

1. *Fourth Amendment.* Privacy advocates have argued that matching of databases containing personal information constitutes a violation of the Fourth Amendment right to security against unreasonable searches. Supporters of computer matching argue that the programs do not search in general, but rather "scan" for records of particular persons who are applying for benefits. That, of course, does not mean that such programs could not be easily modified to search in general.

2. *Privacy Act.* Some claim that computer matching programs violate the Privacy Act of 1974, which provides that personal information collected for one purpose cannot be used for a different purpose without notice to the subject and the subject's consent. However, the Privacy Act has a "routine use" clause that has been used to bypass this consideration. "Congress has in fact authorized most of the ongoing matching programs, overriding whatever protection the Privacy Act afforded" (*Computer Matching,* 1986, p. 97).

3. *Fair Information Practice Principle.* Even if the law is not violated by current computer matching practice, it does violate the fair information practice that information collected for one purpose should not be used for another purpose without due notice and consent. This is reflected in the 1979 ABA resolution: "There must be a way for an individual to prevent information obtained for one purpose from being used or made available for other purposes without his or her consent" (*Computer Matching,* 1986, p. 97).

4. *Due Process.* Violations of "due process" have occurred in computer matching cases. For example, in Massachusetts in 1982, the state matched welfare records against bank accounts and terminated benefits without notice. In several cases, the "matches" were incorrect, and in others there were legitimate reasons for the money in the bank accounts that did not violate welfare restrictions.

5. *Data Security.* Unauthorized access to the databases in which this matching information is stored constitutes a real threat to the personal privacy of those whose records are stored there, and the government has not developed security measures adequate to protect them (*Computer Matching,* 1986, p. 98).

6. *Data Merging.* The government can query any number of files on a citizen; this leads to the possibility of a merged file in a new database containing information from various sources (which could well violate areas 2 and 3). For example, recent rulings allow the IRS to deduct debts owed the government from tax refunds, and the IRS was proposing (in 1986) to establish a "master debtor file" (*Computer Matching,* 1986, p. 98).

7. *Fundamental Privacy Rights.* What is to keep the government from linking personal data on medical records, financial records, reading and viewing preferences, and political and religious activities? This is all unsettlingly reminiscent of Orwell's *1984.* Ronald L. Plesser, who made the presentation to Congress as designee of the American Bar Association, said: "Substantive limits on data linkage have to be established. At some point, privacy and autonomy outweigh government efficiency" (*Computer Matching,* 1986, p. 99; general discussion, pp. 92–103).

When New York City and New Jersey recently compared their welfare databases, they discovered 425 people who were regularly collecting welfare in both areas, using fake IDs, to the tune of about $1 million in unauthorized cost to the welfare system. The system is currently experimenting with using fingerprints as IDs for welfare recipients. Critics complain that it will discourage poor people from getting aid, since it carries with it the stigma of a criminal context. Soon after the fingerprint experiment was implemented, over 3,000 people dropped out of the system.[16]

Some might just say "Good! Three thousand fewer leeches on society." The question comes down to the real purpose of our welfare system. Do we really want to help people in need, or not? A number of the ethical systems we examined would support this as the right thing to do, if one cannot have an ideal society in which there is enough for everyone to prosper. The utilitarian principle is clear: we should do what fosters the greatest good (pleasure and absence of pain) for the greatest number of people. Kant would emphasize that rational beings must be treated as ends in themselves, and this would include awarding them respect and humane treatment, since *they* represent what is intrinsically valuable, not dollars. Certainly it develops virtuous character to be generous. And, on the goods view, we should do what maximizes the highest goods, such as friendship, knowledge, satisfaction, health, and life.

As it is now, people who go for legitimate welfare support, or for temporary unemployment compensation when they unexpectedly lose their jobs in an unstable economy, are made to feel like dirt and are brought back repeatedly to fill out repetitive forms. If we add fingerprint identification, they will surely be made to feel like criminals, as the article suggests. If we *intend* to help those who need help, then we should do it with open hearts and efficient procedures, not grudgingly and in a demeaning way.

The Worst Scenario

We have seen how records on us are kept, analyzed, sold, and transmitted. Most of this information is financial, but there are other records on us as well. *USA Today* estimated recently that the average adult American has computerized files in at least twenty-five different databases. In 1990, the General Accounting Office reported that there were at least 2,006 federal computer databases, 1,656 of which were covered by the Privacy Act. These databases were under the various cabinet departments (Defense, Health and Human Services, Justice, Agriculture, Labor, Treasury, Interior, Transportation, Commerce, Energy, Veterans Affairs, Education, and Housing and Urban Development—in order from most systems to least), and various independent agencies such as the Environmental Protection Agency, NASA, the FCC, the Nuclear Regulatory Commission, and the Federal Reserve System, to name a few. The odds are that your name (and data) shows up in a number of those databases. When the databases start "talking to" each other, they are doing "matching" on you for various purposes.

In the Foreword to David Burnham's *The Rise of the Computer State,* Walter Cronkite wrote:

> Orwell, with his vivid imagination, was unable to foresee the actual shape of the threat that would exist in 1984. It turns out to be the ubiquitous computer and its ancillary communication networks. Without the malign intent of any government system or would-be dictator, our privacy is being invaded, and more and more of the experiences which should be solely our own are finding their way into electronic files that the curious can scrutinize at the punch of a button.
>
> The airline companies have a computer record of our travels—where we went and how long we stayed and, possibly, with whom we traveled. The car rental firms have a computer record of the days and distances we went afield. Hotel computers can fill in a myriad of details about our stays away from home, and the credit card computers know a great deal about the meals we ate, and with how many guests.
>
> The computer files at the Internal Revenue Service, the Census Bureau, the Social Security Administration, the various security agencies such as the Federal Bureau of Investigation and our own insurance companies know everything there is to know about our economic, social and marital status, even down to our past illnesses and the state of our health.
>
> If—or is it when?—these computers are permitted to talk to one another, when they are interlinked, they can spew out a roomful of data on each of us that will leave us naked before whoever gains access to the information. (Burnham, 1983/1980, pp. vii–viii)

Cronkite, Burnham, and many others have seen the threat to our privacy and our autonomy that these systems present. Yet our complex world could not run as it does now without them. It has been suggested that the best way to cripple a country would be to take out its financial networks, and these are now totally dependent on computers. But this leaves us with the question (a very important and a very difficult one) of how we can maintain some level of autonomy and some measure of privacy for ourselves and others in the face of this evergrowing "spider's web" (as Solzhenitsyn described it) of communication and *control.* How can we remain *persons* (with the rights and responsibilities that are entailed) when we are being reduced to mere *numbers* every day?

Dennie Van Tassel wrote a very clever scenario that he devised for the collection he co-edited, *The Compleat Computer* (which is highly recommended reading). The piece is called "Daily Surveillance Sheet, 1989, From a Nationwide Data Bank" (Van Tassel and Van Tassel, 1983/1976, pp. 216–217). In it he describes the "Confidential" report on "Harry B. Slow," which tracks his every move through the use of his many credit cards. All purchases and bank transactions are listed, and from this record the computer analyzes that Harry drinks too much, is probably overweight, has a weakness for young blondes, and is probably having an affair with his secretary (a blonde).

The scenario is amusing, but it is also frightening. We are moving into an age where most of our purchases and activities can be tied to a record with our name (or number) on it, through credit cards, bank accounts, library cards, video rental cards, and other identifiers. We tend not to carry a lot of cash (fear of being robbed, perhaps) and so pay for most items by a traceable credit card. My grocery store has a record of what I buy because, even though I usually pay in cash, to receive their special discounts on items each week, I have to use a special coded card that identifies me as a member of their "Club." Thus they have a record of my buying patterns to analyze and sell to various companies that manufacture the products I buy.

Van Tassel has shown us a picture that is not far from the truth today and that will most likely be very close to the truth in the future. Does this present a moral problem and, if so, is there anything we can do about it? Our political systems should have moral underpinnings, and it is through those political systems that we can try to make a difference. One of the problems is that many of the "technocrats" creating and using the computer systems that are invading privacy are not part of the government and so are not accountable to the public as the government should be.

Some of you will become part of the technological force that creates and maintains elaborate computer systems, and so you, at least, will be aware of the dangers involved and your corresponding responsibilities. Others may not be so aware, and so the answer must lie in education and in making groups accountable. Some impact can come from the public "voting with its feet" and not buying certain products, or making public complaints, such as those against the Lotus Marketplace: Households

project or the Clipper chip. But government must also be sensitized to the threats to the freedoms promised by the Constitution, freedoms which are its responsibility to protect.

What Protections Are There for Privacy?

The United States Constitution, in its Bill of Rights, has two Amendments which might be thought to relate to the privacy issue—the First and the Fourth. The First Amendment guarantees freedom of religion, speech, the press, and assembly. However, none of those freedoms mentions privacy or necessarily entails privacy. The Fourth Amendment says: "The right of the people to be secure in their persons, houses, papers, and effects against unreasonable searches and seizures, shall not be violated." This relates to prohibiting anyone from looking for and/or taking anything from you or your home without a warrant issued upon demonstration of *probable cause*. However, it does not say anything regarding information about you that is not on your person or in your home, but which should be kept private, or at least not made public (such as your tax return, medical records, driving record, or the like). Notice also that your garbage is not considered private; it is no longer in your home, and someone can search it without violating any laws.

The point is that your tax return is no one's business but yours and the IRS's, your medical files are no one's business but yours (or yours and your doctor's), and your driving record is no one's business but yours and the Motor Vehicle Bureau's. No one outside of the offices mentioned has any *need to know*, or any *right to know*, such information about you. Yet there are cases of people working at the IRS "snooping" into people's files (not the ones they are assigned to work on, but those of neighbors, or famous people), of medical information being sold to drug or insurance companies, and of drivers' records being available for a small fee to anyone in thirty-four states.[17] Medical records of political candidates have been compromised to leak stories about psychiatric counseling, suicide attempts, or other damaging information. The press will claim the public's "right to know" in cases of public figures, but the fact remains that a fundamental guarantee of the privacy of information between patient and doctor has been violated.

In the *Roe v. Wade* (410 U.S. 113, 1973, p. 152) abortion decision, justice Harry A. Blackmun stated the opinion:

> The Constitution does not explicitly mention any right of privacy. In a line of decisions, however. . . . the Court has recognized that a right of personal privacy, or a guarantee of certain zones or areas of privacy, does exist under the Constitution. In varying contexts, the Court or individual justices have, indeed, found the roots of that right in the First Amendment, . . . in the Fourth and Fifth Amendments, . . . in the Ninth Amendment, . . . or in the concept of liberty guaranteed by the first section of the Fourteenth Amendment . . . These decisions make it clear that only personal rights can be deemed "fundamental" or "implicit in the concept of ordered liberty" . . . are included in this guarantee of personal privacy. (Cited in Freedman, 1987, p. 73)

If there is any suggestion in the Fifth Amendment, it would have to lie in the right of a person not to be compelled to be a witness against himself (or herself). The Ninth Amendment states: "The enumeration in the Constitution, of certain rights, shall not be construed to deny or disparage others retained by the people." This is too vague or too broad to be helpful. If it is interpreted to support privacy, it could also be construed to support an individual's right to a free car. The Fourteenth Amendment states that all citizens have the rights of citizens, but does not spell these out beyond the rights to life, liberty, and property. It does not seem that a right to privacy can be inferred as strongly from these Amendments (Five, Nine, and Fourteen) as from Amendments One and Four.

Warren and Brandeis Make a Case for Privacy

The beginning of the Court's recognition of the right to privacy lies in the article, entitled "The Right to Privacy," written by Samuel D. Warren and Louis D. Brandeis in 1890.[18] They suggest that the rights to life, liberty, and property as previously interpreted were seen to relate only to the *physical* side of human beings, and do not take into account their *spiritual* side. Gradually this came to be recognized, and "now the right to life has come to mean the right to enjoy life—the right to be let alone; the right to liberty secures the exercise of extensive civil privileges; and the term 'property' has grown to comprise every form of possession—intangible as well as tangible" (Warren and Brandeis, cited in Schoeman, 1984, p. 75).

Recognition of the "legal value of sensations" gave rise to laws against assault, nuisance, libel, and alienation of affections. The rights to property were legally extended to processes of the mind, works of literature and art, good will, trade secrets, and trademarks. They suggest that this development of the law was "inevitable"; the heightened intellect brought about by civilization "made it clear . . . that only a part of the pain, pleasure, and profit of life lay in physical things" (p. 76). Their concern is for the "right to be let alone"—to be free of the intrusions of unauthorized photographs and yellow journalism.

Warren and Brandeis point out that the law of libel only covers broadcasting of information that could injure the person in his or her relations with other people; but there are other personal items of information that no one else should be able to communicate, and libel does not cover this. The very occasion of the article was untoward plying into the lives of Mr. and Mrs. Warren, and the wedding of their daughter, by the Boston newspapers. William L. Prosser, in commenting on privacy in the context of the Warren and Brandeis article, suggests that four torts (wrongful actions for which civil suit can be brought) arose out of their position and subsequent court decisions:

1. Intrusion upon the plaintiff's seclusion or solitude, or into his private affairs.

2. Public disclosure of embarrassing private facts about the plaintiff.

3. Publicity which places the plaintiff in a false light in the public eye.

4. Appropriation, for the defendant's advantage, of the plaintiff's name or likeness. (Prosser, in Schoeman, 1984, p. 107)

Warren and Brandeis close by saying that "the protection of society must come through a recognition of the rights of the individual." Each individual is *responsible* for his or her own actions only; the individual should resist what he or she considers wrong, with a weapon for defense.

> Has he then such a weapon? It is believed that the common law provides him with one, forged in the slow fire of the centuries, and today fitly tempered to his hand. The common law has always recognized a man's house as his castle, impregnable, often, even to its own officers engaged in the execution of its commands. Shall the courts thus close the front entrance to constituted authority, and open wide the back door to idle or prurient curiosity? (Warren and Brandeis, cited in Schoeman, 1984, p. 90)

The subtitle to "The Right to Privacy" is "The Implicit Made Explicit." It would seem that what Warren and Brandeis tried to do, and whose lead most courts subsequently followed, was to point out the strong connection between holding an individual *responsible* for actions and allowing him or her the *privacy* of thought and control of action to exercise such responsibility.

The Warren and Brandeis analysis deals only with the harm that can be done if someone uses information about you, and suggests that merely possessing that information is not a harm. However, one can think of many instances when someone merely possessing private information about you would present, at the very least, an embarrassment. It is analogous to the cases discussed at the beginning of the chapter where, even if you are not aware that you are being monitored, harm is done because you are diminished as a person and a free agent.

Existing Privacy Legislation

The *Fair Credit Reporting Act* (15 U.S.C. 1681) All credit agencies must make their records available to the person whose report it is; they must have established means for correcting faulty information; and they are to make the information available only to *authorized* inquirers.

The *Crime Control Act of 1973* Any state information agency developed with federal funds must provide adequate security for the privacy of the information it stores.

The *Family Educational Right and Privacy Act of 1974* (20 U.S.C. 1232g) Educational institutions must grant students and/or their parents access to student records, provide means for correcting any errors in the records, and make such information available only to authorized third parties.

The *Privacy Act of 1974* (5 U.S.C. 552a) This act restricts the collection, use, and disclosure of personal information, and gives individuals the right to see and correct such information.

Sam Ervin had felt that the legislation required the establishment of a Privacy Commission. The report of the Senate Committee on Government Operations (September 1974) stated:

> It is not enough to tell agencies to gather and keep only data for whatever they deem is in their intended use, and then to pit the individual against government, armed only with the power to inspect his file, and the right to challenge it in court if he has the resources and the will to do so.
>
> To leave the situation there is to shirk the duty of Congress to protect freedom from the incursions by the arbitrary exercise of the power of government and to provide for the fair and responsible use of such power. (U.S. Senate 1976: 9–12; cited in Burnham, 1983/1980, p. 364)

The *Tax Reform Act of 1976* (26 U.S.C. 6103) Tax information must remain confidential and not be released for nontax purposes. (However, there has been an ever-increasing list of exceptions to the release restriction since 1976.)

The *Right to Financial Privacy Act of 1978* (12 U.S.C. 3401) The act establishes some privacy with regard to personal bank records, but provides means for federal agencies to access such records.

The *Protection of Pupil Rights Act of 1978* (20 U.S.C. 1232h)   The act gives parents the right to examine educational materials being used in the schools, and prohibits intrusive psychological testing of students.

The *Privacy Protection Act of 1980* (42 U.S.C. 2000aa)   Government agents may not conduct unannounced searches of news offices or files if no crime is suspected of anyone.

The *Electronic Funds Transfer Act of 1980*   Customers must be notified of any third-party access to their accounts.

The *Debt Collection Act of 1982* (Public Law 97-365)   Federal agencies must observe *due process* (of notification, etc.) before releasing bad-debt data to credit bureaus.

The *Congressional Reports Elimination Act of 1983*   This act eliminated the requirement under the Privacy Act for all agencies to republish all of their systems notices every year.

The *Cable Communications Policy Act of 1984* (Public Law 98-549).   A cable subscriber must be informed of any personal data collected (and when), and the use and availability there will be of such information.[19]

The Importance of Privacy

Not only do all of the databases discussed have information on private citizens that can be "matched" and from which patterns of behavior can be inferred, but there are the problems of *security* of the information (from parties who should not have access to it), whether anyone has a right to that data, and the *accuracy* of the information. . . .

Rothfeder (1989) reports that a GAO survey made in 1990 of the TECS II (Treasury Enforcement Communications Systems, Version II) revealed errors in 59 percent of the records it examined. There is good reason to believe that the other computerized records (in the Justice system, NCIC, voter records, credit bureaus, the IRS, the welfare system, and many more) are also filled with errors. . . .

Thus the problem becomes more than just one of an invasion of privacy; it is also one of "them" having lots of information on individual citizens, which "they" will use for various purposes to manipulate and tax them, but that much of that data is wrong (in small or in large ways).

One objection raised to the demand for privacy says that anyone•who needs privacy must be planning to do something that he or she should not do and so needs the protection of privacy to carry it out. We might call this the "ring of Gyges" objection. Glaucon, in the *Republic,* claimed that if the "just" individual and the "unjust" individual both had a ring of Gyges that would make them navigable at will, they would both behave exactly the same way (taking advantage of others for their own gain). Thus the objectors to demands for privacy say that the only reason anyone would want the "cloak of invisibility" that privacy offers is that she must be up to no good.[20]

It is true that privacy helps to protect the actions of the thief, or the murderer, or the terrorist. But it would be an unfortunate conclusion to draw that therefore no one should be allowed any privacy. Such a world has already been described by George Orwell and others, and it is not a world that anyone would want to live in.

Some can be immune to punishment without needing privacy, if they are sufficiently powerful. Not everyone who wants privacy is planning to do evil; you might, for example, want to plan a surprise birthday party for someone. And not everyone who is planning to do evil needs privacy; Hitler carried out much of his evil in full public view. Many criminals want the notoriety they feel they have earned. Think of examples of hackers like Kevin Mittnick, who seem to glory in the challenge and the recognition.

If we act on the assumption of a world where everyone is selfishly out for personal gain, with no scruples, then we would seem to have no alternative to the society described in Hobbes' *Leviathan.* Then we could let a supercomputer like the one in the movie *Colossus: The Forbin Project* monitor all of our actions and punish misbehavior. But in such a world there would be no creativity, no flowering of the human spirit; we would all become cogs in a big machine, obediently doing what we are told by Colossus. Hopefully, this is not our world, and we do have the human right to exercise our choices.

In the Canadian report on *The Nature of Privacy* by the Privacy and Computer Task Force, the following insightful statement is made:

> If we go about observing a man's conduct against his will the consequence of such observation is that either the man's conduct is altered or his perception of himself as a moral agent is altered. The notion of altering conduct or self-perception against the will of the moral agent is offensive to our sense of human dignity. If, through a monitoring device, we are able to regulate or indeed to follow the conduct of a person it is obvious that we are in effect compromising his responsibility as a chooser of projects in the world, thereby delimiting or influencing the kinds of choices that we make available to the doer. (Weisstaub and Gotlieb, 1973, p. 46)

It is clear that, in order to be a moral agent, in order to be *responsible* for what we do, we must be in control of our own choices, autonomous. If you are being constantly monitored in everything you do, that monitoring will affect your behavior. It is sort of like the Heisenberg Uncertainty Principle in physics; when you try to measure something, you disturb what it is you are trying to measure, and so you do not get a true reading.

The real choices you make are internal, and you need to know that they are truly your own choices (not determined by some external pressure or other). You cannot have that assurance if everything you do is public. If it is, you will always wonder, did I just do that because Dad was watching me? Because I was afraid of being punished if I didn't do it? Then it is not really *my* choice.

Augustine pointed out that it is better to have choice than not to have it, even though that means you may make some bad choices. Similarly, it is better to have privacy than not to have it, even if sometimes others (and even you) misuse it. If we do not have it, just as if we do not truly have choice, we are not fully human, and we cannot fulfill our human potential (which Aristotle

would say is to *choose* the life of understanding, which is a very private thing, though we may choose to share it).

NOTES

1. Ithiel de Sola Pool wrote, in the first chapter of *Technologies of Freedom,* entitled "A Shadow Darkens": "Electronic modes of communication . . . are moving to center stage. The new communication technologies have not inherited all the legal immunities that were won for the old. When wires, radio waves, satellites, and computers became major vehicles of discourse, regulation seemed to be a technical necessity. And so, as speech increasingly flows over those electronic media, the five-century growth of an unabridged right of citizens to speak without controls may be endangered" (Pool, 1983, p. 1) We should be deeply concerned about anything that threatens our right to freedom of speech or our privacy. These are not the same, but we may require privacy to protect our freedom of thought and speech.

2. Charles F. Fried, *An Anatomy of Values* (Cambridge: Harvard University Press, 1970), p. 9.

3. G. Marx, "I'll Be Watching You: The New Surveillance," *Dissent* (Winter 1985), 26.

4. "Sellers of Government Data Thrive," *New York Times,* 26 December 1991, Sec. D, p. 2, col. 2.

5. *Software Engineering Notes* 15, no. 1 (Jan. 1990), 4.

6. *Software Engineering Notes* 16, no. 4 (Oct. 1991), 8.

7. Ibid., p. 12.

8. Ibid., pp. 11–12.

9. *Software Engineering Notes* 17, no. 1 (Jan. 1992), 6–7.

10. "Police Computers Used for Improper Tasks," *New York Times,* 1 November 1992, Sec. 1, p. 38, col. 1.

11. Stephen Barr, "Probe Finds IRS Workers Were 'Browsing' in Files," *The Washington Post,* 3 August 1993, Sec. A, p. 1, col. 1.

12. See the article on CPR by Scott Wallace (1994) and the article by Sheri Alpert (1993) on "Smart Cards, Smarter Policy."

13. 94th Congress, 2nd Session, *Legislative History of the Privacy Act of 1974,* 759. In Eaton, 1986, p. 152.

14. The interested reader is referred to the articles by John Markoff (1991), "Wrestling Over the Key to the Codes," and Steven Levy (1994), "Cypherpunks vs. Uncle Sam: Battle of the Clipper Chip."

15. *The CPSR Newsletter* 11, no. 4, and 12, no. 1 (Winter 1994), 23.

16. Mitch Betts, "Computer Matching Nabs Double-Dippers." *Computerworld* 28, no. 16 (April 28, 1994), 90.

17. Mitch Betts, "Driver Privacy on the Way?", *Computerworld*, 28 February 1994, 29.

18. Brandeis was to serve as an Associate Justice of the Supreme Court from 1916 to 1939.

19. The main source of this list of legislation affecting privacy was Kenneth C. Laudon, *Dossier Society* (1986).

20. There is another side to the story of the ring of Gyges, as you may recall. Socrates says that the truly just individual will behave the same way with or without the ring. One is truly just from within, not because of external sanctions. Kant would tie it to *intentions*. Two individuals may do the same thing, that we view as a just act (such as helping a little old lady across the street), but one does it from ulterior motives (hoping to be remembered in her will) while the other does it from Kant's pure duty—just because it is the right thing to do. Only the second person's act has moral worth. Its worth arose because the person acted autonomously (governing her own actions), *and* acted from a good will. However, she may well value her privacy and not want her act spread over the newspaper headlines.

II.6   HANS MORAVEC

Universal Robots

Humans have long dreamt of a time when machines would take over the more mundane and onerous tasks of life. In this piece, Hans Moravec, Principal Research Scientist at the Robotics Institute of Carnegie Mellon University, discusses how he envisions the future of powerful computer-controlled machines.

These yet-to-be-developed universal robots, claims Moravec, will be able to perceive their environs as they become more powerful and ultimately be able to modify their behavior and actions in the most appropriate way. The completion of remedial activities will be driven by the robot's "desire" to achieve the desired objective. By improving its performance, future robots will become more humanlike in that they will be able to teach themselves and learn.

As Darwin proposed more than 100 years ago, life forms undergo constant change and those new organisms that are better adapted to their environment thrive and may displace older life forms. Similarly, Moravec suggests that the ability of computers will develop in the future as a result of newer technology because they will develop the ability to "learn." This will occur because they will be able to save and modify "conditioning suites," which have proven to be particularly effective and efficient.

Focus Questions

1. How does Moravec see universal robots evolving from today's powerful, affordable computers and in what ways will these future machines differ from industrial robots presently used in industrial and other applications?

2. Compare Moravec's theory of universal robots and how they might serve us with the technologies described by Kurzweil (selection II.8). Do you believe that increasingly humanlike robots of the future might prove to be more a curse than a blessing? Why?
3. If machines continue to become more powerful and intelligent as suggested by this article, do you think we have the foresight to plan for that possible occurrence and the will to ensure that the inevitable changes are beneficial?

Keywords

artificial intelligence, automation, conditioning, evolution, learning, MIPS, robotics, spatial awareness, Turing test

AFFORDABLE COMPUTERS RACED PAST 1 MIPS* in the 1990s, but the benefits have been slow to reach commercial robots. There are hundreds of millions of computers, but only a few hundred thousand robots, many over a decade old. The perceived potential of robotics is limited, and the engineering investment it receives consequently modest. Advanced industrial robots are controlled by last generation's 1- to 10-MIPS computers, less intelligent than an insect. High-speed robot arms use the processing power to precisely plan, measure, and adjust joint motions about one hundred times per second. Mobile robot computers are kept busy tracking a few special navigational features, calculating the robot's position, checking for obstacles and planning and adjusting travel about ten times per second. As with insects, success depends on special properties of the environment: precise location and timing of workspace components for factory arms, correct placement and programming of the navigational features, and absence of too much obscuring clutter for mobile machines. Insects behave more interestingly than present robots because evolutionary competition has drawn them into wickedly risky behavior. Insect survival relies as much on mass reproduction as on individual success; only a tiny, lucky

fraction of each generation lives long enough to produce offspring. Even so, similar limitations surface in both domains. A single misplaced beacon draws a Stanford Hospital robot down a stairwell, and a moth spirals to its death, navigation system fixated on a streetlight rather than the moon. To reduce such risks, $100,000 machines are designed to be plodding dullards, restricted to carefully mapped and marked surroundings.

Robot systems are now installed, debugged, and updated by trained specialists, who measure and prepare the workspace and tailor job- and site-specific control programs. Few jobs are large and static enough to warrant such time-consuming and expensive preparations. If mobile robots for delivery, cleaning, and inspection could be unpacked anywhere and simply trained by leading them once through their task, they would find thousands of times as many buyers. The performance of this decade's experimental robots strongly suggests that 10 MIPS is inadequate to do this sufficiently well. Insectlike 100-MIPS machines, with programs that build coarse 2D maps of their surroundings, or track hundred of points in 3D, might, just possibly, free-navigate tolerably in some circumstances. One thousand MIPS computers, mental matches for the tiniest lizards, can manage multi-million cell 3D grid maps and probably *are* adequate to guide free-roving robots. The basic idea would be to align current maps to old maps stored during training: the more content in the maps, the less chance of error. One thousand MIPS is just about to appear in

From *Robot: Mere Machine to Transcendent Mind* by Hans Moravec. © 1998 by Han Moravec. Used by permission of Oxford University Press, Inc.

*Millions of instructions per second

personal computers, and thus in research robots. It may show up in commercial robots early in the next decade, multiplying their numbers along with their usefulness.

Utility robots for the home could then follow, maybe around 2005, drawn by an assured mass market for affordable machines that could effectively keep a house clean. Early entrants will probably be very specialized, like the conceptual autonomous robot vacuum cleaner. This design senses its world with a triangle of tiny video cameras on each of four sides, is controlled by a 1,000-MIPS computer, and moves in any direction (and scrubs) using three individually steered and driven wheels. About once a second, it stereoscopically measures the range of several thousand points in its vicinity and merges them into a three-dimensional "evidence grid" map. The grid gives the robot a spatial intelligence comparable to a tiny lizard's, but more precise. Taken out of its box and activated in a new home, the robot memorizes its surroundings in 3D. Then, perhaps, it asks "when and how often should I clean this room, and what about the one beyond the door?" Its spatial comprehension would keep it doing its job and out of trouble for years at a stretch. Perhaps it maintains a "web page" by wireless connection, where its maps and schedules can be examined and altered.

Universality

Commercially successful robots will engender a growing industry and more capable successors. The simple vacuum cleaner may be followed by larger utility robots with dusting arms. Arms may become stronger and more sensitive, to clean other surfaces. Mobile robots with dexterous arms, vision and touch sensors, and several thousand MIPS of processing will be able to do various tasks. With proper programming and minor accessories, such machines could pick up clutter, retrieve and deliver articles, take inventory, guard homes, open doors, mow lawns, or play games. New applications will spur further advancements when existing robots fall short in acuity, precision, strength, reach, dexterity, or processing power. Capability, numbers

sold, engineering and manufacturing quality, and cost effectiveness will increase in a mutually reinforcing spiral.

Rossum's Universal Robots was the title of an influential internationally performed play written in 1921 by a Czech playwright, Karel Čapek. At his brother's suggestion, Čapek coined the term "robot" from the Czech word for hard, menial labor. In the play, a universal robot was an artificial human being built to do drudge work of any sort, especially in factories.

In 1935 Alan Turing instantiated David Hilbert's concept of mechanizing mathematics. He designed conceptual machines that moved along a tape, reading and writing discrete symbols according to simple fixed rules, and showed they could do any finite mathematical operation. He also demonstrated that there exist particular machines that interpret the initial contents of their tape as a description of any other machine and proceed, slowly, to simulate this other machine. Such *Universal Turing Machines* inspired some of the first electronic computers and still serve as mathematical tools for studying computation.

Computers are the physical realization of Turing's universal machines, but they are universal only in symbol manipulation—paperwork. A universal *robot* extends the idea into the realm of physical perception and action. Because there is a far greater variety and quantity of physical work to do in the world than paperwork, universal robots are likely to become far more numerous than plain universal computers as soon as their capabilities and costs warrant. Advanced utility robots reprogrammed for various tasks will be a partial step in that direction. Call them the accidental, zeroth generation of universal robot. Subsequent generations will be designed from the start for universality.

First-Generation Universal Robots

Estimated time of arrival: 2010

Processing power: 3,000 MIPS (lizard-scale)

Distinguishing feature: General-purpose perception, manipulation, and mobility

A robot's activities are assembled from its fundamental perception and action repertoire. First-generation robots will exist in a world built for humans, and that repertoire most usefully would resemble a human's. The general size, shape, and strength of the machine should be humanlike, to allow passage through and reach into the same spaces. Its mobility should be efficient on flat ground, where most tasks will happen, but it should somehow be able to traverse stairs and rough ground, lest the robot be trapped on single-floor "islands." It should be able to manipulate most everyday objects, and to find them in the nearby world.

Two-, four-, and six-legged robots of all sizes, able to cross many types of terrain, are becoming common in research. Many, however, are powered externally via wires, and those that carry their own power move slowly and only for short distances on internal power. The mechanics are complex and heavy, with many parts and linkages and at least three motors per leg. Developments in materials, design, motors, power sources, and automated manufacture may ultimately change the economics, but, for the immediate future, legged locomotion cannot compete in performance, cost, or reliability with wheeled vehicles in mostly flat work areas. Typically, a wheeled robot can travel for a day on a battery charge, while a walker, going more slowly, expires in an hour. Yet simple wheels cannot negotiate stairs—a decades-old dilemma for inventors of powered wheelchairs. Among the patented stair-climbing solutions are pivoted tracks, three-spoked wheels ending in smaller wheels, and specialized mechanical feet of many varieties. All have significant costs in weight, efficiency, or maneuverability over plain wheeled vehicles. Robots needed as "frequent climbers" may be configured with such mechanics, but the majority probably will simply roll.

Elevators and ramps mandated for wheelchairs will also provide access to nonclimbing robots. Where such conveniences are lacking, universal robots may be able to lay their own ramps, temporarily dock with stair-climbing mechanisms, or even winch themselves up and down on cables. They have the advantage over humans of being exactly as patient as their control programs specify.

Robots that simply travel have uses, but many jobs call for grasping, transporting, and rearranging ingredients, parts, and tools. Fixed industrial arms, with about six rotary or sliding joints, have good reach and agility but are too large and heavy for mobile robots. NASA, the U.S. space agency, has supported research on lightweight robot arms made of materials like graphite composites, with compact high-torque motors and controls that compensate for flexing in the thin limbs. Cheaper derivatives of these designs could make excellent arms for universal robots. Since many jobs require bringing pairs of objects into contact, robots will probably be able to have several arms, of various sizes.

Human hands are much more complicated than arms, and harder to imitate in robots. Most industrial robot grippers work like miniature vices, others use fixtures shaped for specific jobs, and a few change their "end effectors" from task to task. Inventors worldwide have devised many clever hands that mold themselves to odd objects, but lacking the ability to control their detailed forces, they fail in some grips, and none are used in practice. More elaborate hands, humanlike and otherwise, with multiple individually controlled fingers, have been demonstrated by robotics researchers. With their many segments, linkages, and motors, they tend to be heavy and expensive, and controlling them to sensitively grasp, grip, orient, and fit objects is a difficult area of ongoing research. Because they operate only occasionally, and exert modest forces over short distances, hands can afford to be less energy efficient than mobility systems or arms and so can use types of "muscle" chosen to be more compact than efficient. Particularly compact are "shape-memory" alloys, metals which, easily bent at room temperature, return with great force to their original shape when heated. Given the difficulties, the first generations of universal robot will probably make do with simple, imprecise hands, leaving fine dexterity for the future.

The navigational needs of universal and housecleaning robots are similar. A robot will perceive its surroundings with sensors, probably video cameras configured for stereoscopic vision, and construct a 3D mental map. From the map it will recognize locations, plan trajectories, and detect objects by shape, color, and location. This latter ability will be more important, and thus better developed, in universal robots than in housecleaners. Universal robot maps may be higher resolution, giving them a sharper sense of general spatial awareness. They will probably need an especially fine map of the volume around their hands to precisely locate work objects and visually monitor manipulation. An interesting technique, used successfully in research projects and becoming more practical as cameras shrink, is to put video cameras on the hands themselves, in the palms or on the fingers.

A few thousand MIPS is just enough computing power for a moving robot to maintain a coarse map of its surroundings and use it for locating itself relative to trained itineraries and to plan and control driving. When not traveling, there is power enough to construct a fine map of a manipulator workspace, to locate particular objects, and to plan and control arm motions. Speech and text recognition is advanced enough today that robots of 2010 will surely be able to converse and read. They will also be linked with the Internet, giving them a kind of telepathy. Using it, they will be able to report and take instructions remotely and to download new programs for new kinds of work. Information security will be even more important then than now, because carelessly or maliciously programmed robots will be physically dangerous.

Universal robots may find their very first uses in factories, warehouses, and offices, where they will be more versatile than the older generation of robots they replace. Because of their breadth of applicability, their numbers should grow rapidly and their costs decline. When they become cheap enough for households, they will extend the utility of personal computers from a few tasks in the data world to many in the physical world. Perhaps a program for basic housecleaning will be included with each robot, as word processors were shipped with early personal computers.

As with computers, some applications of robots will surprise their manufacturers. Robot programs may be developed to do light mechanical work (e.g., assembling other robots), deliver warehoused inventories, prepare specific gourmet meals, tune up certain types of cars, hook patterned rugs, weed lawns, run races, play games, arrange earth, stone, and brick, or sculpt. Some tasks will need specialized hardware attachments like tools and chemical sensors. Each application will require its own original software, very complex by today's computer program standards. The programs will contain modules for recognizing, grasping, manipulating, transporting, and assembling particular items, perhaps modules developed via learning programs on supercomputers. In time, a growing library of subtask modules may ease the construction of new programs.

A first-generation robot will have the brain power of a reptile, but most application programs will be so hard pressed to accomplish their primary functions that they will endow the robot with the personality of a washing machine.

Second-Generation Universal Robots

Estimated time of arrival: 2020

Processing power: 100,000 MIPS (mouse-scale)

Distinguishing feature: Accommodation learning

First-generation robots will be rigid slaves to inflexible programs, relentless in pursuing their tasks—or repeating their errors. Their programs will contain the frozen results of learning done on bigger computers under human supervision. Except for specialized episodes like recording a new cleaning route or the location of work objects, they will be incapable of learning new skills or adapting to unanticipated circumstances. Even modest alterations of behavior will require new programming, probably from the original software suppliers.

Second-generation robots, with thirty times the processing power, will learn some of their tricks on the job. Their big advantage is adaptive learning, which "closes the loop" on behavior. Each robot action is repeatedly adjusted in response to measurements of the action's past effectiveness. In the simplest technique, programs will be provided with alternative ways, both in the large and the small, to accomplish steps in a task. Alternatives that succeed become more likely to be invoked in similar circumstances, while alternatives that fail become less probable. "Statistical learning" is another approach, in which a large number of behavior-modifying parameters (e.g., weights in simulated neural nets) are repeatedly tweaked to nudge actual behavior closer to an ideal. Programs for second-generation robots will use many such learning techniques, creating new abilities—and new pitfalls.

Some programs may learn with human assistance. To teach a robot to recognize shoes, its owner might assemble some shoes in a cluttered room, and point them out. The robot, running an object-learning program, will note the shape and color of both the shoes, and of other objects, to train a statistical classifier to distinguish shoes from non-shoes. If the robot later meets a still-ambiguous object, say a gravy boat, it may ask the owner's opinion, to further tune the classifier. Similar programs might learn minor motor skills by first recording movements as the robot is led by hand through the motions, then optimizing the details in practice playbacks. Learned modules, though tedious to create, will probably be easy to package and employ. A general tidying-up program, for instance, could be modified to gather shoes by grafting in a shoe-recognizing module.

Second-generation robots will occasionally be trained by humans, but more often will simply learn from their experiences. The behavior loop is closed in the latter case by a collection of constantly running *conditioning* programs, or modules, that watch out for generally desirable or undesirable situations and generate signals that act on the task-oriented programs that actually control the robot. Each major and minor step in a second-generation application program will have a variety of alternatives: a grasp can be underhand or overhand, harder or softer, an arm movement can be faster or slower, lifting can be done with one arm or two, an object can be sought with one of several recognition modules, two objects can be assembled in a number of locations, and so on. Each alternative will have associated with it a relative probability of being chosen. Whenever a conditioning module issues a signal, the probabilities of recently executed alternatives are altered. Conditioning signals come in two broad categories: positive, which raise the probabilities, and negative, which

lower them. What situations the conditioning modules respond to, and what type and strength of signal they send, is entirely up to the robot's programmers. Some choices seem sensible. Strong negative signals should result from collisions, from objects dropped or crushed, when a task fails or when the robot's batteries are nearly discharged. A near miss, a task completed unusually slowly, or an excessive acceleration might trigger weak negative signals. A rapidly completed task, charged batteries, or an absence of negative signals could produce positive signals. Some conditioning modules may be tied to the robot's speech recognition, generating positive signals for words of praise and negative ones for criticism. Speech recognizers in the 1990s struggle merely to identify the words being spoken. By 2010 they should be able to identify speakers and emotional overtones as well. A second-generation robot with a "general-behavior" program having options for almost any action at every step could probably be slowly trained for new tasks purely through Skinnerian conditioning, like a circus bear. More practical "user-trainable" programs will probably allow the key steps to be directly specified by voice instruction and leading by hand, with the conditioning saved for fine-tuning.

If a first-generation robot working in your kitchen runs into trouble, say, fumbling a key step because a portion of the workspace is awkwardly small, you have the option of abandoning the task, changing its environment, or somehow obtaining altered software that accomplishes the problematic step in a different way. A second-generation robot will make a number of false starts, but most probably will find its own solution. It will adjust to its home in thousands of subtle ways and gradually improve its performance. While a first-generation robot's personality is determined entirely by the sequence of operations in the application program it runs at the moment, a second-generation robot's character is more a product of the suite of conditioning modules it hosts. The conditioning system might, in time, censor an entire application program, if it gave consistently negative results.

Learning is dangerous because it leaps from a few experiences to general rules of behavior. If the experiences happen to be untypical, or the conditioning system misidentifies the relevant conditions, future behavior may be permanently warped. An important element in the ALVINN automatic driving system, which learns to follow a particular type of road by imitating human driving, is a carefully contrived augmentation of the actual camera scenes. Dean Pomerleau's program transforms each real training image and its associated steering command into thirty different ones by geometrically altering them in a way that approximates shifting the truck up to a half lane-width in either direction. Without this stratagem, learned steering is dangerously erratic away from the center of the lane. The program adds other artifacts to teach the system to ignore areas beyond the road edge and distant traffic. Other flexible learning programs, including those in my own research, behave similarly: they are prone to learn dangerous irrelevancies and miss important features if their training experiences are not properly structured. Occasionally, as in the transition from ALVINN to RALPH, enough is known in advance to hardwire in reasonable restraints. More often, though, the necessary information is unavailable at programming time.

Even animals and humans, veterans of tens of millions of years of evolutionary honing, are vulnerable to inappropriate learning. A friend's dog, struck by a car while crossing a road, continued wantonly to cross roads. It would, however, under all circumstances, avoid the region of the sidewalk from which it had set out before the accident. People and animals can be victims of self-reinforcing phobias or obsessions, instilled by a few traumatic experiences or abusive treatment in formative years. A first-generation robot, "trained" off-line under careful factory supervision, will suffer no permanent ill effects from events that interfere with its work but leave it physically undamaged. A second-generation robot, though, could be badly warped by accidents or practical jokes. It might remain impaired until its conditioned memory is cleared, restoring it to naive infancy. Or perhaps, sometimes, robot psychologists could slowly undo the damage. Devising conditioning suites that teach quickly, but resist aberrations, will be among the greatest challenges for programmers of second-generation robots. There is probably no perfect solution, but there are ways to approach the problem.

Second-generation robots of 2020 will have on-board computers as powerful as the supercomputers that learned for first-generation machines a decade before. But by 2020 supercomputers will be proportionally more powerful and will themselves play a background role. The many individual programs of a conditioning suite, each responding to some specific stimulus, interact with one another and with the robot's control programs and environment in ways that will be far too entangled to anticipate accurately. It would be possible to evaluate particular suites by trying them out in robots, the acid test in any case, but that would be a slow and dangerous way to sift a large number of rough candidates. Some would certainly behave in unexpected ways that could damage the robot or even endanger the testers.

Faster and safer initial screenings might be done in factory supercomputer simulations of robots in action. To be of value, simulations would have to be good models, predicting accurately such things as the probability that a given grip can lift a particular object, or that a vision module can find a given something in a particular clutter. Simulating the everyday world in full physical detail will still be beyond computer capacity in 2020, but it should be possible to approximate the results by generalizing data collected from actual robots, essentially to learn from the working experience of real robots how everyday things behave. A large systematic collection effort under human supervision will probably be necessary lest there be too many gaps or distortions. A proper simulator would contain thousands of learned models for various basic interactions (call them *interaction models*), in what amounts to a robotic version of common-sense physics. It would be a perceptual/motor counterpart to the purely verbal framework being collected by the Cyc effort to endow reasoning programs with common sense.

The simulators could be used to automatically find effective conditioning suites, in effect, to learn how to learn. A suite might be evaluated on a simulated robot running a few favorite application programs in a simulated household for a few simulated days. Repeatedly, suites that produced particularly effective and safe work would be saved, modified slightly, and tried again, while those that did poorly would be discarded. This kind of process, called a genetic algorithm, is a computerized version of Darwinian evolution. It is sometimes the most effective way to optimize when the relation between the adjustments (the choice and settings of conditioning modules, in this case) and the quantity to be optimized (robot performance) has no simple model.

Third-Generation Universal Robots

> *Estimated time of arrival:* 2030
>
> *Processing power:* 3,000,000 MIPS *(monkey-scale)*
>
> *Distinguishing feature: World modeling*

Adaptive second-generation robots will find jobs everywhere and may become the largest industry on earth. But teaching them new skills, whether by writing programs or through training, will be very tedious. A third generation of universal robots will have on-board computers as powerful as the supercomputers that optimized second-generation robots. They will learn much faster because they do much trial and error in fast simulation rather than slow and dangerous physicality. Once again, a process done by human-supervised supercomputers at the factory in one robot generation will be improved and installed directly on the next generation, and once again new opportunities and new problems will arise.

With a fast-enough simulator, it will be possible for a robot to maintain a running account of the actual events going on around it—to simulate its world in real time. Doing so requires that almost everything the robot senses be recognized for the kind of object it is, so that the proper interaction models can be called up. Recognizing arbitrary objects by sight is as difficult as knowing how they will interact. It will require modules specially trained for each kind of thing (call them *perception models*). Some perception models may already have been developed for second-generation factory simulators to help automate the tedious job of creating simulations of robot workspaces. An additional ef-

fort to fill gaps and systematize the factory repertoire will surely be necessary to prepare it for fully automatic use in the third generation. Perception models will allow a robot's three-dimensional map of a room to be transformed into a working model where each object is identified and linked with its proper interaction models.

A continuously updated simulation of self and surroundings gives a robot interesting abilities. By running the simulation slightly faster than real time, the robot can preview what it is about to do, in time to alter its intent if the simulation predicts it will turn out badly—a kind of consciousness. On a larger scale, before undertaking a new task, the robot can simulate it many times, with conditioning system engaged, learning from the simulated experiences as it would from physical ones. Consequently well trained for the task, it would likely succeed the first time it attempted it physically—unlike a second-generation machine, which makes all its mistakes out in real life.

When it has some spare time, the robot can replay previous experiences, and try variations on them, perhaps learning ways to improve future performance. A sufficiently advanced third-generation robot, whose simulation extends to other agents—robots and people—would be able to observe a task being done by someone else and formulate a program for doing the task itself. It could imitate.

A third-generation robot might also be induced to invent its own simple programs in response to a specialized conditioning module whose rewards are proportional to how nearly a sequence of robot actions achieves a desired end. Repeated simulations of a general-behavior program with such a "teacher" might gradually shape the program into one that accomplishes the specified result. The teacher can be quite simple compared to the sequence of actions it induces, and could be constructed via voiced commands. The statement *"Put the glass on the table"* might create a conditioning module whose reward is proportional to the distance of the glass bottom from the tabletop. Steered by this, and by standard modules such as ones that generate negative signals if the glass spills or drops, repeated simulations may devise a sequence of arm motions that does the job.

There are complications. A simulator will be dangerously misleading unless it accurately models objects and events. A newly delivered robot is unlikely to have good representations of the personalized knickknacks it freshly encounters and will need some way of learning, perhaps by assigning to new object perception and interaction models from a set of generic classes. Then it would tune the interaction models of particular objects whenever a real event and its simulation differed. Since it would be dangerous to start a robot on a complex task before it had good models of the items involved, third-generation robots will require noncritical "play" periods wherein things are handled, spaces explored, and minor activities attempted, simply to tune up the simulation.

Although they will be able to adapt, imitate, and create simple programs of their own, third-generation robots will still rely on externally supplied programs to do complicated jobs. Since their motor and perceptual functions will be quite sophisticated, and their memories and potential skills large, it will be possible to write wonderfully elaborate control programs for them, accomplishing large jobs, with nuances within nuances. It will be increasingly difficult for human programmers to keep track of the many details and interactions. Fortunately, the task can be largely automated. Shakey, the first computer-controlled mobile robot, had at its heart a reasoning program called STRIPS (Standard Research Institute Problem Solver) that expressed the robot's situation and capabilities as sentences of symbolic logic. STRIPS solved for the sequence of actions that achieved a requested result as a proof of a mathematical theorem. On Shakey's 0.3 MIPS computer, neither the theorem prover nor the sensory processing that fed it could handle the complexity of realistic situations, and Shakey was limited to maneuvering around a few blocks.

Despite Shakey's limitations in 1969, the idea of planning robot actions with a theorem prover was sound. Given a correct description of the initial and desired state of the world, and the robot's abilities, along with enough time and space to work, a theorem prover will find an absolutely correct solution, of arbitrary generality, subtlety, and devilousness, if one exists. By the time of the third universal-robot generation, supercomputers will provide 100,000,000 MIPS, and (thanks to continuing progress in the top-down Artificial Intelligence industry) programs will exist that will be able to perform STRIPS-like reasoning with real-world richness. So factory supercomputers in 2030 will accept complex goals (find a sequence of robot actions that assembles the robot described in the following design database), and compile them via theorem provers into wonderfully intricate control programs for third-generation robots which will, in the field, adapt them to their actual circumstances.

Fourth-Generation Universal Robots

Estimated time of arrival: 2040

Processing power: 100,000,000 MIPS (human-scale)

Distinguishing feature: Reasoning

In the decades while the "bottom-up" evolution of robots is slowly transferring the perceptual and motor faculties of human beings into machinery, the conventional Artificial Intelligence industry will be perfecting the mechanization of reasoning. Since today's programs already match human beings in some areas, those of forty years from now, running on computers a million times as fast as today's, should be quite superhuman. Today's reasoning programs work from small amounts of unambiguous information prepared by human beings. Data from robot sensors such as cameras is much too voluminous and noisy for them to use. But a good robot simulator will contain neatly organized and labeled descriptions of the robot and its world, ready to feed a reasoning program. It could state, for instance, if a knife is on a countertop, or if the robot is holding a cup, or even if a human is angry.

Fourth-generation universal robots will have computers powerful enough to simultaneously simulate the world and reason about the simulation. Like the factory supercomputers of the third generation, fourth-generation robots will be able to devise ultrasophisticated robot programs, for other robots or for themselves. Because of another gift from the Artificial Intelligence industry, they will also be able to understand natural languages. Disembodied language understanders may use a verbal common-sense database similar to the one being developed by the Cyc project, where the meaning of words is defined in reference only to other words. Fourth-generation robots will understand concepts and statements more deeply, through the action of their simulators. When someone tells a robot *"The water is running in the bathtub,"* the robot can update its simulation of the world to include flow into the unseen tub, where a simulated extrapolation would indicate an undesirable overflow later and so motivate the robot to go to turn off the tap. A purely verbal representation might accomplish the same thing if it included the statements such as "A filling bathtub will overflow if its water is not shut off." However, a few general principles in a simulator, interacting in combinations, can substitute for an indefinite number of sentences.

Similarly, a reasoning program, making inferences about physical things, might be enhanced by a simulator. Candidate inferences would be rejected if they failed in a parallel simulation of a typical case, and, conversely, persistent coincidences in the simulation could suggest statements that can be proved or assumed. The robot would be visualizing as it listened, spoke, and reasoned. A modest but very successful version of such an approach was used in one of the earliest Artificial Intelligence programs, a geometry theorem prover by Herbert Gelernter in 1959. Starting with the postulates and rules of inference in Euclid's "Elements," Gelernter's program proved some of the theorems, using algebraic "diagrams" to eliminate false directions in the proofs. Before attempting to prove two triangles congruent in a certain construction, for instance, the program would generate an example of the construction, using random numbers for the unspecified quantities, and measure the resulting triangles. If the specific diagramed triangles did not match within the precision of the arithmetic, the program abandoned the attempt to prove them congruent in general.

Simulator-augmented language understanding and reasoning may be so effective in robots that it will be adopted for use in plain computer programs, "grounding" them in the physical world via the experiences of the robots that tuned the simulators. In time the distinction between robot controllers and disembodied reasoners will diminish, and reasoning programs will sometimes link to robot bodies to interact physically with the world, and robot minds will sometimes retire into large computers to do some intense thinking off-line.

A fourth-generation robot will be able to accept statements of purpose from humans and "compile" them into detailed programs that accomplish the task. With a database about the world at large, the statements could become quite general—things like "earn a living," "make more robots," or "make a smarter robot." In fact, fourth-generation robots will have the general competence of human beings and resemble us in some ways, but in others will be like nothing the world has seen. As they design their own successors, the world will become ever stranger.

Why the Future Doesn't Need Us

When this article by the chief scientist and cofounder of Sun Microsystems was published in *Wired* magazine in April 2000, it created quite a buzz. Joy is clearly no Luddite, but in this reading he issues a stern warning about the dangers that lie ahead for humanity if we continue down the current technological path toward creating super-intelligent, self-replicating machines. The idea that our machines might one day destroy us has been a staple of science fiction books and movies, but the prospect of a race of super-intelligent robots actually displacing human beings as the dominant life-form on the planet has long been dismissed as over-heated fantasy.

In the autobiographical section of his discussion, Joy recounts how he became a technophile and how his own work and that of colleagues have opened up the realistic possibility of creating robots with human-level intelligence by the year 2030. When the potentials of contemporary biotechnology and nanotechnology are examined, Joy thinks we face the prospect of enabling the creation of weapons of mass destruction that could threaten the very existence of life on earth. While contemplating these dangers, Joy recommends that we approach these twenty-first century technological possibilities with a degree of humility and that we learn from the experience of the twentieth century, particularly with respect to nuclear energy, how difficult it is to control the technological genie once it gets out of the bottle. In a personal and almost confessional style, Joy struggles with the question of what kind of future do we humans want for ourselves. After having devoted a career to the pursuit of material progress through science and technology, he is now having second thoughts about whether this is the path that we should be taking.

Focus Questions

1. What is surprising about the long quote that Joy discusses at the beginning of this reading? Is this dystopian vision wholly unrealistic?
2. What is GNR? Why are these technologies different from the NBC technologies of the twentieth century? Explain.
3. What are the important ethical values and principles that Joy believes we need to remember as we contemplate the technological future? Does he believe that "ethical humans" will be able to control the forces that "technological humans" unleash?
4. Compare this selection with those by Jonas (I.9), Kurzweil (II.8), Kass (II.11), and Sagoff (II.12). What are the common themes and issues running through these readings?

Keywords

biotechnology, chaos theory, extinction, genetic engineering, Luddites, nanotechnology, nuclear weapons, robotics, self-replication, terrorism, weapons of mass destruction

FROM THE MOMENT I BECAME INVOLVED in the creation of new technologies, their ethical dimensions have concerned me, but it was only in the autumn of 1998 that I became anxiously aware of how great are the dangers facing us in the 21st century. I

can date the onset of my unease to the day I met Ray Kurzweil, the deservedly famous inventor of the first reading machine for the blind and many other amazing things.

Ray and I were both speakers at George Gilder's Telecosm conference, and I encountered him by chance in the bar of the hotel after both our sessions were over. I was sitting with John Searle, a Berkeley philosopher who studies consciousness. While we were talking, Ray approached and a con-

"Why the Future Doesn't Need Us" © August 4, 2000 by Bill Joy. This article originally appeared in *Wired Magazine*. Reprinted by permission of the author.

versation began, the subject of which haunts me to this day.

I had missed Ray's talk and the subsequent panel that Ray and John had been on, and they now picked right up where they'd left off, with Ray saying that the rate of improvement of technology was going to accelerate and that we were going to become robots or fuse with robots or something like that, and John countering that this couldn't happen, because the robots couldn't be conscious.

While I had heard such talk before, I had always felt sentient robots were in the realm of science fiction. But now, from someone I respected, I was hearing a strong argument that they were a near-term possibility. I was taken aback, especially given Ray's proven ability to imagine and create the future. I already knew that new technologies like genetic engineering and nanotechnology were giving us the power to remake the world, but a realistic and imminent scenario for intelligent robots surprised me.

It's easy to get jaded about such breakthroughs. We hear in the news almost every day of some kind of technological or scientific advance. Yet this was no ordinary prediction. In the hotel bar, Ray gave me a partial preprint of his then-forthcoming book *The Age of Spiritual Machines,* which outlined a utopia he foresaw—one in which humans gained near immortality by becoming one with robotic technology. On reading it, my sense of unease only intensified; I felt sure he had to be understating the dangers, understating the probability of a bad outcome along this path.

I found myself most troubled by a passage detailing a *dys*topian scenario:

The New Luddite Challenge

First let us postulate that the computer scientists succeed in developing intelligent machines that can do all things better than human beings can do them. In that case presumably all work will be done by vast, highly organized systems of machines and no human effort will be necessary. Either of two cases might occur. The machines might be permitted to make all of their own deci-

sions without human oversight, or else human control over the machines might be retained.

If the machines are permitted to make all their own decisions, we can't make any conjectures as to the results, because it is impossible to guess how such machines might behave. We only point out that the fate of the human race would be at the mercy of the machines. It might be argued that the human race would never be foolish enough to hand over all the power to the machines. But we are suggesting neither that the human race would voluntarily turn power over to the machines nor that the machines would willfully seize power. What we do suggest is that the human race might easily permit itself to drift into a position of such dependence on the machines that it would have no practical choice but to accept all of the machines' decisions. As society and the problems that face it become more and more complex and machines become more and more intelligent, people will let machines make more of their decisions for them, simply because machine-made decisions will bring better results than man-made ones. Eventually a stage may be reached at which the decisions necessary to keep the system running will be so complex that human beings will be incapable of making them intelligently. At that stage the machines will be in effective control. People won't be able to just turn the machines off, because they will be so dependent on them that turning them off would amount to suicide.

On the other hand it is possible that human control over the machines may be retained. In that case the average man may have control over certain private machines of his own, such as his car or his personal computer, but control over large systems of machines will be in the hands of a tiny elite—just as it is today, but with two differences. Due to improved techniques the elite will have greater control over the masses; and because human work will no longer be necessary the masses will be superfluous, a useless burden on the system. If the elite is ruthless they may simply decide to exterminate the mass of humanity. If they are humane they may use propaganda or other psychological or biological techniques to reduce the birth rate until the mass of humanity becomes extinct, leaving the world to the elite. Or, if the elite consists of soft-hearted liberals, they may decide to play the role of good shepherds to the rest of the human race. They will see to it that everyone's physical needs are satisfied, that all children are raised under psychologically hygienic conditions, that everyone has a wholesome hobby to keep him busy, and that anyone who may become dissatisfied undergoes "treatment" to cure his "problem." Of course, life will be so purposeless that people will have to be biologically or psychologically engineered either to remove their need for the power process or make them "sublimate" their drive for power into some harmless hobby. These engineered human beings may be happy in such a society, but they will most certainly not be free. They will have been reduced to the status of domestic animals.[1]

In the book, you don't discover until you turn the page that the author of this passage is Theodore Kaczynski—the Unabomber. I am no apologist for Kaczynski. His bombs killed three people during a 17-year terror campaign and wounded many others. One of his bombs gravely injured my friend David Gelernter, one of the most brilliant and visionary computer scientists of our time. Like many of my colleagues, I felt that I could easily have been the Unabomber's next target.

Kaczynski's actions were murderous and, in my view, criminally insane. He is clearly a Luddite, but simply saying this does not dismiss his argument; as difficult as it is for me to acknowledge, I saw some merit in the reasoning in this single passage. I felt compelled to confront it.

Kaczynski's dystopian vision describes unintended consequences, a well-known problem with the design and use of technology, and one that is clearly related to Murphy's law—"Anything that can go wrong, will." (Actually, this is Finagle's law, which in itself shows that Finagle was right.) Our overuse of antibiotics has led to what may be the biggest such problem so far: the emergence of antibiotic-resistant and much more dangerous bacteria. Similar things happened when attempts to eliminate malarial mosquitoes using DDT caused them to acquire DDT resistance; malarial parasites likewise acquired multi-drug-resistant genes.[2]

The cause of many such surprises seems clear: The systems involved are complex, involving interaction among and feedback between many parts. Any changes to such a system will cascade in ways that are difficult to predict; this is especially true when human actions are involved.

I started showing friends the Kaczynski quote from *The Age of Spiritual Machines;* I would hand them Kurzweil's book, let them read the quote, and then watch their reaction as they discovered who had written it. At around the same time, I found Hans Moravec's book *Robot: Mere Machine to Transcendent Mind.* Moravec is one of the leaders in robotics research, and was a founder of the world's largest robotics research program, at Carnegie Mellon University. *Robot* gave me more material to try out on my friends—material surprisingly supportive of Kaczynski's argument. For example:

The Short Run (Early 2000s)

Biological species almost never survive encounters with superior competitors. Ten million years ago, South and North America were separated by a sunken Panama isthmus. South America, like Australia today, was populated by marsupial mammals, including pouched equivalents of rats, deers, and tigers. When the isthmus connecting North and South America rose, it took only a few thousand years for the northern placental species, with slightly more effective metabolisms and reproductive and nervous systems, to displace and eliminate almost all the southern marsupials.

In a completely free marketplace, superior robots would surely affect humans as North American placentals affected South American marsupials (and as humans have affected countless species). Robotic industries would compete vigorously among themselves for matter, energy, and space, incidentally driving their price beyond human reach. Unable to afford the necessities of life, biological humans would be squeezed out of existence.

There is probably some breathing room, because we do not live in a completely free marketplace. Government coerces nonmarket behavior, especially by collecting taxes. Judiciously applied, governmental coercion could support human populations in high style on the fruits of robot labor, perhaps for a long while.

A textbook dystopia—and Moravec is just getting wound up. He goes on to discuss how our main job in the 21st century will be "ensuring continued cooperation from the robot industries" by passing laws decreeing that they be "nice,"[3] and to describe how seriously dangerous a human can be "once transformed into an unbounded superintelligent robot." Moravec's view is that the robots will eventually succeed us—that humans clearly face extinction.

I decided it was time to talk to my friend Danny Hillis. Danny became famous as the cofounder of Thinking Machines Corporation, which built a very powerful parallel supercomputer. Despite my current job title of Chief Scientist at Sun Microsystems, I am more a computer architect than a scientist, and I respect Danny's knowledge of the information and physical sciences more than that of any other single person I know. Danny is also a highly regarded futurist who thinks long-term—four years ago he started the Long Now Foundation, which is building a clock designed to last 10,000 years, in an attempt to draw attention to the pitifully short attention span of our society. . . .

So I flew to Los Angeles for the express purpose of having dinner with Danny and his wife, Pati. I went through my now-familiar routine, trotting out the ideas and passages that I found so disturbing. Danny's answer—directed specifically at Kurzweil's scenario of humans merging with robots—came swiftly, and quite surprised me. He said, simply, that the changes would come gradually, and that we would get used to them.

But I guess I wasn't totally surprised. I had seen a quote from Danny in Kurzweil's book in which he said, "I'm as fond of my body as anyone, but if I can be 200 with a body of silicon, I'll take it." It seemed that he was at peace with this process and its attendant risks, while I was not.

While talking and thinking about Kurzweil, Kaczynski, and Moravec, I suddenly remembered a novel I had read almost 20 years ago—*The White Plague,* by Frank Herbert—in which a molecular biologist is driven insane by the senseless murder of his family. To seek revenge he constructs and disseminates a new and highly contagious plague that kills widely but selectively. (We're lucky Kaczynski was a mathematician, not a molecular biologist.) I was also reminded of the Borg of *Star Trek,* a hive of partly biological, partly robotic creatures with a strong destructive streak. Borg-like disasters are a staple of science fiction, so why hadn't I been more concerned about such robotic dystopias earlier? Why weren't other people more concerned about these nightmarish scenarios?

Part of the answer certainly lies in our attitude toward the new—in our bias toward instant familiarity and unquestioning acceptance. Accustomed to living with almost routine scientific breakthroughs, we have yet to come to terms with the fact that the most compelling 21st-century technologies—robotics, genetic engineering, and nanotechnology—pose a different threat than the technologies that have come before. Specifically, robots, engineered organisms, and nanobots share a dangerous amplifying factor: They can self-replicate. A bomb is blown up only once—but one bot can become many, and quickly get out of control.

Much of my work over the past 25 years has been on computer networking, where the sending and receiving of messages creates the opportunity for out-of-control replication. But while replication in a computer or a computer network can be a nuisance, at worst it disables a machine or takes down a network or network service. Uncontrolled self-replication in these newer technologies runs a much greater risk: a risk of substantial damage in the physical world.

Each of these technologies also offers untold promise: The vision of near immortality that Kurzweil sees in his robot dreams drives us forward; genetic engineering may soon provide treatments, if not outright cures, for most diseases; and nanotechnology and nanomedicine can address yet more ills. Together they could significantly extend our average life span and improve the quality of our lives. Yet, with each of these technologies, a sequence of small, individually sensible advances leads to an accumulation of great power and, concomitantly, great danger.

What was different in the 20th century? Certainly, the technologies underlying the weapons of mass destruction (WMD)—nuclear, biological, and chemical (NBC)—were powerful, and the weapons an enormous threat. But building nuclear weapons required, at least for a time, access to both rare—indeed, effectively unavailable—raw materials and highly protected information; biological and chemical weapons programs also tended to require large-scale activities.

The 21st-century technologies—genetics, nanotechnology, and robotics (GNR)—are so powerful that they can spawn whole new classes of accidents and abuses. Most dangerously, for the first time, these accidents and abuses are widely within the reach of individuals or small groups. They will not require large facilities or rare raw materials. Knowledge alone will enable the use of them.

Thus we have the possibility not just of weapons of mass destruction but of knowledge-enabled mass destruction (KMD), this destructiveness hugely amplified by the power of self-replication.

I think it is no exaggeration to say we are on the cusp of the further perfection of extreme evil, an evil whose possibility spreads well beyond that which weapons of mass destruction bequeathed to the nation-states, on to a surprising and terrible empowerment of extreme individuals.

Nothing about the way I got involved with computers suggested to me that I was going to be facing these kinds of issues.

My life has been driven by a deep need to ask questions and find answers. When I was 3, I was already reading, so my father took me to the elementary school, where I sat on the principal's lap and read him a story. I started school early, later skipped a grade, and escaped into books—I was incredibly motivated to learn. I asked lots of questions, often driving adults to distraction.

As a teenager I was very interested in science and technology. I wanted to be a ham radio operator but didn't have the money to buy the equipment.

Ham radio was the Internet of its time: very addictive, and quite solitary. Money issues aside, my mother put her foot down—I was not to be a ham; I was antisocial enough already.

I may not have had many close friends, but I was awash in ideas. By high school, I had discovered the great science fiction writers. I remember especially Heinlein's *Have Spacesuit Will Travel* and Asimov's *I, Robot,* with its Three Laws of Robotics. I was enchanted by the descriptions of space travel, and wanted to have a telescope to look at the stars; since I had no money to buy or make one, I checked books on telescope-making out of the library and read about making them instead. I soared in my imagination.

Thursday nights my parents went bowling, and we kids stayed home alone. It was the night of Gene Roddenberry's original *Star Trek,* and the program made a big impression on me. I came to accept its notion that humans had a future in space, Western-style, with big heroes and adventures. Roddenberry's vision of the centuries to come was one with strong moral values, embodied in codes like the Prime Directive: to not interfere in the development of less technologically advanced civilizations. This had an incredible appeal to me; ethical humans, not robots, dominated this future, and I took Roddenberry's dream as part of my own.

I excelled in mathematics in high school, and when I went to the University of Michigan as an undergraduate engineering student I took the advanced curriculum of the mathematics majors. Solving math problems was an exciting challenge, but when I discovered computers I found something much more interesting: a machine into which you could put a program that attempted to solve a problem, after which the machine quickly checked the solution. The computer had a clear notion of correct and incorrect, true and false. Were my ideas correct? The machine could tell me. This was very seductive.

I was lucky enough to get a job programming early supercomputers and discovered the amazing power of large machines to numerically simulate advanced designs. When I went to graduate school at UC Berkeley in the mid-1970s, I started staying up late, often all night, inventing new worlds inside the machines. Solving problems. Writing the code that argued so strongly to be written.

In *The Agony and the Ecstasy,* Irving Stone's biographical novel of Michelangelo, Stone described vividly how Michelangelo released the statues from the stone, "breaking the marble spell," carving from the images in his mind.[4] In my most ecstatic moments, the software in the computer emerged in the same way. Once I had imagined it in my mind I felt that it was already there in the machine, waiting to be released. Staying up all night seemed a small price to pay to free it—to give the ideas concrete form.

After a few years at Berkeley I started to send out some of the software I had written—an instructional Pascal system, Unix utilities, and a text editor called vi (which is still, to my surprise, widely used more than 20 years later)—to others who had similar small PDP-11 and VAX minicomputers. These adventures in software eventually turned into the Berkeley version of the Unix operating system, which became a personal "success disaster"—so many people wanted it that I never finished my PhD. Instead I got a job working for Darpa putting Berkeley Unix on the Internet and fixing it to be reliable and to run large research applications well. This was all great fun and very rewarding. And, frankly, I saw no robots here, or anywhere near.

Still, by the early 1980s, I was drowning. The Unix releases were very successful, and my little project of one soon had money and some staff, but the problem at Berkeley was always office space rather than money—there wasn't room for the help the project needed, so when the other founders of Sun Microsystems showed up I jumped at the chance to join them. At Sun, the long hours continued into the early days of workstations and personal computers, and I have enjoyed participating in the creation of advanced microprocessor technologies and Internet technologies such as Java and Jini.

From all this, I trust it is clear that I am not a Luddite. I have always, rather, had a strong belief in the value of the scientific search for truth and in the ability of great engineering to bring material progress. The Industrial Revolution has immeasurably improved everyone's life over the last couple hundred years, and I always expected my career to involve the building of worthwhile solutions to real problems, one problem at a time.

I have not been disappointed. My work has had more impact than I had ever hoped for and has been more widely used than I could have reasonably expected. I have spent the last 20 years still trying to figure out how to make computers as reliable as I want them to be (they are not nearly there yet) and how to make them simple to use (a goal that has met with even less relative success). Despite some progress, the problems that remain seem even more daunting.

But while I was aware of the moral dilemmas surrounding technology's consequences in fields like weapons research, I did not expect that I would confront such issues in my own field, or at least not so soon.

Perhaps it is always hard to see the bigger impact while you are in the vortex of a change. Failing to understand the consequences of our inventions while we are in the rapture of discovery and innovation seems to be a common fault of scientists and technologists; we have long been driven by the overarching desire to know that is the nature of science's quest, not stopping to notice that the progress to newer and more powerful technologies can take on a life of its own.

I have long realized that the big advances in information technology come not from the work of computer scientists, computer architects, or electrical engineers, but from that of physical scientists. The physicists Stephen Wolfram and Brosl Hasslacher introduced me, in the early 1980s, to chaos theory and nonlinear systems. In the 1990s, I learned about complex systems from conversations with Danny Hillis, the biologist Stuart Kauffman, the Nobel-laureate physicist Murray Gell-Mann, and others. Most recently, Hasslacher and the electrical engineer and device physicist Mark Reed have been giving me insight into the incredible possibilities of molecular electronics.

In my own work, as codesigner of three microprocessor architectures—SPARC, picoJava, and MAJC—and as the designer of several implementations thereof, I've been afforded a deep and firsthand acquaintance with Moore's law. For decades,

Moore's law has correctly predicted the exponential rate of improvement of semiconductor technology. Until last year I believed that the rate of advances predicted by Moore's law might continue only until roughly 2010, when some physical limits would begin to be reached. It was not obvious to me that a new technology would arrive in time to keep performance advancing smoothly.

But because of the recent rapid and radical progress in molecular electronics—where individual atoms and molecules replace lithographically drawn transistors—and related nanoscale technologies, we should be able to meet or exceed the Moore's law rate of progress for another 30 years. By 2030, we are likely to be able to build machines, in quantity, a million times as powerful as the personal computers of today—sufficient to implement the dreams of Kurzweil and Moravec.

As this enormous computing power is combined with the manipulative advances of the physical sciences and the new, deep understandings in genetics, enormous transformative power is being unleashed. These combinations open up the opportunity to completely redesign the world, for better or worse: The replicating and evolving processes that have been confined to the natural world are about to become realms of human endeavor.

In designing software and microprocessors, I have never had the feeling that I was designing an intelligent machine. The software and hardware is so fragile and the capabilities of the machine to "think" so clearly absent that, even as a possibility, this has always seemed very far in the future.

But now, with the prospect of human-level computing power in about 30 years, a new idea suggests itself: that I may be working to create tools which will enable the construction of the technology that may replace our species. How do I feel about this? Very uncomfortable. Having struggled my entire career to build reliable software systems, it seems to me more than likely that this future will not work out as well as some people may imagine. My personal experience suggests we tend to overestimate our design abilities.

Given the incredible power of these new technologies, shouldn't we be asking how we can best coexist with them? And if our own extinction is a likely, or even possible, outcome of our technological development, shouldn't we proceed with great caution?

The dream of robotics is, first, that intelligent machines can do our work for us, allowing us lives of leisure, restoring us to Eden. Yet in his history of such ideas, *Darwin Among the Machines,* George Dyson warns: "In the game of life and evolution there are three players at the table: human beings, nature, and machines. I am firmly on the side of nature. But nature, I suspect, is on the side of the machines." As we have seen, Moravec agrees, believing we may well not survive the encounter with the superior robot species.

How soon could such an intelligent robot be built? The coming advances in computing power seem to make it possible by 2030. And once an intelligent robot exists, it is only a small step to a robot species—to an intelligent robot that can make evolved copies of itself.

A second dream of robotics is that we will gradually replace ourselves with our robotic technology, achieving near immortality by downloading our consciousnesses; it is this process that Danny Hillis thinks we will gradually get used to and that Ray Kurzweil elegantly details in *The Age of Spiritual Machines.* . . .

But if we are downloaded into our technology, what are the chances that we will thereafter be ourselves or even human? It seems to me far more likely that a robotic existence would not be like a human one in any sense that we understand, that the robots would in no sense be our children, that on this path our humanity may well be lost.

Genetic engineering promises to revolutionize agriculture by increasing crop yields while reducing the use of pesticides; to create tens of thousands of novel species of bacteria, plants, viruses, and animals; to replace reproduction, or supplement it, with cloning; to create cures for many diseases, increasing our life span and our quality of life; and much, much more. We now know with certainty that these profound changes in the biological sciences are imminent and will challenge all our notions of what life is.

Technologies such as human cloning have in particular raised our awareness of the profound ethical and moral issues we face. If, for example, we were to reengineer ourselves into several separate and unequal species using the power of genetic engineering, then we would threaten the notion of equality that is the very cornerstone of our democracy.

Given the incredible power of genetic engineering, it's no surprise that there are significant safety issues in its use. My friend Amory Lovins recently cowrote, along with Hunter Lovins, an editorial that provides an ecological view of some of these dangers. Among their concerns: that "the new botany aligns the development of plants with their economic, not evolutionary, success." . . . Amory's long career has been focused on energy and resource efficiency by taking a whole-system view of human-made systems; such a whole-system view often finds simple, smart solutions to otherwise seemingly difficult problems, and is usefully applied here as well.

After reading the Lovins' editorial, I saw an op-ed by Gregg Easterbrook in *The New York Times* (November 19, 1999) about genetically engineered crops, under the headline: "Food for the Future: Someday, rice will have built-in vitamin A. Unless the Luddites win."

Are Amory and Hunter Lovins Luddites? Certainly not. I believe we all would agree that golden rice, with its built-in vitamin A, is probably a good thing, if developed with proper care and respect for the likely dangers in moving genes across species boundaries.

Awareness of the dangers inherent in genetic engineering is beginning to grow, as reflected in the Lovins' editorial. The general public is aware of, and uneasy about, genetically modified foods, and seems to be rejecting the notion that such foods should be permitted to be unlabeled.

But genetic engineering technology is already very far along. As the Lovins note, the USDA has already approved about 50 genetically engineered crops for unlimited release; more than half of the world's soybeans and a third of its corn now contain genes spliced in from other forms of life.

While there are many important issues here, my own major concern with genetic engineering is narrower: that it gives the power—whether militarily, accidentally, or in a deliberate terrorist act—to create a White Plague.

The many wonders of nanotechnology were first imagined by the Nobel-laureate physicist Richard Feynman in a speech he gave in 1959, subsequently published under the title "There's Plenty of Room at the Bottom." The book that made a big impression on me, in the mid-'80s, was Eric Drexler's *Engines of Creation*, in which he described beautifully how manipulation of matter at the atomic level could create a utopian future of abundance, where just about everything could be made cheaply, and almost any imaginable disease or physical problem could be solved using nanotechnology and artificial intelligences.

A subsequent book, *Unbounding the Future: The Nanotechnology Revolution*, which Drexler cowrote, imagines some of the changes that might take place in a world where we had molecular-level "assemblers." Assemblers could make possible incredibly low-cost solar power, cures for cancer and the common cold by augmentation of the human immune system, essentially complete cleanup of the environment, incredibly inexpensive pocket supercomputers—in fact, any product would be manufacturable by assemblers at a cost no greater than that of wood—spaceflight more accessible than transoceanic travel today, and restoration of extinct species.

I remember feeling good about nanotechnology after reading *Engines of Creation*. As a technologist, it gave me a sense of calm—that is, nanotechnology showed us that incredible progress was possible, and indeed perhaps inevitable. If nanotechnology was our future, then I didn't feel pressed to solve so many problems in the present. I would get to Drexler's utopian future in due time; I might as well enjoy life more in the here and now. It didn't make sense, given his vision, to stay up all night, all the time.

Drexler's vision also led to a lot of good fun. I would occasionally get to describe the wonders of nanotechnology to others who had not heard of it. After teasing them with all the things Drexler described I would give a homework assignment of my own: "Use nanotechnology to create a vampire; for extra credit create an antidote."

With these wonders came clear dangers, of which I was acutely aware. As I said at a nanotechnology conference in 1989, "We can't simply do our science and not worry about these ethical issues."[5] But my subsequent conversations with physicists convinced me that nanotechnology might not even work—or, at least, it wouldn't work anytime soon. Shortly thereafter I moved to Colorado, to a skunk works I had set up, and the focus of my work shifted to software for the Internet, specifically on ideas that became Java and Jini.

Then, last summer, Brosl Hasslacher told me that nanoscale molecular electronics was now practical. This was *new* news, at least to me, and I think to many people—and it radically changed my opinion about nanotechnology. It sent me back to *Engines of Creation*. Rereading Drexler's work after more than 10 years, I was dismayed to realize how little I had remembered of its lengthy section called "Dangers and Hopes," including a discussion of how nanotechnologies can become "engines of destruction." Indeed, in my rereading of this cautionary material today, I am struck by how naive some of Drexler's safeguard proposals seem, and how much greater I judge the dangers to be now than even he seemed to then. (Having anticipated and described many technical and political problems with nanotechnology, Drexler started the Foresight Institute in the late 1980s "to help prepare society for anticipated advanced technologies"—most important, nanotechnology.)

The enabling breakthrough to assemblers seems quite likely within the next 20 years. Molecular electronics—the new subfield of nanotechnology where individual molecules are circuit elements—should mature quickly and become enormously lucrative within this decade, causing a large incremental investment in all nanotechnologies.

Unfortunately, as with nuclear technology, it is far easier to create destructive uses for nanotechnology than constructive ones. Nanotechnology has clear military and terrorist uses, and you need not be suicidal to release a massively destructive nanotechnological device—such devices can be built to be selectively destructive, affecting, for example, only a certain geographical area or a group of people who are genetically distinct.

An immediate consequence of the Faustian bargain in obtaining the great power of nanotechnology is that we run a grave risk—the risk that we might destroy the biosphere on which all life depends.

As Drexler explained:

"Plants" with "leaves" no more efficient than today's solar cells could out-compete real plants, crowding the biosphere with an inedible foliage. Tough omnivorous "bacteria" could out-compete real bacteria: They could spread like blowing pollen, replicate swiftly, and reduce the biosphere to dust in a matter of days. Dangerous replicators could easily be too tough, small, and rapidly spreading to stop—at least if we make no preparation. We have trouble enough controlling viruses and fruit flies.

Among the cognoscenti of nanotechnology, this threat has become known as the "gray goo problem." Though masses of uncontrolled replicators need not be gray or gooey, the term "gray goo" emphasizes that replicators able to obliterate life might be less inspiring than a single species of crabgrass. They might be superior in an evolutionary sense, but this need not make them valuable.

The gray goo threat makes one thing perfectly clear: We cannot afford certain kinds of accidents with replicating assemblers.

Gray goo would surely be a depressing ending to our human adventure on Earth, far worse than mere fire or ice, and one that could stem from a simple laboratory accident.[6] Oops.

It is most of all the power of destructive self-replication in genetics, nanotechnology, and robotics (GNR) that should give us pause. Self-replication is the modus operandi of genetic engineering, which uses the machinery of the cell to replicate its designs, and the prime danger underlying gray goo in nanotechnology. Stories of run-amok robots like the Borg, replicating or mutating to escape from the ethical constraints imposed on them by their creators, are well established in our science fiction books and movies. It is even possible that self-replication may be more fundamental than we thought, and hence harder—or even impossible—to control. A recent article by Stuart Kauffman in *Nature* titled "Self-Replication: Even Peptides Do It" discusses the discovery that a 32-amino-acid peptide can "autocatalyse its own synthesis." We don't know how widespread this ability is, but Kauffman notes that it may hint at "a route to self-reproducing molecular systems on a basis far wider than Watson-Crick base-pairing."[7]

In truth, we have had in hand for years clear warnings of the dangers inherent in widespread knowledge of GNR technologies—of the possibility of knowledge alone enabling mass destruction. But these warnings haven't been widely publicized; the public discussions have been clearly inadequate. There is no profit in publicizing the dangers.

The nuclear, biological, and chemical (NBC) technologies used in 20th-century weapons of mass destruction were and are largely military, developed in government laboratories. In sharp contrast, the 21st-century GNR technologies have clear commercial uses and are being developed almost exclusively by corporate enterprises. In this age of triumphant commercialism, technology—with science as its handmaiden—is delivering a series of almost magical inventions that are the most phenomenally lucrative ever seen. We are aggressively pursuing the promises of these new technologies within the now-unchallenged system of global capitalism and its manifold financial incentives and competitive pressures.

This is the first moment in the history of our planet when any species, by its own voluntary actions, has become a danger to itself—as well as to vast numbers of others.

It might be a familiar progression, transpiring on many worlds—a planet, newly formed, placidly revolves around its star; life slowly forms; a kaleidoscopic procession of creatures evolves; intelligence emerges which, at least up to a point, confers enormous survival value; and then technology is invented. It dawns on them that there are such things as laws of Nature, that these laws can be revealed by experiment, and that knowledge of these laws can be made both to save and to take lives, both on unprecedented scales. Science, they recognize, grants immense powers. In a flash, they create world-altering contrivances. Some planetary civilizations see their way through, place limits on what may and what must not be done, and safely pass through the time of perils. Others, not so lucky or so prudent, perish.

That is Carl Sagan, writing in 1994, in *Pale Blue Dot,* a book describing his vision of the human future in space. I am only now realizing how deep his insight was, and how sorely I miss, and will miss, his voice. For all its eloquence, Sagan's contribution was not least that of simple common sense—an attribute that, along with humility, many of the leading advocates of the 21st-century technologies seem to lack.

I remember from my childhood that my grandmother was strongly against the overuse of antibiotics. She had worked since before the first World War as a nurse and had a commonsense attitude that taking antibiotics, unless they were absolutely necessary, was bad for you.

It is not that she was an enemy of progress. She saw much progress in an almost 70-year nursing career; my grandfather, a diabetic, benefited greatly from the improved treatments that became available in his lifetime. But she, like many levelheaded people, would probably think it greatly arrogant for us, now, to be designing a robotic "replacement species," when we obviously have so much trouble making relatively simple things work, and so much trouble managing—or even understanding—ourselves.

I realize now that she had an awareness of the nature of the order of life, and of the necessity of living with and respecting that order. With this respect comes a necessary humility that we, with our early-21st-century chutzpah, lack at our peril. The commonsense view, grounded in this respect, is often right, in advance of the scientific evidence. The clear fragility and inefficiencies of the human-made systems we have built should give us all pause; the fragility of the systems I have worked on certainly humbles me.

We should have learned a lesson from the making of the first atomic bomb and the resulting arms race. We didn't do well then, and the parallels to our current situation are troubling.

The effort to build the first atomic bomb was led by the brilliant physicist J. Robert Oppenheimer. Oppenheimer was not naturally interested in politics but became painfully aware of what he perceived as the grave threat to Western civilization from the Third Reich, a threat surely grave because of the possibility that Hitler might obtain nuclear weapons. Energized by this concern, he brought his strong intellect, passion for physics, and charismatic leadership skills to Los Alamos and led a rapid and successful effort by an incredible collection of great minds to quickly invent the bomb.

What is striking is how this effort continued so naturally after the initial impetus was removed. In a meeting shortly after V-E Day with some physicists who felt that perhaps the effort should stop, Oppenheimer argued to continue. His stated reason seems a bit strange: not because of the fear of large casualties from an invasion of Japan, but because the United Nations, which was soon to be formed, should have foreknowledge of atomic weapons. A more likely reason the project continued is the momentum that had built up—the first atomic test, Trinity, was nearly at hand.

We know that in preparing this first atomic test the physicists proceeded despite a large number of possible dangers. They were initially worried, based on a calculation by Edward Teller, that an atomic explosion might set fire to the atmosphere. A revised calculation reduced the danger of destroying the world to a three-in-a-million chance. (Teller says he was later able to dismiss the prospect of atmospheric ignition entirely.) Oppenheimer, though, was sufficiently concerned about the result of Trinity that he arranged for a possible evacuation of the southwest part of the state of New Mexico. And, of course, there was the clear danger of starting a nuclear arms race.

Within a month of that first, successful test, two atomic bombs destroyed Hiroshima and Nagasaki. Some scientists had suggested that the bomb simply be demonstrated, rather than dropped on Japanese cities—saying that this would greatly improve the chances for arms control after the war—but to no avail. With the tragedy of Pearl Harbor still fresh in Americans' minds, it would have been very difficult for President Truman to order a demonstration of the weapons rather than use them as he did—the desire to quickly end the war and save the lives that would have been lost in any invasion of Japan was very strong. Yet the overriding truth was probably very simple: As the physicist Freeman Dyson later said, "The reason that it was dropped was just that nobody had the courage or the foresight to say no."

It's important to realize how shocked the physicists were in the aftermath of the bombing of Hiroshima, on August 6, 1945. They describe a series of waves of emotion: first, a sense of fulfillment that the bomb worked, then horror at all the people that had been killed, and then a convincing feeling that on no account should another bomb be dropped. Yet of course another bomb was dropped, on Nagasaki, only three days after the bombing of Hiroshima.

In November 1945, three months after the atomic bombings, Oppenheimer stood firmly behind the scientific attitude, saying, "It is not possible to be a scientist unless you believe that the knowledge of the world, and the power which this gives, is a thing which is of intrinsic value to humanity, and that you are using it to help in the spread of knowledge and are willing to take the consequences."

Oppenheimer went on to work, with others, on the Acheson-Lilienthal report, which, as Richard Rhodes says in his recent book *Visions of Technology*, "found a way to prevent a clandestine nuclear arms race without resorting to armed world government"; their suggestion was a form of relinquishment of nuclear weapons work by nation-states to an international agency.

This proposal led to the Baruch Plan, which was submitted to the United Nations in June 1946 but never adopted (perhaps because, as Rhodes suggests, Bernard Baruch had "insisted on burdening the plan with conventional sanctions," thereby inevitably dooming it, even though it would "almost certainly have been rejected by Stalinist Russia anyway"). Other efforts to promote sensible steps toward internationalizing nuclear power to prevent an arms race ran afoul either of US politics and internal distrust, or distrust by the Soviets. The opportunity to avoid the arms race was lost, and very quickly.

Two years later, in 1948, Oppenheimer seemed to have reached another stage in his thinking, saying, "In some sort of crude sense which no vulgarity, no humor, no overstatement can quite extinguish, the physicists have known sin; and this is a knowledge they cannot lose."

In 1949, the Soviets exploded an atom bomb. By 1955, both the US and the Soviet Union had tested hydrogen bombs suitable for delivery by aircraft. And so the nuclear arms race began.

Nearly 20 years ago, in the documentary *The Day After Trinity*, Freeman Dyson summarized the scientific attitudes that brought us to the nuclear precipice:

> "I have felt it myself. The glitter of nuclear weapons. It is irresistible if you come to them as a scientist. To feel it's there in your hands, to release this energy that fuels the stars, to let it do your bidding. To perform these miracles, to lift a million tons of rock into the sky. It is something that gives people an illusion of illimitable power, and it is, in some ways, responsible for all our troubles—this, what you might call technical arrogance, that overcomes people when they see what they can do with their minds."[8]

Now, as then, we are creators of new technologies and stars of the imagined future, driven—this time by great financial rewards and global competition—despite the clear dangers, hardly evaluating what it may be like to try to live in a world that is the realistic outcome of what we are creating and imagining.

In 1947, *The Bulletin of the Atomic Scientists* began putting a Doomsday Clock on its cover. For more than 50 years, it has shown an estimate of the relative nuclear danger we have faced, reflecting the changing international conditions. The hands on the clock have moved 15 times and today, standing at nine minutes to midnight, reflect continuing and real danger from nuclear weapons. The recent addition of India and Pakistan to the list of nuclear powers has increased the threat of failure of the nonproliferation goal, and this danger was reflected by moving the hands closer to midnight in 1998.

In our time, how much danger do we face, not just from nuclear weapons, but from all of these technologies? How high are the extinction risks?

The philosopher John Leslie has studied this question and concluded that the risk of human ex-tinction is at least 30 percent,[9] while Ray Kurzweil believes we have "a better than even chance of making it through," with the caveat that he has "always been accused of being an optimist." Not only are these estimates not encouraging, but they do not include the probability of many horrid outcomes that lie short of extinction.

Faced with such assessments, some serious people are already suggesting that we simply move beyond Earth as quickly as possible. We would colonize the galaxy using von Neumann probes, which hop from star system to star system, replicating as they go. This step will almost certainly be necessary 5 billion years from now (or sooner if our solar system is disastrously impacted by the impending collision of our galaxy with the Andromeda galaxy within the next 3 billion years), but if we take Kurzweil and Moravec at their word it might be necessary by the middle of this century.

What are the moral implications here? If we must move beyond Earth this quickly in order for the species to survive, who accepts the responsibility for the fate of those (most of us, after all) who are left behind? And even if we scatter to the stars, isn't it likely that we may take our problems with us or find, later, that they have followed us? The fate of our species on Earth and our fate in the galaxy seem inextricably linked.

Another idea is to erect a series of shields to defend against each of the dangerous technologies. The Strategic Defense Initiative, proposed by the Reagan administration, was an attempt to design such a shield against the threat of a nuclear attack from the Soviet Union. But as Arthur C. Clarke, who was privy to discussions about the project, observed: "Though it might be possible, at vast expense, to construct local defense systems that would 'only' let through a few percent of ballistic missiles, the much touted idea of a national umbrella was nonsense. Luis Alvarez, perhaps the greatest experimental physicist of this century, remarked to me that the advocates of such schemes were 'very bright guys with no common sense.'"

Clarke continued: "Looking into my often cloudy crystal ball, I suspect that a total defense might indeed be possible in a century or so. But the technology involved would produce, as a by-product, weapons so terrible that no one would bother with anything as primitive as ballistic missiles."[10]

In *Engines of Creation,* Eric Drexler proposed that we build an active nanotechnological shield—a form of immune system for the biosphere—to defend against dangerous replicators of all kinds that might escape from laboratories or otherwise be maliciously created. But the shield he proposed would itself be extremely dangerous—nothing could prevent it from developing autoimmune problems and attacking the biosphere itself.[11]

Similar difficulties apply to the construction of shields against robotics and genetic engineering. These technologies are too powerful to be shielded against in the time frame of interest; even if it were possible to implement defensive shields, the side effects of their development would be at least as dangerous as the technologies we are trying to protect against.

These possibilities are all thus either undesirable or unachievable or both. The only realistic alternative I see is relinquishment: to limit development of the technologies that are too dangerous, by limiting our pursuit of certain kinds of knowledge.

Yes, I know, knowledge is good, as is the search for new truths. We have been seeking knowledge since ancient times. Aristotle opened his Metaphysics with the simple statement: "All men by nature desire to know." We have, as a bedrock value in our society, long agreed on the value of open access to information, and recognize the problems that arise with attempts to restrict access to and development of knowledge. In recent times, we have come to revere scientific knowledge.

But despite the strong historical precedents, if open access to and unlimited development of knowledge henceforth puts us all in clear danger of extinction, then common sense demands that we reexamine even these basic, long-held beliefs.

It was Nietzsche who warned us, at the end of the 19th century, not only that God is dead but that "faith in science, which after all exists undeniably, cannot owe its origin to a calculus of utility; it must have originated *in spite of* the fact that the disutility and dangerousness of the 'will to truth,' of 'truth at

any price' is proved to it constantly." It is this further danger that we now fully face—the consequences of our truth-seeking. The truth that science seeks can certainly be considered a dangerous substitute for God if it is likely to lead to our extinction.

If we could agree, as a species, what we wanted, where we were headed, and why, then we would make our future much less dangerous—then we might understand what we can and should relinquish. Otherwise, we can easily imagine an arms race developing over GNR technologies, as it did with the NBC technologies in the 20th century. This is perhaps the greatest risk, for once such a race begins, it's very hard to end it. This time—unlike during the Manhattan Project—we aren't in a war, facing an implacable enemy that is threatening our civilization; we are driven, instead, by our habits, our desires, our economic system, and our competitive need to know.

I believe that we all wish our course could be determined by our collective values, ethics, and morals. If we had gained more collective wisdom over the past few thousand years, then a dialogue to this end would be more practical, and the incredible powers we are about to unleash would not be nearly so troubling.

One would think we might be driven to such a dialogue by our instinct for self-preservation. Individuals clearly have this desire, yet as a species our behavior seems to be not in our favor. In dealing with the nuclear threat, we often spoke dishonestly to ourselves and to each other, thereby greatly increasing the risks. Whether this was politically motivated, or because we chose not to think ahead, or because when faced with such grave threats we acted irrationally out of fear, I do not know, but it does not bode well.

The new Pandora's boxes of genetics, nanotechnology, and robotics are almost open, yet we seem hardly to have noticed. Ideas can't be put back in a box; unlike uranium or plutonium, they don't need to be mined and refined, and they can be freely copied. Once they are out, they are out. Churchill remarked, in a famous left-handed compliment, that the American people and their leaders "invariably do the right thing, after they have examined every other alternative." In this case, however, we must act more presciently, as to do the right thing only at last may be to lose the chance to do it at all.

As Thoreau said, "We do not ride on the railroad; it rides upon us"; and this is what we must fight, in our time. The question is, indeed, Which is to be master? Will we survive our technologies?

We are being propelled into this new century with no plan, no control, no brakes. Have we already gone too far down the path to alter course? I don't believe so, but we aren't trying yet, and the last chance to assert control—the fail-safe point—is rapidly approaching. We have our first pet robots, as well as commercially available genetic engineering techniques, and our nanoscale techniques are advancing rapidly. While the development of these technologies proceeds through a number of steps, it isn't necessarily the case—as happened in the Manhattan Project and the Trinity test—that the last step in proving a technology is large and hard. The breakthrough to wild self-replication in robotics, genetic engineering, or nanotechnology could come suddenly, reprising the surprise we felt when we learned of the cloning of a mammal.

And yet I believe we do have a strong and solid basis for hope. Our attempts to deal with weapons of mass destruction in the last century provide a shining example of relinquishment for us to consider: the unilateral US abandonment, without preconditions, of the development of biological weapons. This relinquishment stemmed from the realization that while it would take an enormous effort to create these terrible weapons, they could from then on easily be duplicated and fall into the hands of rogue nations or terrorist groups.

The clear conclusion was that we would create additional threats to ourselves by pursuing these weapons, and that we would be more secure if we did not pursue them. We have embodied our relinquishment of biological and chemical weapons in the 1972 Biological Weapons Convention (BWC) and the 1993 Chemical Weapons Convention (CWC).[12]

As for the continuing sizable threat from nuclear weapons, which we have lived with now for more than 50 years, the US Senate's recent rejection of the Comprehensive Test Ban Treaty makes it clear relinquishing nuclear weapons will not be politically easy. But we have a unique opportunity, with the end of the Cold War, to avert a multipolar arms race. Building on the BWC and CWC relinquishments, successful abolition of nuclear weapons could help us build toward a habit of relinquishing dangerous technologies. (Actually, by getting rid of all but 100 nuclear weapons worldwide—roughly the total destructive power of World War II and a considerably easier task—we could eliminate this extinction threat.[13])

Verifying relinquishment will be a difficult problem, but not an unsolvable one. We are fortunate to have already done a lot of relevant work in the context of the BWC and other treaties. Our major task will be to apply this to technologies that are naturally much more commercial than military. The substantial need here is for transparency, as difficulty of verification is directly proportional to the difficulty of distinguishing relinquished from legitimate activities.

I frankly believe that the situation in 1945 was simpler than the one we now face: The nuclear technologies were reasonably separable into commercial and military uses, and monitoring was aided by the nature of atomic tests and the ease with which radioactivity could be measured. Research on military applications could be performed at national laboratories such as Los Alamos, with the results kept secret as long as possible.

The GNR technologies do not divide clearly into commercial and military uses; given their potential in the market, it's hard to imagine pursuing them only in national laboratories. With their widespread commercial pursuit, enforcing relinquishment will require a verification regime similar to that for biological weapons, but on an unprecedented scale. This, inevitably, will raise tensions between our individual privacy and desire for proprietary information, and the need for verification to protect us all. We will undoubtedly encounter strong resistance to this loss of privacy and freedom of action.

Verifying the relinquishment of certain GNR technologies will have to occur in cyberspace as well as at physical facilities. The critical issue will be to make the necessary transparency acceptable in a world of proprietary information, presumably by providing new forms of protection for intellectual property.

Verifying compliance will also require that scientists and engineers adopt a strong code of ethical conduct, resembling the Hippocratic oath, and that they have the courage to whistleblow as necessary, even at high personal cost. This would answer the call—50 years after Hiroshima—by the Nobel laureate Hans Bethe, one of the most senior of the surviving members of the Manhattan Project, that all scientists "cease and desist from work creating, developing, improving, and manufacturing nuclear weapons and other weapons of potential mass destruction."[14] In the 21st century, this requires vigilance and personal responsibility by those who would work on both NBC and GNR technologies to avoid implementing weapons of mass destruction and knowledge-enabled mass destruction.

Thoreau also said that we will be "rich in proportion to the number of things which we can afford to let alone." We each seek to be happy, but it would seem worthwhile to question whether we need to take such a high risk of total destruction to gain yet more knowledge and yet more things; common sense says that there is a limit to our material needs—and that certain knowledge is too dangerous and is best forgone.

Neither should we pursue near immortality without considering the costs, without considering the commensurate increase in the risk of extinction. Immortality, while perhaps the original, is certainly not the only possible utopian dream.

I recently had the good fortune to meet the distinguished author and scholar Jacques Attali, whose book *Lignes d'horizons* (*Millennium,* in the English translation) helped inspire the Java and Jini approach to the coming age of pervasive computing. . . . In his new book *Fraternités,* Attali describes how our dreams of utopia have changed over time:

> At the dawn of societies, men saw their passage on Earth as nothing more than a labyrinth of pain, at the end of which stood a door leading, via their death, to the company of gods and to *Eternity.* With the Hebrews and then the Greeks, some men dared free themselves from theological demands and dream of an ideal City where *Liberty* would flourish. Others, noting the evolution of the market society, understood that the liberty of some would entail the alienation of others, and they sought *Equality.*

Jacques helped me understand how these three different utopian goals exist in tension in our society today. He goes on to describe a fourth utopia, *Fraternity,* whose foundation is altruism. Fraternity alone associates individual happiness with the happiness of others, affording the promise of self-sustainment.

This crystallized for me my problem with Kurzweil's dream. A technological approach to Eternity—near immortality through robotics—may not be the most desirable utopia, and its pursuit brings clear dangers. Maybe we should rethink our utopian choices.

Where can we look for a new ethical basis to set our course? I have found the ideas in the book *Ethics for the New Millennium,* by the Dalai Lama, to be very helpful. As is perhaps well known but little heeded, the Dalai Lama argues that the most important thing is for us to conduct our lives with love and compassion for others, and that our societies need to develop a stronger notion of universal responsibility and of our interdependency; he proposes a standard of positive ethical conduct for individuals and societies that seems consonant with Attali's Fraternity utopia.

The Dalai Lama further argues that we must understand what it is that makes people happy, and acknowledge the strong evidence that neither material progress nor the pursuit of the power of knowledge is the key—that there are limits to what science and the scientific pursuit alone can do.

Our Western notion of happiness seems to come from the Greeks, who defined it as "the exercise of vital powers along lines of excellence in a life affording them scope."[15]

Clearly, we need to find meaningful challenges and sufficient scope in our lives if we are to be happy in whatever is to come. But I believe we must find alternative outlets for our creative forces, beyond the culture of perpetual economic growth; this growth has largely been a blessing for several hundred years, but it has not brought us unalloyed happiness, and we must now choose between the pursuit of unrestricted and undirected growth through science and technology and the clear accompanying dangers.

It is now more than a year since my first encounter with Ray Kurzweil and John Searle. I see around me cause for hope in the voices for caution and relinquishment and in those people I have discovered who are as concerned as I am about our current predicament. I feel, too, a deepened sense of personal responsibility—not for the work I have already done, but for the work that I might yet do, at the confluence of the sciences.

But many other people who know about the dangers still seem strangely silent. When pressed, they trot out the "this is nothing new" riposte—as if awareness of what could happen is response enough. They tell me, There are universities filled with bioethicists who study this stuff all day long. They say, All this has been written about before, and by experts. They complain, Your worries and your arguments are already old hat.

I don't know where these people hide their fear. As an architect of complex systems I enter this arena as a generalist. But should this diminish my concerns? I am aware of how much has been written about, talked about, and lectured about so authoritatively. But does this mean it has reached people? Does this mean we can discount the dangers before us?

Knowing is not a rationale for not acting. Can we doubt that knowledge has become a weapon we wield against ourselves?

The experiences of the atomic scientists clearly show the need to take personal responsibility, the danger that things will move too fast, and the way in which a process can take on a life of its own. We can, as they did, create insurmountable problems in almost no time flat. We must do more thinking up front if we are not to be similarly surprised and shocked by the consequences of our inventions.

My continuing professional work is on improving the reliability of software. Software is a tool, and as a toolbuilder I must struggle with the uses to which the tools I make are put. I have always believed that making software more reliable, given its many uses, will make the world a safer and better place; if I were to come to believe the opposite,

then I would be morally obligated to stop this work. I can now imagine such a day may come.

This all leaves me not angry but at least a bit melancholic. Henceforth, for me, progress will be somewhat bittersweet.

NOTES

1. The passage Kurzweil quotes is from Kaczynski's Unabomber Manifesto, which was published jointly, under duress, by *The New York Times* and *The Washington Post* to attempt to bring his campaign of terror to an end. I agree with David Gelernter, who said about their decision:

    "It was a tough call for the newspapers. To say yes would be giving in to terrorism, and for all they knew he was lying anyway. On the other hand, to say yes might stop the killing. There was also a chance that someone would read the tract and get a hunch about the author; and that is exactly what happened. The suspect's brother read it, and it rang a bell.

    "I would have told them not to publish. I'm glad they didn't ask me. I guess."

    (*Drawing Life: Surviving the Unabomber.* Free Press, 1997: 120.)

2. Garrett, Laurie. *The Coming Plague: Newly Emerging Diseases in a World Out of Balance.* Penguin, 1994: 47–52, 414, 419, 452.

3. Isaac Asimov described what became the most famous view of ethical rules for robot behavior in his book *I, Robot* in 1950, in his Three Laws of Robotics: 1. A robot may not injure a human being, or, through inaction, allow a human being to come to harm. 2. A robot must obey the orders given it by human beings, except where such orders would conflict with the First Law. 3. A robot must protect its own existence, as long as such protection does not conflict with the First or Second Law.

4. Michelangelo wrote a sonnet that begins:

    Non ha l' ottimo artista alcun concetto
    Ch' un marmo solo in sè non circonscriva
    Col suo soverchio; e solo a quello arriva
    La man che ubbidisce all' intelletto.

    Stone translates this as:
    The best of artists hath no thought to show
    which the rough stone in its superfluous shell
    doth not include; to break the marble spell
    is all the hand that serves the brain can do.

Stone describes the process: "He was not working from his drawings or clay models; they had all been put away. He was carving from the images in his mind. His eyes and hands knew where every line, curve, mass must emerge, and at what depth in the heart of the stone to create the low relief."

(*The Agony and the Ecstasy*. Doubleday, 1961: 6, 144.)

5. First Foresight Conference on Nanotechnology in October 1989, a talk titled "The Future of Computation." Published in Crandall, B. C. and James Lewis, editors. *Nanotechnology: Research and Perspectives*. MIT Press, 1992: 269. See also *www.foresight.org/Conferences/MNT01/Nano1.html*.

6. In his 1963 novel *Cat's Cradle*, Kurt Vonnegut imagined a gray-goo-like accident where a form of ice called ice-nine, which becomes solid at a much higher temperature, freezes the oceans.

7. Kauffman, Stuart. "Self-replication: Even Peptides Do It." *Nature*, 382, August 8, 1996: 496. See *www.santafe.edu/sfi/People/kauffman/sak-peptides.html*.

8. Else, Jon. *The Day After Trinity: J. Robert Oppenheimer and the Atomic Bomb* (available at *www.pyramiddirect.com*).

9. This estimate is in Leslie's book *The End of the World: The Science and Ethics of Human Extinction*, where he notes that the probability of extinction is substantially higher if we accept Brandon Carter's Doomsday Argument, which is, briefly, that "we ought to have some reluctance to believe that we are very exceptionally early, for instance in the earliest 0.001 percent, among all humans who will ever have lived. This would be some reason for thinking that humankind will not survive for many more centuries, let alone colonize the galaxy. Carter's doomsday argument doesn't generate any risk estimates just by itself. It is an argument for *revising* the estimates which we generate when we consider various possible dangers." (Routledge, 1996: 1, 3, 145.)

10. Clarke, Arthur C. "Presidents, Experts, and Asteroids." *Science*, June 5, 1998. Reprinted as "Science and Society" in *Greetings, Carbon-Based Bipeds! Collected Essays, 1934–1998*. St. Martin's Press, 1999: 526.

11. And, as David Forrest suggests in his paper "Regulating Nanotechnology Development," available at *www.foresight.org/NanoRev/Forrest1989.html*, "If we used strict liability as an alternative to regulation it would be impossible for any developer to internalize the cost of the risk (destruction of the biosphere), so theoretically the activity of developing nanotechnology should never be undertaken." Forrest's analysis leaves us with only government regulation to protect us—not a comforting thought.

12. Meselson, Matthew. "The Problem of Biological Weapons." Presentation to the 1,818th Stated Meeting of the American Academy of Arts and Sciences, January 13, 1999. (*minerva.amacad.org/archive/bulletin4.htm*)

13. Doty, Paul. "The Forgotten Menace: Nuclear Weapons Stockpiles Still Represent the Biggest Threat to Civilization." *Nature*, 402, December 9, 1999: 583.

14. See also Hans Bethe's 1997 letter to President Clinton, at *www.fas.org/bethecr.htm*.

15. Hamilton, Edith. *The Greek Way*. W. W. Norton & Co., 1942: 35.

II.8   RAY KURZWEIL

Promise and Peril

As an inventor who developed the first print-to-speech reading machine in 1976, the music synthesizer in 1982, and a speech-recognition system in 1987, as well as an entrepreneur, author, and artificial intelligence guru, Ray Kurzweil is uniquely qualified to comment on the rate of technological change, especially if computers are involved. In this piece from *Interactive Week*, he expresses concern that many do not appreciate the fact that the pace of change is increasing at a rate far faster than is commonly thought. The "law of accelerating returns" as he calls this phenomena is evident in many areas such as computers, medical care, communication, and biology.

Unlike some other technologists, Kurzweil does not feel it would be appropriate to limit technological development in a particular area because an advance might be used in a way that would ultimately be harmful to humans or the planet. Although getting rid of the bad aspects of a technology might be highly desirable, he feels that it is not possible because of the interdependence of all parts of our technological systems.

However, Kurzweil believes it is necessary that we systematically evaluate the possible future impacts of a technology. Only through such a process can we ensure that the maximum benefit of a technology is obtained while its risks are minimized; and there might be some cases where this is only possible through some level of "relinquishment." Our shared human values and ethics will ultimately decide how we deal with emerging high-risk technologies, which will determine how we live in the future.

Focus Questions

1. What evidence does Kurzweil offer that the rate of technological change is increasing?
2. In considering the possible future impact of technology, what three stages does Kurzweil suggest humans go through?
3. Describe some of the future technologies mentioned in this article that pose potential threats, and in what ways might those same technologies prove to be beneficial to humans?
4. How does the author feel technology might be controlled, and why does he feel this will be very difficult to do?

Keywords

democratization, encryption, "trap door," historical exponential view, intuitive linear view, law of accelerating returns, nanobots, nanotechnology, paradigm shift, pathogen, relinquishment, self-replicating technologies

BILL JOY, COFOUNDER OF SUN MICROSYSTEMS and principal developer of the Java programming language, has recently taken up a personal mission to warn us of the impending dangers from the emergence of self-replicating technologies in the fields of genetics, nanotechnology and robotics, which he aggregates under the label "GNR." Al-though his warnings are not entirely new, they have attracted considerable attention because of Joy's credibility as one of our leading technologists. It reminds me of the attention that George Soros, the currency arbitrager and arch capitalist, received when he made vaguely critical comments about the excesses of unrestrained capitalism.

According to Joy, the day is close at hand when it will be feasible to create genetically altered designer pathogens in college laboratories.

Then, at a later date, we'll have to contend with self-replicating entities created through nanotechnology, the field devoted to manipulating matter

From *Interactive Week,* 10/23/00, Vol. 7, Issue 43, "Promise & Peril: Genetics, nanotechnology and robotics in the 21st century," by Ray Kurzweil. Copyright © 2000 by Ray Kurzweil. Reprinted by permission of the author.

on the scale of individual atoms. Although nano-engineered "self-replicators" are at least one decade, and probably more than two decades, away, the specter that concerns Joy can be described as an unstoppable, nonbiological cancer.

Finally, if we manage to survive these first two perils, we'll encounter robots whose intelligence will rival and ultimately exceed our own. Such robots may make great assistants, but who's to say that we can count on them to remain reliably friendly to mere humans?

Although I am often cast as the technology optimist who counters Joy's pessimism, I do share his concerns regarding self-replicating technologies; indeed, I played a role in bringing these dangers to Bill's attention. In many of the dialogues and forums in which I have participated on this subject, I end up defending Joy's position with regard to the feasibility of these technologies and scenarios when they come under attack by commentators who I believe are being quite shortsighted in their skepticism. Even so, I do find fault with Joy's prescription—halting the advance of technology and the pursuit of knowledge in broad fields such as nanotechnology.

Before addressing our differences, let me first discuss the salient issue of feasibility. Many long-range forecasts of technical feasibility dramatically underestimate the power of future technology for one simple reason: They are based on what I call the "intuitive linear" view of technological progress rather than the "historical exponential view." When people think of a future period, they intuitively assume that the current rate of progress will continue for the period being considered. In fact, the rate of technological progress is not constant, but since it is human nature to adapt to the changing pace, the intuitive view is that the pace will continue at the current rate. It is typical, therefore, that even sophisticated commentators, when considering the future, extrapolate the current pace of change over the next 10 years or 100 years to determine their expectations—the "intuitive linear" view.

But any serious examination of the history of technology reveals that technological change is at least exponential. There are a great many examples of this, including constantly accelerating devel-opments in computation, communication, brain scanning, multiple aspects of biotechnology and miniaturization. One can examine these data in many different ways, on many different time scales and for a wide variety of phenomena. Whatever the approach, we find—at least—double exponential growth.

This phenomenon, which I call the "law of accelerating returns," does not rely on a mere assumption of the continuation of Moore's Law, which predicts, in effect, the quadrupling of computer power every 24 months. Rather, it is based on a rich model of diverse technological processes, a model I have been developing over the past couple of decades.

What it clearly shows is that technology, particularly the pace of technological change, has been advancing at least exponentially since the advent of technology. Thus, while people often overestimate what can be achieved in the short term because there is a tendency to leave out necessary details, we typically underestimate what can be achieved in the long term because exponential growth is ignored.

This observation also applies to rates of paradigm shifts, which are currently doubling approximately every decade. At that rate, the technological progress in the 21st century will be equivalent to changes that in the linear view would require on the order of 20,000 years.

This exponential progress in computation and communication technologies is greatly empowering the individual. That's good news in many ways, because those technologies are largely responsible for the pervasive trend toward democratization and the reshaping of power relations at all levels of society. But these technologies are also empowering and amplifying our destructive impulses. It's not necessary to anticipate all the ultimate uses of a technology to see danger in, for example, every college biotechnology lab's having the ability to create self-replicating biological pathogens.

Nevertheless, I do reject Joy's call for relinquishing broad areas of technology—for example, nanotechnology. Technology has always been a double-edged sword. We don't need to look any further than today's technology to see this. Take biotechnology. We have already seen substantial benefits:

more effective AIDS treatments, human insulin and many others. In the years ahead, we will see enormous gains in overcoming cancer and many other diseases, as well as in greatly extending human longevity, all presumably positive developments—although even these are controversial. On the other hand, the means will soon exist in a routine biotechnology laboratory to create a pathogen that could be more destructive to humans or other living organisms than an atomic bomb.

If we imagine describing the dangers that exist today—enough nuclear explosive power to destroy all mammalian life, just for starters—to people who lived a couple of hundred years ago, they would think it mad to take such risks. On the other hand, how many people in the year 2000 would really want to go back to the short, disease-filled, poverty-stricken, disaster-prone lives that 99 percent of the human race struggled through a couple of centuries ago? We may romanticize the past, but until fairly recently, most of humanity lived extremely fragile lives, in which a single common misfortune could spell disaster. Substantial portions of our species still live this precarious existence, which is at least one reason to continue technological progress and the social and economic enhancements that accompany it.

Cautiously Enriching Life

People often go through three stages in examining the impact of future technology: awe and wonderment at its potential to overcome age-old problems, a sense of dread at a new set of grave dangers that accompany these new technologies, followed, finally and hopefully, by the realization that the only viable and responsible path is to set a careful course that can realize the promise while managing the peril.

Joy eloquently describes the plagues of centuries past and how new, self-replicating technologies, such as mutant bioengineered pathogens or "nanobots" (molecule-sized robots), run amok may bring back the fading notion of pestilence. As I stated earlier, these are real dangers. It is also the case, which Joy acknowledges, that it has been

technological advances, such as antibiotics and improved sanitation, that have freed us from the prevalence of such plagues. Human suffering continues and demands our steadfast attention. Should we tell the millions of people afflicted with cancer and other devastating conditions that we are canceling the development of all bioengineered treatments because there is a risk that these same technologies might one day be used for malevolent purposes? That should be a rhetorical question. Yet, there is a movement to do exactly that. Most people, I believe, would agree that such broad-based relinquishment of research and development is not the answer.

In addition to the continued opportunity to alleviate human distress, another important motivation for continuing technological advancement is economic gain. The continued acceleration of many intertwined technologies are roads paved with gold. (I use the plural here because technology is clearly not a single path.) In a competitive environment, it is an economic imperative to go down these roads. Relinquishing technological advancement would be economic suicide for individuals, companies and nations.

Which brings us to the issue of relinquishment—the wholesale abandonment of certain fields of research—which is Joy's most controversial recommendation and personal commitment. I do feel that relinquishment at the right level is part of a responsible and constructive response to genuine perils. The issue, however, is exactly this: At what level are we to relinquish technology?

Ted Kaczynski, the infamous Unabomber, would have us renounce all of it. This, in my view, is neither desirable nor feasible, and the futility of such a position is only underscored by the senselessness of Kaczynski's deplorable tactics.

Another level would be to forgo certain fields—nanotechnology, for example—that might be regarded as too dangerous. But even these slightly less sweeping strokes of relinquishment are also untenable. Nanotechnology is simply the inevitable result of a persistent trend toward miniaturization that pervades all of technology. It is far from a single, centralized effort, but rather is being pursued by myriad projects with diverse goals.

One observer wrote:

"A further reason why industrial society cannot be reformed . . . is that modern technology is a unified system in which all parts are dependent on one another. You can't get rid of the 'bad' parts of technology and retain only the 'good' parts. Take modern medicine, for example. Progress in medical science depends on progress in chemistry, physics, biology, computer science and other fields. Advanced medical treatments require expensive, high-tech equipment that can be made available only by a technologically progressive, economically rich society. Clearly you can't have much progress in medicine without the whole technological system and everything that goes with it."

The observer I am quoting is Kaczynski. Although one might properly resist him as an authority, I believe he is correct on the deeply entangled nature of the benefits and risks of technology. Where Kaczynski and I clearly part company is in our overall assessment of the relative balance between the two. Joy and I have engaged in dialogues on this issue both publicly and privately, and we concur that technology will and should progress and that we need to be actively concerned with its dark side. If Bill and I disagree, it's on the granularity of relinquishment that is both feasible and desirable.

Abandonment of broad areas of technology will only push these technologies underground where development would continue unimpeded by ethics or regulation. In such a situation, less stable, less responsible practitioners—for example, terrorists—would have a monopoly on deadly expertise.

I do think that relinquishment at the right level needs to be part of our ethical response to the dangers of 21st century technologies. One salient and constructive example of this is the proposed ethical guideline by the Foresight Institute, founded by nanotechnology pioneer Eric Drexler. This guideline would call on nanotechnologists to relinquish the development of physical entities that can self-replicate in a natural environment. Another example is a ban on self-replicating physical entities that contain their own codes for self-replication. In a design that nanotechnologist Ralph Merkle calls the "Broadcast Architecture," such entities would have to obtain such codes from a centralized secure server, which would guard against undesirable replication.

The Broadcast Architecture is impossible in the biological world, which represents at least one way in which nanotechnology can be made safer than biotechnology. In other ways, nanotech is potentially more dangerous because nanobots can be physically stronger than protein-based entities and more intelligent. But it will eventually be possible to combine the two by having nanotechnology provide the codes within biological entities (replacing DNA), in which case we can use the much safer Broadcast Architecture.

Parsing Perils

As responsible technologists, our ethics should include such "fine-grained" relinquishment, among other professional ethical guidelines. Other protections will need to include oversight by regulatory bodies, the development of technology-specific "immune" responses, as well as computer-assisted surveillance by law enforcement organizations. Many people are not aware that our intelligence agencies already use advanced technologies such as automated word spotting to monitor a substantial flow of telephone conversations. As we go forward, balancing our cherished rights of privacy with our need to be protected from the malicious use of powerful 21st century technologies will be one of many profound challenges. This is the reason recent issues of an encryption "trap door," in which law enforcement authorities would have access to otherwise secure information, and the FBI's Carnivore e-mail snooping system have been so contentious.

As a test case, we can take a small measure of comfort from how we have dealt with one recent technological challenge. There exists today a new form of fully nonbiological, self-replicating entity that didn't exist just a few decades ago: the computer virus. When this form of destructive intruder first appeared, strong concerns were voiced that as such viruses became more sophisticated, software pathogens had the potential to destroy the computer network medium in which they live. Yet the "immune system" that has evolved in response to this challenge has been largely effective. Although destructive, self-replicating software entities do cause damage from time to time, the injury is but a small fraction—much less than one-tenth of 1 percent—of the benefit we receive from the computers and communication links that harbor them.

One might counter that computer viruses lack the lethal potential of biological viruses or of destructive nanotechnology. Although true, this strengthens my observation. The fact that computer viruses are not usually deadly to humans only encourages more people to create and release them.

It also means that our response to the danger is relatively relaxed. Conversely, when it comes to self-replicating entities that are potentially lethal on a large scale, our response on all levels will be vastly more intense.

Technology will remain a double-edged sword, and the story of the 21st century has not yet been written. So, while we must acknowledge and deal with the dangers, we must also recognize that technology represents vast power to be used for all humankind's purposes. We have no choice but to work hard to apply these quickening technologies to advance our human values, despite what often appears to be a lack of consensus on what those values should be.

ROBERT WACHBROIT   II.9

Genetic Encores: The Ethics of Human Cloning

In this selection Robert Wachbroit, a bioethicist and research scholar at the Institute for Philosophy and Public Policy at the University of Maryland, discusses the ethical issues surrounding the prospect of human cloning. He attempts to dispel some common fears about cloning and clear up some misunderstandings about this issue. He also outlines a number of scenarios under which it might be argued that cloning a human being would be an ethically acceptable option. He compares the ethics of cloning to that of genetic engineering, which he finds in certain respects to be the more ethically troubling technology.

Focus Questions

1. What is genetic determinism, and why does Wachbroit not believe in it?
2. What are the most important differences between cloning and other forms of artificial or technologically assisted reproduction? Do these differences make an ethical difference?
3. How does Wachbroit's view compare to that of Sagoff (selection II.12) concerning the implications of genetic engineering?

Keywords

asexual reproduction, bioethics, genetic engineering, human cloning

THE SUCCESSFUL CLONING OF AN ADULT SHEEP, announced in Scotland this past February, is one of the most dramatic recent examples of a scientific discovery becoming a public issue. During the last few months, various commentators—scientists and theologians, physicians and legal experts, talk-radio hosts and editorial writers—have been busily responding to the news, some calming fears, others raising alarms about the prospect of cloning a human being. At the request of the President, the National Bioethics Advisory Commission (NBAC) held hearings and prepared a report on the religious, ethical, and legal issues surrounding human cloning. While declining to call for a permanent ban on the practice, the Commission recommended a moratorium on efforts to clone human beings, and emphasized the importance of further public deliberation on the subject.

An interesting tension is at work in the NBAC report. Commission members were well aware of "the widespread public discomfort, even revulsion, about cloning human beings." Perhaps recalling the images of Dolly the ewe that were featured on the covers of national news magazines, they noted that "the impact of these most recent developments on our national psyche has been quite remarkable." Accordingly, they felt that one of their tasks was to articulate, as fully and sympathetically as possible, the range of concerns that the prospect of human cloning had elicited.

Yet it seems clear that some of these concerns, at least, are based on false beliefs about genetic influence and the nature of the individuals that would be produced through cloning. Consider, for instance, the fear that a clone would not be an "individual" but merely a "carbon copy" of someone else—an automaton of the sort familiar from science fiction. As many scientists have pointed out, a clone would not in fact be an identical *copy,* but more like a delayed identical *twin.* And just as identical twins are two separate people—biologically, psychologically, morally and legally, though not genetically—so,

too, a clone would be a separate person from her non-contemporaneous twin. To think otherwise is to embrace a belief in genetic determinism—the view that genes determine everything about us, and that environmental factors or the random events in human development are insignificant.

The overwhelming scientific consensus is that genetic determinism is false. In coming to understand the ways in which genes operate, biologists have also become aware of the myriad ways in which the environment affects their "expression." The genetic contribution to the simplest physical traits, such as height and hair color, is significantly mediated by environmental factors (and possibly by stochastic events as well). And the genetic contribution to the traits we value most deeply, from intelligence to compassion, is conceded by even the most enthusiastic genetic researchers to be limited and indirect.

It is difficult to gauge the extent to which "repugnance" toward cloning generally rests on a belief in genetic determinism. Hoping to account for the fact that people "instinctively recoil" from the prospect of cloning, James Q. Wilson wrote, "There is a natural sentiment that is offended by the mental picture of identical babies being produced in some biological factory." Which raises the question: once people learn that this picture is mere science fiction, does the offense that cloning presents to "natural sentiment" attenuate, or even disappear? Jean Bethke Elshtain cited the nightmare scenarios of "the man and woman on the street," who imagine a future populated by "a veritable army of Hitlers, ruthless and remorseless bigots who kept reproducing themselves until they had finished what the historic Hitler failed to do: annihilate us." What happens, though, to the "pity and terror" evoked by the topic of cloning when such scenarios are deprived (as they deserve to be) of all credibility?

Richard Lewontin has argued that the critics' fears—or at least, those fears that merit consideration in formulating public policy—dissolve once genetic determinism is refuted. He criticizes the NBAC report for excessive deference to opponents of human cloning, and calls for greater public education on the scientific issues. (The Commission in

From "Genetic Encores: The Ethics of Human Cloning" by Robert Wachbroit, *Report from the Institute for Philosophy and Public Policy,* Vol. 17, No. 4 (Fall 1997), pp. 1–7. Reprinted by permission.

fact makes the same recommendation, but Lewontin seems unimpressed.) Yet even if a public education campaign succeeded in eliminating the most egregious misconceptions about genetic influence, that wouldn't settle the matter. People might continue to express concerns about the interests and rights of human clones, about the social and moral consequences of the cloning process, and about the possible motivations for creating children in this way.

Interests and Rights

One set of ethical concerns about human clones involves the risks and uncertainties associated with the current state of cloning technology. This technology has not yet been tested with human subjects, and scientists cannot rule out the possibility of mutation or other biological damage. Accordingly, the NBAC report concluded that "at this time, it is morally unacceptable for anyone in the public or private sector, whether in a research or clinical setting, to attempt to create a child using somatic cell nuclear transfer cloning." Such efforts, it said, would pose "unacceptable risks to the fetus and/or potential child."

The ethical issues of greatest importance in the cloning debate, however, do not involve possible failures of cloning technology, but rather the consequences of its success. Assuming that scientists were able to clone human beings without incurring the risks mentioned above, what concerns might there be about the welfare of clones?

Some opponents of cloning believe that such individuals would be wronged in morally significant ways. Many of these wrongs involve the denial of what Joel Feinberg has called "the right to an open future." For example, a child might be constantly compared to the adult from whom he was cloned, and thereby burdened with oppressive expectations. Even worse, the parents might actually limit the child's opportunities for growth and development: a child cloned from a basketball player, for instance, might be denied any educational opportunities that were not in line with a career in basketball. Finally, regardless of his parents' conduct or attitudes, a child might be burdened by the *thought* that he is a

copy and not an "original." The child's sense of self-worth or individuality or dignity, so some have argued, would thus be difficult to sustain.

How should we respond to these concerns? On the one hand, the existence of a right to an open future has a strong intuitive appeal. We are troubled by parents who radically constrict their children's possibilities for growth and development. Obviously, we would condemn a cloning parent for crushing a child with oppressive expectations, just as we might condemn fundamentalist parents for utterly isolating their children from the modern world, or the parents of twins for inflicting matching wardrobes and rhyming names. But this is not enough to sustain an objection to cloning itself. Unless the claim is that cloned parents cannot help but be oppressive, we would have cause to say they had wronged their children only because of their subsequent, and avoidable, sins of bad parenting—not because they had chosen to create the child in the first place. (The possible reasons for making this choice will be discussed below.)

We must also remember that children are often born in the midst of all sorts of hopes and expectations; the idea that there is a special burden associated with the thought "There is someone who is genetically just like me" is necessarily speculative. Moreover, given the falsity of genetic determinism, any conclusions a child might draw from observing the person from whom he was cloned would be uncertain at best. His knowledge of his future would differ only in degree from what many children already know once they begin to learn parts of their family's (medical) history. Some of us knew that we would be bald, or to what diseases we might be susceptible. To be sure, the cloned individual might know more about what he or she could become. But because our knowledge of the effect of environment on development is so incomplete, the clone would certainly be in for some surprises.

Finally, even if we were convinced that clones are likely to suffer particular burdens, that would not be enough to show that it is wrong to create them. The child of a poor family can be expected to suffer specific hardships and burdens, but we don't thereby conclude that such children shouldn't be born. Despite the hardships, poor children can experience parental love and many of the joys of being alive: the deprivations of poverty, however painful, are not decisive. More generally, no one's life is entirely free of some difficulties or burdens. In order for these considerations to have decisive weight, we have to be able to say that life doesn't offer any compensating benefits. Concerns expressed about the welfare of human clones do not appear to justify such a bleak assessment. Most such children can be expected to have lives well worth living; many of the imagined harms are no worse than those faced by children acceptably produced by more conventional means. If there is something deeply objectionable about cloning, it is more likely to be found by examining implications of the cloning process itself, or the reasons people might have for availing themselves of it.

Concerns About Process

Human cloning falls conceptually between two other technologies. At one end we have the assisted reproductive technologies, such as in vitro fertilization, whose primary purpose is to enable couples to produce a child with whom they have a biological connection. At the other end we have the emerging technologies of genetic engineering—specifically, gene transplantation technologies—whose primary purpose is to produce a child that has certain traits. Many proponents of cloning see it as part of the first technology: cloning is just another way of providing a couple with a biological child they might otherwise be unable to have. Since this goal and these other technologies are acceptable, cloning should be acceptable as well. On the other hand, many opponents of cloning see it as part of the second technology: even though cloning is a transplantation of an entire nucleus and not of specific genes, it is nevertheless an attempt to produce a child with certain traits. The deep misgivings we may have about the genetic manipulation of offspring should apply to cloning as well.

The debate cannot be resolved, however, simply by determining which technology to assimilate cloning to. For example, some opponents of human cloning see it as continuous with assisted reproductive technologies; but since they find those technologies objectionable as well, the assimilation does not indicate approval. Rather than argue for grouping cloning with one technology or another, I wish to suggest that we can best understand the significance of the cloning process by comparing it with these other technologies, and thus broadening the debate.

To see what can be learned from such a comparative approach, let us consider a central argument that has been made against cloning—that it undermines the structure of the family by making identities and lineages unclear. On the one hand, the relationship between an adult and the child cloned from her could be described as that between a parent and offspring. Indeed, some commentators have called cloning asexual reproduction, which clearly suggests that cloning is a way of generating *descendants*. The clone, on this view, has only one biological parent. On the other hand, from the point of view of genetics, the clone is a *sibling*, so that cloning is more accurately described as delayed twinning rather than as asexual reproduction. The clone, on this view, has two biological parents, not one—they are the same parents as those of the person from whom that individual was cloned.

Cloning thus results in ambiguities. Is the clone an offspring or a sibling? Does the clone have one biological parent or two? The moral significance of these ambiguities lies in the fact that in many societies, including our own, lineage identifies responsibilities. Typically, the parent, not the sibling, is responsible for the child. But if no one is unambiguously the parent, so the worry might go, who is responsible for the clone? Insofar as social identity is based on biological ties, won't this identity be blurred or confounded?

Some assisted reproductive technologies have raised similar questions about lineage and identity. An anonymous sperm donor is thought to have no parental obligations towards his biological child. A surrogate mother may be required to relinquish all parental claims to the child she bears. In these cases, the social and legal determination of "who is the parent" may appear to proceed in defiance of profound biological facts, and to subvert attachments that we as a society are ordinarily committed to upholding. Thus, while the *aim* of assisted reproductive technologies is to allow people to produce or raise a child to whom they are biologically connected, such technologies may also involve the creation of social ties that are permitted to override biological ones.

In the case of cloning, however, ambiguous lineages would seem to be less problematic, precisely because no one is being asked to relinquish a claim on a child to whom he or she might otherwise acknowledge a biological connection. What, then, are the critics afraid of? It does not seem plausible that someone would have herself cloned and then hand the child over to her parents, saying, "You take care of her! She's *your* daughter!" Nor is it likely that, if the cloned individual did raise the child, she would suddenly refuse to pay for college on the grounds that this was not a sister's responsibility. Of course, policymakers should address any confusion in the social or legal assignment of responsibility resulting from cloning. But there are reasons to think that this would be *less* difficult than in the case of other reproductive technologies.

Similarly, when we compare cloning with genetic engineering, cloning may prove to be the less troubling of the two technologies. This is true even though the dark futures to which they are often alleged to lead are broadly alike. For example, a recent *Washington Post* article examined fears that the development of genetic enhancement technologies might "create a market in preferred physical traits." The reporter asked, "Might it lead to a society of DNA haves and have-nots, and the creation of a new underclass of people unable to keep up with the genetically fortified Joneses?" Similarly, a member of the National Bioethics Advisory Commission expressed concern that cloning might become "almost a preferred practice," taking its place "on the continuum of providing the best for your child." As a consequence, parents who chose to "play the lottery of old-fashioned reproduction would be considered irresponsible."

Such fears, however, seem more warranted with respect to genetic engineering than to cloning. By offering some people—in all probability, members of the upper classes—the opportunity to acquire desired traits through genetic manipulation, genetic engineering could bring about a biological reinforcement (or accentuation) of existing social divisions. It is hard enough already for disadvantaged children to compete with their more affluent counterparts, given the material resources and intellectual opportunities that are often available only to children of privilege. This unfairness would almost certainly be compounded if genetic manipulation came into the picture. In contrast, cloning does not bring about "improvements" in the genome: it is, rather, a way of *duplicating* the genome—with all its imperfections. It wouldn't enable certain groups of people to keep getting better and better along some valued dimension.

To some critics, admittedly, this difference will not seem terribly important. Theologian Gilbert Meilaender, Jr., objects to cloning on the grounds that children created through this technology would be "designed as a product" rather than "welcomed as a gift." The fact that the design process would be more selective and nuanced in the case of genetic engineering would, from this perspective, have no moral significance. To the extent that this objection reflects a concern about the commodification of human life, we can address it in part when we consider people's reasons for engaging in cloning.

Reasons for Cloning

This final area of contention in the cloning debate is as much psychological as it is scientific or philosophical. If human cloning technology were safe and widely available, what use would people make of it? What reasons would they have to engage in cloning?

In its report to the President, the Commission imagined a few situations in which people might avail themselves of cloning. In one scenario, a husband and wife who wish to have children are both carriers of a lethal recessive gene:

> Rather than risk the one in four chance of conceiving a child who will suffer a short and painful existence, the couple considers the alternatives: to forgo rearing children; to adopt; to use prenatal diagnosis and selective abortion; to use donor gametes free of the recessive trait; or to use the

cells of one of the adults and attempt to clone a child. To avoid donor gametes and selective abortion, while maintaining a genetic tie to their child, they opt for cloning.

In another scenario, the parents of a terminally ill child are told that only a bone marrow transplant can save the child's life. "With no other donor available, the parents attempt to clone a human being from the cells of the dying child. If successful, the new child will be a perfect match for bone marrow transplant, and can be used as a donor without significant risk or discomfort. The net result: two healthy children, loved by their parents, who happen [sic] to be identical twins of different ages."

The Commission was particularly impressed by the second example. That scenario, said the NBAC report, "makes what is probably the strongest possible case for cloning a human being, as it demonstrates how this technology could be used for lifesaving purposes." Indeed, the report suggests that it would be a "tragedy" to allow "the sick child to die because of a moral or political objection to such cloning." Nevertheless, we should note that many people would be morally uneasy about the use of a minor as a donor, regardless of whether the child were a result of cloning. Even if this unease is justifiably overridden by other concerns, the "transplant scenario" may not present a more compelling case for cloning than that of the infertile couple desperately seeking a biological child.

Most critics, in fact, decline to engage the specifics of such tragic (and presumably rare) situations. Instead, they bolster their case by imagining very different scenarios. Potential users of the technology, they suggest, are narcissists or control freaks—people who will regard their children not as free, original selves but as products intended to meet more or less rigid specifications. Even if such people are not genetic determinists, their recourse to cloning will indicate a desire to exert all possible influence over the "kind" of child they produce.

The critics' alarm at this prospect has in part to do, as we have seen, with concerns about the psychological burdens such a desire would impose on the clone. But it also reflects a broader concern about the values expressed, and promoted, by a

society's reproductive policies. Critics argue that a society that enables people to clone themselves thereby endorses the most narcissistic reason for having children—to perpetuate oneself through a genetic encore. The demonstrable falsity of genetic determinism may detract little, if at all, from the strength of this motive. Whether or not clones will have a grievance against their parents for producing them with this motivation, the societal indulgence of that motivation is improper and harmful.

It can be argued, however, that the critics have simply misunderstood the social meaning of a policy that would permit people to clone themselves even in the absence of the heartrending exigencies described in the NBAC report. This country has developed a strong commitment to reproductive autonomy. (This commitment emerged in response to the dismal history of eugenics—the very history that is sometimes invoked to support restrictions on cloning.) With the exception of practices that risk coercion and exploitation—notably baby-selling and commercial surrogacy—we do not interfere with people's freedom to create and acquire children by almost any means, for almost any reason. This policy does not reflect a dogmatic libertarianism. Rather, it recognizes the extraordinary personal importance and private character of reproductive decisions, even those with significant social repercussions.

Our willingness to sustain such a policy also reflects a recognition of the moral complexities of parenting. For example, we know that the motives people have for bringing a child into the world do not necessarily determine the manner in which they raise him. Even when parents start out as narcissists, the experience of childrearing will sometimes transform their initial impulses, making them caring, respectful, and even self-sacrificing. Seeing their child grow and develop, they learn that she is not merely an extension of themselves. Of course, some parents never make this discovery; others, having done so, never forgive their children for it. The pace and extent of moral development among parents (no less than among children) is infinitely variable. Still, we are justified in saying that those who engage in cloning will not, by virtue of this fact, be immune to the transformative effects of parenthood—even if it is the case (and it won't always be) that they begin with more problematic motives than those of parents who engage in the "genetic lottery."

Moreover, the nature of parental motivation is itself more complex than the critics often allow. Though we can agree that narcissism is a vice not to be encouraged, we lack a clear notion of where pride in one's children ends and narcissism begins. When, for example, is it unseemly to bask in the reflected glory of a child's achievements? Imagine a champion gymnast who takes delight in her daughter's athletic prowess. Now imagine that the child was actually cloned from one of the gymnast's somatic cells. Would we have to revise our moral assessment of her pleasure in her daughter's success? Or suppose a man wanted to be cloned and to give his child opportunities he himself had never enjoyed. And suppose that, rightly or wrongly, the man took the child's success as a measure of his own untapped potential—an indication of the flourishing life he might have had. Is this sentiment blamable? And is it all that different from what many natural parents feel?

Conclusion

Until recently, there were few ethical, social, or legal discussions about human cloning via nuclear transplantation, since the scientific consensus was that such a procedure was not biologically possible. With the appearance of Dolly, the situation has changed. But although it now seems more likely that human cloning will become feasible, we may doubt that the practice will come into widespread use.

I suspect it will not, but my reasons will not offer much comfort to the critics of cloning. While the technology for nuclear transplantation advances, other technologies—notably the technology of genetic engineering—will be progressing as well. Human genetic engineering will be applicable to a wide variety of traits; it will be more powerful than cloning, and hence more attractive to more people. It will also, as I have suggested, raise more troubling questions than the prospect of cloning has thus far.

JUDY WAJCMAN   II.10

Reproductive Technology: Delivered into Men's Hands

In this reading, taken from her book *Feminism Confronts Technology,* Judy Wajcman argues that "certain kinds of technology are inextricably linked to particular institutionalized patterns of power and authority, and the case of reproductive technologies is no exception." She illustrates this thesis by means of an examination of the historical transformation of childbirth from what was at one time a natural process managed by women and midwives into an increasingly medicalized process managed by men and scientists.

The point of view taken by the author may strike some readers as unduly feminist in its orientation. However, this reading can be usefully compared to that of Corlann Gee Bush (selection I.5) who emphasizes the importance of considering the cultural context of technologies, and that of Freeman Dyson (selection I.10) who discusses the differing impacts that technological innovation has on patterns of social power and equality. In the end, the reader will have to decide for herself or himself whether the reproductive technologies Wajcman discusses have been a been a boon to women's liberation, or as some writers have argued, have simply increased the control by men over women's lives and bodies.

Focus Questions

1. What are the factors that Wajcman identifies as having been mainly responsible for the medicalization of childbirth?
2. Wajcman refers to Winner's idea that technologies can embody political values (selection I.7). How is this notion illustrated in reference to the technologies of artificial or assisted human reproduction that Wajcman discusses?
3. How does the perspective on birth control developed in this reading compare with that discussed by Hardin (selection II.13)? Specifically, what are the "valences" of different methods of birth control? How do these valances relate to the problem of controlling the growth of the human population?

Keywords

biotechnology, birth control, contraception, genetic research, human embryo research, infertility, in vitro fertilization, reproductive technology, women's liberation

NOWHERE IS THE RELATIONSHIP between gender and technology more vigorously contested than in the sphere of human biological reproduction. Women are the bearers, and in most societies the primary nurturers, of children. This means that reproductive technologies are of particular significance to them. Birth control has been a major issue for all movements for women's equality, and much feminist scholarship has been devoted to uncovering women's struggle throughout history against the appropriation of medical knowledge and practice by men.

Central to this analysis and of increasing relevance today is the perception that the processes of pregnancy and childbirth are directed and controlled by ever more sophisticated and intrusive technologies. Implicit in this view is a concept of reproduction as a natural process, inherent in women alone, and a theory of technology as patri-archal, enabling the male domination of women and nature.

The burgeoning debate about these issues has largely been conducted within the feminist movement on the one hand and within the fundamentalist Right on the other. Interestingly, socialists have generally been silent on recent developments in reproductive technology, perhaps because they primarily affect women, or perhaps because they do not concern workplace production, the Left's traditional obsession. But these are the technologies of life, raising complex moral issues about the role of human intervention in the world of living beings. This chapter will explore feminist perspectives on reproductive technologies, placing them in the wider context of the growing supremacy of technology in medicine.

Feminist Perspectives on Reproductive Technology

The literature on reproductive technology is rife with technological determinist arguments which assume that changes in technology are the most important cause of changes in society.[1] Perhaps here

From "Reproductive Technology: Delivered into Men's Hands," *Feminism Confronts Technology* by Judy Wajcman. University Park: The Pennsylvania State University Press, 1991, p. 51–80. Copyright © 1991 Judy Wajcman. Reproduced by permission of the publisher. References have been omitted.

more than elsewhere, major technological advances are seen as having directly transformed women's lives for the better. The technologies of pregnancy and childbirth are said to have put an end to the dangerous and painful aspects of giving birth. Healthy pregnancies and healthy babies are attributed to the wonders of modern antenatal care, now a highly medicalized and technologized process. The new sophisticated techniques for monitoring foetal development in the early stages of pregnancy mean that some "defective" foetuses can be aborted. Infertile women who previously had no options can now embark on infertility programmes that promise the chance of conceiving "naturally." And, most common of all, advances in the technologies of fertility control are seen as the key to the massive social changes that have occurred for women's equality. The widespread availability of reliable contraception and abortion, a right often fought for by women, have meant that for the first time in human history women are in control of their own bodies.[2]

TECHNOLOGY AS THE KEY TO WOMEN'S LIBERATION

In the early period of the contemporary women's movement, reproductive technology was seen as particularly progressive because it opened up the potential for finally severing the link between sexuality and reproduction. The much-cited advocate of the use of high technology to liberate women was Shulamith Firestone. In *The Dialectic of Sex* (1970) she emphasized the need to develop effective contraceptive and birth technologies in order to free women from the "tyranny of reproduction" which dictated the nature of women's oppression. Patriarchy was seen to be fundamentally about the control of women's bodies, especially their sexuality and fertility, by men. This view located women's oppression in their own biology and posited a technological fix in the shape of ectogenesis. The application of a neutral technology would bring an end to biological motherhood and thus make sexual equality possible.

Since then, feminist analysis has not shared Firestone's enthusiasm for the artificial womb as the key to women's liberation. Instead, feminists have recently been more concerned either to oppose the experimentation on women's bodies that the development of these techniques entails or to harness these techniques in the interests of fulfilling women's maternal desires.

Genetic research, biotechnology, and infertility treatment are now making such dramatic advances that Firestone's ideas no longer seem to belong in the realm of fantasy. The organic unity of foetus and mother can no longer be assumed now that human eggs and embryos can be moved from body to body or out of and back into the same female body. The major proponents of the possibilities of reproductive technologies are the scientists and medical practitioners developing the techniques as well as women who have benefited from them. Leading infertility doctors argue that embryo research promises the possibility of eliminating some of the most crippling forms of hereditary disease and most importantly, gives hope to previously childless couples. As one Member of Parliament recently put it:

> The object of our interest in medical research into embryology and human fertilisation is to help humanity. It is to help those who are infertile and to help control infertility. . . . The researchers are not monsters, but scientists. They are medical scientists working in response to a great human need. We should be proud of them. The infertile parents who have been helped are grateful to them. (Pfeffer, 1987, p. 81)

However, all over the world, the use of human embryos in scientific research is becoming a major source of controversy. Governments are under pressure to impose tighter regulations and define the limits of what is permissible. Ethical and religious objections have been strongly voiced to the inexorable advance of science and technology into the sacred realms of creation. The "right to life" lobby calls for legislation to ban research in human embryology and the practice of in-vitro fertilization. Just as they oppose abortion as an unnatural interference with procreation, their concern is for the life and soul of the foetus. The intense public debate is centred around the question of which, if any, of the procedures and experimental programmes should be licensed and given resources.

In Australia, Europe, and North America there is growing debate among feminists over the impact that these novel reproductive and genetic technologies will have on women's lives. This is a very divisive area for feminists. Whereas abortion and contraception were about challenging the traditional definition of femininity which equated it with motherhood, by contrast these new technologies are about fulfilling, rather than rejecting, the traditional feminine role.

A shared concern is that techniques such as in-vitro fertilization coexist with a powerful ideology of motherhood. Many feminists argue that the in-vitro fertilization programme reinforces the definition of motherhood as a biological imperative rather than a social relationship. As Christine Crowe (1987, p. 84) observes: "IVF does *not* cure infertility; it provides (and for a few women only) an avenue to biological motherhood through technological intervention."[3] It is a "technological fix" in the sense that it does not at any point address the initial causes of infertility. Doctors and the media describe these technologies as enhancing women's "natural need" to mother, and infertile women as desperate. Much of the feminist discussion centres on the notion of choice and whether the right to choose to have an abortion can be equated with the right to choose to have a child.[4] As we shall see below, feminist support for techniques such as in-vitro fertilization is founded in the belief that these technologies increase women's choices and that women do indeed have the right to reproduce.

REPRODUCTIVE TECHNOLOGY AS PATRIARCHAL DOMINATION

Most vocal in their opposition to the development and application of genetic and reproductive engineering are a group of radical feminists who in 1984 formed FINRRAGE (Feminist International Network of Resistance to Reproductive and Genetic Engineering). Represented by authors such as Gena Corea (1985), Jalna Hanmer (1985), Renate D. Klein (1985), Maria Mies (1987) and Robyn Rowland (1985), they see the development of reproductive technologies as a form of patriarchal exploitation of women's bodies.

Whereas Firestone saw women's reproductive role as the source of their oppression, FINRRAGE writers want to reclaim the experience of motherhood as the foundation of women's identity. For, as Robyn Rowland (1985, p. 78) expresses it: "the qualities of mothering or maternal thinking stand in opposition to the destructive, violent and self-aggrandizing characteristics of men." The previously celebrated technological potential for the complete separation of reproduction from sexuality is now seen as an attack on women. Radical feminist theory sees these techniques as an attempt to appropriate the reproductive capacities which have been, in the past, women's unique source of power. It is about removing "the last woman-centred process from us." For Jalna Hanmer (1985, p. 103), "The dominant mode of [patriarchal] control is changing hands from the individual male through marriage to men as a social category, through science and technology. . . . The locus of control and struggle is shifting from sexuality to reproduction and childcare, i.e. motherhood."

For this group of feminists, who have criticized the ways in which patriarchal society has ignored or sanctioned sexual and domestic violence against women, the new reproductive and gene technologies are "violence against women in yet another form." "Genetic and reproductive engineering is another attempt to end self-determination over our bodies." According to this theory, techniques such as in-vitro fertilization, egg donation, sex predetermination and embryo evaluation offer a powerful means of social control because they will become standard practice. Just as other obstetric procedures were first introduced for "high risk" cases and are now used routinely on most birthing women, these authors fear that the new techniques will eventually be used on a large proportion of the female population.

FINRRAGE sees reproductive technologies as inextricably linked with genetic engineering and eugenics. It is techniques such as in-vitro fertilization which provide researchers with the embryos on which to do scientific research. A parallel is drawn between the way in which men have been increasingly controlling the reproduction of animals to improve their stock by experimenting on them, and the extension of this form of experimentation to women. The female body is being expropriated, fragmented, and dissected as raw material, or providing "living laboratories" as Renate Klein puts it, for the technological production of human beings.

The most powerful statement of this is Gena Corea's image of "the reproductive brothel" which extrapolates from the way animals are now used like machines to breed, to a future in which women will become professional breeders, "the mother machine" at men's command. Some writers argue that these techniques will actually replace natural reproduction, guaranteeing the fabrication of genetically perfect babies. According to this futuristic dystopia, men will achieve ultimate control of human creation and women will be redundant.

Many feminists have explained the patriarchal desire for control over reproduction in psychoanalytic or psychological terms, associating it with male fear of female procreativity and the quest for immortality. The potential of this technology to disconnect the foetus from a woman's body is seen as a specific form of the ancient masculine impulse "to confine and limit and curb the creativity and potentially polluting power of female procreation" (Oakley, 1976, p. 57), in short, male womb envy. Embedded in this approach, and most explicit in the work of Maria Mies, is a conception of science and technology as intrinsically patriarchal. FINRRAGE states that they want a new feminist science based on "a non-exploitative relationship between nature and ourselves." Clearly, feminist philosophical theorizing about the masculinist character of scientific objectivity and rationality is being heavily drawn on in current debates about reproductive technologies.

Mies argues that it makes absolutely no difference whether it is women or men who apply and control this technology; this technology is intrinsically an instrument of domination, "a new stage in the patriarchal war against women." Technology is not neutral but is always based on "exploitation of and domination over nature, exploitation and subjection of women, exploitation and oppression of other peoples" (1987, p. 37). Mies argues that this is the very logic of the natural sciences and its model is the machine. For her the method of technical progress is the violent destruction of natural links

between living organisms, the dissection and analysis of these organisms down to their smallest elements, in order to reassemble them, according to the plans of the male engineers, as machines. The goal of the enterprise is to become independent of the "moods" of nature and of the women out of whom life still comes. Reproductive and genetic technologies are about conquering the "last frontier" of men's domination over nature.

REPRODUCTIVE TECHNOLOGY AS NEUTRAL

Rather than seeing reproductive technologies as a sustained attack on women, another group of feminist commentators emphasize the ambivalent effects that reproductive technologies have on the lives of women. According to Michelle Stanworth (1987, p. 3), a blanket rejection of these innovations is inadequate as many of them "offer indispensable resources upon which women seek to draw according to their circumstances." These new technologies are seen as having the potential to empower, as well as to disempower, women and the discussion is couched in terms of "the costs and the benefits."

These authors argue that the women's movement has largely ignored the problems of infertility and treated women who participate in these high-tech research programmes as "blinded by science" and as passive victims of pronatal conditioning. According to them, most of the authors associated with FINRRAGE fail to consider women as active agents who have generated demands for such technologies because of their authentic desire to bear children. As a result, feminist opposition to these technologies has a tendency to "confuse masculine rhetoric and fantasies with actual power relations, thereby submerging women's own response to reproductive situations in the dominant (and victimizing) masculine text" (Petchesky, 1987, p. 71). Reproductive technologies may be the only opportunity infertile women have to fulfil this need and therefore we should support their "right of reproductive choice."

This group of writers take issue with the radical feminist view that technologies in themselves have patriarchal political properties. Instead, they problematize the institutional setting in which these medical/technical procedures occur. Whereas the FINRRAGE authors are against these innovations because they inevitably disempower women, according to Rosalind Pollack Petchesky, "we need to separate the power relations within which reproductive technologies . . . are applied from the technologies themselves" (1987, p. 79). Similarly, for Michelle Stanworth, the problem is not technology but the way "these technologies draw their meaning from the cultural and political climate in which they are embedded" (1987, p. 26).

The feminist debate about the new reproductive technologies reviewed here is a relatively recent one and, as a result, it is characterized by more sensitivity to "the politics of difference" than some of the earlier feminist literature. There is now a much clearer realization that gender, that what it is to be a woman, is experienced everywhere through such mediations as sexual orientation, age, race, class, history, and colonialism. The recognition that new technologies may have very different implications for Third World and First World women, within and between countries, is a strength of much of the literature.

The real dangers for women that accompany medical and scientific advances in the sphere of reproduction are directly related to the different circumstances of women's position in society. Access to the benefits of expensive techniques such as in-vitro fertilization is heavily related to the ability to pay. Women who are poor and vulnerable will not have access to these techniques and furthermore, they will be least able to resist abuses of medical power and techniques. For example, ethical issues over sex predetermination have a special urgency given evidence that the technique of amniocentesis is currently being used to preselect female fetuses for abortion in India. Sterilization and drugs such as Depo-Provera, as well as hazardous experiments, have been particularly targeted at coloured women.

The potential use of increasingly sophisticated forms of genetic screening is likely to influence the definition of a "genetic defect" and may have implications for the way disability is seen in society. Research such as Wendy Farrant's (1985) shows that the medical management of prenatal screening in Britain has taken the form of gaining women's consent for termination as a condition for being allowed the amniocentesis test. In this context, these techniques are about population control rather than about enabling women to make more informed choices about reproduction.

There is broad agreement among feminists about these dangers. For those feminists who dispute the FINRRAGE analysis, these dangers are seen not as a function of the technologies themselves, but of their abuse. This position is summed up by Stanworth (1987, p. 15), when she says that these technologies have been "a double-edged sword. On the one hand, they have offered women a greater technical possibility to decide if, when and under what conditions to have children; on the other, the domination of so much reproductive technology by the medical profession and the state has enabled others to have an even greater capacity to exert control over women's lives." From this perspective, therefore, the feminist critique of reproductive technologies goes no further than demanding access to knowledge and resources so that women are able "to shape the experience of reproduction according to their own definitions."

An aspect of the politics of reproductive technology left out by this account is that the technologies redefine what counts as illness. "Infertility" now becomes not a biological state to which the woman must adapt her life, but a medical condition—a problem capable of technological intervention. The very existence of the technologies changes the situation even if the woman does not use them. Her "infertility" is now treatable, and she must in a sense actively decide not to be treated. In this way the technologies strengthen the maternal function of all women, and reinforce the internalization of that role for each woman.

Indeed, the emphasis placed on women's right to use these technologies to their own ends tends to obscure the way in which historical and social relations are built into the technologies themselves. While recognizing the social shaping of women's choices in the sense of motivations, few participants in the debate see that the technologies from which women choose are themselves shaped socially.[5]

Techniques such as in-vitro fertilization, egg donation, artificial insemination, and surrogacy have the potential to place the whole notion of genetic parenthood, and thus family relationships, in jeopardy. However, only those technologies that reinforce the value of having one's "own" child, one that is genetically related to oneself, are being developed and, as Patricia Spallone (1987, pp. 173–4) argues, these values determined the Warnock Committee's assessment of "acceptable" risks to women's health. Despite the dangers, the Committee approved the use of in-vitro fertilization, where egg donation provides an offspring which is genetically related to the husband. Yet the technique of egg donation by uterine lavage (embryo flushing or surrogate embryo transfer) was rejected on the basis of physical risks. The medical risks involved in this procedure are no greater, but it carries the risk of unwanted pregnancy in the donor woman. Two women would then be sharing a pregnancy and the existence of this donor mother-to-be would challenge the usual categories of motherhood. This technology was rejected, not on the grounds that it endangers women's health, but because of its socially disruptive character to the identification of blood ties with the family.

Women are in fact selecting from the very restricted range of technological options which are available to them. This is glossed over by the feminist critics of the FINRRAGE position. By focusing on the sexual politics in which the new reproductive technologies are embedded, they pay insufficient attention to the technology itself. In adopting, implicitly or explicitly, the use/abuse model of technology, they fail to appreciate the extent to which technologies have political qualities. This is where the strength of the FINRRAGE analysis lies. In my view, FINRRAGE are right to argue that gender relations have profoundly structured the form of reproductive technologies that have become available.

To make this claim, however, one does not need to conceptualize it in terms of a monolithic male conspiracy. As Langdon Winner (1980, p. 125) has said: "to recognize the political dimensions in the shapes of technology does not require that we look for conscious conspiracies or malicious intentions." Nor does it imply that men are a homogeneous group. While it is evident that all the stages in the career of a medical technology, from its inception and development, through to consolidation as part of routine practice, are a series of interlocking male activities, the male interests involved are specifically those of white middle-class professionals. The division of labour that produces and deploys the reproductive technologies is both sexual and professional: women are the patients, while the obstetricians, gynaecologists, molecular biologists and embryologists are men.

If we regard technology as neutral but subject to abuse we will be blinded to the consequences of artifacts being designed and developed in particular ways. To make sense of reproductive technology we need to examine the social and economic forces that drive research forward or that inhibit more progressive developments. Throughout this book I have argued that certain kinds of technology are inextricably linked to particular institutionalized patterns of power and authority, and the case of reproductive technologies is no exception. Men's appropriation of technology here, as in the other areas we have examined, has been decisive in attempts to create and maintain control over women. This can best be demonstrated by looking at the emergence of specific technologies and how they figure in the historical establishment of male hegemony in Western medicine.

The Medicalization and Mechanization of Childbirth

DELIVERED INTO MEN'S HANDS

A major focus of feminist historians of medicine has been to document the central role of women healers and midwives before the rise of modern medicine. Up until the close of the seventeenth century attendance on childbirth had always been the preserve of women, traditionally providing a livelihood for the wife and widow. It was midwives who came to women in labour and who assisted women in the process of giving birth. Their experience and knowledge about birthing and about birth assistance was passed from one generation of women to the next. Throughout the eighteenth century a bitter and well documented contest took place between female midwives and the emerging male-dominated medical profession, as to who would have control over intervention in the birth process (Ehrenreich and English, 1979 and Donnison, 1977). It emerges from these accounts that a particular technology played a crucial role in determining the outcome.

In England from the 1720s onwards an increasing number of men were entering midwifery in direct competition with women. Before that time, surgeons (an exclusively male occupation) had only been called in for difficult cases where natural delivery was not possible. They had carved out this work in the thirteenth century by forming surgeons' guilds which gave them the exclusive right to use surgical instruments. Before the invention of forceps however there was little they could do except to remove the infant piece-meal by the use of hooks and perforators, or to perform a Caesarian section on the body of the mother after her death (Donnison, 1977). Obstetric forceps were introduced by the Scottish apothecary William Smellie by the 1730s.

The forceps enabled its user to deliver live infants in cases where previously either child or mother would have died, and also to shorten tedious labour. According to custom, midwives were not allowed to use instruments as an accepted part of their practice. The use of forceps thus became the exclusive domain of physicians and surgeons, and was associated with the emerging profession of medicine. The introduction of forceps gave these men the edge over female midwives who were adept at the manual delivery of babies and who had all the practical knowledge about birth and birthing. As soon as this technology was introduced it was seized upon by physicians, who used it far too often, even in the contemporary opinion of the inventor himself. The outcome of the struggle that ensued was that the midwives lost their monopoly on birthing intervention, which became the province of the profession of medicine. For the first time in history childbirth, which had always been "women's business," had been captured by men.

Clearly the ascendancy of male obstetrics was the result of a number of interrelated factors, a critical element being the movement of childbirth from home into the newly established lying-in hospitals. However, the invention of one of the first technological aids to birthing provided a crucial resource for male medical practitioners. It is telling that the public debate precipitated by the entry of men into midwifery pivoted around the use of instruments such as obstetric forceps: "the doctors' practice of midwifery was becoming distinguishable by its very technical aspect" (Faulkner, 1985, p. 93). Young male midwives were often incompetent and frequently used instruments unnecessarily to hasten the birth and save their time, often damaging the mother and killing the child. The misuse of instruments was still common enough to attract the following criticism from a leading medical practitioner, a James Blundell of Guy's Hospital, who wrote in 1834 that some men seemed to suffer from "a sort of instinctive impulse to put the level and the forceps into the vagina" (Donnison, 1977, p. 50). Thus technical intervention rapidly became the hallmark of male medical practice.

This is not to say that birthing women were necessarily hostile to increased technical intervention. In the early decades of this century there was considerable feminist agitation in favour of the use of anaesthesia during labour, which male physicians were then opposing. Women took up the cause of drug-induced "twilight sleep" because they saw it as "the newest and finest technique available" to relieve the acute pain of childbirth. Physicians' objections to its use took various forms but ultimately they were defending their professional prerogative to determine the patient's treatment. As Judith Walzer Leavitt shows, this episode is a good example of the complexity of arguments about control. The doctors were resisting a process that would have reinforced *their* control over childbirth and the women were demanding the right to be unconscious during delivery! Although the twilight-sleep movement was motivated by a desire to increase women's control over the birthing process, it paradoxically "helped change the definition of birthing from a natural home event, as it was in the nineteenth century, to an illness requiring hospitalization and physician attendance" (1986, p. 140).

Nowadays, in Western societies, childbirth is generally experienced in hospital and is associated with increased and routine technological intervention. Under the aegis of the predominantly male medical profession, the trend has been towards the routine use of anaesthesia, the common resort to forceps, the standard practice of episiotomy, and the increase in births artificially induced as well as Caesarian sections.[6] Perhaps the most vivid image of women's treatment is "the rack-like delivery bed on which a mother is strapped, flat on her back with her legs in stirrups, in a position which might have been deliberately designed to make her own efforts to bear a child as ineffectual as possible" (Donnison, 1977, p. 198). A number of feminist authors, including Ann Oakley, have argued that this medical "management" of pregnancy and childbirth by a powerful professional male elite has reduced women to the status of reproductive objects, engendering adverse emotional experiences for childbearing women. Contemporary feminists have been particularly critical of the extent to which birth has been transformed from a natural process into a pathological one.

Until fairly recently it was generally assumed that maternal and neonatal deaths were reduced as a direct result of the increased proportion of hospital confinements and the application of technology in pregnancy, labour, and birth. This belief explains women's apparent tolerance for a system that some have argued has transformed birth into a passive and alienating experience. It is now widely acknowledged however that in many, if not in most, cases, massive technological intervention in childbirth is unnecessary. With the exception of risky births and women who need Caesarian sections, such intervention is not a biological necessity; rather, it reflects the structure of power and decision making within obstetrical situations.

Recent sociological and medical literature has been reevaluating the contribution of medical technology to the health of mothers and babies, in comparison with social factors such as the standard of nutrition and sanitation. As Jill Rakusen and Nick Davidson (1982, p. 152) put it: "The single most significant contribution to a cut in the death and handicap rate among newborn babies would be a comprehensive anti-poverty programme."[7] Indeed, the women whose welfare might be most enhanced by these medical technologies have least access to them.

The strength of the feminist critique of professional medical care is not only its dissection of medical-technological treatments but its analysis of the way scientific and medical knowledge is itself gendered. To understand the medical treatment of birth, it is important to recognize that in the development of Western thought and medicine, the body came to be regarded as a machine. The Cartesian model of the body as a machine and the physician as technician or mechanic emerged in the seventeenth century and was integral to the development of the biomedical sciences. This mechanical metaphor continues to dominate modern medical practice and underlies the propensity to apply technology and to see surgery as the appropriate cure.

Gender symbolism and representations of sexual difference were central to the scientific and medical texts of the eighteenth and nineteenth centuries. In contrast to the male norm, women's bodies were depicted as frail and prone to physical and mental disease, the prime objects of medical intervention. Ludi Jordanova's recent book *Sexual Visions* contains fascinating material on the depiction of the differences between women and men in the biomedical sciences between the eighteenth and twentieth centuries. These sciences were associated with the idea of the unveiling of nature, and woman, as the personification of nature and "the other," was thus the appropriate corpse for the male practice of anatomy. (Although imagery of women's bodies was predominant, the unveiling of "otherness" also took a racial form.) Jordanova argues that gender is still a central medical metaphor and by examining advertisements in a contemporary medical magazine she explores the ways in which illnesses are visually tagged as "male" or "female." "Depression, anxiety, sleeplessness and migraine are likely to be associated with women, while disorders that can inhibit full movement and strenuous sporting activities are associated, metaphorically, with masculinity" (1989, p. 144).

The language of the biomedical sciences today is no less suffused with implicit assumptions about and imagery of sexual difference. Through a detailed comparison of medical writings on the female reproductive system with those on the male equivalent, Emily Martin (1987) found that the cultural grammar was radically distinct. Whereas the dominant metaphors used of the female system are negative and demeaning to women, by contrast those used of the male system suggested power and positive qualities. The images contained in medical descriptions of menstruation and menopause are characteristically in terms of failed production, breakdown, and decay; sperm is depicted as "amazing . . . in its sheer magnitude."[8] In obstetric literature, the uterus is regarded as the machine that produces the baby and the woman is the labourer supervised and managed by the doctor. Even in the act of conception the language of medicine assigns a passive role to women and an active role to the male. Propelled by a powerful tail, sperm, that "nuclear war-head of paternal genes," actively swims upstream to fertilize the waiting egg.

The profound gender-bias in the way medical science views women's and men's bodies, in its very way of seeing problems, has consequences both in the rate and kind of technological intervention. This is exemplified in the differential treatment of reproductive disorders in women and men. Infertility treatment is primarily aimed at women and male infertility is hardly visible or even acknowledged. "Unlike the female reproductive system, which is served by gynaecology, there is no medical specialty for the male reproductive system" (Pfeffer, 1985, p. 35). Far from being a sign of neglect, this is symptomatic of the medical profession's refusal to see the male reproductive system as defective.

Much medical technology has no doubt been of physical benefit to women, particularly in terms of pain relief, and this has been under-emphasized in the feminist literature, which is highly critical of modern, hospital-based obstetric practices. This view equates the increase in technological intervention with a corresponding loss of women's power and control over a dehumanized birth process. The history of reproductive technology is thus seen in terms of the oppression of women by science and medicine. Modern practices are compared unfavourably with explicit or implicit conceptions of what childbirth was like in earlier periods or in primitive societies. It is presumed or asserted that

until the advent of male medical control, childbirth was a safe, non-alienating, and purely "natural" physiological process; that women midwives and relatives attended in a sympathetic and supportive role.

However, as Sally Macintyre (1977, p. 18) points out: "Childbirth is, of course, socially controlled in all societies." Far from women themselves being individually in control, childbirth is invariably surrounded by rules, customs, prescriptions and sanctions. Indeed, historically and cross-culturally it is evident that women commonly police the process themselves, not simply deferring to the expectant mother's own wishes. To counterpose masculine technologized childbirth to women's "natural" ways begs the question. The issue is not what childbirth was or would be like for women without the controls imposed by modern technology, but why the technologies we have take the form they do. Thus we need to look at the social context in which the new reproductive technologies have developed.

TECHNOLOGY AND PROFESSIONALIZATION

In all professions, claiming expert technical knowledge has been favoured as a way of legitimating specialization. The unequal power relations between medical practitioners and their female patients are based on a combination of factors, predominantly those of professional qualification and gender. Oakley argues that the technological imperative within reproductive medicine is intrinsic to the defence of doctors' claims of professionalism. "Indeed, retention of absolute control over technical procedures is clearly an absolute necessity for the survival of modern medical power" (Oakley, 1987, p. 46). The term "technological imperative" was originally used by Fuchs (1968) to suggest that the addition of any new technology generates an increase in further use by its very existence, and this in turn generates still more technology.

There are a number of interlocking socioeconomic factors which generate the development and use of medical technologies before their appropriateness and efficiency are determined, even before the grounds for their increased use are established (McKinlay, 1981). What are the dynamics of this process in accounting for the massive expansion of medical machinery? Technology is central to claims of professionalism and this has two important related aspects: having power in the doctor–patient relationship and having power within the profession. Let us turn to the doctor–patient relationship first.

The professional hierarchy means that doctors are regarded as experts who possess technical knowledge and skill that lay people don't have. The doctor–patient relationship is also often a class one, with a meeting between a middle-class, highly educated professional and a working-class patient. As well as being gendered, the relationship is often characterized by racial inequalities. Technology plays a major role in consolidating this distancing of the doctor from a necessarily passive patient, leading to the dehumanization of health care. The growing supremacy of technology in contemporary medical practice is not by any means confined to obstetrics, and both male and female patients find it an alienating experience.

In modern Western medicine, technological advances have transformed the methods of diagnosing illness, and these new methods have in turn altered the relationship between physician and patient.[9] The ubiquitous stethoscope has its origins in the doctor's wish to keep the patient at a distance, overlaid with the requirements of modesty as between men and women. According to the apocryphal story, the stethoscope was invented in 1816 by Laennec, during the examination of a young woman who had a baffling heart disorder. Restrained by the patient's youth and sex from placing his ear to her heart he recalled that sound travelled through solid bodies. From rolling some sheets of paper into a cylinder on this occasion he went on to construct the first wooden stethoscope (Reiser, 1978, p. 25). The human ear was supplanted by the stethoscope not because of any technical deficiency but because of prevailing social mores.[10]

Broadly speaking, since the nineteenth century there have been three stages in the historical development of the methods used to diagnose illness. Physicians have moved "from direct communication with their patients' experiences, based upon a verbal technique of information gathering, to direct connection with the patients' bodies through tech-

niques of physical examination, to indirect connection with both the experience and bodies of their patients through machines and technical experts" (Reiser, 1978, p. 227).

During the course of the twentieth century doctors have increasingly come to rely on technologically generated evidence at the expense of physical examination and history-taking. Machines inexorably direct the attention of both the doctor and the patient away from experiential or "subjective" factors and towards the measurable aspects of illness. Moreover, Reiser argues that many of the modern diagnostic machines which have supplanted the more traditional manual methods and simple instruments are of little real value. The fact that they are so commonly used is not an indication of the reliability of the "objective" evidence they produce but rather a result of doctors' insecurity and corresponding dependence on them. The skills involved in medicine may actually be declining as a result of this overdependence on technology as doctors become less willing to make independent clinical judgements based upon their own abilities and experience.

Obstetrics is a special case because the patients are uniformly women, they are generally not ill, and it is clearly an area where male doctors can have no personal experience of the "condition" being treated. So their claims to expertise might appear tenuous to women. Oakley argues that technology is particularly attractive to obstetricians because techniques such as the stethoscope and foetal monitoring enable male doctors to claim to know more about women's bodies than the women themselves.

Once the technology is available women as patients may well want and expect high-technology treatment. This does not make women the passive victims of reproductive technologies and the male doctors who wield them. Within limits, women who are already advantaged in the social structure may even experience "a sense of greater control and self-empowerment than they would have if left to 'traditional' methods or 'nature'" (Petchesky, 1987, p. 72).

However, the routine use of ultrasound imaging in pregnancy continues despite scepticism as to its medical benefits. Indeed the basic technique of ultrasound was not designed for obstetric purposes at all. Its origins date from attempts to detect submarines through soundwaves during the First World War. The subsequent development of ultrasound as a medical technology was as an offshoot of a major research project on acoustics at MIT financed by the US Navy (Yoxen, 1987). The concentration on pregnancy came several years after its use in other clinical diagnostic fields and the interest in foetal abnormality and rates of growth, with which it is now mainly associated, came even later. The procedure serves to discredit and then displace women's own experience of the progress of the foetus in favour of scientific data on the monitor. Some feminist critics fear that these techniques turn women into mere spectators of their own medically-managed pregnancy. As such they represent the ultimate appropriation by men of women's knowledge and expertise.

Within Western medicine, the high technology activities are not only a key to power at the level of doctor–patient relations, but also to power within the profession. Status, money, and professional acclaim within the medical profession are distributed according to the technological sophistication of the speciality. To be seen to be developing and expanding high technology procedures signals success in the competition for scarce resources—as between specialists, between hospitals, and between individuals. "Medical specialization and technological innovation have a special feature: they are parallel and interactive. Medical specialization leads to technological innovation; then, as a given technology is used, physicians, and industrial designers collaborate to improve it. As it is defined, that process leads to ever more specialization and associated work and procedures" (Fagerhaugh et al., 1987, pp. 7–8).

The evolution of the new techniques of in-vitro fertilization and embryo transfer illustrate this process. On the face of it, the current enthusiasm for the new techniques seems curious. After all, in-vitro fertilization and embryo transfer have proceeded without much further work on establishing causes of infertility or improving other treatments. Given their low success rate, and the level of physical danger and psychological distress that accompany these new reproductive technologies, why the current

concentration on in-vitro fertilization among infertility specialists? How does it happen that resources are allocated to this "unsuccessful" technology?

Whilst it is true that new technologies generally have a high failure rate until perfected, it is also the case that "many roads" are not taken in science. There is as yet no detailed description of the stages in the origination of these procedures and techniques. We might ask, with Edward Yoxen (1985, p. 143), what set of career choices led Edwards and Steptoe into their collaboration, or why their interpretation of the risk studies in animals was much less cautious than anyone else's, or why there are so few data on the effects of the drugs and invasive procedures used in in-vitro fertilization, or why there are so few data on the causes of infertility. Questions of inventive success and failure can be made sense of only by reference to the goals of the people involved.

Professional interests explain a great deal about the development of these techniques. Before the introduction of in-vitro fertilization and embryo transfer, the investigation and treatment of infertility had long been afforded low status in the medical hierarchy. Many of the procedures were carried out by general practitioners, as they required little special knowledge. Naomi Pfeffer (1987) argues that the new techniques of in-vitro fertilization and embryo transfer provide gynaecologists with an exciting, high-status area of research as well as a technically complex practice which only they can use. Status and substantial financial reward are to be had, as well as job satisfaction.

By 1982 in Britain, the Royal College of Obstetricians and Gynaecologists was already claiming that their fields had expanded so much that it should be divided into four sub-specialities. "The pressures towards sub-specialization within gynaecology and obstetrics, then, constitute another incentive for medical personnel involved in the treatment of infertility to lay claim to new areas of expertise" (Pfeffer, 1987, p. 88). Official recognition of sub-specialization would attract financial support for training and research. In many ways therefore it is apparent that professional interests play a central role in determining the type and tempo of technological innovation in this area.

There are however wider economic forces at work. The commercial interests of the vast biotechnology industry are particularly influential. Much has been written about the "new medical–industrial complex" and the way in which resources are systematically channelled into profitable areas that often have no connection with satisfying human needs. There is as yet little detailed information about the financial interests of medical biotechnology corporations in the development of the new reproductive technologies. Furthermore the potential commercial applications of the products are as yet unclear, at least to the general public.[11] What is clear is that the needs of infertile women play only a small part in the research agenda envisaged. Embryos are a unique source of information about human genetics, embryonic development, and foetal growth. As Professor Robert Winston, of the Hammersmith Hospital, West London, explained: "We think that in-vitro fertilization is merely the first step. In the long term the embryo could be removed for a few hours and then be replaced. This suggestion is not pie in the sky" (quoted in *The Guardian*, 1 January 1989).

By March 1989, male embryos had been distinguished from female embryos within days of conception. The potential for genetic screening is now immense and with it the possibility for gene transplant experiments, known as "gene therapy." The ultimate aim, which has attracted vast research funding in North America, Europe, and Japan is to unravel all the instructions contained in the human genetic code.

Some commentators have likened the scope of the biotechnology revolution to that of the microelectronic revolution, seeing it as the next technology-based phase of capitalist development.[12] Already we can see that the human body is caught up in commerce in new ways, with human organs such as kidneys, eyeballs, frozen foetuses, and gametes being traded on the international market. Whatever one's position on the ethics of embryo research it is clear that it is always structured by relations of exploitation based on race, class, and gender. The traffic in Korean foetuses for American military research into biological warfare is a case in point.

Although women are the prime targets of medical experimentation, reproductive technology cannot be analysed in terms of a patriarchal conspiracy. Instead a complex web of interests has been woven here—those of professional and capitalist interests overlaid with gender. It is more specifically to the operation of gender divisions that we now turn. The next section will examine the dynamics of a technology less recent and better documented than those referred to above. Nowhere are sexual relations more profoundly formative of a set of technologies than in the sphere of contraception.

The Sexual Relations of Contraceptive Technology

The perspectives from which most histories of fertility control are written are redolent of technological determinism. The conventional view shared by historians and demographers is that in preindustrial societies women were the victims of their own fecundity.[13] There is a tendency to look back from our current "Pill Era" and regard birth control as a nineteenth-century invention, representing the triumph of the progressive forces of technology over ignorance and prejudice. The Pill, a technical invention, is credited with enabling women for the first time to control their fertility, and the massive social changes for women that accompanied its introduction are attributed to it.[14]

It is assumed that earlier generations were prevented from practising birth control because they lacked the necessary technology. Many accounts of the history of birth control begin with the invention of the condom, arguing that it was only in the nineteenth century with the manufacture of rubber devices that effective contraception was made possible (McLaren, 1984, p. 5). On closer analysis it is apparent that the extent and openness with which birth control is practised, and the form it takes, is as much dependent on a society's attitude to sex, children, and the status of women, as it is on effective technology. "For the use of birth control requires a morality that permits the separation of sexual intercourse from procreation, and is related to the extent to which women are valued for roles other than those of wife and mother" (Greenwood and King, 1981, p. 169).[15] Birth control has always been a matter of social and political acceptability rather than of medicine and technology. Like childbirth, its prevention has always been subject to elaborate regulation and ritual.

In her book on birth control in America, Linda Gordon (1977) argues that social institutions and cultural values, rather than medical or technical considerations, have shaped modern contraceptive technology. Like most feminists, Gordon began with the premise that birth control represented the single most important contribution to the material basis of women's emancipation in the last century. However, she was quickly led to ask why the technology of contraception developed when it did, and why, in our generation, the invention of the Pill is seen as the key to liberation. For her, birth control was as much symptom as cause of larger social changes in the relations between the sexes and in the economic organization of society.

The ability to transcend biology was present in the earliest known societies. "There is a prevalent myth, in our technological society, that birthcontrol technology came to us with modern medicine. This is far from the truth, as modern medicine did almost nothing, until the last twenty years, to improve on birth control devices that were literally more than a millennium old" (Gordon, 1977, p. 25). In fact, most of our present methods have had precursors in societies far less technologically sophisticated than ours. There is evidence from old medical texts and from anthropological studies that women have almost universally sought to control their fertility. Far from being invented by scientists or doctors, effective forms of birth control were devised and administered by women in nearly all ancient societies.

Reproductive knowledge and practice has always been part of women's folklore and culture. The relatively recent establishment of the male hegemony in medicine has obscured the existence of earlier methods that were more under women's control. Traditionally, knowledge about techniques for birth control, like remedies for other complaints, was developed and practised by wisewomen and midwives

and handed down from generation to generation. A wide array of birth-control techniques were practised in the ancient world and in modern pre-industrial societies including magic, herbal potions, infanticide, abortion, coitus interruptus, vaginal sponges, douches, and pessaries.

Not only did these techniques vary in their effectiveness, but they had very different implications for sexual relations. Some techniques are more amenable than others to being used independently and even secretly by women; some give full control to men; others are more likely to be used co-operatively. The point that needs to be emphasized is that women and men might have conflicting concerns and goals in mind when contemplating fertility control and these are reflected in the different techniques available. We will return to this point later.

Gordon argues that it is only by looking at this heritage of birth control customs that we can comprehend the emergence of the birth control movement, for that movement took its strength from women's understanding that traditional methods of fertility control were being suppressed. In particular, while abortion had hitherto been the subject of moral controversy, it was not until the nineteenth century that it was actually criminalized. These abortion laws were intended to eliminate doctors' rivals such as midwives and to undermine traditional forms of reproductive control. The result of the medical and legal intervention in this crucial form of birth control was a decline in women's ability to effectively limit their pregnancies. What was new in the nineteenth century, then, was not the technology to control fertility but the emergence of a political movement that campaigned for the right to use contraception.

However, reproductive self-determination for women was not the primary catalyst of the birth control movement. Equally important were the populationist movements inspired by Malthusian theories which sought population control as the cure for poverty.

During the twentieth century, contraception and to a lesser extent abortion have become respectable, and largely regulated by the medical profession. However the influence of population-control ideol-

ogy is still central to modern birth control programmes. Since the 1950s, birth prevention has become a major international industry and it is linked
with the politics of state intervention in population
planning. Populationist ideology, not scientific discovery, was the catalyst for the major financial
investment in research on birth-prevention methods and, according to Elkie Newman (1985), influenced the specific techniques which have become
available. The technological prerequisites for the
development of an oral hormonal contraceptive had
existed by 1938 but popular morality and pronatalist
policies delayed its development until the late 1950s.
According to Newman, it was the sudden and popular fear of a world population explosion which le-
gitimated work on the Pill and resulted in family
planning services becoming a major part of aid
packages to the Third World.[16]

How then do we explain the emphasis on hormonal contraceptives and, by contrast, the heavy
neglect of barrier methods, which are classed as
old-fashioned? "Considering how much time,
money, and energy is now spent on birth-control
research, we might expect to be able to choose
from among, say, ten different kinds of barrier
methods or perhaps a range of 'morning-after'
methods. Instead, our options are confined to essentially two barrier methods, the various hormonal methods, a few IUDs and abortion techniques, and a small but increasing number of
sterilization techniques" (Newman, 1985, p. 135).

Although the Pill is the most reliable method of
contraception, it is associated with dangerous
health risks and side effects for women. Nevertheless doctors favour the Pill because it helps to avoid
the ethical dilemmas of dealing with unwanted
pregnancy and abortion, and it requires a minimum of time and skill while keeping contraception
firmly under their control. From the doctor's point
of view, the fact that this method does not require
many visits to the clinic, and does not need to be
explained at great length to the patient are additional advantages. It is also important not to underestimate the significance of the Pill's profitability. It
is economical to produce and market and needs to
be taken daily, thus generating vast profits for the
pharmaceutical industry that supplies it.

Apart from the corporate interests involved,
most of the research into medical contraceptive
methods is done by men on techniques for use by
women. Interestingly, the incentive for the development of the condom was not birth control but
rather men's need for protection from venereal disease. Given that women and men have different
patterns of sexual behaviour, might not these differences be reflected in the design of contraceptive
technologies? Indeed, Pollack (1985, p. 76) argues
that these technologies "are developed from a patriarchal perspective, emphasizing the sexual enjoyment of men and underestimating the costs to
women. Male sexual pleasure is the most significant
factor taken into account in the methods which become available, and in the ways in which contraceptives are used."

Certainly men prefer methods that "interfere"
least with their experience of sex, even at the expense of women's health and enjoyment. The
reluctance of heterosexual men to either wear con-
doms (even in the AIDS era) or to have a vasec-
tomy indicates the primacy of their sexual feelings
over the medical risks women are taking. While
some medical techniques for men have been developed, the dangerous effects tend to be played
down far less than is the case with female methods.[17] "In fact men have been very reluctant to vol-
unteer for experiments with male methods of any
kind, just as they have been generally reluctant to
be sterilized. The World Health Organization recently decided not to put much money into research on male methods in the future—they simply
cannot persuade enough men to try them!" (Newman, 1985, pp. 141–2).

The Pill is also the technology favoured by
women. As women still have the prime responsibility for pregnancy, the Pill is chosen for its high degree of protection and for the control that women
can exercise over its use. Many women feel uneasy
about touching parts of their own bodies and this
is often linked to their anxieties about sexual activity. Using this method does not involve touching
one's genitals, does not require male cooperation
or even knowledge, and it allows for "spontaneous" sex. The Pill has the additional psychological advantage of separating contraception from

sexual activity, both in time and anatomically. It does not interfere with what is considered to be "normal" romantic heterosexual sex, that is, for men to be lustful and assertive and for women merely to surrender. By comparison, the fitting of caps or diaphragms does require some skill, and to use it one has to admit to a man and to oneself that one is planning to have sex.

The definition of sexual activity as heterosexual intercourse involving penetration provides the context in which contraceptives are researched, developed, distributed and used. Contraceptive methods are designed to fit in with male-defined sex. Freed from the responsibility and the practices involved in using the sheath or withdrawal, men have been able to concentrate more on their enjoyment of sex. For women too the Pill has meant more effective birth control which in turn has been translated into more possibilities of sexual pleasure for women. However, women's increased sexual independence has been at a high health cost. If the gains for women outweigh their losses it is because of the achievements of the women's movement and not the technology *per se*. The Pill has not brought about women's liberation; women have gained control over their lives through social and political mobilization.

The purpose of this section has been to suggest that sexual relations in combination with population policies and market forces have shaped contraceptive technology. And, in turn, the design or form of the technology has been crucial to its use. In order to understand why particular technologies have the effects they do, this chapter has provided an account of the context in which reproductive technologies have developed and diffused. We have seen the role that technology has had in the medicalization and mechanization of medicine in general and in the area of human reproduction in particular. While the overall effect of this has been the masculinization of an area that was previously a women's sphere, women who are already advantaged in society have been in a position to benefit from recent reproductive techniques. In this area as elsewhere, technologies operate within and reinforce pre-existing social inequalities.

NOTES

1. See Stanworth (1987, pp. 10–11) for a categorization of the various technologies that are grouped under the term "reproductive technologies."

2. As Michelle Stanworth pointed out to me, the pro-interventionist position is also endorsed by the historian Edward Shorter (1983) who shares with Firestone a belief that women are the victims of their bodies and that twentieth-century medical technology has released them to be equal to men.

3. According to a recent estimate (Rowland, 1988), the success rate of in-vitro fertilization schemes is only about 10 per cent.

4. Of course, the belief that the maternal instinct is normal does not apply to single women or to lesbians. The Warnock Committee in Britain (set up to advise the UK Government on reproductive technologies) for example recommended restricting such techniques as in-vitro fertilization, egg donation, embryo donation and artificial insemination to stable, cohabiting heterosexual couples.

5. I would like to draw the reader's attention to McNeil, et al. (1990) which does locate reproductive technologies within the sociology of technology. The collection only came into my hands as this book went to press.

6. Feminists have also been concerned to expose the increase in hysterectomy, particularly for black and Third World women, as a form of involuntary sterilization or as "a simple solution to everything from backaches to contraception" (Homans, 1985, p. 5).

7. See also Arney (1982) and Richards (1978).

8. Martin (1987, p. 48). Although this negative medical imagery pervades women's own images of their bodies, involving extreme fermentation of the self, women also resist. By analysing the different speech women use according to their class and race, Martin provides examples of how women generate their own more self-respecting meanings for menstruation, menopause, and birth. Interestingly she discovered that white middle-class women were far more likely to uncritically accept the hegemonic medical model of their bodies than working-class women, black or white.

9. This account is drawn from Reiser (1978). See also Foucault (1973) and Jewson (1976).

10. This is not to deny that subsequently the stethoscope did become technically "superior."

11. It recently emerged that American insurance firms are taking a keen interest in the development of genetic screening for its potential use in the recruitment of employees.

12. In fact, Haraway (1985) and Yoxen (1986) argue that this biotechnology revolution is also a cultural revolution, in that the very meaning of life is being transformed. With the development of genetic engineering, the dominant image of nature becomes one of organisms as information-processing systems that can be reprogrammed. "Thus our image of nature is coming more and more to emphasise human intervention through a process of design" (Yoxen, 1986, p. 30).

13. The classic study is Himes (1936).

14. Even Rosenberg (1979, p. 50), normally such an astute critic of technological determinism, falls into this trap: ". . . one might therefore well argue that the women's liberation movement is essentially due to the combination of declining fertility (in turn partly attributable to a more effective technology of contraception), on the one hand, and the electrification of the household chores, on the other. One need not be a technological determinist to argue that the social benefits of the new-found freedom of women in American society are, in large measure, the product of technological innovation."

15. That the invention of reproductive technologies often long predate their widespread use is evidenced by, for example, artificial insemination. Although we think of this as a radical new means of separating conception from sex, it was actually first performed in 1776 (McLaren, 1984, p. 13).

16. See also Doyal (1979), especially chapter 7 on "Medicine and Imperialism."

17. This point is well made in a parody of a new contraceptive technique for men reprinted in *Spare Rib* (Vol. 93, April 1980, p. 9) . . .

LEON KASS   II.11

Preventing a Brave New World

In this article, Leon Kass, Addie Clark Harding Professor at the Committee on Social Thought at the University of Chicago, and Chairman of the President's Commission on Bioethics, argues that modern medical science is poised to cross an ethical boundary that will have momentous consequences for the future of humanity. Harking back to the dystopian vision of Aldous Huxley's classic *Brave New World* (1932), Kass argues that "the technological imperative, compassionate humanitarianism, moral pluralism, and free markets" are leading us down a path that places us at risk of losing our humanity. Kass argues that we should enact a worldwide ban on human cloning as a means of deterring "renegade scientists" from engaging in the practice. His proposed ban would apply to both reproductive and therapeutic cloning of human embryos, because he believes that banning only reproductive cloning would prove impossible to enforce. Kass believes that we have the power to exercise control over the technological project but can only do so if we muster the political will to just say "no" to human cloning.

Focus Questions

1. What are the three main factors that Kass identifies as limiting our ability to control the onward march of the biomedical project? What other factors contribute to our inability to avoid the dangers that Kass is concerned about?

2. What reasons does Kass give for "drawing the line" at human reproductive cloning by prohibiting the practice? Are these reasons convincing? Do the same arguments apply with equal force to therapeutic cloning?

3. Why does Kass believe that employing cloning or genetic engineering techniques to produce human children is "profoundly dehumanizing, no matter how good the product"?

4. Compare Kass' arguments to those offered by Wachbroit (selection II.9) and Sagoff (selection II.12). Is there a moral difference between applying genetic engineering techniques to humans and to nonhuman plants and animals? Explain.

Keywords

dehumanization, genetic determinism, infertility, reproductive cloning, reproductive freedom, somatic cell nuclear transfer

I.

The urgency of the great political struggles of the twentieth century, successfully waged against totalitarianisms first right and then left, seems to have blinded many people to a deeper and ultimately darker truth about the present age: all contemporary societies are travelling briskly in the same utopian direction. All are wedded to the modern technological project; all march eagerly to the drums of progress and fly proudly the banner of modern science; all sing loudly the Baconian anthem, "Conquer nature, relieve man's estate." Leading the triumphal procession is modern medicine, which is daily becoming ever more powerful in its battle against disease, decay, and death, thanks especially to astonishing achievements in biomedical science and technology—achievements for which we must surely be grateful.

Yet contemplating present and projected advances in genetic and reproductive technologies, in neuroscience and psychopharmacology, and in the development of artificial organs and computer-chip implants for human brains, we now clearly recognize new uses for biotechnical power that soar beyond the traditional medical goals of healing disease and relieving suffering. Human nature itself lies on the operating table, ready for alteration, for eugenic and psychic "enhancement," for wholesale re-design. In leading laboratories, academic and industrial, new creators are confidently amassing their powers and quietly honing their skills, while on the street their evangelists are zealously prophesying a post-human future. For anyone who cares about preserving our humanity, the time has come to pay attention.

Some transforming powers are already here. The Pill. In vitro fertilization. Bottled embryos. Surrogate wombs. Cloning. Genetic screening. Genetic manipulation. Organ harvesting. Mechanical spare parts. Chimeras. Brain implants. Ritalin for the young, Viagra for the old, Prozac for everyone. And, to leave this vale of tears, a little extra morphine accompanied by Muzak.

Years ago Aldous Huxley saw it coming. In his charming but disturbing novel, *Brave New World* (it appeared in 1932 and is more powerful on each re-reading), he made its meaning strikingly visible for all to see. Unlike other frightening futuristic novels of the past century, such as Orwell's already dated *Nineteen Eighty-Four*, Huxley shows us a dystopia that goes with, rather than against, the human grain. Indeed, it is animated by our own most humane and progressive aspirations. Following those aspirations to their ultimate realization, Huxley enables us to recognize those less obvious but often more pernicious evils that are inextricably linked to the successful attainment of partial goods.

Huxley depicts human life seven centuries hence, living under the gentle hand of humanitarianism rendered fully competent by genetic manipulation, psychoactive drugs, hypnopaedia, and high-tech amusements. At long last, mankind has succeeded in eliminating disease, aggression, war, anxiety, suffering, guilt, envy, and grief. But this victory comes at the heavy price of homogenization, mediocrity, trivial pursuits, shallow attachments, debased tastes, spurious contentment, and souls without loves or longings. The Brave New World has achieved prosperity, community, stability, and nigh-universal contentment, only to be peopled by creatures of human shape but stunted humanity. They consume, fornicate, take "soma," enjoy "centrifugal bumble-puppy," and operate the machinery that makes it all possible. They do not read, write, think, love, or govern themselves. Art and science, virtue and religion, family and friendship are all passe. What matters most is bodily health and immediate gratification: "Never put off till tomorrow the fun you can have today." Brave New Man is so dehumanized that he does not even recognize what has been lost.

Huxley's novel, of course, is science fiction. Prozac is not yet Huxley's "soma"; cloning by nuclear transfer or splitting embryos is not exactly "Bokanovskification"; MTV and virtual-reality parlors are not quite the "feelies"; and our current safe and consequenceless sexual practices are not universally as loveless or as empty as those in the novel. But the kinships are disquieting, all the more so since our technologies of bio-psycho-engineering are still in their infancy, and in ways that make all too clear what they might look like in their full maturity. Moreover, the cultural changes that technology has already wrought among us should make us even more worried than Huxley would have us be.

In Huxley's novel, everything proceeds under the direction of an omnipotent—albeit benevolent—world state. Yet the dehumanization that he portrays does not really require despotism or external control. To the contrary, precisely because the society of the future will deliver exactly what we most want—health, safety, comfort, plenty, pleasure, peace of mind and length of days—we can reach the same humanly debased condition solely on the basis of free human choice. No need for World Controllers. Just give us the technological imperative, liberal democratic society, compassionate humanitarianism, moral pluralism, and free markets, and we can take ourselves to a Brave New World all by ourselves—and without even deliberately deciding to go. In case you had not noticed, the train has already left the station and is gathering speed, but no one seems to be in charge.

Some among us are delighted, of course, by this state of affairs: some scientists and biotechnologists, their entrepreneurial backers, and a cheering claque of sci-fi enthusiasts, futurologists, and libertarians. There are dreams to be realized, powers to be exercised, honors to be won, and money—big money—to be made. But many of us are worried, and not, as the proponents of the revolution self-servingly claim, because we are either ignorant of science or afraid of the unknown. To the contrary, we can see all too clearly where the train is headed, and we do not like the destination. We can distinguish cleverness about means from wisdom about ends, and we are loath to entrust the future of the race to those who cannot tell the difference. No friend of humanity cheers for a post-human future.

Yet for all our disquiet, we have until now done nothing to prevent it. We hide our heads in the sand because we enjoy the blessings that medicine keeps supplying, or we rationalize our inaction by declaring that human engineering is inevitable and we can do nothing about it. In either case, we are complicit in preparing for our own degradation, in some respects more to blame than the bio-zealots who, however misguided, are putting their money where their mouth is. Denial and despair, unattractive outlooks in any situation, become morally reprehensible when circumstances summon us to keep the world safe for human flourishing. Our immediate ancestors, taking up the challenge of their time, rose to the occasion and rescued the human future from the cruel dehumanizations of Nazi and Soviet tyranny. It is our more difficult task to find ways to preserve it from the soft dehumanizations of well-meaning but hubristic biotechnical "re-creationism"—and to do it without undermining biomedical science or rejecting its genuine contributions to human welfare.

Truth be told, it will not be easy for us to do so, and we know it. But rising to the challenge requires recognizing the difficulties. For there are indeed many features of modern life that will conspire to frustrate efforts aimed at the human control of the biomedical project. First, we Americans believe in technological automatism: where we do not foolishly believe that all innovation is progress, we fatalistically believe that it is inevitable ("If it can be done, it will be done, like it or not"). Second, we believe in freedom: the freedom of scientists to inquire, the freedom of technologists to develop, the freedom of entrepreneurs to invest and to profit, the freedom of private citizens to make use of existing technologies to satisfy any and all personal desires, including the desire to reproduce by whatever means. Third, the biomedical enterprise occupies the moral high ground of compassionate humanitarianism, upholding the supreme values of modern life—cure disease, prolong life, relieve suffering—in competition with which other moral goods rarely stand a chance. ("What the public wants is not to be sick," says James Watson, "and if we help them not to be sick, they'll be on our side.")

There are still other obstacles. Our cultural pluralism and easygoing relativism make it difficult to reach consensus on what we should embrace and what we should oppose; and moral objections to this or that biomedical practice are often facilely dismissed as religious or sectarian. Many people are unwilling to pronounce judgments about what is good or bad, right and wrong, even in matters of great importance, even for themselves—never mind for others or for society as a whole. It does not help that the biomedical project is now deeply entangled with commerce: there are increasingly powerful economic interests in favor of going full steam ahead, and no economic interests in favor of going slow. Since we live in a democracy, moreover, we face political difficulties in gaining a consensus to direct our future, and we have almost no political experience in trying to curtail the development of

any new biomedical technology. Finally, and perhaps most troubling, our views of the meaning of our humanity have been so transformed by the scientific-technological approach to the world that we are in danger of forgetting what we have to lose, humanly speaking.

But though the difficulties are real, our situation is far from hopeless. Regarding each of the aforementioned impediments, there is another side to the story. Though we love our gadgets and believe in progress, we have lost our innocence regarding technology. The environmental movement especially has alerted us to the unintended damage caused by unregulated technological advance, and has taught us how certain dangerous practices can be curbed. Though we favor freedom of inquiry, we recognize that experiments are deeds and not speeches, and we prohibit experimentation on human subjects without their consent, even when cures from disease might be had by unfettered research; and we limit so-called reproductive freedom by proscribing incest, polygamy, and the buying and selling of babies.

Although we esteem medical progress, biomedical institutions have ethics committees that judge research proposals on moral grounds, and, when necessary, uphold the primacy of human freedom and human dignity even over scientific discovery. Our moral pluralism notwithstanding, national commissions and review bodies have sometimes reached moral consensus to recommend limits on permissible scientific research and technological application. On the economic front, the patenting of genes and life forms and the rapid rise of genomic commerce have elicited strong concerns and criticisms, leading even former enthusiasts of the new biology to recoil from the impending commodification of human life. Though we lack political institutions experienced in setting limits on biomedical innovation, federal agencies years ago rejected the development of the plutonium-powered artificial heart, and we have nationally prohibited commercial traffic in organs for transplantation, even though a market would increase the needed supply. In recent years, several American states and many foreign countries have successfully taken political action, making certain practices illegal and placing others under moratoriums (the creation of human embryos solely for research; human germ-line genetic alteration). Most importantly, the majority of Americans are not yet so degraded or so cynical as to fail to be revolted by the society depicted in Huxley's novel. Though the obstacles to effective action are significant, they offer no excuse for resignation. Besides, it would be disgraceful to concede defeat even before we enter the fray.

Not the least of our difficulties in trying to exercise control over where biology is taking us is the fact that we do not get to decide, once and for all, for or against the destination of a post-human world. The scientific discoveries and the technical powers that will take us there come to us piece-meal, one at a time and seemingly independent from one another, each often attractively introduced as a measure that will "help [us] not to be sick." But sometimes we come to a clear fork in the road where decision is possible, and where we know that our decision will make a world of difference—indeed, it will make a permanently different world. Fortunately, we stand now at the point of such a momentous decision. Events have conspired to provide us with a perfect opportunity to seize the initiative and to gain some control of the biotechnical project. I refer to the prospect of human cloning, a practice absolutely central to Huxley's fictional world. Indeed, creating and manipulating life in the laboratory is the gateway to a Brave New World, not only in fiction but also in fact.

"To clone or not to clone a human being" is no longer a fanciful question. Success in cloning sheep, and also cows, mice, pigs, and goats, makes it perfectly clear that a fateful decision is now at hand: whether we should welcome or even tolerate the cloning of human beings. If recent newspaper reports are to be believed, reputable scientists and physicians have announced their intention to produce the first human clone in the coming year. Their efforts may already be under way.

The media, gawking and titillating as is their wont, have been softening us up for this possibility by turning the bizarre into the familiar. In the four years since the birth of Dolly the cloned sheep, the tone of discussing the prospect of human cloning has gone from "Yuck" to "Oh?" to "Gee whiz" to "Why not?" The sentimentalizers, aided by leading bioethicists, have downplayed talk about eugenically cloning the beautiful and the brawny or the best and the brightest. They have taken instead to defending clonal reproduction for humanitarian or compassionate reasons: to treat infertility in people who are said to "have no other choice," to avoid the risk of severe genetic disease, to "replace" a child who has died. For the sake of these rare benefits, they would have us countenance the entire practice of human cloning, the consequences be damned.

But we dare not be complacent about what is at issue, for the stakes are very high. Human cloning, though partly continuous with previous reproductive technologies, is also something radically new in itself and in its easily foreseeable consequences—especially when coupled with powers for genetic "enhancement" and germline genetic modification that may soon become available, owing to the recently completed Human Genome Project. I exaggerate somewhat, but in the direction of the truth: we are compelled to decide nothing less than whether human procreation is going to remain human, whether children are going to be made to order rather than begotten, and whether we wish to say yes in principle to the road that leads to the dehumanized hell of *Brave New World*.

. . .

For we have here a golden opportunity to exercise some control over where biology is taking us. The technology of cloning is discrete and well defined, and it requires considerable technical know-how and dexterity; we can therefore know by name many of the likely practitioners. The public demand for cloning is extremely low, and most people are decidedly against it. Nothing scientifically or medically important would be lost by banning clonal reproduction; alternative and non-objectionable means are available to obtain some of the most important medical benefits claimed for (nonreproductive) human cloning. The commercial interests in human cloning are, for now, quite limited; and the nations of the world are actively seeking to prevent it. Now may be as good a chance as we will ever have to get our hands on the wheel of the runaway train now headed for a post-human world and to steer it toward a more dignified human future.

II.

What is cloning? Cloning, or asexual reproduction, is the production of individuals who are genetically identical to an already existing individual. The procedure's name is fancy—"somatic cell nuclear transfer"—but its concept is simple. Take a mature but unfertilized egg; remove or deactivate its nucleus; introduce a nucleus obtained from a specialized (somatic) cell of an adult organism. Once the egg begins to divide, transfer the little embryo to a woman's uterus to initiate a pregnancy. Since almost all the hereditary material of a cell is contained within its nucleus, the re-nucleated egg and the individual into which it develops are genetically identical to the organism that was the source of the transferred nucleus.

An unlimited number of genetically identical individuals—the group, as well as each of its members, is called "a clone"—could be produced by nuclear transfer. In principle, any person, male or female, newborn or adult, could be cloned, and in any quantity; and because stored cells can outlive their sources, one may even clone the dead. Since cloning requires no personal involvement on the part of the person whose genetic material is used, it could easily be used to reproduce living or deceased persons without their consent—a threat to reproductive freedom that has received relatively little attention.

Some possible misconceptions need to be avoided. Cloning is not Xeroxing: the clone of Bill Clinton, though his genetic double, would enter the world hairless, toothless, and peeing in his diapers, like any other human infant. But neither is cloning just like natural twinning: the cloned twin will be identical to an older, existing adult; and it will arise not by chance but by deliberate design; and its entire genetic makeup will be preselected by its parents and/or scientists. Moreover, the success rate of cloning, at least at first, will probably not be very high: the Scots transferred two hundred seventy-seven adult nuclei into sheep eggs, implanted twenty-nine clonal embryos, and achieved the birth of only one live lamb clone.

For this reason, among others, it is unlikely that, at least for now, the practice would be very popular; and there is little immediate worry of mass-scale production of multicopies. Still, for the tens of thousands of people who sustain more than three hundred assisted-reproduction clinics in the United States and already avail themselves of in vitro fertilization and other techniques, cloning would be an option with virtually no added fuss. Panos Zavos, the Kentucky reproduction specialist who has announced his plans to clone a child, claims that he has already received thousands of e-mailed requests from people eager to clone, despite the known risks of failure and damaged offspring. Should commercial interests develop in "nucleus-banking," as they have in sperm-banking and egg-harvesting; should famous athletes or other celebrities decide to market their DNA the way they now market their autographs and nearly everything else; should techniques of embryo and germline genetic testing and manipulation arrive as anticipated, increasing the use of laboratory assistance in order to obtain "better" babies—should all this come to pass, cloning, if it is permitted, could become more than a marginal practice simply on the basis of free reproductive choice.

What are we to think about this prospect? Nothing good. Indeed, most people are repelled by nearly all aspects of human cloning: the possibility of mass production of human beings, with large clones of look-alikes, compromised in their individuality; the idea of father-son or mother-daughter "twins"; the bizarre prospect of a woman bearing and rearing a genetic copy of herself, her spouse, or even her deceased father or mother; the grotesqueness of conceiving a child as an exact "replacement" for another who has died; the utilitarian creation of embryonic duplicates of oneself, to be frozen away or created when needed to provide homologous tissues or organs for transplantation; the narcissism of those who would clone themselves, and the arrogance of others who think they know who deserves to be cloned; the Frankensteinian hubris to create a human life and increasingly to control its destiny; men playing at being God. Almost no one finds any of the suggested reasons for human cloning compelling, and almost everyone anticipates its possible misuses and abuses. And the popular belief that human cloning cannot be prevented makes the prospect all the more revolting.

Revulsion is not an argument; and some of yesterday's repugnances are today calmly accepted—not always for the better. In some crucial cases, however, repugnance is the emotional expression of deep wisdom, beyond reason's power completely to articulate it. Can anyone really give an argument fully adequate to the horror that is father–daughter incest (even with consent), or bestiality, or the mutilation of a corpse, or the eating of human flesh, or the rape or murder of another human being? Would anybody's failure to give full rational justification for his revulsion at those practices make that revulsion ethically suspect?

I suggest that our repugnance at human cloning belongs in this category. We are repelled by the prospect of cloning human beings not because of the strangeness or the novelty of the undertaking, but because we intuit and we feel, immediately and without argument, the violation of things that we rightfully hold dear. We sense that cloning represents a profound defilement of our given nature as procreative beings, and of the social relations built on this natural ground. We also sense that cloning is a radical form of child abuse. In this age in which everything is held to be permissible so long as it is freely done, and in which our bodies are regarded as mere instruments of our autonomous rational will, repugnance may be the only voice left that speaks up to defend the central core of our humanity. Shallow are the souls that have forgotten how to shudder.

III.

Yet repugnance need not stand naked before the bar of reason. The wisdom of our horror at human cloning can be at least partially articulated, even if this is finally one of those instances about which the heart has its reasons that reason cannot entirely know. I offer four objections to human cloning: that it constitutes unethical experimentation; that it threatens identity and individuality; that it turns procreation into manufacture (especially when understood as the harbinger of manipulations to come); and that it means despotism over children and perversion of parenthood. Please note: I speak only about so-called reproductive cloning, not about the creation of cloned embryos for research. The objections that may be raised against creating (or using) embryos for research are entirely independent of whether the research embryos are produced by cloning. What is radically distinct and radically new is reproductive cloning.

Any attempt to clone a human being would constitute an unethical experiment upon the resulting child-to-be. In all the animal experiments, fewer than two to three percent of all cloning attempts succeeded. Not only are there fetal deaths and stillborn infants, but many of the so-called "successes" are in fact failures. As has only recently become clear, there is a very high incidence of major disabilities and deformities in cloned animals that attain live birth. Cloned cows often have heart and lung problems; cloned mice later develop pathological obesity; other live-born cloned animals fail to reach normal developmental milestones.

The problem, scientists suggest, may lie in the fact that an egg with a new somatic nucleus must re-program itself in a matter of minutes or hours (whereas the nucleus of an unaltered egg has been prepared over months and years). There is thus a greatly increased likelihood of error in translating the genetic instructions, leading to developmental defects some of which will show themselves only much later. (Note also that these induced abnormalities may also affect the stem cells that scientists hope to harvest from cloned embryos. Lousy embryos, lousy stem cells.) Nearly all scientists now agree that attempts to clone human beings carry massive risks of producing unhealthy, abnormal, and malformed children. What are we to do with them? Shall we just discard the ones that fall short of expectations? Considered opinion is today nearly unanimous, even among scientists: attempts at human cloning are irresponsible and unethical. We cannot ethically even get to know whether or not human cloning is feasible.

If it were successful, cloning would create serious issues of identity and individuality. The clone may experience concerns about his distinctive identity not only because he will be, in genotype and in appearance, identical to another human being, but because he may also be twin to the person who is his "father" or his "mother"—if one can still call them that. Unaccountably, people treat as innocent the homey case of intra-familial cloning—the cloning of husband or wife (or single mother). They forget about the unique dangers of mixing the twin relation with the parent-child relation. (For this situation, the relation of contemporaneous twins is no precedent; yet even this less problematic situation teaches us how difficult it is to wrest independence from the being for whom one has the most powerful affinity.) Virtually no parent is going to be able to treat a clone of himself or herself as one treats a child generated by the lottery of sex. What will happen when the adolescent clone of Mommy becomes the spitting image of the woman with whom Daddy once fell in love? In case of divorce, will Mommy still love the clone of Daddy, even though she can no longer stand the sight of Daddy himself?

Most people think about cloning from the point of view of adults choosing to clone. Almost nobody thinks about what it would be like to be the cloned child. Surely his or her new life would constantly be scrutinized in relation to that of the older version. Even in the absence of unusual parental expectations for the clone—say, to live the same life, only without its errors—the child is likely to be ever a curiosity, ever a potential source of deja vu. Unlike "normal" identical twins, a cloned individual—copied from whomever—will be saddled with a genotype that has already lived. He will not be fully a surprise to the world: people are likely always to compare his doings in life with those of his alter ego, especially if he is a clone of someone gifted or famous. True, his nurture and his circumstance will be different; genotype is not exactly destiny. But one must also expect parental efforts to shape this new life after the original—or at least to view the child with the original version always firmly in mind. For why else did they clone from the star basketball player, the mathematician, or the beauty queen—or even dear old Dad—in the first place?

Human cloning would also represent a giant step toward the transformation of begetting into making, of procreation into manufacture (literally,

"handmade"), a process that has already begun with in vitro fertilization and genetic testing of embryos. With cloning, not only is the process in hand, but the total genetic blueprint of the cloned individual is selected and determined by the human artisans. To be sure, subsequent development is still according to natural processes; and the resulting children will be recognizably human. But we would be taking a major step into making man himself simply another one of the man-made things.

How does begetting differ from making? In natural procreation, human beings come together to give existence to another being that is formed exactly as we were, by what we are—living, hence perishable, hence aspiringly erotic, hence procreative human beings. But in clonal reproduction, and in the more advanced forms of manufacture to which it will lead, we give existence to a being not by what we are but by what we intend and design.

Let me be clear. The problem is not the mere intervention of technique, and the point is not that "nature knows best." The problem is that any child whose being, character, and capacities exist owing to human design does not stand on the same plane as its makers. As with any product of our making, no matter how excellent, the artificer stands above it, not as an equal but as a superior, transcending it by his will and creative prowess. In human cloning, scientists and prospective "parents" adopt a technocratic attitude toward human children: human children become their artifacts. Such an arrangement is profoundly dehumanizing, no matter how good the product.

Procreation dehumanized into manufacture is further degraded by commodification, a virtually inescapable result of allowing baby-making to proceed under the banner of commerce. Genetic and reproductive biotechnology companies are already growth industries, but they will soon go into commercial orbit now that the Human Genome Project has been completed. "Human eggs for sale" is already a big business, masquerading under the pretense of "donation." Newspaper advertisements on elite college campuses offer up to $50,000 for an egg "donor" tall enough to play women's basketball and with SAT scores high enough for admission to Stanford; and to nobody's surprise, at such prices there are many young coeds eager to help shoppers obtain the finest babies money can buy. (The egg and womb-renting entrepreneurs shamelessly proceed on the ancient, disgusting, misogynist premise that most women will give you access to their bodies, if the price is right.) Even before the capacity for human cloning is perfected, established companies will have invested in the harvesting of eggs from ovaries obtained at autopsy or through ovarian surgery, practiced embryonic genetic alteration, and initiated the stockpiling of prospective donor tissues. Through the rental of surrogate-womb services, and through the buying and selling of tissues and embryos priced according to the merit of the donor, the commodification of nascent human life will be unstoppable.

Finally, the practice of human cloning by nuclear transfer—like other anticipated forms of genetically engineering the next generation—would enshrine and aggravate a profound misunderstanding of the meaning of having children and of the parent-child relationship. When a couple normally chooses to procreate, the partners are saying yes to the emergence of new life in its novelty—are saying yes not only to having a child, but also to having whatever child this child turns out to be. In accepting our finitude, in opening ourselves to our replacement, we tacitly confess the limits of our control.

Embracing the future by procreating means precisely that we are relinquishing our grip in the very activity of taking up our own share in what we hope will be the immortality of human life and the human species. This means that our children are not our children: they are not our property, they are not our possessions. Neither are they supposed to live our lives for us, or to live anyone's life but their own. Their genetic distinctiveness and independence are the natural foreshadowing of the deep truth that they have their own, never-before-enacted life to live. Though sprung from a past, they take an uncharted course into the future.

Much mischief is already done by parents who try to live vicariously through their children. Children are sometimes compelled to fulfill the broken dreams of unhappy parents. But whereas most parents normally have hopes for their children, cloning parents will have expectations. In cloning, such

overbearing parents will have taken at the start a decisive step that contradicts the entire meaning of the open and forward-looking nature of parent-child relations. The child is given a genotype that has already lived, with full expectation that this blueprint of a past life ought to be controlling the life that is to come. A wanted child now means a child who exists precisely to fulfill parental wants. Like all the more precise eugenic manipulations that will follow in its wake, cloning is thus inherently despotic, for it seeks to make one's children after one's own image (or an image of one's choosing) and their future according to one's will.

Is this hyperbolic? Consider concretely the new realities of responsibility and guilt in the households of the cloned. No longer only the sins of the parents, but also the genetic choices of the parents, will be visited on the children—and beyond the third and fourth generation; and everyone will know who is responsible. No parent will be able to blame nature or the lottery of sex for an unhappy adolescent's big nose, dull wit, musical ineptitude, nervous disposition, or anything else that he hates about himself. Fairly or not, children will hold their cloners responsible for everything, for nature as well as for nurture. And parents, especially the better ones, will be limitlessly liable to guilt. Only the truly despotic souls will sleep the sleep of the innocent.

IV.

The defenders of cloning are not wittingly friends of despotism. Quite the contrary. Deaf to most other considerations, they regard themselves mainly as friends of freedom: the freedom of individuals to reproduce, the freedom of scientists and inventors to discover and to devise and to foster "progress" in genetic knowledge and technique, the freedom of entrepreneurs to profit in the market. They want largescale cloning only for animals, but they wish to preserve cloning as a human option for exercising our "right to reproduce"—our right to have children, and children with "desirable genes." As some point out, under our "right to reproduce" we already practice early forms of unnatural, artificial, and extra-marital reproduction, and we already practice early forms of eugenic choice. For that reason, they argue, cloning is no big deal.

We have here a perfect example of the logic of the slippery slope. The principle of reproductive freedom currently enunciated by the proponents of cloning logically embraces the ethical acceptability of sliding all the way down: to producing children wholly in the laboratory from sperm to term (should it become feasible), and to producing children whose entire genetic makeup will be the product of parental eugenic planning and choice. If reproductive freedom means the right to have a child of one's own choosing by whatever means, then reproductive freedom knows and accepts no limits.

Proponents want us to believe that there are legitimate uses of cloning that can be distinguished from illegitimate uses, but by their own principles no such limits can be found. (Nor could any such limits be enforced in practice: once cloning is permitted, no one ever need discover whom one is cloning and why.) Reproductive freedom, as they understand it, is governed solely by the subjective wishes of the parents-to-be. The sentimentally appealing case of the childless married couple is, on these grounds, indistinguishable from the case of an individual (married or not) who would like to clone someone famous or talented, living or dead. And the principle here endorsed justifies not only cloning but also all future artificial attempts to create (manufacture) "better" or "perfect" babies.

The "perfect baby," of course, is the project not of the infertility doctors, but of the eugenic scientists and their supporters, who, for the time being, are content to hide behind the skirts of the partisans of reproductive freedom and compassion for the infertile. For them, the paramount right is not the so-called right to reproduce, it is what the biologist Bentley Glass called, a quarter of a century ago, "the right of every child to be born with a sound physical and mental constitution, based on a sound genotype . . . the inalienable right to a sound heritage." But to secure this right, and to achieve the requisite quality control over new human life, human conception and gestation will need to be brought fully into the bright light of the laboratory, beneath which the child-to-be can be fertilized,

nourished, pruned, weeded, watched, inspected, prodded, pinched, cajoled, injected, tested, rated, graded, approved, stamped, wrapped, sealed, and delivered. There is no other way to produce the perfect baby.

If you think that such scenarios require outside coercion or governmental tyranny, you are mistaken. Once it becomes possible, with the aid of human genomics, to produce or to select for what some regard as "better babies"—smarter, prettier, healthier, more athletic—parents will leap at the opportunity to "improve" their offspring. Indeed, not to do so will be socially regarded as a form of child neglect. Those who would ordinarily be opposed to such tinkering will be under enormous pressure to compete on behalf of their as yet unborn children—just as some now plan almost from their children's birth how to get them into Harvard. Never mind that, lacking a standard of "good" or "better," no one can really know whether any such changes will truly be improvements.

Proponents of cloning urge us to forget about the science-fiction scenarios of laboratory manufacture or multiple-copy clones, and to focus only on the sympathetic cases of infertile couples exercising their reproductive rights. But why, if the single cases are so innocent, should multiplying their performance be so off-putting? (Similarly, why do others object to people's making money from that practice if the practice itself is perfectly acceptable?) The so-called science-fiction cases—say, Brave New World—make vivid the meaning of what looks to us, mistakenly, to be benign. They reveal that what looks like compassionate humanitarianism is, in the end, crushing dehumanization.

V.

Whether or not they share my reasons, most people, I think, share my conclusion: that human cloning is unethical in itself and dangerous in its likely consequences, which include the precedent that it will establish for designing our children. Some reach this conclusion for their own good reasons, different from my own: concerns about distributive justice in access to eugenic cloning; worries about the genetic effects of asexual "inbreeding"; aversion to the implicit premise of genetic determinism; objections to the embryonic and fetal wastage that must necessarily accompany the efforts; religious opposition to "man playing God." But never mind why: the overwhelming majority of our fellow Americans remain firmly opposed to cloning human beings.

For us, then, the real questions are: What should we do about it? How can we best succeed? These questions should concern everyone eager to secure deliberate human control over the powers that could re-design our humanity, even if cloning is not the issue over which they would choose to make their stand. And the answer to the first question seems pretty plain. What we should do is work to prevent human cloning by making it illegal.

We should aim for a global legal ban, if possible, and for a unilateral national ban at a minimum—and soon, before the fact is upon us. To be sure, legal bans can be violated; but we certainly curtail much mischief by outlawing incest, voluntary servitude, and the buying and selling of organs and babies. To be sure, renegade scientists may secretly undertake to violate such a law, but we can deter them by both criminal sanctions and monetary penalties, as well as by removing any incentive they have to proudly claim credit for their technological bravado.

Such a ban on clonal baby-making will not harm the progress of basic genetic science and technology. On the contrary, it will reassure the public that scientists are happy to proceed without violating the deep ethical norms and intuitions of the human community. It will also protect honorable scientists from a public backlash against the brazen misconduct of the rogues. As many scientists have publicly confessed, free and worthy science probably has much more to fear from a strong public reaction to a cloning fiasco than it does from a cloning ban, provided that the ban is judiciously crafted and vigorously enforced against those who would violate it.

. . .

. . . I now believe that what we need is an all-out ban on human cloning, including the creation of embryonic clones. I am convinced that all halfway measures will prove to be morally, legally, and strategically flawed, and—most important—that they will not be effective in obtaining the desired result. Anyone truly serious about preventing human reproductive cloning must seek to stop the process from the beginning. Our changed circumstances, and the now evident defects of the less restrictive alternatives, make an all-out ban by far the most attractive and effective option.

Here's why. Creating cloned human children ("reproductive cloning") necessarily begins by producing cloned human embryos. Preventing the latter would prevent the former, and prudence alone might counsel building such a "fence around the law." Yet some scientists favor embryo cloning as a way of obtaining embryos for research or as sources of cells and tissues for the possible benefit of others. (This practice they misleadingly call "therapeutic cloning" rather than the more accurate "cloning for research" or "experimental cloning," so as to obscure the fact that the clone will be "treated" only to exploitation and destruction, and that any potential future beneficiaries and any future "therapies" are at this point purely hypothetical.)

The prospect of creating new human life solely to be exploited in this way has been condemned on moral grounds by many people—including *The Washington Post,* President Clinton, and many other supporters of a woman's right to abortion—as displaying a profound disrespect for life. Even those who are willing to scavenge so-called "spare embryos"—those products of in vitro fertilization made in excess of people's reproductive needs, and otherwise likely to be discarded—draw back from creating human embryos explicitly and solely for research purposes. They reject outright what they regard as the exploitation and the instrumentalization of nascent human life. In addition, others who are agnostic about the moral status of the embryo see the wisdom of not needlessly offending the sensibilities of their fellow citizens who are opposed to such practices.

But even setting aside these obvious moral first impressions, a few moments of reflection show why an anti-cloning law that permitted the cloning of embryos but criminalized their transfer to produce a child would be a moral blunder. This would be a law that was not merely permissively "pro-choice" but emphatically and prescriptively "anti-life." While permitting the creation of an embryonic life, it would make it a federal offense to try to keep it alive and bring it to birth. Whatever one thinks of the moral status or the ontological status of the human embryo, moral sense and practical wisdom recoil from having the government of the United States on record as requiring the destruction of nascent life and, what is worse, demanding the punishment of those who would act to preserve it by (feloniously!) giving it birth.

But the problem with the approach that targets only reproductive cloning (that is, the transfer of the embryo to a woman's uterus) is not only moral but also legal and strategic. A ban only on reproductive cloning would turn out to be unenforceable. Once cloned embryos were produced and available in laboratories and assisted-reproduction centers, it would be virtually impossible to control what was done with them. Biotechnical experiments take place in laboratories, hidden from public view, and, given the rise of high-stakes commerce in biotechnology, these experiments are concealed from the competition. Huge stockpiles of cloned human embryos could thus be produced and bought and sold without anyone knowing it. As we have seen with in vitro embryos created to treat infertility, embryos produced for one reason can be used for another reason: today "spare embryos" once created to begin a pregnancy are now used in research, and tomorrow clones created for research will be used to begin a pregnancy.

Assisted reproduction takes place within the privacy of the doctor-patient relationship, making outside scrutiny extremely difficult. Many infertility experts probably would obey the law, but others could and would defy it with impunity, their doings covered by the veil of secrecy that is the principle of medical confidentiality. Moreover, the transfer of embryos to begin a pregnancy is a simple procedure (especially compared with manufacturing the embryo in the first place), simple enough that its final steps could be self-administered by the woman, who would thus absolve the doctor of blame for having "caused" the illegal transfer. (I have in mind something analogous to Kevorkian's suicide machine, which was designed to enable the patient to push the plunger and the good "doctor" to evade criminal liability.)

Even should the deed become known, governmental attempts to enforce the reproductive ban would run into a swarm of moral and legal challenges, both to efforts aimed at preventing transfer to a woman and—even worse—to efforts seeking to prevent birth after transfer has occurred. A woman who wished to receive the embryo clone would no doubt seek a judicial restraining order, suing to have the law overturned in the name of a constitutionally protected interest in her own reproductive choice to clone. (The cloned child would be born before the legal proceedings were complete.) And should an "illicit clonal pregnancy" be discovered, no governmental agency would compel a woman to abort the clone, and there would be an understandable storm of protest should she be fined or jailed after she gives birth. Once the baby is born, there would even be sentimental opposition to punishing the doctor for violating the law—unless, of course, the clone turned out to be severely abnormal.

For all these reasons, the only practically effective and legally sound approach is to block human cloning at the start, at the production of the embryo clone. Such a ban can be rightly characterized not as interference with reproductive freedom, nor even as interference with scientific inquiry, but as an attempt to prevent the unhealthy, unsavory, and unwelcome manufacture of and traffic in human clones.

. . .

I appreciate that a federal legislative ban on human cloning is without American precedent, at least in matters technological. Perhaps such a ban will prove ineffective; perhaps it will eventually be shown to have been a mistake. (If so, it could later be reversed.) If enacted, however, it will have achieved one overwhelmingly important result, in addition to its contribution to thwarting cloning: it will place the burden of practical proof where it belongs. It will require the proponents to show very clearly what great social or medical good can be had only by the cloning of human beings. Surely it is only for such a compelling case, yet to be made or even imagined, that we should wish to risk this major departure—or any other major departure—in human procreation.

Americans have lived by and prospered under a rosy optimism about scientific and technological progress. The technological imperative has probably served us well, though we should admit that there is no accurate method for weighing benefits and harms. And even when we recognize the unwelcome outcomes of technological advance, we remain confident in our ability to fix all the "bad" consequences—by regulation or by means of still newer and better technologies. Yet there is very good reason for shifting the American paradigm, at least regarding those technological interventions into the human body and mind that would surely effect fundamental (and likely irreversible) changes in human nature, basic human relationships, and what it means to be a human being. Here we should not be willing to risk everything in the naive hope that, should things go wrong, we can later set them right again.

Some have argued that cloning is almost certainly going to remain a marginal practice, and that

we should therefore permit people to practice it. Such a view is shortsighted. Even if cloning is rarely undertaken, a society in which it is tolerated is no longer the same society—any more than is a society that permits (even small-scale) incest or cannibalism or slavery. A society that allows cloning, whether it knows it or not, has tacitly assented to the conversion of procreation into manufacture and to the treatment of children as purely the projects of our will. Willy-nilly, it has acquiesced in the eugenic re-design of future generations. The humanitarian superhighway to a Brave New World lies open before this society.

But the present danger posed by human cloning is, paradoxically, also a golden opportunity. In a truly unprecedented way, we can strike a blow for the human control of the technological project, for wisdom, for prudence, for human dignity. The prospect of human cloning, so repulsive to contemplate, is the occasion for deciding whether we shall be slaves of unregulated innovation, and ultimately its artifacts, or whether we shall remain free human beings who guide our powers toward the enhancement of human dignity. The humanity of the human future is now in our hands.

MARK SAGOFF   II.12
_____

Genetic Engineering and the Concept of the Natural

In the past several years there has been a furor generated over the use of genetically modified organisms (GMOs) in the world food supply. Particularly in Europe, but also in several other countries, there are active consumer movements whose goal is to rid the supermarket shelves of any trace of GMO ingredients. The controversy has ignited a trade war between the United States, which has a rather laissez-faire attitude toward GMO crops, and its European trading partners, whose consumers are demanding GMO labeling, if not a complete ban, on GMO foods.

In this selection, philosopher Mark Sagoff takes a look at food labeling in general; he argues that the consumer's preference for "all natural" foods has been stimulated in large part by the food industry itself, which has decided to sell its products along with the fantasy that our food is produced without technological intervention. Sagoff distinguishes four senses in which something may be said to be "natural" and argues that part of the problem with the food industry is that it equivocates on the meaning of this term and tries to have it both ways. Illustrating the different senses of "natural" with passages from Shakespeare's *The Winter's Tale*, Sagoff artfully reminds us that there are moral, aesthetic, and cultural value aspects to the debate over genetically engineered foods, and that trade-offs between these values and those of convenience and consumerism can be papered over but not avoided by advertising claims made by corporate agribusiness.

Focus Questions

1. Why does Sagoff think that the current practice of advertising foods as "natural" is an example of consumer constructivism?
2. What are the four senses of "natural" that Sagoff distinguishes? Which of these senses correctly apply to genetically engineered foods? Which don't? Explain.
3. Is it possible to give consumers what they want with no trade-offs, as industry spokespersons suggest? Why or why not?
4. Compare this reading to that of Strong (selection I.12) and Lovins (selection II.16). In what sense has modern technology subverted the concept of nature?

Keywords

agribusiness, consumerism, genetic engineering, GMOs, labeling, multinational corporations, nature

WHY DO MANY CONSUMERS view genetically engineered foods with suspicion? I want to suggest that it is largely because the food industry has taught them to do so. Consumers learn from advertisements and labels that the foods they buy are all natural—even more natural than a baby's smile. "The emphasis in recent years," *Food Processing* magazine concludes, "has been on natural or nature-identical ingredients." According to *Food Product Design*, "the desire for an all natural label extends even to pet food."

The food industry, I shall argue, wishes to embrace the efficiencies offered by advances in genetic engineering. This technology, both in name and in concept, however, belies the image of nature or of the natural to which the food industry constantly

and conspicuously appeals. It should be no surprise that consumers who believe genetically modified foods are not "natural" should for that reason regard them as risky or as undesirable. If they knew how much technology contributes to other foods they eat, they might be suspicious of them as well.

All-Natural Technology

Recently, I skimmed through issues of trade magazines, such as *Food Technology* and *Food Processing*, that serve the food industry. In full-page advertisements, manufacturers insist the ingredients they market come direct from primordial Creation or, at least, that their products are identical to nature's own. For example, Roche Food Colours runs in these trade magazines a full-page ad that displays a bright pink banana over the statement: "When nature changes her colours, so will we." The ad continues:

From "Genetic Engineering and the Concept of the Natural" by Mark Sagoff, *Philosophy and Public Policy Quarterly, Spring/ Summer 2001*, Vol. 21 (2/3), pp 2–10. Copyright © 2001 Institute for Philosophy and Public Policy. Reprinted by permission.

Today more and more people are rejecting the idea of artificial colours being used in food and drink. . . .

Our own food colours are, and always have been, strictly identical to those produced by nature.

We make pure carotenoids which either singly or in combination achieve a whole host of different shades in the range of yellow though orange to red.

And time and time again they produce appetising natural colours, reliably, economically, and safely.

Just like nature herself.

Advertisement after advertisement presents the same message: food comes directly from nature or, at least, can be sold as if it did. Consider, for example, a full-page advertisement that McCormick and Wild, a flavor manufacturer, runs regularly in *Food Processing*. The words "BACK TO NATURE" appear under a kiwi fruit dripping with juice. "Today's consumer wants it all," the advertisement purrs, "great taste, natural ingredients, and new ideas. . . . Let us show you how we can put the world's most advanced technology in natural flavors at your disposal. . . ."

This advertisement clearly states the mantra of the food industry: "Today's consumer wants it all." Great taste. Natural ingredients. New ideas. The world's most advanced technology. One can prepare the chemical basis of a flavor, for example, benzaldehyde—almond—artificially with just a little chemical know-how, in this instance, by mixing oil of clove and amyl acetate. To get exactly the same compound as a "natural" flavor, one must employ far more sophisticated technology to extract and isolate benzaldehyde from peach and apricot pits. The "natural" flavor, an extract, contains traces of hydrogen cyanide, a deadly poison evolved by plants to protect their seeds from insects. Even so, consumers strongly prefer all-natural to artificial flavors, which sell therefore at a far lower price.

In its advertisements, the Haarmann & Reimer Corporation (H&R) describes its flavor enhancers as "HypR Clean Naturally." With "H&R as your partner, you'll discover the latest advances in flavor technology" that assure "the cleanest label pos-

sible." A "clean" label is one that includes only natural ingredients and no reference to technology. In a competing advertisement, Chr. Hansen's Laboratory announces itself as the pioneer in "culture and enzyme technologies. . . . And because our flavors are completely natural, you can enjoy the benefits of 'all-natural' labeling." Flavor manufacturers tout their stealth technology—i.e., technology so advanced it disappears from the consumer's radar screen. The consumer can be told he or she is directly in touch with nature itself.

The world's largest flavor company, International Flavors & Fragrances (IFF) operates manufacturing facilities in places like Dayton, New Jersey, an industrial corridor of refineries and chemical plants. Under a picture of plowed, fertile soil, the IFF Laboratory, in a full-page display, states, "Where Nature is at work, IFF is at work." The text describes "IFF's natural flavor systems." The slogan follows: "IFF technology. In partnership with Nature." Likewise, MEER Corporation of Bergen, New Jersey, pictures a rainforest under the caption, "It's A Jungle Out There!" The ad states that "true-to-nature" flavorings "do not just happen. It takes . . . manufacturing and technical expertise and a national distribution network . . . for the creation of natural, clean label flavors."

Food colors are similarly sold as both all natural and high tech. "VegetoneH colors your foods *naturally* for a healthy bottom line," declares Kalsec, Inc., of Kalamazoo, Michigan. Its ad shows a technician standing before a computer and measuring chemicals into a test tube. The ad extols the company's "patented natural color systems." The terms "natural" and "patented" fit seamlessly together in a conceptual scheme in which there are no trade-offs and no compromises. The natural is patentable. If you think any of this is contradictory, you will not get far in the food industry.

Organic TV Dinners

As a typical American suburbanite, I can buy not just groceries but "Whole Foods" at Fresh Fields and other upscale supermarkets. I am particularly impressed by the number of convenience foods that are advertised as "organic." Of course, one might think that any food may be whole and that all foods are organic. Terms like "whole" and "organic," however, appeal to and support my belief that the products that carry these labels are less processed and more natural—closer to the family farm—than are those that are produced by multinational mega-corporations, such as Pillsbury or General Foods.

My perusal of advertisements in trade magazines helped disabuse me of my belief that all-natural, organic, and whole foods are closer to nature in a substantive sense than other manufactured products. If I had any residual credulity, it was removed by an excellent cover story, "Behind the Organic-Industrial Complex," that appeared in a recent issue of the *New York Times Magazine*. The author, Michael Pollan, is shocked, shocked to find that the prepackaged microwavable all-natural organic TV dinners at his local Whole Foods outlet are not gathered from the wild by red-cheeked peasants in native garb. They are highly-processed products manufactured by multinational corporations. Contrary to the impression created by advertisements, organic and other all-natural foods are often fabricated by the same companies—using comparable technologies—as those that produce Velveeta and Miracle Whip. And the ingredients come from as far away as megafarms in Chile—not from local farmers' markets.

Reformers who led the organic food movement in the 1960s wished to provide an alternative to agribusiness and to industrial food production, but some of these reformers bent to the inevitable. As Pollan points out, they became multimillionaire executives of Pillsbury and General Mills in charge of organic food production systems. This makes sense. A lot of advanced technology is needed to produce and market an all-natural or an organic ready-to-eat meal. Consumers inspect food labels to ward off artificial ingredients; yet they also want the convenience of a low-priced, pre-prepared, all-natural dinner.

At General Mills, as one senior vice president, Danny Strickland, told Pollan, "Our corporate philosophy is to give consumers what they want with no trade-offs." Pollan interprets the meaning of this statement as follows. "At General Mills," Pollan explains, "the whole notion of objective truth has

been replaced by a value-neutral consumer constructivism, in which each sovereign shopper constructs his own reality."

Mass-marketed organic TV dinners do not compromise; they combine convenience with a commitment to the all-natural, eco-friendly, organic ideology. The most popular of these dinners are sold by General Mills through its subsidiary, Cascadian Farms. The advertising slogan of Cascadian Farms, "Taste You Can Believe In," as Pollan observes, makes no factual claims of any sort. It "allows the consumer to bring his or her personal beliefs into it," as the Vice President for Marketing, R. Brooks Gekler, told Pollan. The absence of any factual claim is essential to selling a product, since each consumer buys an object that reflects his or her particular belief system.

What is true of marketing food is true of virtually every product. A product will sell if it is all-natural and eco-friendly and, at the same time, offers the consumer the utmost in style and convenience. A recent *New York Times* article, under the title, "Fashionistas, Ecofriendly and All-Natural," points out that the sales of organic food in the United States topped $6.4 billion in 1999 with a projected annual increase of 20 percent. Manufacturers of clothes and fashion accessories, such as solar-powered watches, are cashing in on the trend. Maria Rodale, who helps direct a publishing empire covering "natural" products, founded the women's lifestyle magazine *Organic Style*. Rodale told the *Times* that women want to do the right thing for "the environment but not at the cost of living well." Advances in technology give personal items and household wares an all-natural eco-friendly look that is also the last word in fashion. Consumers "don't want to sacrifice anything," Ms. Rodale told a reporter. Why should there be a trade-off between a commitment to nature and a commitment to the good life? "Increasingly there are options that don't compromise on either front."

The food industry does not sell food any more than the fashion industry sells clothes or the automobile industry sells automobiles. They sell imagery. The slogan, "Everything the consumer wants with no trade-offs," covers all aspects of our dreamworld. Sex without zippers, children without zits, lawns without weeds, wars without casualties, and food without technology. Reality involves trade-offs and rather substantial ones. For this reason, if you tried to sell reality, your competitor would drive you out of business by avoiding factual claims and selling fantasy—whatever consumers believe in—instead. Consumers should not be confused or disillusioned by facts. They are encouraged to assume that they buy products of Nature or Creation. In view of this fantasy, how could consumers view genetic engineering with anything but suspicion?

Nature's Own Methods

Genetic engineering, with its stupendous capacity for increasing the efficiencies of food production in all departments, including flavors and colorings, raises a problem. How can genetic recombination be presented to the consumer as completely natural—as part of nature's spontaneous course—as have other aspects of food technology? A clean label would tell consumers there is nothing unnatural or inauthentic about genetically engineered products. Industry has responded in two complementary ways to this problem.

First, the food industry has resisted calls to label bioengineered products. Gene Grabowski of the Grocery Manufacturers Association, for example, worries that labeling "would imply that there's something wrong with food, and there isn't." Michael J. Phillips, an economist with the Biotechnology Industry Organization, adds that labeling "would only confuse consumers by suggesting that the process of biotechnology might in and of itself have an impact on the safety of food. This is not the case."

Second, manufacturers point out that today's genetic technologies do not differ, except in being more precise, from industrial processes that result in the emulsifiers, stabilizers, enzymes, proteins, cultures, and other ingredients that do enjoy the benefits of a clean label. Virtually every plant consumed by human beings—canola, for example—is the product of so much breeding, hybridization, and modification that it hardly resembles its wild ancestors. This is a good thing, too, since these wild ancestors were barely edible if not downright poisonous. Manufacturers argue that genetic engineering differs from conventional breeding only because it is more accurate and therefore changes nature less.

For example, Monsanto Corporation, in a recent full-page ad, pictures a bucolic landscape reminiscent of a painting by Constable. The headline reads, "FARMING: A picture of the Future." The ad then represents genetic engineering as all natural—or at least as natural as are conventional biotechnologies that have enabled humanity to engage successfully in agriculture. "The products of biotechnology will be based on nature's own methods," the ad assures the industry. "Monsanto scientists are working with nature to develop innovative products for farmers of today, and of the future."

In this advertisement, Monsanto applies the tried-and-true formula to which the food industry has long been committed—presenting a technology as revolutionary, innovative, highly advanced, and as "based on nature's own methods." *Everything* is natural. Why not? As long as there are no distinctions, there are no trade-offs. Consumers can buy what they believe in. A thing is natural if the public believes it is. "There is something in this more than natural," as Hamlet once said, "if philosophy could find it out."

Four Concepts of the Natural

If consumers reject bioengineered food as "unnatural," what does this mean? In what way are foods that result from conventional methods of genetic mutation and selection, which have vastly altered crops and livestock, more "natural" than those that depend in some way on gene splicing? Indeed, is anything in an organic TV dinner "natural" other than, say, the rodent droppings that may be found in it? Since I am a philosopher, not a scientist, I am particularly interested in the moral, aesthetic, and cultural—as distinct from the chemical, biological, or physical—aspects of the natural world. I recognize that many of us depend in our moral, aesthetic, and spiritual lives on distinguishing those things for which humans are responsible from those that occur as part of nature's spontaneous course.

Philosophers have long pondered the question whether the concept of the natural can be used in a normative sense—that is, whether to say that a practice or a product is "natural" is somehow to imply that it is better to that extent than one that is not. Why should anyone assume that a product that is "natural" is safer, more healthful, or more aesthetically or ethically attractive than one that is not? And why is technology thought to be intrinsically risky when few of us would survive without quite a lot of it?

Among the philosophers who have questioned the "naturalistic fallacy"—the assumption that what is natural is for that reason good—the nineteenth-century British philosopher John Stuart Mill has been particularly influential. In his "Essay on Nature," Mill argues that the term "nature" can refer either to the totality of things ("the sum of all phenomena, together with the causes which produce them") or to those phenomena that take place "without the agency . . . of man." Plainly, everything in the world—including every technology—is natural and belongs equally to nature in the first sense of the term. Mill comments:

> To bid people to conform to the laws of nature when they have no power but what the laws of nature give them—when it is a physical impossibility for them to do the smallest thing otherwise than through some law of nature—is an absurdity. The thing they need to be told is, what particular law of nature they should make use of in a particular case.

Of nature in the second sense—that which takes place without the agency of man—Mill has a dour view. "Nearly all the things which men are hanged or imprisoned for doing to one another, are nature's every day performances," Mill wrote. Nature may have cared for us in the days of the Garden of Eden. In more recent years, however, humanity has had to alter Creation to survive. Mill concludes, "For while human action cannot help conforming to nature in one meaning of the term, the very aim and object of action is to alter and improve nature in the other meaning."

Following Mill, it is possible to distinguish four different conceptions of nature to understand the extent to which bioengineered food may or may not be natural. These four senses of the term include:

1. *Everything in the universe.* The significant opposite of the "natural" in this sense is the "supernatural." Everything technology produces has to be completely natural because it conforms to all of nature's laws and principles.

2. *Creation in the sense of what God has made.* The distinction here lies between what is sacred because of its pedigree (God's handiwork) and what is profane (what humans produce for pleasure or profit).

3. *That which is independent of human influence or contrivance.* The concept of "nature" or the "natural" in this sense, e.g., the "pristine," is understood as a privative notion defined in terms of the absence of the effects of human activity. The opposite of the "natural" in this sense is the "artificial."

4. *That which is authentic or true to itself.* The opposite of the "natural" in this sense is the specious, illusory, or superficial. The "natural" is trustworthy and honest, while the sophisticated, worldly, or contrived is deceptive and risky.

These four conceptions of nature are logically independent. To say that an item or a process—genetic engineering, for example—is "natural" because it obeys the laws of nature, is by no means to imply it is "natural" in any other sense. That genetically manipulated foods can be found within (1) the totality of phenomena does not show that they are "natural" in the sense that they are (2) part of primordial Creation; (3) free of human contrivance; or (4) authentic and expressive of the virtues of rustic or peasant life.

The problem of consumer acceptance of biotechnology arises in part because the food industry sells its products as natural in the last three senses. The industry wishes to be regulated, however, only in the context of the first conception of nature, which does not distinguish among phenomena on the basis of their histories, sources, or provenance. The industry argues that only the biochemical properties of its products should matter to regulation;

the process (including genetic engineering) is irrelevant to food safety and should not be considered.

The food industry downplays the biochemical properties of its products, however, when it advertises them to consumers. The industry—at least if the approach taken by General Mills is typical—tries to give the consumer whatever he believes in. If the consumer believes in a process by which rugged farmers on the slopes of the Cascades raise organic TV dinners from the soil by sheer force of personality, so be it. You will see the farm pictured on the package to suggest the product is close to Creation, free of contrivance, and authentic or expressive of rural virtues. What you will not see on any label—if the industry has its way—is a reference to genetic engineering. The industry believes regulators should concern themselves only with the first concept of nature—the scientific concept—and thus with the properties of the product. Concepts related to the process are used to evoke images that "give consumers what they want with no trade-offs."

Shakespeare on Biotechnology

I confess that, as a consumer, I find organic foods appealing and I insist on "all-natural" ingredients. Am I just foolish? You might think that I would see through labels like "all natural" and "organic"—not to mention "whole" foods—and that I would reject them as marketing ploys of a cynical industry. Yet like many consumers, I want to believe that the "natural" is somewhat better than the artificial. Is this just a fallacy?

Although I am a professional philosopher (or perhaps because of this), I would not look first to the literature of philosophy to understand what may be an irrational—or at least an unscientific—commitment to buying "all natural" products. My instinct would be to look in Shakespeare to understand what may be contradictory attitudes or inexplicable sentiments.

Shakespeare provides his most extensive discussion of biotechnology in *The Winter's Tale,* one of his comedies. In Act IV, Polixenes, King of Bohemia, disguises himself to spy upon his son, Florizel, who has fallen in love with Perdita, whom all believe to be a shepherd's daughter. In fact, though raised as a shepherdess, Perdita is the castaway daughter of the King of Sicily, a close but now estranged friend of Polixenes. Perdita welcomes the disguised Polixenes and an attendant lord to a sheep shearing feast in late autumn, offering them dried flowers "that keep/ Seeming and savour all winter long." Polixenes merrily chides her: "well you fit our ages/ With flowers of winter."

She replies that only man-made hybrids flourish so late in the fall:

> . . . carnations, and streak'd gillyvors,
> Which some call nature's bastards. Of that kind
> Our rustic garden's barren; and I care not
> To get slips of them.

Polixenes asks why she rejects cold-hardy flowers such as gillyvors, a dianthus. She answers that they come from human contrivance, not from "great creating nature." She complains there is "art" in their "piedness," or variegation. Polixenes replies: "Say there be;

> Yet nature is made better by no mean
> But nature makes that mean; so over that art
> Which you say adds to nature, is an art
> That nature makes. . . . This is an art
> Which does mend nature—change it rather; but
> The art itself is nature.

The statement, "The art itself is nature" anticipates the claim made by Monsanto that "The products of biotechnology will be based on nature's own methods." Polixenes, Mill, and Monsanto remind us that everything in the universe conforms to nature's own principles, and relies wholly on nature's powers. From a scientific perspective, in other words, all nature is one. The mechanism of a lever, for example, may occur in the physiology of a wild animal or in the structure of a machine. Either way, it is natural. One might be forced to agree, then, that genetic engineering applies nature's own methods and principles; in other words, "the art itself is nature."

The exchange between Perdita and Polixenes weaves together the four conceptions of nature I identified earlier in relation to John Stuart Mill. When Polixenes states, "The art itself is nature," he uses the term "nature" to comprise everything in the Universe, that is, everything that conforms to physical law. Second, Perdita refers to "great creating nature," that is, to Creation, i.e., the primordial origin and condition of life before the advent of human society. Third, she contrasts nature to art or artifice by complaining that hybrids do not arise spontaneously but show "art" in their "piedness." Finally, Perdita refers to her "rustic garden," which, albeit cultivated, is "natural" in the sense of simple or unadorned, in contrast to the ornate horticulture that would grace a royal garden. The comparison between the court and the country correlates, of course, with the division that exists in Perdita herself—royal in carriage and character by her birth, yet possessed of rural virtues by her upbringing.

Shakespeare elaborates this last conception of "nature" as the banter continues between Perdita and the disguised Polixenes. To his assertion, "The art itself is nature," Perdita concedes, "So it is." Polixenes then drives home his point: "Then make your garden rich in gillyvors,/ And do not call them bastards."

To which Perdita responds:

I'll not put
The dibble in earth to set one slip of them;
No more than were I painted I would wish
This youth should say 'twere well, and only therefore
Desire to breed by me.

Besides comparing herself to breeding stock—amusing in the context, since she speaks to her future father-in-law in the presence of his son—Perdita reiterates a fourth and crucial sense of the "natural." In this sense, what is "natural" is true to itself; it is honest, authentic, and genuine. This conception reflects Aristotle's theory of the "nature" of things, which refers to qualities that are spontaneous because they are inherent or innate.

Perdita stands by her insistence on natural products—from flowers she raises to cosmetics she uses—in spite of Polixenes' cynical but scientific reproofs. Does this suggest Perdita is merely a good candidate for Ms. Rodale's organic chic? Should she receive a free introductory copy of *Organic*

Style? Certainly not. There is something about Perdita's rejection of biotechnology that withstands this sort of criticism. Why have Perdita's actions a moral authority or authenticity that the choices consumers make today may lack?

Having It Both Ways

Perdita possesses moral authority because she is willing to live with the consequences of her convictions and of the distinctions on which they are based. By refusing to paint herself to appear more attractive, for example, Perdita contrasts her qualities, which are innate, to those of the "streak'd gillyvor," which owe themselves to technological meddling. This comparison effectively gives her the last word because she suits the action to it: she does not and would not paint herself to attract a lover. Similarly, Perdita does not raise hybrids, though she admits, "I would I had some flow'rs" that might become the "time of day" of the youthful guests at the feast, such as Florizel.

Perdita does not try to have it both ways—to reject hybrids but also to grow cold-hardy flowers. She ridicules those who match lofty ideals with ordinary actions—whose practice belies their professed principles. For example, Camillo, the Sicilian lord who attends Polixenes, compliments Perdita on her beauty. He says, "I should leave grazing, were I of your flock,/ And only live by gazing." She laughs at him and smartly replies, "You'd be so lean that blasts of January/ Would blow you through and through."

Many people today share Perdita's affection for nature and her distaste for technology. Indeed, it is commonplace to celebrate Nature's spontaneous course and to condemn the fabrications of biotechnology. Jeremy Rifkin speaks of "Playing Ecological Roulette with Mother Nature's Designs"; Ralph Nader has written the foreword to a book titled, *Genetically Engineered Food: Changing the Nature of Nature*. The Prince of Wales, in a tirade against biotechnology, said, "I have always believed that agriculture should proceed in harmony with nature, recognising that there are natural limits to our ambitions. We need to rediscover a reverence for the natural world to become more aware of the relationship between God, man, and creation."

While consumers today share Perdita's preference for the natural in the sense of the authentic and unadorned and spurn technological meddling, they do not share her willingness to live with the consequences of their commitment. They expect to enjoy year round fruits and vegetables of unblemished appearance, and consistent taste and nutritional quality. Gardeners wish to plant lawns and yards with species that are native and indigenous, and they support commissions and fund campaigns to throw back the "invasions" of exotic and alien species. Yet they also want lawns that resist drought, blight, and weeds, and—to quote Perdita again—to enjoy flowers that "come before the swallow dares, and take/The winds of March with beauty." In other words, the consumer wants it both ways. Today's consumers, as Ms. Rodale knows, "don't want to sacrifice anything." Today's consumers insist, as did Perdita, on the local, the native, the spontaneous. Yet they lack her moral authority because they are unwilling to live with the consequences of their principles or preferences. Consumers today refuse to compromise; they expect fruits and flowers that survive "the birth/ Of trembling winter" and are plentiful and perfect all year round.

Naked Lunch

Those who defend genetic engineering in agriculture are likely to regard as irrational consumer concerns about the safety of genetically manipulated crops. The oil and other products of Roundup Ready soybeans, according to this position, pose no more risks to the consumer than do products from conventional soybeans. Indeed, soybean oil, *qua* oil, contains neither DNA nor protein and so will be the same whether or not the roots of the plant are herbicide resistant. Even when protein or DNA differs, no clear argument can be given to suppose that this difference—e.g., the order of a few nucleotides—involves any danger. Crops are the outcome of centuries or millennia of genetic crossing, selection, mutation, breeding, and so on.

Genetic engineering adds but a wrinkle to the vast mountains of technology that separate the foods we eat from wild plants and animals.

The same kind of argument may undermine consumer beliefs that "natural" colors and flavors are safer or more edible than artificial ones. In fact, chemical compounds that provide "natural" and "artificial" flavors can be identical and may be manufactured at the same factories. The difference may lie only in the processes by which they are produced or derived. An almond flavor that is produced artificially, as I have mentioned, may be purer and therefore safer than one extracted from peach or apricot pits. Distinctions between the natural and the artificial, then, need not correspond with differences in safety, quality, or taste—at least from the perspective of science.

Distinctions consumers draw between the natural and the artificial—and preferences for the organic over the engineered—reflect differences that remain important nonetheless to our cultural, social, and aesthetic lives. We owe nature a respect that we do not owe technology. The rise of objective, neutral, physical and chemical science invites us, however, to disregard all such moral, aesthetic, and cultural distinctions and act only on facts that can be scientifically analyzed and proven. Indeed, the food industry, when it is speaking to regulators rather than advertising to consumers, insists on this rational, objective approach.

In an essay titled, "Environments at Risk," Mary Douglas characterizes the allure of objective, rational, value-neutral, science:

> This is the invitation to full self-consciousness that is offered in our time. We must accept it. But we should do so knowing that the price is William Burroughs' *Naked Lunch*. The day when everyone can see exactly what it is on the end of everyone's fork, on that day there is no pollution and no purity and nothing edible or inedible, credible or incredible, because the classifications of social life are gone. There is no more meaning.

Advances in genetic engineering invite us to the full self-consciousness that Douglas describes and aptly analogizes to the prison life depicted in *Naked*

Lunch. It is the classifications of social life—not those of biological science—that clothe food and everything else with meaning. Genetic engineering poses a problem principally because it crosses moral, aesthetic, or cultural—not biological—boundaries. The fact that the technology exists and is successful shows, indeed, that the relevant biological boundaries (i.e., between species) that might have held in the past now no longer exist.

Given advances in science and technology, how can we maintain the classifications of social life—for example, distinctions between natural and artificial flavors and between organic and engineered ingredients? How may we, like Perdita, respect the difference between the products of "great creating nature" and those of human contrivance? Perdita honors this distinction by living with its consequences. Her severest test comes when Polixenes removes his disguise and threatens to condemn her to death if she ever sees Florizel again. Florizel asks her to elope, but she resigns herself to the accident of their origins—his high, hers (she believes) low—that separates them forever. Dressed up as a queen for the festivities, Perdita tells Florizel: "I will queen it no further. Leave me, sir; I will go milk my ewes and weep."

Perdita, of course, both renounced her cake and ate it, too. In Act IV, she gives up Florizel and his kingdom, but in Act V she gets them. Her true identity as a princess is eventually discovered, and so the marriage happily takes place. If you or I tried to live as fully by our beliefs and convictions—if we insisted on eating only those foods that come from great creating nature rather than from industry—we would not be so fortunate. "You'd be so lean that blasts of January/Would blow you through and through."

Perdita is protected by a playwright who places her in a comedy. Shakespeare allows her to live up to her convictions without compromising her lifestyle. This is exactly what the food industry promises to do—"to give consumers what they want with no trade-offs." It is exactly what Ms. Rodale offers—to protect the environment "but not at the cost of living well." The food, fashion, and other industries work off stage to arrange matters so that

consumers can renounce genetic engineering, artificial flavors, industrial agriculture, and multinational corporations. At the same time, consumers can enjoy an inexpensive, all-natural, organic, TV dinner from Creation via Cascadian Farms.

Perdita lives in the moral order of a comedy. In that moral order, no compromises and no trade-offs are necessary. You and I are not so fortunately situated. Indeed, we must acknowledge the tragic aspect of life—the truth that good things are often not compatible and that we have to trade off one for the sake of obtaining the other. The food industry, by suggesting that we can have everything we believe in, keeps us from recognizing that tragic truth. The industry makes all the compromises and hides them from the consumer.

This article is based on a presentation made at the National Agricultural Biotechnology Council's annual meeting, "High Anxiety and Biotechnology: Who's Buying, Who's Not, and Why?," held May 22–24, 2001. A version of this article is forthcoming in NABC Report 13 symposium proceedings.

The author acknowledges the support of the National Human Genome Research Institute program on Ethical, Legal, and Social Implications of Human Genetics, Grant R01HG02363; also the National Science Foundation, Grant 9729295.

Sources: *Food Processing,* February 1988. Lucy Saunders, "Selecting an Enzyme," *Food Product Design* (May 1995), online at: http://www.foodproductdesign.com/archive/1995/0595AP. html; Michael Pollan, "Behind the Organic-Industrial Complex," *New York Times Magazine* (May 13, 2001); Ruth La Ferla, "Fashionistas, Ecofriendly and All-Natural," *New York Times* (July 15, 2001); Bill Lambrecht, "Up To 50%+ of Crops Now Genetically Modified," *St. Louis Post-Dispatch,* Washington Bureau (August 22, 1999), and available on-line at http:// www.healthresearchbooks.com/articles/labels2.htm; Jim Wilson, "Scientific Food Fight," in *Popular Mechanics* on-line, which is available at http://popularmechanics.com/popmech/ sci/0002STRSM.html; John Stuart Mill, "Nature" in *Three Essays on Religion* (New York, Greenwood Press, 1969), reprint of the 1874 ed.; Jeremy Rifkin, "The Biotech Century: Playing Ecological Roulette with Mother Nature's Designs," in *E Magazine* (May/June 1998); Martin Teitel and Kimberly A. Wilson, *Genetically Engineered Food: Changing the Nature of Nature: What You Need to Know to Protect Yourself, Your Family, and Our Planet* (Vermont: Inner Traditions, Int'l, Ltd., 1999); "Seeds of Disaster: An Article by The Prince of Wales," *Daily Telegraph* (June 8, 1998); Mary Douglas, "Environments at Risk," in *Implicit Meanings: Essays in Anthropology* (London: Routledge & Kegan Paul, 1975).

GARRETT HARDIN   II.13

The Tragedy of the Commons

This article addresses the question of how to deal with the expected growth of the human population in the twenty-first century. Garrett Hardin argues in this selection that the problem of controlling human population growth has no technical solution. This is true, he argues, because of a general class of problems that arise from allowing individuals the freedom to act so as to maximize their individual self-interests by exploiting resources held in common. Problems of this kind can produce tragic results because they have the paradoxical effect of eventually bringing ruin to all those who are seeking to maximize their own interests in the belief that doing so will produce "the greatest happiness for the greatest number." The solution to such problems, he suggests, can only be one that sets limits on the individual pursuit of self-interest or on the freedom of the commons.

Focus Questions

1. What does Hardin mean by "the tragedy of the commons"? How does this problem arise?
2. What are some examples of how "Freedom in a commons brings ruin to all"? Can you think of other examples of this general phenomenon?
3. How does the perspective of this reading relate to those developed by Robert McGinn (selection I.11) and Robert Kates (selection II.15)? If the population problem has no technical solution, what kind of solutions, if any, does it have?

Keywords

commons, ethical egoism, game theory, National Parks, over-fishing, population control, rational self-interest, utilitarianism

AT THE END OF A THOUGHTFUL article on the future of nuclear war, J. B. Wiesner and H. F. York concluded that: "both sides in the arms race are . . . confronted by the dilemma of steadily increasing military power and steadily decreasing national security. *It is our considered professional judgment that this dilemma has no technical solution.* If the great powers continue to look for solutions in the area of science and technology only, the result will be to worsen the situation."[1]

I would like to focus your attention not on the subject of the article (national security in a nuclear world) but on the kind of conclusion they reached, namely that there is no technical solution to the problem. An implicit and almost universal assumption of discussions published in professional and semi-popular scientific journals is that the problem under discussion has a technical solution. A technical solution may be defined as one that requires a change only in the techniques of the natural

From *Managing the Commons* by Garrett Hardin and John Baden. Copyright © 1977 by W. H. Freeman and Company. Used with permission.

sciences, demanding little or nothing in the way of change in human values or ideas of morality.

In our day (though not in earlier times) technical solutions are always welcome. Because of previous failures in prophecy, it takes courage to assert that a desired technical solution is not possible. Wiesner and York exhibited this courage; publishing in a science journal, they insisted that the solution to the problem was not to be found in the natural sciences. They cautiously qualified their statement with the phrase, "It is our considered professional judgment. . . ." Whether they were right or not is not the concern of the present article. Rather, the concern here is with the important concept of a class of human problems which can be called "no technical solution problems," and more specifically, with the identification and discussion of one of these.

It is easy to show that the class is not a null class. Recall the game of tick-tack-toe. Consider the problem, "How can I win the game of tick-tack-toe?" It is well known that I cannot, if I assume (in keeping with the conventions of game theory) that my opponent understands the game perfectly. Put another way, there is no "technical solution" to the problem. I can win only by giving a radical meaning to the word "win"; I can hit my opponent over the head; or I can falsify the records. Every way in which I "win" involves, in some sense, an abandonment of the game, as we intuitively understand it. (I can also, of course, openly abandon the game and refuse to play it. This is what most adults do.)

The class of "no technical solution problems" has members. My thesis is that the "population problem," as conventionally conceived, is a member of this class. How it is conventionally conceived needs some comment. It is fair to say that most people who anguish over the population problem are trying to find a way to avoid the evils of overpopulation without relinquishing any of the privileges they now enjoy. They think that farming the seas or developing new strains of wheat will solve the problem—technologically. I try to show here that the solution they seek cannot be found. The population problem cannot be solved in a technical way, any more than can the problem of winning the game of tick-tack-toe.

What Shall We Maximize?

Population, as Malthus said, naturally tends to grow "geometrically," or, as we would now say, exponentially. In a finite world this means that the per-capita share of the world's goods must decrease. Is ours a finite world?

A fair defense can be put forward for the view that the world is infinite; or that we do not know that it is not. But, in terms of the practical problems that we must face in the next few generations with the foreseeable technology, it is clear that we will greatly increase human misery if we do not, during the immediate future, assume that the world available to the terrestrial human population is finite. "Space" is no escape.[2]

A finite world can support only a finite population; therefore, population growth must eventually equal zero. (The case of perpetual wide fluctuations above and below zero is a trivial variant that need not be discussed.) When this condition is met, what will be the situation of mankind? Specifically, can Bentham's goal of "the greatest good for the greatest number" be realized?

No—for two reasons, each sufficient by itself. The first is a theoretical one. It is not mathematically possible to maximize for two (or more) variables at the same time. This was clearly stated by von Neumann and Morgenstern,[3] but the principle is implicit in the theory of partial differential equations, dating back at least to D'Alembert (1717–1783).

The second reason springs directly from biological facts. To live, any organism must have a source of energy (for example, food). This energy is utilized for two purposes: mere maintenance and work. For man, maintenance of life requires about 1600 kilocalories a day ("maintenance calories"). Anything that he does over and above merely staying alive will be defined as work, and is supported by "work calories" which he takes in. Work calories are used not only for what we call work in common speech; they are also required for all forms of enjoyment, from swimming and automobile racing to playing music and writing poetry. If our goal is to maximize population it is obvious what we must do: We must make the work calories per person approach as close to zero as possible. No gourmet meals, no vacations, no sports, no music, no literature, no art.

. . . I think that everyone will grant, without argument or proof, that maximizing population does not maximize goods. Bentham's goal is impossible.

In reaching this conclusion I have made the usual assumption that it is the acquisition of energy that is the problem. The appearance of atomic energy has led some to question this assumption. However, given an infinite source of energy, population growth still produces an inescapable problem. The problem of the acquisition of energy is replaced by the problem of its dissipation, as J. H. Fremlin has so wittily shown.[4] The arithmetic signs in the analysis are, as it were, reversed; but Bentham's goal is unobtainable.

The optimum population is, then, less than the maximum. The difficulty of defining the optimum is enormous; so far as I know, no one has seriously tackled this problem. Reaching an acceptable and stable solution will surely require more than one generation of hard analytical work—and much persuasion.

We want the maximum good per person; but what is good? To one person it is wilderness, to another it is ski lodges for thousands. To one it is estuaries to nourish ducks for hunters to shoot; to another it is factory land. Comparing one good with another is, we usually say, impossible because goods are incommensurable. Incommensurables cannot be compared.

Theoretically this may be true; but in real life incommensurables are commensurable. Only a criterion of judgment and a system of weighting are needed. In nature the criterion is survival. Is it better for a species to be small and hideable, or large and powerful? Natural selection commensurates the incommensurables. The compromise achieved depends on a natural weighting of the values of the variables.

Man must imitate this process. There is no doubt that in fact he already does, but unconsciously. It is when the hidden decisions are made explicit that the arguments begin. The problem for the years ahead is to work out an acceptable theory of weighting. Synergistic effects, nonlinear variation, and difficulties in discounting the future make the intellectual problem difficult, but not (in principle) insoluble.

Has any cultural group solved this practical problem at the present time, even on an intuitive level? One simple fact proves that none has: there is no prosperous population in the world today that has, and has had for some time, a growth rate of zero. Any people that has intuitively identified its optimum point will soon reach it, after which its growth rate becomes and remains zero.

Of course, a positive growth rate might be taken as evidence that a population is below its optimum. However, by any reasonable standards, the most rapidly growing populations on earth today are (in general) the most miserable. This association (which need not be invariable) casts doubt on the optimistic assumption that the positive growth rate of a population is evidence that it has yet to reach its optimum.

We can make little progress in working toward optimum population size until we explicitly exorcise the spirit of Adam Smith in the field of practical demography. In economic affairs, *The Wealth of Nations* (1776) popularized the "invisible hand," the idea that an individual who "intends only his own gain," is, as it were, "led by an invisible hand to promote . . . the public interest."[5] Adam Smith did not assert that this was invariably true, and perhaps neither did any of his followers. But he contributed to a dominant tendency of thought that has ever since interfered with positive action based on rational analysis, namely, the tendency to assume that decisions reached individually will, in fact, be the best decisions for an entire society. If this assumption is correct it justifies the continuance of our present policy of laissez faire in reproduction. If it is correct we can assume that men will control their individual fecundity so as to produce the optimum population. If the assumption is not correct, we need to reexamine our individual freedoms to see which ones are defensible.

Tragedy of Freedom in a Commons

The rebuttal to the "invisible hand" in population control is to be found in a scenario first sketched in a little-known pamphlet in 1833 by a mathematical amateur named William Forster Lloyd (1794–1852).[6] We may well call it "the tragedy of the commons," using the word "tragedy" as the philosopher Whitehead[7] used it. "The essence of dramatic tragedy is not unhappiness. It resides in the solemnity of the remorseless working of things." He then goes on to say, "This inevitableness of destiny can only be illustrated in terms of human life by incidents which in fact involve unhappiness. For it is only by them that the futility of escape can be made evident in the drama."

The tragedy of the commons develops in this way. Picture a pasture open to all. It is to be expected that each herdsman will try to keep as many cattle as possible on the commons. Such an arrangement may work reasonably satisfactorily for centuries because tribal wars, poaching, and disease keep the numbers of both man and beast well below the carrying capacity of the land. Finally, however, comes the day of reckoning, that is, the day when the long-desired goal of social stability becomes a reality. At this point, the inherent logic of the commons remorselessly generates tragedy.

As a rational being, each herdsman seeks to maximize his gain. Explicitly or implicitly, more or less consciously, he asks, "What is the utility to me of adding one more animal to my herd?" This utility has one negative and one positive component.

1. The positive component is a function of the increment of one animal. Since the herdsman receives all the proceeds from the sale of the additional animal, the positive utility is nearly +1.

2. The negative component is a function of the additional overgrazing created by one more animal. Since, however, the effects of overgrazing are shared by all the herdsmen, the negative utility for any particular decision-making herdsman is only a fraction of –1.

Adding together the component partial utilities, the rational herdsman concludes that the only sensible course for him to pursue is to add another animal to his herd. And another. . . . But this is the conclusion reached by each and every rational herdsman sharing a commons. Therein is the tragedy. Each man is locked into a system that compels him to increase his herd without limit in a world that is limited. Ruin is the destination toward which all men rush, each pursuing his own best interest in a society that believes in the freedom of the commons. Freedom in a commons brings ruin to all.

Some would say that this is a platitude. Would that it were! In a sense, it was learned thousands of years ago, but natural selection favors the forces of psychological denial.[8] The individual benefits as an individual from his ability to deny the truth even though society as a whole, of which he is a part, suffers. Education can counteract the natural tendency to do the wrong thing, but the inexorable succession of generations requires that the basis for this knowledge be constantly refreshed.

A simple incident that occurred a few years ago in Leominster, Massachusetts, shows how perishable the knowledge is. During the Christmas shopping season the parking meters downtown were covered with plastic bags that bore tags reading: "Do not open until after Christmas. Free parking courtesy of the mayor and city council." In other words, facing the prospect of an increased demand for already scarce space, the city fathers reinstituted the system of the commons. (Cynically, we suspect that they gained more votes than they lost by this retrogressive act.)

In an approximate way, the logic of the commons has been understood for a long time, perhaps since the discovery of agriculture or the invention of private property in real estate. But it is understood mostly only in special cases which are not sufficiently generalized. Even at this late date, cattlemen leasing national land on the Western ranges demonstrate no more than an ambivalent understanding, in constantly pressuring federal authorities to increase the head count to the point where overgrazing produces erosion and weed-dominance. Likewise, the oceans of the world continue to suffer from the survival of the philosophy of the commons. Maritime nations still respond automatically to the shibboleth of the "freedom of the seas." Professing to believe in the "inexhaustible resources of the oceans," they bring species after species of fish and whales closer to extinction.[9]

The National Parks present another instance of the working out of the tragedy of the commons. At present, they are open to all, without limit. The parks themselves are limited in extent—there is only one Yosemite Valley—whereas population seems to grow without limit. The values that visitors seek in the parks are steadily eroded. Plainly, we must soon cease to treat the parks as commons or they will be of no value to anyone.

What shall we do? We have several options. We might sell them off as private property. We might keep them as public property, but allocate the right to enter them. The allocation might be on the basis of wealth, by the use of an auction system. It might be on the basis of merit, as defined by some agreed-upon standards. It might be by lottery. Or it might be on a first-come, first-served basis, administered to long queues. These, I think, are all objectionable. But we must choose—or acquiesce in the destruction of the commons that we call our National Parks.

Pollution

In a reverse way, the tragedy of the commons reappears in problems of pollution. Here it is not a question of taking something out of the commons, but of putting something in—sewage, or chemical, radioactive, and heat wastes into water; noxious and dangerous fumes into the air; and distracting and unpleasant advertising signs into the line of sight. The calculations of utility are much the same as before. The rational man finds that his share of the cost of the wastes he discharges into the commons is less than the cost of purifying his wastes before releasing them. Since this is true for everyone, we are locked into a system of "fouling our own nest," so long as we behave as independent, rational, free-enterprisers.

The tragedy of the commons as a food basket is averted by private property, or something formally like it. But the air and waters surrounding us cannot readily be fenced, and so the tragedy of the commons as a cesspool must be prevented by different means, by coercive laws or taxing devices that make it cheaper for the polluter to treat his pollutants than to discharge them untreated. We have not progressed as far with the solution of this problem as we have with the first. Indeed, our particular con-

cept of private property, which deters us from exhausting the positive resources of the earth, favors pollution. The owner of a factory on the bank of a stream—whose property extends to the middle of the stream—often has difficulty seeing why it is not his natural right to muddy the waters flowing past his door. The law, always behind the times, requires elaborate stitching and fitting to adapt it to this newly perceived aspect of the commons.

The pollution problem is a consequence of population. It did not much matter how a lonely American frontiersman disposed of his waste. "Flowing water purifies itself every ten miles," my grandfather used to say, and the myth was near enough to the truth when he was a boy, for there were not too many people. But as population became denser, the natural chemical and biological recycling processes became overloaded, calling for a redefinition of property rights.

How to Legislate Temperance

Analysis of the pollution problem as a function of population density uncovers a not generally recognized principle of morality, namely: *the morality of an act is a function of the state of the system at the time it is performed*.[10] Using the commons as a cesspool does not harm the general public under frontier conditions, because there is no public; the same behavior in a metropolis is unbearable. One hundred fifty years ago a plainsman could kill an American bison, cut out only the tongue for his dinner, and discard the rest of the animal. He was not in any important sense being wasteful. Today, with only a few thousand bison left, we would be appalled at such behavior.

In passing, it is worth noting that the morality of an act cannot be determined from a photograph. One does not know whether a man killing an elephant or setting fire to the grassland is harming others until one knows the total system in which his act appears. "One picture is worth a thousand words," said an ancient Chinese, but it may take ten thousand words to validate it. It is as tempting to ecologists as it is to reformers in general to try to persuade others by way of the photographic shortcut. But the essence of an argument cannot be photographed: it must be presented rationally—in words.

That morality is system-sensitive escaped the attention of most codifiers of ethics in the past. "Thou shalt not . . ." is the form of traditional ethical directives which make no allowance for particular circumstances. The laws of our society follow the pattern of ancient ethics, and therefore are poorly suited to governing a complex, crowded, changeable world. Our epicyclic solution is to augment statutory law with administrative law. Since it is practically impossible to spell out all the conditions under which it is safe to burn trash in the back yard or to run an automobile without smog-control, by law we delegate the details to bureaus. The result is administrative law, which is rightly feared for an ancient reason—*Quis custodiet ipsos custodes?*—Who shall watch the watchers themselves? John Adams said that we must have a "government of laws and not men." Bureau administrators, trying to evaluate the morality of acts in the total system, are singularly liable to corruption, producing a government by men, not laws.

Prohibition is easy to legislate (though not necessarily easy to enforce); but how do we legislate temperance? Experience indicates that it can be accomplished best through the mediation of administrative law. We limit possibilities unnecessarily if we suppose that the sentiment of *Quis custodiet* denies us the use of administrative law. We should rather retain the phrase as a perpetual reminder of fearful dangers we cannot avoid. The great challenge facing us now is to invent the corrective feedbacks that are needed to keep custodians honest. We must find ways to legitimate the needed authority of both the custodians and the corrective feedbacks.

Freedom to Breed Is Intolerable

The tragedy of the commons is involved in population problems in another way. In a world governed solely by the principle "dog eat dog"—if indeed there ever was such a world—how many children a family had would not be a matter of public concern. Parents who bred too exuberantly would leave fewer descendants, not more, because they would be unable to care adequately for their chil-

dren. David Lack and others have found that such a negative feedback demonstrably controls the fecundity of birds.[11] But men are not birds, and have not acted like them for millenniums, at least.

If each human family were dependent only on its own resources; *if* the children of improvident parents starved to death; *if,* thus, overbreeding brought its own "punishment" to the germ line— *then* there would be no public interest in controlling the breeding of families. But our society is deeply committed to the welfare state,[12] and hence is confronted with another aspect of the tragedy of the commons.

In a welfare state, how shall we deal with the family, the religion, the race, or the class (of indeed any distinguishable and cohesive group) that adopts overbreeding as a policy to secure its own aggrandizement?[13] To couple the concept of freedom to breed with the belief that everyone born has an equal right to the commons is to lock the world into a tragic course of action.

Unfortunately this is just the course of action that is being pursued by the United Nations. In late 1967, some thirty nations agreed to the following: "The Universal Declaration of Human Rights describes the family as the natural and fundamental unit of society. It follows that any choice and decision with regard to the size of the family must irrevocably rest with the family itself, and cannot be made by anyone else."[14]

It is painful to have to deny categorically the validity of this right; denying it, one feels as uncomfortable as a resident of Salem, Massachusetts, who denied the reality of witches in the seventeenth century. At the present time, in liberal quarters, something like a taboo acts to inhibit criticism of the United Nations. There is a feeling that the United Nations is "our last and best hope," that we shouldn't find fault with it; we shouldn't play into the hands of the arch conservatives. However, let us not forget what Robert Louis Stevenson said: "The truth that is suppressed by friends is the readiest weapon of the enemy." If we love the truth we must openly deny the validity of the Universal Declaration of Human Rights, even though it is promoted by the United Nations. We should also join with Kingsley Davis[15] in attempting to get Planned

Parenthood–World Population to see the error of its ways in embracing the same tragic ideal.

Conscience Is Self-Eliminating

It is a mistake to think that we can control the breeding of mankind in the long run by an appeal to conscience. Charles Galton Darwin made this point when he spoke on the centennial of the publication of his grandfather's great book. The argument is straightforward and Darwinian.

People vary. Confronted with appeals to limit breeding, some people will undoubtedly respond to the plea more than others. Those who have more children will produce a larger fraction of the next generation than those with more susceptible consciences. The differences will be accentuated, generation by generation.

In C. G. Darwin's words: "It may well be that it would take hundreds of generations for the progenitive instinct to develop in this way, but if it should do so, nature would have taken her revenge, and the variety *Homo Contracipiens* would become extinct and would be replaced by the variety *Homo progenitivus*."[16]

The argument assumes that conscience or the desire for children (no matter which) is hereditary—but hereditary only in the most general formal sense. The result will be the same whether the attitude is transmitted through germ cells, or exosomatically, to use A. J. Lotka's term. (If one denies the latter possibility as well as the former, then what's the point of education?) The argument has here been stated in the context of the population problem, but it applies equally well to any instance in which society appeals to an individual exploiting a commons to restrain himself for the general good—by means of his conscience. To make such an appeal is to set up a selective system that works toward the elimination of conscience from the race.

Pathogenic Effects of Conscience

The long-term disadvantage of an appeal to conscience should be enough to condemn it; but it has serious short-term disadvantages as well. If we ask a

man who is exploiting a commons to desist "in the name of conscience," what are we saying to him? What does he hear?—not only at the moment but also in the wee small hours of the night when, half asleep, he remembers not merely the words we used but also the nonverbal communication cues we gave him unawares? Sooner or later, consciously or subconsciously, he senses that he has received two communications, and that they are contradictory: 1. (intended communication) "If you don't do as we ask, we will openly condemn you for not acting like a responsible citizen"; 2. (the unintended communication) "If you *do* behave as we ask, we will secretly condemn you for a simpleton who can be shamed into standing aside while the rest of us exploit the commons."

Everyman then is caught in what Bateson has called a "double bind." Bateson and his co-workers have made a plausible case for viewing the double bind as an important causative factor in the genesis of schizophrenia.[17] The double bind may not always be so damaging, but it always endangers the mental health of anyone to whom it is applied. "A bad conscience," said Nietzsche, "is a kind of illness."

To conjure up a conscience in others is tempting to anyone who wishes to extend his control beyond the legal limits. Leaders at the highest level succumb to this temptation. Has any president during the past generation failed to call on labor unions to moderate voluntarily their demands for higher wages, or to steel companies to honor voluntary guidelines on prices? I can recall none. The rhetoric used on such occasions is designed to produce feelings of guilt in noncooperators.

For centuries it was assumed without proof that guilt was a valuable, perhaps even an indispensable, ingredient of the civilized life. Now, in this post-Freudian world, we doubt it.

Paul Goodman speaks from the modern point of view when he says: "No good has ever come from feeling guilty, neither intelligence, policy, nor compassion. The guilty do not pay attention to the object but only to themselves, and not even to their own interests, which might make sense, but to their anxieties."[18]

One does not have to be a professional psychiatrist to see the consequences of anxiety. We in the

Western world are just emerging from a dreadful two-centuries-long Dark Ages of Eros that was sustained partly by prohibition laws, but perhaps more effectively by the anxiety-generating mechanisms of education. Alex Comfort has told the story well in *The Anxiety Makers*;[19] it is not a pretty one.

Since proof is difficult, we may even concede that the results of anxiety may sometimes, from certain points of view, be desirable. The larger question we should ask is whether, as a matter of policy, we should ever encourage the use of a technique, the tendency (if not the intention) of which, is psychologically pathogenic. We hear much talk these days of responsible parenthood; the coupled words are incorporated into the titles of some organizations devoted to birth control. Some people have proposed massive propaganda campaigns to instill responsibility into the nation's (or the world's) breeders. But what is the meaning of the word conscience? When we use the word *responsibility* in the absence of substantial sanctions are we not trying to browbeat a free man in a commons into acting against his own interest? Responsibility is a verbal counterfeit for a substantial quid pro quo. It is an attempt to get something for nothing.

If the word responsibility is to be used at all, I suggest that it be in the sense Charles Frankel uses it.[20] "Responsibility," says this philosopher, "is the product of definite social arrangements." Notice that Frankel calls for social arrangements—not propaganda.

Mutual Coercion Mutually Agreed Upon

The social arrangements that produce responsibility are arrangements that create coercion, of some sort. Consider bank robbing. The man who takes money from a bank acts as if the bank were a commons. How do we prevent such action? Certainly not by trying to control his behavior solely by a verbal appeal to his sense of responsibility. Rather than rely on propaganda we follow Frankel's lead and insist that a bank is not a commons; we seek the definite social arrangements that will keep it

from becoming a commons. That we thereby infringe on the freedom of would-be robbers we neither deny nor regret.

The morality of bank robbing is particularly easy to understand because we accept complete prohibition of this activity. We are willing to say "Thou shalt not rob banks," without providing for exceptions. But temperance also can be created by coercion. Taxing is a good coercive device. To keep downtown shoppers temperate in their use of parking spaces we introduce parking meters for short periods, and traffic fines for longer ones. We need not actually forbid a citizen to park as long as he wants to; we need merely make it increasingly expensive for him to do so. Not prohibition, but carefully biased options are what we offer him. A Madison Avenue man might call this persuasion; I prefer the greater candor of the word *coercion*.

Coercion is a dirty word to most liberals now, but it need not forever be so. As with the four-letter words, its dirtiness can be cleansed away by exposure to the light, by saying it over and over without apology or embarrassment. To many, the word *coercion* implies arbitrary decisions of distant and irresponsible bureaucrats; but this is not a necessary part of its meaning. The only kind of coercion I recommend is mutual coercion, mutually agreed upon by the majority of the people affected.

To say that we mutually agree to coercion is not to say that we are required to enjoy it, or even to pretend we enjoy it. Who enjoys taxes? We all grumble about them. But we accept compulsory taxes because we recognize that voluntary taxes would favor the conscienceless. We institute and (grumblingly) support taxes and other coercive devices to escape the horror of the commons.

An alternative to the commons need not be perfectly just to be preferable. With real estate and other material goods, the alternative we have chosen is the institution of private property coupled with legal inheritance. Is this system perfectly just? As a genetically trained biologist I deny that it is. It seems to me that, if there are to be differences in individual inheritance, legal possession should be perfectly correlated with biological inheritance—that those who are biologically more fit to be the custodians of property and power should legally inherit more. But genetic recombination continually makes a mockery of the doctrine "like father, like son" implicit in our laws of legal inheritance. An idiot can inherit millions, and a trust fund can keep his estate intact. We must admit that our legal system of private property plus inheritance is unjust—but we put up with it because we are not convinced, at the moment, that anyone has invented a better system. The alternative of the commons is too horrifying to contemplate. Injustice is preferable to total ruin.

It is one of the peculiarities of the warfare between reform and the status quo that is thoughtlessly governed by a double standard. Whenever a reform measure is proposed it is often defeated when its opponents triumphantly discover a flaw in it. As Kingsley Davis has pointed out,[21] worshipers of the staus quo sometimes imply that no reform is possible without unanimous agreement, an implication contrary to historical fact. As nearly as I can make out, automatic rejection of proposed reforms is based on one of two unconscious assumptions: (1) that the status quo is perfect; or (2) that the choice we face is between reform and no action; if the proposed reform is imperfect, we presumably should take no action at all, while we wait for a perfect proposal.

But we can never do nothing. That which we have done for thousands of years is also action. It also produces evils. Once we are aware that the status quo is action, we can then compare its discoverable advantages and disadvantages with the predicted advantages and disadvantages of the proposed reform, discounting as best we can for our lack of experience. On the basis of such a comparison, we can make a rational decision which will not involve the unworkable assumption that only perfect systems are tolerable.

Recognition of Necessity

Perhaps the simplest summary of this analysis of man's population problems is this: the commons, if justifiable at all, is justifiable only under conditions of low-population density. As the human population has increased, the commons has had to be abandoned in one aspect after another.

First we abandoned the commons in food gathering, enclosing farm land and restricting pastures and hunting and fishing areas. These restrictions are still not complete throughout the world.

Somewhat later we saw that the commons as a place for waste disposal would also have to be abandoned. Restrictions on the disposal of domestic sewage are widely accepted in the Western world; we are still struggling to close the commons to pollution by automobiles, factories, insecticide sprayers, fertilizing operations, and atomic energy installations.

In a still more embryonic state is our recognition of the evils of the commons in matters of pleasure. There is almost no restriction on the propagation of sound waves in the public medium. The shopping public is assaulted with mindless music, without its consent. Our government has paid out billions of dollars to create a supersonic transport which would disturb 50,000 people for every one person whisked from coast to coast 3 hours faster. Advertisers muddy the airwaves of radio and television and pollute the view of travelers. We are a long way from outlawing the commons in matters of pleasure. Is this because our Puritan inheritance makes us view pleasure as something of a sin, and pain (that is, the pollution of advertising) as the sign of virtue?

Every new enclosure of the commons involves the infringement of somebody's personal liberty. Infringements made in the distant past are accepted because no contemporary complains of a loss. It is the newly proposed infringements that we vigorously oppose; cries of "rights" and "freedom" fill the air. But what does "freedom" mean? When men mutually agreed to pass laws against robbing, mankind became more free, not less so. Individuals locked into the logic of the commons are free only to bring on universal ruin; once they see the necessity of mutual coercion, they become free to pursue other goals. I believe it was Hegel who said, "Freedom is the recognition of necessity."

The most important aspect of necessity that we must now recognize is the necessity of abandoning the commons in breeding. No technical solution can rescue us from the misery of overpopulation. Freedom to breed will bring ruin to all. At the moment, to avoid hard decisions many of us are tempted to propagandize for conscience and responsible parenthood. The temptation must be resisted, because an appeal to independently acting consciences selects for the disappearance of all conscience in the long run, and an increase in anxiety in the short.

The only way we can preserve and nurture other and more precious freedoms is by relinquishing the freedom to breed, and that very soon. "Freedom is the recognition of necessity"—and it is the role of education to reveal to all the necessity of abandoning the freedom to breed. Only so, can we put an end to this aspect of the tragedy of the commons.

NOTES

1. J. B. Wiesner and H. F. York, *Scientific American* 211 (No. 4), 27 (1964).

2. G. Hardin, *Journal of Heredity* 50, 68 (1959); S. von Hoernor, *Science* 137, 18 (1962).

3. J. von Neumann and O. Morgenstern, *Theory of Games and Economic Behavior* (Princeton University Press, Princeton, N.J., 1947), p. 11.

4. J. H. Fremlin, *New Scientist*, No. 415 (1964), p. 285.

5. A. Smith, *The Wealth of Nations* (Modern Library, New York, 1937), p. 423.

6. W. F. Lloyd, *Two Lectures on the Checks to Population* (Oxford University Press, Oxford, England, 1833).

7. A. N. Whitehead, *Science and the Modern World* (Mentor, New York, 1948), p. 17.

8. G. Hardin, Ed., *Population, Evolution, and Birth Control* (Freeman, San Francisco, 1964), p. 56.

9. S. McVay, *Scientific American* 216 (No. 8). 13 (1966).

10. J. Fletcher, *Situation Ethics* (Westminster, Philadelphia, 1966).

11. D. Lack, *The Natural Regulation of Animal Numbers* (Clarendon Press, Oxford, England, 1954).

12. H. Girvetz, *From Wealth to Welfare* (Stanford University Press, Stanford, Calif., 1950).

13. G. Hardin, *Perspectives in Biology and Medicine* 6, 366 (1963).

14. U. Thant, *International Planned Parenthood News*, No. 168 (February 1968), p. 3.

15. K. Davis, *Science* 158, 730 (1967).

16. S. Tax, Ed., *Evolution After Darwin* (University of Chicago Press, Chicago, 1960), vol. 2, p. 469.

17. G. Bateson, D. D. Jackson, J. Haley, J. Weakland. *Behavioral Science* 1, 251 (1956).

18. P. Goodman, *New York Review of Books* 10 (8), 22 (23 May 1968).

19. A. Comfort, *The Anxiety Makers* (Nelson, London, 1967).

20. C. Frankel, *The Case for Modern Man* (Harper & Row, New York, 1955), p. 203.

21. J. D. Roslansky, *Genetics and the Future of Man* (Appleton-Century-Crofts, New York, 1966), p. 177.

II.14   KEVIN E. TRENBERTH

Stronger Evidence of Human Influence on Climate—The 2001 IPCC Assessment

It is not surprising to hear talk about the "crazy" or "strange" weather and how it seems to be so different than in the past. Even though most people have not done extensive research into the history of our planet's weather patterns, there seems to be general agreement that the weather is different than before. Although there is ample evidence that fluctuations in many factors related to weather have changed over the years, there is little agreement among scientists about whether those changes have been random or induced by humans.

There is no disagreement, however, about the fact that humans have always had an impact on their environment—beginning with our distant relatives fighting to survive in a hostile world to the present-day high levels of consumption of fossil fuels in many developed, affluent countries. Based on recent research, even the myth of the "noble savage" living in harmony with nature has come into question. Although there were certainly far fewer early humans in the ancient world than today, and their technological capabilities were limited, they left behind indicators of their negative impact on their surroundings, even though it was minimal compared to modern humans. Human environmental impact cannot be denied, although the link between humans and modification of the climate has not been proved.

Although the debate over global warming is not likely to be solved soon, many scientists are discussing a variety of issues related to that topic. The author of this article, Kevin Trenberth, head of the Climate Analysis Section, National Center for Atmospheric Research, feels that, given the level of technological power at our disposal today, it is critical that we carefully consider ways in which to responsibly deal with the mounting evidence that we have influenced the global climate. According to Trenberth, sophisticated analytical models indicate that the projected rates of climate change "exceed anything seen in nature for the past 10,000 years," a fact that should be of concern to not only scientists but all who call this planet home.

Focus Questions

1. What are some of the major factors and their sources that appear to influence climate change?
2. What climate conditions are mentioned by Trenberth, and how have they shifted over time?
3. Discuss the "greater climate system" and the various factors influencing it.
4. What role do "feedbacks" play in climate modification related to heating and cooling changes?

Keywords

CFCs, climate change, El Niño, feedbacks, global warming, greenhouse gases, hydrological cycle, IPCC, Kyoto Protocol, mean climate, natural climate variability, paleo-climate records, solar radiation

THE INTERGOVERNMENTAL PANEL ON CLIMATE Change (IPCC) reports on the evolving science of global climate change, focusing special attention on the ways in which human activities affect the climate. IPCC reviews the evidence for climate change and the possible causes and considers how the climate system responds to various agents of change. Because our climate models are simplified versions of the real world and are still being improved upon, IPCC evaluates the ability of models to describe the processes involved in the climate system and the functioning of the system as a whole. The panel seeks to attribute recent observed

From "Stronger Evidence of Human Influence on Climate," by Kevin E. Trenberth, *Environment Magazine, Vol. 43* (May, 2001), pp. 10–19. Reprinted with permission of the Helen Dwight Reid Educational Foundation. Published by Heldref Publications, 1319 Eighteenth St., N.W. Washington, D.C. 20036-1802. Copyright © 2001.

changes to possible causes, especially the human influences, and then, using climate models, projects future change from those causes.

Climate changes have occurred in the past naturally for various reasons, over periods ranging from decades to millennia. Fluctuations in the sun's energy output and other factors that influence the amount and fate of the energy that reaches the Earth's surface have caused natural climate change. And now, by greatly changing the composition of the atmosphere, humankind is performing an enormous geophysical experiment.[2] Human actions alter the Earth's environment in ways that cause climate change.[3] Legitimate debates go on about the extent and rate of change and what, if anything, can be done about it, but that the experiment is underway is not in doubt.

Land use (e.g., farming and building cities), storage and use of water (e.g., dams, reservoirs, and irrigation), generation of heat (e.g., furnaces), and the use of fossil fuels are the human-induced environmental changes that most influence the climate. The use of fossil fuels introduces visible particulate pollution (called aerosols) and gases such as carbon dioxide (CO_2) into the atmosphere, both of which alter the balance of radiation on Earth. These gases are relatively transparent to incoming solar radiation, yet they absorb and reemit outgoing infrared radiation. The resulting blanketing effect is known as the greenhouse effect, and the gases involved are called greenhouse gases. Not all greenhouse gases are the result of human activities. There is a large natural greenhouse effect that makes the Earth habitable. The increase in CO_2 levels over the last century or two from human activities, as well as the introduction of other greenhouse gases more recently, mean that more energy stays in the system. Global warming and the associated climate change are the expected results.

Observed Climate Change

Records of surface temperature show that a global mean warming of about 0.7°C has occurred over the past 100 years. IPCC reports this change as 0.6 ±0.2°C, but this is a linear fit to what is obviously not a linear trend. . . . Temperatures increased most noticeably from the 1920s to the 1940s; they then leveled off from the 1950s to the 1970s and took off again in the late 1970s. The 1990s mark the warmest decade on record, and 1998 is by far the warmest year on record, exceeding the previous record held by 1997. Preliminary annual global mean temperatures in the year 2000 were about the same as for 1999. Synthesis of information from tree rings, corals, ice cores, and historical data further indicates that the 1990s are the warmest decade in at least the past 1,000 years for the Northern Hemisphere, which is as far back as annual-resolution hemispheric estimates of temperatures can be made.[4] The melting of glaciers over most of the world and rising sea levels confirm the reality of the global temperature increases.

There is good evidence from measurements of sea level pressure, wind, and temperature over the twentieth century for decadal changes in the atmospheric circulation and some evidence for similar ocean changes. For instance, these include changes in winds over the North Atlantic and Europe related to the phenomenon known as the North Atlantic Oscillation and changes in El Niño.[5] Such observations signal that increases in temperature are not uniform or monotonic. For example, some places warm more than the average, while other places cool. Changes in precipitation and other components of the hydrological cycle also vary considerably geographically. For instance, it is likely that precipitation has increased by perhaps 1 percent per decade during the twentieth century over most mid- and high-latitude continents of the Northern Hemisphere. Changes in climate variability are also being seen and changes in extremes are beginning to emerge. Perhaps of greatest note are the observed increases in the heat index (which measures humidity and temperature effects on comfort) and the observed trend toward more intense precipitation events.

One persistent controversy in climate change science has been the discrepancy between the trend seen in the so-called satellite temperature record and that seen in the temperature record from the Earth's surface. The controversy stems in part from the fact that the two data sets do not measure the same phenomenon. The satellite record, which begins in 1979, measures microwave radiation from the lowest 8 kilometers of the Earth's atmosphere and thus depicts temperatures in that part of the atmosphere, which are quite different from those at the surface. Climate models that assess the scenario of increasing greenhouse gases suggest that warming in the lower atmosphere should be greater than that at the surface. But here is the point of contention for skeptics: The observed satellite record shows less warming from 1979–1999. Consequently, doubt has been cast on the veracity of both the surface temperature record and the models. However, when the observed stratospheric ozone depletion is included in the models, the models predict that the surface and tropospheric temperatures increase at about the same rate. In fact, this is what has happened from about 1960 to the present based on balloon observations, which replicate the satellite record after 1979. Because the satellite record includes only two decades, the influence of El Niño and the eruption of Mt. Pinatubo in 1991 leads to a disproportionate relative downward trend in temperatures observed in the lower atmosphere. Other effects, such as changes in cloud cover, have not been accounted for by the models and may also affect the two records differently. Accordingly, the different short-term trend in the satellite record is not at odds with the warming in the surface record.

The Climate System and Its Driving Forces

Because we humans live in and breathe the atmosphere, it is natural for us to focus on the atmospheric changes. But the atmosphere is only one element of a greater climate system that involves interactions among various internal components and external forcings. The internal, interactive components include the atmosphere, the oceans, sea ice, the land and its features (including the vegetation, albedo, biomass, and ecosystems), snow cover, land ice, and the hydrology of the land (including rivers, lakes, and surface and subsurface water). The factors that are normally regarded as external to the system include the sun and its output, the

Earth's rotation, sun-Earth geometry and the slowly changing orbit, the physical components of the Earth system such as the distribution of land and ocean, the topographic features on the land, the ocean-bottom topography and basin configurations, and the mass and basic composition of the atmosphere and the oceans. These factors determine the mean climate, which may vary from natural causes. Climate variations arise naturally when the atmosphere is influenced by and interacts with other internal components of the system and "external" forcings.

The continual flow of radiation from the sun provides the energy that drives the Earth's climate. About 31 percent of that radiation gets reflected back into space by molecules, tiny airborne particles (aerosols), clouds, or by the Earth's surface and thus plays no part in the climate. The sun's massive energy input leads to warming. To maintain a balance, the Earth radiates back into space, in the form of "long-wave" or infrared radiation, roughly the same amount of energy that it receives. The amount of radiation lost from the top of the atmosphere to space corresponds to a global mean surface temperature of about –19°C, much colder than the annual average global mean temperature of about 14°C. The higher mean temperature of the Earth, given the amount of energy radiated from its surface, can be explained by the existence of the atmosphere. The Earth's atmosphere intercepts the bulk of energy emitted at the surface and, in turn, reemits energy both toward space and back to the Earth. The energy that escapes into space is emitted from the tops of clouds at various atmospheric levels (which are almost always colder than the surface) or by atmospheric gases that absorb and emit infrared radiation. These greenhouse gases, notably water vapor and CO_2, produce a blanketing effect known as the natural greenhouse effect. Water vapor gives rise to about 60 percent of the current greenhouse effect and CO_2 accounts for about 26 percent.[6] Clouds also absorb and emit infrared radiation and have a blanketing effect similar to that of the greenhouse gases. But because clouds also reflect solar radiation, they act to cool the surface. Though on average the two opposing effects offset one another to a large degree, the net global effect of clouds in our current climate, as determined by space-based measurements, is a small cooling of the surface.

Human Influences

The amount of CO_2 in the atmosphere has increased by about 31 percent since the beginning of the Industrial Revolution, from 280 parts per million (ppm) by volume to 367 ppm. This increase is due mainly to combustion of fossil fuels and the removal of forests. Projections of future CO_2 concentrations suggest that, in the absence of controls, the rate of increase may accelerate and thus double the concentrations of CO_2 from pre-industrial levels within the next 50 to 100 years. Human activities (especially biomass burning; agriculture; animal husbandry; fossil fuel extraction, distillation, and use; and the creation of landfills and rice paddies) have increased the atmospheric concentrations of several other greenhouse gases (methane, nitrous oxide, chlorofluorocarbons [CFCs]) and tropospheric ozone. These other greenhouse gases tend to reinforce the changes caused by increased CO_2 levels. However, the observed decreases in lower stratospheric ozone since the 1970s, caused principally by human-introduced CFCs and halocarbons, contribute a small cooling effect.

Aerosols enter the atmosphere naturally when they are blown off the surface of deserts or dry regions, blasted into the atmosphere during volcanic eruptions, or released during forest fires. They impact climate in various ways. For instance, the aerosols introduced into the atmosphere during the eruption of Mt. Pinatubo in the Philippines in June 1991 blocked enough radiation for two years to cause observable cooling. Human activities contribute to aerosol particle formation mainly through emissions of sulfur dioxide (SO_2) (a major source of acid rain), particularly from coal-burning power stations and through biomass burning. Sulfate aerosols, visible as a milky, whitish haze from airplane windows, reflect a fraction of solar radiation back to space and hence work to cool the Earth's surface. Some aerosols, like soot, absorb solar radiation and lead to local warming of the atmosphere. Other aerosols absorb and reemit infrared radiation. Aerosols play still another role. By acting as the nuclei on which cloud droplets condense, they affect the number and size of droplets in a cloud and thereby alter the reflective and absorptive properties of clouds.[7] Aerosols from human activities are mostly introduced near the Earth's surface and are often washed out of the atmosphere by rain. They typically remain aloft for only a few days near their sources. Aerosols therefore have a very strong regional affect on the climate, usually producing cooling.

The determination of the climatic response to the changes in heating and cooling is complicated by feedbacks. Some of these feedbacks amplify the original warming (positive feedback) and others serve to reduce warming (negative feedback). If, for instance, the amount of CO_2 in the atmosphere were suddenly doubled while all other factors remained constant, the amount of energy absorbed by the atmosphere would increase. With additional energy trapped in the system, a new balance would have to be reached. To accomplish this balance the atmosphere would have to warm up. In the absence of other changes, the warming at the surface and throughout the troposphere would be about $1.2°C$.[8] In reality, many other factors could change as a result of doubled CO_2 concentrations, and various feedbacks would come into play. When the positive and negative feedbacks are considered, the best IPCC estimate of the average global warming for doubled CO_2 is $2.5°C$. The net effect of the feedbacks is positive and, in fact, roughly doubles the global mean temperature increase otherwise expected. Increases in water vapor that accompany warming contribute the strongest positive feedback.

Modeling of Climate Change

To quantify the response of the climate system to changes in forcing, the complex interactions and feedbacks among the components must be accounted for. . . . Numerical models of the climate system based upon sound, well-established physical principles are the tools used to estimate climate change. Experiments can be run with climate models in which concentrations of greenhouse gases or other influences, like aerosols, are varied. The best models capture the current understanding of the physical processes involved in the climate system, the interactions among the processes, and the performance of the system as a whole. The predictive powers of a model can be tested by running the model with known forcings from the past through it and then comparing the results to actual climate records. Though models are exceedingly useful tools for carrying out numerical climate experiments, they do have limitations and must be used carefully.[9] The latest models have been able to reproduce the climate of the past century or so with increasing accuracy. . . . Thus the global mean temperature record is well replicated within limits imposed by natural fluctuations merely by specifying the changes in atmospheric composition and changes in the sun.

Detection and Attribution

Two main issues that must be settled before politicians are likely to take action: First, it must be discerned whether the recent climate has changed more than expected from natural variability; second, observed climate changes must be attributed to various causes, including human influences. Several key points that emerged from the recent IPCC assessment address these issues:

- The magnitude and rate of change of mean surface temperature globally, or at least in the Northern Hemisphere, over the past few decades is outside the range of anything deduced from paleo-climate records of the last 1,000 years. Data are inadequate before that.
- Estimates of internal climate variability (how much climate can vary from natural causes not including changes in the sun) derived from models are reasonably consistent with the pre-industrial variability deduced from paleo-climate data. Together, the estimates from model and paleo-climate observations provide more reliable estimates of the natural variability.
- Consequently, given the better sense of natural climate variability, detection of climate change is much clearer now than it was five years ago.

Hence, it is very unlikely that recent climate change is natural in origin.
- The natural forcing agents (e.g., solar and volcanoes) over the last two to four decades are likely to have had a net cooling effect and, thus, cannot be a cause of the recent increase in temperature.
- A combination of internal climate variability, natural forcing, and perhaps small anthropogenic forcing can account for the increases in the observed globally averaged surface temperature up until about 1970. Increases in solar radiation may account, in part (perhaps 0.15 to 0.2°C), for the warming between about 1920 and 1940, even though solar changes are poorly known before 1979 when satellite observations began. . . . However, it is also probable that a natural component related to changes in North Atlantic Ocean circulation may have played a role.
- The rate and magnitude of the warming over the last few decades cannot be explained unless the net human influence is one of warming over the last 30 years. Uncertainties in cooling by aerosol forcing (especially the effects on clouds) are therefore constrained.
- The nearer the "balance" or the offset between positive anthropogenic greenhouse gas forcing and negative anthropogenic aerosol forcing over the last 50 years, the larger the climate responsiveness needs to be to explain warming over recent decades. For instance, if the net warming is small, the climate system must be quite sensitive to that warming to produce the observed temperature change. But if the warming is larger, the climate system must be less sensitive to produce the same temperature change. This has implications for future predictions.

The line of argument shown by these points is open to the criticism that there is some circular reasoning involved. The objective of attributing climate change to specific causes is to account for the change in temperature, but the temperature change itself is invoked as part of the argument. Ideally, only the knowledge of forcings and responsiveness of the system, as given by models, are used to replicate the observed temperature. Neither the forcings nor the true sensitivity of the systems are known well enough to proceed in this manner. Climate modelers attempt to avoid such a trap by basing their models on sound physical principles. However, many parameters have to be chosen when developing models. Although the choices are based on knowledge of the processes, and the parameters are physically based, there is ample scope for unintentional tuning. For example, the brightness of clouds depends on the size and number of cloud droplets but varies from cloud to cloud and is not known well. Choice of a particular value for the model clouds may compensate for shortcomings in the amount of clouds in the model. Inevitably, running a model with two different sets of parameters yields different results, and the set that brings the model into best agreement with observations is chosen for further use in the model. It is important, therefore, to recognize that the procedure is not as objective as it might appear and that uncertainties remain.

The most contentious section in the *Summary for Policy Makers* proved to be the concluding paragraph on attribution. After much debate, a carefully crafted statement was agreed upon: "In the light of new evidence, and taking into account the remaining uncertainties, most of the observed warming over the last 50 years is likely to have been due to the increase in greenhouse gas concentrations." Moreover, although not highlighted by IPCC, increasing evidence suggests that the signal of human influence on climate emerged from the noise of natural variability in about 1980 and will only get larger.

The implications of these findings may be felt in the near future. The models predict that global temperature increases of 0.1 to 0.2°C over the next decade are likely unless volcanic eruptions interfere.[10] Time will tell whether the assessment is correct, perhaps within a decade.

Prediction of Climate Change

Climate models have been used to project the effects of future global warming to the year 2100. Because human activities are not predictable in any deterministic sense, "predictions" based on human influences necessarily contain a "what if" emissions scenario. IPCC presumes that these predictions will be used for planning purposes, including actions to prevent undesirable outcomes, consistent with the Framework Convention on Climate Change. Such actions, which are a consequence of the prediction, may change the outcome and thus make the prediction wrong. Accordingly, they are not truly predictions but rather projections that are tied to particular emissions scenarios. This is an important point, because some skeptics have ignored the distinction and misused it to challenge findings. For example, in 1990, only scenarios with increasing greenhouse gases were used. Then, in 1995, the first primitive scenarios with aerosols were included, which produced a cooling. Some skeptics, pointing to this difference, claimed that the models had changed and were therefore suspect, when, in fact, it was the scenarios that had changed, not the models. In addition, for a given scenario, the rate of temperature increase depends on the model used and how, for instance, the model depicts features such as clouds. It is for this reason that a range of possible outcomes exists. About half of the spread in range of values at 2100 is due to uncertainties in models. The spread in values is unrelated to the scenarios and should not be considered as representative of anything real. The rest of the spread in range can be accounted for by the different scenarios.

In 2001, the future emissions scenarios were set up by the *Special Report on Emissions Scenarios* (SRES)[11] . . . and included 35 scenarios. . . . For each emissions scenario, IPCC calculates expected concentrations of CO_2. In the year 2100, the projected values range from about 550 ppm to almost 1,000 ppm, compared with 367 ppm at present. . . . When the range of uncertainties is factored in and the projections for 2100 across all 35 scenarios are analyzed, there is an increase in the global mean temperature from 1.4°C to 5.8°C. . . . Most increases fall between 2°C to 4°C. These numbers exceed those in the 1995 IPCC report, which showed temperature changes ranging from about 1°C to 3.5°C.[12] The increase is higher mainly because the new emissions scenarios include lower sulfur emissions (which are likely to be reduced for air quality reasons). The 35 scenarios also expand the range of possibilities from the last report and contribute to the range in temperature projected in 2100. Modifications in carbon cycle models that convert emissions to concentrations and in climate models account for less than 20 percent of the deviation between the 1995 IPCC report and this year's report and thus do not account for much change in the range.

. . . Because heat penetrates slowly into the voluminous oceans, sea-level rise is expected to be manifested over a longer period of time than temperature change. Because the heat inputs that have already occurred will only work their way through the system slowly, even in the unlikely scenario of a massive reduction in greenhouse gas emissions, sea-level rise will continue unabated. Note again that though these projections include crude estimates of the effects of sulfate aerosol, they deliberately omit other possible human influences, such as changes in land use.[13] A major concern is that the projected rates of climate change . . . exceed anything seen in nature in the past 10,000 years.

An increase in global mean temperature logically follows increased heating. But temperature increase, often thought of as the sole indicator of "global warming," is not the only possible outcome. For example, rising concentrations of greenhouse gases enhance the hydrological cycle by furnishing additional energy for evaporation of surface moisture. Because the water-holding capacity of the atmosphere is greater at higher temperatures, increased atmospheric moisture should accompany global temperature increases. Because water vapor is also a powerful greenhouse gas, it contributes a strong positive feedback, amplifying global warming. Naturally occurring droughts are also liable to be exacerbated by enhanced drying. Thus droughts, such as those set up by El Niño, are likely to take hold more quickly, wilt plants sooner, and become more extensive and longer-lasting with global warming. When the land is dry, the energy that would ordinarily drive the hydrological cycle goes into raising temperatures, bringing on sweltering heat waves. Further, globally there will have to be an increase in precipitation to balance the enhanced evaporation. More moisture in the atmosphere implies stronger moisture flow converging into all

precipitating weather systems—such as thunderstorms or extratropical rain or snow storms—and rain or snow events of greater intensity.[14]

For any change in mean climate, there is likely to be an amplified change in extremes. Because of the wide range of natural variability associated with day-to-day weather, most small climate changes will probably go unnoticed; the extremes, however, will be easily detected. Extremes play an exceedingly important role for natural and human systems and infrastructure. All living organisms are adapted to a range of natural weather variations. New extremes could be devastating to ecosystems. Extremes that exceed tolerances of a system can cause nonlinear effects: the so-called "straw that breaks the camel's back." For instance, floods that historically have had an expected return period of 100 years may now recur in 50 or 30 years.[15] More frequent extreme floods may overstress dams and levees, causing breaks and the consequent damage to infrastructure, loss of human life, and contamination of drinking water.

The changes in extremes of weather and climate observed to date have only recently been compared to the changes projected by models, many of which agree with recent observed trends. Models project that higher maximum temperatures, more hot days, and more heat waves are all likely. The largest temperature increases are expected mainly in areas where soil moisture decreases are apt to occur. Increases of daily minimum temperatures are projected to occur over most land areas and are generally larger where snow and ice retreat. A decreased number of frost days and cold waves is likely. Changes in surface air temperature and surface humidity will mean increases in the heat index and increased discomfort. Increases in surface air temperature will lead to a greater number of days during which cooling (such as from air conditioning) might be considered desirable for comfort and fewer days during which space heating is required for comfort. Precipitation extremes are expected to increase more than the mean, as will the frequency of extreme precipitation events. A general drying is projected for the midcontinental areas during summer, as a result of higher temperatures and increased drying not offset by increased precipitation in these regions. Theoretical and modeling studies project increases in the upper limit of intensity of tropical cyclones in addition to appreciable increases in their average and peak precipitation intensities. Changes in El Niño are also likely, but their nature is quite uncertain.[16]

Humans Are Changing the Climate

In 1995, the IPCC assessment concluded that "the balance of evidence suggests a discernible human influence on global climate."[17] Since then the evidence has become much stronger—the recent record warmth of the 1990s, the historical context provided by the improved paleo-record, improved modeling and simulation of the past climate, and improved statistical analysis. Thus the headline in the new IPCC report states, "There is new and stronger evidence that most of the warming observed over the last 50 years is attributable to human activities."[18] The best assessment of global warming is that the human contribution to climate change first emerged from the noise of background variability in the late 1970s. Hence, climate change is expected to continue into the future. The amplification of extremes is likely to cause the greatest impact. Although some changes arising from global warning may be benign or even beneficial, the economic effects of more extreme weather will be substantial and clearly warrant attention in policy debates.

Because of the long lifetime of CO_2 in the atmosphere and the slow heat penetration and equilibration of the oceans, there is already a substantial commitment to further global climate change, even in the absence of further emissions of greenhouse gases. IPCC considered implications for stabilizing CO_2 and greenhouse gases at various concentrations up to four times pre-industrial levels and concluded that substantial reductions in emissions, well below current levels, would be required sooner or later in all cases. Even full implementation of the Kyoto Protocol would merely slow the time of doubling of CO_2 concentrations from pre-industrial values by perhaps 15 years (for instance

from 2060 to 2075).[19] Moreover, these projections emphasize that even stabilizing concentrations would not stop climate change because of the slow response of the system; for this reason, temperature increases and especially sea-level rise would continue for many decades thereafter. As we begin to understand that our geophysical experiment might turn out badly, we are also discovering that it cannot be turned off abruptly.

The IPCC report provides the evidence that global warming is happening and now the question arises, *What, if anything, should be done about these findings?* The options include: do nothing, mitigate or stop the problem, adapt to the changes as they happen, or find some combination of these options. Different value systems come into play in deciding how to proceed. Considerations include those of population growth, equity among developed and developing countries, intergenerational equity, stewardship of the planet, and the precautionary principle ("better to be safe than sorry"). Those with vested interests in the current situation frequently favor the first option, extreme environmentalists favor the second, and those who have a belief that technology can solve all problems might favor the third. In rationally discussing options, it is helpful to recognize the legitimacy of these different points of view. This problem is truly a global one because the atmosphere is a global commons. These immense problems cannot be solved by one nation acting alone. Unfortunately, to date, international progress toward mitigating and preparing for the possible outcomes of global warming is inadequate.

The evidence presented by the IPCC report suggests that there is a strong case for slowing down the projected rates of climate change caused by human influences. Any climate change scenario is fraught with uncertainties. But a slowing in the warming process would allow researchers to improve projections of climate change and its impacts. Actions taken to slow down climate change would provide time to better prepare for and adapt to the changes as they appear. Natural systems and human systems, many of which have long amortization lifetimes (e.g., power stations, dams, and buildings), are then less likely to be dislocated or become obsolete quickly. Therefore, we must plan ahead. Greater energy efficiency and expanding use of renewable resources, such as solar power, are clearly key steps toward slowing the rate of climate change.

NOTES

1. IPCC, *Climate Change 2001: The Scientific Basis,* J. T. Houghton et al., eds. (Cambridge, U.K.: Cambridge University Press. 2001) (in press).

2. R. Revelle and H. E. Suess, "Carbon Dioxide Exchange between Atmosphere and Ocean and Question of an Increase of Atmospheric CO_2 during the Past Decades." *Tellus* 9 (1957): 18–27.

3. F. S. Rowland, "Climate Change and Its Consequences: Issues for the New U.S. Administration," *Environment,* March 2001, 28–34.

4. Reconstructions of temperature and rainfall make use of multiple proxy indicators at individual sites around the world but have to be merged, reconciled, and combined to give regional and larger area averages. Sufficient data with annual resolution now exist to do this for the Northern Hemisphere for the past 1,000 years but not for the Southern Hemisphere or for beyond the past millennium. See M. E. Mann, R. S. Bradley, and M. K. Hughes, "Global-scale Temperature Patterns and Climate Forcing over the Past Six Centuries," *Nature* 392, 23 April 1998, 779–87; and M. E. Mann, R. S. Bradley, and M. K. Hughes, "Northern Hemisphere Temperatures during the Past Millennium: Inferences, Uncertainties, and Limitations," *Geophysical Research Letters* 26 (1999): 759–62.

5. J. W. Hurrell, "1995: Decadal Trends in the North Atlantic Oscillation Regional Temperatures and Precipitation," *Science* 269 (1995): 676–9; K. E. Trenberth and T. J. Hoar, "The 1990–1995 El Niño-Southern Oscillation Event: Longest on Record," *Geophysical Research Letters* 23 (1996): 57–60; and K. E. Trenberth and T. J. Hoar, "El Niño and Climate Change," *Geophysical Research Letters* 24 (1997): 3057–60.

6. J. T. Kiehl and K. E. Trenberth, "Earth's Annual Global Mean Energy Budget," *Bulletin of the American Meteorological Society* 78 (1997): 197–208.

7. Recent evidence highlights the possible importance of this effect, although the magnitude is very uncertain. See J. M. Hansen, M. Sato, A. Lacis, and R. Ruedy, "The Missing Climate Forcing," *Philosophical Transactions of the Royal Society of London* 352 (1997): 231–40.

8. K. E. Trenberth, J. T. Houghton, and L. G. Meira Filho, "The Climate System: An Overview," in J. T. Houghton et al., eds., *Climate Change 1995: The Science of Climate Change* (Cambridge, U.K.: Cambridge University Press, 1996), 51–64.

9. K. E. Trenberth, "The Use and Abuse of Climate Models in Climate Change Research," *Nature* 386, 13 March 1997, 131–33.

10. IPCC, note 1 above.

11. IPCC, *Special Report on Emissions Scenarios, Summary for Policy Makers* (2000).

12. IPCC, *Climate Change 1995: The Science of Climate Change,* J. T. Houghton et al., eds. (Cambridge, U.K.: Cambridge University Press, 1996). For a review of the second IPCC assessment, see *Climate Change 1995: The Science of Climate Change,* reviewed by W. C. Clark and J. Jälger, *Environment,* November 1997, 23–8; *Climate Change 1995: Impacts, Adaptations, and Mitigation,* reviewed by R. W. Kates, *Environment,* November 1997, 29–33; and *Climate Change 1995: Economic and Social Dimensions,* reviewed by T. O'Riordan, *Environment,* November 1997, 34–39.

13. It is estimated that conversion from forests to agriculture in the United States makes the surface much brighter, especially in the late summer and fall after crops are harvested. This means more solar radiation is reflected, which results in cooling.

14. K. E. Trenberth, "Atmospheric Moisture Residence Times and Cycling: Implications for Rainfall Rates with Climate Change," *Climatic Change* 39 (1998): 667–94.

15. K. E. Trenberth, "The Extreme Weather Events of 1997 and 1998," *Consequences* 5 (1999): 2–15.

16. The 1997–1998 El Niño is the biggest recorded event by several measures. The last two decades have been marked by unusual El Niño activity. See Trenberth and Hoar, 1996 and 1997, note 5 above. A key question is how is global warming influencing El Niño? Because El Niño is involved with movement of heat in the tropical Pacific Ocean, it is conceptually easy to see how increased heating from the build up of greenhouse gases might interfere. Climate models certainly show changes with

global warming, but none simulate El Niño with sufficient fidelity to have confidence in the results. So the question of how El Niño may change with global warming is a current research topic.

17. Trenberth, note 14 above.

18. IPCC, note 1 above.
19. T. M. L. Wigley, "The Kyoto Protocol: CO_2 [CH_4] and Climate Implications," *Geophysical Research Letters* 25 (1998): 2285–8.

II.15   LESTER R. BROWN AND CHRISTOPHER FLAVIN

A New Economy for a New Century

As the president and senior vice-president respectively of the Worldwatch Institute, a Washington, DC-based research group concerned with environmental issues, the authors of this article have considered many ways in which human actions threaten both our lives and the planet on which we live. Even though many people have the optimistic view that technology can solve all of our problems, there is evidence that our recently integrated world economy often behaves in ways not in the best interest of the environment.

Unlike our present economic system, one that is environmentally sustainable ensures that the science of ecology is as important as the traditional sciences that are employed in the business world. Even though there is widespread faith in technology, the authors are concerned that the massive changes that have taken place in the past century, including the move to a market-driven world economy, are placing demands on our environment and its resources that cannot be continued into the future. Increasing requirements for energy, food, building materials, and space, all characteristics of the globalization process, must be rethought if major problems are to be avoided.

Until the terrorist attacks against the United States on September 11, 2001, there were some indications of economic problems on the horizon, although most believed that the economies of many if not all countries would continue to grow, perhaps at an even faster rate than previously. Those who proposed a more-careful approach to future development were often either ignored or derided as "techno-pessimists," running around warning that "the sky is falling."

Brown and Flavin remind us that our future depends totally on the state of the natural world, and it is in everyone's best interests to operate in a way that recognizes that subordination rather than attempting to bend nature to our will, regardless of the long-range cost. The global economy is of paramount concern to many, but its health should not be placed before that of the environment.

Focus Questions

1. What relationships do the authors see between the economy and the environment, and why do they feel these are important?
2. Give some examples of the "acceleration of history" and why we should be concerned about this phenomenon.
3. What impact is the global economy placing on our eco-system, and how might it be mitigated?

4. How do the points made in this article relate to the concept of environmental steward-ship presented by Hardin (selection II.13)?

Keywords

economy, environmental deterioration, environmental limits, environmentally sustain-able, human rights, integrated world economy, rich-poor gap, social cohesion, throwaway economy

IN THE 1890S, THE AMERICAN PRESS ASSOCIATION brought together the country's "best minds" to ex-plore the shape of things to come in the twentieth century. As they looked ahead, the country's "futur-ists" were almost universally optimistic. Among the predictions that have held up well are the wide-spread use of electricity and telephones, the open-ing of the entire world to trade, and the emancipa-tion of women.

Other forecasts proved to be naïve, including the notion that people would live to be 150 and that air pollution would be eliminated. The dark sides of the twentieth century—two world wars, the de-velopment of chemical and nuclear weapons, the emergence of global threats to the stability of the natural world, and a billion people struggling just to survive—were predicted by no one.

Today, as compared to a century ago, faith in technology and human progress is almost as preva-lent in the writings of leading economic com-mentators. Their easy optimism is bolstered by the extraordinary achievements of the twentieth cen-tury—including developments such as jet aircraft, personal computers, and genetic engineering—that go well beyond anything predicted by the most imaginative futurists of the 1890s.

But like their predecessors, today's futurists look ahead from a narrow perspective—one that ignores some of the most important trends now shaping our world. And in their fascination with the Infor-mation Age, many observers seem to have forgotten that our modern civilization, like its forerunners, is totally dependent on its ecological foundations.

Overcoming Adversity

Since our emergence as a species, human popula-tions have continually run up against local environ-mental limits: the inability to find sufficient game, grow enough food, or harvest enough wood has led to sudden collapses in human numbers and, in some cases, to the disappearance of entire civilizations. Al-though it may seem that advancing technology and the emergence of an integrated world economy have ended this age-old pattern, they may have simply transferred the problem to the global level.

Oceanic fisheries, for example, are being pushed to their limits and beyond, water tables are falling on every continent, rangelands are deteriorating from overgrazing, many remaining tropical forests are on the verge of being wiped out, and carbon dioxide concentrations in the atmosphere have reached the highest level in 160,000 years. If these trends continue, they could make the turning of the millennium seem trivial as a historic moment, for they may be triggering the largest extinction of life since a meteorite wiped out the dinosaurs some 65 million years ago.

The Western economic model—the fossil-fuel-based, automobile-centered, throwaway econ-omy—that so dramatically raised living standards for part of humanity during this century is in trou-ble. If it were to become the global model, and if world population were to reach ten billion during the next century, as the United Nations projects, the effect would be startling.

Source: Worldwatch Institute, State of the World 1999, copy-right 2002, www.worldwatch.org.

If in 2050, for example, the world has one car for every two people, as in the United States today, there would be five billion cars. Given the congestion, pollution, and the fuel, material, and land requirements of the current global fleet of 501 million cars, a global fleet of five billion is difficult to imagine. If petroleum use per person were to reach the current U.S. level, the world would consume 360 million barrels per day, compared with current production of 67 million barrels.

Or consider a world of ten billion with everyone following an American diet, centered on the consumption of fat-rich livestock products. Ten billion people would require nine billion tons of grain, the harvest of more than four planets at Earth's current output levels. With massive irrigation-water cutbacks in prospect as aquifers are depleted, and with the dramatic slowdown in the rise in land productivity since 1990, achieving even relatively modest gains is becoming difficult.

An economy is environmentally sustainable only if it satisfies the principles of sustainability—principles that are rooted in the science of ecology. In a sustainable economy, the fish catch doesn't exceed the sustainable yield of fisheries, the amount of water pumped from underground aquifers doesn't exceed aquifer recharge, soil erosion doesn't exceed the natural rate of new soil formation, tree cutting doesn't exceed tree planting, and carbon emissions don't exceed the capacity of nature to fix atmospheric carbon dioxide. A sustainable economy doesn't destroy plant and animal species faster than new ones evolve.

We are entering a new century, then, with an economy that cannot take us where we want to go. The challenge is to design and build a new one that can sustain human progress without destroying its support systems—and that offers a better life to all. The shift to an environmentally sustainable economy may be as profound a transition as was the Industrial Revolution that led to the current dilemma.

The Acceleration of History

Although the specific turning point that will be observed on January 1, 2000, is a purely human creation, flowing from the calendar introduced by Julius Caesar in 45 BCE, the three zeros that will appear on that day are powerful reminders of the passage of time—of how the pace of change has accelerated since the last such turning point, in the Middle Ages. The sweeping developments in the past century have all occurred in a period that represents just 1 percent of the time since humans first practiced agriculture.

The accelerating pace of change can be seen in virtually every field of human activity. In many ways, however, the defining economic development of this century is the harnessing of the energy in fossil fuels. In 1900, only a few thousand barrels of oil were used daily. By 1997, that figure had reached 72 million barrels.

We have also seen a vast increase in the use of materials, including growth in the use of metals from 20 million tons annually to 1.2 billion tons. The use of paper increased six times from 1950 to 1996, reaching 281 million tons. Production of plastics, largely unheard of in 1900, reached 131 million tons in 1995. The human economy now draws on all ninety-two naturally occurring elements in the periodic chart, compared with just twenty in 1900.

Among the most obvious accelerating trends is the increase in human mobility—a development the forecasters in the 1890s didn't anticipate. In 1900 there were only a few thousand automobiles in use worldwide; today there are 501 million. During the first half of this century, we went from the pioneering flight by the Wright Brothers in 1903 at Kitty Hawk, North Carolina, to jet aircraft that could fly faster than sound.

Engineers built the first electronic computers in 1946; in 1949, *Popular Mechanics* predicted that "computers in the future may have only 1,000 tubes and perhaps weigh only one and a half tons." Today, the average five-pound laptop computer can process data faster than the largest mainframes available at mid-century.

The explosive growth of the Internet—expanding from 376,000 host computers in 1990 to more than 30 million in 1998—has far surpassed the growth of heavy industry during its heyday. In the United States, an important threshold was crossed recently when the market capitalization of Microsoft passed that of General Motors, signifying the dominance of a new generation of technology. The number of telephone lines leapt from 89 million in 1960 to 742 million in 1996, while cellular phone subscribers rose from ten million in 1990 to 135 million in 1996. At the end of 1998, the world's first affordable satellite telephones went on the market, bringing the world's most remote regions into the ubiquitous information web. And the number of households with televisions went from four million in 1950 to just under one billion as the century closes, bringing the latest news and cultural trends to a global community. One outgrowth of the Information Age is what *Economist* editor Frances Cairncross describes as "the death of distance."

Aside from the growth of population itself, urbanization is the dominant demographic trend of the century now ending. In 1900, some sixteen cities had a million people or more and roughly 10 percent of humanity lived in cities. Today, 326 cities have at least that many people and there are fourteen megacities—those with ten million or more residents. If cities continue to grow as projected, more than half of us will be living in them by 2010, making the world more urban than rural for the first time in history.

Our growing population has required ever greater quantities of food, and growing incomes have led many societies to diversify and enrich their diets. These burgeoning food demands have been met by a continuing proliferation of new technologies, including the development of more productive crop varieties, the expanded use of fertilizer and irrigation, and the mechanization of agriculture. Grain use has increased nearly fivefold since the century began, while water use has quadrupled.

On the darker side, the twentieth century has also been the most violent in human history, thanks in part to technological "advances" such as airplanes and automatic weapons. Some 26 million people were killed in World War I; 53 million in World War II. Combined with other war deaths since the century began, the total surpasses the war casualty figure from the beginning of civilization until 1900.

Another major change that distinguishes the twentieth century is globalization—the vast economic and information webs that now tie together disparate parts of the world. By 10,000 years ago, our ancestors migrating out of Africa had settled not only the vast Eurasian continent but the Americas, Australia, and other remote corners of the world. It took most of the time since then, until the European Age of Exploration in the 1500s, for the world's distant peoples to be brought into more immediate contact with one another. And it was not until late in the nineteenth century that the development of steam-powered ships dramatically increased international trade. World trade has grown from $380 billion in 1950 to $5.86 trillion in 1997—a fifteenfold increase.

With the acceleration of history has come escalating pressures on the natural world—on which we remain utterly dependent, even in the Information Age. History will undoubtedly continue to accelerate, but if our descendants are to prosper, historical trends will have to move in a new direction early in the twenty-first century.

Rethinking Progress

As we approach the new millennium, many respected thinkers seem to believe that we are in for a period of inevitable economic and technological progress. Even the recent economic crisis that has spread misery from Indonesia to Russia is seen as a brief pause in an unending upward climb for *Homo sapiens.*

In a special double issue on the economy in the twenty-first century, *Business Week* ran a headline proclaiming, "You Ain't Seen Nothing Yet," forecasting even faster rates of economic progress in the century ahead. The magazine's editors expect the global economy to ride a wave of technology in the decades to come, solving all manner of social problems, as well as adding to the investment portfolios of its readers.

This view of the future, fueled by heady advances in technology, is particularly prevalent in the information industry. It reflects a new conception of the human species, one in which human societies are seen as free of dependence on the natural world. Our information-based economy is thought capable of evolving independently of the Earth's ecosystem.

The complacency reflected in this view overlooks our continued dependence on the natural world and the profound vulnerabilities this represents. It concentrates on economic indicators while largely overlooking the environmental indicators that measure the Earth's physical deterioration. This view is dangerous because it threatens to discourage the restructuring of the economy needed if economic progress is to continue.

If we are to build an environmentally sustainable economy, we have to go beyond traditional economic indicators of progress. If we put a computer in every home in the next century but also wipe out half of the world's plant and animal species, that would hardly be an economic success. And if we again quadruple the size of the global economy but many of us are hungrier than our hunter-gatherer ancestors, we won't be able to declare the twenty-first century a success.

Learning to Walk

One of the first steps in redefining progress is to recognize that our generation is the first whose actions can affect the habitability of the planet for future generations. We have acquired this capacity not by conscious design but as a consequence of a global economy that is outgrowing its environmental support systems.

In effect, we have acquired the capacity to alter Earth's natural systems but have refused to accept responsibility for doing so. We live in a world that has an obsessive preoccupation with the present. Focused on quarterly profit-and-loss statements, we are behaving as though we have no children. In short, we have lost our sense of responsibility to future generations.

Parents everywhere are concerned about their children. In their efforts to ensure a better life for their children, parents invest in education and medical care. But unless we now also assume responsibility for the evolution of the global economy, these short-term investments in our children's future may not amount to much; our principal legacy to them will be a world that is deteriorating ecologically, declining economically, and disintegrating socially.

Building an environmentally sustainable global economy depends on a cooperative global effort. No country acting alone can stabilize its climate. No country acting alone can protect the diversity of life on Earth. These goals can be achieved only through global cooperation that recognizes the interdependence of countries.

Unless the poorer nations' need for food, sanitation, cooking fuels, and other basic requirements are being met, the world's more affluent nations can hardly expect them to contribute to solving long-term global problems, such as climate change. The challenge is to reverse the last decade's trends of rising international inequalities and shrinking aid programs. In short, we can no longer separate efforts to build an environmentally sustainable economy from efforts to meet the needs of the world's poor.

According to various estimates, some 841 million people in the world are malnourished, 1.2 billion lack access to clean water, 1.6 billion are illiterate, and two billion don't have access to electricity. *Forbes* magazine estimates that the 225 richest people in the world now have a combined wealth of more than $1 trillion—a figure that approaches the combined annual incomes of the poorest one-half of humanity. Indeed, the assets of the three richest individuals exceed the combined annual economic output (measured at the current exchange rate) of the forty-eight poorest countries.

It is now becoming obvious that the widening gap between rich and poor is untenable in a world where resources are shared. In the absence of a concerted effort by the wealthy to address the problems of poverty and deprivation, building a sustainable future may not be possible.

Efforts to restore a stable relationship between the economy and its environmental support systems depends on social cohesion within societies as well. As at the international level, this cohesion is also influenced by the distribution of wealth. As communications improve and severely deprived people everywhere come to understand better their relative economic position, they are likely to take action to achieve a more equitable share of the economic pie.

In October 1998, the disenfranchised in the economically depressed southern part of Nigeria began taking over oil wells and pumping stations to protest their government's failure to use its vast flow of oil wealth to benefit people in the region. A villager noted that, even though oil had flowed out of the area for thirty years, his village still had "no school, no clinic, no power, and little hope."

Developing an Attitude

The trends of recent years suggest that we need a new moral compass to guide us into the twenty-first century—a compass that is grounded in the principles of meeting human needs sustainability. Such an ethic of sustainability would be based on a concept of respect for future generations.

The challenge may be greatest in the United States, where the per capita use of grain, energy, and materials is the highest in the world, and where in the 1990s half of all adults are overweight, houses and cars have continued to get larger, and driving has continued to increase, overwhelming two decades' worth of efficiency improvements. The world's ecosystems have largely survived 270 million people living like this in the twentieth century, but they won't survive eight billion or more doing so in the twenty-first century.

At issue is a change in understanding what values will support a restructuring of the global economy so that economic progress can continue. Although such a transformation may seem farfetched, the end-of-century perspective offers hope.

The past 100 years have seen vast changes in ethics and standards. The concept of human rights, for example, has flowered in the twentieth century. The basic principles of human rights have been around for several hundred years, but only in 1948—a mere half-century ago—did governments adopt a complex body of national and international laws that recognize these rights.

Another example of changing attitudes and values, one that has occurred even faster, is the growing understanding of the effects of cigarette smoking on health. This recognition has led to a sea change in public attitudes and policies toward smoking within a few decades.

A Blueprint for Success

Once it becomes clear that the existing industrial development model is not viable over the long term, the question becomes: what would an environmentally sustainable economy look like? Because we know the fundamental limits the world now faces and some of the technologies that are available, we can describe this new economy in broad outline, if not in detail.

Its foundation is a new design principle—one that shifts from the one-time depletion of natural resources to one that is based on renewable energy and that continually reuses and recycles materials. It is a solar-powered, bicycle/rail-centered, reuse/recycle economy—one that uses energy, water, land, and materials much more efficiently and wisely than we do today.

Although solar energy in its various forms has been widely considered a fringe source, it is now moving toward center stage. The use of solar cells to supply electricity is spreading rapidly, with sales climbing 17 percent annually. As of the end of 1998, some 500,000 homes—most of them in developing-world villages not yet connected to an electrical grid—were getting their electricity from solar cells.

Technologically, the most exciting advance comes from solar roofing material developed in the past few years. These solar tiles and shingles are made of photovoltaic cells that convert sunlight to electricity. They promise not only to create rooftops that become the power plants for buildings but to revolutionize electricity generation worldwide.

In 1997, British Petroleum announced that it was taking the threat of global warming seriously and was putting $1 billion into solar and other renewable energy resources. Royal Dutch Shell followed shortly thereafter, announcing a commitment of $500 million to renewable energy resources, with additional funds likely to follow. For energy companies interested in growth, it is not likely to be in petroleum, since, due to resource limits, oil production is projected to peak in the next five to twenty years and then begin declining.

As the cost of electricity from solar sources falls, it will become economical to electrolyze water, producing hydrogen. Hydrogen thus becomes a way of both storing and transporting renewable energy. A device called a fuel cell efficiently turns hydrogen back into electricity in automobiles or small power plants located in homes or office buildings. Several major oil and gas companies, including Royal Dutch Shell and Gasunie in the Netherlands, have begun to take an interest in hydrogen, while Daimler-Chrysler, Ford, General Electric, and Toyota are all investing in fuel cells. By the middle of the next century, hydrogen produced from solar electricity from the deserts of Arizona may be sent by pipeline to distant cities.

The notion of transport systems centered on bicycles and railroads may seem primitive at first, but this is because governments everywhere have assumed that the auto-centered transportation system was the only one to consider seriously. The unfolding reality, however, is quite different.

In 1969, the world produced 25 million bicycles and 23 million cars. And although car production was expected shortly to overtake that of bicycles, it actually fell further and further behind. In recent years, annual production of bicycles has averaged 105 million while that of automobiles has averaged 37 million. In contrast to the United States, where most bicycles sold are for recreational use, most of the 105 million bicycles sold each year worldwide are for basic transportation.

There are many reasons why bicycles have gained in popularity a century after the automobile was invented. One is that the number of people who can afford a bicycle is far greater than the number who can afford a car—and this is likely to be true for some decades to come. Cities are turning to them because they require little land, do not pollute, and reduce traffic congestion and noise.

In China, a group of prominent scientists has challenged the central government's decision to build an auto-centered transportation system, arguing that the country doesn't have enough land

both to feed its people and to build the roads, highways, and parking lots needed for cars. The new economy will not exclude the automobile, because in many situations it is indispensable, but it is unlikely to be the centerpiece of the transportation system as it is in many nations today.

Replacing a throwaway economy with a reduce/reuse/recycle economy is perhaps more easily understood than restructuring the transportation system because of the progress already made in recycling. Nonetheless, even with substantial recycling gains, the flow of garbage into landfills is still increasing almost everywhere in the world. We still have a long way to go in increasing material efficiency.

Some argue that it is possible to reduce materials use by a factor of four. Indeed, the Organization for Economic Cooperation and Development is investigating ways to reduce the use of materials in modern industrial societies by 90 percent. The overall challenge in manufacturing is to follow a new design principle, with services rather than goods as the focus. For example, Interface—an Atlanta-based firm operating in twenty-six countries—sells carpeting services to its clients, systematically recycling the worn-out carpets, leaving nothing for the landfill. The key is to gradually reduce the material throughout the economy, reducing energy use and pollution in the process. A concept known as eco-efficiency, with the goal of maximizing production while minimizing or, in some cases, eliminating effluents, is being pursued by companies around the world.

To the Future and Beyond

It is difficult to overstate the urgency of reversing the trends of environmental deterioration. Archeologists study the remains of civilizations that irreparably undermined their ecological support systems. These societies found themselves on a population or economic path that was environmentally unsustainable and were not able to make the economic adjustments to avoid a collapse. Unfortunately, archeological records don't reveal whether these ancient civilizations failed to understand the need for change or saw the problem but couldn't agree on the steps needed to stave off economic decline.

Today, the adjustments we need to make are clear. We know what we need to do. We have a vision of a restructured economy—one that will sustain economic and social progress. The challenge is to mobilize public support for the economic transformation. No challenge is greater or more satisfying than building an environmentally sustainable global economy—one where economic and social progress can continue not only in the twenty-first century but many centuries beyond. The question remaining is whether we can meet that challenge in time.

AMORY B. LOVINS, L. HUNTER LOVINS, AND PAUL HAWKEN   II.16

A Road Map for Natural Capitalism

The first two authors of this reading, Amory and Hunter Lovins, are the founders and directors of the Rocky Mountain Institute (*www.rmi.org*), a Colorado-based environmental policy think tank, and Paul Hawken is the founder of the Smith & Hawken retail and catalogue company. In this reading, which originally appeared in *Harvard Business Review,* they describe some ways for businesses to rethink their current wasteful and inefficient strategies and replace them with more profitable and sustainable alternatives.

The popular mindset of most businesses today is to utilize natural resources as if they were unlimited, ignoring the long-term implications caused by these actions. However, this article provides several examples of ways in which natural design alternatives have proved to be more profitable in the long run. The authors argue that businesses should strive to increase the productivity of natural resources and utilize production systems modeled on biological ones. Businesses should emphasize creating solutions, not products.

The authors believe that technological innovation, not government regulation, will produce technological solutions that will enable us to both better protect the biosphere, provide for a higher standard of living, and also produce profits for entrepreneurs. The key to making industrial capitalism sustainable is to transform it into "natural capitalism" that reinvests in and expands "the planet's ecosystems so that they can produce their vital services and biological resources even more abundantly."

Focus Questions

1. What are the four key elements of "natural capitalism" as the authors describe it?
2. The authors give several examples of designers who have implemented "whole-system design" technologies that have netted substantial savings over conventional designs. Do you think these examples can be generalized to other kinds of technology? Discuss the potential for this new approach in several industry sectors.
3. Compare the view of the authors of this reading with those of Postrel (selection II.2) and Feenberg (selection I.8). Do you think it likely that environmental values can provide the basis for the development of more sustainable technological solutions, or is it

necessary to impose regulations that force industries to limit damage to the environment? Discuss.

Keywords

biomimicry, capitalism, closed-loop manufacturing, ecosystems, industrialism, innovation, pollution, regulation, whole-system design

ON SEPTEMBER 16, 1991, A SMALL group of scientists was sealed inside Biosphere II, a glittering 3.2-acre glass and metal dome in Oracle, Arizona. Two years later, when the radical attempt to replicate the earth's main ecosystems in miniature ended, the engineered environment was dying. The gaunt researchers had survived only because fresh air had been pumped in. Despite $200 million worth of elaborate equipment, Biosphere II had failed to generate breathable air, drinkable water, and adequate food for just eight people. Yet Biosphere I, the planet we all inhabit, effortlessly performs those tasks every day for 6 billion of us.

Disturbingly, Biosphere I is now itself at risk. The earth's ability to sustain life, and therefore economic activity, is threatened by the way we extract, process, transport, and dispose of a vast flow of resources—some 220 billion tons a year, or more than 20 times the average American's body weight every day. With dangerously narrow focus, our industries look only at the exploitable resources of the earth's ecosystems—its oceans, forests, and plains—and not at the larger services that those systems provide for free. Resources and ecosystem services both come from the earth—even from the same biological systems—but they're two different things. Forests, for instance, not only produce the resource of wood fiber but also provide such ecosystem services as water storage, habitat, and regulation of the atmosphere and climate. Yet companies that earn income from harvesting the wood fiber resource often do so in ways that damage the forest's ability to carry out its other vital tasks.

Unfortunately, the cost of destroying ecosystem services becomes apparent only when the services start to break down. In China's Yangtze basin in 1998, for example, deforestation triggered flooding that killed 3,700 people, dislocated 223 million, and inundated 60 million acres of cropland. That $30 billion disaster forced a logging moratorium and a $12 billion crash program of reforestation.

The reason companies (and governments) are so prodigal with ecosystem services is that the value of those services doesn't appear on the business balance sheet. But that's a staggering omission. The economy, after all, is embedded in the environment. Recent calculations published in the journal *Nature* conservatively estimate the value of all the earth's ecosystem services to be at least $33 trillion a year. That's close to the gross world product, and it implies a capitalized book value on the order of half a quadrillion dollars. What's more, for most of these services, there is no known substitute at any price, and we can't live without them.

This article puts forward a new approach not only for protecting the biosphere but also for improving profits and competitiveness. Some very simple changes to the way we run our businesses, built on advanced techniques for making resources more productive, can yield startling benefits both for today's shareholders and for future generations.

This approach is called *natural capitalism* because it's what capitalism might become if its largest category of capital—the "natural capital" of ecosystem services—were properly valued. The journey to natural capitalism involves four major shifts in business practices, all vitally interlinked:

- *Dramatically increase the productivity of natural resources.* Reducing the wasteful and destructive flow of resources from depletion to pollution represents a major business opportunity. Through fundamental changes in both production design and technology, farsighted companies are developing ways to make natural resources—energy, minerals, water, forests—stretch 5, 10, even 100 times further than they do today. These major resource savings often yield higher profits than small resource savings do—or even saving no resources at all would—and not only pay for themselves over time but in many cases reduce initial capital investments.

- *Shift to biologically inspired production models.* Natural capitalism seeks not merely to reduce waste but to eliminate the very concept of waste. In closed-loop production systems, modeled on nature's designs, every output either is returned harmlessly to the ecosystem as a nutrient, like compost, or becomes an input for manufacturing another product. Such systems can often be designed to eliminate the use of toxic materials, which can hamper nature's ability to reprocess materials.

- *Move to a solutions-based business model.* The business model of traditional manufacturing rests on the sale of goods. In the new model, value is instead delivered as a flow of services—providing illumination, for example, rather than selling lightbulbs. This model entails a new perception of value, a move from the acquisition of goods as a measure of affluence to one where well-being is measured by the continuous satisfaction of changing expectations for quality, utility, and performance. The new relationship aligns the interests of providers and customers in ways that reward them for implementing the first two innovations of natural capitalism—resource productivity and closed-loop manufacturing.

- *Reinvest in natural capital.* Ultimately, business must restore, sustain, and expand the planet's ecosystems so that they can produce their vital services and biological resources even more abundantly. Pressures to do so are mounting as human needs expand, the costs engendered by deteriorating ecosystems rise, and the environmental awareness of consumers increases. Fortunately, these pressures all create business value.

Natural capitalism is not motivated by a current scarcity of natural resources. Indeed, although many biological resources, like fish, are becoming scarce, most mined resources, such as copper and oil, seem ever more abundant. Indices of average commodity prices are at 28-year lows, thanks partly to powerful extractive technologies, which are often subsidized and whose damage to natural capital remains unaccounted for. Yet even despite these artificially low prices, using resources manyfold more productively can now be so profitable that pioneering companies—large and small—have already embarked on the journey toward natural capitalism.[1]

Still the question arises—if large resource savings are available and profitable, why haven't they all been captured already? The answer is simple: scores of common practices in both the private and public sectors systematically reward companies for wasting natural resources and penalize them for boosting resource productivity. For example, most companies expense their consumption of raw materials through the income statement but pass resource-saving investment through the balance sheet. That distortion makes it more tax efficient to waste fuel than to invest in improving fuel efficiency. In short, even though the road seems clear, the compass that companies use to direct their journey is broken. Later we'll look in more detail at some of the obstacles to resource productivity—and some of the important business opportunities they reveal. But first, let's map the route toward natural capitalism.

Dramatically Increase the Productivity of Natural Resources

In the first stage of a company's journey toward natural capitalism, it strives to wring out the waste of energy, water, materials, and other resources throughout its production systems and other operations. There are two main ways companies can do this at a profit. First, they can adopt a fresh approach to design that considers industrial systems as a whole rather than part by part. Second, companies can replace old industrial technologies with new ones, particularly with those based on natural processes and materials.

IMPLEMENTING WHOLE-SYSTEM DESIGN

Inventor Edwin Land once remarked that "people who seem to have had a new idea have often simply stopped having an old idea." This is particularly true when designing for resource savings. The old idea is one of diminishing returns—the greater the resource saving, the higher the cost. But that old idea is giving way to the new idea that bigger savings can cost less—that saving a large fraction of resources can actually cost less than saving a small fraction of resources. This is the concept of expanding returns, and it governs much of the revolutionary thinking behind whole-system design. Lean manufacturing is an example of whole-system thinking that has helped many companies dramatically reduce such forms of waste as lead times, defect rates, and inventory. Applying whole-system thinking to the productivity of natural resources can achieve even more.

Consider Interface Corporation, a leading maker of materials for commercial interiors. In its new Shanghai carpet factory, a liquid had to be circulated through a standard pumping loop similar to those used in nearly all industries. A top European company designed the system to use pumps requiring a total of 95 horsepower. But before construction began, Interface's engineer, Jan Schilham, realized that two embarrassingly simple design changes would cut that power requirement to only 7 horsepower—a 92% reduction. His redesigned system cost less to build, involved no new technology, and worked better in all respects.

What two design changes achieved this 12-fold saving in pumping power? First, Schilham chose fatter-than-usual pipes, which create much less friction than thin pipes do and therefore need far less pumping energy. The original designer had chosen thin pipes because, according to the textbook method, the extra cost of fatter ones wouldn't be

justified by the pumping energy that they would save. This standard design trade-off optimizes the pipes by themselves but "pessimizes" the larger system. Schilham optimized the *whole* system by counting not only the higher capital cost of the fatter pipes but also the *lower* capital cost of the smaller pumping equipment that would be needed. The pumps, motors, motor controls, and electrical components could all be much smaller because there'd be less friction to overcome. Capital cost would fall far more for the smaller equipment than it would rise for the fatter pipe. Choosing big pipes and small pumps—rather than small pipes and big pumps—would therefore make the whole system cost less to build, even before counting its future energy savings.

Schilham's second innovation was to reduce the friction even more by making the pipes short and straight rather than long and crooked. He did this by laying out the pipes first, *then* positioning the various tanks, boilers, and other equipment that they connected. Designers normally locate the production equipment in arbitrary positions and then have a pipe fitter connect everything. Awkward placement forces the pipes to make numerous bends that greatly increase friction. The pipe fitters don't mind: they're paid by the hour, they profit from the extra pipes and fittings, and they don't pay for the oversized pumps or inflated electric bills. In addition to reducing those four kinds of costs, Schilham's short, straight pipes were easier to insulate, saving an extra 70 kilowatts of heat loss and repaying the insulation's cost in three months.

This small example has big implications for two reasons. First, pumping is the largest application of motors, and motors use three-quarters of all industrial electricity. Second, the lessons are very widely relevant. Interface's pumping loop shows how simple changes in design mentality can yield huge resource savings and returns on investment. This isn't rocket science; often it's just a rediscovery of good Victorian engineering principles that have been lost because of specialization.

Whole-system thinking can help managers find small changes that lead to big savings that are cheap, free, or even better than free (because they make the whole system cheaper to build). They can do this because often the right investment in one part of the system can produce multiple benefits throughout the system. For example, companies would gain 18 distinct economic benefits—of which direct energy savings is only one—if they switched from ordinary motors to premium-efficiency motors or from ordinary lighting ballasts (the transformer-like boxes that control fluorescent lamps) to electronic ballasts that automatically dim the lamps to match available daylight. If everyone in America integrated these and other selected technologies into all existing motor and lighting systems in an optimal way, the nation's $220-billion-a-year electric bill would be cut in half. The after-tax return on investing in these changes would in most cases exceed 100% per year.

The profits from saving electricity could be increased even further if companies also incorporated the best off-the-shelf improvements into their building structure and their office, heating, cooling, and other equipment. Overall, such changes could cut national electricity consumption by at least 75% and produce returns of around 100% a year on the investments made. More important, because workers would be more comfortable, better able to see, and less fatigued by noise, their productivity and the quality of their output would rise. Eight recent case studies of people working in well-designed, energy-efficient buildings measured labor productivity gains of 6% to 16%. Since a typical office pays about 100 times as much for people as it does for energy, this increased productivity in people is worth about 6 to 16 times as much as eliminating the entire energy bill.

Energy-saving, productivity-enhancing improvements can often be achieved at even lower cost by piggybacking them onto the periodic renovations that all buildings and factories need. A recent proposal for reallocating the normal 20-year renovation budget for a standard 200,000-square-foot glass-clad office tower near Chicago, Illinois, shows the potential of whole-system design. The proposal suggested replacing the aging glazing system with a new kind of window that lets in nearly six times more daylight than the old sun-blocking glass units. The new windows would reduce the flow of heat and noise four times better than traditional windows do. So even though the glass costs slightly more, the overall cost of the renovation would be reduced because the windows would let in cool, glare-free daylight that, when combined with more efficient lighting and office equipment, would reduce the need for air-conditioning by 75%. Installing a fourfold more efficient, but fourfold smaller, air-conditioning system would cost $200,000 less than giving the old system its normal 20-year renovation. The $200,000 saved would, in turn, pay for the extra cost of the new windows and other improvements. This whole-system approach to renovation would not only save 75% of the building's total energy use, it would also greatly improve the building's comfort and marketability. Yet it would cost essentially the same as the normal renovation. There are about 100,000 twenty-year-old glass office towers in the United States that are ripe for such improvement.

Major gains in resource productivity require that the right steps be taken in the right order. Small changes made at the downstream end of a process often create far larger savings further upstream. In almost any industry that uses a pumping system, for example, saving one unit of liquid flow or friction in an exit pipe saves about ten units of fuel, cost, and pollution at the power station.

Of course, the original reduction in flow itself can bring direct benefits, which are often the reason changes are made in the first place. In the 1980s, while California's industry grew 30%, for example, its water use was cut by 30%, largely to avoid increased wastewater fees. But the resulting reduction in pumping energy (and the roughly tenfold larger saving in power-plant fuel and pollution) delivered bonus savings that were at the time largely unanticipated.

To see how downstream cuts in resource consumption can create huge savings upstream, consider how reducing the use of wood fiber disproportionately reduces the pressure to cut down forests. In round numbers, half of all harvested wood fiber is used for such structural products as lumber; the other half is used for paper and cardboard. In both cases, the biggest leverage comes from reducing the amount of the retail product used. If it takes, for example, three pounds of harvested trees to produce one pound of product, then saving one pound of product will save three pounds of trees—plus all the environmental damage avoided by not having to cut them down in the first place.

The easiest savings come from not using paper that's unwanted or unneeded. In an experiment at its Swiss headquarters, for example, Dow Europe cut office paper flow by about 30% in six weeks simply by discouraging unneeded information. For instance, mailing lists were eliminated and senders of memos got back receipts indicating whether each recipient had wanted the information. Taking those and other small steps, Dow was also able to increase labor productivity by a similar proportion because people could focus on what they really needed to read. Similarly, Danish hearing-aid maker Oticon saved upwards of 30% of its paper as a by-product of redesigning its business processes to produce better decisions faster. Setting the default on office printers and copiers to double-sided mode reduced AT&T's paper costs by about 15%. Recently developed copiers and printers can even strip off old toner and printer ink, permitting each sheet to be reused about ten times.

Further savings can come from using thinner but stronger and more opaque paper, and from designing packaging more thoughtfully. In a 30-month effort at reducing such waste, Johnson & Johnson saved 2,750 tons of packaging, 1,600 tons of paper, $2.8 million, and at least 330 acres of forest annually. The downstream savings in paper use are multiplied by the savings further upstream, as less need for paper products (or less need for fiber to make each product) translates into less raw paper, less raw paper means less pulp, and less pulp requires fewer trees to be harvested from the forest. Recycling paper and substituting alternative fibers such as wheat straw will save even more.

Comparable savings can be achieved for the wood fiber used in structural products. Pacific Gas and Electric, for example, sponsored an innovative design developed by Davis Energy Group that used engineered wood products to reduce the amount of wood needed in a stud wall for a typical tract house by more than 70%. These walls were stronger, cheaper, more stable, and insulated twice as well.

Using them enabled the designers to eliminate heating and cooling equipment in a climate where temperatures range from freezing to 113°F. Eliminating the equipment made the whole house much less expensive both to build and to run while still maintaining high levels of comfort. Taken together, these and many other savings in the paper and construction industries could make our use of wood fiber so much more productive that, in principle, the entire world's present wood fiber needs could probably be met by an intensive tree farm about the size of Iowa.

ADOPTING INNOVATIVE TECHNOLOGIES

Implementing whole-system design goes hand in hand with introducing alternative, environmentally friendly technologies. Many of these are already available and profitable but not widely known. Some, like the "designer catalysts" that are transforming the chemical industry, are already runaway successes. Others are still making their way to market, delayed by cultural rather than by economic or technical barriers.

The automobile industry is particularly ripe for technological change. After a century of development, motorcar technology is showing signs of age. Only 1% of the energy consumed by today's cars is actually used to move the driver: only 15% to 20% of the power generated by burning gasoline reaches the wheels (the rest is lost in the engine and drive-train) and 95% of the resulting propulsion moves the car, not the driver. The industry's infrastructure is hugely expensive and inefficient. Its convergent products compete for narrow niches in saturated core markets at commoditylike prices. Auto making is capital intensive, and product cycles are long. It is profitable in good years but subject to large losses in bad years. Like the typewriter industry just before the advent of personal computers, it is vulnerable to displacement by something completely different.

Enter the Hypercar. Since 1993, when Rocky Mountain Institute placed this automotive concept in the public domain, several dozen current and potential auto manufacturers have committed billions of dollars to its development and commercialization. The Hypercar integrates the best existing technologies to reduce the consumption of fuel as much as 85% and the amount of materials used up to 90% by introducing four main innovations.

First, making the vehicle out of advanced polymer composites, chiefly carbon fiber, reduces its weight by two-thirds while maintaining crashworthiness. Second, aerodynamic design and better tires reduce air resistance by as much as 70% and rolling resistance by up to 80%. Together, these innovations save about two-thirds of the fuel. Third, 30% to 50% of the remaining fuel is saved by using a "hybrid-electric" drive. In such a system, the wheels are turned by electric motors whose power is made onboard by a small engine or turbine, or even more efficiently by a fuel cell. The fuel cell generates electricity directly by chemically combining stored hydrogen with oxygen, producing pure hot water as its only by-product. Interactions between the small, clean, efficient power source and the ultralight, low-drag auto body then further reduce the weight, cost, and complexity of both. Fourth, much of the traditional hardware—from transmissions and differentials to gauges and certain parts of the suspension—can be replaced by electronics controlled with highly integrated, customizable, and upgradable software.

These technologies make it feasible to manufacture pollution-free, high-performance cars, sport utilities, pickup trucks, and vans that get 80 to 200 miles per gallon (or its energy equivalent in other fuels). These improvements will not require any compromise in quality or utility. Fuel savings will not come from making the vehicles small, sluggish, unsafe, or unaffordable, nor will they depend on government fuel taxes, mandates, or subsidies. Rather, Hypercars will succeed for the same reason that people buy compact discs instead of phonograph records: the CD is a superior product that redefines market expectations. From the manufacturers' perspective, Hypercars will cut cycle times, capital needs, body part counts, and assembly effort and space by as much as tenfold. Early adopters will have a huge competitive advantage—which is why dozens of corporations, including most automakers, are now racing to bring Hypercar-like products to market.[2]

In the long term, the Hypercar will transform industries other than automobiles. It will displace about an eighth of the steel market directly and most of the rest eventually, as carbon fiber becomes far cheaper. Hypercars and their cousins could ultimately save as much oil as OPEC now sells. Indeed, oil may well become uncompetitive as a fuel long before it becomes scarce and costly. Similar challenges face the coal and electricity industries because the development of the Hypercar is likely to accelerate greatly the commercialization of inexpensive hydrogen fuel cells. These fuel cells will help shift power production from centralized coal-fired and nuclear power stations to networks of decentralized, small-scale generators. In fact, fuel-cell-powered Hypercars could themselves be part of these networks. They'd be, in effect, 20-kilowatt power plants on wheels. Given that cars are left parked—that is, unused—more than 95% of the time, these Hypercars could be plugged into a grid and could then sell back enough electricity to repay as much as half the predicted cost of leasing them. A national Hypercar fleet could ultimately have five to ten times the generating capacity of the national electric grid.

As radical as it sounds, the Hypercar is not an isolated case. Similar ideas are emerging in such industries as chemicals, semiconductors, general manufacturing, transportation, water and wastewater treatment, agriculture, forestry, energy, real estate, and urban design. For example, the amount of carbon dioxide released for each microchip manufactured can be reduced almost 100-fold through improvements that are now profitable or soon will be.

Some of the most striking developments come from emulating nature's techniques. In her book, *Biomimicry,* Janine Benyus points out that spiders convert digested crickets and flies into silk that's as strong as Kevlar without the need for boiling sulfuric acid and high-temperature extruders. Using no furnaces, abalone can convert seawater into an inner shell twice as tough as our best ceramics. Trees turn sunlight, water, soil, and air into cellulose, a sugar stronger than nylon but one-fourth as dense. They then bind it into wood, a natural composite with a higher bending strength than concrete, aluminum alloy, or steel. We may never become as skillful as spiders, abalone, or trees, but smart designers are already realizing that nature's environmentally benign chemistry offers attractive alternatives to industrial brute force.

Whether through better design or through new technologies, reducing waste represents a vast business opportunity. The U.S. economy is not even 10% as energy efficient as the laws of physics allow. Just the energy thrown off as waste heat by U.S. power stations equals the total energy use of Japan. Materials efficiency is even worse: only about 1% of all the materials mobilized to serve America is actually made into products and still in use six months after sale. In every sector, there are opportunities for reducing the amount of resources that go into a production process, the steps required to run that process, and the amount of pollution generated and by-products discarded at the end. These all represent avoidable costs and hence profits to be won.

Redesign Production According to Biological Models

In the second stage on the journey to natural capitalism, companies use closed-loop manufacturing to create new products and processes that can totally prevent waste. This plus more efficient production processes could cut companies' long-term materials requirements by more than 90% in most sectors.

The central principle of closed-loop manufacturing, as architect Paul Bierman-Lytle of the engineering firm CH2M Hill puts it, is "waste equals food." Every output of manufacturing should be either composted into natural nutrients or remanufactured into technical nutrients—that is, it should be returned to the ecosystem or recycled for further production. Closed-loop production systems are designed to eliminate any materials that incur disposal costs, especially toxic ones, because the alternative—isolating them to prevent harm to natural systems—tends to be costly and risky. Indeed, meeting EPA and OSHA standards by eliminating harmful materials often makes a manufacturing process cost less than the hazardous process it re-

placed. Motorola, for example, formerly used chlorofluorocarbons for cleaning printed circuit boards after soldering. When CFCs were outlawed because they destroy stratospheric ozone, Motorola at first explored such alternatives as orange-peel terpenes. But it turned out to be even cheaper—and to produce a better product—to redesign the whole soldering process to that it needed no cleaning operations or cleaning materials at all.

Closed-loop manufacturing is more than just a theory. The U.S. remanufacturing industry in 1996 reported revenues of $53 billion—more than consumer-durables manufacturing (appliances; furniture; audio, video, farm, and garden equipment). Xerox, whose bottom line has swelled by $700 million from remanufacturing, expects to save another $1 billion just by remanufacturing its new, entirely reusable or recyclable line of "green" photocopiers. What's more, policy makers in some countries are already taking steps to encourage industry to think along these lines. German law, for example, makes many manufacturers responsible for their products forever, and Japan is following suit.

Combining closed-loop manufacturing with resource efficiency is especially powerful. DuPont, for example, gets much of its polyester industrial film back from customers after they use it and recycles it into new film. DuPont also makes its polyester film ever stronger and thinner so it uses less material and costs less to make. Yet because the film performs better, customers are willing to pay more for it. As DuPont chairman Jack Krol noted in 1997, "Our ability to continually improve the inherent properties [of our films] enables this process [of developing more productive materials, at lower cost, and higher profits] to go on indefinitely."

Interface is leading the way to this next frontier of industrial ecology. While its competitors are "down cycling" nylon-and-PVC-based carpet into less valuable carpet backing, Interface has invented a new floor-covering material called Solenium, which can be completely remanufactured into identical new product. This fundamental innovation emerged from a clean-sheet redesign. Executives at Interface didn't ask how they could sell more carpet of the familiar kind; they asked how they could create a dream product that would best meet their customers' needs while protecting and nourishing natural capital.

Solenium lasts four times longer and uses 40% less material than ordinary carpets—an 86% reduction in materials intensity. What's more, Solenium is free of chlorine and other toxic materials, is virtually stainproof, doesn't grow mildew, can easily be cleaned with water, and offers aesthetic advantages over traditional carpets. It's so superior in every respect that Interface doesn't market it as an environmental product—just a better one.

Solenium is only one part of Interface's drive to eliminate every form of waste. Chairman Ray C. Anderson defines waste as "any measurable input that does not produce customer value," and he considers all inputs to be waste until shown otherwise. Between 1994 and 1998, this zero-waste approach led to a systematic treasure hunt that helped to keep resource inputs constant while revenues rose by $200 million. Indeed, $67 million of the revenue increase can be directly attributed to the company's 60% reduction in landfill waste.

Subsequently, president Charlie Eitel expanded the definition of waste to include all fossil fuel inputs, and now many customers are eager to buy products from the company's recently opened solar-powered carpet factory. Interface's green strategy has not only won plaudits from environmentalists, it has also proved a remarkably successful business strategy. Between 1993 and 1998, revenue has more than doubled, profits have more than tripled, and the number of employees has increased by 73%.

Change the Business Model

In addition to its drive to eliminate waste, Interface has made a fundamental shift in its business model—the third stage on the journey toward natural capitalism. The company has realized that clients want to walk on and look at carpets—but not necessarily to own them. Traditionally, broadloom carpets in office buildings are replaced every decade because some portions look worn out. When that happens, companies suffer the disruption of shutting down their offices and removing their furniture. Billions of pounds of carpets are re-

moved each year and sent to landfills, where they will last up to 20,000 years. To escape this unproductive and wasteful cycle, Interface is transforming itself from a company that sells and fits carpets into one that provides floor-covering services.

Under its Evergreen Lease, Interface no longer sells carpets but rather leases a floor-covering service for a monthly fee, accepting responsibility for keeping the carpet fresh and clean. Monthly inspections detect and replace worn carpet tiles. Since at most 20% of an area typically shows at least 80% of the wear, replacing only the worn parts reduces the consumption of carpeting material by about 80%. It also minimizes the disruption that customers experience—worn tiles are seldom found under furniture. Finally, for the customer, leasing carpets can provide a tax advantage by turning a capital expenditure into a tax-deductible expense. The result: the customer gets cheaper and better services that cost the supplier far less to produce. Indeed, the energy saved from not producing a whole new carpet is in itself enough to produce all the carpeting that the new business model requires. Taken together, the 5-fold savings in carpeting material that Interface achieves though the Evergreen Lease and the 7-fold materials savings achieved through the use of Solenium deliver a stunning 35-fold reduction in the flow of materials needed to sustain a superior floor-covering service. Remanufacturing, and even making carpet initially from renewable materials, can then reduce the extraction of virgin resources essentially to the company's goal of zero.

Interface's shift to a service-leasing business reflects a fundamental change from the basic model of most manufacturing companies, which still look on their businesses as machines for producing and selling products. The more products sold, the better—at least for the company, if not always for the customer or the earth. But any model that wastes natural resources also wastes money. Ultimately, that model will be unable to compete with a service model that emphasizes solving problems and building long-term relationships with customers rather than making and selling products. The shift to what James Womack of the Lean Enterprise Institute calls a "solutions economy" will almost always improve customer value *and* providers' bottom lines because it aligns both parties' interest, offering rewards for doing more and better with less.

Interface is not alone. Elevator giant Schindler, for example, prefers leasing vertical transportation services to selling elevators because leasing lets it capture the savings from its elevators' lower energy and maintenance costs. Dow Chemical and Safety-Kleen prefer leasing dissolving services to selling solvents because they can reuse the same solvent scores of times, reducing costs. United Technologies' Carrier division, the world's largest manufacturer of air conditioners, is shifting its mission from selling air conditioners to leasing comfort. Making its air conditioners more durable and efficient may compromise future equipment sales, but it provides what customers want and will pay for—better comfort at lower cost. But Carrier is going even further. It's starting to team up with other companies to make buildings more efficient so that they need less air-conditioning, or even none at all, to yield the same level of comfort. Carrier will get paid to provide the agreed-upon level of comfort, however that's delivered. Higher profits will come from providing better solutions rather than from selling more equipment. Since comfort with little or no air-conditioning (via better building design) works better and costs less than comfort with copious air-conditioning, Carrier is smart to capture this opportunity itself before its competitors do. As they say at 3M: "We'd rather eat our *own* lunch, thank you."

The shift to a service business model promises benefits not just to participating businesses but to the entire economy as well. Womack points out that by helping customers reduce their need for capital goods such as carpets or elevators, and by rewarding suppliers for extending and maximizing asset values rather than for churning them, adoption of the service model will reduce the volatility in the turnover of capital goods that lies at the heart of the business cycle. That would significantly reduce the overall volatility of the world's economy. At present, the producers of capital goods face feast or famine because the buying decisions of households and corporations are extremely sensitive to fluctuating income. But in a continuous-flow-of-services economy, those swings would be greatly reduced, bringing a welcome stability to businesses.

Excess capacity—another form of waste and source of risk—need no longer be retained for meeting peak demand. The result of adopting the new model would be an economy in which we grow and get richer by using less and become stronger by being leaner and more stable.

Reinvest in Natural Capital

The foundation of textbook capitalism is the prudent reinvestment of earnings in productive capital. Natural capitalists who have dramatically raised their resource productivity, closed their loops, and shifted to a solutions-based business model have one key task remaining. They must reinvest in restoring, sustaining, and expanding the most important form of capital—their own natural habitat and biological resource base.

This was not always so important. Until recently, business could ignore damage to the ecosystem because it didn't affect production and didn't increase costs. But that situation is changing. In 1998 alone, violent weather displaced 300 million people and caused upwards of $90 billion worth of damage, representing more weather-related destruction than was reported through the entire decade of the 1980s. The increase in damage is strongly linked to deforestation and climate change, factors that accelerate the frequency and severity of natural disasters and are the consequences of inefficient industrialization. If the flow of services from industrial systems is to be sustained or increased in the future for a growing population, the vital flow of services from living systems will have to be maintained or increased as well. Without reinvestment in natural capital, shortages of ecosystem services are likely to become the limiting factor to prosperity in the next century. When a manufacturer realizes that a supplier of key components is overextended and running behind on deliveries, it takes immediate action lest its own production lines come to a halt. The ecosystem is a supplier of key components for the life of the planet, and it is now falling behind on its orders.

Failure to protect and reinvest in natural capital can also hit a company's revenues indirectly. Many companies are discovering that public perceptions of environmental responsibility, or its lack thereof, affect sales. MacMillan Bloedel, targeted by environmental activists as an emblematic clear-cutter and chlorine user, lost 5% of its sales almost overnight when dropped as a U.K. supplier by Scott Paper and Kimberly-Clark. Numerous case studies show that companies leading the way in implementing changes that help protect the environment tend to gain disproportionate advantage, while companies perceived as irresponsible lose their franchise, their legitimacy, and their shirts. Even businesses that claim to be committed to the concept of sustainable development but whose strategy is seen as mistaken, like Monsanto, are encountering stiffening public resistance to their products. Not surprisingly, University of Oregon business professor Michael Russo, along with many other analysts, has found that a strong environmental rating is "a consistent predictor of profitability."

The pioneering corporations that have made reinvestments in natural capital are starting to see some interesting paybacks. The independent power producer AES, for example, has long pursued a policy of planting trees to offset the carbon emissions of its power plants. That ethical stance, once thought quixotic, now looks like a smart investment because a dozen brokers are now starting to create markets in carbon reduction. Similarly, certification by the Forest Stewardship Council of certain sustainably grown and harvested products has given Collins Pine the extra profit margins that enabled its U.S. manufacturing operations to survive brutal competition. Taking an even longer view, Swiss Re and other European reinsurers are seeking to cut their storm-damage losses by pressing for international public policy to protect the climate and by investing in climate-safe technologies that also promise good profits. Yet most companies still do not realize that a vibrant ecological web underpins their survival and their business success. Enriching natural capital is not just a public good—it is vital to every company's longevity.

It turns out that changing industrial processes so that they actually replenish and magnify the stock of natural capital can prove especially profitable because nature does the production; people need to just step back and let life flourish. Industries that

directly harvest living resources, such as forestry, farming, and fishing, offer the most suggestive examples. Here are three:

- Allan Savory of the Center for Holistic Management in Albuquerque, New Mexico, has redesigned cattle ranching to raise the carrying capacity of rangelands, which have often been degraded not by overgrazing but by undergrazing and grazing the wrong way. Savory's solution is to keep the cattle moving from place to place, grazing intensively but briefly at each site, so that they mimic the dense but constantly moving herds of native grazing animals that coevolved with grasslands. Thousands of ranchers are estimated to be applying this approach, improving both their range and their profits. This "management-intensive rotational grazing" method, long standard in New Zealand, yields such clearly superior returns that over 15% of Wisconsin's dairy farms have adopted it in the past few years.

- The California Rice Industry Association has discovered that letting nature's diversity flourish can be more profitable than forcing it to produce a single product. By flooding 150,000 to 200,000 acres of Sacramento valley rice fields—about 30% of California's rice-growing area—after harvest, farmers are able to create seasonal wetlands that support millions of wildfowl, replenish groundwater, improve fertility, and yield other valuable benefits. In addition, the farmers bale and sell the rice straw, whose high silica content—formerly an air-pollution hazard when the straw was burned—adds insect resistance and hence value as a construction material when it's resold instead.

- John Todd of Living Technologies in Burlington, Vermont, has used biological Living Machines—linked tanks of bacteria, algae, plants, and other organisms—to turn sewage into clean water. That not only yields cleaner water at a reduced cost, with no toxicity or odor, but it also produces commercially valuable flowers and makes the plant compatible with its residential neighborhood. A similar plant at the Ethel M Chocolates factory in Las Vegas, Nevada, not only handles difficult industrial wastes effectively but is showcased in its public tours.

Although such practices are still evolving, the broad lessons they teach are clear. In almost all climates, soils, and societies, working with nature is more productive than working against it. Reinvesting in nature allows farmers, fishermen, and forest managers to match or exceed the high yields and profits sustained by traditional input-intensive, chemically driven practices. Although much of mainstream business is still headed the other way, the profitability of sustainable, nature-emulating practices is already being proven. In the future, many industries that don't now consider themselves dependent on a biological resource base will become more so as they shift their raw materials and production processes more to biological ones. There is evidence that many business leaders are starting to think this way. The consulting firm Arthur D. Little surveyed a group of North American and European business leaders and found that 83% of them already believe that they can derive "real business value [from implementing a] sustainable-development approach to strategy and operations."

A Broken Compass?

If the road ahead is this clear, why are so many companies straying or falling by the wayside? We believe the reason is that the instruments companies use to set their targets, measure their performance, and hand out rewards are faulty. In other words, the markets are full of distortions and perverse incentives. Of the more than 60 specific forms of misdirection that we have identified,[3] the most obvious involve the ways companies allocate capital and the way governments set policy and impose taxes. Merely correcting these defective practices would uncover huge opportunities for profit.

Consider how companies make purchasing decisions. Decisions to buy small items are typically based on their initial cost rather than their full life-cycle cost, a practice that can add up to major

wastage. Distribution transformers that supply electricity to buildings and factories, for example, are a minor item at just $320 apiece, and most companies try to save a quick buck by buying the lowest-price models. Yet nearly all the nation's electricity must flow through transformers, and using the cheaper but less efficient models wastes $1 billion a year. Such examples are legion. Equipping standard new office-lighting circuits with fatter wire that reduces electrical resistance could generate after-tax returns of 193% a year. Instead, wire as thin as the National Electrical Code permits is usually selected because it costs less up-front. But the code is meant only to prevent fires from overheated wiring, not to save money. Ironically, an electrician who chooses fatter wire—thereby reducing long-term electricity bills—doesn't get the job. After paying for the extra copper, he's no longer the low bidder.

Some companies do consider more than just the initial price in their purchasing decisions but still don't go far enough. Most of them use a crude payback estimate rather than more accurate metrics like discounted cash flow. A few years ago, the median simple payback these companies were demanding from energy efficiency was 1.9 years. That's equivalent to requiring an after-tax return of around 71% per year—about six times the marginal costs of capital.

Most companies also miss major opportunities by treating their facilities costs as an overhead to be minimized, typically by laying off engineers, rather than as profit center to be optimized—by using those engineers to save resources. Deficient measurement and accounting practices also prevent companies from allocating costs—and waste—with any accuracy. For example, only a few semiconductor plants worldwide regularly and accurately measure how much energy they're using to produce a unit of chilled water or clean air for their clean-room production facilities. That makes it hard for them to improve efficiency. In fact, in an effort to save time, semiconductor makers frequently build new plants as exact copies of previous ones—a design method nicknamed "infectious repetitis."

Many executives pay too little attention to saving resources because they are often a small percentage of total costs (energy costs run to about 2%

in most industries). But those resource savings drop straight to the bottom line and so represent a far greater percentage of profits. Many executives also think they already "did" efficiency in the 1970s, when the oil shock forced them to rethink old habits. They're forgetting that with today's far better technologies, it's profitable to start all over again. Malden Mills, the Massachusetts maker of such products as Polartec, was already using "efficient" metal-halide lamps in the mid 1990s. But a recent warehouse retrofit reduced the energy used for lighting by another 93%, improved visibility, and paid for itself in 18 months.

The way people are rewarded often creates perverse incentives. Architects and engineers, for example, are traditionally compensated for what they spend, not for what they save. Even the striking economics of the retrofit design for the Chicago office tower described earlier wasn't incentive enough actually to implement it. The property was controlled by a leasing agent who earned a commission every time she leased space, so she didn't want to wait the few extra months needed to refit the building. Her decision to reject the efficiency-quadrupling renovation proved costly for both her and her client. The building was so uncomfortable and expensive to occupy that it didn't lease, so ultimately the owner had to unload it at a firesale price. Moreover, the new owner will for the next 20 years be deprived of the opportunity to save capital cost.

If corporate practices obscure the benefits of natural capitalism, government policy positively undermines it. In nearly every country on the planet, tax laws penalize what we want more of—jobs and income—while subsidizing what we want less of—resource depletion and pollution. In every state but Oregon, regulated utilities are rewarded for selling more energy, water, and other resources, and penalized for selling less, even if increased production would cost more than improved customer efficiency. In most of America's arid western states, use-it-or-lose-it water laws encourage inefficient water consumption. Additionally, in many towns, inefficient use of land is enforced through outdated regulations, such as guidelines for ultrawide suburban streets recommended by 1950s civil-defense

planners to accommodate the heavy equipment needed to clear up rubble after a nuclear attack.

The costs of these perverse incentives are staggering: $300 billion in annual energy wasted in the United States, and $1 trillion already misallocated to unnecessary air-conditioning equipment and the power supplies to run it (about 40% of the nation's peak electric load). Across the entire economy, unneeded expenditures to subsidize, encourage, and try to remedy inefficiency and damage that should not have occurred in the first place probably account for most, if not all, of the GDP growth of the past two decades. Indeed, according to former World Bank economist Herman Daly and his colleague John Cobb (along with many other analysts), Americans are hardly better off then they were in 1980. But if the U.S. government and private industry could redirect the dollars currently earmarked for remedial costs toward reinvestment in natural and human capital, they could bring about a genuine improvement in the nation's welfare. Companies, too, are finding that wasting resources also means wasting money and people. These intertwined forms of waste have equally intertwined solutions. Firing the unproductive tons, gallons, and kilowatt-hours often makes it possible to keep the people, who will have more and better work to do.

Recognizing the Scarcity Shift

In the end, the real trouble with our economic compass is that it points in exactly the wrong direction. Most businesses are behaving as if people were still scarce and nature still abundant—the conditions that helped to fuel the first Industrial Revolution. At that time, people were relatively scarce compared with the present-day population. The rapid mechanization of the textile industries caused explosive economic growth that created labor shortages in the factory and the field. The Industrial Revolution, responding to those shortages and mechanizing one industry after another, made people a hundred times more productive than they had ever been.

The logic of economizing on the scarcest resource, because it limits progress, remains correct.

But the pattern of scarcity is shifting: now people aren't scarce but nature is. This shows up first in industries that depend directly on ecological health. Here, production is increasingly constrained by fish rather than by boats and nets, by forests rather than by chain saws, by fertile topsoil rather than by plows. Moreover, unlike the traditional factors of industrial production—capital and labor—the biological limiting factors cannot be substituted for one other. In the industrial system, we can easily exchange machinery for labor. But no technology or amount of money can substitute for a stable climate and a productive biosphere. Even proper pricing can't replace the priceless.

Natural capitalism addresses those problems by reintegrating ecological with economic goals. Because it is both necessary and profitable, it will subsume traditional industrialism within a new economy and a new paradigm of production, just as industrialism previously subsumed agrarianism.

The companies that first make the changes we have described will have a competitive edge. Those that don't make that effort won't be a problem because ultimately they won't be around. In making that choice, as Henry Ford said, "Whether you believe you can, or whether you believe you can't, you're absolutely right."

NOTES

1. Our book, *Natural Capitalism,* provides hundreds of examples of how companies of almost every type and size, often through modest shifts in business logic and practice, have dramatically improved their bottom lines.
2. Nonproprietary details are posted at http://www.hypercar.com.
3. Summarized in the report "Climate: Making Sense *and* Making Money" at http://www.rmi.org/catalog/climate.htm.

Bibliography

Aiken, W. E. (1977). *Technocracy and the American Dream: The Technocratic Movement 1900–1941.* Berkeley: University of California Press.

Appleyard, B. (1998). *Brave New Worlds: Staying Human in the Genetic Future.* New York: Viking Press.

Arterton, F. C. (1987). *Teledemocracy: Can Technology Protect Democracy?* London: Sage.

Baden, J. A., Noonan, D. S., and Ruckelshaus, W. D. (Eds.) (1998). *Managing the Commons,* 2nd ed. Bloomington: Indiana University Press.

Barnet, R. J., and Cavanagh, J. (1994). *Global Dreams: Imperial Corporations and the New World Order.* New York: Touchstone.

Bartlett, D., and Steele, J. (1992). *America: What Went Wrong?* Kansas City, MO: Andrews and McMeel.

Beniger, J. (1986). *The Control Revolution: Technological and Economic Origins of the Information Society.* Cambridge, MA: Harvard University Press.

Bijker, W. E., Hughes, T. P., and Pinch, T. (1990). *The Social Construction of Technological Systems.* Cambridge, MA: MIT Press.

Bolter, J. D. (1984). *Turing's Man.* Chapel Hill: University of North Carolina Press.

Boorstin, D. J. (1978). *The Republic of Technology.* New York: Harper & Row.

Borgmann, A. (1984). *Technology and the Character of Contemporary Life: A Philosophical Inquiry.* Chicago: University of Chicago Press.

Brand, S. (1987). *The Media Lab: Inventing the Future at MIT.* New York: Viking.

Braun, E. (1984). *Wayward Technology.* Westport, CT: Greenwood Press.

Bright, C. (1998). *Life Out of Bounds: Bioinvasion in a Borderless World.* New York: Norton.

Brod, C. (1984). *Techno Stress: The Human Cost of the Computer Revolution.* Reading, MA: Addison-Wesley.

Brook, J., and Boal, I. A. (Eds.) (1995). *Resisting the Virtual Life: The Culture and Politics of Information.* San Francisco: City Lights Books.

Brown, L., et al. (1998). *State of the World 1998: A Worldwatch Institute Report on Progress Toward a Sustainable Society.* New York: Norton.

Brzezinski, Z. (1989). *The Grand Failure: The Birth and Death of Communism in the Twentieth Century.* New York: Scribner's.

Burke, J., and Ornstein, R. (1997). *The Axmaker's Gift: Technology's Capture and Control of Our Minds and Culture.* New York: Putnam Group.

Bush, C. G. (1983). *Machina Ex Dea.* New York: Teacher's College Press.

Carnegie Commission on Science, Technology, and Government. (1992) *Enabling the Future: Linking Science and Technology to Societal Goals.* New York: Carnegie Commission on Science, Technology, and Government.

Carson, R. (1962). *Silent Spring.* Boston: Houghton Mifflin.

Chandler, A. D., Jr. (1977). *The Visible Hand: The Management Revolution in American Business.* Cambridge, MA: Belknap Press.

Chomsky, N. (1996). *World Orders Old and New.* New York: Columbia University Press.

Commoner, B. (1971). *The Closing Circle: Nature, Man and Technology.* New York: Knopf.

Corn, J. (Ed.) (1986). *Imagining Tomorrow: History, Technology, and the American Future.* Cambridge, MA: MIT Press.

Cowan, R. S. (1983). *More Work for Mother: The Ironies of Household Technology from the Open Hearth to the Microwave.* New York: Basic Books.

Cowan, R. S. (1997). *A Social History of American Technology.* New York: Oxford University Press.

Cross, G. (1993). *Time and Money: The Making of Consumer Culture.* New York: Routledge.

Daly, H. E., and Cobb, J. B., Jr. (1994). *For the Common Good: Redirecting the Economy Toward Community, the Environment, and a Sustainable Future.* New York: Beacon Press.

Dawkins, R. (1990). *The Selfish Gene.* Oxford: Oxford University Press.

Desmond, K. (1986). *The Harwin Chronology of Inventions, Innovations, Discoveries.* London: Constable.

Diamond, Jared. (1999). *Guns, Germs, and Steel: The Fates of Human Societies.* New York: Norton.

Donaldson, T. (1989). *The Ethics of International Business.* New York: Oxford University Press.

Douglas, M., and Wildavsky, A. (1982). *Risk and Culture: The Selection of Technical and Environmental Dangers.* Berkeley: University of California Press.

Dreyfus, H. (1979). *What Computers Can't Do: The Limits of Artificial Intelligence,* 2nd ed. New York: Basic Books.

Dreyfus, H. (1992). *What Computers Still Can't Do: A Critique of Artificial Reason.* Cambridge, MA: MIT Press.

Drucker, P. (1993). *Post-Capitalist Society.* New York: HarperCollins.

Dunn, L. (1965). *A Short History of Genetics.* New York: Plenum Press.

Durning, A. (1989). *Action at the Grassroots: Fighting Poverty and Environmental Decline.* Washington, DC: Worldwatch Institute.

Dyson, F. (1985). *Origins of Life.* Cambridge: Cambridge University Press.

Dyson, F. (1999). *The Sun, the Genome, and the Internet: Tools of Scientific Revolutions.* New York: Oxford University Press.

Dyson, G. B. (1997). *Darwin Among the Machines: The Evolution of Global Intelligence.* New York: Perseus.

Easton, T. A. (Ed.). (1998). *Taking Sides: Clashing Views of Controversial Issues in Science, Technology, and Society,* 3rd ed. Guilford, CT: Dushkin/McGraw-Hill.

Edgar, S. (1997). *Morals and Machines: Perspectives in Computer Ethics.* New York: Jones and Bartlett.

Ellul, J. (1964). *The Technological Society,* J. Wilkenson trans. New York: Knopf.

Elster, J. (1983). *Explaining Technical Change.* Cambridge: Cambridge University Press.

Ermann, M. D., Williams, M., and Shauf, M. (Eds.). (1997). *Computers, Ethics, and Society,* 2nd ed. New York: Oxford University Press.

Feenberg, Andrew. (1999). *Questioning Technology.* New York: Routledge.

Feenberg, A., and Hannay, A. (Eds.). (1995). *Technology and the Politics of Knowledge.* Bloomington: Indiana University Press.

Feeré, F. (1995). *Philosophy of Technology.* Athens: University of Georgia Press.

Fox, M. (1992). *Superpigs and Wondercorn: The Brave New World of Biotechnology and Where It May Lead.* New York: Lyons and Burford.

Frenkel, S. (Ed.) (1999). *On the Front Line: Organization of Work in the Information Age.* Ithaca, NY: Cornell University Press.

Friedman, T. L. (1999). *The Lexus and the Olive Tree.* New York: Farrar, Straus & Giroux.

Gates, Bill. (1995). *The Road Ahead.* New York: Viking Penguin.

Gimpel, J. (1977). *The Medieval Machine: The Industrial Revolution of the Middle Ages.* New York: Penguin.

Gordon, D. (1996). *Fat and Mean: The Corporate Squeeze of Working Americans and the Myth of Managerial "Downsizing."* New York: Kessler Books.

Hardin, G. (1993). *Living Within Limits: Ecology, Economics, and Population Taboos.* New York: Oxford University Press.

Hardison, O. B., Jr. (1989). *Disappearing Through the Skylight: Culture and Technology in the Twentieth Century.* New York: Viking.

Heidegger, M. (1977). *The Question Concerning Technology and Other Essays,* W. Lovitt, trans. New York: Harper & Row.

Henry, D. (1989). *From Foraging to Agriculture.* Philadelphia: University of Pennsylvania Press.

Hofstetter, R. (1997). *Mobius.* New York: Vantage Press.

Hughes, T. P. (1989). *American Genesis: A Century of Invention and Technological Enthusiasm.* New York: Viking.

Ihde, D. (1990). *Technology and the Lifeworld: From Garden to Earth.* Bloomington: Indiana University Press.

Jonas, H. (1974). *Philosophical Essays: From Ancient Creed to Technological Man.* Englewood Cliffs, NJ: Prentice-Hall.

Jonas, H. (1984). *The Imperative of Responsibility: In Search of an Ethics for the Technological Age.* Chicago: University of Chicago Press.

Karliner, J. (1997). *The Corporate Planet: Ecology and Politics in the Age of Globalization.* San Francisco: Sierra Club Books.

Kennedy, P. (1993). *Preparing for the Twenty-first Century.* New York: Random House.

Kevles, D. (1995). *In the Name of Eugenics: Genetics and the Uses of Human Heredity.* Cambridge, MA: Harvard University Press.

Keynes, J. (1989). *General Theory of Employment, Interest and Money*. New York: Harcourt Brace.

Kidder, T. (1982). *The Soul of a New Machine*. London: Allen Lane.

Kitcher, P. (1996). *The Lives to Come: The Genetic Revolution and Human Possibilities*. New York: Touchstone.

Koestler, A. (1964). *The Act of Creation*. New York: Macmillan.

Korten, D. C. (1995). *When Corporations Ruled the World*. West Hartford, CT: Kumarian Press.

Kuhn, T. (1970). *The Structure of Scientific Revolutions,* 2nd ed. Chicago: University of Chicago Press.

Kurzweil, R. (1990). *The Age of Intelligent Machines*. Cambridge, MA: MIT Press.

Kurzweil, R. (1999). *The Age of Spiritual Machines: When Computers Exceed Human Intelligence*. New York: Viking.

Landes, D. (1983). *Revolution in Time: Clocks and the Making of the Modern World*. Cambridge, MA: Harvard University Press.

Latour, B. (1987). *Science in Action*. Cambridge, MA: Harvard University Press.

Lovins, A. B. (1977). *Soft Energy Paths: Towards a Durable Peace*. Cambridge, MA: Ballinger.

Lyons, J., and Gorner, P. (1966). *Altered Fates: Gene Therapy and the Retooling of Human Life*. New York: Norton.

Mackenzie, D., and Wajcman, J. (Eds.). (1999). *The Social Shaping of Technology*. Philadelphia: Open University Press.

Maisels, C. (1990). *The Emergence of Civilization: From Hunting and Gathering to Agriculture, Cities, and the State in the Near East*. London: Routledge and Kegan Paul.

Marx, L. (1964). *The Machine in the Garden: Technology and the Pastoral Ideal in America*. New York: Oxford University Press.

McCorduck, P. (1979). *Machines Who Think*. San Francisco: Freeman.

McGee, G. (1997). *The Perfect Baby: A Pragmatic Approach to Genetics*. Lanham, MD: Rowman & Littlefield.

McLuhan, M. (1964). *Understanding Media: The Extensions of Man*. New York: McGraw-Hill.

McPhee, J. (1989). *The Control of Nature*. New York: Farrar, Straus & Giroux.

Mesthene, E. (1970). *Technological Change: Its Impact on Man and Society*. New York: New American Library.

Meyerowitz, J. (1985). *No Sense of Place: The Impact of Electronic Media on Sociable Behavior*. New York: Oxford University Press.

Mills, S. (Ed.). (1997). *Turning Away from Technology: A New Vision for the 21st Century*. San Francisco: Sierra Club Books.

Mitcham, C. (1994). *Thinking Through Technology: The Path Between Engineering and Philosophy*. Chicago: University of Chicago Press.

Mitcham, C., and Mackey, R. (Eds.). (1973). *Biography of the Philosophy of Technology*. Chicago: University of Chicago Press.

Mitcham, C., and Mackey, R. (Eds.). (1983). *Philosophy and Technology: Readings in Philosophical Problems of Technology*. New York: Free Press.

Morevec, H. (1989). *MindChildren: The Future of Robot and Human Intelligence*. Cambridge, MA: Harvard University Press.

Morevec, H. (1999). *Robot: Mere Machine to Transcendent Mind*. New York: Oxford University Press.

Mumford, L. (1934). *Technics and Civilization*. New York: Harcourt, Brace, and World.

Mumford, L. (1966). *Technics and Human Development*. New York: Harcourt Brace Jovanovich.

Naisbitt, J. (1984). *Megatrends: Ten New Directions Transforming Our Lives*. New York: Warner Books.

Negroponte, N. (1995). *Being Digital*. New York: Vintage Books.

Noble, D. F. (1979). *America by Design: Science, Technology, and the Rise of Corporate Capitalism*. New York: Oxford University Press.

Noble, D. F. (1984). *Forces of Production: A Social History of Industrial Automation*. New York: Knopf.

Noble, D. F. (1997). *The Religion of Technology: The Divinity of Man and the Spirit of Invention*. New York: Knopf.

Nye, D. E. (1994). *American Technological Sublime*. Cambridge, MA: MIT Press.

Oakley, A. (1984). *The Captured Womb: A History of the Medical Care of Pregnant Women*. Oxford: Blackwell.

Pacey, A. (1983). *The Culture of Technology*. Cambridge, MA: MIT Press.

Perrin, N. (1979). *Giving Up the Gun: Japan's Reversion to the Sword, 1543–1879*. Boston: David R. Godine.

Petrovski, H. (1985). *To Engineer Is Human: The Role of Failure in Successful Design*. New York: St. Martin's Press.

Petrovski, H. (1996). *Invention by Design: How Engineers Get from Thought to Thing*. Cambridge, MA: Harvard University Press.

Pitt, Joseph C. (2000). *Thinking About Technology: Foundations of the Philosophy of Technology*. New York: Seven Bridges Press.

Pool, R. (1997). *Beyond Engineering: How Society Shapes Technology*. New York: Oxford University Press.

Postman, N. (1985). *Amusing Ourselves to Death: Public Discourse in the Age of Show Business*. New York: Viking.

Postman, N. (1992). *Technopoly: The Surrender of Culture to Technology*. New York: Knopf.

Postrel, V. (1998). *The Future and Its Enemies: The Growing Conflict over Creativity, Enterprise, and Progress*. New York: Free Press.

Reich, R. (1992). *The Work of Nations: Preparing Ourselves for 21st Century Capitalism*. New York: Random House.

Renner, M. (1996). *Fighting for Survival: Environmental Decline, Social Conflict, and the New Age of Insecurity*. Washington, DC: Worldwatch Institute.

Rheingold, H. (1991). *Virtual Reality*. New York: Summit Books.

Rifkin, J. (1983). *Algeny*. New York: Viking.

Rifkin, J. (1995). *The End of Work: The Decline of the Global Labor Force and the Dawn of the Post-Market Era*. New York: Putnam.

Roberts, J. M. (1993). *A Short History of the World.* New York: Oxford University Press.

Rosenberg, N. (1982). *Inside the Black Box: Technology and Economics.* Cambridge: Cambridge University Press.

Roszak, T. (1994). *The Cult of Information: A Neo-Luddite Treatise on High Tech, Artificial Intelligence, and the True Art of Thinking,* 2nd ed. Berkeley: University of California Press.

Russo, E., and Cove, D. (1995). *Genetic Engineering: Dreams and Nightmares.* New York: Viking.

Rybczynski, W. (1985). *Taming the Tiger: The Struggle to Control Technology.* New York: W. H. Freeman.

Sahal, D. (1981). *Patterns of Technological Innovation.* Cambridge: Cambridge University Press.

Schick, K. D., and Toth, N. (1993). *Making Silent Stones Speak: Human Evolution and the Dawn of Technology.* New York: Simon & Schuster.

Schor, J. (1991). *The Overworked American: The Unexpected Decline of Leisure.* New York: Basic Books.

Schumacher, E. F. (1973). *Small Is Beautiful: Economics as if People Mattered.* New York: Harper & Row.

Sclove, R. E. (1995). *Democracy and Technology.* New York: Guilford Press.

Shaiken, H. (1985). *Work Transformed: Automation and Labor in the Computer Age.* New York: Holt, Rinehart & Winston.

Shrader-Frechette, K., and Westra, L. (Eds.). (1997). *Technology and Values.* Totowa, NJ: Rowman and Littlefield.

Silver, L. (1997). *Remaking Eden: Cloning and Beyond in a Brave New World.* New York: Avon Books.

Simons, G. (1992). *Robots: The Quest for Living Machines.* New York: Sterling.

Smith, A. (1937). *An Inquiry into the Nature and Causes of the Wealth of Nations.* New York: Modern Library.

Stover, C. (Ed.). (1963). *The Technological Order: Proceedings of the Encyclopaedia Brittanica Conference.* Detroit: Wayne State University Press.

Strasser, S. (1989). *Satisfaction Guaranteed: The Making of the American Mass Market.* New York: Pantheon.

Strobel, F. (1993). *Upward Dreams, Downward Mobility: The Economic Decline of the American Middle Class.* Lanham, MD: Rowman and Littlefield.

Strong, D. (1995). *Crazy Mountains: Learning from Wilderness to Weigh Technology.* Albany: State University of New York Press.

Teich, A. H. (1997). *Technology and the Future,* 7th ed. New York: St. Martin's Press.

Tenner, E. (1997). *Why Things Bite Back: Technology and the Revenge of Unintended Consequences.* Cambridge, MA: Harvard University Press.

Thurow, L. C. (1996). *The Future of Capitalism: How Today's Economic Forces Shape Tomorrow's World.* New York: William Morrow.

Tiles, M., and Oberdiek, H. (1995). *Living in a Technological Culture: Human Tools and Human Values.* New York: Routledge.

Toffler, A. (1970). *Future Shock*. New York: Random House.

Toffler, A., and Toffler, H. (1990). *Powershift*. New York: Bantam Books.

Turkle, S. (1982). *The Second Self: The Human Spirit in a Computer Culture*. New York: Simon & Schuster.

Turney, J. (1998). *Frankenstein's Footsteps: Science, Genetics and Popular Culture*. New Haven, CT: Yale University Press.

Van Creveld, M. (1989). *Technology and War: From 2000 BC to the Present*. New York: Free Press.

Volti, R. (1992). *Society and Technological Change*, 2nd ed. New York: St. Martin's Press.

Wajcman, J. (1991). *Feminism Confronts Technology*. University Park: Pennsylvania State University Press.

White, L., Jr. (1966). *Medieval Technology and Social Change*. New York: Oxford University Press.

Wilson, E. O. (1998). *Consilience: The Unity of Knowledge*. New York: Knopf.

Winner, L. (1977). *Autonomous Technology: Technics-Out-of-Control as a Theme in Political Thought*. Cambridge, MA: MIT Press.

Winner, L. (1986). *The Whale and the Reactor: A Search for Limits in an Age of High Technology*. Chicago: University of Chicago Press.

Wolman, W., and Colamosca, A. (1997). *The Judas Economy: The Triumph of Capital and the Betrayal of Work*. New York: Addison-Wesley.

Wresch, W. (1996). *Disconnected: Haves and Have-Nots in the Information Age*. New Brunswick, NJ: Rutgers University Press.

Wright, L. (1964). *Home Fires Burning: The History of Domestic Heating and Cooking*. London: Routledge and Kegan Paul.

Zuboff, S. (1988). *In the Age of the Smart Machine: The Future of Work and Power*. New York: Basic Books.

Timeline of Significant Technological Innovations
(continued from front of book)

Event	Date	Event	Date
Fire (human made)	30000 BC	LEGO toys	1932
First mammals	65 MYA	Lens (convex)	300 BC
Fork	600	Life (bacteria)	2.75 BYA
Formation of Earth	5 BYA	Life (earliest forms)	1.5 BYA
Fuel cell	1839	Lighthouse (Pharos)	300 BC
GPS	1970	Linotype (typesetting)	1884
Genetic engineering	1973	Lock/Key	400 BC
Germs theory (infection)	1850s	Loom (earliest)	2000 BC
Glassblowing	100 BC	Loom (punch cards)	1805
Glasses (eye)	1286	Mammals	65 MYA
Gravity explained	1687	Mammogram	1913
Great Wall of China	300 BC	Map	2300 BC
Guitar (electric)	1931	McDonalds (hamburgers)	1948
Gum (chewing/bubble)	1870/1928	Measurement (foot)	2100 BC
Gun	1288	Microscope	1660
Gunpowder/Fireworks	1280	Microwave oven	1953
Hair drier (electric)	1902	Mirror (metal)	2500 BC
Harness (horse)	300 BC	Motion pictures (silent/sound)	1888/1927
Helicopter (theory)	1500	Mouse (computer)	1968
Helicopter (practical flight)	1939	Mummification	2600 BC
Heliocentric theory	1543	Musical instruments	30000 BC
Hieroglyphics	3300 BC	Numerical controlled machines	1952
Hole (donut)	1850	NMR imaging	1968
Homo Erectus	2 MYA	Neanderthals	300000 BC
Homo Habilis	2.4 MYA	Needle	20000 BC
Homo Sapiens	90000 BC	Newspaper (printed)	1590
Horseshoe	900	Nuclear reaction	1942
Humanoids	15 MYA	Nylon	1934
Human flight	1783	Oil lamp	250 BC
Human Genome Project	1989	Oil tanker (ship)	1872
Ink jet printer	1976	Organ transplant (kidney/heart)	1953/1967
Interchangeable parts	1430	Oven	40000 BC
Internal combustion engine	1877	Pacemaker (external/internal)	1958/1959
Irrigation	2400 BC	Pap test	1928
Knife (electric)	1938	Paper	140 BC
L P record	1948	Paperback book	1937
Lamp (incandescent/fluorescent)	1841/1938	Parachute (demonstrated)	1783
Laser	1958	Parchment	250 BC
Lathe	1500	Pasteurization	1856